M000087402

# A SACRED SPACE IS NEVER EMPTY

# A Sacred Space Is Never Empty

## A HISTORY OF SOVIET ATHEISM

*Victoria Smolkin*

PRINCETON UNIVERSITY PRESS
PRINCETON & OXFORD

Published by Princeton University Press,
41 William Street, Princeton, New Jersey 08540

In the United Kingdom: Princeton University Press,
6 Oxford Street, Woodstock, Oxfordshire OX20 1TR

press.princeton.edu

Jacket design by Amanda Weiss



ISBN 978-0-691-17427-3

Library of Congress Control Number: 2018935161

British Library Cataloging-in-Publication Data is available

This book has been composed in Miller

Printed on acid-free paper. ∞

Printed in the United States of America

10 9 8 7 6 5 4 3 2

For my family

# CONTENTS

# ACKNOWLEDGMENTS

EVERY BOOK REQUIRES a tremendous mobilization of resources and support—intellectual, material, and moral. I am grateful to finally have the chance to thank those institutions and individuals that made this book possible.

First, there are the many and diverse forms of intellectual support. This project was born at the University of California, Berkeley, where I was fortunate enough to work with many remarkable and inspiring scholars over the course of my graduate studies, including Thomas Brady, John Connelly, Victoria Frede, Thomas Laqueur, Olga Matich, Yuri Slezkine, Edward Walker, and the late Viktor Zhivov. Thomas Brady's course on "Immanence and Transcendence" stimulated me to consider how the story of Soviet atheism's attempts to grapple with existential questions is both particular and universal. John Connelly has been a rare model of academic discipline and human empathy. Victoria Frede was generous in sharing her expertise on the intellectual history of Russian atheism. Thomas Laqueur's visionary work was an inspiration. Olga Matich was an invaluable guide into the Russian and Soviet cultural imagination. The late Viktor Zhivov opened up the world of Russian Orthodoxy and inspired me to compare disciplinary regimes, both religious and ideological, across time and space. Edward Walker continuously challenged me to articulate why any of this actually matters. Finally, my advisor, Yuri Slezkine, who has been at the foundation of this project from the beginning, taught me the value of asking big questions and showed me that good history can also be a good story. I am grateful to him for his constant support—of the scholarship, but also of the scholar.

In the process of working on this project, I have presented my ideas at many conferences and workshops. The valuable and challenging feedback I received on each occasion has undoubtedly improved the book. In particular, I would like to thank the organizers and participants of the Russian History Workshop at the University of Pennsylvania; Russian and East European Reading Group at Yale University; Shelby Cullom Davis Center at Princeton University; Leonard E. Greenberg Center for the Study of Religion in Public Life at Trinity College; research group on "Religious Cultures in 19th and 20th Century Europe" at the Center for Advanced Studies of the Ludwig Maximilians Universität in Munich, Germany; Virginia and Derrick Sherman Endowed Emerging Scholar Lecture at the University of North Carolina at Wilmington; and UC Berkeley Institute of Slavic, East European, and Eurasian Studies, which has remained an intellectual home, hosting me on multiple occasions, including its Carnegie Seminar on Ideology and Religion and, of course, the Russian history *kruzhok*.

This project has also benefited from the expertise and assistance of many exceptional archivists, librarians, research assistants, and colleagues, without whom this book would have been impossible. I would like to thank the archivists at the State Archive of the Russian Federation (GARF); Russian State Archive of Social and Political History (RGASPI), including the Komsomol Archive; Russian State Archive of Recent History (RGANI); State Museum of the History of Religion (GMIR); Central State Archives of Public Organizations of Ukraine (TsDAGO); Central State Archive of Supreme Bodies of Power and Government of Ukraine (TsDAVo); and Lithuanian Special Archives (LYA). I am also grateful to the talented librarians of the European Reading Room at the Library of Congress, the Firestone Library at Princeton University, the Woodrow Wilson Center, and the Olin Library at Wesleyan University. Likewise, I am grateful for the help of many excellent research assistants, including Samantha Aibinder, Bulat Akhmetkarimov, Massimo Beloni, Gabriel Finkelstein, Aaron Hale-Dorrell, Emily Hoge, Misha Iakovenko, Joseph Kellner, Jacob Lassin, Joel Michaels, James Reston, Elyas Saif, Kathryn Sobchenko, Kayla Stoler, and Olga Yakushenko. My transcribers, Lyudmila Mironova and Valerii Lubiako, were models of professionalism and efficiency.

I am also grateful to the many people who shared their professional expertise and offered encouragement, especially Cynthia Buckley, Tatiana Chumachenko, Michael Froggatt, Aleksei Gaidukov, Nadiezda Kizenko, Sonja Luehrmann, Nikolai Mitrokhin, Mikhail Odintsov, Mikhail Smirnov, Anna Sokolova, Alexander Titov, Catherine Wanner, and Viktor Yelensky. I am grateful to my interview subjects for their insights, as well as their trust. I am also indebted to my students at Wesleyan; this project has profited a great deal from our discussions. Finally, I would especially like to thank the noble souls who read and offered critical feedback on the manuscript. Some—Emily Baran, David Brandenberger, Paul Bushkovitch, Justin Charron, John Connelly, Nicole Eaton, Christine Evans, Victoria Frede, Susanne Fusso, Anna Geltzer, Michael Gordin, Joseph Kellner, Nadiezda Kizenko, Sonja Luehrmann, Nikolai Mitrokhin, Alexis Peri, Ethan Pollock, Justine Quijada, Peter Rutland, Magda Teter, Helena Toth, Todd Weir, and Viktor Zhivov—read parts. Some—Richard Elphick, Denis Kozlov, and Erik Scott—read the entire manuscript. And the unlucky—Yuri Slezkine and Paul Werth—read the entire manuscript multiple times. On each occasion, I benefited tremendously from their insights and challenges. The faults and mistakes that remain are likely there because I did not take their advice.

Then, there is the material support without which the research and writing of this book would have been impossible. I am grateful to the Department of History and the Program in Eurasian and East European Studies at the University of California, Berkeley; Social Science Research Council (SSRC)

Pre-Dissertation Research Fellowship; Fulbright-Hays Doctoral Dissertation Research Abroad Fellowship; American Councils (ACTR/ACCELS) Advanced Research Fellowship; UC Berkeley Dean's Normative Time Dissertation Fellowship; and Woodrow Wilson Foundation Newcombe Dissertation Fellowship in Religion and Ethics, for providing the resources to complete the dissertation, which was the first incarnation of this project. Several organizations provided the support that allowed me to continue thinking, writing, and revising the dissertation into the book it has become. The Social Science Research Council Eurasia Post-Doctoral Research Award allowed me to do essential additional research. The Shelby Cullom Davis Center for Historical Studies at Princeton University, under the exemplary leadership of Philip Nord, offered a stimulating and productive atmosphere for developing this project. The Woodrow Wilson Center's Kennan Institute offered the perfect space to put academic ideas in conversation with the world beyond.

Wesleyan University has been a wonderful environment for this project to mature. I am grateful to my colleagues, both past and present, who have helped make my time at Wesleyan so productive, especially in the History Department, College of Social Studies, and Russian, East European, and Eurasian Studies Program. I have also been fortunate in having the guidance of wise and generous mentors, especially Susanne Fusso, Bruce Masters, Peter Rutland, Gary Shaw, and Magda Teter. I have also benefited from the university's generous research support. In particular, I would like to express my gratitude to the History Department and its Colonel Return Jonathan Meigs First (1740–1823) Grant, which made possible several trips to Russia, Ukraine, and Lithuania to do additional archival research and interviews, and the Center for the Humanities, which, under Ethan Kleinberg's model guidance, has offered a wonderful place to think and write.

I am also deeply indebted to the people who participated in the development, revision, and production of this book. I am grateful to my developmental editor, Madeleine Adams, for her early interventions. Without her insight that I was trying to write two books simultaneously, and her insistence that I had to pick one, I might still be writing in circles. I am also grateful to Princeton University Press for its support, and for being patient with the detours along the way. In particular, I would like to thank the editor, Brigitta van Rheinberg, for her faith in the project; the assistant editors, Quinn Fusting and Amanda Peery, for their great feedback and professionalism; and the production editor, Karen Carter, for her expert oversight of the process. I would also like to thank Cindy Milstein and Joseph Dahm for their careful copyediting, and Carolyn Sherayko for her work with the index, and Christopher Chenier for his assistance with the images.

This book includes material that was first published in the following publications: "'Sviato mesto pusto ne byvaet': Ateisticheskoe vospitanie v

Sovetskom Soiuze, 1964–1968," *Neprikosnovennyi zapas: debaty o politike i kul'ture* 3, no. 65 (Summer 2009): 36–52; "The Contested Skies: The Battle of Science and Religion in the Soviet Planetarium," in *Soviet Space Culture: Cosmic Enthusiasm in Socialist Societies*, ed. Eva Maurer, Julia Richers, Monica Rüthers, and Carmen Scheide (Basingstoke: Palgrave Macmillan, 2011), 57–78; "Cosmic Enlightenment: Scientific Atheism and the Soviet Conquest of Space," in *Into the Cosmos: Space Exploration and Soviet Culture in Post-Stalinist Russia*, ed. James T. Andrews and Asif A. Siddiqi (Pittsburgh: University of Pittsburgh, 2011), 159–94; and "The Ticket to the Soviet Soul: Science, Religion and the Spiritual Crisis of Late Soviet Atheism," *Russian Review* 73, no. 2 (April 2014): 171–97. I am grateful for the permission to reproduce this material in the book. I am also grateful to the ITAR-TASS News Agency, State Museum of the History of Religion (GMIR), and Central Archive of Moscow (GBU "TsGA Moskvy") for permission to reproduce the images in this book.

Finally, there is the moral support, without which it is hard to imagine having the endurance required to finish a book. My research in Russia and Ukraine would not have been as memorable and rewarding without the companionship of friends and colleagues, especially Molly Brunson, Nicole Eaton, Christine Evans, Mayhill Fowler, Faith Hillis, Alexis Peri, Kristin Romberg, and Erik Scott, and I am grateful that in the years since our paths keep bringing us together. I have also been fortunate enough to have people in my life who make it wonderful, and I would like to thank all the friends who said the right thing at the right time, or did not say the wrong thing at the wrong time—especially Pasha Belasky, Karl Boulware, La Mott Raymond Britto Jr., Molly Brunson, Christine Evans, Anna Geltzer, Michael Goodman, Emilie Miller, Sarah Morhaim, Colin Pierce, Julie Pierce, Inna Razumova, Sasha Rudensky, and Sarah Thompson. Kevin Rothrock contributed a great deal to this project, for which I am also grateful.

Above all, I would like to thank my family, big and small, who have been beside me—in body and spirit—over the course of this project. My grandparents and their stories have always kept human experience at the forefront of my thinking about history. I am sorry that my grandmother Alla and my grandfather Peter did not live to see this book completed, but they always knew that it would be, even when I did not, and that is a comfort. My parents, Diana and Oleg, always had faith, and always knew when to intervene: my mother, with her constant and generous efforts to shoulder some of the burden, and my father with his jokes and stories, which brought much-needed laughter and made the burden seem less heavy. My brother, Vladislav, has consistently been a model of creative energy and the most tireless of cheerleaders, reinjecting vitality into the book and its author in critical moments. Finally, I want to thank my daughter, Sophia, for her patience, curiosity, and love. She was born with this book, and has patiently shared her mother with it. Ever since she became aware that her mother was writing a book, she has been checking the mailbox to see if it had come. I had to finish it, so that the book she has been waiting for would finally arrive.

# ABBREVIATIONS

| | |
|---|---|
| AON | Academy of Social Sciences (Akademiia obshchestvennykh nauk), 1946–91 |
| CARC | Council on the Affairs of Religious Cults (Sovet po delam religioznykh kul'tov), 1944–65 |
| CAROC | Council on the Affairs of the Russian Orthodox Church (Sovet po delam russkoi pravoslavnoi tserkvi), 1943–65 |
| CRA | Council for Religious Affairs (Sovet po delam religii), 1965–91 |
| GMIR/A | Leningrad State Museum of Religion [and Atheism] (Gosudarstvennyi muzei istorii religii [i ateizma]), 1931–present |
| INA | Institute of Scientific Atheism (Institut nauchnogo ateizma), 1964–91 |
| KGB | Committee for State Security (Komitet gosudarstvennoi bezopasnosti) |
| NKGB | People's Commissariat for State Security (Narodnyi komissariat gosudarstvennoi bezopasnosti) |
| NKVD | People's Commissariat for Internal Affairs (Narodnyi komissariat vnutrennikh del) |
| OGPU | Joint State Political Directorate (Ob'edinennoe gosudarstvennoe politicheskoe upravlenie pri SNK SSSR) |
| RSFSR | Russian Soviet Federal Socialist Republic (Rossiiskaia Sovetskaia Federativnaia Sotsialisticheskaia Respublika) |
| SSR | Soviet Socialist Republic (Sovetskaia Sotsialisticheskaia Respublika) |
| TsDNT | N. K. Krupskaia Central House of Folk Arts (Tsentral'nyi Dom Narodnogo Tvorchestva imeni N. K. Krupskoi) |
| TsK KPSS | Central Committee of the Communist Party of the Soviet Union (Tsentral'nyi Komitet Kommunisticheskoi Partii Sovetskogo Soiuza) |
| VChK | All-Russian Extraordinary Commission for the Struggle with Counter-Revolution and Sabotage (Vserossiiskaia chrezvychainaia komissia po bor'be s kontrrevoliutsiei i sabotazhem) |

VOOPIiK All-Russian Society for the Preservation of Monuments of History and Culture (Vserossiiskoe Obshchestvo Okhrany Pamiatnikov Istorii i Kul'tury)

VTsIK All-Union Central Executive Committee (Vsesoiuznyi Tsentral'nyi Ispolnitel'nyi Komitet)

ZAGS Bureau for the Registration of Acts of Civil Status (Zapis' aktov grazhdanskogo sostoianiia)

Znanie Society for the Dissemination of Political and Scientific Knowledge (Obshchestvo po rasprostraneniiu politicheskikh i nauchnykh znanii), 1947–present

# A SACRED SPACE IS NEVER EMPTY

# INTRODUCTION

> Issues such as good and evil, conscience, justice, and retribution found a reflection in the historical mission of religion. . . . This is why people do not grow tired of it for 1000 years. Marxism also presented itself as a general theory of humanity, a new civilization, the image of the new man. The bid was certainly serious, but life revealed its problems. All the reproaches made about socialism-communism found their reflection in the authority and standing of atheism. Atheism [was] the new civilization's calling card.
>
> —S. A. KUCHINSKII, DIRECTOR OF THE LENINGRAD STATE MUSEUM OF THE HISTORY OF RELIGION AND ATHEISM (1989)

ON APRIL 29, 1988, at the height of perestroika, the general secretary of the Soviet Communist Party, Mikhail Gorbachev, made the unanticipated decision to meet with Patriarch Pimen (Izvekov) and the Synod of Bishops of the Russian Orthodox Church. This was the first official meeting between the leader of the Soviet Communist Party and the hierarchs of the Orthodox Church since 1943, when Joseph Stalin summoned three Orthodox metropolitans to the Kremlin in the middle of the night to inform them that after more than two decades of repression, the Orthodox Church could return to Soviet life with the benediction of the state. The direct impetus for Gorbachev's meeting with the patriarch was the approaching millennium of the Christianization of Rus'—an event commemorating Grand Prince Vladimir's adoption of Christianity in 988 as the official religion of Kievan Rus', which gathered his diverse lands and peoples into a unified state. Gorbachev's motives for meeting with the patriarch were not unlike Stalin's—which is to say, they were political. Just as Stalin had broken with two decades of antireligious policy in order to mobilize patriotism at home and appeal to allies abroad in the midst of a catastrophic war, Gorbachev was attempting to harness Orthodoxy's moral capital at home and court political favor with Cold War adversaries in order to regain control over perestroika—which by early 1988 was not only losing popular support but also being challenged from within the Soviet political establishment by Communist Party conservatives as well as nationalists across the Soviet Union's titular republics, including Russia itself.

In his address, Gorbachev noted that his meeting with the patriarch was taking place "on the threshold of the 1000th anniversary of the introduction of Christianity in Rus." This event, he announced, was now going to be commemorated "not only in a religious but also a sociopolitical tone, since it was a significant milestone in the centuries' long path of the development of the fatherland's history, culture, and Russian statehood." Gorbachev acknowledged the deep "worldview differences" between the Soviet Communist Party and Russian Orthodox Church, but emphasized that Orthodox believers were nevertheless "Soviet people, working people, patriots," and, as such, entitled to all the rights of Soviet citizenship "without restrictions," including "the full right to express their convictions with dignity." During the meeting, Gorbachev also called on the church to play a role in the moral regeneration of Soviet society, "where universal norms and customs can help our common cause."[1] Finally, Gorbachev promised the church unprecedented concessions: the return of religious buildings and property that had been nationalized by the Bolsheviks following the October Revolution, permission for religious instruction of children and charity work, the elimination of restrictions on the publication of religious literature and the Bible, and the liberalization of the restrictive laws that had governed Soviet religious life since the revolution. The new legal framework, adopted in 1990, endowed religious organizations with juridical and property rights, and restricted state interference in religious affairs. But what turned out to be the most consequential revision was the new prohibition on the Soviet state's funding of atheism—a provision that effectively ended the long marriage between Communism and atheism in the Soviet Union.[2]

Gorbachev's meeting with the patriarch transformed the Russian Orthodox millennium from a narrowly religious event marginal to Soviet public life into a national celebration sanctioned by the Soviet state. This unexpected and dramatic shift in the Soviet position on religion turned out to be consequential, and raises a number of questions: Why did Soviet Communism abandon its commitment to atheism? Was there a relationship between the two political divorces that took place in the Soviet Union's final years—the divorce of Communism and atheism, and the divorce of the Soviet state from the Communist Party?

*A Sacred Space Is Never Empty* is a history of Soviet atheism from the Bolshevik Revolution of 1917 until the return of religion to public life in the Soviet Union's final years. The Bolsheviks imagined Communism as a world without religion. The Soviet experiment was the first attempt to turn this vision into reality. When the Bolsheviks seized power in October 1917, they promised to liberate the people from the old world—to overcome exploitation with justice, conflict with harmony, superstition with reason, and religion with atheism. As they set out to build the new Communist world, they rejected all previous sources of authority, replacing the autocratic state with Soviet power, religious morality with class morality, and backward superstition with an enlightened, rational, and modern way of life. In their effort to remake the world, the Bolsheviks sought to remove religion from the "sacred spaces" of Soviet life. They renounced traditional religious institutions, theologies, and ways of life, offering in their place the Communist Party and Marxism-Leninism—a party that claimed a monopoly on power and truth, and an ideology that promised

FIGURE I.1. Mikhail Gorbachev meets Patriarch Pimen (Izvekov) in the Kremlin to discuss the upcoming celebration of the millennium of the adoption of Christianity in Rus'. April 29, 1988, Moscow. Image no. 1042407, Yuri Lizunov and Alexander Chumichev for ITAR-TASS, used with permission.

to give new meaning to collective and individual life. Yet despite the secularization of the state, the party's commitment to atheism, the vision of radical social transformation through cultural revolution, and several antireligious and atheist campaigns, Soviet Communism never managed to overcome religion or produce an atheist society. Indeed, as Gorbachev's ultimate reversal on religion and atheism makes clear, religion remained a problem for the Soviet project until the end—a problem that atheism proved unable to solve.

This book argues that in order to understand why religion posed a problem for Soviet Communism, we need to shift our attention from religion to atheism. It is certainly true that the official Soviet position on religion remained remarkably consistent from the Bolshevik Revolution until the USSR's dissolution. Atheism, however, was reimagined in fundamental ways, with critical consequences for the Communist Party and the Marxist-Leninist ideology in which it grounded its legitimacy: from the antireligious repression and "militant atheism" of the early Soviet period, to Stalin's rapprochement with religion in 1943, to Nikita Khrushchev's remobilization of the campaign against religion and turn to "scientific atheism," to Leonid Brezhnev's retreat from ideological utopianism in the late Soviet period, to Gorbachev's break with atheism and return of religion to public life in 1988. The book follows how the Soviet state's definition of religion informed its production of atheism, and how the engagement with both religion and atheism transformed how the state understood Soviet Communism. Soviet atheism, then, has its own history—one that is intertwined with, yet distinct from, the history of religion.

But what is "religion"? Scholars of religion have suggested that no definition remains stable across time and space—a claim that extends beyond the Soviet case. Indeed, since the nineteenth century, when scholars began to study religion as a distinct attribute of human experience, the definition of religion has transformed from the assertion that it is a universal fact that exists in different forms in all human societies to the proposition that religion does not exist beyond the scholar's own imagination.[3] The customary understanding of religion, born in the modern age, locates it within individual belief (rather than, for example, in ritual practice, tradition, or the authority of religious institutions and clergy).[4] But definitions of religion are neither neutral nor universal. As Jonathan Z. Smith observes, religion is not a "native category" but instead one "imposed from the outside"—historically, from the position of Christian Europe.[5] Religion, then, is defined by history as well as by those who deployed the category for distinct analytic—and often also political—purposes.

For the history of Soviet atheism, however, the theoretical questions about the definition of religion are secondary, since regardless of whether or not religion is a human universal, those who comprised the Soviet atheist apparatus—party and government officials, ideology theorists and propaganda cadres, social scientists, cultural workers, and enlightenment activists, among others—took for granted that religion existed, and that it was antithetical to Communism, posed a danger to the Communist project, and therefore needed to be exorcized from Soviet life. Their engagement with religion, and their evolving understanding of what it meant about the Soviet path to Communism, needs to be analyzed. Although various definitions remain significant for understanding Soviet atheism (including religion as belief in the supernatural, a force that binds and integrates communities, or a disciplinary instrument), what is most relevant to this history is that the atheist apparatus positioned religion as something alien and rooted in the old world: the ideology of a former sociopolitical order, false worldview, and obsolete way of life. For Soviet atheism, religion—inasmuch as it survived in the new world—was a problem that needed to be solved, although how the atheist apparatus understood the problem changed over time in critical ways and with significant consequences.

This book argues that for Soviet Communism, religion represented, above all, an obstacle to its monopoly on political, ideological, and spiritual authority. Over the course of the Soviet period, the atheist apparatus learned that in order to bring about a world without religion, it was not enough to simply exorcize religion from the center of political, social, cultural, and everyday life. It was also necessary to fill Soviet Communism's sacred space with positive meaning. To analyze the process through which the meaning and function of this sacred space was produced, contested, and revised, the book is organized around three sets of oppositions: the *political* opposition between the party's commitment to ideological purity and state's pursuit of effective governance; the *ideological* opposition between religion, superstition, and backwardness and science, reason, and progress; and the *spiritual* opposition between emptiness and indifference and fullness and conviction. These three oppositions can be seen as a set of critical problems that Soviet Communism had to solve as it did the work of building the new world.

The political opposition—between ideological purity and effective governance—forced the party to answer the question of what kind of state Soviet Communism should produce. As the oscillations between ideological and pragmatic commitments throughout Soviet history show, this question was never answered definitively. With regard to religion in particular, Stalin provisionally reconciled this opposition in 1943, when, after more than two decades of erratic antireligious and atheist campaigns, his rapprochement with religious institutions was a compromise on ideological purity for the sake of political security and social mobilization during the war. The ideological opposition—between religion and science—highlights the party's effort to answer the question of what kind of society Soviet Communism should produce, and dominated the debates of the Khrushchev era. Whereas "building socialism" under Stalin was above all a political project to create the economic infrastructure and social cohesion of a modern socialist state, "building Communism" under Khrushchev was an ideological project to produce a rational, harmonious, and morally disciplined Communist society. Within this framework, religion, which had been passively tolerated since the war, again became a problem, though the nature of the problem changed. Religion was no longer a political enemy; it was an ideological opponent. Finally, the spiritual opposition—between indifference and conviction—reflects the party's effort to define what kind of person Soviet Communism should produce. This question haunted the Soviet project from its inception, but it became the central preoccupation of the atheist apparatus beginning in the mid-1960s, when Brezhnev's rise to power brought an end to Khrushchev's ideological utopianism. Soviet atheists became aware that the sacred space they fought so hard to liberate from the old faiths, rather than becoming atheist, simply remained empty. How to fill this sacred space with atheist conviction was the fundamental question facing the atheist apparatus for the rest of the Soviet period.

In the late Soviet period, atheists also became aware of a new phenomenon: ideological indifference. Atheists saw symptoms of indifference in the growing political apathy, ideological hypocrisy, moral decay, and philistine individualism that they believed were spreading through Soviet society, especially among the youth. Indifference seemed more pervasive than any commitments Soviet citizens had either to the old faiths or to Communism, and it was harder to fight because it did not have institutions, clergy, or dogma. As atheists tried to understand why indifference had become a mass phenomenon, the stakes of their inability to produce atheist conviction came into focus: if they failed to fill the sacred space at the center of Soviet Communism, it would be filled by alien ideologies and commitments—since, as the Russian proverb goes, "a sacred space is never empty." Atheism, then, was a mirror that reflected Soviet Communism back to itself by forcing it to contend with the significance of religion for the Soviet project over the course of its historical development.

## *Communism and Religion*

Ideologies have long been compared to religion. In this respect, Soviet Communism, while distinct, is not unique. Already after the French Revolution, the French historian Alexis de Tocqueville observed that despite its antireligious rhetoric, revolutionary ideology "assumed all aspects of a religious revival"—so much so that "it would perhaps be truer to say that it developed into a species of religion, if a singularly imperfect one, since it was without a God, without a ritual, or promise of a future life."[6] Much like Tocqueville, many of those who have compared ideologies to religion were critics who used the analogy to condemn revolutionary projects as radical and irrational.[7] In interwar Europe, intellectuals who opposed the rise of Communism, fascism, and Nazism produced the concept of "political religion" to underscore that these new ideologies embodied a qualitatively different breed of politics: a politics that demanded a total commitment of body and soul.[8]

Communism was at the center of this narrative.[9] With regard to Soviet Communism in particular, its religious—or more precisely, antireligious—aspect was considered one of its central features. Indeed, from the Vatican's 1937 denunciation of "atheistic Communism" to the Cold War mobilization against "godless Communism," atheism has often been cast not just as a component part of Communism but as its very essence.[10] It should be surprising, then—given the prominence of the comparison of Communism to religion and centrality of the Soviet case to that narrative—that we still have few studies that explain why the Soviet position on religion and atheism changed over time.[11]

How scholars have interpreted the history of religion and atheism in the Soviet Union itself has a history—one that reflects both the historical and academic context in which scholarship was produced. Since the Second World War, when Soviet studies began to take shape, scholars have produced three narratives about religion and atheism under Soviet Communism. The first narrative, dominant during the Cold War, focuses on antireligious repression; the second, prevalent in the years immediately following the dissolution of the USSR, examines the role of atheism in the broader project of utopianism and cultural revolution; and the third construes Soviet religious policy as a form of secular modernity. These three narratives cast Soviet Communism as a totalitarian "political religion," a failed utopia, or a variant of secularism. In this sense, they are about more than religion and atheism; they speak to questions about the very nature of Soviet Communism.

The first narrative, produced in the first years following the October Revolution, largely by foreign observers visiting the Soviet Union and Russian émigrés set the parameters of how Soviet Communism would come to be understood, especially during the Cold War.[12] Even before the October Revolution, the Russian religious intelligentsia decried the millenarianism of Russian revolutionaries and denounced socialism as a false faith.[13] After 1917, Russian émigrés—perhaps most prominently the religious philosophers Nikolai Berdiaev (1874–1948), Sergei Bulgakov (1871–1944), and Nikolai Trubetskoi (1890–1938)—continued to frame Soviet Communism in religious terms.[14] In his influential book *The Origin of Russian Communism*, originally published in 1937, Berdiaev wrote that Communism's "militant atheism" and "implacably hostile attitude" to religion was "no accidental phenomenon," but "the very essence of the communist general outlook on life." The fact that it professed "to answer the religious questions of the human soul and to give a meaning to life" made Communism more than a "social system" or "scientific, purely intellectual theory." With its ambition to encompass the totality of human experience, Communism was "intolerant and fanatical," and as "exclusive" as any religious faith.[15]

The writer René Fülöp-Miller, reflecting on his journey to the USSR in the early 1920s, observed that while "Bolshevism has almost always been regarded purely as a political problem," the problem extended "far beyond the narrow horizon of political sympathies and antipathies." He noted that Bolshevik "doctrines offer not the vague hope of consolation in another and better world of the future, but precepts for the immediate and concrete realization of this better world." For Fülöp-Miller, the party's radical intolerance of other creeds—including and perhaps especially religion—was "a specifically sectarian characteristic." The "furious hostility" of Bolshevism to other creeds was "one of the surest proofs that Bolshevism itself may be treated as a sort of religion and not as a branch of science." Indeed, Fülöp-Miller contended, it was precisely in the Bolsheviks' "war against religion" that "the religious character of Bolshevism [could] be most clearly discerned." This made the Bolsheviks not a political party but rather a millenarian sect.[16] Narratives shaped by these early encounters with Bolshevism cast a long shadow, and shaped the image of Soviet Communism through much of the twentieth century.[17]

Many of the early academic studies of religion in the USSR focused on the repression of religious institutions and believers—and for good reason.[18] Soviet Communism devastated religious life in the USSR. The Bolsheviks destroyed religious institutions, nationalized religious property, imprisoned and murdered clergy and believers, uprooted religious communities, and confined religious life to an increasingly narrow private sphere. Still, in focusing on the repression of religion, these studies paid less attention to how atheism was imagined as a distinct political, ideological, and spiritual project. Studies of religious repression therefore tell us a great deal about the destructive impact of the Soviet state's engagement with religion, but much less about its productive side—how the Soviet project sought to address the functions and questions it inherited from religion, and how it assessed the successes and failures of antireligious and atheist strategies for producing an alternative cosmology and way of life.

A second wave of literature—largely produced in the late and post-Soviet period, when the Soviet archives were finally opened to researchers—turned its attention to atheism.[19] Influenced by the "cultural turn" in the humanities and social sciences, these studies examined atheism within the broader framework of Bolshevik utopianism. At stake was the bigger question of the degree to which the party and its ideology penetrated the Soviet soul.[20] To get at this, studies centering on religion and atheism explored the institutions and cadres charged with producing and disseminating ideology—the Communist Party, the Communist Youth League (Komsomol), and the League of the Militant Godless—and how these organizations conceptualized and inculcated atheism. What they show is that despite the mobilization of institutions and propaganda for the atheist project in the 1920s and 1930s, militant atheism made little impact on how ordinary people imagined and lived their lives. These studies are essential to revealing both the logic and the limitations of the atheist project in its early stages. Their focus, however, was on the early Soviet period, whereas the postwar and particularly post-Stalin periods—when Soviet atheism was developed as a theoretical discipline and institutionalized on a mass scale—remained largely unexamined. Some recent studies have offered valuable insight into the distinct spiritual landscape of the late Soviet period,[21] yet most work that extends into the postwar era has concentrated less on the ideological transformations within the Soviet project than on how the Soviet project affected specific religious groups.[22]

The third wave of scholarship on religion and atheism in the USSR has shifted attention from antireligious repression and atheist propaganda to looking at Soviet Communism through the lens of secularism.[23] These studies draw an important distinction between secularization as a social process and secularism as a political project.[24] Moreover, rather than considering the Soviet project in isolation, this research analyzes it comparatively alongside various models of the secular, from the French *laïcité* to secularism in Turkey and India. Informed by the theoretical claims of anthropology, sociology, and religious studies, these studies characterize secularism as a disciplinary project concerned with effective governance and the formation of rational citizen-subjects.[25] They propose that whereas the modern secular state presents secularism as neutral with regard to religion, the secular is in fact a productive category grounded in both Christian tradition and European history. When deployed by the state, secularism defines and regulates religion by delineating the proper boundaries between private passions and public order. Within this framework, religion becomes—as Talal Asad argues—something "anchored in personal experience, expressible as belief-statements, dependent on private institutions, practiced in one's spare time, [and] *inessential* to our common politics, economy, science, and morality."[26]

In conversation with this literature on secularism, scholars of the Soviet case frame it as a variant of secular modernity.[27] Even as they note its peculiarity, they point to the shared foundation of both liberal and Communist engagements with religion as *political* projects: both assume religion is backward and irrational, and is therefore a threat to political and social stability—especially when it transgresses beyond the private sphere, which secularism delineates as its proper realm.[28] Indeed, the liberal assumptions of secularism are the backdrop against which illiberal ideologies like Communism have been understood—which returns us to the concept of political religion. What made Communism peculiar to early observers like Fülöp-Miller and Berdiaev—which is to say, what made it like religion—was precisely the violation of the boundaries established by the modern liberal state, in which (irrational) religious passions were to be kept out of (rational) politics, and hence out of public life.

Finally, Soviet atheism has also remained marginal in the flourishing scholarship on late socialism, which seeks to understand socialist society's gradual loss of faith in the Communist project, while at the same time complicating the depiction of late socialism as an era of "stagnation."[29] These studies stress the creativity and dynamism of late socialist culture, and analyze the complex subjectivities it produced. Still, inasmuch as this literature is interested in Soviet ideology, the focus has been largely on discourse and consumption rather than on ideological production.[30] Scholars of the early Soviet period have recently shifted attention from ideological discourse to the institutions and mechanisms of ideological production in the Stalin era.[31] But ideological production in the late Soviet period is only now beginning to be explored.[32]

At stake in the investigation of Soviet ideology is the question of whether or not ideology mattered to the Soviet project and experience, and the picture that emerges suggests that by the late Soviet period, it largely did not. To be sure, by the Brezhnev era official ideology appeared ossified, with scientific atheism arguably the most stagnant dogma of all. Yet if we examine the debates within the ideological apparatus, which often took place behind closed doors, we get a different view. By revealing the architecture and internal logic of ideological production, this book suggests that ideology in general and atheism in particular mattered—even in the late Soviet period, when most Soviet people no longer took it seriously. Indeed, as this book shows, they mattered precisely *because* most Soviet people were indifferent to Soviet atheism as a worldview and Soviet Communism as an ideology, presenting the party with a serious political dilemma.

To return to the history of Soviet atheism, the three stories scholars have told about the relationship between ideology, religion, and atheism in the USSR—that the Soviet project was a political religion, failed utopia, or particular version of secular modernity—when taken separately are incomplete, and when taken together confirm, but do not illuminate, the transformations in Soviet approaches to religion and atheism. Without a doubt, these narratives highlight essential features of the Soviet project: the Soviet project was repressive from beginning to end, though the objects of repression changed; Soviet utopianism, including its atheist component, indeed failed if measured by the Soviet state's own definition of success; and the Soviet project did produce the kinds of secular institutions and subjects that make the Soviet state comparable to other modern states. Yet seeing these narratives as distinct rather than entangled stories masks the complexities and obscures the contradictions that, this book argues, are critical to understanding how the Soviet state approached its engagements with religion and atheism, and why these approaches changed over time. By examining how the Soviet state conceptualized and deployed "religion" and "atheism" in different historical contexts for different political, social, and cultural projects, this book unpacks the contradictions that shaped, and ultimately undermined, the coherence of Soviet Communism.

## *What Is Religion?*

The founders of Soviet Communism—Karl Marx (1818–83) and Vladimir Lenin (1870–1924)—did not write much about religion. What they did write was folded into the greater story of humanity's progress toward Communism. For Marx, history was the unfolding narrative of humanity's interaction with nature, and historical materialism—the philosophical foundation of Marxism—explicitly rejected religious explanations of historical development. Marx argued that whereas religion offered transcendent falsehoods to explain earthly misery, historical materialism unveiled the political, economic, and social origins underpinning the injustices of the existing order. "Once the other-world of truth has vanished," Marx wrote, the task of history was to "establish the truth of this world." Philosophy worked "in the service of history" to overcome human alienation and offer answers to the questions about life in this world. In this way, "the criticism of Heaven turns into the criticism of Earth, the criticism of religion into the criticism of law, and the criticism of theology into the criticism of politics."[33] But philosophy was not enough. As Marx put it, "The philosophers have only *interpreted* the world, in various ways; the point, however, is to *change* it."[34]

Marx did not so much reject religion as propose a new world in which religion was unnecessary. Religion, for Marx, was an early form of consciousness, and therefore a false consciousness.[35] As Marx put it, "Man makes religion, religion does not make man." Religion, therefore, was "the self-consciousness and self-feeling of man who has either not yet found himself or has lost himself again." It was a reflection of the world, and because the old world itself was "reversed," its reflection—religion—was "a reversed world-consciousness."[36] For the ruling classes, religion was a tool to subjugate the working masses. For the masses, it was, "at one and the same time, the *expression* of real suffering and a *protest* against real suffering," and therefore also a balm that alleviated their agony. It was "the sigh of the oppressed creature, the heart of a heartless world and the soul of soulless conditions," and in this sense—in Marx's famous formulation—"the opium of the people."[37] Yet in alleviating people's agony, religion blinded the masses to their own human dignity and agency. Once humanity became conscious of its true essence, it would discard religious illusions, since "to call on [the people] to give up their illusions about their condition is to call on them to *give up a condition that requires illusions.*" To abolish religion as the "*illusory* happiness of the people" was, in actuality, "the demand for their *real* happiness." By "discard[ing] his illusions," a person would "move around himself as his own true sun."[38] Communism, then, would bring an end to the economic misery and political injustice that lay at the heart of all conflict, alienation, and suffering—the social roots of religion—and create a just and harmonious world where the powerful could not oppress, and the people would have no need for an illusory balm to alleviate their pain.

In many ways, Marxism's dismissal of religion reflected a broader nineteenth-century optimism—embodied in the era's new ideologies in general and socialism in particular—about the liberating potential of science, especially as it could be applied to society. The new ideologies considered religion to be a philosophical framework for making sense of the world that reflected a specific stage of historical development. Science, however, had revealed that religion was no longer an adequate explanation of how the world works (nature) or how to live in harmony with others (culture). The emergence of the social sciences in the nineteenth century was intimately connected with a faith that they could explain how the world worked and humanity's place in it better than religion. These new sciences—from Auguste Comte's (1798–1857) positivism, to the "utopian socialism" of Charles Fourier (1772–1837) and Robert Owen (1771–1858), to the "scientific socialism" of Marx and Friedrich Engels (1820–95)—were not just political but also moral projects.[39] Comte saw positivism as a "religion of humanity" that could solve the problem of human conflict by figuring out a scientific—and hence rational—approach to achieving social harmony once and for all.[40] As Gareth Stedman Jones argues, "'Socialism' in its different varieties presented itself as the universal replacement for the old religions of the world built upon a new 'science'-based cosmology and a new ethical code," so that Marxism was "designed both to complete and replace Christianity."[41] For Marx and his followers, socialism was a new truth, a better answer to the world's questions, a better solution to social problems, and a better way for the individual to overcome alienation and achieve moral actualization. The problem with religion, then, was not that it claimed to offer universally true answers to life's questions. The problem was that it offered the wrong answers, which left humanity in a subjugated and alienated state.

In sum, Marx at the same time took religion seriously, since he saw the criticism of religion as "the premise of all criticism"—and not seriously enough, since he considered the criticism of religion as "in the main complete" and therefore not a problem that required further philosophical engagement.[42] As Marx and Engels—put it in the *Communist Manifesto*, "The charges against communism" made from a religious, philosophical, and, more generally, idealistic position were "not deserving of serious examination," since it did not "require deep intuition" to understand that consciousness was the product of material conditions.[43] The religious problem was, at its foundation, socioeconomic, and so was its solution.

Lenin was less concerned than Marx with religion as a philosophical or social phenomenon. His approaches to religion were above all dictated by political objectives. In "Socialism and Religion" (1905), his most developed statement on the subject, Lenin followed Marx in casting religion as a form of "spiritual oppression" that was "merely a product and reflection of the economic yoke within society."[44] Like Marx, Lenin decried the passivity fostered by the religious promise of heavenly reward, because it blinded the proletariat to its agency and thus the path to revolution. "Rather than being drowned in 'spiritual booze,'" Lenin wrote, "the slave should be conscious of his slavery and rise to struggle for his emancipation."[45] But Lenin made an important distinction between the state's and party's position on religion. He insisted on the secular separation of church and state as a necessary component of modernization: "Complete separation of church and state is what the socialist proletariat demands of the modern state and the modern church. . . . The Russian revolution must put this demand into effect as a necessary component of political freedom." He envisioned religious communities as "absolutely free associations of like-minded citizens, associations independent of the state." The state, in short, was to be indifferent to religion, so long as religion remained "a private affair."[46] Lenin juxtaposed the state's indifference to religion with the party's demand that party members not only reject religion but also profess atheist conviction. "So far as the party of the socialist proletariat is concerned," Lenin argued, "religion is not a private affair." The party was "an association of class-conscious, advanced fighters for the emancipation of the working class," and as such "cannot and must not be indifferent to lack of class-consciousness, ignorance or obscurantism in the shape of religious beliefs."[47]

Yet even as Lenin demanded strict ideological discipline of party members, he was, above all, concerned with politics and maintaining the party's hold on power. Though he allowed that "science can be enlisted in the battle against religion," he explicitly spoke out against repression and discrimination on religious grounds. Instead, he demanded that Bolsheviks help believers see through the "religious fog" with "purely ideological and solely ideological weapons." For Lenin, Marxism was an ideology grounded in reason, and he saw propaganda as the means for spreading Communism and bringing forth a world without religion. But propaganda was only an *aid* to the political revolution, which would, in transforming the economic and political base, in turn transform the social order as well as the people's consciousness and way of life. "No number of pamphlets and no amount of preaching can enlighten the proletariat, if it is not enlightened by its own struggle against the dark forces of capitalism," Lenin wrote. "Unity in this really revolutionary struggle of the oppressed class for the creation of a paradise on earth is more important to us than unity of proletarian opinion on paradise in heaven." The party, in Lenin's view, had to weigh the benefits of ideological purity against the imperative of expanding party ranks and securing political power. Indeed, Lenin instructed party members to avoid prioritizing the religious question, and not "allow the forces of the really revolutionary economic and political struggle to be split up on account of third-rate opinions or senseless ideas, *rapidly losing all political importance*, rapidly being swept up as rubbish by the very course of economic development."[48] The main task was making revolution in the name of Communism; once Communism was constructed, religion would simply wither away.

For Lenin, moreover, Communism was, emphatically, *not* a religion. In his polemic with the so-called God-builders—a group that included prominent Russian Marxists like Aleksandr Bogdanov (1873–1928), a member of the Central Committee of the Russian Social Democratic Workers' Party; the writer Maxim Gorky (1868–1936); and Anatolii Lunacharskii (1875–1933), the future head of the Soviet Commissariat of Enlightenment—Lenin denounced the effort to construct a socialist "religion of humanity" as a despicable "flirtation" with God (*koketnichan'e s bozhen'koi*).[49] As Lenin put it in his 1913 letter to Gorky, "God-seeking differs from God-creating or God-making and other things of the kind, much as a yellow devil differs from a blue." Since all religion, "however pure, ideal, or spontaneous," was an "ideological plague," any Bolshevik who "preached against God-seeking" by offering workers a socialist God was "prostitut[ing] himself in the worst way" and engaging in "necrophilia" (*trupolozhstvo*).[50] As Lenin saw it, the distinction between Communism and religion was not trivial. Whereas religion was an irrational illusion, Communism was a science grounded in reason; whereas religion appealed to the supernatural to reveal the wonders of the universe, Communism relied on materialism to explain the workings of nature; whereas religion turned to the transcendent to solve the problems of this world, Communism placed agency in the hands of people. Communism was not a religion, form of politics, or philosophy because it transcended religion, politics, and philosophy, and transformed the world in its totality through revolution.

## *What Is Atheism?*

As faithful Marxists-Leninists, the Bolsheviks did not anticipate religion to be a serious obstacle to their project of revolutionary transformation. They understood, of course, that seizing political power would not immediately transform society, but they had faith in the Marxist model of historical development according to which religion would inevitably wither away. From the outset, however, there was a distinct tension between the Bolsheviks as Marxists committed to atheism, and the Bolsheviks as modernizers for whom secularization was a central tool for building a modern state. Whereas the Bolshevik Party Charter required an atheist conviction of party members, Lenin's first goal, following the Bolshevik seizure of power, was to establish a secular state in which religion was separate from politics, education, economics, medicine, and the law. Lenin saw the old regime's confessional order as a feudal holdover that underscored Russia's backwardness vis-à-vis Europe. For Lenin, the new order had to become secular (and therefore modern) before it could become atheist (and therefore Communist). The consolidation of political power and construction of a socialist economic base were the preconditions for the creation of a modern Communist order.

But what of atheism? If Marx and Lenin wrote little about religion, they wrote even less about atheism—largely because they considered it unimportant to the revolutionary unfolding of history. For both Marx and Lenin, religion had no autonomous power: since it was part of the "superstructure," its existence depended on the economic and political "base" that nourished it. Without the capitalist foundation and religious institutions that exploited the masses in its service, religion would simply disappear—along with private property, class divisions, the family, and the entire bourgeois capitalist edifice. Neither Marx nor Lenin ascribed much significance to atheism as a philosophical position, since appeals to reason could have no effect on the masses as long as they were trapped in miserable conditions and blinded by religious illusions.[51] Only eliminating the socioeconomic roots of those conditions that required illusions would lead the masses to atheism. Atheism, then, was always the product of Communism; it did not produce it.

How, then, did the Bolsheviks imagine the disappearance of religion and arrival of atheism after the revolution? In theory, the Bolshevik understanding of religion and atheism in the new Communist order was remarkably simple. In his book *How Gods and Goddesses Are Born, Live, and Die* (1923), Emelian Iaroslavskii (1878–1943)—who, as the founder of the League of the Militant Godless and editor of the journal *Bezbozhnik* (*Godless*), became the leading Bolshevik voice of Soviet atheism—saw atheism as the final chapter in the story people told themselves about the world and their place in it. Following the nineteenth-century German philosopher Ludwig Feuerbach (1804–72), whose anthropological conception of religion was also the basis of Marx's thinking, Iaroslavskii argued that religion always had "earthly roots," and deities were simply the reflection of the human communities that produced them. As communities became more complex, so did their stories, which also reflected their more advanced stage of development. For this reason, different peoples across the world without direct contact with each other (but in comparable stages of development) produced similar gods. Iaroslavskii posited that whereas in its early history humanity had trembled in ignorance at nature's power and created gods to make sense of and tame the elements, soon the time would come when humanity would recognize itself as the ultimate source of authority, and then it would no longer need to populate the heavens with powerful supernatural deities. Just as "there was a time when people did not know any religion," Iaroslavskii explained, "now the time has come when millions of people are breaking with religion and rejecting it."[52] Religion, then, was not eternal or transcendent but instead the product of history. It had been born, lived through its historical stage, and under Communism would die.

What became clear after the October Revolution was that religion was not going to die a natural death. The unfolding of history would require the active involvement of the Bolshevik Party. The Bolsheviks understood religion as a phenomenon that consisted of three components: the political, grounded in religious institutions; the ideological, embodied in a false worldview based on the belief in the supernatural; and the spiritual, encompassed in the values, practices, and customs that made up the ineffable dimension of everyday life, or *byt*.[53] The party's engagements with religion reflected this understanding. To address religion as a political phenomenon, the party deployed a militant anticlerical approach that used administrative regulation and political repression to circumscribe the autonomy of religious institutions, marginalize religion in public life, and undermine its political power. To address religion as an ideological problem, the party relied on propaganda, education, and enlightenment to inculcate a scientific materialist worldview. Finally, to address religion as a spiritual problem, it used the tools of cultural revolution to transform traditional ways of life into the new Communist byt (*novyi kommunisticheskii byt*).

At the same time, relying on Marxist-Leninist theory to make sense of how and why Soviet approaches to religion and atheism changed over time obscures the specific historical circumstances in which the party had to make decisions and form policies. While it is a truism to say that the Communist revolution did not come with a blueprint, it is nevertheless worth underscoring that the Soviet project had to work out its relationship to religion and atheism not just in theory but also in history. Marx was dead, Lenin died in 1924, but the Soviet project endured for another seven decades. Marxism-Leninism constituted the conceptual framework through which Soviet atheists made sense of religion, but they were also influenced by their own experiences with religion on the ground. As history moved forward and the revolution receded ever farther into the past, Soviet atheists had to figure out how Marxism-Leninism could help them answer the questions and solve the problems of their immediate reality, which remained contradictory and imperfect.

Over the course of the Soviet period, the party's three conceptions of religion—as politics, ideology, and spiritual culture—coexisted, but not without tensions and contradictions. In part, this was because Soviet priorities changed over time, and in part it was because Soviet power managed religion and atheism through different institutions, which operated according to their own distinct logics. Indeed, behind its monolithic façade, Soviet power was a complex edifice comprising party, government, security, and cultural organizations. The party's mandate was to guide the political development of the Soviet project according to Marxist-Leninist ideology, as well as to cultivate political discipline and ideological consciousness among party cadres, and the Soviet masses more broadly. The task of the government bureaucracy was to execute the will of the party through the state's administrative apparatus. The charge of the security organs was to police political and ideological orthodoxy in order to protect the system from internal and external enemies. The work of cultural institutions was to shape Soviet society by cultivating enlightened, rational, and disciplined subjects.

Each of these institutional frameworks—party, government, security, and culture—had different objectives when it came to religion and atheism, and different strategies for achieving those goals. The party's ultimate goal, made explicit in its charter, was to produce an atheist society free of religion. The task of government organs—most prominently, the government councils on religious affairs—was to manage the relationship between religious institutions and the state, as well as to manage religion on the ground using legal and administrative means.[54] The task of security organs was to neutralize opposition, which included religious organizations and believers perceived to be anti-Soviet through extralegal means, including terror.[55] But the primary focus of this book is on the cultural organizations that managed both the theoretical and practical aspects of atheist work. Concentrating on the theoretical side of atheist production were institutions such as the Leningrad State Museum of Religion and Atheism (Gosudarstvennyi muzei istorii religii i ateizma, or GMIRA), founded in 1931; the departments of Scientific Atheism created in the country's top universities and institutes under Khrushchev; and, after its establishment in 1964, the Institute of Scientific Atheism (Institut nauchnogo ateizma, or INA) of the Central Committee's Academy of Social Sciences (Akademiia obshchestvennykh nauk pri TsK KPSS, or AON). The practical work of disseminating atheism fell to enlightenment organizations such as the League of the Militant Godless (Soiuz voinstvennykh bezbozhnikov), which functioned from 1925 until 1941, and the Society for the Dissemination of Political and Scientific Knowledge (Obshchestvo po rasprostraneniiu politicheskikh i nauchnykh znanii, or Znanie), which was established in 1947 in part to take over the atheist work of the league. In pursuing their distinct objectives, these institutions often worked against each other, and sometimes even against broader Soviet aims. Even if party, government, security, and cultural organizations had the same overarching goal—building Soviet Communism—they had different priorities. Their specific objectives—ideological purity, effective governance, neutralizing opposition, and cultural transformation—competed with one another, which made Soviet engagements with religion and atheism inconsistent, and frequently counterproductive to the success of the Soviet project.

Finally, it is worth noting that when the party used "religion" as a general term, it was often implicitly speaking about Orthodox Christianity and the Russian Orthodox Church. This was both because Orthodox Christianity was the majority confession, constituting about 70 percent of the population at the turn of the century, and because of the deep historic ties between the Orthodox Church and the Russian state.[56] Other religious groups—Muslims, Jews, Baptists, Buddhists, Catholics, or any of the numerous other religious confessions present in the USSR—were typically named explictly. Much as Russians were the Soviet Union's unmarked ethnic group, Russian Orthodoxy was the unmarked religion.[57] This is significant because it informed the logic of Soviet atheism's internal development, leading Soviet atheists, for example, to shift attention from combatting the church and its dogma to replacing religious rites and rituals—a sphere that is particularly significant in Orthodox Christianity, but considerably less so in many of the USSR's other confessions. Because of the centrality of Russian Orthodoxy to the party's engagements with religion and atheism, critical themes—specifically, the connection between religion and nationalism inside the USSR, and the role of religion in the international context, especially during the Cold War—are less prominent in this book, though they are, of course, ever-present in the Soviet Union's history.

## *Communism's Calling Card*

*A Sacred Space Is Never Empty* begins by tracing how the Bolsheviks approached religion under Lenin and Stalin, from the revolution in 1917 until

Stalin's death in 1953, using legal and administrative regulation, extralegal repression and terror, and militant atheist propaganda. It argues that against the background of the Bolsheviks' claims about building a new world, remaking society, and transforming human nature, religion remained, in the early Soviet period, above all a political problem. While in theory militant atheism was considered an important weapon on the religious front, in practice it consistently remained secondary to other objectives: political consolidation, economic modernization, and social stability. Religion mattered to the Bolsheviks inasmuch as it constituted a threat to Soviet power, and by the end of the 1930s—with the political power of the Orthodox Church as an institution nearly destroyed—they believed that threat to have been effectively neutralized. From this point, the continued existence of religion in the Soviet Union would be on the state's terms. Stalin set those terms in 1943, when his wartime reversal on the religious question and creation of a government bureaucracy to manage religious affairs formalized a new framework for Soviet engagements with religion that remained in place for the rest of the Soviet period. Stalin's last decade in power was a period of relative stability on the religious front, whereas the decline of political support for atheism made it largely invisible in public life.

The book then follows how the revolution's promise to remake the world mapped onto the revolution's "second act," when, following Stalin's death, Khrushchev sought to place the Soviet project on new foundations by announcing that the USSR had entered the new stage of "Building Communism." For Khrushchev, political de-Stalinization, economic modernization, and ideological mobilization were all part of the effort to return revolutionary vitality to Marxist-Leninist ideology. Communism's arrival, Khrushchev proclaimed, was imminent; the "grandchildren" of the revolution—the young people coming of age in the 1960s—would live to see it. Yet religion remained a stain on Soviet modernity, an alien ideology inside Soviet Communism. Since religion remained a fact of Soviet life, and since Khrushchev, a true Communist, believed it to be fundamentally incompatible with Communism, atheism returned to Soviet life. Under Khrushchev, the party mobilized an extensive antireligious campaign, closing nearly half the country's religious spaces, instituting repressive constraints on the autonomy of religious organizations and clergy, and investing unprecedented resources into creating a centralized atheist apparatus. Moreover, Soviet atheism was redefined: since religious institutions were now considered politically loyal and even patriotic, religion became an ideological problem, a "survival" to be eradicated from Soviet consciousness through enlightenment. In the Khrushchev era, then, the militant atheism of the early Soviet period was renounced in favor of a scientific atheism.

In the Brezhnev era, the continued failure of religion to "die out," even after the party's best efforts to hurry the process along with antireligious measures, forced atheists to confront the complex reality of lived religiosity, and to reconsider their definition of religion and approaches to atheist work—again. The atheist apparatus had to recognize that even if, in theory, Communism embraced individual life from the cradle to the grave, what this meant in practice—in Soviet lived experience—still remained unclear. In the late Soviet period, atheists increasingly came to see religion not just as a political and ideological problem but also as a spiritual problem. They believed that this lived religion, deeply embedded in worldviews and ways of life, could be overcome only with a spiritual atheism that addressed not just institutions and beliefs but also morality, emotions, aesthetics, rituals, and community experience. While initially the Soviet definition of atheism was simply what was left once the gods were chased out, the atheist apparatus came to realize that it had to move beyond a negative definition and produce a positive atheism that could fill the empty space left behind.

But the paradox of Soviet atheism is that despite its centrality to Communism in theory, in practice it was never clear what it was, how important it was, or who exactly was in charge of defining it and spreading it to the masses. As unwitting caretakers of the Soviet soul, Soviet atheists found themselves continuously searching for new answers to the religious question. In the process, Soviet Communism's battle *against* religion came to be seen as a battle *for* atheism. In this sense, Soviet Communism tried to transform atheism into its opposite: a set of positive beliefs and practices with a coherent spiritual center.

Atheism, at its core, rejects the idea that transcendent or supernatural forces have power over the natural world. In the Soviet context, atheism underpinned Communism's most radical and utopian premise: the promise that humanity could master the world, and that injustice and evil could be overcome in this life rather than the next. But Soviet atheism was also about power, a tool for undermining competing sources of political, ideological, and spiritual authority—political institutions that were not the Communist Party, ideologies that were not Marxism-Leninism, communities that were not the Soviet people, and ways of life that were not the Soviet way of life. In contesting competing claims to truth and authority, Soviet Communism assumed the burden of providing its own answers to life's questions and solutions to life's problems. In this way, atheism became the battleground on which Soviet Communism engaged with the existential concerns at the heart of human existence: the meaning of life and death.

Soviet atheism's effort to compete with and ultimately transcend religion sheds light on how Soviet Communism framed the battle between the old and the new, and how this conception shaped approaches to winning Soviet minds, hearts, and souls. This book, then, is about how the party discovered that it had to become a church and the revolutionary attempt to turn an ideology into a religion—not just in theory, but also in history. Following the particular meanings and functions of atheism through Soviet history makes visible the broader significance of atheism to Soviet Communism. Atheism was Communism's "calling card" because it was the precondition for its arrival: a testament of individual conviction in Communism's political, ideological, and spiritual truth and authority. If atheist conviction did not fill the sacred space of Soviet Communism, the commitment of Soviet citizens to Communism would remain provisional, and the Soviet project incomplete.

CHAPTER ONE

# The Religious Front

## MILITANT ATHEISM UNDER LENIN AND STALIN

ON THE EVE of the 1917 revolution, the Russian imperial autocracy was an Orthodox Christian state mapped onto a multiconfessional empire. It covered a sixth of the world's landmass, and its more than 130 million subjects included Orthodox Christians, Muslims, Jews, Buddhists, Catholics, Lutherans, and various Protestant confessions as well as followers of numerous indigenous traditions. To govern this large and diverse population, the imperial autocracy relied on what historian Paul Werth calls the "multiconfessional establishment," using religious institutions to extend its reach—both out to the borders of the expanding empire and deeper into the lives of ordinary subjects whose worlds remained far from the center of tsarist authority.[1] Through religious institutions, the state projected its power, unified its diverse peoples, governed its growing number of "foreign" confessions, and disciplined individual morality.[2] The Orthodox Church had a privileged place at the top of the empire's confessional hierarchy and had historically performed an essential political role for the Russian state alongside its spiritual mission, providing transcendent legitimation for the tsar's earthly authority. Orthodoxy's position as the first among equals was formalized in the middle of the nineteenth century with "Official Nationality," a tripartite ideological formula for imperial power that encompassed Orthodoxy (*pravoslavie*); autocracy (*samoderzhavie*); and nationality (*narodnost'*), a term that implies that the people's "nation-mindedness," encompassed in their obedience to the tsar and devotion to the Orthodox Church.[3] In short, religion—and Orthodoxy in particular—was doing a lot of work for the old regime.

Whereas the Russian autocracy was an Orthodox Christian state mapped onto a multiconfessional empire, the Bolsheviks were an atheist party that sought to create a modern secular state to build a new Communist order. To do this, the Bolsheviks first had to deal with the institutions, ideologies, and cultural frameworks that they inherited from imperial Russia, and displace religion from the center of politics, ideology, society, culture, and everyday life. Once in power, the Bolsheviks used different channels to turn their vision into reality, from education, enlightenment, and cultural reforms to administrative regulation, political repression, and terror and violence. Yet despite their antireligious sloganeering at home and the image of godless atheism that quickly spread beyond Soviet borders, the immediate reality was that the Bolsheviks had neither a systematic approach to managing religion nor a clear consensus about the nature and purpose of atheism in the Soviet project. Rather than being guided by a coherent vision of atheism's role in forging the new Communist world, Soviet policies were improvised, dictated by competing objectives, and constrained by the political and social realities on the ground. In their drive to preserve the revolution and consolidate power, the Bolsheviks often had to choose between ideological purity or effective governance, cultural revolution or social stability. The question of how the Bolshevik Party's commitment to atheism should shape Soviet engagements with religion remained without a definitive answer long after the revolution, producing the oscillations and contradictions that shaped political, social, and spiritual life under Lenin and Stalin.

## *The Old World*

For Russia, the story of the "old world" begins in 988, with the Baptism of Rus'. According to the *Primary Chronicle* the "land of Rus'" came into being when Grand Prince Vladimir's adoption of Christianity unified his lands and peoples. Before 988, Vladimir had already tried to build a pantheon to the multiple pagan gods of the eastern Slavs living in his realm in an effort to consolidate power, but when the pantheon failed to do this political work, Vladimir turned to the monotheistic faiths of his neighbors. In 986, the story goes, he received emissaries from the Muslim Bulgars of the Volga, the Jews of Khazaria, the Western Christians of Rome, and the Eastern Christians of Constantinople. Impressed by what he heard about Constantinople, Vladimir sent his own emissaries to Byzantium, who, upon their return, reported that Constantinople's St. Sophia Cathedral was so magnificent that they "did not know whether we were in heaven or earth."[4] Vladimir became a Christian, destroyed the pagan pantheon, and forcibly baptized his people. And so, in 988, the land of the Rus' became Christian, and in becoming Christian, it became a state with a history.

The story of the Baptism of Rus' is as much about the consolidation of political power as it is about spiritual salvation. From the beginning, Russian statehood and political identity were inextricably connected with Orthodox Christianity. In part, this was because of growing tensions between the Latin West and the Byzantine East, which eventually split Christendom in the Great

Schism of 1054. Kievan Rus', which had been converted not long before, remained under the authority of Byzantium. Byzantium declined over the next two centuries, and compromised with the Latin Church by recognizing papal authority at the 1438 Council of Florence, in exchange for assistance against the Ottoman threat. The Orthodox Church in Russia, unwilling to make the same compromise, became de facto independent of the Byzantine Church.[5] When Constantinople fell in 1453, Muscovite Russia positioned itself as the only politically independent Orthodox state, which endowed Muscovite ideology with considerable political capital. As Muscovy consolidated political power, the Orthodox Church too became more assertive, establishing its own patriarchate in 1589. The relationship between church and state, then, was reciprocal. Just as the Orthodox Church depended on the Russian state to defend its ecclesiastical autonomy, the Russian state depended on Orthodoxy for its political legitimacy. The theoretical foundation of Russia's statehood was formulated by ecclesiastical writers, and the authority of the Orthodox ruler was grounded in his ability to protect and defend the true faith. Russian rulers, therefore, depended on Orthodoxy for its symbolic investment of the political order with sacred meaning.

The thread that runs through Russian history is that Russia's salvation rests in power, and, more specifically, in the state's capacity to contain two perennial threats to its territorial and cultural sovereignty: domestic disunity and foreign occupation. A strong state—or, perhaps more importantly, the image of a strong state—was considered essential to this enterprise. Russian history is punctuated by political salvation from recurring crises. Indeed, the Romanov dynasty, which ruled Russia for more than three hundred years, was founded in 1613 in the aftermath of the "Time of Troubles," a period when political disunity and social disintegration opened the state to foreign invasion. It was under the threat of being ruled by a Polish (and Catholic) prince that the Orthodox Church and the Muscovite political elite came together to elect the first Romanov tsar, Mikhail Fedorovich (r. 1613–45), after decades of political infighting. Young and pious—he was only sixteen when he became tsar—Mikhail was dominated by his father, Feodor Nikitich Romanov (c. 1544–1633), who became, in 1619, Filaret, Patriarch of the Church. The origin of Russia's old regime, then, lay in the shared power of church and state.

Russia's old regime was a traditional political order: the ruler was autocratic, and the people were subjects, not citizens. At the same time, beginning with the rule of Tsar Peter the Great (r. 1682–1725), the Russian imperial autocracy became part of a broader European process that saw the rise and consolidation of the state. To mobilize resources and govern most effectively, the early modern European state enlisted the church as a partner in the project of disciplining its subjects. Peter's vision of a rational state placed Russia within this broader European pattern,[6] and like elsewhere in Europe, the political consolidation of the imperial Russian state was carried out at the expense of religious authority. The Russian state's precarious grasp on power and tenuous reach into local governance meant that it always saw the church as both an ally and threat—a competing authority that could both support and undermine the state. Peter, growing up in the wake of the Old Believers schism that marked the tumultuous rule of his father, Tsar Aleksei Mikhailovich (r. 1645–76), had witnessed the devastation that competing centers of authority could inflict, and believed that the consolidation of state power depended on the state's ability to incorporate the church into the work of government. With his church reforms, Peter placed the church under the oversight of the Holy Synod, a new government body headed by a layperson. This strengthened the bureaucratic and political reach of the state by institutionalizing the record keeping of births, marriages, and deaths (to be carried out through local parishes), disciplining "superstition," making annual confession mandatory, and obligating the clergy to report the content of confession if it was construed as a political threat.[7] Indeed, from the perspective of an autocrat governing a geographically vast and confessionally diverse land, the work of defining and regulating correct conduct was far too important to be left outside the state's authority.[8] Indeed, as Viktor Zhivov argues, "Peter did not aspire to any form of revived piety. In general, for Russian rulers discipline was immeasurably more important than any kind of religious values."[9] But the purpose of Peter's church reforms was not just to place the political authority of the state above that of the church; it was to appropriate the church's spiritual charisma. Indeed, the primary value of Orthodoxy, for Peter, was its ability to buttress state ideology. As Vera Shevzov notes, Peter's Spiritual Regulation (1721) was intended to make clear to his subjects—who "imagine[d] that such a [church] administrator is a second Sovereign, a power equal to that of the Autocrat, or even greater than he"—the distinction between political and spiritual authority, and primacy of the former over the latter.[10] During the imperial period, then, the Russian state and Orthodox Church worked, in the words of Nadieszda Kizenko, "hand in hand," both governing the people and directing their spiritual salvation.[11]

The autocracy reached its apogee during the reign of Tsar Nicholas I (r. 1825–55), but before long, Tsar Alexander II's (r. 1855–81) Great Reforms of the 1860s, in the spheres of jurisprudence, economy, military, and education, began to strain Russia's traditional order.[12] Perhaps the most significant reform undertaken by the imperial autocracy was the emancipation of the serfs in 1861, which gave Russia's peasants new freedoms, including the right to move in search of better opportunities. By the end of the nineteenth century, Russia's economic transformation, and industrialization in particular, meant that these opportunities were concentrated in the empire's urban centers. As peasants moved to the cities and became workers, their worlds expanded beyond the village, with the factory and the new urban culture they encountered beyond it shaping their worldviews. In the city, these new workers also encountered modern politics and the revolutionary intelligentsia, who organized political "circles" to make workers conscious of their misery and teach them what they could do to better their lot.[13]

At the same time, even as the empire modernized, much that was customary persisted, including religious culture. Indeed, the concept of religion—in the modern definition of the term, as something grounded in belief that happened in a specially designated time and space—would have remained unfamiliar for most people. Rather than being relegated to a distinct sphere, religion extended far beyond the church and its dogma. Religion remained at the core of politics, bureaucracy, culture, and education, and continued to be embedded in the places and practices of everyday life, ordering space and time, separating work and rest, shaping communal bonds around a shared history, and forming the foundation of individual and group identity. Through religion, communities came together to make pilgrimages, celebrate feasts, observe fasts, and mark births, marriages, and deaths. Religion was less about belief than about experience, encompassing values and customs that most simply took for granted.[14] Even as the links between the worker and the village grew weaker, they rarely disappeared.

By the beginning of the twentieth century, under imperial Russia's last ruler, Tsar Nicholas II (r. 1894–1917), the autocratic order was breaking down under the pressures of modernization. During the revolution of 1905, the people's political demands forced the tsar to concede certain civil rights and political freedoms, including religious toleration, which made it legal for individuals to leave the Orthodox Church.[15] In this newly pluralistic religious marketplace, the Orthodox Church, the established church, found it difficult to compete with confessions that had control over their own affairs.[16] This was especially the case with regard to the various "sects" that were becoming more numerous and vocal.[17] At the same time, religion was so central to the political, social, and cultural framework of the empire that even liberal reformers were wary of placing the Russian state on secular foundations—both administratively, by establishing a secular bureaucracy, and ideologically, by fully institutionalizing the "freedom of conscience" promised by the tsar in his October Manifesto.[18] Indeed, the Edict of Toleration underscored the contradictions of the modernizing autocracy, since it fell short of true freedom of conscience by only permitting conversion to (but not away from) Christian confessions, and not allowing for confessionlessness or unbelief.[19]

Russian statesmen also worried that without religion as a foundation, the growing chasm between the state and people—who, in the state's view, remained superstitious, irrational, and thus potentially subversive and ungovernable—would become unbridgeable. Conservative officials feared that removing religion from the political and ideological foundation of the imperial order would lead to atheism, and atheism would bring about moral collapse and undermine the state. But even liberal reformers committed to freedom of conscience in principle acknowledged that the Russian state lacked the bureaucratic capacity to do without the multiconfessional establishment. Finally, for much of the revolutionary intelligentsia, the intimate relationship between the Russian autocratic state and Orthodox Church made the latter, and religion more broadly, into the enemy of all that was good, just, and enlightened. Atheism, which, as Victoria Frede argues, had not been "thinkable" even among the educated elite in the early nineteenth century, had become by the twentieth century a means of asserting moral and political autonomy in opposition to both the church and state.[20]

In the period between the Great Reforms and the Bolshevik Revolution, then, Russia's traditional order came to be burdened with many contradictions. The regime was faced with the proliferation of new sects and "foreign" faiths, mounting demands for civil rights by an increasingly urban and educated population, and new conceptions of religion as a matter of individual conscience rather than group belonging—all of which clashed with the autocracy's continued reliance on the political, ideological, and administrative functions of religion. Modernization strained the autocratic regime and presented it with questions and problems that it could not afford to ignore. Nevertheless, until the end, the tsar continued to see his people as subjects rather than citizens. The people, however, increasingly understood themselves beyond the traditional categories of estate and confession, identifying as members of ethnic and national groups and classes, as well as individuals endowed with freedoms and rights.

This, then, was the political, social, and cultural landscape that the Bolsheviks inherited when they seized power in October 1917.

## *The Bolsheviks as Leninists*

The Marxist-Leninist framework within which the Bolsheviks understood religion followed a clear telos. Since religion was considered to be the product of oppressive political structures and unjust economic relations, the revolution could not be considered complete until religion was exorcized from the body politic. Marx believed that religion would disappear of its own accord with the eradication of the political and economic base in which it was rooted. Engels added to this an emphasis on scientific enlightenment, which would cure the people of false and primitive ideas about the world. Lenin's emphasis on the vanguard role of the Bolshevik Party demanded of every Bolshevik an active struggle against religion in all its forms—although, like Marx, he advocated against offending religious feelings, since doing so could turn passive believers into active counterrevolutionaries. For the Bolsheviks, overcoming religion was a process: religious institutions had to be neutralized before religious beliefs could be eradicated, and worldviews had to be freed from religious beliefs before everyday life could be transformed. The first step, then, was to solve religion as a political problem.

Following the October Revolution, the Bolsheviks found themselves surrounded by hostile powers abroad and embroiled in a civil war at home (1917–21), and their first priority was to stay in power. For Lenin, the success of the revolution depended on the modernization of the state, and he considered the subjugation of religion to state authority to be an essential component of a modern political order. As he argued in "Religion and Socialism" (1905), only the secularization of religion would "bring an end to [Russia's] shameful and cursed past, wherein the church was enserfed to the state, and the people were enserfed to the state church. . . . The full separation of the church from the state—this is what the socialist proletariat demands of the modern state and the modern church."[21] Following this logic, the Bolsheviks, immediately passed a series of decrees to establish the foundations for a modern secular state. The "Decree on Land" (October 26, 1917) nationalized all monastic and church land.[22] Another decree, "On Civil Marriage, Children, and on the Registration of Acts of Civil Status" (December 18, 1917), created a secular bureaucracy—the office for the registration of acts of civil status (Zapis' aktov grazhdanskogo sostoianiia, or ZAGS)—to take over the registration of births, marriages, deaths, and divorces from religious institutions.[23] Finally, a third decree, "On the Separation of Church from State and School from Church" (January 23, 1918), deprived religious organizations of their status as juridical entities and removed religion from government and education.[24] Besides disenfranchising the church, the Bolsheviks also took the administration and control of religious life out of the clergy's hands. No longer allowed to own property, parishes now had to lease church buildings from the state. The clergy became employees of the parish "twenties" (*dvadsatki*), groups of lay parishioners that registered as a religious congregation and administered parish affairs. Together, these measures dramatically reduced the autonomy of religious institutions and made the state the final authority over religious life.

For the Bolsheviks, what was at stake in the secularization of the state was, above all, the removal of religion from politics and public life. The 1918 Soviet Constitution endowed the individual with "freedom of conscience," defined as the right to profess any religion or none at all, as well as the right to fulfill religious "needs," defined as liturgical. Soviet law also stipulated that the activities of government and social organizations could no longer to be accompanied by public religious rituals or ceremonies, and private rituals could be performed only "inasmuch as they do not disturb the social order and did not infringe on the rights of citizens of the Soviet republic."[25] Atheism, however, had no restrictions on its entry into the public sphere. Religion thus became something that happened on the margins—within an individual, in private, and in a distinct time and space—whereas atheism was cast as the normative center of the new Soviet order.

At the same time, Lenin was a politician, and he understood that the party's prospects for turning Communism into reality depended on its ability not just to make a revolution but also to stay in power. If in theory Bolshevik approaches to religion were shaped by ideological tenets, in practice they were determined by immediate priorities and exigencies. The Bolsheviks took religion seriously when it posed a political threat, and since the Orthodox Church presented the most serious threat to Soviet power, their first priority was to neutralize its influence.[26] Whereas the Bolsheviks could dismiss private religiosity as a sign of cultural backwardness doomed to extinction, they saw in the Orthodox Church a powerful institution with symbolic and material capital that could be transformed into a political weapon, fomenting religious opposition abroad and mobilizing religious activism at home. The Bolsheviks—not without reason—feared that the Orthodoxy could transform private religiosity into public action.

Bolshevik policies, therefore, did not have the same impact on all confessions. Whereas they drastically limited the privileges to which the Orthodox Church, as the established church of the old regime, had grown accustomed, they granted other confessions new rights. The Bolsheviks understood that while their hold on power was precarious, they could not afford to alienate those who could help them liberate political and social life from Orthodox influence. Indeed, to weaken the Orthodox Church, the party was willing to forge alliances with those religious groups that had been persecuted under the imperial autocracy. Sectarians, for example, initially found the new order more congenial than the old regime.[27] This was partly due to Lenin's affinity for Russian sectarians, whom he saw as hardworking, rational, collective minded, and sober. Their religious dissent, Lenin wrote in 1899, was not the typical "Russian revolt, pointless and merciless" (*russkii bunt, bessmyslennyi i bezposhchadnyi*) but rather political protest voiced in a religious idiom.[28] Vladimir Bonch-Bruevich (1873–1955)—the godfather of Bolshevik atheism and himself a historian of religious sectarianism—presented sectarians as potential allies whose discontent could be channeled to support the revolutionary cause.[29] The Bolsheviks were also reluctant to pursue militant antireligious policies in the borderlands, where religion was intimately connected with nationalism, since they were mindful of exacerbating already volatile separatist movements. Therefore, even if the Bolsheviks considered religion in general to be a tool for the exploitation of the proletarian masses, their early antireligious measures were aimed above all at the Orthodox Church.

The party's support of reformers within the Orthodox Church was another temporary strategy intended to divide and undermine the church. The revolution had deepened internal divisions between Orthodox reformers and conservatives, which had been brewing for decades and had come to the surface during the Church Council of 1917–18.[30] The anathema on the Bolsheviks and excommunication of the "open and secret enemies of the church" issued by Patriarch Tikhon (Belavin) on January 18, 1918, only sharpened this division.[31] Whereas Orthodox conservatives denounced cooperation with the Bolsheviks, Orthodox reformers, the Renovationists (*Obnovlentsy*), viewed reforms as a necessary step in what they believed to be a much-needed modernization of Orthodoxy and saw the potential for common ground with the new regime. The Bolsheviks, eager to manipulate these internal divisions, supported the Renovationists in the early 1920s.[32]

During the Civil War, as the Bolsheviks fought for survival, they put aside their commitment to secular norms and turned to extralegal measures against those they perceived to be hostile to Soviet power. In February 1922, they used the devastating famine produced by Bolshevik economic policies—which claimed close to seven million lives—to engage the church in an open conflict by demanding that it give up property to be sold for famine relief.[33] Recognizing the vulnerability of the church, Patriarch Tikhon agreed to cooperate, but the Bolsheviks found his stipulation that the church would be in charge of the relief efforts unacceptable. However, as Bolsheviks began to requisition church property by force, they were met with resistance from locals unwilling to turn over sacred objects. This conflict over the requisition of church valuables came at a moment when Soviet power was especially precarious. Not only had the civil war devastated the countryside and strained urban infrastructure, leading to outbreaks of famine, crime, and disease, but the Bolsheviks were also losing their social base—a fact painfully revealed by the uprising of the Kronstadt sailors in 1921.

For Lenin, popular resistance to Bolshevik attempts to confiscate church valuables was intolerable—not because it actually managed to stop the requisitions (it did not), but because it mobilized the masses against Bolshevik power. Behind this resistance, Lenin saw the work of the clergy, which meant that the church was no longer just a reactionary force but also an active agent of counterrevolution, and therefore a political actor. In a secret letter written to the Bolshevik Politburo on March 19, 1922, Lenin announced that the Soviet regime was declaring a "ruthless battle against the black-hundreds clergy" (*besposhchadnoe srazhenie chernosotennomu dukhovenstvu*), and opined that "the greater number of representatives of the reactionary clergy and reactionary bourgeoisie we manage to shoot on this basis the better."[34] Lenin's letter—unknown during the Soviet period, and published only in 1990—set off a new militant phase in the Bolsheviks' war against religion.

Yet even as Lenin cast the church and clergy as political enemies that needed to be neutralized, he continued to caution against aggressive antireligious agitation among the masses, which he warned would politicize the religious question. Shortly before sending his letter, Lenin had written "On the Meaning of Militant Materialism," an essay that has come to be regarded as his "philosophical testament," in which he wrote that even though the party had seized power, the revolution would fall without allies outside party ranks.[35] "One of the biggest mistakes made by Communists," Lenin declared, "is the idea that a revolution can be made by revolutionaries alone."[36] At the same time, he pointed to the danger that many among the non-Bolshevik intelligentsia were apologists for religion and other "prejudices of bourgeois reaction."[37] To "expose and indict" these "overeducated lackeys of clericalism" (*diplomirovannykh lakeev popovshchiny*), Lenin called for the liberation of the masses from religious darkness through the preaching of militant materialism.[38] To reach the "millions of people . . . who have been condemned by all modern society to darkness, ignorance, and superstition," Bolsheviks had to use any available tool and method, especially atheist literature and the natural sciences. "It would be the biggest and most grievous mistake a Marxist could make to think [that the masses] can extricate themselves from this darkness only through a purely Marxist education."[39] Instead, the masses had to be enlightened with "the most varied atheist propaganda material [and] approached this way and that, so as to get them interested, to wake them from their religious slumber, to shake them from every possible angle and using any possible method."[40] Together, these two documents—Lenin's letter calling for an assault against the clergy and his article advocating militant materialism as a tool of enlightenment—capture Lenin's thinking about religion and atheism and provide the context for the turn away from the passive secular approaches adopted immediately after the revolution toward a more militant atheism.

For the Bolsheviks, the campaign to requisition religious property also had the benefit of sowing deeper divisions within the church, since Patriarch Tikhon's opposition to the requisitions gave the Renovationists the opportunity to depose him. In April 1922, Tikhon was arrested and held at the Donskoi Monastery, and the Bolsheviks openly backed the Renovationists. The Orthodox laity was likewise divided on Soviet power, with many choosing to go underground into the "catacombs" rather than recognize the authority of the Renovationists.[41] After Tikhon's death in 1925 and the Bolsheviks' abolition of the patriarchate in 1926, the question that faced Orthodoxy was whether the future of the faith lay in the underground church or compromise with Soviet power, which now looked like it was there to stay. In 1927, Metropolitan Sergii (Stragorodskii), the guardian of the vacant patriarchal throne and acting head of the church, issued an open declaration of loyalty to the Soviet state. In it, he joined the fate of the Orthodox Church to that of the Soviet project, stating, "We want to be Orthodox, and at the same time to acknowledge the Soviet Union as our civic Motherland, whose joys and successes are also ours, and whose woes are our woes."[42] Sergii's profession of loyalty to Soviet power granted Orthodoxy a limited "right to citizenship" in the Soviet Union, but also pushed more believers underground, which in turn made Orthodoxy more suspect. For the Bolsheviks, who perceived what were in fact diverse religious movements as a monolithic counterrevolutionary force, the existence of a religious underground was a political threat that they answered with administrative restrictions and terror,[43] using the existence of the religious underground as a pretext for repression of the legally functioning Orthodox Church.[44]

Overall, the first decade of Soviet engagements with religion was driven by the Bolsheviks' belief that to stay in power, they had to establish a state infrastructure that could withstand the pressures of war, civil war, economic backwardness, and social unrest. Therefore, while the Bolsheviks were fighting for the regime's survival and establishing the institutions that would go on to define the Soviet system, religious policy was driven more by the established anticlericalism of the radical intelligentsia than any serious engagement with atheism. Because the Bolsheviks saw secularization as a fundamental part of modernization (as well as a step on the path to forging an atheist society), they initially deployed legal and administrative measures to manage religion. Indeed, the first—and, until the establishment of the Cult Commission under the Central Executive Committee (Vsesoiuznyi Tsentral'nyi Ispolnitel'nyi Komitet, or VTsIK) in 1929, the only—organization officially charged with governing religion was the eighth department of the People's Commissariat of Justice, which operated from 1918 until 1924.[45] At the same time, since they believed that secularization had divorced religion from politics, the Bolsheviks perceived clergy and believers who violated the new boundaries between private and public religiosity, church and state, as political versus religious actors, who were being persecuted not for their religious beliefs but rather for their counterrevolutionary politics. The secular face of the Soviet state depended on the support of extralegal security organs, which always operated behind the scenes to help the party achieve its goals.

## *The Bolsheviks as Agents of Enlightenment*

According to Marxist-Leninist theory, the revolution created the conditions for a bright Communist future that was inherently atheist. The Bolshevik Party, however, still had a central role to play in the revolutionary drama. As the political vanguard and a beacon of class morality, its role was to bring the revolution's "human material" to Communist consciousness. For the party, the end of the civil war and the transition to the New Economic Policy (NEP) meant that the revolution had moved from fighting for its survival to the work of building the new world. As the Bolshevik theorist Lev Trotsky (1879–1940), one of the party's most articulate proponents of cultural revolution and the new Communist byt, wrote in his essay, "A Person Does Not Live by Politics Alone,"

> The prerevolutionary history of our party was a history of revolutionary politics. Party literature, party organizations, everything around us stood under the slogan of "politics." . . . After the conquest of power and

> its consolidation as a result of the Civil War, our main goals have moved into the sphere of economic and cultural construction. . . . [They have become] more complicated, more scattered, more focused on details and in some ways more "prosaic."[46]

The religiosity of the masses was, of course, among the most prosaic aspects of life. Since there was no room for religion in the new Communist world, the party would have to tackle religiosity in culture and the sphere of everyday life, or byt.

In principle, popular religiosity—if it stayed within the secular parameters established after the revolution—should not have been perceived as a problem. Why should it matter to the party if Soviet people had icons in their home, celebrated Easter, or baptized their children? After all, none of these practices violated Soviet laws and indeed were among the rights accorded to citizens by the Soviet Constitution. But for the Bolsheviks, secularization was not the goal of the revolution but only the precondition for birth of the new Communist order. Once religious institutions had been deprived of their political support and economic power, and once the people had been liberated from the influence of the clergy and enlightened, the Bolsheviks had no doubt that the masses would embrace atheism. Especially if the Bolshevik Party guided the process and sped it along.

For the Bolsheviks, popular religiosity was the product of a backwardness, and Bolshevik logic held that education and enlightenment would lift the veil of superstition from the eyes of the masses and show them the light of reason. They believed in the transformative power of propaganda, education, and enlightenment, and enlisted these as essential tools of cultural transformation. The first strategy, antireligious propaganda, fell under the purview of party and Komsomol activists, who were also aided by members of the League of the Godless (after 1929, the League of the Militant Godless). Militant atheists saw themselves as warriors fighting on the religious front, and their primary objective was to destroy religion's authority and influence among the population by undermining the church and unmasking the clergy. In practice, this meant requisitioning and destroying religious spaces and property, persecuting and "unmasking" the clergy (as duplicitous enemy agents or immoral swindlers who took advantage of simple folk for personal gain), and undermining belief in the supernatural (especially its material manifestations, like relics and miraculous icons).[47] The party also believed in the power of the word to spread the message and deployed numerous publications—the journals *Revolution and Church* (*Revoliutsia i tserkov'*) (1919) and *Under the Banner of Marxism* (*Pod znamenem marksizma*) (1921), and the newspapers *Atheist* (*Bezbozhnik*) (1921) and *Atheist at the Workbench* (*Bezbozhnik u stanka*) (1922), among others—to depict religion as a backward, reactionary force in the service of counterrevolution. But above all, the Bolsheviks relied on visual propaganda. In a country where much of the population was still barely literate, newspapers and pamphlets could carry the atheist message only so far, and the Bolsheviks realized quickly that the effective transmission of Communist ideology depended on captivating visual aids conveyed in a familiar idiom.[48] Antireligious posters and caricatures became a staple in the arsenal of militant atheism (see figure 1.1).

If the goal of administrative repression and militant atheist propaganda was to relegate religion to the margins of public life, the goal of education and enlightenment was to transform individual worldviews and bring consciousness into the light of scientific materialism. Unlike militant antireligious propaganda aimed at the church and clergy, education and enlightenment targeted the Soviet masses, casting them as victims of backwardness. In the tradition of nineteenth-century reformers, the Bolsheviks believed education was central for turning individuals into conscious agents capable of changing the world.[49] Lunacharskii, head of the Soviet Commissariat of Enlightenment—the institution in charge of education—saw the school as a vehicle of cultural transformation that could "take fresh, small hearts and bright, open, little minds [and make], given the right education approach, a true miracle . . . a real human being."[50] Teachers, therefore, had a "sacred calling" in the project of human emancipation.[51] Yet curiously, religion was so far outside his vision of education that Lunacharskii—like Marx, Engels, and Lenin—did not, at the outset, see the need for an explicitly antireligious curriculum in the classroom; it was enough to remove religious instruction and spread enlightenment.

In the early Soviet period, the idea that Soviet schools should become temples of atheism did not materialize. As historian Larry Holmes points out, people continued to perceive the school as "a conduit for useful information" as opposed to a vehicle for cultural transformation.[52] Given scarce resources and massive absenteeism, teachers prioritized instruction in reading, writing, and arithmetic over antireligious agitation, seeing it as "a luxury no one could afford."[53] Those teachers who tried to press the antireligious agenda found themselves without support from above and facing hostility from below, as parents resisted the removal of religion from the classroom, sometimes threatening teachers with violence.[54] Moreover, even if religion did disappear from the classroom over time, it was not replaced by atheism. The Soviet school had become an irreligious, but not an atheist, space.

Beyond the classroom, the Soviet masses were to be transformed through cultural institutions in which they would encounter and internalize the narrative of scientific progress, with science as the untiring enemy of a religious establishment committed to thwarting human emancipation.[55] This narrative embedded religion in the story of human attempts to overcome powerlessness in the face of nature, and cast atheism as the inevitable product of people's growing understanding of the sublime forces that governed the universe. As human understanding evolved, materialism would replace religious explanations of the world. This tale of progress concluded with the human triumph

FIGURE 1.1. Nikolai Kogout, "Consubstantial Trinity" (*Troitsa edinosuchshnaia*). Moscow: Gublit, Mospoligraf, 1926. Soviet Anti-Religious Propaganda Collection, Saint Louis University Libraries Special Collections, Saint Louis, MO.

over nature, which included everything from liberating humanity from the plight of drought and hunger, to colonizing other planets and overcoming death.

The most common spaces for both atheist propaganda and scientific enlightenment were new institutions like reading huts, cultural clubs, and antireligious museums. Cultural clubs were envisioned as centers for enlightenment activities (reading and political discussion groups) and entertainment (dances, amateur theater, and film screenings). Clubs were channels through which the party could disseminate political and cultural enlightenment, and were intended to replace the church as the centers of community life. Indeed, local activists would often turn the local church into the village club, thereby recasting it as a secular space. In more populated towns, the Bolsheviks created antireligious museums.[56] Like schools, antireligious museums also fell under the jurisdiction of the Commissariat of Enlightenment and were run by activists from the local party or League of Militant Godless cell. The exhibits consisted of antireligious posters and religious objects from recently closed churches, mosques, and synagogues, and were considered most effective when they occupied religious spaces that had been repurposed for atheist use. Indeed, the most prominent antireligious museums were established on the grounds of some of the country's most important monasteries and churches: the Moscow Antireligious Museum in the Donskoi Monastery (1927), Central Antireligious Museum in Moscow's Strastnoi Monastery (1928), State Antireligious Museum in Leningrad's St. Isaac's Cathedral (1931), and Museum of the History of Religion in Leningrad's Kazan Cathedral (1932). This museumification of religion transformed sacred objects and spaces into sanitized cultural artifacts. To underscore their commitment to scientific enlightenment, the Bolsheviks also invested significant resources to construct two monuments to scientific materialism in the center of Moscow. The first, the Donskoi Crematorium (1927), built on the grounds of the Donskoi Monastery, promoted a sanitized view of death that left no space for the soul or an afterlife.[57] The second and far more successful of the two was the Moscow Planetarium (1929), which presented science as the triumph of reason over nature.[58]

The Moscow Planetarium was the first planetarium in the Soviet Union, and was the product of the Commissariat of Enlightenment's proposal to create "a new type of enlightenment institution."[59] Designed by constructivist architects Mikhail Barshch and Mikhail Siniavskii according to the most progressive principles in construction and city planning, and armed with the latest German equipment, the planetarium concentrated the hopes of the Soviet enlightenment project.[60] Indeed, considering the material constraints of the USSR in the 1920s, the Bolsheviks' dedication of resources for the construction of a planetarium is evidence of their faith in the transformative potential of scientific enlightenment.[61] The planetarium's location, next to the Moscow Zoo, was emblematic of the didactic vision it was meant to embody: in one trip, a visitor, with the guidance of educational lectures, could follow the path of evolution and uncover the material nature of the universe.

Highlighting its transformative power, the constructivist artist Aleksey Gan described the planetarium as "an optical scientific theater" whose primary function was to "foster a love for science in the viewer." In general, Gan saw the theater as a regressive rather than progressive force. The theater, Gan wrote, was simply "a building in which religious services are held," a space to satisfy the people's primitive instinct for spectacle—an instinct that would persist "until society grows to the level of a scientific understanding [of the world], and the instinctual need for spectacle comes up against the real phenomena of the world and technology." The planetarium, then, would satisfy the instinct for spectacle, but shift it "from servicing religion to servicing science." In this new type of theater, the workings of the universe would be revealed to the masses; everything was "mechanized" and people had a chance to direct "one of the world's most technologically complicated machines." This experience helped the viewer "a scientific understanding of the world and rid himself of the fetishism of a savage, priestly prejudices, and the civilized Europeans' pseudoscientific worldview."[62]

When the planetarium opened its doors in Moscow in November 1929, the confidence that the light of science would defeat the darkness of religion was paramount.[63] Indeed, Iaroslavskii invested the planetarium with tremendous ideological potential, stating that "priestly fables about the universe turn to dust in the face of scientific conclusions, which are supported by the kind of picture of the world provided by the planetarium."[64] In the 1930s, the planetarium hosted over eighteen thousand lectures and eight million visitors. It organized a young astronomer's club; a "star theater" that staged plays about Galileo, Copernicus, and Giordano Bruno; and a "stratospheric committee" that counted among its members the mechanical engineer and "tireless space crusader" Fridrikh Tsander as well as the father of the Soviet space program, Sergei Korolev.[65] The main question that worried atheists was not *if* the assault of scientific materialism on religion would ultimately be victorious but *when* and through what means victory would finally be achieved.

## *The Bolsheviks as World Builders*

The final frontier in the party's war against religion was byt. Whereas religious institutions were irredeemable, and therefore subject to antireligious repression and militant atheist propaganda, popular religiosity proved to be more complicated. As Trotsky wrote, "Owing to its dialectical flexibility, communist theory develops political methods that guarantee its influence under any conditions. But a political idea is one thing, byt is another. Politics is flexible, but byt is immobile and stubborn. This is why there are so many conflicts over byt among workers, when consciousness comes up against tradition."[66] In theory, the Bolsheviks believed cultural revolution and enlightenment would empower humanity to reclaim agency and overcome alienation. In practice, they consistently encountered the "stubborn" religiosity of the masses.[67]

The problem of byt had long been a contested issue for both the political and creative intelligentsia. The Russian creative intelligentsia had been engaged in a "battle with byt" (*bor'ba s bytom*), to borrow the writer Andrei Bely's phrase, since the turn of the twentieth century, seeing bourgeois byt as the embodiment of the old world's philistinism and corruption.[68] Byt was, in the words of the theorist Roman Jakobson, "a stagnating slime, which stifles life in its tight, hard mold," and the revolution was an aesthetic project that would shed this "slime" and liberate the creative power of the people.[69] For the Bolsheviks, on the other hand, the revolution, including its cultural dimension, was less an aesthetic project than a civilizing mission. The Bolsheviks waged war against what they perceived to be the vestiges of the old byt among the masses—poor work ethic, foul language, spitting, drunkenness, and sexual promiscuity—by inculcating "culturedness" (*kul'turnost'*): literacy, hygiene, sobriety, and correct public conduct.[70] Issues like marriage and sexuality, ethics and morality—and of course religion—were discussed in party meetings, the press, and Communist study circles, as the party tried to work out the contours of the new Communist byt and the correct Bolshevik approach to everyday life, and especially to the home and the family.[71]

Trotsky was one of the few among the Bolshevik elite to really acknowledge the power of byt.[72] In his writings on the subject, he emphasized that in the battle against byt, antireligious campaigns and enlightenment measures were not enough. He argued that since the religiosity of the masses was not a consciously held belief but rather set of habits and customs taken for granted, atheist propaganda that appealed to reason would have little effect. "Religiosity among the Russian working classes does not really exist in practice," Trotsky wrote. "The Orthodox Church was a daily custom and a government institution. It was never successful in penetrating deeply into the consciousness of the masses, nor in blending its dogmas and canons with the inner emotions of the people." Popular religiosity remained reflexive, the habit "of the street sight-seer who on occasion does not object to joining a procession or pompous ceremony, listening to singing, or waving his arms." Religion was the background of life (see figure 1.2). The masses turned to the church because of its "social-aesthetic attractions," Trotsky argued. "Icons still hang in the home just because. Icons decorate the walls; they would be bare without them; people would not be used to it." The scent of incense, the brilliant light, the beautiful singing, offered "a break in the monotony of ordinary life." If the Bolsheviks hoped to "liberate the common masses from their habitual rituals and ecclesiasticism," they had to provide "new forms of life, new amusements, new and more cultured theaters."[73]

In his reflections on the problem of byt, Trotsky noted the power of rituals, and rites of passage in particular, in keeping religion in people's lives. Even as Trotsky proclaimed that "the worker's state has rejected church ceremony,

FIGURE 1.2. Nikolai Kogout, "How they beat religion into a person" (*Kak vkolachivaiut v cheloveka religiiu*). Moscow: Gublit, Mospoligraf, 1926. Soviet Anti-Religious Propaganda Collection, Saint Louis University Libraries Special Collections, Saint Louis, MO.

and informed its citizens that they have the right to be born, marry, and die without the mysterious gestures and exhortations of persons clad in cassocks, gowns, and other ecclesiastical vestments," he also warned that if the Bolsheviks hoped to build a new world without religion, they could not ignore rituals.[74] "How is marriage to be celebrated or the birth of a child in the family?" he asked. "How is one to pay the tribute of affection to the beloved dead? It is on this need of marking the principal signposts along the road of life that church ritual depends."[75] Trotsky underscored the emotional component of ritual as an important part of human experience noting that, "It is much easier for the state to do without rituals than for everyday life." Those who believed they could bring forth a new way of life without rituals were going to extremes, and "in the battle with the old byt would break their forehead, nose, and other essential organs."[76]

In theory, then, the Bolsheviks sought to transform the backward masses into new Soviet people.[77] Yet in practice, the forms of the new Communist byt remained vague through the 1920s and 1930s, the stuff of debates among the creative intelligentsia and party theorists rather than the lived experience of the masses.

For the Bolsheviks, there was also the question of how Communist ideology should shape the morality and byt of the party's own cadres. With the adoption of the NEP, as the party retreated from Marxism-Leninism in politics and economy, the struggle for ideological purity moved into the sphere of byt, codes of Communist behavior and morality. Historian Michael David-Fox observes that "a preoccupation with the 'revolutionary everyday' came to the fore as a way of transforming the NEP 'retreat' into a cultural advance," especially as byt increasingly came to be seen as a marker of "one's relationship to the revolution" and "a badge of political affiliation, staking out the boundaries of the revolutionary and the reactionary."[78] Bolsheviks agreed that the Leninist conception that morality was grounded in class and rejected the purportedly universal morality of the old faiths, which served only the interests of the exploiting class. Anything that advanced the revolution was inherently moral.[79] Over the course of the 1920s and early 1930s, morality and byt turned into instruments to discipline rank-and-file party members, who regularly found themselves under review for various infractions of Communist norms.

One of the problems with the Leninist thesis that the party was the vanguard of the revolution was that, in theory, each party member had to be a model of political consciousness and living embodiment of the new byt. For this reason, nowhere are the contradictions between Communist ideology and Soviet reality more apparent than in the party's effort to discipline its own cadres. After the revolution the party expanded its ranks, and grew even larger following Lenin's death in 1924 with the "Lenin Levy." As the party grew, the Bolshevik old guard found itself having to define and often defend the ideological purity of the party. It also had to balance its commitment to ideological purity with the need to become the party of the masses, for whom the active atheist position required of party members frequently presented an obstacle.

In the first years after the revolution, the Central Committee regularly received letters from party cells asking for guidance on how to treat the religiosity of party members: Should party members who baptized their children or got married in a church be expelled? For the Bolshevik old guard, the answer was ideologically simple but politically complicated. Leading Bolshevik theorists—Iaroslavskii, Lunacharskii, Trotsky, Ivan Skvortsov-Stepanov (1870–1928), and Nikolai Bukharin (1888–1938)—argued that religion was associated with powerlessness, weakness, and passivity, whereas atheism meant agency, strength, and creativity.[80] To be an atheist was to shed comfortable illusions and take charge of one's fate. To be an atheist also meant to shed the individualistic fear of death and concern with personal salvation and embrace collective immortality, which could be attained only by giving all of oneself to the revolution and creation of the new world. A party member who held onto religious commitments—whether in the form of belief in supernatural forces or the observance of rituals and traditions—was, in the words of Aron Sol'ts, the party theorist of Communist ethics, "a deserter from the byt front [*bytovoi front*]."[81] To build the new world, Bolsheviks had to be atheists.

The Second Party Program, adopted at the Eighth Party Congress held March 18 to 23, 1919, made explicit that with regard to religion, the party was not satisfied by the "bourgeois democratic" separation of religion from the state and education, which had been decreed in 1918. Rather, the party demanded that members work toward "the complete destruction of the ties between the exploiting classes and the organization of religious propaganda, [by] effecting the liberation of the masses from prejudices and organizing the broadest scientific-enlightenment and antireligious propaganda."[82] As Bukharin and Evgenii Preobrazhenskii (1886–1937) stated in *The ABC of Communism* (1919), a pamphlet that popularized the new party program for the party rank and file, religion was incompatible with the calling of a Communist, but personal unbelief, while necessary, was not sufficient. A true Communist had to actively work to eradicate religion and spread atheism.[83] Neither the party program nor *The ABC of Communism*, however, made explicit what exactly was required of each party member to liberate the masses from religion, nor did it make explicit the consequences for violating Bolshevik directives, leaving unanswered questions about how exactly the Bolshevik party program should be brought into the lives of rank-and-file party cadres.

The person who took it on himself to guide the party on this issue was Iaroslavskii. In a two-part *Pravda* series titled "A Tribute to Prejudices" (1919), Iaroslavskii laid out the Bolshevik position on religiosity among party cadres.[84]

In the first article, Iaroslavskii made it clear that for the Bolsheviks religion was not a "private affair" but a political position in open violation of the Party Charter. "In order to carry out antireligious propaganda among others," Iaroslavskii wrote, "party members themselves have to be free of religious prejudices." After all, a Bolshevik could not be a convincing atheist agitator if he continued to "pay tribute" to religion.[85] But Iaroslavskii's logical reasoning generated heated debate among the rank and file, and the Central Committee received numerous letters from both party cadres and ordinary Soviet people asking for clarification on the party's position on religion.

Iaroslavskii laid out the crux of the debate in a second article, which he organized around three letters: one from a twelve-year-old named Vendrovskii, and the others from two individuals who signed off as "The Russian" (*Russkii*) and "A Speculator on the Way to Moscow" (*Edushchii v Moskvu spekuliant*). The chief objections to the party's demand that all members be active atheists, Iaroslavskii summarized, fell into three categories: that Point 13 of the Party Charter contradicts the Soviet Constitution, which guarantees all citizens the right to conduct religious and antireligious propaganda; that the party will have to take religious prejudices into consideration if it does not want to "put the lives of many Communists in the village and in the city in a very difficult family situation"; and that it is "necessary to differentiate between those who observe the prejudices of others, and those who observe their own prejudices."[86] To the first point regarding the contradiction between the secular constitution of the state and atheist obligation of the party, Iaroslavskii clarified that the party was a voluntary organization, which meant that whereas the program was "not obligatory for 'all citizens,' for Communists it is." For Iaroslavskii, it was "completely childish" to appeal to the constitution in this matter, "as if every Communist is first a citizen of the Soviet republic, and only after, a member of the party," as if "the party is just a part of the state," rather than the "vanguard division" of the revolution. The party had "strictly established codes of conduct that are mandatory for all members." Those who "still do not understand this, and want the Communist Party to open its doors for any interested person, regardless of their convictions," need to be reminded that the party, as a voluntary organization, had the right to "demand that members break with everything that gets in the way of completely accepting the Communist program."[87] Iaroslavskii also reminded party cadres that Bolsheviks operating in the underground before the revolution "had to definitive[ly] break with families that were against our revolutionary activity"—a situation that for many continued after the revolution as well. Iaroslavskii conceded that this put some party members in a difficult situation within their families, but he was unforgiving with regard to those who observed religious rites and traditions simply to avoid domestic strife. "These people have no belief, they are called hypocrites," Iaroslavskii asserted. "It's not for them to bring the Communist program to life."[88] Communists needed to be moral models since the masses, and especially the peasant masses, "are very sensitive for the deeds of the Communist not to depart from his words."[89] In 1921, the party issued a decree "On the Organization of Antireligious Propaganda and the Violation of Point 13 of the Party Program," which again reminded cadres of the party's expectations.[90]

The party's efforts to discipline religion were further exacerbated when the party opened its ranks, following Lenin's death on January 21, 1924, to new cadres with no experience in the revolutionary underground and little schooling in Marxist-Leninist theory. When Iaroslavskii addressed the question of party discipline shortly after Lenin's death, he found himself facing the swollen ranks of the party's Lenin Levy, consisting of workers and peasants, many of whom saw no contradiction between Communism and religion, and did not understand why they had to give up their customary ways.[91] In an article titled "Is It Possible to Live without God?," Iaroslavskii observed that in every party meeting, the religious question was an obstacle for workers. "There have been almost no instances when workers would express disagreement with some other point of our Communist program: they accept it wholesale," Iaroslavskii wrote. "But the question of religion, gods, icons, the observance of rituals . . . not infrequently is the hardest of all to figure out for the workers, especially the women workers." To help new recruits see their way through this dilemma, Iaroslavskii reminded them of Lenin's position on religion:

> There can be no doubt that Lenin was for propaganda, that is, for the preaching of godlessness, that Lenin considered religious beliefs a sign of a lack of consciousness, darkness, or obscurantism, a weapon of bourgeois class rule. And can we be indifferent to the lack of consciousness, to darkness, to obscurantism? This is the question to which each Leninist must give an answer. And if he thinks his words through to their logical conclusion, then, of course, he will not be able to accept half-measures, that cowardly decision, that says to him: you can remain a Communist, you can remain a Leninist, but you can throw aside Lenin's thoughts on religion and consider Lenin's position on the religious question mistaken and unacceptable. No, our program on the religious question is completely tied up with the entire program of our party.[92]

The Communist program, Iaroslavskii concluded, "is founded on the scientific worldview [and] has no room for gods, angels, devils, or any other fabrications of human fantasy." Religion was thus irreconcilable with the calling of a Bolshevik. "To be a true Leninist means to accept the entire program, all of the understandings of society and nature that our program provides, which has no need for gods, devils, or priests, regardless of the guise in which they are presented [*pod kakim by sousom oni ne prepodnosilis'*]."[93] Communists have no need for the consolations of religion, for dreams about immortality, Iaroslavskii proclaimed, because their commitment was to "creat[ing] a life full of joy on Earth."

> Marx has died. Lenin has died. But we say: Marx lives in the minds of millions of people, in their thoughts, in their struggle; Lenin lives in each Leninist, in the millions of Leninists, in the entirety of the proletariat's battle, in the Leninist party fulfilling Lenin's testament and leading the working class in its battle for the construction of the new world. This is immortality; and we Communists only think about this type of immortality; not in the air, not in the skies, not on the clouds, which we will leave for the priests and the birds happily and free of charge, but on the Earth on which we live, rejoice, suffer, and fight for Communism.
>
> It is not only possible to live without belief in god; it is possible to live joyously, to fight with conviction, to act with courage.
>
> One cannot be a Leninist and believe in God.[94]

For the Bolshevik old guard, party members who believed in or even "paid tribute" to religious prejudices were not true Communists since their loyalties were divided or—worse yet—undetermined.

At the same time, Iaroslavskii acknowledged the tremendous power religion still exercised in the home and in the family.[95] In "domestic byt," Iaroslavskii wrote, "there is not one event, beginning with birth, that happens without the clergy. The priest gets involved in all even remotely significant life events." For the masses, life without "this priest, his prayers, the splashing of 'holy water' . . . without all this sorcery" is "deprived of meaning." For the peasant masses in particular, "everything that a priest says is the holy truth."[96] To build the new Communist order, the Bolsheviks believed they had to transform the family as an institution; but in the meantime, the Bolsheviks recognized that their task was to help party cadres navigate their actual families.

Party cadres from the provinces wrote to the center asking for guidance on their domestic conflicts which Iaroslavskii shared on the pages of *Prarda*. A peasant named Suravegin recounted how, following an argument, his wife gouged out the eyes of the portraits of party leaders he had hung up in their home, after which he threw her icon of the Mother of God on the floor, breaking it into pieces. In another family, the Communist husband and children burned the religious wife's icons in her absence, after which she burned down their "atheist corner" (*ugolok bezbozhnika*).[97] "What should a Leninist do if his family is still religious, does not permit taking down the icons, takes the children to church, and so on?" asked a rural party member named Glukhov. "Can icons be hung in his home against his will and desire? Should he force his family to submit to his views, even if it brings the matter to divorce?"[98] Glukhov's own position was categorical. If the family did not submit to his views, then it was necessary to "break with the family," since it was "impermissible for icons to hang in the home of a Leninist, for a priest to baptize a Leninist's children, and for a Leninist's children to go to church."[99]

Iaroslavskii approached the matter more pragmatically. He noted that, with the gender ratio in the Bolshevik party being eight to one, if male Bolsheviks wanted to avoid family discord over ideological issues, then "male communists could only marry female communists," which meant that only one male party member out of eight would be able to get married and the rest would be consigned to bachelorhood."[100] Instead, Iaroslavskii suggested a softer and more gradual approach to family disagreements over religion. Rather than break with his family, a Leninist should strive to enlighten. "If a wife hangs icons," he suggested, a worker should say to her, "You insult me as a communist. I can hang antireligious posters next to your icons, which you won't like."[101] More generally, the task of a Leninist, Iaroslavskii posited, was to work on the moral upbringing and political consciousness of family members, making sure that his children are brought into the party ranks through the pioneers and the Komsomol.

As the Soviet system became more stable and the party's power more secure, the personal conduct of party cadres again became of critical interest to the guardians of Bolshevik orthodoxy.[102] Addressing the question of what the party demanded of Communists in their personal conduct and whether the party should interfere in their personal lives, Iaroslavskii clarified that the inner "convictions" of party members could not be considered their "private affair" (*chastnoe delo*).[103] The Soviet government, Iaroslavskii pointed out, "does not demand of anyone that he belongs to the [League of the Militant Godless] or that he break with religion." On the contrary, the government "guarantees every citizen full freedom" whether to believe or not, to belong to a religious community or the League of the Militant Godless. "But the party is another matter," Iaroslavskii wrote. "The party demands of all members not only to break with religion, but to actively participate in antireligious propaganda." For the party, therefore, "the kind of family a Communist makes was not 'all the same.'" Iaroslavskii noted that even if these questions were not explicitly addressed in party documents, "it is self-evident that a Communist, in his personal byt and in his family life, has to be an example for all the nonparty masses, whom he calls onto the path of the new life, the path of the restructuring of all human relations."[104] Nevertheless, the question of how to incorporate Communist morality and byt beyond the party, into the lives of the masses, long remained unanswered.

The Bolshevik Party's neglect of private life in the early Soviet period was a symptom of the ascetic revolutionary milieu in which it had been forged—a milieu that renounced personal ties in order to single-mindedly devote all intellectual, physical, and emotional resources to the revolution. For the Bolsheviks, true meaning was never to be found in private life, since it was in the public sphere that the important questions would be worked out. Once in power, though, the Bolsheviks were faced with the question of how their revolutionary asceticism could or should be translated into cultural policy for the masses. The fact that in the early Soviet period, byt always remained secondary to other concerns—political, economic, social, and even cultural—is a reflection of how the Bolsheviks understood the process of transforming the old world they had set out to destroy into the new world in the name of which they made a revolution.

Bolsheviks recognized that, having transformed into a party of the masses, they could not demand that all party members renounce familial ties, even when these ran counter to party ethics. At the same time, they were unwilling to abandon the domestic sphere to the forces of backwardness. Individual morality, byt, and the family remained central concerns, though whether the party was active or passive in its engagement with these issues changed over time and depended on numerous external factors. But ultimately, if the Soviet project was to succeed, the party had to conquer the home and the family since these remained the central site of reproduction—reproduction that was not only demographic also but cultural, ideological, and political.

## *The Bolsheviks as Stalinists*

The secular framework adopted immediately after the revolution undermined the juridical, economic, and political power of the Orthodox Church, but the church nevertheless remained "a very powerful social corporation" through the 1920s.[105] While the Bolsheviks could read Metropolitan Sergii's declaration of loyalty to Soviet power as a political victory, they had no illusions that the people had given up faith or tradition. Until collectivization, however, the Bolsheviks were concerned primarily with subordinating the church as an institution, leaving local religious life more or less intact.[106] In part this was a political strategy, since rather than subduing religious communities, Bolshevik repression instead often mobilized religious activism.[107] Indeed, historian Glennys Young shows that over the course of the early Soviet period, religiosity became increasingly politicized. For example, Young traces the transformation of the word *tserkovnik* in the Soviet press, noting that whereas in the mid-1920s, journalists "tended to use *tserkovnik* as a synonym for 'clergy,'" the term gradually "ceased to be a solely religious category."[108] When religious activists began to influence rural politics by joining local soviets, the rhetorical tserkovnik "became a political as well as a religious actor" whose "identity [was] associated with the frustration of Soviet goals and expectations."[109] By the early 1930s, the term *tserkovnik* had become "a synonym for a factional politician of the rural world."[110] Indeed, as Gregory Freeze shows, often the Bolsheviks came to see religious activists as a greater threat to Soviet power than the church and clergy because they had support from nationalists, rich peasants, and other anti-Soviet groups.[111]

As the Bolsheviks mobilized for the First Five-Year Plan (1928–32), party leaders like Bukharin were describing the religious question as a "front in class war," and religion itself as an "enemy of socialist construction [that] fights us on the cultural front."[112] This shift in antireligious rhetoric toward denouncing religion in general, rather than religious institutions in particular, was a sign that the project of socialist construction had entered a new phase. With the First Five-Year Plan, the Bolsheviks sought to mobilize all resources toward industrialization, collectivization, and cultural revolution. The antireligious campaign was an important part of the broader cultural revolution, since the cultural revolution was about class war, and religion was a class enemy. The party marshaled all the means at its disposal—atheist propaganda, legal and administrative restrictions, and extralegal repression—to prevent religion from becoming an obstacle to constructing "socialism in one country."

Before making the change of course public, the party worked behind the scenes. On January 24, 1929, a secret party circular titled "On Measures for the Intensification of Antireligious Work" declared that "religious organizations are the only legally existing counterrevolutionary organizations" in the USSR, which made it imperative to wage "a merciless war" against them. The resolution called on the League of the Militant Godless (which now had "militant" added to its name) to intensify atheist propaganda and become a more powerful force in local politics.[113] Shortly after, on April 8, 1929, the Council of People's Commissars (Sovnarkom) and VTsIK issued the decree "On Religious Organizations," which formalized the Bolshevik plan to remove religion from politics and public life by radically narrowing its "borders of legality."[114] The 1929 law was intended to bring all aspects of religious life under state control by repealing numerous provisions established in 1918: it outlawed the religious education of children and charity work, closed monasteries, and dictated that religious communities had to register with local government organs. To make sure the league faced no competition, the Bolsheviks revoked the right to "religious propaganda" from the fourth article of the Constitution of the Russian Soviet Federal Socialist Republic (RSFSR), which had, until then, guaranteed Soviet citizens "freedom of religious and antireligious propaganda."[115] It was not enough, moreover, to marginalize religion; public life also had to be made visibly Soviet.[116] In effect, the only right Soviet citizens retained was the right to worship inside the confines of specifically designated religious spaces.

Given the centrality of religion to Russian rural life and primacy of collectivization to Stalin's modernization program, the First Five-Year Plan demanded a solution to the religious question. In June 1929, at the Second Congress of the League, the Leningrad atheist Iosif Eliashevich called for a "godless five-year plan" (*bezbozhnuiu piatiletku*), and local cells were instructed to "take measures for the mass exit of laborers from religious communities."[117] As Iaroslavskii declared at a 1930 league meeting, "The process of full collectivization is tied with the liquidation of a significant part of churches."[118] In practice, collectivization often began with the forced closure of the local church, which was followed by popular protest. This scenario was common enough that on March 14, 1930, the party issued a decree against so-called excesses in antireligious measures. This, of course, had little to do with a commitment to legality, and everything to do with the fact that starting a collectivization campaign by closing the village church prevented effective implementation. Rather than a change of policy, the decree was a warning about strategy. Churches continued to be closed, repurposed, or destroyed, and religious communities were dissolved.[119]

The Second Five-Year Plan (1933–37) brought with it the aim to "liquidate capitalist elements and classes" and produce a classless society, which made the place of religion even more precarious. On the one hand, from the perspective of socialist ideology, religion had no future in the Soviet Union; the only question was how much political effort the party should exert in hastening its demise. On the other hand, vehement international opposition to Soviet antireligious repression hamstrung the Soviet state, which aspired to recognition on the world stage. But by the mid-1930s—as the 1934 murder of Sergei Kirov, a Leningrad Bolshevik whose popularity made him a potential rival of Stalin, raised the pitch of class warfare and political terror—there was a growing consensus among the Bolsheviks that religious institutions in general and the Orthodox Church in particular remained politically dangerous, and therefore needed to be definitively neutralized.[120]

In 1937, at the height of the Great Terror, the Bolshevik political elite discussed the idea of a Soviet Union completely free of religion. The party accused the Orthodox Church of collaborating with the religious underground at home and counterrevolutionary agents abroad,[121] and cast the 1929 law as too permissive for allowing the continued existence and even proliferation of religion.[122] In 1937 alone, the Bolsheviks closed more than eight thousand churches (with another six thousand in 1938), and arrested thirty-five thousand "servants of religious cults."[123] The Bolsheviks also exiled or murdered much of the Orthodox Church hierarchy. The historian Mikhail Shkarovskii argues that by 1938 the Orthodox Church was "on the whole, destroyed."[124] Local organs charged with managing religion were liquidated as unnecessary, thereby "eliminating even the possibility of contact between the state and the church."[125] By the end of the 1930s, the only institution that was still charged with managing religious affairs was the People's Commissariat for Internal Affairs (NKVD).

Yet what the statistics of church closures obscure—but what was of course evident to the Bolsheviks—is the fact that religion continued to mobilize popular resistance. The Bolsheviks had few illusions that religion had been exorcized from Soviet life. Ethnographers studying rural life, such as N. M. Matorin (1898–1936) and V. G. Bogoraz-Tan (1865–1936), produced studies of "lived religion" (*zhivaia religiia*) and "folk Orthodoxy" (*narodnoe pravoslavie*) that attested to the continued religiosity of the countryside throughout the 1920s and 1930s.[126] The results of the 1937 Soviet census also made clear that religion was a social fact.[127] The census, which was developed by Soviet ethnographers and curated by Stalin personally, included a question on "Religion" (*Religiia*), added to the final draft on Stalin's initiative.[128] As the instructions to the census officials clarified, the question was intended to indicate belief rather than confessional belonging, and the results revealed that of the 98,412 people surveyed, more than half (56.17 percent) identified as believers, and this proportion rose to two-thirds in the countryside. The official response to the census was to blame the poor state of antireligious work and annul the results, but the Bolsheviks could not ignore the fact that more than half the country still felt an allegiance to religion, and continuing antireligious policies would alienate this base from the Soviet project.[129] Another census, conducted in 1939, tried to circumvent the problem by removing the religious question but actually further underscored the cost of antireligious policies when some answered the question "Citizen of which state" with "Christian" or "Orthodox."[130]

In some ways, popular resistance to being assimilated into the Soviet project arose because the Bolsheviks, in proclaiming their plan to transform the world, positioned Soviet Communism as the antithesis of the traditional order, which for many made it suspect. An anticollectivization pamphlet cited by Lynn Viola in her study of peasant rebellion under Stalin illustrates the peasants' perception of collective farms and Soviet power as fundamentally evil:

> In the [collective farm] there will be a special branding iron, [they] will close all the churches, not allow prayer, dead people will be cremated, the christening of children will be forbidden, invalids and the elderly will be killed, there won't be any husbands or wives, [all] will sleep under a 100-metre blanket. . . . Children will be taken from their parents, there will be wholesale incest: brothers will live with sisters, sons with mothers, fathers with daughters, etc. The [collective farm]—this means beasts in a single shed, people under a single blanket.[131]

Another telling example of popular attitudes is the rumor that Soviet passports, which were being introduced in the cities, had the mark of the Antichrist. In the popular imagination, the Soviet order was an antiworld that was governed by an inverted moral code.

On the eve of the Second World War, the Bolsheviks faced a complex situation. They had nearly destroyed the church as an institution—of the more than fifty thousand Orthodox churches on the territory of the RSFSR in 1917, fewer than a thousand were left in 1939.[132] But they had neither broken the people's ties with Orthodoxy nor created a compelling atheist narrative that reached beyond public life, into the home. Even as the political elite was having conversations about the prospects of a country free of religion, it was also signaling another course. In 1936, Article 124 of the new Stalin Constitution affirmed the rights of Soviet citizens to "observe religious cults" (*otpravliat' religioznye kul'ty*), which, given the devastation of the recent antireligious campaign, was read by some clerics and believers as a sign of better times ahead.[133] Stalin also signaled a new course to the Soviet political establishment. In 1937, historian Sergei Bakhrushin (1882–1950) published a revisionist article titled "On the Issue of the Christianization of Rus'" in the journal *Marxist Historian* (*Istorik-Marksist*), arguing that Grand Prince Vladimir's adoption of Christianity, rather than a tool of oppression, was a savvy political decision that consolidated the state.[134] In his article, Bakhrushin criticized existing narratives of the Christianization of Rus' in 988, which, he argued, falsely privileged the psychological element of Vladimir's conversion or attributed the event to the efforts of foreign missionaries. Instead, he presented the adoption of Christianity as a conscious political decision made by Rus' political elites that should be seen as part of the history of Russia's state formation. Though presented in the narrow framework of academic history, Bakhrushin's article was an ideological departure in that it presented religion as a progressive historical factor that facilitated the consolidation of the state. Bakhrushin's article emerged in the aftermath of a government commission convened to formulate rules for writing high school history textbooks, which had decided to bring religion back into the historical narrative by positing that "the introduction of Christianity was progressive in comparison with pagan barbarism."[135] The Bolsheviks' reconsideration of religion's historical role speaks to the broader shift observed by the historian David Brandenberger, within the ideological establishment of the "propaganda state."[136]

Over the course of the 1930s, governance began to compete with ideology in directing Stalinist religious policy. In order to consolidate society and promote Soviet patriotism for the coming war with capitalist imperialism that Stalin thought inevitable, the party receded from the ideological iconoclasm of the cultural revolution, and returned to traditional values and a populist idiom.[137] In part, this shift took place because the institutional power of the Orthodox Church had been broken, and religion was no longer perceived as a serious political threat. But it also came because the antireligious campaign had proven to be a fiasco, undermining social stability while achieving little to advance the atheist mission. The Cult Commission, which had been formed in April 1929 to implement the new law on religion, spent its time not just on taxing and closing churches, confiscating religious property, and persecuting clergy, but also on trying to contain the disorder that resulted from these policies.[138] The atheist apparatus, meanwhile, was a bureaucratic chimera, a "Potemkin village of atheism," to borrow the phrase of the historian Daniel Peris, the influence of which did not extend far beyond sloganeering.[139] The league boasted a membership of over five million "godless" (a figure greater than that of the Bolshevik Party itself), but its loud propaganda campaigns and inflated membership statistics masked its inefficacy and thin presence on the ground.[140] But perhaps the more important issue is that its message was not so much *atheist* as antireligious and, more specifically, anticlerical. As Peris notes, "A distinction needs to be made between the regime's effective and brutal suppression of external religious manifestations and the league as an agent of atheism."[141] On the whole, the Bolsheviks devoted much more energy to debating how to eradicate religion than to producing a positive atheist program.[142]

At the same time, at end of the 1930s, the party came as close as it ever would to eradicating religion, and although its efforts had not been successful, it did manage to neutralize the church as a political institution and, in the words of Shkarovskii, "create the appearance of a godless state."[143] It was an illusion, however, that the Bolsheviks soon realized was too costly to maintain.

## *The Church Patriotic*

When the war finally came to the USSR, Stalin faced a decision: whether to continue the antireligious status quo, or turn to the Orthodox Church and deploy it for the benefit of the Soviet state. Several factors made the benefits of partnership with the church appear to outweigh the costs. First, wartime allies were alienated by Soviet religious repression. Second, in the occupied territories, German forces were effectively using religion against Soviet power, currying favor with local populations by opening churches. Third, there was also a noticeable religious revival among Soviet citizens, even in unoccupied territories, evident in their increased petitions to open local churches.[144] The Orthodox Church's active support of the Soviet war effort offered proof of its political loyalty as well as its use to Soviet power. Indicative of the new course is the limited reentry of the church into public life. For instance, following the Nazi invasion on June 22, 1941, the Soviet people were addressed by Metropolitan Sergii before they were addressed by Stalin. In his radio address, Sergii stressed the church's historical role in mobilizing the Russian people against "the pitiful progeny of the enemies of Orthodox Christianity, who are trying again to bring our people to our knees before untruth, and to brutally force them to sacrifice the welfare and wholeness of the motherland." Sergii reminded the people that even though their ancestors had been through even worse trials, their spirits had not fallen because they thought not about their own safety and profit but rather "their sacred duty to the motherland and the faith—and they emerged victors."[145] Shortly after, in summer 1941, churches began to be reopened on Russian territory. Throughout the war, the church held prayer services for Soviet victory and raised money for the defense, including funding its own Dmitri Donskoi tank division.[146] For Stalin, the church's wartime mobilization was proof of not just its loyalty but also its potential value to the Soviet state. After destroying the Orthodox Church as an institution and political actor, Stalin decided to reverse course.[147]

In 1943, when it seemed likely that the Soviet Union would survive the war, and that it would also keep the western territories it had annexed in 1939, Stalin introduced a new model for managing Soviet religious affairs. On September 4, 1943, he called a meeting at his summer residence outside Moscow, attended by Georgii Malenkov (a member of the Party Secretariat), Lavrentii Beria (head of the NKVD), and Georgii Karpov, an NKVD colonel who had been in charge of counterintelligence operations, including those that concerned religion. The meeting turned out to be Karpov's interview for a new position. During their conversation, Stalin asked Karpov about the history and contemporary state of the church as well as its connections with religious organizations abroad. He also inquired about the character of several Orthodox metropolitans, asking about their political loyalties, material circumstances, and authority within the church.[148] Stalin then informed Karpov that a special organization was being established to manage church-state relations—to be called the Council on the Affairs of the Russian Orthodox Church (CAROC)—and appointed Karpov to lead it. He told Karpov to call Metropolitan Sergii and invite him, along with Metropolitans Aleksii (Simanskii) and Nikolai (Iarushevich), to a meeting at the Kremlin. The meeting took place later that evening, attended by the metropolitans, Karpov, Vyacheslav Molotov, and Stalin himself. Stalin informed the church hierarchs that the patriarchate was being restored and that the church could now count on the state's support.[149] Finally, Stalin instructed Karpov to begin the process of establishing CAROC, but also warned him first, that the council should not undermine the image of the church's autonomy and independence, and second, that Karpov's new position did not make him into a new overprocurator of the Holy Synod, the powerful government institution that managed church-state affairs under the imperial autocracy.[150] By all accounts, no one—including the NKVD and Orthodox Church hierarchs—anticipated Stalin's reversal on the religious question.

On September 8, 1943, the Orthodox Church convened a council composed of nineteen bishops, sixteen of whom had just been released from prison camps, and elected Metropolitan Sergii as the patriarch of the Russian

Orthodox Church. On September 14, 1943, two days after the patriarch was enthroned, the Council of People's Commissars (Sovet narodnykh komissarov, or Sovnarkom) established CAROC. On May 19, 1944, CAROC was followed by the creation of the Council on the Affairs of Religious Cults (Sovet po delam religioznykh kul'tov, or CARC), which was tasked with managing relations with non-Orthodox confessions. Shortly after being established, CAROC and CARC began the work of reopening religious spaces and registering religious communities.[151]

It is worth noting that the councils were established as advisory organs within the government rather than the security apparatus. Even though the KGB's oversight of the councils' work was tacitly acknowledged at home and openly decried abroad, the councils' position as a government organ communicated a shift in Soviet religious policy from an extralegal to a legal foundation. This is noteworthy because, between the disbanding of the Cult Commission in 1938 and the establishment of the councils, the security organs were the only organization that managed religious affairs. The political significance of the new framework was underscored by the effort to make a visible wall between the councils and the KGB. On July 7, 1945, the KGB issued a secret order clarifying to its local branches that with the establishment of "special organs" to manage religious affairs, the functions of the security apparatus were to be "limited to the interests of intelligence and counterintelligence work."[152] Local cadres were instructed on the division of labor between their work and that of the plenipotentiaries of CAROC and CARC. KGB officers were not to confuse the activities of the two organizations, discuss the work of the councils with their informants, or share work spaces with CAROC and CARC plenipotentiaries. In one instance, a KGB cadre was reprimanded for using "internal channels" to forward a letter from his informant to Karpov, since by doing this he "underscored in the eyes of the informant the connection of the NKGB with the Council of the Affairs of the Russian Orthodox Church."[153] Cadres were also reminded that the councils did not report to them but rather to the Council of Ministers, and that "the open and direct use of the institution of the plenipotentiary for one's own goals can lead to the undesirable conviction among the *tserkovniki* that [the councils] are filial branches of the NKGB organs."[154]

The fact that the decision to bring religion back into Soviet life came from Stalin personally suggests that he perceived the political threat of religion to be effectively neutralized.[155] This opened the way for religious institutions to become partners in reconstruction and governance after the war. Moreover, with the annexation of the Baltic states (Estonia, Latvia, and Lithuania), Moldova, and the western regions of Ukraine and Belarus—none of which had gone through either the militant atheist campaigns or the collectivization to which the rest of the Soviet Union had been subjected in the 1920s and

1930s—the Soviet Union now had thousands of new churches, clergy, and believers within its expanded borders. Whereas the number of open churches in the unoccupied territories of the RSFSR had been reduced from 3,617 (in 1936) to around 950 (in 1939) before the war, after the annexations there were 8,279 Orthodox churches inside Soviet borders as well as thousands of communities belonging to other confessions—Roman Catholics, Ukrainian (Eastern Rite, or Greek) Catholics, and sectarians—whose loyalty to the Soviet regime Stalin questioned.[156] Stalin found himself with a new religious problem at home, and he saw the Orthodox Church as a tool for regaining control over the western borderlands, where Soviet power was most tenuous, and even buttressed it to weaken the locally dominant confessions, such as Lithuanian Catholics and Ukrainian Greek Catholics.[157] To this end, Stalin dissolved and outlawed the Ukrainian Greek Catholic Church and transferred its property to the Orthodox Church shortly after the war. Stalin also saw the Orthodox Church as a foreign policy tool on the world stage, a counterweight to the Vatican's influence in Europe and a diplomatic tool in the emerging Cold War.[158]

The new Soviet model of church-state relations had more than a family resemblance to church-state relations under the imperial order. Indeed, Ivan Polianskii, a KGB colonel and the new chairperson of CARC, explicitly referenced what he understood to be the Orthodox Church's traditional relationship as a junior partner to the state, with no political ambitions of its own. As he reported to the party's Department of Propaganda and Agitation in 1947,

> The overwhelming majority of the religiously inclined citizens confess Orthodoxy and therefore are under certain influence of the Russian Orthodox Church, which due to its historically evolved doctrine, never laid claim and does not lay claim to a role of the first-rate political player, but always followed in the trail of state politics. The hierarchical organizational structure of the Orthodox Church is more perfect than the structure of any other cult, which allows us to control and regulate its internal life with greater flexibility and effectiveness.[159]

Following the incorporation of the Orthodox Church into the Soviet state, Stalin pursued a similar strategy with other confessions. Just as he had restored the Orthodox patriarchate in order to create a centralized and hierarchical governing body for Russian Orthodoxy, he also created an analogous institution for Islam, the Spiritual Administration of the Muslims of Central Asia and Kazakhstan in 1943.[160] He also allowed the establishment of the Union of Evangelical Christian Baptists in order to bring the Baptists out of the underground and under CARC control, in the process producing a schism between those who were willing to exist legally within the framework of the state, and those who chose to remain unregistered and underground.[161]

## *All Quiet on the Atheist Front*

Was Stalin's wartime rapprochement with the Orthodox Church and shift on the religious question more broadly a rupture in the party's understanding and management of religion? Certainly, the new framework lent itself to multiple interpretations among contemporaries, and disoriented both ordinary Soviet citizens, who drew diverse conclusions about the place of religion in the postwar order, and party cadres, who saw the new status quo as a betrayal of ideological purity.[162] In his study of wartime religious revival, Peris notes that many of the religious interpreted Stalin's reversal as a return to the "natural" order of affairs. "The religious, long accustomed to a state which claimed responsibility for all spheres of activity and thought, now believed that the care for their Orthodox souls fell under the state's purview." Indeed, some interpreted CAROC as a revived Holy Synod, and addressed their appeals to both the patriarch and Karpov, using "a mix of pre-revolutionary and Soviet terminology suggesting a union of church and state."[163] As Peris writes, "Stalin's comment to Karpov at the September 1943 meeting that [Karpov] was not to become the church's over-procurator . . . rang hollow. Almost overnight, many elements of the pre-Revolutionary relationship between church and state were established."[164]

The "activist core" of the party, on the other hand, felt alienated by the new status quo.[165] To party cadres who had spent the 1930s closing churches, repressing clergy, and ferreting out underground religious communities, the sanctioned return of religion alongside the virtual disappearance of atheism was disorienting.[166] Indeed, Shkarovskii notes that many officials expressed their discomfort about the "drawing closer" (*sblizhenie*) of state and church.[167] But ideological puritans made up a relatively small cohort, since most party cadres did not have a deep mastery of Marxist or Leninist theory. Stalinist ideology, moreover, had already undergone major shifts in the 1930s as the party struggled to formulate an official narrative that remained within the parameters of Marxism-Leninism, while also appealing to an audience broader than its most devoted followers.[168] Most party cadres therefore were relatively untroubled by the return of religion and disappearance of atheism. As Peris observes, they "assumed that a resurgent church would occupy its 'natural' position as a subordinate unit of the state."[169]

Some scholars have emphasized continuities with early Soviet policy, noting that the Bolsheviks were consistent in privileging politics over ideology on the religious question. The historian Arto Luukkanen, in his study of the Cult Commission, argues that Soviet policy was always dictated more by political exigencies than by ideological motives.[170] Shkarovskii sees in Stalin a political pragmatist whose contradictory religious policies masked his consistency in prioritizing effective governance and security above other concerns. Shkarovskii observes a process of the "statization" (*ogosudartsveleniia*) of the

Orthodox Church between 1943 and 1948, as the state mobilized it for both foreign and domestic objectives. All this suggests that Stalin prioritized politics over ideological commitments. As Shkarovskii writes, "Both in atheism and in religion [Stalin] saw social phenomena that had to serve his system, each in its own way."[171]

Stalin's abandonment of atheism in the same period would support this analysis. The wartime religious revival on both the territories occupied by the German army and those that remained under Soviet control revealed that militant atheism was a thin veneer that could be easily shed.[172] Indeed, by the end of the 1930s, official support for militant atheism was gone, though atheists themselves did not yet seem to realize it. In 1939, Fedor Oleshchuk, a priest's son and the deputy head of the league, published an article in the party journal *Bolshevik* calling for an intensification of militant atheism. "Every priest, even the most Soviet one, is an obscurantist, reactionary, and an enemy of socialism," wrote Oleshchuk, and the party could not rest until Soviet people were "made into atheists."[173] But while lone atheist voices continued to proclaim their commitment to the atheist mission, the new political climate did not bode well for militant atheism. In fact, even before Stalin formalized the new church-state partnership by restoring the patriarchate and creating CAROC to manage church-state relations, he made several decisions that signaled a course that privileged governance over ideology. With the start of the war, atheist periodicals and publishing houses were shut down, most antireligious museums were closed, and most of the institutions charged with atheist work were dissolved. Indeed, when Iaroslavskii died in 1943, one could say that militant atheism died as well.

After the war, Stalin was much more concerned with effectively managing religion—using the councils and the KGB—than with spreading atheism. The party never explicitly renounced atheism, but to the frustration of its most ideologically committed cadres, it no longer invested it with political value or resources.[174] Eventually, atheists understood the party's signals and receded into the background.

## *Conclusion*

In the early Soviet period, the Bolsheviks engaged with religion above all as a political problem. This prioritization of the political threat posed by religious institutions and clergy helps make sense of oscillations in Soviet approaches to religion and atheism before the war. The Bolshevik Party's multiple objectives—modernization and governance, ideological mobilization and cultural revolution—produced antireligious policies that often worked against each other and rarely produced the intended results. The meaning and importance of atheism, as a field of ideological work distinct from the regulation and repression of religion, was contested over the course of the 1920s and 1930s, but atheist work as such remained secondary to political concerns, which decided the fate of both religion and atheism.

That religion was taken seriously above all when it posed a threat to Bolshevik power is most clear from the fate of the Orthodox Church under Lenin and Stalin. Lenin considered the church, as the confession of the majority of Soviet citizens with deep roots in Russia's history and culture, a serious threat to Bolshevik power, which remained tenuous through the 1920s. Stalin's consolidation of power throughout the 1930s, however, secured Bolshevik rule and broke the political power of the church. As priorities shifted during the war, the church became increasingly attractive as an ally, both in mobilizing patriotism at home and as a diplomatic vehicle for the Soviet state's ambitions abroad. CAROC and CARC, as bureaucracies whose task was to manage relations between religious organizations and the state, were intended to serve as the neutral face of Soviet legality that masked the state's control over religious affairs—a point underscored by the effort to make a visible wall between the work of the councils and extralegal activities of the NKVD. The fate of the Orthodox Church also highlights the main distinction between the Leninist and Stalinist approaches to religion: to preserve Soviet power, Lenin expelled religion from politics and public life, whereas Stalin recognized that its political power could be used to serve the state.

On the religious front, Stalin's last decade in power—from 1943, when the new model of church-state relations was introduced, until his death in 1953—was a period of relative stability in church-state relations and even a limited religious revival in Soviet society. Atheism, on the other hand, disappeared from public life until Stalin's successor, Khrushchev, opened the door for atheism's return.

CHAPTER TWO

# The Specter Haunting Soviet Communism

## ANTIRELIGIOUS CAMPAIGNS UNDER KHRUSHCHEV

> Creating the new person is a complicated and lengthy process. It is impossible to mechanically transfer people from the kingdom of capitalism into the kingdom of Communism. We cannot bring into Communism a person overgrown with the moss of capitalist prejudices. First, we need to liberate him from the baggage of the past. The battle with capitalist survivals in people's consciousness that was begun by our revolution, the transformation of the habits and customs built up my millions of people over the centuries, is a prolonged and complicated task. Survivals of the past are a dreadful power that, like a nightmare, weigh on the minds of the living. They root themselves in the byt and consciousness of millions of people, long after the economic conditions that gave birth to them have vanished.
>
> —NIKITA KHRUSHCHEV, SPEECH AT THE TWENTY-SECOND CONGRESS OF THE SOVIET COMMUNIST PARTY, OCTOBER 17, 1961

IN WINTER 1956—shortly before the opening of the Twentieth Party Congress (February 14–25, 1956)—the Communist Party Central Committee's Propaganda Department received a report about a curious incident: in Kuibyshev (now Samara), a large industrial city on the Volga, a young Komsomol girl named Zoia Karnaukhova had reportedly been turned to stone, "punished by God for blasphemy."[1] The events took place at 84 Chkalov Street, where a group of friends had gathered for a birthday party.[2] While her friends danced, Zoia waited for a young man named Nikolai, and when he did not show up, she declared that she would instead dance with the icon of Nikolai the Miracle Worker hanging in the "red corner" of the house. She climbed up on a chair, grabbed the icon, and dancing around the room, exclaimed, "If there is a God, then let him punish me!" Suddenly, the report concluded, "thunder thundered, lightning flashed, and smoke surrounded the young woman." When the smoke lifted, the report concluded, "the young woman had been turned into a pillar of stone, [grasping] the icon in her hands."[3]

News of the miracle—or, in the words of the party report, the "preposterous fable" (*nelepaia skazka*)—quickly spread through Kuibyshev, and people gathered on Chkalov Street to see the girl who had been turned to stone for blasphemy. Over the course of January 19, 20, and 21, the report noted, "the crowd reached several hundred people," and the police, who had already sent militia to Chkalov Street, soon had to "intensify the post" with another detachment on horseback. Meanwhile local officials had "intervened in the affair too late," waiting several days to condemn the incident in the local newspaper. Titled "A Bizarre Incident" (*Dikii sluchai*), the article argued that the "savage and embarrassing" events on Chkalov Street were a reprimand of the district party committee. "Let the ugly grimace of the old byt, which many of us witnessed in those days, become for them a lesson and a warning."[4] Local party officials heard the warning and soon "designed measures to intensify natural scientific propaganda."[5] Their enlightenment measures, however, were overshadowed by the spontaneous mobilization around Stone Zoia, which turned Chkalov Street into a pilgrimage destination for Soviet people—both the pious and those who were simply curious—eager to witness the miracle for themselves.

Stone Zoia was certainly a sensational story, but as a manifestation of popular religiosity it was neither unique nor new. Indeed, CAROC and CARC regularly filed reports that contained similarly "bizarre" stories of "superstition" from around the country that ranged from renewed icons and appearances of the Virgin Mary, to accusations of witchcraft that ended in murder.[6] More problematic than sensational incidents like Stone Zoia were the less sensational and much more common signs of postwar religious revival, such as rises in the governments figures on church income, attendance, and rites. And more troubling than the signs of the sanctioned religious revival were the manifestations of unsanctioned popular religiosity—group baptisms, pilgrimages to holy sites, the veneration of miraculous icons, and recourse to the services of faith healers—that moved religiosity beyond the walls of the church. Why, then, was the story of Stone Zoia—a Komsomol girl from Kuibyshev turned to stone after blasphemously dancing with an Orthodox icon—important enough to make it all the way up to the Central Committee? Why did the Soviet state disturb the postwar stability of church-state relations and again see religion as a problem? And why did Khrushchev bring atheism back after Stalin had cast it aside?

## *The Ugly Grimace of the Old Way of Life*

The Khrushchev era brought a new wave of antireligious and atheist campaigns, first in the so-called Hundred Days campaign in the summer of 1954, and then again in a much more extensive campaign that began in 1958 and continued until Khrushchev's forced retirement in 1964.[7] The story of the Khrushchev era antireligious campaigns is part of the bigger story about

Khrushchev's efforts to redefine the course of Soviet Communism after Stalin's death. Stalin's death created an ideological and political vacuum at the heart of Soviet Communism, and shook Soviet society to its foundations. As historian Stephen Bittner writes, "A universe of meaning was thrown into disarray, a process that was akin to the 'cosmic reorganization' that followed the collapse of communism."[8] What did Soviet Communism mean without Stalin? For Stalin's successors, providing an answer to this question became the mechanism for defining the course of Soviet development and consolidating political power. Ultimately, the person who emerged victorious from the struggle for power that followed Stalin's death was Khrushchev, and he did this by redefining the meaning of Soviet Communism for the new era.

On February 25, 1956, at the Twentieth Party Congress, Khrushchev gave a "Secret Speech" in which he condemned Stalin's "cult of personality" as a deviation from Leninism, and denounced Stalinist coercion, violence, and terror as a betrayal of the party and its ideology. As Soviet society reeled from Khrushchev's revelations about Stalin, the party struggled to contain the fallout. In order to redeem the people's faith in the Soviet project, Khrushchev needed to relegitimate the party and its revolutionary ideology.[9] If de-Stalinization was the negative side of Khrushchev's platform, then the Third Party Program, announced at the Twenty-Second Party Congress (October 17–31, 1961), was its positive side: the return to ideological purity, party leadership, and material progress toward the Communist future.[10] Khrushchev told Soviet citizens that the country had entered a new era of building Communism—an era marked by the party's commitment to material welfare, individual development, and moral regeneration. He declared that Soviet economic growth would overtake the West within a decade and promised the Soviet people that they would see Communism built in their lifetime.[11] On October 31, 1961, the last day of the Twenty-Second Party Congress, Khrushchev ordered the removal of Stalin's body from the mausoleum on Moscow's Red Square, where it had lain next to Lenin's since 1953.

The degree of Khrushchev's personal involvement in the antireligious campaign is difficult to determine.[12] Indeed, Khrushchev's own recollections as well as the memoirs of his son Sergei Khrushchev and son-in-law Aleksei Adzhubei are all conspicuously silent on the topic.[13] Nevertheless, Khrushchev made several public pronouncements on religion. When prodded by foreign journalists to express his position on religion in the Soviet Union, Khrushchev spoke of his personal unbelief, argued against the notion that an atheist was less moral than a religious believer, and generally stressed the hypocrisy of religious institutions and officials. At the same time, Khrushchev, mindful of the political importance of the religious question in international affairs, asserted that in the Soviet Union, religious belief remained an issue of individual conscience rather than state policy. As he put it in a 1957 interview with the

French newspaper *Le Figaro*, "The question of who believes in God and who does not is not a question that should give rise to conflicts—it is the personal affair of each individual. Therefore let us not discuss the subject in detail."[14]

Yet while Khrushchev's specific role in the antireligious campaign is unclear, there is no question about his investment in the construction of Communism—a project that was inherently connected to the eradication of religious "survivals" and inculcation of a scientific atheist worldview in Soviet society. Over the course of his tenure, Khrushchev's pronouncements on religion became more explicit and aggressive. In a 1958 *Pravda* article, he stated, "I think that there is no God. I have long ago freed myself from such an idea. I am an advocate of the scientific worldview. Science and belief in supernatural forces are incompatible and mutually exclusive views."[15] By the early 1960s, when the Soviet Union claimed global primacy in science and technology, especially after sending the first person to space, Khrushchev was jokingly asking Soviet cosmonauts to keep an eye out for God during their space travels. Indicative of the antireligious mood of the time are two statements attributed to Khrushchev that circulated in popular culture: that soon, religion would exist only in museums, and that Khrushchev would show the Soviet people the last priest on television.[16] While Khrushchev's revival of the antireligious campaign may seem peculiar in the context of the era's political liberalization and cultural "thaw," it was consistent with the mission of cleansing Communism of corruption, which included Stalin's accommodation with religion and retreat from atheism.

The question that haunted Soviet Communism during the Khrushchev era was why religion remained a part of Soviet life decades after the October Revolution. With the construction of socialism, the economic and social roots of religion had ostensibly been eradicated. Moreover, with Stalin's subjugation of religious institutions to the government apparatus, religion was considered effectively neutralized as an autonomous political agent that could influence Soviet society or shape Communism's historical development. Yet Marxist claims about the disappearance of religion with the arrival of Communism clashed with revelation that religious survivals were far more prevalent and tenacious than the ideological model had prophesied.

Taking place a month before the Twentieth Party Congress, the peculiar story of Stone Zoia was an uncomfortable reminder that religion remained a social fact. To be sure, the continued existence of religion had always been a problem for the world's first socialist country, but in the new era of Communist construction, religion became a new kind of problem. Stone Zoia—a public demonstration of religiosity around a Komsomol girl turned to stone for blasphemy—surely sounded a dissonant chord against the background of Khrushchev's promises about scientific and technological progress and the imminent arrival of Communism. Khrushchev's optimism was thus tempered by the acknowledgment that forty years after the October Revolution, vestiges of the old world were still part of Soviet life. As Khrushchev himself admitted at the Twenty-Second Party Congress, "survivals" of the old world continued to "hold sway over the minds of living creatures like a nightmare, long after the economic conditions that gave birth to them have vanished."[17] In this framework, the only ideologically coherent explanation for the continued existence of religion in the Soviet Union was that it was a stubborn vestige of a former worldview and way of life. Under Khrushchev, then, the party realized that it was not enough to eliminate the political and economic base of religion. In order to transform the Soviet society of the present into the Communist society of the future, religion had to be eradicated not just from Soviet politics and public life but also from Soviet people's consciousness.

## *Atheism's Return: The Campaign of 1954*

Between the Bolshevik seizure of power in 1917 and Stalin's declaration that socialism had been constructed in the USSR during the "Congress of Victors" (Seventeenth Party Congress) in 1934, the Soviet Union had transformed from a polity teetering on the brink of survival, run by a small revolutionary party, and shunned by the outside world, into a functioning, internationally recognized state.[18] Stalin's consolidation of power in the mid-1930s was accompanied by the rejection of revolutionary utopianism in favor of traditionalism and more immediate political priorities. In particular, his need to mobilize resources and gain support for the Soviet war effort, both at home and abroad, precipitated a reevaluation of the Soviet position on religion. Following Stalin's 1943 concordat with the Orthodox Church, religion again became part of Soviet life—albeit heavily regulated and largely silent.

After the war, the Orthodox Church rebuilt the infrastructure that had been nearly destroyed by the antireligious campaigns of the early Soviet period. The patriarchate was restored, more than ten thousand churches were reopened, and priests returned from labor camps.[19] Young men were recruited into the seminaries in order to address the severe shortage of clergy, with the number of applicants rising every year, from 269 in 1950 to 560 in 1953.[20] Believers continuously petitioned the state to allow more churches to be opened and for services to be held more regularly. Atheist work, on the other hand, stagnated, especially in the culturally conservative atmosphere of the late Stalin era. While late Stalinist propaganda maintained a commitment to enlightenment, the emphasis was on literacy, hygiene, and the cultivation of "culturedness." Even in scientific enlightenment, the stress on atheism was cast aside.

Indicative of the shift away from atheist propaganda toward a broader conception of enlightenment is the establishment of Znanie in 1947. Founded as a voluntary association of intelligentsia committed to the enlightenment of the masses, Znanie took over the functions of the dissolved League of the Militant Godless. Its mandate was considerably broader, though, and included popular science, Marxist-Leninist theory, domestic politics, and international affairs.[21] While atheism was technically folded into the broader category of scientific enlightenment, it occupied only a small fraction of Znanie's work until after Stalin's death. Veteran *bezbozhniki* occasionally lectured and published pamphlets on science and religion, but on the whole, atheist work came to a standstill.[22] At the Nineteenth Party Congress held in 1952, shortly before Stalin's death, atheism was not even discussed.[23] In the 1940s and early 1950s, the ideological establishment and atheist cadres tacitly understood the low priority of atheist work.

Stalin's death destabilized the precarious calm in postwar religious life.[24] After the war, Soviet religious policy had privileged governance over ideology. If religion was a social fact, then the state's role was to forge a partnership with religious institutions, and CAROC and CARC were created to "normalize" relations with religious institutions and believers. Stalin's death put the mission of the councils in question. In June 1953, three months after Stalin's death, the head of CAROC, Karpov, sent a note to the Central Committee requesting guidance on religious policy, and asking "what line should be followed, what principles and methods are permissible."[25] Karpov suggested that, keeping in mind the religious revival, CAROC should focus on maintaining a working relationship with the church—an objective to which he believed CAROC's informal yet intimate connection with the KGB continued to present a problem.[26] Over the course of 1953 and early 1954, CAROC continued to send notes to both state and party organs, but its inquiries remained unanswered, even when petitions were personally addressed to the heads of both institutions, Malenkov and Khrushchev.[27] Cautious not to act without direction from above, CAROC's work came to a halt.

For party purists, who saw the postwar rapprochement with religion as a departure from Leninist principles, and watched with trepidation as religion revived and atheism stagnated, Stalin's death was an opportunity. Vladimir Bonch-Bruevich—a prominent figure in the atheist old guard—seized the chance to put atheism back on the agenda.[28] Bonch-Bruevich pointed out that Leningrad's State Museum of the History of Religion (Gosudarstvennyi Muzei Istorii Religii, or GMIR) was the only atheist institution that survived the war. Founded in 1932 and housed in the Kazan Cathedral on Nevsky Prospect, Leningrad's central thoroughfare, GMIR was almost closed after the war, having suffered serious damage during the wartime blockade of Leningrad. What saved GMIR from the fate of other early Soviet atheist museums, which had been closed before the war, was that unlike other atheist museums, whose primary purpose was propaganda, it was conceived as a research institution and therefore housed under the Soviet Academy of Sciences rather than the Ministry of Culture or Commissariat of Enlightenment.[29] In 1946, Bonch-Bruevich became the museum's new director. Like the museum itself, Bonch-Bruevich was one of the few remaining links with the militant atheism of the early Soviet period. Since the cathedral that housed GMIR was so damaged, the museum remained closed to visitors until 1951, and Bonch-Bruevich stayed in Moscow, where he held a position at the Institute of History of the Academy of Sciences. There, he devoted himself to the project that consumed him until his death in 1955: reviving Soviet atheism.[30] To put atheism back on the political agenda, Bonch-Bruevich tried to generate academic interest by creating the History of Religion and Atheism sector at the academy's Institute of History in 1947. Yet even this limited initiative lacked the ingredients critical to success: the support of his academic colleagues and patronage of party elites. Until Stalin's death, the sector was barely active.[31]

The first sign of a shift in the political fortune of Soviet atheism was Bonch-Bruevich's success in adding the word "atheism" to the name of the museum, which in January of 1954 became the State Museum of Religion and Atheism (Gosudarstvennyi Muzei Istorii Religii i Ateizma, or GMIRA). As Bonch-Bruevich reported in a letter to a colleague, "Now, for the first time in the existence of the Soviet Academy of Sciences, the word 'atheism' has been officially incorporated into the name of an academic institution. . . . I consider this event pretty significant in our battle."[32] Shortly after, certain high-ranking party cadres began to signal their interest in revisiting the religious question. In March, Dmitrii Shepilov, the editor of *Pravda*, sent Khrushchev a letter sharing that the newspaper's correspondents reported that there was a "serious reactivation of church functionaries and various kinds of sectarians, [and] of the poor state of scientific atheist propaganda." Shepilov further pointed out that there were 18,609 functional churches, mosques, and synagogues in the USSR, and more than 18,000 registered clerics in the USSR—a significant increase from the prewar period.[33]

On March 27, 1954, two Central Committee departments—propaganda and science—followed up with a report titled "On Major Insufficiencies in Natural-Scientific, Antireligious Propaganda," which likewise drew Khrushchev's attention to the dangers of ideological passivity.[34] In spring 1954, then, atheism finally found its party patrons: the head of the Central Committee Culture Department, Aleksei Rumiantsev; Central Committee Secretary Piotr Pospelov; the head of the propaganda department, Mikhail Suslov; Minister of Culture Ekaterina Furtseva; as well as Shepilov and Aleksandr Shelepin, both part of a new Komsomol cohort gathering around Khrushchev. Someone, however, was needed to guide the campaign, and Bonch-Bruevich—with his scholarly and revolutionary pedigree—became the vehicle for atheism's return. In a flurry of internal reports, phone calls, and meetings throughout May and June, Bonch-Bruevich's party patrons signaled that a new antireligious campaign was imminent.[35]

On July 7, 1954, the Central Committee issued a decree, "On Great Insufficiencies in the Propagation of Scientific Atheism and on Measures for Its Improvement," one of Khrushchev's first ideological pronouncements. Having been developed in the closed circles of the party apparatus, the decree caught everyone—religious organizations, ordinary Soviet citizens, and even CAROC and CARC—off guard.[36] It proceeded from the position that religion and Communism were incompatible, and that the continued existence of religion in socialist conditions was the product of the intensified activism of religious organizations, on the one hand, and the party's neglect of atheism since the war, on the other. Party cadres were criticized for their ideological passivity and called to actively participate in atheist work. But the call for improvement in atheist work extended beyond the party, and included the Ministries of Culture and Education as well as Znanie, among others. The decree called on the Ministry of Education to strengthen atheist programs in schools; the Komsomol to intensify atheist work targeting the youth; the state publishing house Gospolitizdat to publish better atheist literature; and Znanie to publish *Science and Religion* (*Nauka i religiia*), an atheist monthly aimed at the masses.

The antireligious campaign was not just about cleansing Communist ideology of corruption but also about modernization. Khrushchev viewed religion as a predominantly rural problem, and one of the campaign's goals was to eliminate popular religious practices that undermined agricultural productivity, such as pilgrimages and feast days, which party propaganda depicted as debaucheries that disrupted the work of collective farms and often ended in violence.[37] "As a result of the activation of the church," the decree stated, "the number of citizens who observe religious holidays and rituals has increased [and] pilgrimages to so-called holy places are reviving. . . . Celebrations of religious holidays (which are often accompanied by drunkenness that lasts many days and mass killings of livestock) damage the national economy, distract thousands of people from work, [and] undermine labor discipline."[38] Regional CAROC plenipotentiaries reported on labor lost when collective farmers took off work to celebrate religious holidays, and lamented that these celebrations often happened with the tacit approval of local officials, and sometimes even with their participation.[39] A report on celebrations of feast days at a collective farm in the Kostroma region emphasized the economic and moral cost of such popular practices:

> Until very recent times, every locale celebrated many religious holidays, among them one, and sometimes two, feast days. All in all, thirty-nine [holidays] were commemorated in the villages. Party organs and the directors of the collective farm decided to take stock of how much all these holidays are costing the association. It was established that each religious holiday was celebrated by an average of five hundred people,

> and the celebrations lasted three to four days. Because of this, the collective farm lost around eighty thousand workdays every year. Therefore, just from collective farmers not showing up to work, the enterprise underproduced by three million rubles (according to the old system). But there were also casualties that do not easily lend themselves to being counted—and these are moral casualties. . . . [M]ass drunkenness could be observed, accompanied by hooliganism, debauchery, and fights with serious consequences.[40]

While community celebrations involving drinking and merrymaking had long been traditional forms of leisure in the Russian countryside, they were now categorized as deviant and backward, and therefore an obstacle to the Soviet goal of bridging the material and cultural differences between city and country.

Much as in the early Soviet period, the media were assigned priority in the battle against religion. Publishers and journalists were criticized for neglecting atheist topics in the postwar period, and thick journals like *Communist* (*Kommunist*), *New World* (*Novyi mir*), and *October* (*Oktiabr'*) were cited as not having published even one atheist article between 1945 and 1954. Newspapers had done little better. The party's newspaper, *Pravda*, had put out only one atheist article in almost a decade, and even the Komsomol's newspaper, *Komsomol'skaia Pravda*, typically on the front lines of ideological campaigns, had published only five atheist articles in the same period.[41] Publishing houses were called on to publish atheist literature, including foreign classics like Giovanni Boccaccio, Voltaire, and Anatole France, and the works of Soviet authors like Anton Chekhov, Gorky, Aleksandr Serafimovich, and Vladimir Maiakovsky, that engaged with anticlerical and atheist themes.[42] Journalists and editors were also instructed to produce new atheist works that spoke to contemporary audiences, and to modernize atheist content by placing a heavy emphasis on scientific and technological feats. Finally, the party underscored the need to engage the masses through television and radio, noting that the radio was a particularly effective tool because it reached rural areas.[43]

Newspapers, meanwhile, published articles that relied on old tropes—like the familiar drunk, immoral, and rapacious clergy—but also introduced new themes, such as the danger of superstition.[44] Soviet readers were treated to cautionary tales, like the one about Natasha Shichalina, who had the misfortune of falling for the "dreamy, always silent" Gavril, a young Baptist who murdered her because she tried to resist "the demands of his sect."[45] Readers were also told the story of Gera Borodin, a young boy who went temporarily blind playing with homespun rockets. Rather than put their faith in modern Soviet medicine, Gera's simple mother and grandmother took him to the village church to pray to Saint Panteleimon the Healer, promising the saint that if he restored Gera's vision they would continue to take him to church. This decision, *Komsomol'skaia Pravda* concluded, "was the first step to Gera's ruin," isolating him from his peers and ultimately leading him to commit suicide.[46]

The press also attacked provincial party and Komsomol officials for being passive about atheist work, arguing that they were also responsible for the persistence of religion under socialist conditions. Party directives criticized local cadres for "blindly follow[ing] the clergy" (*idut na povodu u tserkovnikov*), and reports even cited incidents where local officials went to the church for financial assistance or, conversely, used Soviet resources to assist the church (such as when one party official lent the local monastery ten collective farm workers for three days).[47] *Komsomol'skaia Pravda* reported on villages in Ulianovsk where rumors of a large "ghost woman" who "brazenly" wandered around town spread among the inhabitants, clearing out the streets and village club.[48] Shortly after the ghost woman was exposed as a prank, an icon was reported to have "renewed" in a local woman's home, and visitors filled "half a bucket of copper and silver pieces in one day alone." The Komsomol, meanwhile, ignored atheist work, even though the region had four pilgrimage sites to which believers "thronged" in the summer, all "under the noses of district leaders."[49] Another article decried a similar state of affairs in Kursk Province, where "even young people can be seen among those who go to 'holy places' for 'cures' and religious festivals," while the provincial Komsomol committee "remains a dispassionate observer of what is going on."[50] Another *Komsomol'skaia Pravda* feature on religion in the Gorky region noted with alarm that the clergy were winning the war over Soviet hearts and minds. As the author noted, "The Old Believer priest tells parents to hang crosses around their children's necks and to teach them psalms and prayers, while Komsomol propagandists remain silent."[51] The Komsomol, he argued, was "obligated to protect all youth from the influence of church and sect members and to carry on antireligious propaganda among the entire public," since the clergy "do not act in heavenly space, but on earth, among the public," spreading "opium" among the villagers. In light of this, the party called on each Komsomol member to combat religion, spread atheism, and explain to the masses that religion was incompatible with both science and Communism.[52]

Church officials responded to the July decree with concern, dismayed by the return of administrative measures against clerics and believers as well as press slander that cast priests and believers as politically unreliable elements. In a conversation with his local CAROC plenipotentiary, Archpriest Medvedevskii of Leningrad complained that the church did not have the opportunity to respond to atheist attacks in the press. He also insisted that the church was not responsible for the drunkenness and hooliganism that took place during religious feast days, objecting that on the contrary, clergy called on believers to "pass the holidays in a worthy manner." The church, he argued, was being scapegoated. When local officials failed to fulfill the plan, they blamed the church "to cover up the true reasons for their lagging behind."[53] Others, however, did not see the antireligious campaign as a threat. In secret reports sent to CAROC, the KGB noted that there were even priests who dismissed and mocked atheist efforts. In Latvia, Orthodox priests were reported to have remarked that the quality of Soviet atheism was so low that they had little to worry about: "They talk a lot and say there is no God. But if there is no God, then there is no reason to agitate about it so much and try to break through an open door. This kind of propaganda does not leave an impression on believers."[54]

Reports from the regions showed that ordinary people interpreted the new antireligious campaign in different ways. In summer 1954, CAROC was flooded with letters asking whether the press campaign was the prelude to mass church closures and arrests. Rumors of impending church closures incited mass protests, and Soviet people hurried to religious objects and baptize their children.[55] The intensification of antireligious propaganda in the press, CAROC reported, actually produced a sudden increase in demand for religious rites, especially baptisms. In October 1954, both councils sent the Central Committee a joint letter in which they pointed to the counterproductive results of the campaign. As Karpov and Polianskii wrote, "These mistakes and distortions have angered not thousands but millions of Soviet citizens who draw inflammatory conclusions from them. Individual church leaders from Eastern Europe also draw such conclusions. Leading national religious representatives in the USSR, who daily receive almost all foreign delegations that arrive in our country, and church officials who travel abroad, are placed in a difficult position."[56] In this way, Karpov and Polianskii tried to show that the campaign undermined social cohesion and political stability, and threatened to damage the image of the Soviet Union abroad. Finally conceding that the 1954 campaign was a fiasco, the party retreated.

The November 10, 1954, decree "On Errors in the Conduct of Scientific Atheist Propaganda among the Population" addressed the fallout of the summer's antireligious campaign, and tried to repair the damage. Unlike the July decree, which was intended for internal consumption, the November decree was published in *Pravda* and broadly disseminated. Also unlike the July decree, which had been produced by a small group of propaganda specialists within the party apparatus, the November decree was the product of consultations with both CAROC and CARC, and reflected greater awareness of the Soviet religious landscape and a shift in the party's understanding of religion.[57] The November decree's primary message was that in the present historical context, religion was to be addressed with ideological rather than political mechanisms. It is well known, the decree explained, that before the revolution the church exploited the masses by serving the autocratic regime, and after the revolution supported counterrevolutionary elements at home and imperialist ambitions abroad. Yet party cadres were now to understand that since the social roots of religion were eliminated, the battle against religion had moved into "the ideological struggle of the scientific, materialist worldview against the antiscientific, religious worldview."[58] Religion had become an ideological rather than a political problem.

To be sure, the decree clarified, some religions continued to be political problems. In the USSR's western borderlands, for example, where confession mapped onto nationality and mobilized nationalist resistance, religion continued to exercise political power. Likewise, sectarians, especially those considered to be foreign (such as Jehovah's Witnesses or Seventh-day Adventists), found themselves under greater suspicion, not just for their stark refusal to accommodate Soviet power, but also for their alleged connections with their coreligionists abroad.[59] But religious institutions that operated legally, the decree explained, were patriotic. It was therefore incorrect to see the clergy and believers as internal enemies, rather than citizens whose rights and feelings had to be respected. Religion was no longer a political enemy to be repressed, but an alien ideology to be eradicated through enlightenment. The battle was with the belief, not the believer.

Shortly after issuing the November decree, the Central Committee gauged popular reception.[60] As with the July decree, popular responses were varied and often surprising. While the party had initially feared that the more liberal line would encourage religious activity, local CAROC plenipotentiaries shared that church attendance actually declined once believers stopped fearing church closures. The November decree, they reported, "brought to believers a calm about the fate of their churches, which expressed itself in a certain decline, in various locations of the Soviet Union, in the number of church attendees even during such a venerated holiday as Christmas." In Riga, Latvia, "even those who constantly attended church services were lazy about showing up to every mass during these Christmas holidays, while before they would have never missed them." In the Krasnodar region, priests had predicted that church attendance would rise, since believers "would no longer be embarrassed," yet these expectations "did not turn out to be justified." In general, popular responses to the more liberal party line were positive, and believers expressed "satisfaction" that the Central Committee had now "warned everyone that no one can violate the constitutional rights of Soviet citizens."[61]

During local party meetings, people asked whether Communists who lived with religious family members were permitted to keep icons in their homes, why so many Soviet army officers went to church, why Communists who observed religious rites were not excluded from the party, whether the new decree meant that all young people were now permitted to marry in the church, why there were still open seminaries in the Soviet Union at all, and why the state could not just close all the churches and be done with it.[62] At the same time, reports also noted that some local officials seemed to "understand the decree incorrectly." One worker expressed this sentiment specifically in terms of the right to participate in religious rituals: "Recently, there has been a lot of writing in newspapers that judges those who have been godparents or baptized their child in church. What business is this of anyone's? As long as one works honestly, this is an affair of each person's conscience, which is written about in our constitution. We need to clarify for people their incorrect worldview, but we should not persecute them for this." Others were criticized for falling into the other extreme and "understand[ing] the decree as the freedom of practicing various religious beliefs by party members." A collective farmer from Lipetsk named Marenkov bristled at the thought of having to respect the rights of the clergy: "Why do we fuss over the priests? We should gather them together and get control over them. And if we cannot do this, we can at least give directives to the patriarch, so that he would issue a command to all the priests so that they would cease their work. Because otherwise it turns out that two ideologies exist among us simultaneously."[63] Overall, the 1954 campaign sent mixed messages and created confusion. The existence of "two ideologies at the same time" allowed for a broad spectrum of opinions about the meaning and place of religion in Soviet life.

Following the contradictory results of the 1954 antireligious campaign, the party retreated from the religious front. But the Soviet reengagement with religion is illuminating not so much for the questions it answered as for those it raised. To paraphrase the words of the Latvian priest, why was the party trying to break through an open door? In other words, why—given the political loyalty of most religious organizations and the party's faith in Marxism-Leninism—did religion again become a problem after Stalin's death? To answer this question, it is helpful to return to Bonch-Bruevich. Speaking at a meeting at the Academy of Sciences shortly after the promulgation of the November decree, Bonch-Bruevich decried the party's retreat from atheism. He recounted a recent visit to Leningrad, where he was "astounded" by the "enormous number" of churches being restored, but when he went to the regional party committee to ask about the "pious city" (*bogomol'nyi gorod*) under construction, local officials were evasive. "It turns out," Bonch-Bruevich continued, "that the patriarch, through his people on the State Inspection on the Preservation of Monuments got permission to restore these churches as objects of special value." What made the situation especially offensive to Bonch-Bruevich was that he was lobbying the very same commission to renovate the Kazan Cathedral that housed GMIRA, but was "categorically refused." For Bonch-Bruevich, there was something fundamentally wrong with a scenario in which churches were restored while the atheist museum was neglected. That the atheist museum would remain in disrepair while churches were being restored so outraged Bonch-Bruevich that he threatened to write to Khrushchev and Malenkov to "tell them about the disgraceful behavior of this organization, which from the point of view of an old Bolshevik, should be disbanded, since only the devil knows who is in it. . . . They probably wear crosses under their vests, but we are supposed to defer to them."[64]

In the end, the 1954 campaign was largely a press affair that had limited immediate impact on Soviet religious life. Despite the militant rhetoric, few churches were actually closed. Whereas in 1953 there were 13,508 Orthodox churches, 60 monasteries, and 12,089 priests, in 1954 the numbers had shrunk only slightly to 13,422 churches, 59 monasteries, and 11,912 priests, and in 1955 to 13,376 churches, 57 monasteries, and 10,863 priests. The statistics did not begin to change dramatically until 1961.[65] Given the fact that the antireligious decree was not openly disseminated at the time and had a relatively limited impact on religious life, its primary purpose was to send a signal to party, government, and religious officials about the change of course on the religious question.

## *Two Ideologies among Us*

The new party line on religion produced a range of interpretations about the future of religion in the USSR. The start of de-Stalinization in 1956 also contributed to the confusion, since neither religious nor state officials had clear guidance on how religious and atheist policy should map onto political developments. With the onset of de-Stalinization, the number of active Orthodox priests increased substantially as those who had been imprisoned or exiled were amnestied or rehabilitated. Rescinding an earlier prohibition, CAROC now allowed local plenipotentiaries to register clergy who had been imprisoned, so that by the end of the 1950s, 30 percent of clergy in Latvia and Lithuania, 45 percent in Belarus, and 80 percent in Ukraine had been imprisoned.[66] Religious literature was also allowed greater print runs, and in 1956, Bibles were printed in Russian for the first time in Soviet history, with a print run of twenty-eight thousand.[67] The religious question also remained a factor in foreign policy, as Khrushchev tried to establish greater contact with the world beyond Soviet borders. Orchestrated displays of religious vitality in the USSR earned the Soviet Union valuable political capital abroad, and the party made sure that foreign tourists were taken to churches to witness Soviet religious freedom.[68] During the 1957 Moscow Youth Festival, Soviet young people even held debates with religious visitors from England about the respective value of socialist and Christian morality.[69]

Over the course of 1955 to 1957, the Soviet political establishment was also faced with more immediate political problems, from managing the course of de-Stalinization to the power struggles among the political elite. Between 1955 and 1958, the religious question receded to the background, and religious life returned. The councils continued to collect data on religion, keeping track of the number of open churches and active clergy, church and clergy finances, holiday church attendance, popular religiosity, and the observance of rites—especially baptisms, marriages, and funerals, which were considered a major source of income for the church and the best indication of religious vitality. Orthodox Church income, largely from fees charged for officiating rites and the sale of candles, continued to increase. In Ukraine, for example, church income increased from 130 million to 145 million rubles between 1955 and 1956.[70] Overall, CAROC attributed the church's improved financial situation not only to the more liberal atmosphere but also to the increased standard of living, observing that "the size of church and clergy income reveal that the believers care for the church is not weakening but growing, and that at this point a religious community can expend serious means on the capital improvement of its religious buildings."[71]

Much of the increase in church income was attributed to rising observance of religious rites. The Leningrad CAROC plenipotentiary F. V. Fedoseev reported that comparing the first quarters of 1956 and 1957, the number of baptisms increased from 2,697 to 3,769, marriages from 70 to 111, and funerals from 1,955 to 1,958, with church income increasing accordingly, from 85,768 to 94,894 rubles.[72] Holiday church attendance also continued to rise. In large cities, churches were full on major religious holidays, especially Christmas and Easter. Moscow officials noted that when religious holidays fell on weekends or vacation days, churches were filled to capacity, some with as many as four thousand people.[73] Overall, the end of the antireligious campaign of 1954, combined with the significant economic growth of the mid-1950s, brought substantial gains for religion, but few for atheism.[74]

Believers interpreted de-Stalinization as a signal that political liberalization extended to the Soviet position on religion. The CAROC plenipotentiary in Moscow, Aleksei Trushin, reported that after the Twentieth Party Congress, believers' petitions to open churches increased.[75] He also relayed that petitioners connected their requests to open churches and register religious communities with contemporary political developments, citing the party's new emphasis on socialist legality, the meeting of Nikolai Bulganin—chair of the Council of Ministers—with Patriarch Aleksii, and press coverage of foreign church delegations visiting the USSR.[76] As one petitioner wrote, "Before we did not bother about opening churches because we thought that it would all be in vain. But now, when we learned from Bulganin's and Khrushchev's pronouncements in India that we have full freedom of conscience, we took this task on ourselves."[77]

Confusion about the status of religion in the Soviet Union even led some to posit a "third way" forward that put religion in the service of Communism. Boris Roslavlev, the self-professed "voice of believers within the intelligentsia," sent CAROC an extensive proposal about religion in contemporary conditions, which CAROC passed along to the Central Committee. In it, Roslavlev focused on the positive role that religion, and especially religious morality, could play in a period when Soviet society found itself on the "threshold of Communism" (*v nashem preddverii k kommunizmu*). He noted that the "believing intelligentsia" was attracted to religion because it saw in it "the improvement of human morality." Sometimes, Roslavlev wrote, "One wants to be alone with oneself, face-to-face with one's own conscience. And to see an image toward which one should strive. That image is Christ. It is said that it is possible to turn away from man's judgment, but not from that image [of Christ]."[78] Roslavlev questioned whether Communist morality could affect individuals as profoundly as the prospect of religious judgment, and wondered if perhaps Soviet people had not yet reached the moral purity that would make them fitting Communist citizens. He proposed that the Soviet state needed the Russian Orthodox Church (which, Roslavlev noted, represented the majority of Soviet citizens) to build the ideal Communist society. "Communism demands total development, total spiritual purity, the elevation of morality, and the most spiritual relations among people," Roslavlev wrote. "And the church, the true church, can very much help us on the threshold to Communism, in the spiritual strengthening of the right and the just." Communist morality, Roslavlev argued, was not fit for the task:

> They will tell us—we have Communist morality—that this is what should be inculcated into the human masses. True. But this demands an enormous amount of education; it demands many decades and a great deal of work. We can plan on this, which is what our government is doing, but to say that we will definitely and completely achieve this. . . . We cannot say this. There are many conditions that have not yet been overcome, as a result of which many will remain outside this elevated and great plan, outside the educational system. If we speak about the broad masses of people, it is easier to approach the soul and the conscience. Therefore, it is likely that we can be more successful at improving morality with the help of Christ. Especially if we see (and we undoubtedly see) that religion is not so easy to emasculate [*vykholostit'*].[79]

In noting the numerous shortcomings of both Soviet reality and Communist morality, Roslavlev pointed to Soviet Communism's inability to rob religion of its power, and proposed that religion persisted in the USSR not only because of what it offered but also because of what Soviet Communism failed to provide: material well-being and spiritual nourishment. For the Communist Party, of course, Roslavlev's solution—to put religion in the service of Communism—was not an option, since under Khrushchev religion was redefined as an alien ideology that threatened to undermine Communist construction. As the party solidified its ideological platform, attempts to reconcile religion with Communism—whether they came from ordinary citizens, government officials, the clergy, or the intelligentsia—became less welcome.

Finally, de-Stalinization also placed the institutions charged with maintaining "normal" relations with religious organizations, CAROC and CARC, in a precarious position, since the two frameworks guiding their work—the Stalinist model that privileged governance, and the Khrushchev era model that emphasized ideology—often worked against one another. Over the course of 1956 and 1957, CAROC struggled with internal disagreements about its missions, leading it to seek guidance from the party.[80] In a note to the Central Committee addressed to Pospelov, I. Ivanov, head of CAROC's Division of Inspectors, asked for clarification about the party line on religion in light of the Twentieth Party Congress.[81] Following the council's original mandate to maintain stability and control over religious affairs, Ivanov argued that denying believers' petitions to open churches, which violated their constitutional right to "observe religious cults," undermined the council's task to provide a "safety valve" for grievances.[82] In another letter, Ivanov's deputy, V. Spiridonov, proposed that in order to "successfully execute the decisions of the Twentieth Party Congress and the quick movement forward toward Communism," the council "should not turn into a headquarters of the political war with religion, and not do anything that would violate normal relations between the church and the state." CAROC's primary objective, Spiridonov argued, was to support the church in its "active battle for peace and its support for the affairs of the party and government in the country [and] not inventing some kind of strategic and tactical actions in the war against religion."[83] The party, Spiridonov concluded, should work with the church in the service of shared foreign and domestic objectives, and should fight religion "by the word only."[84]

In the context of Khrushchev's ideological mobilization, however, CAROC's emphasis on governance and stability no longer made sense. Moreover, by 1957, the party was becoming impatient. Nevertheless, much depended on the balance of power within the Soviet political establishment between the party apparatus and government institutions.[85] When Khrushchev eventually triumphed over his political rivals in the so-called Antiparty Group in 1957, the struggle for power was decided in favor of the party. Taking over the guidance of religious policy, the party informed the councils that their role was not to "normalize" religious life but rather to limit the influence of religion on Soviet society. Shortly after, antireligious articles reappeared in the press.[86]

In 1958, then, several factors came together to mobilize the party for a renewed offensive against religion: anxiety about religious revival, a more activist Orthodox Church and laity, and a shift in the balance of power within the Soviet political elite in favor of the party.[87] When these developments reached the party's ideological establishment—Suslov, Furtseva, Pospelov, and Leonid Il'ichev as well as Komsomol enthusiasts like Shelepin, Adzhubei, Sergei Pavlov, and Vladimir Semichastnyi—it was read as an intolerable deviation from the Communist model. Before long, it became clear that the party, rather than government organs, would direct Soviet religious policy. Finally, the antireligious campaign that had been building behind closed doors began, and the attempts to disguise it were no longer considered necessary.[88]

## *A Great Danger: The Campaign of 1958–64*

The revived antireligious campaign was ignited by a letter, sent to Suslov, the guardian of party orthodoxy, on April 15, 1958, by V. Shapovnikova, a special correspondent of *Literary Gazette* (*Literaturnaia gazeta*).[89] In it, Shapovnikova described her shock when she first encountered religion during a recent trip she had taken to the countryside to report on Baptist prayer meetings. What she witnessed, as well as the considerable reader response to her article, opened her eyes to the fact that a "great force stands behind the preacher" and she warned Suslov that "we are very weakly armed against such a force." Shapovnikova suggested that for the urban intelligentsia, religion was a blind spot. "We cannot even say with certainty the extent of the danger before us," she wrote. "I am convinced that the danger is great."[90] The absence of an effective atheist apparatus in the face of a robust and visible religion was a serious problem, and she noted that the organizations charged with atheist work—GMIRA and Znanie—did not seem to understand the consequences of their inactivity.

Shapovnikova's letter sounded an alarm within the party. Suslov ordered an investigation of the religious situation, and in April 1958, the Central Committee organized a conference that brought together the institutions involved in religious and atheist affairs. The conference produced a report addressed to the Central Committee's Agitation and Propaganda Department on the shortcomings of atheist work, and shortly after, government and party organs began to issue decrees to limit the influence of religion on Soviet society.[91] More specifically, two secret decrees issued in fall 1958 signaled the onset of the new campaign. The first, issued on October 4, 1958, by the Central Committee, addressed deficiencies of atheist work, while the second, issued on October 16, 1958, by the Council of Ministers, introduced even more prohibitive taxes on churches and monasteries, including tax increases on important sources of income like candles.[92] The clergy began to be harassed for activities that until then, while restricted, were often tacitly tolerated, such as performing religious rites in people's homes, charitable work, religious education, and purchasing real estate and transportation intended for religious use. The church was ordered to close more churches and monasteries, and CAROC officials were instructed to discourage and deny believers' petitions for registrations and church openings.[93] "Socialist legality"—which had initially led some citizens to petition for the legal rights of the church and believers as well as appeal to freedom of conscience—was now interpreted as a tool to limit religious activity. In short, as historian Tatiana Chumachenko writes, "Everything that was permitted by special legislative acts, resolutions, and instructions of the government in the 1940s and 1950s was now declared a violation of Soviet law."[94]

Khrushchev's antireligious campaign was connected to other issues that concerned the party, including youth, education, morality, and byt. Antireligious measures were intended to limit the influence of religion on children and young people, especially since after the demographic devastation of the war, the new generation was quickly becoming a majority of the adult population.[95] CAROC noted that the fate of religion in the Soviet Union depended on its ability to reproduce itself in the next generation. As a report on rising church attendance observed, "the increase in church attendance is not only on account of elderly people, but, to a considerable degree, on account of the youth. The rise in religious weddings and baptisms is evidence, since only young people get married and baptize children."[96] Religion would not disappear as long as the next generation remained under its influence. The Komsomol press began an extensive discussion around atheism, publishing readers' letters that asked questions like whether Komsomol members could go to church, and linking atheism to the broader issue of "new and healthy byt."[97] The church was instructed to limit the number of applicants accepted into seminaries and raise the age for application from eighteen to thirty. Sometimes, Komsomol and party activists physically blocked the path of grandmothers trying to take their grandchildren to church.

Soviet officials linked youth religiosity to problems in other areas, especially education and the family. They criticized schools for ignoring atheist upbringing, and urged teachers to be more vigilant about the family lives of their students and exert more influence on the worldviews of those in their care.[98] CAROC reported that teachers were often unwilling to engage with religion, excusing their avoidance of atheist work by arguing that the scientific emphasis of Soviet education would organically lead students to atheist conclusions. The council pointed out that leaving the subject of religion and atheism unaddressed left room for a dangerous amount of family influence at home. As one seventh grader explained at a school meeting on atheist education:

> In school, teachers tell us to listen to our parents. At home, parents tell us to respect and listen to our teachers. Once each year, either before or after Easter, teachers tell us not to go to church, but our mothers and fathers tell us every day to pray to God and go to church. Teachers tell us that they will lower the grades of those who go to church, while parents tell us if we do not go to church they will throw us out of the house. So, who should we listen to? It is essential for all adults, for our teachers and parents, to come to an agreement among themselves.[99]

In the context of the intensified antireligious campaign, the competing influences of family and school became even more apparent.

Finally, an important innovation of the new antireligious campaigns was the party's attention to popular religiosity and folk practices, which were now folded into the broader definition of religion.[100] Under Lenin and Stalin, when religion was defined primarily in political terms, neutralizing religious institutions and officials required direct action. Eradicating popular religiosity, on the other hand, was seen as a long-term process that would develop organically under the influence of education, enlightenment, and modernization. Under Khrushchev, the party began to focus on practices that, until then, had not been the primary target of antireligious policy: pilgrimages, the commemoration of local saints, feast days, and holy sites. This collapse of the difference between organized religion and popular religiosity portrayed both as a form of superstition.[101] As anthropologist Sergei Shtyrkov points out, there was "a sudden broadening of the sphere to which the term 'religion' was applied. Much of that, which had previously been understood as local or ethnic tradition or custom, became 'religious' and, consequently, had to be rooted out."[102] Popular religiosity and local traditions became the object of atheist work.[103]

The press, as usual, played an important role in this reframing of religion, deploying what Shtyrkov terms "denunciatory ethnography" (*oblichitel'naia etnografiia*).[104] In the newspaper *Socialist Ossetia*, for example, a local journalist, M. Snegirev, published an exposé about local party members who, along with the rest of the town's inhabitants, did not show up to work during the three-day celebration of the local feast day. Instead of "battling this evil," Snegirev wrote, Communists were themselves "imprisoned by the obsolete traditions." In another village, "three or four old people" organized a procession to the cemetery, where they made a ritual sacrifice to "call forth rain." These elderly people managed to "stupefy" the entire town, including impressionable youth, while party officials, collective farm directors, and teachers stood idly by. Snegirev also shared a story about the "deadbeat opportunist" Zakaria Khasonov, who organized a "talisman factory" in his home. Khasonov claimed that the talismans, containing "some sort of mysterious signs [that] are incomprehensible to Khasonov himself," would bring good fortune and love, protect from illness, and ensure the birth of male children. As "simpletons" flocked to purchase the talismans, Khasonov's courtyard filled with various household items that villagers brought as payment, as well as "a river of laborers' rubles." Even the brigadier of the collective farm had fallen for Khasonov's machinations. These exposés were meant to communicate that "superstitious" behavior was unacceptable in the present historical stage, especially among Soviet officials and party members.[105]

The party saw the church as the impetus behind such manifestations of popular religiosity, but the campaign against superstition was in fact an area where the interests of the state converged with the interests of the church.[106] On September 10, 1958, before the new antireligious campaign became public, and even before the secret decrees issued by party and government institutions, Karpov had been sent to Odessa to meet with Patriarch Aleksii.[107] Karpov's mission was delicate: to inform the patriarch of the coming campaign and secure his cooperation, while at the same time assuring him that the state remained committed to "normal" relations with the church. However, when Karpov informed the patriarch about the party's intention to close the Kiev Monastery of the Caves, the patriarch threatened to step down from his post—a development that would have been completely unacceptable to CAROC, which always had one eye on the foreign reception of domestic religious affairs. Karpov managed to defuse the crisis and convince the patriarch that he had "no reason to doubt the [state's] sincerity toward him," and turned the conversation to a topic on which the two could compromise: the effort to eradicate superstition. Karpov asked the patriarch to address the problem of the so-called *klikushi*—a term used to refer to female believers possessed by demons who were a regular presence in Orthodox life.[108] In his report on the meeting, Karpov noted that whereas the patriarch said the situation with the Monastery of the Caves was "complicated," he told Karpov that the church considered *klikushestvo* a form of superstition, describing the *klikushi* as "charlatans," "thieves," and "deranged, sick people." Since the church saw superstition as a sin and the "fruit of ignorance," the patriarch assured Karpov that he had already instructed the clergy that they were not to participate in pilgrimages to any "so-called 'holy' trees, wells, and springs," and that he would issue instructions against *klikushestvo*.

On November 28, 1958, the Presidium of the Communist Party adopted the resolution "On Measures for Stopping Pilgrimages to So-Called 'Holy Sites.'"[109] Over the course of the campaign, holy sites were seized and either closed or appropriated for other uses. Holy wells were filled with concrete, their closure justified by claiming that they were unhygienic and spread malaria and venereal disease.[110] Sometimes holy sites were turned into a youth camp.[111] At other times, they became pig farms. The new campaign also denounced self-appointed religious leaders (*samochintsy*), such as local women who, in the absence of institutional religion, were often seen as repositories of religious knowledge, or unregistered priests and mullahs who performed services and rites, sometimes wandering the countryside from village to village to avoid persecution. Even on the eve of the most antagonistic period in Soviet church-state relations, the two sides could agree on certain definitions and objectives, such as the opposition of backwardness to enlightenment, and legitimate and illegitimate authority. The antireligious campaign, then, was also a disciplinary project: in order to control religion, religion was redefined to exclude those elements that were not institutionalized and grounded in individual belief. In this sense, the church's interest in reinforcing the line between religion and superstition coincided with Khrushchev's agenda, in which fighting superstition was part of a broader project of producing a rational and modern Soviet society.

In January 1960, shortly after the Central Committee issued a decree "On Measures for Liquidating Violations of Soviet Law on Cults by the Clergy," Karpov sent a letter to Khrushchev. In it, he argued for the necessity of preserving "normal" relations with the church, especially since the Soviet Union "was not yet in a position to do away with the well-known use of church organizations abroad to achieve our state's political interests."[112] However, with the aggressive antireligious measures now under way, Karpov's position became increasingly untenable. Shortly after sending the letter, Karpov was dismissed from his post and much of the CAROC "old guard" purged, sending the message that the council's mission was not to normalize church-state relations but instead to serve the party in the antireligious campaign.

Karpov's letter and the party's reaction to it underscored the growing divide between the old guard, shaped by the Stalinist emphasis on governance, and the new generation shaped by Khrushchev ideological mobilization. Indicative of this shift is the appointment of Vladimir Kuroedov, a career party cadre, to replace Karpov. Kuroedov, who went on to serve as the head of the council for the next twenty-five years, had made a career in the party apparatus, and over the course of it, had served as the head of the Propaganda Department of the Lithuanian Communist Party, secretary of the Sverdlov and Gorky regional party organs, and editor of the Gorky regional newspaper. Before becoming the chair of CAROC, he worked in the party apparatus in Moscow. In 1960, Furtseva, then the curator of religion within the Central Committee, invited Kuroedov for a meeting and informed him that he was proposed as Karpov's replacement.[113] Kuroedov had no expertise or experience with religious affairs; as he recalled later, managing religion was "completely unknown" to him and he was not "enthusiastic" about the prospect. Nevertheless, the next day Kuroedov was called to a meeting of the Ideological Commission, where Suslov informed him that his post was confirmed and debriefed him that the church had been taking too many liberties and it was time to "restore order." The mood was militant, and the ideological establishment seemed confident that the USSR was on the threshold of a "final rooting out of religion."[114]

Under Kuroedov, the functions of the council changed, as it was instructed to use all available administrative and ideological measures to limit religion's influence on Soviet society.[115] In 1961, secret instructions outlined the expanded responsibilities of local CAROC plenipotentiaries. As before, they had to inform the center about the clergy's attitudes to political developments and current events; keep tabs on local believers; record how much money the church donated to the Soviet Peace Fund, which had been established in 1961 as part of the USSR's peace campaign, and how much income was generated by the sale of candles, crosses, and wreaths; and gather information on religious property, the makeup of the parish councils, and registered and unregistered communities. But CAROC plenipotentiaries were also assigned additional duties. They now had to organize atheist work, inculcate new socialist rituals, and help priests who had broken with religion find new employment. On March 16, 1961, the USSR Council of Ministers issued the decree "On the Intensification of Control over the Observance of Religious Cults," which empowered local officials to interfere in the affairs of religious communities. In this, they were also aided by the newly established Commissions for Support of Council Plenipotentiaries—volunteer groups that helped monitor things like how religious property was used, or who observed religious rites.

Finally, in what was perhaps the campaign's most consequential strategy, the party used CAROC to pressure the Orthodox Church to adopt internal reforms that would limit the economic power and social autonomy of the clergy. Priests were forbidden from taking part in any administrative or financial decisions and became salaried employees of the parish, dependent on the will of the parish councils. In particular, these reforms targeted religious rites, which the party sought to prevent by introducing various disincentives. The party believed that priests, in becoming salaried employees, would lose their material incentive to perform religious rites, since their earnings would remain the same no matter how many infants they baptized.[116] Meanwhile, Soviet citizens were now required to provide their passport at the time of the rite, and their personal information would be recorded and could be passed along—to local officials, schools, and workplaces—which could then result in expulsion, demotion, or termination. In these ways, the party sought to keep religion within church walls, and the Soviet people out of the church.

An antireligious campaign of this scale was bound to produce results, but not necessarily those intended by the party. Over the course of the Khrushchev era, five out of the Soviet Union's eight theological seminaries were closed, and the number of functioning monasteries, which had reached one hundred in 1945, was reduced from sixty-three in 1959 to eighteen by the mid-1960s.[117] The number of functioning churches and chapels was reduced from around thirteen thousand in 1960 to between seven and eight thousand in the mid-1960s. To put these figures in context, by 1964, there were just over half as many functioning churches as there had been in 1947.[118]

Yet union-wide statistics hid a more complicated picture, especially in terms of the campaign's effect on local religious life in the regions. In the Krasnoiarsk region, for example, central directives produced unexpected outcomes.[119] As elsewhere, the 1954 campaign had little impact on Orthodoxy, and was followed by a period of religious revival between 1955 and 1957.[120] With the revival of the campaign in 1958, nine of the region's sixteen parishes were closed, and the economic activity of the church was further restricted.[121] Despite efforts to limit religious life and stifle the economic activity of the church, however, the overall income of the Orthodox Church in the Krasnoiarsk region increased from 327,583 rubles in 1960 to 383,997 rubles in 1965.[122] Soviet religious life also became increasingly urban as believers from areas that were now "churchless" went to the city to address religious needs.[123] Furthermore, following church closures, religiosity moved into ever more clandestine corners and therefore beyond the state's control. On the whole, then, despite the statistics pointing to a decline in the number of open churches, the party had to acknowledge the dynamism, flexibility, and tenacity of religion, and could no longer maintain the illusion that administrative restrictions would bring about religion's inevitable extinction.

This troubling state of affairs was brought home to the Central Committee in 1964 by the deputy head of the KGB's Chief Directorate, Fedor Shcherbak, in a secret report titled "On Facts of Administrative Measures against Believers on the Part of Local Organs on the Territory of the RSFSR."[124] Local authorities, Shcherbak reported, closed churches, prayer houses, and mosques, fired religious believers from work, and expelled students from universities for observing religious rites.[125] Most of these antireligious measures, he stressed, were illegal and led to undesirable consequences: increased religious "fanaticism," as well as the growth of unregistered religious groups and their movement underground, where authorities could no longer monitor their activities. In Briansk, local officials closed several Baptist prayer houses "without taking into account protests on the part of believers." This led believers to "a semilegal situation" (with services taking place in private residences), and ultimately created a religious community that was both more robust and more dispersed—and hence more difficult to regulate. Whereas previously the congregation had two hundred members, one presbyter, and three pastors, Shcherbak shared that even though the prayer houses were closed, the number of pastors had increased to twenty-four and the number of believers to three hundred.[126]

Shcherbak went on to list numerous examples of counterproductive antireligious measures. On one occasion, the Briansk police and volunteer groups disbanded a Baptist meeting, threw the believers out of the prayer house, confiscated their Bible, arrested and fined some of them, and got another fired from her job. The result, Shcherbak noted, was that "the sectarians offered her material assistance and used this fact as an example of the unjust treatment of believers by the state."[127] In the Bashkir autonomous region, a local mullah was called in by the district soviet and asked to stop holding services at the local mosque, with the offer that if he agreed, the pension for his son who had died at the front would be increased from twenty-eight to thirty-five rubles. In Kalinin and Tambov, the local officials accompanied church closures with atheist campaigns where "specially chosen groups of atheists walked from home to home of the collective farmers and members of the [parish] twenties . . . and demanded that they reject their membership in the religious congregations, threatening that if they did not, their private plots would be reduced, their pensions taken away, and they would be fired." In Tomsk, local authorities confiscated the vacation voucher of a local Jehovah's Witness, which his union had given him for exemplary work, and then proceeded to conduct atheist work with him, which, the report wryly observed, consisted of a local Communist "coming to his apartment in an unsober state and trying, with various unworthy methods, to 'educate' him."[128]

Such "crude deviations" in antireligious work, Shcherbak concluded, led to "various undesirable phenomena": popular dissatisfaction with local authorities as well as the "activation and the growth of religious fanaticism" of religious groups that had previously been effectively monitored by the state. As religious groups grew in size and moved underground, it became more difficult for the KGB "to control them and conduct prophylactic work." Religious communities were also becoming more active. Large groups traveled to Moscow to petition central authorities, with the "hostile" (*vrazhdebno nastroeny*) among them even "trying to penetrate into foreign consulates or contact foreigners in order to pass along tendentious information about the situation of the church in our country." In the Altai region, local Baptists relentlessly petitioned the local authorities after their congregation was disbanded and threated to go to foreign consulates if their petitions were not addressed. In July 1964, a group of Baptists from Tatarstan, Chuvashiia, and Mari El arrived in Moscow, and demanded to be received in the Presidium of the Supreme Council of the USSR, Central Committee, and Council on the Affairs of Religious Cults.[129] Overall, Shcherbak argued that repressive antireligious policies raised the political visibility of religion, especially abroad, while doing little to achieve atheist goals at home.

Reflecting on the antireligious campaign in 1966, Ivan Brazhnik—the deputy chair of the Council for Religious Affairs (CRA), which, in 1965, succeeded CAROC and CARC by bringing the regulation of all religious confessions under the roof of one institution—also noted that "the illegal, rushed closure of churches" under Khrushchev had only increased religiosity. Brazhnik informed the audience that in a recent CRA report to the party's Central Committee, the council had to present some troubling statistics: in the Dnepropetrovsk region, where 129 churches (83.5 percent) had been closed between 1961 and 1966, the previous year had shown that "there were 217 percent more rites conducted in the remaining 20 churches than had been conducted in 150 [churches]."[130] Meanwhile in the Vologda region, where no churches had been closed, the number of religious baptisms, marriages, and funerals declined. More than half of Moldova's churches had been closed since 1961, but "nevertheless, or more exactly, despite this—or perhaps even more exactly, because of this—the level of the population's religiosity is not declining but growing." In Moldova, 31 percent were buried according to church ritual in 1963, whereas in 1965 the figure increased to more than 40 percent. The income of the Russian Orthodox Church in Moldova was 1 million rubles in 1962, but by 1964 had increased to 1.8 million. To illustrate his point, Brazhnik shared that in the Tiraspol' region, where all the churches had been closed, a thousand newborns had been baptized.[131] "We should not present the patterns in such a linear fashion; we understand what it means to have churches and how this facilitates ritual observance," Brazhnik stated. "But let the comrades from Dnepropetrovsk and Moldova explain the figures on church closures."[132]

In the face of such results, both the KGB and CRA recommended that the party scale back administrative policies. This, of course, did not mean that the

Soviet political establishment questioned atheism as a goal, but it lost confidence that administrative methods would bring about an atheist society.

## *Conclusion*

In 1848, Marx and Engels famously opened their *Communist Manifesto* with the statement: "A spectre is haunting Europe—the spectre of Communism."[133] By the Khrushchev era, it was Communism itself that was being haunted by a specter—the specter of religion. At the outset of Khrushchev's antireligious campaign, the party was confident in the prospect of overcoming religion and building an atheist society. This confidence rested largely in the faith that history had a logic, that this logic was the movement toward Communism, and that therefore religion would inevitably wither away. This optimism is captured in a 1961 report filed by V. G. Furov, the recently appointed deputy head of CAROC, about a conversation he had with Patriarch Aleksii. The patriarch, Furov wrote, "looks at many things from the position of a former person, and it would be worthwhile to clarify for him certain general issues about the development of our society: the country is building Communism, science is flourishing, the people are becoming more cultured. . . . Aren't the prospects of the church in, say, twenty or thirty years—when people, because of the laws of social development and educational work, will be atheists—clear?"[134] By the end of the Khrushchev era, such naïveté was rare.

The existence of religion in the Soviet Union had always presented a problem for those who saw the USSR as the beacon of world Communism, but in the context of Khrushchev's utopian ambitions to build Communism within decades, religion became an intolerable stain that needed to be eradicated. At the same time, even as public life was filled with optimistic proclamations about progress and Communist construction, Soviet society was always aware of the contradictions and shortcomings of Soviet reality.[135] Indeed, Khrushchev's promises—that the Soviet economy would "bury" the United States by 1970, or that the current generation of Soviet youth would live to see Communism—required no less of a leap of faith than the belief in a transcendent God that turned a blasphemous girl into a pillar of stone. Behind closed doors, therefore, confidence about the Soviet Union's progress toward Communism was more measured, and religion was increasingly seen as a marker of the distance between the Soviet present and the arrival of Communism.

The ambition of the Khrushchev era antireligious campaigns was to exorcize Soviet life of religion. The party mobilized significant resources in pursuit of this goal, and by certain measures succeeded in advancing the atheist mission. By 1964, it had closed half the country's religious spaces and placed heavy restraints on the autonomy of religious institutions. It also made religiosity increasingly private by monitoring, disrupting, and destroying religious sites and events and undermining popular religious practices. The party also made the observance of religious rites more difficult and the repercussions of observing them more significant. Finally, Soviet public life was filled with antireligious and atheist propaganda, whereas religious organizations had practically no public voice or access to mass media. Inasmuch as religion appeared in public, it was as an object of fear, condescension, or ridicule in Soviet newspapers, radio programs, and films.

At the same time, despite the undeniable fact that the antireligious campaign had a devastating effect on religious institutions and communities, atheists considered it a failure. Even with administrative restrictions in place, Marxist-Leninist predictions about the withering away of religion clashed with the fact that religion remained a fact of Soviet life, made evident by the continuous increases in church income and religious rites. The diverse popular responses to the antireligious campaign also revealed that the idea that religion had no place in Soviet Communism was by no means obvious to everyone. As one party report put it, "With increasing frequency one can hear: 'We believe in God, Lenin, and Khrushchev,' [and] it is not rare to find, in the home of a believer, a prayer book lying next to the Program of the Communist Party."[136] Whereas official ideology presented religion and Communism as inherently irreconcilable, many people—and even some party members—did not see the contradiction or understand the stakes of the atheist project. Some atheists continued to enthusiastically recount isolated success stories, but most lamented that in their battle against religion, they were making little progress.

The Soviet reengagement with religion under Khrushchev forced the party to reconsider its definition of religion and approach to atheism. Religion was no longer considered a political enemy, but an ideological opponent, making believers into patriotic Soviet citizens—albeit ones who needed to be rescued from their own superstition and backwardness. As religion became an ideological problem, a worldview grounded in a false conception of the universe that needed to be placed on scientific materialist foundations, Soviet atheism had to renounce its militant origins and become scientific.

CHAPTER THREE

# Cosmic Enlightenment

## SOVIET ATHEISM AS SCIENCE

> The sky!—Ostap said.—The sky is becoming desolate. It is no longer that epoch, that slice of time. Now, the angels want to come down to Earth, where it is nice, where there are municipal services, where there is a planetarium and one can look at the stars while listening to an antireligious lecture.
>
> —OSTAP BENDER, *THE GOLDEN CALF*

ON MAY 6, 1962, during a widely publicized visit to the Seattle World's Fair, the Soviet cosmonaut German Titov—the second person to go to space after cosmonaut number one, Yuri Gagarin—made international headlines by stating that he had not seen "God or angels" during his seventeen orbits of Earth. The comment was in reply to a reporter's question about whether traveling to space had changed his worldview, and Titov's response reflected the radical humanism that accompanied Soviet scientism: "Up to our first orbital flight by Yuri Gagarin no god helped build our rocket," Titov announced. "The rocket was made by our people. I do not believe in god. I believe in man, his strength, his possibilities and his reason."[1] Titov's pronouncement provoked a powerful reaction in the American public: letters from ordinary people poured into newspapers, religious figures like Billy Graham expressed indignation about Titov's attack on God, and the astronaut John Glenn responded directly, stating that the God he believed in was "not so small that I thought I would run into Him [in outer space]."[2]

That cosmonauts and astronauts should make public pronouncements on a subject usually left to theologians might seem strange, but the space race, of course, was never a purely scientific or technological competition.[3] Set in the political context of the Cold War, space travelers were used to declare political, economic, and technological supremacy, but their testimonies about the heavens also carried significant ideological weight.[4] In this Cold War drama, then, cosmonauts and astronauts played central parts, and in many ways, the mythologies surrounding them had much in common.[5] Both astronauts and cosmonauts were cast as patriotic, brave, and relatable—ordinary people and, at the same time, superheroes.[6] Yet there was one key difference: whereas astronauts were God-fearing, cosmonauts were godless.

John F. Kennedy and Khrushchev, the leaders of the two Cold War superpowers, had been exchanging views on the philosophical implications of human space travel since April 12, 1961, when Gagarin became the first person in space. As Khrushchev told the US press shortly after Titov's trip, the Soviet Union had asked Titov to keep an eye out for the God and paradise so much talked about by the priests, just to make sure. "After all, Gagarin was up there only an hour and a half," Khrushchev joked. "So he might have missed Paradise." Titov, however, flew for an entire day, and confirmed that "there was nothing there."[7] Kennedy, meanwhile, chose the Presidential Prayer Breakfast—itself a Cold War institution introduced during Dwight D. Eisenhower's mobilization of what the historian Jonathan Herzog calls the "spiritual-industrial complex"—to tell those gathered that religion was "the basis of the issue that separates us from those that make themselves our adversary."[8]

The resonance of Titov's statement at the Seattle World's Fair, and space travelers' pronouncements on religion more generally, was a critical, if peculiar, product of the two culture wars that reached their apogee in the 1950s and 1960s: the war between science and religion, and the Cold War rivalry of the godly West and godless Communism. In fact, the Seattle World's Fair was itself the product of this tension: originally conceived as a mechanism to raise the public esteem for science in light of the fact that, as John W. Campbell, the editor of the journal *Astounding Science-Fiction* put it, "The American people have been thoroughly scared witless by the accomplishments of science"—the atomic bomb, *Sputnik*, and the prospect of actual Soviets transgressing the heavens and invading the American skies.[9] Yet whereas the fair began as a response to the challenge posed by Soviet scientific-technological achievements, it quickly became an ideological battleground as religious groups showcased their response to scientific triumphalism in the competing Christian Witness Pavilion situated across from the Space Needle and next to the Science Pavilion.

The Soviets capitalized on Soviet space firsts to proclaim the truth of scientific materialism, arguing that atheism removed the hurdles to technological achievements that still constrained the capitalist world. The United States countered Soviet attempts to marry space exploration with atheism by underscoring the religious faith of the astronauts—a process that culminated on Christmas 1968, when the astronaut Jim Lovell's reading of Genesis was broadcast to Earth from the US spaceship circling the moon. As the standoff between Communism and capitalism escalated, both sides sought platforms to express the impact of the "scientific appropriation of a realm that had once been the preserve of mystery and religion" on human life.[10] Their differences on these issues were cast as central indicators of their opposing worldviews and ways of life, and therefore each side's claims to moral and political legitimacy.

At the same time, despite political and ideological differences, both sides were also firmly embedded in the broader narrative of secular modernity, which held that the march of progress—industrialization, bureaucratization, the development of the welfare state, and humanity's mastery over nature through science and technology—would make religion increasingly irrelevant not just in politics and public life but even in the minds and lives of individuals. Science, within this framework, not only undermined religion's claims to truth; it also made modern miracles like space travel possible. Scientific miracles, however, raised existential questions about humanity's place in the universe, and nothing had the potential to enact this more dramatically than the story of humans who traveled to the frontiers of technological possibility and philosophical imagination.

Debates about the philosophical implications of space travel and impact of the scientific-technological revolution on humanity were prominent features of public life in both the socialist world and its capitalist counterpart.[11] Indeed, the argument that scientific and technological advances exorcised the supernatural from everyday life—leaving a cosmos that, in the words of the sociologist Peter Berger, "became amenable to systematic, rational penetration, both in thought and activity"—was a shared response to the remarkable breakthroughs of the space age. As Berger observed, the scientific conquest of the heavens collapsed the "sacred canopy," leaving a "sky empty of angels" that became "open to the intervention of the astronomer, and, eventually, of the astronaut."[12] In the 1960s, then, as cosmonauts and astronauts raced to space, debates about the implications for religion were a central feature of both Soviet and American public life, even if in the West the conversation was about "religious crisis," whereas in the USSR it was about Communism overcoming religion.[13]

Alongside the global context of the Cold War, the Soviet veneration of science and space conquest also played an important domestic role under Khrushchev: filling the ideological vacuum created by Stalin's death. Whereas the Bolshevik old guard had forged a bridge across Lenin's death by producing a robust cult around the dead leader and his teachings, Khrushchev's desacralization of both Stalin and Stalinism compounded the political crisis by shaking the ideological foundations of Soviet Communism. In part, the party tried to fill this empty ideological space with the cults of science, space travel, and the cosmonaut—sometimes quite literally, as when a Vostok rocket took the place formerly occupied by a statue of Stalin in the newly renamed Kosmos Pavilion at Moscow's Exhibition of Economic Achievements (Vystavka dostizhenii narodnogo khoziastva, or VDNKh).[14] Indeed, that the purpose of cosmic enthusiasm was more to awe and mobilize the masses than to educate them is underscored as well by the fact that exhibitions of space technology deliberately camouflaged the technical details of the Soviet space program in order to protect technological advantage over the Cold War adversary.

For Soviet Communism, cosmonauts were utopianism made flesh—Socialist Realist heroes come to life—and Socialist Realism and socialist reality were never closer than during the Soviet space age.[15] The relationship between cosmonauts and Communism, moreover, was reciprocal, as Gagarin dedicated his historic space flight in 1961 to the upcoming Twenty-Second Party Congress. Within the framework of the Soviet Union's transition from socialism to Communism, cosmonauts became prototypes of the new Soviet person, the citizen of the Communist future proclaimed to be imminent by Khrushchev. In the Marxist-Leninist utopia, cosmonauts bridged the distance between the scientific and philosophical, the real and ideal. Their fearlessness and positive, life-affirming attitude made them icons of the limitless human potential that Marxism-Leninism promised to all Soviet citizens. Their voyages, both in life and to space, were put forth as a counterexample and antidote to the fear and weakness that atheists claimed were cultivated by religion.

Popular enthusiasm for Soviet space conquest, and the cosmonauts who personified it, made it clear that the ideological capital of cosmic conquest reached beyond the material. Surely, Soviet space conquests proved that humankind was guided not by a supernatural God but rather by the power of reason. If cosmic enthusiasm could be channeled into atheist work, the logic went, then science could deal the final blow to religion. In the model atheist conversion narrative, scientific advances—with space conquest as the apogee of scientific possibility—should have turned believers into atheists. But the embrace of science extended beyond the natural sciences. In the turn to a more technocratic style of governance, the party also mobilized the social sciences, turning to disciplines like ethnography and sociology in order to gather data about Soviet society and "bring theory closer to life," to borrow the terminology of the time. What the party learned when social scientists studied Soviet religious worlds was that the responses of ordinary Soviet citizens to scientific enlightenment did not necessarily follow the model conversion narrative in which science overcame religion. The truth proclaimed by science ran up against the facts revealed by social science, ultimately leading Soviet atheism to new questions.

## *Heaven Is Empty!*

In October 1962—five years after the Soviet Union launched *Sputnik*, the first artificial satellite of Earth, on October 4, 1957, and a year and a half after Gagarin completed the first staffed space flight on April 12, 1961—the Soviet Union's new atheist journal *Science and Religion* published a lengthy article taking stock of the "First Cosmic Five-Year Plan."[16] Titled "Five Years of Storming the Heavens," the article marveled at Soviet accomplishments in human space travel, which had until recently existed only in the realm of fantasy.[17] It also posed the question that had been haunting the global imagination since *Sputnik*: How did it come to be that the Soviet Union managed to do what "tsarist Russia could not even dream about," namely, "the accomplishment of such heroic feats in the fight for progress, the competition with more technologically and economically developed countries"?[18] Why was it that *Soviet* cosmonauts managed to fulfill humanity's long-cherished dream, when humanity "ceased to envy the bird" and flew, "relying not on the power of muscles, but on the power of his reason"?[19] And finally, what did it mean that the first man who "stormed the heavens" was "Gagarin—steel worker, son of a steel worker, from a peasant family, Russian, Soviet, Communist, [and] 'godless'"?[20]

In the Cold War opposition of two world systems, Gagarin's alleged godlessness was symbolically significant. The editorial claimed that Soviet supremacy in space had a direct connection to the system's "scientific, materialist, and therefore . . . atheist worldview"—indeed, that it expressed "the logic of modern history." Humanity's path to the cosmos was lined with the "fierce resistance of religion," yet "he chased out the mythical god from the boundaries of the earth," made nature submit to his will, and "became a giant, victorious over the elements, directing the laws of nature and society." Lastly, when he mastered Earth, man began his conquest of the heavens, the "holy of holies." Material objects "created by the sinful hands of the godless" broke through to the celestial spheres, and "man, whose insignificance the clergy has reiterated for centuries, is accomplishing space flights, creating and controlling artificial planets, and conquering the cosmos."[21] This narrative left little room for doubt; it called for believers to abandon their "dark superstitions" and urged atheists to combat religion, which remained an obstacle in the path to enlightened Communist society. The Soviet cosmonauts' conquest of the heavens was to shine "the sun of Reason" on those who lagged behind the march of human progress.[22] As Gagarin's autobiography *Path to the Cosmos* put it, "The fact that a human being had flown to the cosmos was a bitter blow to the church public. I was delighted to read accounts of how believers, under the influence of scientific achievements, had turned away from god, assented to the fact that there was no god and that everything associated with his name was rubbish and nonsense."[23]

Pronouncements attributed to Gagarin about the cosmos being devoid of God and angels took on a life of their own. Meanwhile, Titov's actual statement at the Seattle World's Fair turned him into the public face of scientific atheism—a role that Titov seemed to embrace and indeed even cultivate.[24] Shortly after he became the second person in space, Titov published an editorial in *Science and Religion* the title of which reflected a question that he was asked often: "Did I Meet God?" His answer, of course, was no. The universe opened up to mankind, Titov observed, not to "a ghostly inhabitant of the heavens." He wrote that during his flight, he heard a radio program in Japan that was discussing "god, saints, and other sly things." He wanted to send them a greeting, but then thought, "What's the point? What if they think that it's true, that God does exist?" Regardless, Titov continued, "the prayers of believers will never reach God, if only because there is no air in that place where he is supposed to exist. So whether you pray or you do not, God will not hear you. I never met anyone in space, and of course, it is impossible that I could have."[25]

Stories that conformed to this narrative of scientific enlightenment—that Soviet space travels destroyed the boundary between the terrestrial and celestial, and converted religious belief into atheist conviction—were widely publicized through the press, radio, and television.[26] With the explosion of cosmic enthusiasm after successful Soviet space missions, letters about the effect of space achievements on religious worldviews poured into newspapers and journals as well as the mailboxes of cosmonauts themselves.[27] *Science and Religion* published letters from former believers—often elderly women, but sometimes "sectarians" and even priests—who described how space travel and scientific progress more generally led them to doubt their religious faith. Even before Gagarin became the first person in space, *Science and Religion* published a letter from a worker from the Cherkassy region, Ivan Dovgal, who argued that the penetration of artificial satellites into outer space was a powerful argument against religious belief. Dovgal wrote that "the persistent religious beliefs of his coworkers truly made him incredulous; he could not understand how they could continue to believe in a heaven after death in light of the fact that Soviet satellites circling the Earth at great heights have not discovered any heaven, that the Soviet rocket, flying around the Sun, likewise did not discover heaven."[28] Such rhetoric became much more common after Gagarin's flight, when humans who had traveled to space could report on what they saw (or did not see) in the heavens. An editorial in the central state newspaper, *Izvestiia*, exclaimed, "Iurii Gagarin really has given a terrible headache to believers! He flew right through the heavenly mansions and did not run into anyone: neither the Almighty, nor Archangel Gabriel, nor the angels of heaven. It seems, then, that heaven is empty!"[29]

One letter—from E. Danilova, a seventy-three-year-old woman from the Kuibyshev region—fit the atheist conversion narrative so perfectly that it was not only printed in *Izvestiia* but also reproduced in numerous later publications, lectures, and even party meetings.[30] Written in a folksy tone, Danilova's letter described her experience of Gagarin's flight:

> On the 12th of April, in the morning, I was sitting on a little stool and heating the oven. Suddenly I hear the call sign on the radio. My heart stopped: could something have happened? . . .
>
> And suddenly I hear: Man is in space! My God! I stopped heating up the oven, sat next to the radio receiver, afraid to step away even for a minute. And how much I reconsidered over the course of these minutes. . . .

> How can this be?—Man wants to be higher than God! But we were always told that God is in the heavens, so how can a man fly there and not bump into Elijah the Prophet or one of God's angels? How can it be that God, if he is all-powerful, allow such a breach of his authority? . . . What if God punishes him for his insolence? But on the radio they say he has landed! Thank God—he is alive and well! I could not hold myself back and crossed myself.
>
> Now I am convinced that God is Science, is Man.
>
> Iurii Gagarin overcame all belief in heavenly powers that I had in my soul. He himself inhabits the skies, and there is no one in the sky more powerful than him. Glory to you, Soviet man, conqueror of the skies![31]

Nikolai Rusanov, a priest who wrote to the party journal *Kommunist* to share how he broke with the church as a result of Gagarin's flight, also portrayed his conversion as liberation from religious darkness through science. In his 1962 letter, Rusanov cast himself as a "'prodigal son' who has returned, after his delusions, to the unified Soviet family."[32] Rusanov characterized himself in the twenty years of his previous (religious) life as having been "removed from the world, bringing no benefit to myself, to society, or the government." It was only after he opened his eyes to the disgraceful, scandalous lives of the clergy along with the "glaring" contradictions between the Bible and science that he lost his belief. "Is it even possible," Rusanov asks, "in this century of the atom, of artificial satellites, the century of the conquest of the cosmos, of flights to the stars, to believe in [the idea] that somewhere there is a God, angels, devils, an afterlife?"[33] Science, Rusanov writes, makes religious belief impossible, and the only explanation for the clergy continuing to serve the church is that there is money to be made off the simple people. Rusanov depicted religious life as fundamentally corrupt and hypocritical, and religious belief as inherently deluded and antisocial. Atheist work for him therefore had a missionary urgency:

> The people want to know the truth about religion, especially now, when it is becoming clear to many that religion is a lie and many cease to believe in God. It is in this period that it is necessary to make antireligious propaganda more aggressive, to have more individual conversations with believers, more accessible lectures that would force the believer to think about his situation, so that he understands the harm of religion, so that he knows how he is deceived by the clergy, so that he is convinced that man's life is guided not by God but by man himself. It is man who, without the help of God, builds a new and joyous life. The believer should not wait for a heavenly paradise, because it does not and will not exist, but an earthly paradise, which will be built within

> the next fifteen to twenty years here, in our godless Soviet country. The name of this paradise is Communism.[34]

Like other infamous priests turned atheists—such as the theology professor Aleksandr Osipov, and the seminary instructor Evgraf Duluman—Rusanov became an atheist lecturer, traveling around the country to share his conversion story.

The scientific enthusiasm at the heart of these atheist conversion narratives was neither rationalized nor disenchanted; it did not propose, in Max Weber's words, a world without "mysterious incalculable forces" that could, in principle, be mastered by calculation. Indeed, these narratives are striking in their conflation of the scientific and magical elements. Danilova's story, for example, was imbued with an exalted language that replaced religious faith with faith in the redemptive potential of science, and substituted one charismatic figure in the heavens (God) with another (Gagarin). Rusanov, with his faith in an imminent Communist paradise, likewise traded the "heavenly paradise" for the "earthly paradise" of Soviet Communism. The object of devotion changed, but not the mode of thinking.

Atheist conversions, however, were not widespread or representative, and thus prescriptive versus descriptive. At the same time, they were useful for illustrating to the masses how science should bring them to atheism. This was most prominent in the use of visual tools like cartoons and posters, where rockets and cosmonauts regularly assaulted the heavens and mocked various deities, usually represented in the typical repertoire of cherubs, angels, and old bearded men. One cartoon in the satirical magazine *Crocodile* (*Krokodil*)

FIGURE 3.1. "Let's trade: I'll give you my halo, and you give me your helmet. . . ." E. Gurov, *Krokodil*, no. 9 (1965): 3.

showed God floating in space alongside a cosmonaut, offering the cosmonaut his halo in exchange for the cosmonaut's helmet (see figure 3.1).[35] Another set of cartoons, in a 1961 issue of the Ukrainian atheist journal *Militant Atheist* (*Voiovnichii ateist*), showed a group of disappointed angels on a cloud, looking on as a rocket hit God on the head and sped off into the skies, with the caption,

FIGURE 3.2. Boris Starchikov, "The Connection Is Broken!" (*Sviaz' prervana!*). Moscow: Plakat, 1970s.

FIGURE 3.3. Vladimir Men'shikov, "There Is No God!" (*Boga net!*). Leningrad: Izd-vo "Khudozhnik RSFSR," 1975. GMIR, Inv. no. A-6156/1-IV, used with permission.

"When will he get it through his head that matter exists?," as well as another cartoon that showed God on a cloud, sitting behind a desk with a sign marked "Heavenly Affairs," as a cosmonaut pulls up on a rocket and asks him to "Hand the affairs over, old man!"[36]

Other images presented science, embodied in space technology, breaking the connection between the old world and the new. One poster depicted a young woman praying to icons under the direction of her forbidding, darkly clad grandmother in the background, while in the foreground the same young woman threw out icons as she watched a rocket flying through the skies on a television. The caption read, "Grandmother told me sternly that there is no path without god, but the bright light of science has proven that there is no god!" Another showed a priest trying to call God on the phone, but rockets speeding through the skies have broken the cord between them, with the caption reading, "The connection is broken!" (see figure 3.2). But the image with the most direct message simply showed a cosmonaut in a red suit waving to the viewer as he floats in the sky above a church, synagogue, and mosque—all of which are tilted to the side as if falling over—and the caption reads, "There is no god!" (see figure 3.3).

Even if many atheist cadres acknowledged that the image of cosmonauts chasing the gods out of the heavens was simplistic and even crude, its pervasiveness speaks to how Soviet propaganda used the trope to communicate what was scientific about scientific atheism in a popular idiom. At the same time, the question of what would fill the heavens once science and technology (or rockets and cosmonauts) chased out the old gods remained. Could scientific atheism fill the sacred space?

## *A Planetarium for Believers*

With the mobilization of the Khrushchev era antireligious campaign, Znanie received new resources for coordinating atheist work. The society finally began to publish an atheist journal, *Science and Religion* (which had originally been proposed in 1954), and the first issue came out in September 1959. The journal's mission was to disseminate the party's position on religion, showcase Soviet scientific achievements, and proclaim humankind's triumph over nature along with Communism's superiority to all ways of understanding and organizing the world. Unsurprisingly, space achievements featured prominently and often on the journal's pages from the first issue, which proudly displayed the blueprint for the monument to Soviet space program planned for construction at Moscow's VDNKh.[37] Space heroes were the most compelling and effective way of generating genuine reader interest, and as Soviet scientific victories continued to astound the world, the party called on both *Science and Life* and *Science and Religion* to use cosmic enthusiasm to make atheist propaganda more appealing, especially to the youth.[38] Accordingly, both journals' circulation grew considerably over the course of the Khrushchev era, with *Science and Religion* increasing from seventy thousand in 1959 to two hundred thousand in 1965 (though its circulation was still modest in comparison with the more popular *Science and Life*).[39]

In spring 1959, Znanie also received a new atheist institution: the Moscow Planetarium. As the Znanie leadership stated, "This government decision gives the society the ability to use the planetarium as a base for a considerable expansion and improvement of natural scientific and scientific atheist propaganda."[40] The purpose of transferring the planetarium from the Moscow city administration (Mosgorispolkom) to the All-Union Znanie Society was to turn it into a more effective tool in the "propaganda of natural scientific knowledge on the structure of the universe."[41] The Moscow Planetarium was to become the coordinating center of Soviet atheism. Indeed, if cosmonauts were the saints of scientific atheism, then the planetarium was the temple.

In the Khrushchev period, the planetarium was considered the most effective space for atheist work, admired for its aesthetically pleasing and intellectually engaging methodology that emphasized the experiential component of education. Yet despite an auspicious beginning under Stalin, Moscow's planetarium had remained the only one in the Soviet Union for years. With Khrushchev's remobilization of the antireligious campaign, however, faith in the atheist potential of the planetarium returned, and the state began to invest resources into the construction of new planetariums (despite the fact that as late as 1959, even the Moscow Planetarium continued to operate at a loss).[42] Under Khrushchev, the number of planetariums grew, and the scope of their atheist work expanded. The thirteen planetariums that existed in the USSR in the early 1950s were considered insufficient, and atheists called for a planetarium in every major Soviet city.[43] By 1973, there were more than seventy planetariums, the majority constructed over the course of the Khrushchev era.[44]

While the Moscow Planetarium was constructed from the ground up according to avant-garde principles of constructivist architectural design, it was, in this respect, almost unique. Many of the planetariums constructed after the war—in Gorky (Nizhnii Novgorod), Kiev, Riga, Barnaul, and others—occupied former church spaces—a fact that had both practical and ideological significance.[45] Planetariums hosted enlightenment lectures, film screenings, question-and-answer sessions and debates, youth astronomy clubs, and, most prominently, enlightenment lectures with titles like "why I broke with religion," "sects and their reactionary essence," "man, the cosmos, and god," "science and religion on the universe," "how religion accommodates itself to science," "the atheist significance of space flights," "space flights and religion," and "the sky and religious holidays" (see figure 3.4).[46] These lectures were conducted by permanent employees of the Moscow Planetarium, including the prominent atheist author Viktor Komarov, who wrote prolifically about how the planetarium could be used in atheist work.[47] Planetariums also provided a captivating forum for visiting lecturers like Aleksei Chertkov, a former priest and prominent public atheist.[48] Most of all, the planetarium was the perfect place to mobilize the enthusiasm generated by the Soviet space program, and the most popular lecturers were, of course, Soviet cosmonauts.

FIGURE 3.4. "Moscow Planetarium lecturer N. I. Zhulukov demonstrates model illustrating the movement of the Earth and the Moon around the sun's orbit at the Central House of Culture of Labor Reserves." October 10, 1959. GBU "TsGA Moskvy," no. 1-3094, used with permission.

Audiences were drawn in with technologically advanced equipment and especially the opportunity to hear about what cosmonauts encountered in their celestial journeys.[49]

Planetariums were attractive because they not only invited believers to attend lectures but also brought the planetarium to believers. The so-called mobile planetarium could organize lectures and exhibits beyond the confines of its central location, on "agitation bus" trips to Houses of Culture, pioneer camps, retirement homes, military complexes, student dorms, schools, libraries, red corners, parks of leisure and culture, factories, and even local housing administration offices. Using the mobile planetarium, lecturers went to collective farms in a mass populist drive to educate the rural population that began in the late 1950s. There they would attract an audience by combining the chance to use a telescope and learn about the most recent achievements of Soviet cosmonauts as well as by giving workers the opportunity to take a break from farm work. After listening to a lecture, audiences could relax in the field, listen to festive music coming from the planetarium's loudspeakers, and even conclude the night with dancing.[50]

By 1963, the Moscow Planetarium was selling nearly 280,000 tickets annually to its lectures, question-and-answer meetings, and visits to the observatory, and its field trips outside the main planetarium space increased attendance rates to 278,000 listeners for mass lectures and 517,083 for educational lectures.[51] Over the course of the year, the Moscow Planetarium dedicated fifty-three evenings to atheism specifically, which made up 18.8 percent of all planetarium lectures—an increase from 14.4 percent in 1962. The Moscow Planetarium reported that atheist programs left an effect on the audience; visitors wrote that "in the planetarium, one truly understands the absurdity and inadequacy of religious fairy tales," "having visited the planetarium, one can successfully conduct an argument with believers," "it is necessary to attract more and more believers to the planetarium; it is a truly great school for dethroning god," and "the planetarium had an enormous effect on our consciousness and helped us make sense of many unclear issues; the knowledge we received in the planetarium has definitively convinced us that God did not, does not, and cannot exist."[52]

At a conference convened in Moscow in May 1957, shortly before the USSR launched *Sputnik*, the Marxist-Leninist philosopher and academician Mark Mitin (1901–87), then the chair of the All-Union Znanie Society, stressed that since the battle with religion had moved from politics into ideology, atheists had to be mindful of the new tactics deployed by their opponent. Religious organizations "prefer not to openly speak out against science, [and] to present themselves as 'friends' of science, striving to 'prove' the connections between science and religion, the possibility of unifying the two, based on mutual respect and 'noninterference,' . . . and seek to prove that science and religion are not opposed to each other, but on the contrary, need one another."[53] Atheist cadres were instructed to make clear why science and religion were irreconcilable—to stress that while the religious worldview proclaimed the finite nature of the universe, scientific materialism revealed its infinity in both space and time.[54] As the Estonian astronomer Gustav Naan put it, once it was taken as fact that the cosmos followed the same laws as Earth, "Nothing heavenly really remained in the 'heavens.'"[55]

Yet the experience of atheists on the ground suggested that the thinking of a believer did not necessarily follow this same logic, and atheists themselves noted that the atheist component of scientific enlightenment was not without problems. Atheist work in the planetarium was criticized for relying almost exclusively on the natural sciences and avoiding "worldview" issues.[56] It was not enough to deliver lectures on chemistry and physics, the argument went, without explicitly addressing their atheist significance by tying them to religion and idealism. In 1955, B. L. Laptev brought attention to the importance of making clear the *atheist* significance of lectures on the natural sciences, pointing out that without this, scientific enlightenment could not be used effectively in the battle against religion. "We conducted [scientific enlightenment] lectures for years," Laptev said, "and it still took a Central Committee decree to reveal to us that we do not conduct scientific atheist propaganda."[57]

Such criticism was especially directed at cadres, as not all planetarium lecturers seemed to understand the significance of explicitly connecting atheism to, for example, lectures on astronomy or physics. This was a common complaint about scientists, who in offering their expertise in the service of mass enlightenment were often unwilling to exploit the opportunity to agitate explicitly against religion.[58] To illustrate the repercussions of avoiding direct battle against religion, Laptev described a planetarium lecture he had read at a collective farm on astronomy. When he was done, he asked his audience whether they liked the lecture, which was accompanied by audio and visual materials. His listeners answered that they did, but when asked what they liked about it, they informed him, "We liked how gloriously God constructed the universe."[59]

This was not the first time that Soviet atheists encountered the idea that scientific enlightenment did not necessarily constitute atheist propaganda, but given the long hiatus in atheist work under Stalin and the acknowledged shortcomings of atheist work under Khrushchev, it was a point that needed reiterating. To teach atheist cadres how to exploit the planetarium, Znanie met with the veteran planetarium lecturer, Ivan Shevliakov, to discuss his lectures on "Science and Religion on the Universe" and "The Atheist Significance of Discoveries in Astronomy and Cosmonautics."[60] Shevliakov had worked at the Moscow Planetarium for over forty years, and he observed that over the course of that time, both the audience and religion itself had changed. The audience knew much more about science and much less about religion.

> If in the first years after the revolution, we had to prove that Earth is round and other elementary things and had an auditorium that knew the Bible, the Gospels, the Old and New Testaments, the commandments, the Apostles' Creed, and so forth, then now even the clergy say that the audience knows almost nothing [about religion], and we propagandists are reaping the fruits of this revolution in the consciousness of the new generation, which began life after the October Revolution, after the separation of church and state, and church and education.[61]

The church, meanwhile, was also no longer the same opponent. It had moved away from its opposition to science—something that atheists could see for themselves, Shevliakov noted, if they leafed through the pages of the *Journal of the Moscow Patriarchate* (*Zhurnal Moskovskoi Patriarkhii*).

Indeed, Shevliakov pointed out to his colleagues that religion had long sought to accommodate science. Even in his prerevolutionary school days, "no one defended Bible stories in the literal sense that they are put forward." He recalled how, having learned in science class that Earth was six billion years old, he wondered how to reconcile this with the Bible's teaching that the world was created in six days. Yet when he asked the priest whether this was "a contradiction between science and religion," the priest informed him, "There is no contradiction—what for God is one day, is a billion years for man," and told him to sit back down.[62] "And this is not today, but in 1916," Shevliakov pointed out. He also told his audience that during an early visit to the Moscow Planetarium, Nadezhda Krupskaia, Lenin's widow as well as a central figure in the sphere of Soviet education, had noted that enlightenment lectures needed to make atheism more explicit. After listening to an "inexperienced" lecturer speak about the structure of the universe, Krupskaia observed that if an astronomy lecture did not draw out atheist conclusions, "every believer will leave, cross himself, and in his soul say that God's world is great and beautiful." Astronomy alone, Shevliakov concluded, was not enough to "demolish the religious worldview."[63]

Over the course of the antireligious campaign, atheists across the Soviet Union encountered obstacles in their crusade against religion. An atheist from the Tambov region reported that while their mobile planetarium attracted visitors of all ages during trips to the countryside, the atheist conclusions often did not come across. He described a ninety-five-year-old man in one village who "could not be removed from the apparatus for thirty minutes" because, as the old man explained, "I'm going to die soon, and I refuse to go to the other world until I see what's there."[64] Another lecturer reported that their mobile planetarium was popular with collective farmers, and especially sectarians, yet during planetarium visits, sectarians would try to "corner the lecturer [and] if they [got] the last word, they consider[ed] it a victory."[65] The reactions of planetarium visitors brought to light a phenomenon that atheists should not have found so surprising—namely, that the cosmological connection that they assumed between astronomy, space exploration, and atheism was neither necessary nor obvious to their audience. On the contrary, the history of science provided numerous examples where the elegant construction of the universe was indeed taken to prove the existence, rather than absence, of an all-powerful creator.

## *Bibles for Cosmonauts*

Marxism-Leninism outlined a clearly materialist conception of the world, but beneath propaganda, the relationship between the material and spiritual, the profane and sacred, turned out to be far more complicated. In rejecting religious cosmology, Soviet atheists were left to see if scientific materialism—which laid bare the constitution of the natural world—could mobilize the enthusiasm and belief that had been cultivated and harnessed by religion. Indeed, while they generally saw Marxism-Leninism as a repudiation of metaphysics, they learned that the questions they inherited from religion were as much philosophical as scientific. The question facing Soviet atheism was whether scientific materialism could be infused with a spiritual component yet remain scientific and materialist.

The experience of efforts to spread scientific atheism brought to light the degree to which most atheists lacked even a basic understanding of religion, and as a result did not reach their intended audience. In fact, one of the most frequent criticisms of atheist propaganda was that it spent too much energy preaching to the choir of unbelievers, and not enough entering into a productive dialogue with believers.[66] At a 1963 Central Committee conference on atheism, Osipov—the theology professor turned atheist—argued that one of the difficulties of atheist work was finding the right tone for a diverse audience. "Every propagandist encounters both [types of] people," Osipov noted. "Three days ago, in Kiev, [I] simultaneously [received] two notes [from the audience]: 'What do you think about Feuerbach's theory of atheism?' And next to it [another note], 'So tell me, former priest, do witches exist in the world?' " The Central Committee broke out in laughter. "So that," Osipov concluded, "is our range."[67] As Soviet atheists reconsidered strategies, they became aware that they needed to understand both religion and religiosity.

Speaking at the same party conference, cosmonaut Titov shared that during the many occasions when he was expected to speak about the cosmos to waiting audiences, he encountered the same problem.

> The fact that ordinary inhabitants of Earth have been to the heavens, the holy of holies of all religions, the space of god, has an enormous effect on believers, does not leave any one of them indifferent, and forces them to deeply think about their views and convictions. And many believers are struck by the fact that god did not manifest in response to the fact that ordinary mortals intruded into his estate.
>
> I would also like to cite one letter that a sixty-seven-year-old inhabitant of Kazan wrote to us. He sent it simply to the address "Cosmonaut." He writes this: "I am already sixty-seven years old, I am illiterate, and yet I nonetheless would like to be taken on a cosmic flight. I understand that I can contribute nothing from the point of view of science, so to speak. But yet, it is said, that there is no god. I believe that there is no god, but all the same, as the years wear on, I would like to make certain that god does not exist."
>
> [Animation and laughter in the hall.]
>
> Il'ichev: trust, but verify.[68]

More generally, Titov complained that he felt unprepared for atheist work. In general, he admitted, cosmonauts could not make the atheist significance of their cosmic missions clear in their lectures, and their responses to audience questions, such as whether they had encountered God in space, were unconvincing to believers. Titov observed that cosmonauts were fundamentally unfamiliar with religion, and therefore lacked the religious literacy that would give their claims power.

> I do not know even one prayer and have never even heard one, because I, like all my cosmonaut friends, grew up in our socialist reality and studied in our Soviet schools. Later, in university, and now at the academy, no one ever spoke to me about this religion—and it seems to me that the situation is similar in all educational institutions. And if by chance I came across some [atheist] books, then, with rare exception . . . these books were so boring that unless there was a real necessity, one does not really want to read them. [Laughter in the hall, applause.]
>
> We consulted with our boys, the cosmonauts, . . . and we realized we had to petition the ideological department to help us acquire bibles. [Laughter.] Now we have received them, and I have a bible in my library, because when I speak in public, especially abroad, we find ourselves in difficult situations. This is why we discussed whether cosmonauts, in the course of their studies and training, should somehow be informed a little about all this god and religion business.[69]

In a revealing inversion, Titov's request for Bibles for cosmonauts underscored the basic fact that atheist work could not be effective if cadres were unfamiliar with religion. Enlightenment work highlighted the *scientific* achievements of Soviet space flights, Titov concluded, but did not yet mobilize the philosophical significance of space exploration for the atheist mission. The unexpected and contradictory reactions of both ordinary believers and the church to scientific achievements forced atheists to question their understandings of religion as well as their predictions about its future in modern society. They also forced them to reconsider their belief that science was atheism's most powerful weapon.

## *Not by* Sputnik *Alone*

Behind model atheist conversion narratives, Soviet atheists discovered that the effect of cosmic conquests on religion was less linear than they had imagined, and their reports often relayed their frustration with what they saw as stubborn superstition. One atheist relayed his conversation with a sectarian in Irkutsk, who when told that a rocket was being launched to the moon, replied, "This never happened and will never happen. God will not allow a foreign body to come to the moon." When asked whether she would renounce religious belief if a rocket actually went to the moon, she responded only, "This never happened and will never happen, because it is impossible."[70]

Sociological research on religious cosmologies conducted in Tretie Levye Lamki, a village in the Tambov region, also revealed that many believers saw no contradiction between their faith and enthusiasm for Soviet space achievements. One fifty-two-year-old woman, Anna Dobrysheva, answered most of the researcher's questions with "Who knows?," and did not understand, even after repeated explanations, the contradiction between science and religion. As the researcher noted in his report, Dobrysheva "believes in space flights, but cannot seem to understand why [atheists] don't believe in God, and why they oppose science and religion."[71] In her view, "If we [believers] believe you [atheists], then you need to believe us as well."[72] One of the more unbelieving interview subjects was Petr Meshukov, categorized as "not belonging to a religion although he keeps icons [in his home]." Meshukov was described as a science enthusiast who "fully support[ed Charles] Darwin's theories about the origins of man, which when he is in an unsober state, provokes him to call people who offend him 'a degenerate product of simian genealogy'"[73] When asked about his understanding of the natural world, the researcher recorded that Meshukov "has some vague notion, although is certain that 'god has as much connection to them as the tail of a crocodile does to a person.'"[74] Overall, the position of the villagers was best summed up by Matrena Arkhipova, who stated that "Communists are good in every way, except that they don't believe in God, [and] that is bad."[75] In what became a perennial thorn in the side of Soviet atheists, believers, even when they embraced Soviet scientific achievements and space conquest, still managed to reconcile these with their religious worldviews.

Problematically, for Soviet atheists, so did the church. At a conference on the evolving relationship between science and religion, atheists emphasized the danger of the church's "accommodation" of science and religion's efforts to "adapt" to modernity. Research on sermons in the Vladimir region described clergy who either dismissed the atheist component of space conquests, or, worse yet, presented Soviet space achievements in a religious framework. A CARC report, for instance, described a Catholic priest in Belarus who refuted the notion that space achievements provided proof of God's nonexistence: "Nature has not yet been fully studied by man, [and man] is not yet able to control it. Then there exists some sort of power that controls nature. Sending satellites and people to space does not mean that there is no God. God exists, but he is invisible and not in man's likeness."[76] Archpriest Taranovskii was purported to proclaim, "Flights to space are new proof of God's great power, and the idea that cosmonauts did not notice God, well, it is not as if he sits in one place. One cannot see God; he is a spirit. And if life on other planets is discovered, then their existence also involved the participation of God; he is all-powerful. Even if God walked on the shores of the river Kliazma, people still would not believe that this is God."[77] Archbishop Onisim of the Vladimir-Suzdal diocese even urged the clergy to speak about the great achievements of the Soviet space program, particularly among the rural population.

Many atheists complained that the church was more difficult to combat when it denied the opposition between religion and science, or even co-opted scientific progress, painting it as a manifestation of God's will. According to this position, God's plan worked through unbelievers, and "the unbelieving Gagarin flew to space because it was advantageous to our God."[78] Yet what worried Soviet atheists even more was when religion responded to science by making the boundary between the material and spiritual more defined, and claiming for religion a "monopoly" over spiritual life.[79]

The Khrushchev era atheist campaign produced two distinct yet related results. On the one hand, the trials and errors of atheist agitators initiated a reconsideration of ideological positions on the nature and future of religion. The failure of religion to wither away—even under the seemingly conclusive blow dealt to religious cosmologies by scientific progress in general and Soviet space exploration in particular—needed a better explanation and more effective approach. While the beginning of the Khrushchev era atheist campaign was driven by a view of religion as a set of unenlightened beliefs and primitive practices that continued as a result of a kind of historical inertia, Soviet atheists soon realized that the essence and dynamics of religious belief had been transformed. Indeed, they came to suspect that it was their own theories and methods that were primitive, and as such, needed to be modernized to keep pace.

But when they attempted to fight faith with fact, they often encountered people who were untroubled by the contradictions that atheist propaganda so ardently unmasked, and instead reconciled scientific and religious cosmologies in unexpected ways. The worldviews Soviet atheists found on the ground ranged from unsystematic to eclectic to what might be called dualist—that is, worldviews that relied on science for explanations of the material world and religion for explanations of the spiritual realm. Indicative in this respect are the responses of Ul'iana Lukina from the Ivanovo region to a 1964 sociological survey titled "The Contemporary Believer's Perceptions of God." When asked how she combines, in her mind, the idea of God with the laws of the universe, Lukina replied that "she never occupies herself with speculations about the universe." When asked what she thought about the fact that spaceships had flown to space, Lukina answered, "So they flew, so what? There was a time when I barely made it from here to Ufa, and now it is possible to go twice a week. God has nothing to do with it. God, after all, is within us." When asked for her thoughts on the subject in general, Lukina concluded, "What is the point of thinking about this? It's just somehow more peaceful with God."[80]

Attempts to understand religious modernization continued to occupy atheists, as various hypotheses about the persistence of religion were found wanting, and atheist methods were tested without producing the desired results. In the Khrushchev era, new theories about the nature of religion led to new methods in atheist propaganda, so that atheists increasingly came to see philosophy as a critical weapon in the atheist arsenal. This shift put in question the assumptions at the foundation of scientific atheism and made atheists aware of the spiritual vacuum that opened up when scientific atheism tried to contest religious cosmologies.

## *Conclusion*

Soviet atheism sought to offer its own epistemological and moral positions, and initially cast the real and symbolic force of Soviet space achievements as the most powerful weapon in atheist work. But the entanglements of cosmic enthusiasm and scientific atheism also highlight transformations in how religion was understood and approached. Cosmonauts occupied the space between utopia and reality, and became a vehicle for the management of desire, longing, and faith. Through the cosmonauts' charisma, an ordinary Soviet person could tap into the ideological enthusiasm that was habitually required in Soviet citizens and perhaps even be converted by the experience. Yet as ideological models, cosmonauts remained removed from the Soviet masses by an impenetrable curtain, and the path to the heavens was available to the few, not the many. Soviet space achievements were presented as material proof of the great strides the country was making toward Communist modernity, but the persistence of religion in Soviet life as well as the efforts to exorcise it with more and better atheist work cast light on the distance that still separated the model Soviet person paraded on the world stage (and embodied in the figure of the cosmonaut) and the ordinary Soviet people in the audience. Not only did Soviet space conquest fail to produce atheist convictions, it also revealed the ideological blind spots of Marxism-Leninism.

In the end, Soviet scientific atheism faced the same problem of scientism everywhere: the problem of how to address the spiritual. Weber eloquently captured this predicament in his 1918 speech "Science as a Vocation," a foundational document for the social-scientific efforts to make sense of religion, science, and the nature of secularity.[81] "The fate of our times," Weber famously observed, "is characterized by rationalization and intellectualization and, above all, by the 'disenchantment of the world.'" But even if science "disenchanted" the material world, it remained outside the realm of morality and spiritual life. Science, Weber argued, was not "the 'way to true being,' the 'way to true art,' the 'way to true nature,' the 'way to true God,' the 'way to true happiness.'" Which is to say that even if science was useful, it was not necessarily meaningful. Invoking Lev Tolstoy's tortured engagements with the questions at the center of modern existence, Weber pointed out that Tolstoy believed science to be meaningless because it gave no answer to the ultimate question that concerned humanity: "What shall we do and how shall we live?" Weber conceded that religion remained an option to those in search of religious devotion and transcendent meaning, but only if they were ready to make an "intellectual sacrifice": "To the person who cannot bear the fate of the times like a man, one must say: may he rather return silently [to] the arms of the old churches [which] are opened widely and compassionately for him."[82]

For Soviet Communism, however, the retreat of Soviet citizens into the compassionate arms of the church could be interpreted only as defeat. The goal, after all, was to produce the new Soviet person who fully embraced reason—a person whose total commitment to the Communist project was made manifest through a full-throated atheist conviction that rejected all competing claims of authority and meaning. That scientific miracles and cosmic conquests failed to convert the masses to atheism and create atheist conviction forced Communist ideologists to confront the idea that chasing the gods and angels out of the heavens with rockets and cosmonauts was not enough, and that Soviet scientific atheism had to also fill the empty space with its own positive meaning. Atheists realized that if they wanted to reach the Soviet soul, they would have to turn not to science but to morality, and engage not just the rational but also the spiritual.

CHAPTER FOUR

# The Ticket to the Soviet Soul

## SOVIET ATHEISM AS WORLDVIEW

"Doesn't that mean then, that you think God exists?"

"He doesn't exist, yet He does. There's no pain in the stone, but there's pain in the fear of the stone. God is the pain of the fear of death. He who conquers pain and fear—will become God. Then a new life will dawn; there'll be a new man; everything will be new. . . . History will be divided into two parts: from the gorilla to the destruction of God, and from the destruction of God to . . ."

"To the gorilla?"

". . . to the physical transformation of the earth and of man. Man will become God and he will be changed physically. The world will be changed, and things will be changed, all thoughts and all feelings."

—FYODOR DOSTOEVSKY, *DEVILS*

ON JANUARY 18, 1960, at the height of Khrushchev's antireligious campaign, Znanie convened a conference to take stock of the renewed offensive against religion. The mood was bleak. Nikolai Gubanov, a prominent atheist, painted an especially pessimistic picture. Atheists had misunderstood and underestimated religion, Gubanov lamented, and atheism was not making inroads into the Soviet soul. Religion was not dying out but persisting—often flourishing—even in the inhospitable conditions of socialist modernity. To illustrate the atheists' predicament, Gubanov reminded his audience of a comic short story by Chekhov: "There were two civil servants, one an old man, the other a young man. And there was [an orator] who, on all special occasions—weddings and funerals—would roll out the speeches. When the civil servant died, [the orator] gave a speech. But he thought that the old man had died, when in fact it was the young one who had died. So he gave a speech in memory of the old civil servant, who was standing next to him and was very pleased to hear his own eulogy."[1] Gubanov was mistaken about the details of the story, but he was right about the main point: if socialism was not, in fact, burying religion, then Soviet atheists were premature in their eulogizing.

When atheists encountered lived religiosity, they found that—contrary to the patterns of development outlined by Marxism-Leninism—religion was not disappearing under the pressure of socialist construction and scientific progress. Customary explanations for the persistence of religion—economic expla-

FIGURE 4.1. "In the shade," A. Kanevskii, *Krokodil*, no. 3 (1962): cover.

nations about continued social inequalities, political explanations about the subversive strategies of reactionary religious organizations, theories about the lag between material development and the transformation of consciousness, or the notion that religiosity was the product of ignorance and backwardness—all failed to explain the complex spiritual landscape on the ground. Ordinary people, it turned out, were not necessarily troubled by contradictions between science and religion, and religion was not a socially marginal holdover of sectarians and old women but rather a flexible and dynamic phenomenon that was rooted in contemporary Soviet life. Indeed, Gubanov pointed out that many Soviet people used the leisure time and material welfare made possible by Khrushchev era economic reforms and populist social policies to attend church, observe religious rites, and contribute to their local religious communities. To illustrate this, Gubanov recounted a conversation he had with an elderly woman while lecturing in the provinces. The woman admitted that her family's lot had improved in the late 1950s, but when Gubanov asked how these improvements had changed her attitude toward religion, she told him, "Well, I suppose now I can go to church and can give more to the priest."[2] What atheists were learning, then, was that antireligious measures were inadequate to the task of producing an atheist society—or as Gubanov put it, "In our scientific atheist propaganda, we bury the wrong civil servant."[3]

## *Producing Soviet Communism*

The party's reengagement with religion was critical to shaping ideological production in the Khrushchev era, and remained so for the rest of the Soviet period. Between the Twentieth Party Congress, when Khrushchev initiated the process of de-Stalinization, and the Twenty-Second Party Congress, when he announced the Third Party Program (the first revision of the Communist ideological platform since 1919), Khrushchev consolidated both his personal power and the political project that would become his legacy: building Communism.[4] As the new party program outlined, with the transition from socialism to Communism, Soviet society would come to be governed by Communist morality and ethics, not the administrative apparatus of the state.[5] Within this framework, the moral and spiritual character of the Soviet people—not just their political loyalty, but also their worldview and way of life—gained a new significance. The ideological transformations of the Khrushchev era, then, were not just about the content of ideology—about replacing Stalinism with a new Communist dogma—but also about form, reflecting a new conception of the work that ideology was supposed to do.[6] No longer just a tool for policing orthodoxy, ideology was now envisioned as an instrument of spiritual transformation through which the real Soviet person of the present was supposed to become the model Communist person of the future.

The project to produce the new Communist person was not a Khrushchev era invention, but had been central to the Communist project from inception. Marx had famously proclaimed that the Communist world would be one in which "nobody has one exclusive sphere of activity but each can become accomplished in any branch he wishes." Since Communism would regulate production and liberate society from managing economic needs, people would be able to devote themselves to personal development. Under Communism, Marx wrote, it would become possible "to do one thing today and another tomorrow, to hunt in the morning, fish in the afternoon, rear cattle in the evening, criticize after dinner . . . without ever becoming hunter, fisherman, shepherd or critic."[7] However, despite Marx's noble vision of human emancipation, Soviet Communism continued to exist in the space between ideological proclamations and the everyday struggles that continued to define Soviet experience. As a woman from the Rostov region wrote to the Central Committee in 1963, it was hard to believe that while Soviet cosmonauts were conquering the heavens, her village still had no radio, and some of her neighbors had never seen a movie.[8] What changed under Khrushchev was that the party believed the time had come to address the gap between Communist ideology and Soviet reality. Since the material base of Communism had been built, it was now possible to tackle the final stage of Communist construction: the spiritual transformation of Soviet society.

The new role of ideology was evident in the increased attention that the party devoted to ideological work. When, in 1956, Khrushchev initiated the process of drafting the new party program, he gathered party theorists, academics, and propaganda cadres to study Soviet people's worldviews and byt in order to theorize the transition from socialism to Communism.[9] Soviet people, on their end, responded enthusiastically to the party's apparent interest in their views, flooding the Central Committee with proposals about the correct path to Communism.[10] To make sense of this unprecedented flow of information about Soviet society, the party expanded the ideological apparatus. Academic disciplines that had been marginal since the 1930s, like sociology and ethnography, were revived, and new institutions—such as *Komsomol'skaia Pravda*'s Institute of Public Opinion and the Leningrad State University's Laboratory of Sociological Research—were created to study Soviet society.[11] Khrushchev also established new "ideological commissions" within the party's Central Committee, charging them with charting the new course in the spheres of propaganda, science, culture, literature, art, mass media, and education.[12]

The Third Party Program and its "Moral Code of the Builders of Communism" were the party's road map for the transition from socialism to Communism, combining early Soviet revolutionary fervor with the postwar promise of material abundance. Khrushchev introduced numerous reforms aimed at improving the Soviet standard of living, from a massive housing campaign to provide Soviet families with individual apartments to the increase of consumer goods.[13] Still, while raising the standard of living was seen as a necessary precondition to building Communism, material improvement was not the end goal. Indeed, Khrushchev explicitly connected Soviet material conditions with Communism's spiritual promise. As Khrushchev put it in a 1961 speech, "We cannot just promise the people a beautiful future." There had been enough "frivolous" talk about prospects; now it was time to do "everything necessary" to reach production goals, so that "people have meat, milk, and other goods today." Khrushchev pointed out that whereas religion promised heavenly rewards, Communism promised abundance and justice in this world. "The priests say that those who suffer more on this earth will reach the kingdom of heaven after death. We have no right to be like these priests. We have to always be communists; people who stand firmly on this earth, who provide people with earthly goods rather than promise them heavenly rewards."[14] Material welfare was necessary to produce the "all-around developed individual"—the new person in whose name the party had made the revolution.[15] In crucial ways, then, the party tied the political legitimacy of the Soviet project with its ability to address not just material, but also spiritual needs.

Although the new "Moral Code of the Builders of Communism" listed the central virtues of Communist morality—from collectivism, internationalism, and patriotism to work ethic and family values—religion and atheism did not appear explicitly. They did, however, feature prominently in the ideological establishment's closed discussions.[16] In a preparatory document for the new party program, Aleksandr Shishkin (1902–77), a philosopher of ethics and chair of the Philosophy Department at the Moscow State Institute of International Relations, cast religion as Communism's moral antithesis.[17] "The enemies of Communism often say that Communists reject universal morality. But in reality, [Communists] only reject hypocritical bourgeois morality, which appealing to the commandments of God, serves the mercenary interests of the exploiters," Shishkin explained. Since only Communist morality was "truly humane" and "serve[d] the goal of human progress," the party's practical task of "creating well-rounded developed people" was "indivisible from all other tasks of Communist construction." To build Communism, it was necessary to "overcome the remains of outdated views on labor [and] religious survivals, and liquidate all amoral behavior."[18] Once the vestiges of the old world were expelled, the people would live "in a Communist way" and would be "guided by the principles of Communist morality," in both labor and everyday life. Their labor, moreover, would not be oppressive but "creative," becoming the "primary need of life," the path toward spiritual fulfillment. The Soviet people of the Communist future would take part in "material production," but still "have sufficient time for science, art, sport, or something else toward which he feels drawn." Under Communism, the human personality would finally "blossom" and the new Communist person would harmoniously combine "spiritual wealth, moral purity, and physical perfection."[19]

This ideal of the harmonious, well-rounded, disciplined, and moral Communist person echoed across citizens' letters about the new party program. One writer proposed that the goal of ideological work was "the creation of the Communist person, a person with the hands of a worker, the head of a scholar, the eyes of a painter and sculptor, the soul of a poet and composer, the prose of a writer, and the body of a gymnast."[20] As a party member from Perm wrote, "It is necessary for all laborers to understand the full absurdity and foolishness of religious delusions in our century—the century of cosmonauts [and] marvelous discoveries. Our marvelous Soviet person cannot . . . enter Communism alongside the priests and pastors."[21]

The project of building Communism reframed religion as a specifically ideological problem. As the new party program stated, "The party considers the main goal of ideological work at the present stage to be the upbringing of all laborers in the spirit of high ideological consciousness and devotion to Communism, a Communist approach to labor and the economy, the full overcoming of survivals of bourgeois views and morals, the all-around, harmonious development of the personality, the creation of a true wealth of spiritual culture." Communist upbringing needed to educate people "in the spirit of the scientific materialist worldview" in order to "overcome religious prejudices"—without, of course, "offending the feelings of believers."[22] The party viewed "the battle with manifestations of bourgeois ideology, morality, [and] superstitions" as a constituent part of its work. Its task was to remove the obstacles that stood in the way of the Communist future.

But the party also realized that meeting spiritual needs was a subtler task than addressing material shortages. While party propaganda intended for mass consumption presented a clear and optimistic program for Communist construction, discussions about ideological production behind the scenes were more fraught. Indeed, what the prominence of ideology in Soviet public life obscures is that ideology was not a monolithic narrative effectively delivered by a coordinated apparatus, but produced and disseminated by specific individuals, among whom there was often little consensus about goals and strategies. The historian Nikolai Mitrokhin argues that the "high priests" (*ideologicheskie zhretsy*) of Soviet ideology were shaped less by Marxist-Leninist theory than by their own notions about what constituted correct "Soviet" values and norms.[23] For many, he notes, Marxism "remained on the level of something learned long ago in university and forgotten," which also left room for confusion, interpretation, and debate.[24]

Under Khrushchev, The Central Committee issued directives intended for party cadres in a new register, emphasizing shortcomings and underscoring the need for new approaches in ideological work. A January 9, 1960, decree, "On the Tasks of Party Propaganda in Contemporary Conditions," criticized party propaganda for dogmatism, which it cast as a holdover from "the period of Stalin's cult of personality."[25] The Central Committee instructed cadres to abandon ineffective approaches that were "separate[ed] from life," and to focus on the "main practical task" of creating "the new communist person with communist character traits, habits, and morals." But the problem with propaganda was not just that it was too dogmatic, but that it was not reaching the masses. The decree noted that whereas previous propaganda efforts focused on party members and the intelligentsia, the "present stage of development" required that *all* Soviet people "have mastery of the ideas of Marxism-Leninism," since with the transition from "socialist governance" to "communist societal self-management," individual consciousness would become the main form of regulating Soviet society. "Certain groups of the population," the decree noted, "are completely outside daily ideological-political influence," and party cadres could not remain passive in the face of "idealistic, anti-Marxist-Leninist, religious ideology." They had to "make their way to every Soviet person" and "concretely fight against survivals of capitalism in the[ir] consciousness."[26] Ideological work had to move beyond public spaces like factories, libraries, museums, and cultural clubs, and reach the Soviet person at home.

But even when the ideological establishment turned its attention to atheism, it remained unclear what constituted a "scientific-atheist worldview" and how it could be inculcated in practice. To spread the atheist worldview among the masses required effective institutions to produce and direct it, persuasive narratives to make it compelling, and trained cadres to disseminate it—an organized and effective atheist apparatus—and when Khrushchev embarked on the project of building Communism and overcoming religion, such an atheist apparatus did not exist.

To get a sense of the state of atheist work at the start of Khruschev's antireligious campaign, it is instructive to examine the party's publishing house, Gospolitizdat, as a space of atheist production. On March 21, 1958—shortly before the party and government issued the decrees that initiated the antireligious campaign—Gospolitizdat's editorial board met to discuss its role in the production of atheist material. Although the specific agenda for the meeting was the upcoming publication of the *Atheist's Reference Guide* (*Spravochnik Ateista*), the conversation quickly turned to the broader problems facing Soviet atheism. Atheists were aware, for example, that atheist work that focused on anticlerical propaganda was ineffective. In a revealing outburst, one atheist asked, "How long are we going to talk about the burning of Giordano Bruno?!" He noted that while atheists were busy unmasking religion, their opponent was focusing elsewhere: on undermining the opposition between religion and Communism, even claiming that "Marxist teaching is the development of early Christianity."[27] Atheists were also aware that they had a serious cadre problem, in terms of both quantity and quality. The "old atheist" Liutsian Klimovich (1907–89), a specialist on Islam whose atheist pedigree dated to the League of the Militant Godless in the 1920s, noted that the party's ambivalent position on religion and retreat of atheism after the war created confusion among both party cadres and believers about the relationship of religion to Communism. "It is no secret that [propaganda cadres] think of the church almost as a government institution," he observed. "This question really demands to be clarified."[28] The new generation of atheist cadres needed to be "armed" with knowledge about the Bible and the Koran, since "they have to criticize them, but they cannot even get their hands on them."[29] Meanwhile, among Soviet believers, "the mood is that religion and Communism get on very well, that it is possible to enter into Communism with religion. We tell them that this is harmful, [but it is necessary to explain] what is harmful and why. So far, we have not offered a convincing answer, just generalities."[30]

The discussions within Gospolitizdat suggest that the ideological establishment was well aware that it lacked the resources to carry out the party's will. In fact, to fulfill their mandate, Gospolitizdat's editors found themselves in the peculiar position of studying party, CAROC, CARC, and KGB reports on the religious situation in the USSR; seeking out new authors, especially believers who had broken with religion, whose narratives were perceived to be especially effective at communicating the atheist message; going to bookstores to find out which atheist titles were in demand and why; and even visiting churches to listen to sermons and learn more effective strategies for reaching and engaging the masses from the clergy. In short, the ambitions of the antireligious campaign revealed to the ideological establishment that it lacked the resources, institutions, and cadres to conduct atheist work. Having virtually dismantled the atheist apparatus under Stalin, the party now had to rebuild it.

In order to disseminate the atheist message to the people, the ideological establishment also recognized that it needed to recruit the scientific and creative intelligentsia to produce compelling atheist material, from books, plays, and films, to radio and television programs. But above all, it understood that it needed atheist cadres and the institutions to coordinate their work. When the religious question returned under Khrushchev, the number of cadres who had knowledge of or experience with religion was insignificant. When the party became interested not just in regulating and repressing religion but also in understanding it, it turned to the limited number of experts working within the structures of the Central Committee's Academy of Social Sciences, the Academy of Sciences, and the newly established departments of scientific atheism in the country's major higher education institutions. It also turned to the "old atheists," the former members of the dispersed League of Militant Godless. Finally, it turned to "apostates," former clergy who had publicly broken with religion and embraced atheism: most famously, Evgraf Duluman, a former student at the Moscow Theological Academy and instructor at the Saratov seminary, and Aleksandr Osipov, a former professor of theology at the Leningrad Theological Academy, both of whom had made their crisis of faith public by publishing articles in the newspaper *Komsomol'skaia Pravda*.[31]

When the party set out to make the Soviet masses atheist, then, it could turn to militant atheists, religious experts, and apostates, but each of these categories came with its own set of problems. Whereas the generation of old atheists—who, like Klimovich, had been forged in the militant campaigns of the early Soviet period—had a foundation in Marxist theory and were committed to the mission, their militancy and dogmatism were out of sync with the post-Stalinist ideological climate. The religious experts, meanwhile, had religious knowledge but little enthusiasm for spreading the atheist message. The apostates, on their end, could relay the message that religion was darkness by unmasking theological contradictions and the inner workings of the church, but they were not only few in number, but remained, in a fundamental sense, alien to the majority of Soviet people, especially the younger generation. What the party needed was an army of "new atheists" who were trained, enthusiastic, and relatable. What it actually had was a cohort of cadres who had little experience with atheist work and lacked even basic knowledge of religion, and who often found themselves in the sphere of atheist work by pure chance, and so lacked the desired expertise, commitment, and enthusiasm.

## *Bringing Atheism to the Masses*

After the dissolution of the League of the Militant Godless during the war, Znanie was established in 1947 and became the primary organization charged with atheist work. Like most Soviet institutions, Znanie was a centralized organization that reached from the All-Union Znanie Society in Moscow down to the republican, regional, and local levels. Its members included academics, members of the scientific and creative intelligentsia, professionals—doctors, agronomists, engineers, teachers—and propaganda cadres who combined Znanie activities with their work in the party and Komsomol. Under Khrushchev, its activities and membership grew exponentially. Whereas the society organized 83,000 lectures in 1948, its first full year of operations, by 1957 the number of lectures grew to 3,217,000, and by 1962 to 12,757,000.[32]

In the new era of building Communism, the demands placed on Znanie's "Academy of Millions" were especially high.[33] As the antireligious campaign gained momentum, an internal Znanie report explained that the successful construction of Communism depended on the "ideological conviction" and "moral characteristics" of the people. This required overcoming capitalist survivals in people's consciousness, with religion being "one of the most significant."[34] The Communist Party, the report noted, was grounded in science and had "always been irreconcilable with religion, which plays the role of spiritual moonshine, poisoning people's consciousness." Whereas Communism promoted agency in this life, religion "preach[ed] resignation to fate, the passive waiting for heavenly life in the next world." Rather than a harmless tradition, religion threatened the Soviet project since religiosity was "often accompanied by violations in labor and government discipline," was "detrimental to agriculture," and left people "spiritually desolate."[35]

Previously the primary target of atheist work was the believer; now Znanie instructed atheists to cast a wider net: "Life demands that scientific-atheist propaganda approach the broad masses of laborers. We must get to every industrial brigade, production department, dormitory, housing administration, [and] courtyard."[36] As the Znanie leadership explained, "The propaganda of scientific-atheist knowledge is needed by everyone: for some, it will help strengthen them against the influence of religious ideology; for [others], it will help them become knowledgeable agitators against religion."[37] Every lecture was to have an atheist "pointedness," and lectures on all subjects—from the natural sciences to foreign affairs, from art to literature—needed to make their atheist conclusions explicit.

To reach the masses, Znanie also adopted new forms and methods of atheist work, establishing new atheist clubs, atheist evening schools, atheist museum exhibits, atheist corners in libraries, and even atheist amateur theater and dance collectives. It also focused on cadre training, organizing classes and workshops in institutes, party schools, and "people's universities" in the provinces, as well as conferences and seminars at Znanie's central atheist institutions, such as Moscow's Planetarium and House of Scientific Atheism (see figure 4.2).[38] Atheist work became more varied as atheists turned to new pedagogical aids—visuals, debates, plays—to engage the audience. In one atheist club, for example, cadres organized an atheist event on "Science and Superstition" that combined pedagogy with entertainment, and included a question-and-answer session with representatives of the local intelligentsia (the school principal, teachers, doctors, and journalists), an amateur theater troupe performance of Sergei Mikhalkov's play *Darkness* (*Temnota*), and a viewing of the film *On the Threshold of Consciousness* (*U Poroga Soznaniia*).[39]

Discussions of successful models of atheist work, like the club above, dominated Znanie meetings. While ritualistic in form, these had the dual function of disseminating effective strategies and marking progress. At a 1960 seminar, for example, a Znanie lecturer and instructor from Moscow's Institute of Culture named Shevchenko shared the story of Ivanteevka, a small town near Moscow, as a model of atheist work. While "certain comrades reasoned that the roots of religion have been torn out, that religion is a dying survival, that all people are educated, and only go to the movies, dances, and to lectures about whether there is life on Mars," Shevchenko observed, religion was still very much a part of Soviet life—though, with the right approach, it did not have to be.[40] Shevchenko asked his audience to "imagine a textile industry town [where] many have lost their fathers, husbands, and sons during the Great Patriotic War." Many of the men who remained had moved to Moscow or worked in a nearby collective farm, leaving "many single mothers, who have a difficult time bringing up their children."[41] The town church was filled with women, he continued whose shadows darted back and forth among the many candles. Before Easter, boys and girls lined up outside the church, sent by their grandmothers to have their Easter cakes blessed. Then a new Orthodox priest, Father Vasilii, arrived. Father Vasilii was educated, a reserve major in the army, and showed an "exceptional maneuverability" in his capacity to "adapt to modern conditions."[42] He also charged a "solid fee" for religious rites.

FIGURE 4.2. Meeting of a study group at the Moscow House of Scientific Atheism. Moscow House of Scientific Atheism, November 21, 1963. GBU "TsGA Moskvy," no. 1-48741, used with permission.

Soon, religion began to find its way into the lives of Ivanteevka residents. A retired teacher decided to lead the parish administration. She put her students in touch with the priest, who told them that if they did not go to church, then they were "against peace, and therefore, against the politics of Soviet power."[43] Before long, "little crosses began to sparkle on the necks of many children." Young people flocked to the newly repaired church for Christmas services, where the choir sang, a tree was lit up, and the priest handed out gifts. Soon, the crowds of believers could no longer fit inside the church, and the "velvety voice" of Father Vasilii could be heard on loudspeakers outside.[44] Of course, Shevchenko noted, "our organizations, even if belatedly, sounded the alarm." Letters of indignant workers appeared in the regional newspaper. The bishop transferred Father Vasilii to another parish and replaced him with a "meek and manageable little old man." But the problem could not be resolved so easily. For months after Father Vasilii's transfer, "the fanatical devotees of the departed, a handsome man in his prime, [picketed] outside of the church, [wrote] letters everywhere demanding the return of their idol, and [would not] allow the old man to even approach the threshold. The church is closed!" So even though the Ivanteevka church was closed, "the damage was done."[45]

To address the situation, Shevchenko met with local activists to remind them of the importance of ideological work. The Ivanteevka party cell placed the best agitators in the homes of Ivanteevka families in order to conduct "individual work." Clubs hosted public lectures, question-and-answer sessions, and an antireligious film festival. Teachers tried to "passionately convince" believing parents to stop "crippling the souls" of their children, the "people of the epoch of Communism."[46] Posters appeared around town announcing lectures and debates on "crucial worldview questions" such as "The Truth about Happiness, the Meaning of Life, and the Future" and "Does the Bible Teach Goodness?" Shevchenko shared that during his lectures, he often received notes from the audience asking whether atomic bombs could destroy humanity, so he organized a lecture series around science fiction themes, which also appealed to the youth. Instead of a future filled with fear about the Apocalypse, he offered his listeners "an emotional and impassioned truth about the future . . . a future of light, joy, [and] the daring of Man the Creator—a vision of that which, in the words of [Konstantin] Tsiolkovskii, is 'impossible today' but will become 'possible tomorrow.' "[47] By the end of the campaign, several students had renounced religion, and even managed to interest their mothers in atheism "with captivating stories about adventures in interplanetary space travel." Under the influence of their children, parents began to "reconsider the 'heavenly firmament' and the reality of the 'heavenly kingdom,' having been filled with respect for great Soviet science."[48]

Another innovation of the Khrushchev era was the so-called "People's University," a continuing education program aimed at the enlightenment of the working classes. At the Fourth All-Union Znanie Congress held in 1963, Znanie leadership held up the People's University in Tartu, Estonia, which had been established in 1959, as an exemplary model of atheist work, and invited A. M. Mitt, a physics teacher and atheist lecturer, to report on the program's success.[49] Mitt relayed that the Tartu people's university, intended largely for agricultural workers, benefitted from its proximity to the University of Tartu, one of the oldest universities in the Soviet Union. But he also stressed that in setting up the atheist program, local atheists had to start from scratch. They established a two-year program for students comprising twenty-five lectures read every other Sunday evening, four question-and-answer sessions, three thematic evenings, and excursions that included a visit to an atheist film festival and a trip to the GMIRA in Leningrad. Mitt clarified that while registered students were usually atheists, the program also attracted a large number of

FIGURE 4.3. Outdoor atheist lecture organized by the Moscow House of Scientific Atheism. Moscow House of Scientific Atheism, 1963. GBU "TsGA Moskvy," no. 1-48745, used with permission.

visitors, many of them religious. As a sign of success, Mitt reported that even though it was held the day after Christmas, their event on "Religious Miracles in Light of Science" still gathered an audience of three hundred. Similarly, their atheist film festival deliberately held during Easter week attracted eight thousand viewers, or around 10 percent of the population of Tartu.[50] In part, Mitt attributed the success of Tartu's People's University to the fact that lectures were often read by professors from the University of Tartu, which was much esteemed in the community. The proximity also brought numerous established academic and cultural figures to the area—prominent biologists, astrophysicists, and even the famous Orthodox apostate Osipov—to lecture in the program. Atheist instruction also included excursions to the Geological and Zoological Museum, astronomical observatory, university's computing center, and Museum of Ethnography.

After completing the atheist program, Mitt shared, students and visitors became "convinced that atheism is not the whimsy of 'professional blasphemers' but the direct and incontrovertible consequence of scientific achievements."[51] The number of religious rituals in Tartu had declined significantly, with baptisms and confirmations falling by 90 percent, and funerals by 50 percent between 1957 and 1963.[52] Two churches had been closed "due to the absence of attendees," and the number of sectarians declined steadily, with one even joining the atheist program's academic council. Finally, Mitt highlighted the program's most remarkable graduate, an eighty-year-old man "with the beard of the venerable Abraham," who had spent the last thirty years of his life as a Seventh-day Adventist. After completing the program, Mitt relayed, he "declared that he had wasted half of his life, and is grateful to us, that we finally helped him make sense of all of life's questions." Mitt shared that the department's lectures "force[d] people to . . . decide, in their own conscience, the main question—where is truth, in science or religion? Where does one look for it—at church with the priests or in the House of Culture with the scientists?"[53] Mitt even had to begin having office hours for people to "come bare their souls and ask me to clarify questions that have become critical for them [*kotorye u nikh naboleli*] and to which they seek answers."[54]

Atheist success was measured by conversion: when a believer renounced religion and fully embraced Soviet Communism, which in practice meant joining a typically Soviet organization, like the Komsomol or an amateur arts group. Such conversions, Znanie proposed, could be achieved by expanding the scope and depth of the individual atheist's personal engagement with the believer. A Znanie lecturer from Stavropol, for instance, relayed his work with a local believer whose child had fallen ill. She wanted to take her son to a local "healer" (*znakharka*), but the atheist visited her and told her of a child from a neighboring village who had died as a result of homespun treatment. Yet his work did not stop with this attempt to convince her by way of argument and evidence. He followed up on the situation by coming to the woman's home with a horse, and bringing her and her son to a doctor in a nearby town. Then he continued to visit the family twenty more times until the husband and wife broke with religion. This kind of personal attention and individual work, he explained, helped him convert almost two hundred people to atheism.[55]

But such atheist successes were just a drop in the bucket. In 1964, when Znanie atheists again gathered to take stock of progress, they framed their work explicitly as a competition with the church—a competition in which they were the weaker party. To explain their predicament, Shevchenko (who had shared the story of atheist work in Ivanteevka) highlighted the relative power of the opposing sides. He pointed out that the USSR had 15,000 religious organizations, 10,500 of which belonged to the Orthodox Church. Half of those—5,000—were on the territory of the RSFSR. Bringing the focus closer to home, he noted that the Moscow region had 100 Orthodox churches, in which there took place about 500,000 "so-called religious acts" including "marriages, baptisms, confessions, sermons, and so forth, from mass to individual ones" in 1963 alone. Znanie, meanwhile, had organized only 3,900 atheist lectures, and these made up just 3 percent of its lecture program. Atheists, Shevchenko conceded, were right to be "worried that the clergy are beating us with their strength, and especially the strength of their theological knowledge," and agreed that it was "difficult to argue with these seemingly well-qualified clerics." But he also pointed out that by confining themselves to "strictly atheist" activities, atheists were not using the full arsenal of available resources. Yes, there were 5,000 Orthodox churches in the RSFSR, he acknowledged, but there were also 60,000 clubs, 1,000 libraries, 369 museums, 282 theaters, and over 100 planetariums and observatories, as well as folk theaters, bookstores, and houses of culture. Moreover, he noted, Soviet people had purchased 1.5 million radios and 1.5 million televisions in the first six months of 1963 alone, opening up another channel through which to have "a big influence." If atheists mobilized the entire arsenal of Soviet secular culture for atheist work, they could free people from "the horrible manacles of religiosity."[56]

The party continued to exert pressure on religious institutions and believers, and Znanie pressed on with atheist work, but the results—despite the success stories recited in Znanie reports—were mixed at best.[57] Znanie also continued to rely overwhelmingly on lecture propaganda, citing statistics about continuing increases in lectures, even as it decried the limitation of the form. By now, however, such recitations created more questions than answers. As one atheist lecturer in Moscow put it, "What is the difference if I say that we have increased the number of lectures by 100–200–500 percent in comparison with the previous year" when Communists themselves lacked "militancy" and a "Leninist attitude toward religion?"[58] To illustrate his point, he shared a note he received during a recent lecture for five hundred propaganda workers in Moscow: "During Easter, by tradition, we eat Easter cakes and paint eggs in our home. But we do not believe in God. I am a Communist, my brother is in the Komsomol, and my father is a party candidate. Is it really so very bad?"[59]

## *Clubs and Lectures against Churches and Sermons*

Over the course of the Khrushchev era, the party tried to communicate that a Communist who painted Easter eggs—or went to church, or observed religious rites--was indeed "very bad." As the Ideological Commission noted, "There are many signals that party organizations do not devote the necessary attention to the atheist education of laborers, have a conciliatory attitude toward the activities of churchmen and sectarians, [and] do not actively battle survivals of the past. Not infrequently, Communists reconcile themselves to the fact that religious rituals are conducted in their families, and sometimes even participate in them themselves."[60] None of this, of course, was new, but the project of building Communism gave these customary complaints about failures in party discipline a new urgency. The Party Charter made explicit that passivity on religion was intolerable, and obligated party members to battle religion actively.[61]

Internal reports consistently mentioned the failure of party members to serve as model atheists. An atheist lecturer named Rudenko, for example, relayed an exchange he had with a regional party secretary on a train on their way to a party conference.[62] "We know you atheists," the party secretary had mocked Rudenko, "you read lectures to yourselves." Rudenko used the party secretary's derision to point out that "Communist" and "atheist" did not always overlap, and shared an anecdote to illustrate that local cadres were especially dismissive of atheism:

> We were in one district helping the party *obkom* work on scientific atheist propaganda in connection with the latest Central Committee resolution. One district secretary says, let us go check the situation in the families of Communists, in their byt. We checked all the villages at the same time. We walked into [the home of] each Communist, and struck dumb, stared at the iconostasis. I will not speak of percentages, but there were not a few people with icons. So how did they explain themselves, these Communists? "These aren't mine, they are my grandmother's, or my auntie's," and when we reported this to the city party secretary, he said that we should ask them whether in ideological questions they are guided by the instructions of the party or their grandmothers and aunties. [Meanwhile] we [atheists] do not give lectures for Communists [and] Soviet state functionaries.[63]

Rudenko noted that the above incident, "while not characteristic," was not rare. "If you look among yourselves," he remarked, "I think you will find a similar phenomenon."[64] The ideological establishment interpreted the ideological passivity of party cadres as proof that religion remained pervasive in Soviet life. The fact that the Soviet home was not necessarily a Communist home, and that a Communist was not necessarily an atheist, was a sign of the distance between the Soviet present and the Communist future. The "naïve" and "unmilitant" attitudes among party members meant that Communists did not appreciate atheism's ideological and political significance.

Znanie also pointed to the danger of direct engagements with priests and believers, noting that when atheists confronted religion directly, they usually found themselves at a disadvantage (see figure 4.4). One cadre described an atheist event in Vladivostok, where the leader of a local Pentecostal community informed the audience that they had listened to "slander" and insisted that he could prove the historical reality of Christ and "biblical myths" like the great flood with scientific evidence. Instead of achieving atheist objectives, the Vladivostok lecture showed that "unhealthy encounters of believers with unbelievers could not but enflame religious fanaticism."[65] Atheists were warned that believers could use the occasion of an atheist lecture as a "tribune for

— Если они будут так работать, на клубе поставим крест.  Рисунок А. ЦВЕТКОВА

FIGURE 4.4. "If they keep working like this, we can put a cross on the club" (*Esli oni budut tak rabotat', na klube postavim krest*). A. Tsvetkov, *Krokodil*, no. 10 (April 10, 1962): 13.

the propaganda of the religious worldview." To compete with religion, atheists needed practical training that was "connected to life." Indeed, an atheist named Uskov drew a direct analogy between the training of atheist cadres and the preparation of priests.

> Why is it that in seminaries homiletics—the art of preaching—is taught as one of the most important subjects, while among us, no one ever speaks about how one should communicate, what language to use, how one should comport themselves based on the audience? After all, a lecturer is not only that person who wrote the lecture and knows the subject. Besides this, he must speak clearly, accessibly, understandably, so that [the lecture] would reach the consciousness of the masses. In religion, after all . . . the lecturer must excite people's emotions. . . . This is the main art—the ability to communicate with the masses.

Uskov also stressed the importance of proper training for lecturers by showing the dangers of direct confrontations with believers. He described a recent Moscow lecture provocatively titled "Does God Exist?" that ended in a "big embarrassment." Faced with an audience of three hundred people—an audience of precisely "those whom we must service," specifically elderly people and believers—the lecturer quickly revealed his lack of preparation as "old ladies assaulted him with questions," and he only "mumbled and could not respond." Uskov insisted that atheists had to pay attention not only to theory but also to "the lecturer's ability to simply, accessibly, and most important, convincingly communicate his knowledge in such a difficult and important sphere of our propaganda."[66]

The pitfalls of poorly trained atheist cadres were likewise highlighted by a veteran atheist named Vinogradov, who had been involved in atheist work since 1928. Antireligious propaganda, he observed, was "the most difficult kind of propaganda." It demanded "enormous tact, methodological mastery and serious knowledge," all of which were especially tested when the lecture took place in the countryside.

> Let us say you are lecturing about Christ, then immediately after such a lecture you are asked a question: So who created the Earth and the sun? Why don't people today come from monkeys? Why does the priest in the village of Volchakovka offer free suppers, but in the Soviet teahouse it costs money? When a lecturer says he will not answer such questions, he loses authority. If in a village a lecturer is asked a question that does not relate to his topic, and he does not answer the question, then they say—he cannot make sense of a question like this, and he comes here to talk about God.[67]

Indeed, Vinogradov proposed that the most important part of a lecture was not the lecture itself, but the question-and-answer session. This was where most lecturers floundered, especially in rural areas "where all lectures turned into conversations."[68] Atheists had to improve their approaches, since even philosophers, doctors, and biologists were "stumped" when confronted by "biblical experts." Moreover, Vinogradov argued, that in order to be effective, party members first had to "put their own homes in order" by getting rid of icons and disciplining those who observed religious rites. He pointed to the stereotypes that party members sometimes resorted to in order to avoid responsibility for such behaviors, describing a young Komsomol member who blamed the icon in his home on his wife. His wife, the young worker had lamented, was a believer, and he was unable to "reeducate" her. Yet when Vinogradov approached the wife, pointing out to her that it was unseemly for a young Soviet woman to have an icon in her home, she answered, "I told that fool forty times to take it down." Instead of such "domestic atheists," Vinogradov called for militant atheists.[69]

Finally, Vinogradov also urged atheists to devote personalized attention to believers, arguing that this individualized approach was the foundation of

FIGURE 4.5. "Ascension" (*Voznesenie*). Caption: "–Why are you lifting me up?—For bad atheist lectures!" (*–Za chto voznosite?—Za plokhie ateisticheskie lektsii!*), Kukryniksy, *Krokodil*, no. 17 (June 20, 1962): 5.

religion's power. He described a village where, in 1958, there were several hundred baptisms, one hundred of which were people between the ages of sixteen and twenty. For Vinogradov, the high number baptisms, and especially adult baptisms, was evidence that the clergy and sectarians were reaching out to the local community.

> It is no secret that sectarians visit people in their homes, speak with them. Does the party secretary visit people's homes? What about the chairman of the regional division [of Znanie]? I know of an incident where the executive committee refused to repair a roof, and the sectarians took care of it—meaning, they win over people's hearts. Sectarians employ all means and approach each person individually. . . . It seems to me that the strongest effect can be achieved by way of individual conversations . . . in order to sow at least a grain of doubt.[70]

Vinogradov proposed that atheist work should not be confined simply to religious questions. He noted that during his lectures, he met many people whom he continued to visit: "They write to me—you spoke to us about morality, but our chairman curses at us every day. Another writes that there is no day care, and she needs help placing her child. A lecturer in the village must go to the district committee [and] the executive committee about such issues."[71] In effect, then, Vinogradov proposed that atheist work was not just about argument but about care, drawing a parallel between the work of an atheist and the pastoral role of a priest.

Aleksandr Gagarin, professor of philosophy at Moscow State University and chair of Znanie's RSFSR bureau of scientific atheism, also criticized atheist work as too abstract, and urged atheists to appeal to emotion.[72] Yet as he outlined shortcomings, atheist cadres asked Gagarin to elucidate how the new approach to atheist work with believers looked in practice. "I do it in the following way," Gagarin explained. "I live with people and I clarify [things] for them. . . . [It is necessary] to win them over, to enter into their confidence, the same way that the priest, in his time, won them over. This work is difficult, and honorariums are not paid for it, but this work is revolutionary, and it will play an enormous role."[73] Like Gagarin, atheist theorists in the ideological establishment began to argue that atheist work did not stop at the end of a lecture. In order to achieve results, atheists had to participate in the daily lives of their audience, to understand their experiences, and to address their problems. Such calls to improve atheism by borrowing the tools and strategies of atheism's religious opponents are revealing.[74] Certainly, old methods continued to be used, but atheists increasingly urged local cadres to approach their work with a pastoral mission. Indeed, at an atheist conference, Gagarin characterized the "communist atheist" as a kind of spiritual guide. While "bourgeois atheists" were content to leave the individual in a precarious state of "indifference," unanchored in an ideological position, atheists had to guide the individual who had "departed from the shores of religion" but had not yet "arrived at the shore of atheism."[75]

On May 9, 1963, Znanie held a conference on the "Formation and Development of the Spiritual Life of Communist Society."[76] The focus of the conference, convened to discuss the production of the five-volume *Socialism and Communism*, was on the spiritual development of Soviet society in the transition from socialism to Communism. Religion played a prominent role in the conversation as participants explored the role of social psychology and public opinion in religiosity along with concrete measures for developing the new Communist personality and inculcating the scientific atheist worldview. Those present acknowledged that appeals to reason and science did not make Soviet people into atheists.[77] As former explanations for the continued existence of religion were found wanting, some argued that what prevented success was that the ideological establishment lacked a clear picture of the emotional world and byt of Soviet people. As one speaker declared, "The primary object of ideological work must be Man—the world of his thoughts and emotions, the cultivation in him of all the best thoughts and emotions. . . . [W]e must keep each human being in our field of vision, to see and know how he actually is not only in production, but in social spaces, in his family, in everyday life."[78]

To highlight the complexity of byt, the artist Boris Nemenskii recounted his conversation with the principal of a village school. "Come visit our homes," the school principal told him. "Take a look at how our technological intelligentsia spends its leisure time, which our government is trying to increase as much as possible. They play dominoes. We must make it so that this [leisure] time is used for the spiritual development of our people."[79] The neglect of the family and everyday life in ideological work became all the more grievous as the material conditions of the country improved, and Soviet people had more time and space to themselves. Nevertheless, while the conference participants identified a problem, they were still at a loss for how to treat the "spiritual world of Soviet Man" with any degree of specificity.[80] Znanie continued to discuss the obstacles that had to be overcome in order to make the transition to Communism, but struggled to produce concrete strategies for addressing Soviet spiritual life. As one speaker eloquently put it, "It has been correctly noted that whereas formerly we were in the period where we spoke about what *will not be* under Communism, now the time has come to discuss what *will be* under Communism."[81]

## *Worldviews at War*

The most active of Khrushchev's ideological commissions was headed by Leonid Il'ichev, a Khrushchev protégé whose influence on ideological matters was second only to that of Mikhail Suslov, the guardian of party orthodoxy.[82] The work of the commission, established in 1962, peaked in 1963, with two Central Committee plenums—in June and November—on the critical role of the scientific-materialist worldview in the system of Communist upbringing (*kommunisticheskoe vospitanie*).

If building Communism was the ideological project of the Khrushchev era, the center of that project was the inculcation of the scientific atheist worldview. This discourse about worldview had roots in nineteenth-century European socialism, within which the transformation of worldviews was the mechanism of cultural and political revolution.[83] Although the ideological debates of the Khrushchev era did not make this genealogy explicit, the Soviet use of worldview echoed the German conception of *weltanschauung*, which, as historian Todd Weir writes, embodied "a systematic understanding of the world [conceived] as a meaningful totality that formed the basis of a community," and was expected not only to explain "the present state of the social and physical world" but also "to contain a normative system and a program of salvation on many fronts."[84] As Il'ichev explained at a meeting of the Ideological Commission, worldview was "a rather broad complex of diverse ideas and impressions about the essence of the world, and on the relationship of man to this world." It encompassed a range of political, economic, philosophical, natural scientific, ethical, and aesthetic ideas, and if, within this complex, "religious ideas dominate over all of the others, then the worldview is religious, the inverse of the scientific worldview."[85]

The Central Committee's June Plenum, held on June 18–24, 1963, was convened to work out the positive definition of the scientific atheist worldview. It was the first party plenum devoted exclusively to ideological work, and it underscored that during the new phase of the transition from socialism to Communism—when the Soviet Union, a country that began by "lag[ging] behind in every respect," had climbed to "the heights of socioeconomic progress"—the war between the two dominant world systems had become concentrated in the sphere of ideology.[86] Il'ichev warned that the modern world had become the arena of a "fierce battle of two opposite ways of life," and the "imperialists" counted on the "ideological erosion" of Soviet society. Indeed, the "outright gangsterism of imperialist ideologists" played on human weakness and concentrated on the party's inability to transform the Soviet soul and produce the new Communist personality.[87] In this battle of worldviews, religion played a central role. Il'ichev argued that once it lost authority over the mysteries of the natural world to science, it began to concentrate on monopolizing the "spiritual-moral" sphere, shifting the field of battle with religion into the realm of worldviews. To fortify Soviet citizens against the "virus" of capitalism, the party saw "the education of the new person as the most difficult task of Communist transformation."[88]

Despite the call to arms, however, the Ideological Commission offered little by way of concrete measures for fighting the war of worldviews. When it again convened in the fall of 1963 to discuss "the means for implementing the decisions regarding atheist development of the June Plenum," Il'ichev asserted that the fear of secularization had led religious institutions to modernize.[89] Rather than oppose scientific progress and remain apart from life in this world, religion now sought to adapt to modern science and politics. Christianity, long assumed to be "dying out," was going on the offensive—a development that undermined the Marxist platform that religion was inherently retrograde, reactionary, and incapable of modernization. As the Second Vatican Council (1962–65) made evident, religious organizations were not content to stay on the margins, and continued to make claims on both individual and social life.

At its October 31, 1963, meeting, the Ideological Commission openly discussed the shortcomings of the antireligious campaign's "battle with religious ideology." Il'ichev offered several explanations for why, despite social and scientific progress, religion retained its influence over "hundreds of millions of people." First, he pointed out that while religion's loyalty to Soviet power during the war "strengthened its authority" among believers, the state had not counteracted the return of religion to Soviet life by intensifying atheist propaganda. As Il'ichev explained, "It is no secret that exactly in that moment when the church . . . strengthened its positions, atheist work basically ceased, up until the well-known Central Committee decrees of 1954." As a result, "some people perceived the changes in the position of the church almost as a reconsideration of our position on religious ideology." Indeed, it was precisely because religion was no longer considered a political problem that it had become a serious ideological problem. Second, Il'ichev proposed that "secularization" was an intermediate phase that allowed contradictory beliefs to coexist in the mind of the individual. "Believers build Communism alongside atheists. Many of them sincerely try to combine in their consciousness socialist ideas with religious beliefs. It is not uncommon to find in the home of a believer a prayer book next to the program of the Communist Party." Finally, what the party found most threatening was religion's turn away from claims about the origins and nature of the world toward moral and social questions. Even Khrushchev's platform of "peaceful coexistence" with the capitalist world, Il'ichev observed, had led to the "clericalization" of Communism.[90] Religion's emphasis on a "social doctrine" undermined Communism's claim to be the sole salvation of the weak and oppressed. In the Soviet Union, where religious institutions were no longer cast as a reactionary political threat, believers saw no contradiction between their religious commitments and loyalty to the Soviet state. Indeed, many of those surveyed considered Communism to be the manifestation of Christian ideals.

To reach the masses, atheists had to connect Marxism-Leninism to the issues that concerned ordinary Soviet people. Il'ichev criticized atheists who "turned the Marxist postulate about the social roots of religion and the reasons for [religious] survivals into a dead dogma." To underscore the grave state of atheist work, Il'ichev shared that while the antireligious campaign decreased the number of functioning Orthodox churches by 34 percent between 1960 and 1962, the number of religious rites observed in that period had "decreased insignificantly."[91] In Ukraine, 40 percent of children born were baptized; in many regions of the RSFSR, the number was 30 to 40 percent; and in Moldova as many as 47 percent were baptized. Religiosity remained high in the Baltics; in Lithuania, religious rites accompanied 68 percent of births, 50 percent of marriages, and 70 percent of funerals. In certain regions of the USSR, religious rites had even increased. Most problematic was the fact that even the intelligentsia and party members often observed religious rituals. For party members this was an especially egregious offense, and Il'ichev noted that the "high principles characteristic of our party" demanded that the party hold to account "those Communists who not only avoid the battle with religious survivals demanded by our Party Charter but in practice themselves support these survivals, [since] among the baptized, there are many children of Communists and Komsomol members."[92] Alongside "objective" conditions for the continued survival of religion in socialist society, then, there were also "subjective" reasons for the continued existence of religion in the Soviet Union that were the product of deficiencies in party work.

Il'ichev denounced the ideological "duality and duplicity [*razdvoenost', dvoedushie*]" of the Soviet intelligentsia. "There are still those members of the 'intelligentsia,'" Il'ichev explained, "who not only do not participate in the scientific atheist education of laborers but themselves go to church, baptize their children, get married with a priest, [and] bake Easter cakes. At work, [he] pretends to be an atheist, but at home [he] observes all rituals. . . . To get along with his pious mother-in-law, he parts with all the firm convictions that are most dear to mankind—with [socialist] ideals [and] scientific truth." The creative intelligentsia contributed little to the atheist project and keeping in mind its prominence in Soviet public life, the intelligentsia's "spiritual duplicity" was "far from harmless."[93]

The clergy, on the other hand, managed to attract people to religion despite the fact, as Il'ichev pointed out, that the church had no access to the press, radio, or television.[94] This was because the church never forgot the individual person, following each life from the cradle to the grave. For the party, conversely, the individual often fell out of view, especially once he or she was no longer part of the work collective. Il'ichev offered the archetype of the Soviet worker who is forgotten by the factory collective after retirement and gets "pulled into" religion. "It's bitter to be forgotten by one's comrades in old age," Il'ichev stressed. "There is nothing more dangerous for society, and more hurtful to a person, than falling into oblivion." This was a betrayal of the promise of Communism. The Communist promise, after all, was that the collective would be "penetrated with care about [each person's] well-being, to serve as a firm support in life from birth until extreme old age." The collective should, Il'ichev argued, "provide a person with essential spiritual harmony, security in the future, and the ability to withstand life's difficulties and hardships." Atheists had to focus their efforts not on lectures, debates, or pamphlets but rather on individual work with Soviet people. "You cannot beat religion simply with lectures. In order to squeeze out god, it is first necessary to become truly human." The true atheist, Il'ichev put forward, "is a person who is in his marrow concerned with the fates of those who have become victims of religious ideology; . . . a person who bravely invades a person's life and brings the warmth of his heart to the people; a humanist who is battling for people's souls."[95]

Religion, then, was "a parasite on the unsettled questions of [Communist] construction, various difficulties in our forward progress, disorders in people's personal lives, and much else." In sermons, Communism's "ideological enemies from the religious camp" provided answers to "the most important human problems": the meaning of life, conscience, and morality; the individual's place in and obligations to society; and joy, and suffering, and death. "In short," Il'ichev concluded, "religion speculates on those problems that worry the mind and heart of Man, and thrust their own interpretations on both believers and unbelievers. We often limit ourselves to the negative estimate of religion, and do not often offer believers our own positive solution to life's problems. Communists could win the "war over the minds of all mankind" only if they did not isolate themselves from these existential questions, and did not "leave churchmen and sectarians any loophole to people's souls."[96] The continued existence of religion in the Soviet Union was thus also the product of Communism's blind spots—the questions it was not answering, and needs it was not meeting.

Above all, the persistence of religion was perceived to be a result of its psychological, aesthetic, and emotional dimensions, which Marxism-Leninism and scientific atheism did not address sufficiently. Reports from the field showed that people's attachment to religion was frequently based on the aesthetic and emotional components of religious experience, as well as on traditions and rituals. Echoing debates from the early Soviet period, Il'ichev put forth that "religiosity reveals itself, above all, in the sphere of byt. Believers seek to accompany such events as the birth of a child, marriage, or the death of loved ones with religious rituals."[97] Until Soviet Communism provided its own answers and rituals for these occasions, people would continue to be tied to the church and religion, if not by conviction, then by tradition. It was imperative that atheists fill the void left by negative antireligious propaganda with a positive atheist worldview and rituals.

In November 1963, the Ideological Commission met again to discuss atheist work in light of Il'ichev's article on "The Formation of the Scientific

Worldview and Atheist Education." In the article, Il'ichev argued that atheist propaganda appeals to reason but loses sight of emotions; the clergy and sectarians, Il'ichev wrote, "aim to act not only, and not so much, on reason, as on emotions. . . . We ourselves need to not only understand the meaning of the emotional factor but to make practical use of it."[98] To get to byt, the commission zeroed in on the family as a site of ideological intervention.[99] The family, long considered the conservative repository of religiosity, became one of the battlegrounds for the Soviet soul.[100] In order to transform religious beliefs into atheist worldviews, it was necessary to break the family's ties with the church. In this project, rituals played a critical role, since they not only brought people to the church but also transmitted religion across generations. "Orthodox hierarchs declare that while praying in the church the believer—and here I cite—'seeks and satisfies their religious mood [and] aesthetic sensibility in the splendor of the cathedral and the beauty of the service.' How does our antireligious propaganda satisfy in this respect? Does it satisfy aesthetic sensibilities?" The response to Il'ichev's question, recorded in the meeting transcript, was "animation" and "laughter," but Il'ichev pushed his audience to consider whether it was time "to think seriously about our civic rituals, about endowing them with more solemnity, making them more attractive."[101]

The reports that the party received on religious life across the country also underscored the importance of the pastoral function of religion—its ability to console in times of pain and grief. In this respect in particular, Soviet atheism fell short, and Sergey Pavlov, head of the Komsomol, highlighted the implications of this oversight. Pavlov argued that "spiritual traumas" can be manipulated by the church to bring people to religion.

> Why does this happen? Because behind our various undertakings . . . we overlook the human being, such as he is, with all his big internal difficulties. The most difficult art is the art of working with people. Not everyone is blessed with this ability. . . . We need to keep in mind that religious forms and traditions have accumulated over centuries.
>
> Some Komsomol organizations have already begun to do something about this, but what is lacking is knowledge, experience, and the plain ability to make sense of the difficulties of human fate and find the most correct solution. Let's take an example. It's difficult to imagine that a young person would come to our club in order to get some advice on matters of the heart. Even if he did come, [the director] would say: "Listen, maybe you should go to the infirmary, because it seems that you are not well." This kind of thing happens often.
>
> But the church is both the external and internal. . . . [A] person comes to church . . . because someone will sit with him, there will be

> a heart-to-heart . . . and good advice. And there won't be mockery or some trivial, commonplace truths. But let's even take the external. So a church—believers go in and so do we, . . . and whether you want to or not, you will take your hat off anyway, because the circumstances somehow bring you to it. But then take our clubs. . . .[102]

To address this problem, the ideal Soviet atheist was supposed to approach the Soviet person as an individual, take an interest in the joys and worries that accompany life, and intervene when help was needed. As Il'ichev summed it up, "The battle with religion should be connected with the battle for improving the conditions of people's lives, the transformation of their byt. This battle should be conducted in such a way, that the believer would see in the atheist a close friend who wishes him good, and not evil."[103] To be successful, it was not enough to place administrative restrictions on religious life and fill Soviet newspapers and lecture halls with enlightenment propaganda. Atheism needed its own clerical caste capable of doing the pastoral work that would bring Soviet people to atheism.

The emphasis on the need for a "human approach" was echoed by the writer Vladimir Tendriakov (1924–83), who had authored a number of works on the difficulties posed by religion in rural communities, most prominently in his 1958 novella *The Miracle Worker* (*Chudotvornaia*). The most prominent figure among the creative intelligentsia to participate in the atheist project, Tendriakov spoke out against the administrative repression of religion and insisted that without the human approach, "no propaganda will help."[104] To stress the significance of religious emotions, Tendriakov described the powerful "illusion of humaneness" of a Baptist meeting he had recently attended. Believers referred to one another as "brother" and "sister," creating the sense of an intimate community that, Tendriakov proposed, was more important than religious dogma and belief. As one woman at the meeting told him, she really did not care whether God exists; she would remain religious since "because of [religion], [life] is much easier for me than for you."[105]

Tendriakov used this episode to express his reservations about atheist approaches: "We cannot forget that one does not cure the sick with a stick and that man's spiritual world cannot remain unfilled—if we do not fill it, it will be filled by those whose views are foreign to us. A sacred space never remains empty."[106] Il'ichev concluded that the traditional Marxist dogma, though "correct" and "unshakable," was no longer sufficient; in the new era of building Communism, it was necessary to proceed to "concrete, real reality." In what became the refrain of atheist discussions, Il'ichev warned that "if we only destroy an idea and do not put in its place our Soviet idea, our Soviet way of thinking, our Soviet way of life, we will accomplish nothing."[107] The sacred space would remain empty.

## *Soviet Atheism beyond Science and Religion*

On August 31, 1964, shortly before Khrushchev was forcefully retired from his position as the general secretary of the Soviet Communist Party, Vasilii Zaichikov, deputy chair of the All-Union Znanie Society, and Vladimir Mezentsev, the new editor of *Science and Religion*, wrote to the Central Committee requesting permission to reform the journal. The authors noted that in the five years since it began publication in 1959, the country's only atheist periodical had "played its own positive role," but the time had come to address shortcomings.[108]

> So that we do not miss the mark, the journal should answer all those questions that arise among the broad masses of Soviet people, including believers—questions to which the church provides its own answers. These are the most diverse issues of contemporary life—issues that extend far beyond the relationship of science and religion: the meaning of life, happiness and solace, the moral and immoral in human behavior, truth and conscience, good and evil, the upbringing of children, the preservation of traditions, and how to understand contemporary events.[109]

Zaichikov and Mezentsev argued that *Science and Religion* must turn to "life questions" (*k zhiteiskoi tematike*), since it was precisely such "moral-ethical" issues that had become central to contemporary religious discourse. Because the success of atheism depended on the journal's ability to reach a mass audience, *Science and Religion* had to become a "popular philosophical journal of a kind we do not yet have." Yet as the first five years of publication had shown, the atheist message was not making inroads into the Soviet soul. Mezentsev shared with his colleagues that he "did not like hearing at the [Central Committee's] Ideological Department that we do not know how to propagandize our worldview, and do very little to popularize it. . . . After all, at conferences, readers very reasonably say to us: you take away our faith, but what do you give us in return?"[110]

*Science and Religion* was Soviet atheism writ small, and as such, it reflected the ups, downs, and contradictions of the atheist project. Conceived during Khrushchev's "Hundred Days" antireligious campaign of 1954, the plan for the atheist journal initially went nowhere and, much like the 1954 campaign itself, was shelved for several years, not to be revived until the end of the 1950s. When *Science and Religion* finally began publication in 1959, it was to be a tool for disseminating atheism to both atheist cadres and believers, the journal's two primary audiences.[111] It was, however, envisioned as distinct from the militant atheism of early Soviet publications like *Bezbozhnik* (though it struggled to break free from this militant tradition).[112]

Initially, the journal reflected the two main approaches of the antireligious campaign: the anticlerical approach of unmasking religious institutions, clergy, and dogma as politically reactionary, corrupt, and fanatical, and the enlightenment approach of spreading scientific and technological knowledge in order to disseminate the truth of scientific materialism. By the end of the Khrushchev era, though, *Science and Religion* found itself having to address new themes, largely in response to questions and concerns posed by its readers. It had become clear that rather than focusing on "negative" antireligious propaganda, the journal needed to emphasize atheism's "positive" elements—to speak to life questions as well as appeal to the reader's emotions and everyday concerns.

Much of the debate about the mission of *Science and Religion* revolved around the journal's title. Zaichikov and Mezentsev argued that the title *Science and Religion* "did not facilitate dissemination among the masses [and] was [no longer] justified," since it upheld the very binary—the opposition between science and religion—that atheists were beginning to question.[113] The journal's title positioned science as the best weapon against religion, but atheists were losing confidence that science could provide the answers that would bring atheism into the home—and heart—of ordinary Soviet people.[114] But if not science, then what? The initial titles proposed—*Light (Svet)*, *Knowledge and Faith* (*Znanie i vera*), and even *Life and Religion* (*Zhizn' i religiia*)—were a variation in nuance, but they still upheld the binary opposition of light, science, reason, and life, on the one hand, and religious darkness, irrationality, and death, on the other.

By the time the editorial board met to discuss the future of *Science and Religion* in 1964–65, atheists had come to see religion not so much as a political or ideological problem but rather a spiritual one. Mezentsev argued that the Communist answer to religion was not science, or even philosophy, but instead the Marxist-Leninist worldview: "Religion, after all, is a worldview, not a body of knowledge, [and] we need to title the journal more appropriately. It is more correct to say 'Marxism-Leninism and Religion.'" In order to rise to religion's challenge, "we can and we must give our views on the world, our Communist worldview," and since "the battle is being waged along moral lines, we must take moral issues to be our foundation." Mezentsev proposed more titles that better reflected the journal's new mission: *Spring* (*Rodnik*), *Knowledge for All* (*Znania dlia vsekh*), *Torch of Truth* (*Svetoch*), *Man and the World* (*Chelovek i mir*), and the slight (yet significant) variation, *World of Man* (*Mir cheloveka*).[115] The debate around *Science and Religion*, reflected the broader transformations taking place in late Soviet ideology. The fact that the proposals for the journal's new title did not include either "science" or "religion," and the proposition that *World of Man* best reflected the journal's new vision of atheism, reveals a shift in Soviet thinking about the nature of religion and mission of atheism.

Znanie's conference on *Science and Religion* was a referendum on the approaches of the Khrushchev era and raised critical questions about the future development of Soviet atheism. "Will we move away from atheism or not?" asked Aleksandr Okulov, director of the INA. "If we approach this from the point of view of the title, then it seems that the journal will move away from it; if from the point of view of the content, then, conversely, the journal will move toward the person. Human relations—this is the main thing! The church played on this even before. And we need to legitimize that attention to the problem of human relations on earth as a very important question." Okulov observed that rather than targeting religious institutions and dogma, atheists needed to address the spiritual concerns of contemporary believers. What atheism needed, he insisted, was "a journal dedicated to human beings and human relations."[116]

Yet while there was a consensus about the new direction, crucial questions remained: How could *Science and Religion* communicate the new vision of a positive atheism to the reader? And who was the intended audience? The editors noted that the materials aimed at the journal's two target audiences—religious believers and atheist cadres—frequently undermined one another. "It is clear that each of these [audiences] has its own needs—in terms of themes, level of education, or form of delivery—and [these needs] are often absolutely incompatible. For example, a believer can only be repulsed by various methodological materials [aimed at propagandists] discussing approaches to believers [and] methods of tearing [believers] away from religion, while for the propagandist, these materials are essential."[117] Znanie leaders complained about the burden of the journal's "dual nature," and argued that the journal had to make a decision about whether it would be a specialist publication intended for atheist cadres or mass publication aimed at the conversion of Soviet believers to the scientific atheist worldview.[118]

In light of the new demands placed on ideological work, attracting converts seemed much more critical than preaching to the atheist choir. But even if there was consensus on turning *Science and Religion* into a popular publication, the masses remained out of reach. Okulov observed that "even in such large cities as Voronezh, many people do not read newspapers, do not listen to the radio, [and] do not even go to the movies." Pointing out that there were twenty-three million people in the RSFSR with only an elementary education, he asked, "What do newspapers do for these people in the spiritual sense?"[119] The historian of philosophy Movses Grigorian agreed that atheists had to find a way into the lives of these "barely literate people." He argued against seeing the reform of the journal as a betrayal of the atheist mission: "We need to confirm our understanding of the world with a popular, entertaining language, so that [it becomes] another spiritual support. We should not see this as a departure from the problem of atheism."[120]

However, even as atheists agreed that their success hinged on their ability to reach the masses, they also agreed that "reform must be done very carefully."[121] Dmitri Ugrinovich, chair of the Philosophy Department at Moscow State University, observed that *Science and Religion* would become the first Soviet publication to take up spiritual concerns. Whereas the popular science journal *Science and Life* built on a long tradition of popular science publications that made science accessible to the masses, atheism had yet to find a common language with ordinary Soviet people. In effect, the journal faced a problem endemic to Soviet ideology: how to manage the tension between popular demand and ideological purity, to cater to consumer taste while performing a political and pedagogical function.[122] Atheists needed to produce a journal that addressed spiritual concerns and answered existential questions in order to bring the reader to the ideologically correct conclusion about the place of religion and atheism in Soviet life.

Atheists also worried that in appealing to the masses, they would abandon atheist cadres, since for atheist cadres, *Science and Religion* was one of the few sources, indeed sometimes the only source, for atheist material. As V. M. Chertikhin, head of Gospolitizdat's atheism section, noted in seeking a wider readership, the journal "might forget about the level of scientific propaganda, which might decline [and then] there will be little benefit from the journal."[123] P. I. Sumarev, professor of philosophy at the Institute of Railroad Transport, observed, "Atheist propaganda is complicated. It is conducted in universities and among believers in Houses of Culture [and] reading huts, but there is no one center, and we do not know what is going on elsewhere."[124] In the mid-1960s, existing centers of atheist work—the Moscow Planetarium, the Moscow House of Scientific Atheism, GMIRA in Leningrad, and the new INA—were only beginning to coordinate atheist work on a union-wide scale. The reality was that for most provincial atheist cadres, Moscow and Leningrad remained out of reach. Indeed, the party and Znanie regularly received complaints from provincial cadres about the need for systematic training along with more and better atheist material. Even with its modest circulation, then, *Science and Religion* was still the only widely accessible atheist publication in the Soviet Union.

A forum for atheist cadres was also necessary because mistakes were endemic. I. K. Panchin of the Department of Atheism at the Moscow Food Industry Institute argued that few atheists had moved beyond "the tradition of the twenties and thirties," and many continued to "divide people into atheists and believers."[125] Iurii Stel'makov, a graduate student at Moscow State University's recently founded Department of Scientific Atheism and representative of the Komsomol propaganda department, also insisted that atheism had to move beyond simple contradictions and denunciations, to understand the complex dynamics of religiosity through individual psychology and experience. He reminded his colleagues that the standard formula used to explain religiosity—"a person falls on hard times and is dragged into a sect"—was "a harmful primitivism," and rather than being manipulated by devious clergy, "a person must [first] develop such a need, and then . . . the person is not dragged in but himself joins a sect." Stel'makov denounced atheist propaganda that used "elementary contradictions . . . in the spirit of—since cosmonauts have gone to space, then there is no God, since [they] did not see him there, and so forth." Instead, he urged atheists to embrace the complexity of human experience: "In . . . the journal there is a good letter that says, 'The Bible is as contradictory as life itself.' This is good, because it reflects the imperfection of human reason. And this is the point often made by progressive believers. In response to all of our arguments about contradictions, they just laugh . . . and say that the cosmonaut was constrained by the walls of his spaceship and could not see God, [or] that God is in the heart or in infinity." At the end of the day, he concluded, "we try to replace the truth of life with the truth of facts."[126]

But the real danger of "primitive" atheism was that it repelled its intended audience and ultimately alienated precisely those people whom atheists sought to reach: "We have one atheist lecturer, former KGB, who looks at even the most ordinary Baptist as an enemy. . . . We tend to look at believers as politically unreliable, dangerous individuals. In these conditions, no atheist work is possible. . . . After [such atheist measures] believers would say, we accept Communism, but not this form of Communism."[127] Another cadre noted that Soviet atheists were raising worldview issues "for the first time," whereas religions "have long since occupied themselves with these questions." Nevertheless, what particularly worried him was that the spiritual component of Marxism-Leninism lacked substance. When believers asked what atheists offered "in exchange for religion," he explained, atheists offered only "scientific statistics or philosophy, and other than this we give nothing."[128]

Communism offered bright prospects, but the inner world of Soviet people remained full of contradictions and everyday difficulties. Boris Mar'ianov, the journal's executive secretary, noted that more needed to be written about "the tragedy of the spiritual world."[129] It was not enough to address the individual in general; atheists had to speak to particular spiritual experiences. As Sumarev put it, "*World of Man* is indeed a more fitting title. . . . But such a thing as 'man' in general does not exist. Rather, there are concrete human beings, toward whom we will address ourselves. We often discuss believers, but we forget that in our society, the believer does not exist in isolation. If his surroundings march in step with [Soviet] life, then it will be easier to tear him away from religion and educate him in the spirit of our Communist morality." Sumarev implied that the shortcomings of Soviet atheism were emblematic of broader deficiencies within the Soviet system. Sumarev also urged atheists to work on the "emotional intensity" of atheist propaganda. "The problem with atheist propaganda is that we have absolutely desiccated it," he observed. "It is impoverished in the emotional sense, whereas a believer lives by his emotions."[130]

Producing a positive atheism was not just a theoretical concern. It extended into the very fabric of everyday life, as every act of administrative indifference worked to undermine the promises of Soviet Communism. A. T. Moskalenko of the Siberian division of the Academy of Sciences stressed that the journal had to bring attention to the subjective experience of Soviet life.

> The title *World of Man* is good. There is a world of man, but we ignored it for many years. Believers say that we are only interested in international issues, we do not look into a person's soul, [and] man's soul has never interested [us]. I can bring an example: a woman comes to the party obkom, asks for help, and is refused. Prior to this, the woman already went to all the sects, but was nowhere able to find the truth, and thought she might find it at the obkom of the party. But even there no one helped her. And now a person does not even know where to seek truth. . . . We sometimes do not understand the worries of our Soviet person, and do not take them into account. As a result, [we have] such examples as when a person worked at an enterprise for twenty to thirty years, [and then] retires, falls ill, and before death asks for a priest. Having been a party member for a long time, [he] hands back his party card and joins a sect. And we are afraid to say that we have such defects. Let us also try to remember the subjective worries of man. We speak too often about objective [conditions] and forget the subjective worries.[131]

Soviet atheism, then, fell short in two ways: in everyday life, as local organs failed to address individual grievances (leading the Soviet woman to lose faith in Soviet institutions and appeal to the sect), and in providing answers to existential questions, as when an exemplary worker, a longtime party member, asks for a priest before death, or even "hands back his party card and joins a sect." Considering the stakes of the Soviet atheist enterprise, Moskalenko's outline of the problem in Dostoevskian terms is revealing: just as Ivan Karamazov's handing back his ticket was a rejection of the irreconcilable contradictions of religion, the party member's "handing back his ticket" on the threshold of death was a rejection of the Soviet cosmos.

At its ideological foundation, the Communist project promised human emancipation by harmonizing social relations and redeeming the individual from alienation. It was the secular redemption offered by Communism that was supposed to eliminate the need for religion, since Communist society would be so just and humane that the opiate of religion would be unnecessary. But in the late 1960s, even as the new Communist person became the centerpiece of Soviet ideology, real Soviet people continued to turn to religion—raising the heretical possibility that the roots of religion were located in Soviet socialism itself. As long as the local administration continued to fail the woman in Moskalenko's testimony, religion would remain an obstacle to the desired convergence of Soviet citizens and Communist ideology. At the final hour, even the most exemplary Soviet citizen might hand back his ticket.

The discussion that emerged in the editorial offices of *Science and Religion* both reflected and changed the course of Soviet atheism. Studies of Soviet religiosity revealed a "modernized" religion, and made clear the flaws in simply opposing it with science and portraying it as a politically reactionary force. The interest of ordinary people in spiritual questions, moreover, directed the journal to shift its focus to worldview questions so that by the 1970s, the exposition of positive atheism came to be one of the journal's most important functions.[132] As Anatolii Ivanov, the journal's editor from 1968 until 1982, reflected:

> Man—his place in the world, the meaning of his existence, the purpose of his life—stands in the center of the battle of religion and atheism on moral issues. These "eternal questions" have always concerned people, and continue to worry them, regardless of whether or not they believe in God. Religion offers a certain life program that indicates how a person is to build relationships with others, departing from the acknowledgment of constant divine interventions into his thoughts and affairs.[133]

Since the journal's new mission was to show Soviet readers "the vitality of Communist moral norms [and] greatness of the moral world of the Soviet person," the journal introduced new rubrics on themes like "The Meaning of Life."[134] To be sure, the journal continued to devote a great deal of attention to scientific enlightenment and the criticism of religion, with rubrics such as "Nature and Reason," "Scientific Horizons," "Theology and Science," and "Inside Scientific Laboratories," as well as material devoted to the scientific technological revolution and Cold War stories about clerical propaganda efforts to subvert the USSR through religious channels. Nevertheless, the journal's new engagement with worldview questions reflected the broader transformation of Soviet atheism.

## *Conclusion*

Over the course of the Khrushchev era, the party's reengagement with religion—from its imposition of severe administrative restrictions on religious life to its proclamation that science had triumphed over religion—revealed the limits of atheist work. It became clear that ideology dissipated on the threshold of the Soviet home, whereas religion remained embedded in many Soviet people's lives, shaping worldviews and byt. When the party embarked on the project of "building Communism," it saw that the door to the Soviet home—and hence to the Soviet soul—remained closed, and when it opened, it revealed newspapers extolling technological feats and Soviet cosmonauts, but also icons and baptized children. While Soviet people often failed to see the contradictions in these competing narratives, or why their commitment to both would prevent them from being full members of Soviet society, the party increasingly perceived these contradictions as a problem. The ideological establishment became aware that to produce the new Communist person—to transform not just political behavior but worldviews and ways of life—ideology in general, and atheism in particular, had to answer new kinds of questions, solve new kinds of problems, and reach new kinds of spaces.

Indeed, with the transition from socialism to Communism under way, the project of transforming byt—which had been part of Communist discourse since the revolution, but had remained largely within the framework of party discipline—was extended to the whole Soviet population. Paradoxically, it was the party's effort to improve the material conditions of Soviet life that made the ideological problem of byt more acute, since, following Khrushchev's housing campaign and labor reforms, more Soviet people got leisure time and private housing—that is, time and space that placed them farther out of the party's reach. Ideological work had to move beyond the familiar platforms of mass media, work meetings, and recreational lectures, and find a way into the home. Since the success of the Communist project depended on moral and spiritual transformation, the party had to reach the Soviet soul. To put it another way, to reach Communism, Soviet society had to become the Communist Party writ large.

The story of Znanie, and its flagship journal *Science and Religion*, provides a lens into the ideological landscape of the late Soviet period. The ideological confidence and mobilization at the start of the Khrushchev era turned into disappointments and produced new questions. At the same time, this crisis of ideological confidence also created a new generation of atheist cadres who did not just reproduce the official doctrine but questioned comfortable assumptions and reevaluated customary approaches. Underneath the official veneer, late Soviet ideology transformed. The experiences of Khrushchev era antireligious campaigns made the ideological establishment aware of the disconnect between atheist theory and practice—a problem they continued to grapple with long after Khrushchev's departure from the political stage.

Soviet atheists found themselves looking to Marxist-Leninist ideology to understand the new political, material, and social conditions of late Soviet modernity. Official philosophers continued to publicly extol the truth of the doctrine. As Iurii Frantsev and Iurii Filonovich proclaimed in an *Izvestiia* editorial, "We have in our hands a truly miraculous method of transformation, our 'philosopher's stone'—the philosophy of Marxism-Leninism."[135] But while official pronouncements still offered Marxism-Leninism as a roadmap to the bright Communist future, the late Soviet ideological establishment was more ambivalent about Communism's prospects. The party, moreover, was aware that formulaic ideological slogans, with their emphasis on labor, production, and individual sacrifice for the collective, were beginning to ring hollow in a modernizing society increasingly invested in individual consumption in both its material and spiritual forms.

Moreover, in the battle of opposing worldviews, Soviet atheists found themselves consciously mirroring their opponent. Noting the diverse and dynamic varieties of lived religion, they decried religion's turn away from arguments about the competing truth claims of science and theology toward moral and spiritual concerns. Yet even as atheists criticized religious modernization as hypocrisy and opportunism (*prisposoblenchestvo*), they nevertheless worried that this adaptability accounted for religion's continued vitality. Conversely, Soviet atheism's failure to address these questions remained a persistent obstacle. Indeed, atheism was weak precisely where religion thrived—a fact that the party feared was not lost on the Cold War adversary. The experience of the antireligious campaigns made Soviet atheists aware of the stakes of failure. As the philosopher Boris Grigorian, then the deputy editor of *Science and Religion*, put it at a 1964 conference, the task of atheist work was "to show the constructive work and positive foundations—scientific, historical, [and] philosophical—that can fill the vacuums that form as a result of a person's liberation from religious conceptions and beliefs."[136] This effort to make sense of religion's continued existence under socialism and produce a positive atheism reveals the ideological establishment's active engagement with the "spiritual" as a category.

Finally, the repeated warnings that Soviet atheism needed to address the aesthetic, emotional, communal, and ritual sides of human experience became the impetus for the expansion of atheist work in the late Soviet period. Looking ahead, atheists recognized that they needed to concentrate their work on two problems. First, they needed to better understand the disconnect between the dictates of Marxism-Leninism and the Soviet reality they encountered on the ground. Second, they needed to transform atheism from a didactic tool that appealed to reason into an emotionally and spiritually robust positive program. To address the first problem, the party turned to the social sciences, establishing new institutions to study religion and produce atheism. To address the second, the party called on academic, government, enlightenment, and cultural organizations to create and disseminate socialist rituals that could address Soviet people's aesthetic, emotional, and spiritual needs. These two projects—the social-scientific project to understand religion and the spiritual project to replace it—occupied the atheist apparatus for the rest of the Soviet period.

CHAPTER FIVE

# "We Have to Figure Out Where We Lost People"

## SOVIET ATHEISM AS SOCIAL SCIENCE

> Between "God exists" and "God does not exist" there lies an enormous field, which a wise man crosses only with great effort.
>
> —ANTON CHEKHOV, *NOTEBOOKS*

THE INA—housed within the Central Committee's AON, the party's highest organ charged with the production of ideology—was the Soviet Communist Party's most explicit effort to address the vacuum left behind by the primary ideological mobilizations of the Khrushchev era: de-Stalinization and the campaign against religion. The primary tasks of the institute, founded by the January 2, 1964, Central Committee resolution "On Measures for Strengthening the Atheist Education of the Population," were to develop a more sophisticated theoretical understanding of religion and atheism, centralize atheist work in the country by coordinating it on a union-wide level with local research institutes and party organs, and train a new cohort of cadres who had both theoretical and practical expertise in atheist work. By 1964, the ideological establishment was aware that atheism needed to address a modernized religion that did not necessarily oppose science or even Communism but rather spoke to social and moral questions.[1] As the AON rector, Frantsev, put it in one of the INA's first meetings, the new task of atheist work was to focus "*not* on how believers imagine God, with a mustache and beard or without them, but instead on the role that believers attribute to supernatural powers in human life [and] in the life of contemporary society."[2] Frantsev, who earlier in his career had written extensively on religion and had even served as GMIR's director from 1937 until 1942—insisted that if atheists did not develop a more sophisticated understanding of religion, they had no hope of producing an effective atheist program.[3]

Though the direct product of Khrushchev's ideological mobilization, the INA was emblematic of atheist work in the Brezhnev era (1964–82), when the state became more technocratic in its approach to both ideology and governance. The atheist apparatus mobilized the social sciences in order to map patterns of Soviet secularization and understand religious modernization. Yet in turning to the social sciences to solve ideological problems, Soviet atheists had to negotiate the tension between two forms of truth that could not easily be reconciled; in effect, the scientific method was supposed to lead them to the truth proclaimed by Marxism-Leninism. Yet what they found on the ground challenged the narrative of Marxist-Leninist patterns of development, which in turn forced atheists to reconsider their understanding of religion and its place in Soviet life. As atheists turned to disciplines like ethnography, psychology, and sociology, to understand religion, they made an unexpected discovery: rather than positioning themselves as either believers or unbelievers, many Soviet people were instead growing indifferent to both religion *and* atheism, and indeed to ideological concerns more broadly. Over the course of the late Soviet period, as the institute established itself as the center of religious and atheist studies in the Soviet Union, the atheist apparatus came to see not belief but rather indifference as the most significant ideological problem that Soviet Communism had to address.

## *Ideology as Social Science*

The ideologically temperate climate of the Brezhnev era has led some to see it as a period of "stagnation"—a label famously introduced by Gorbachev to characterize the state of affairs under his predecessors, and maintained by many scholars since.[4] Certainly, in comparison with the tumultuous administrative and ideological transformations of the Khrushchev period that preceded it, as well as the Gorbachev period that followed, the Brezhnev era was marked by stability, if not lethargy, in many areas. Yet beneath the seemingly stagnant surface, the sphere of Soviet ideology was transforming in critical ways. Even in the most dogmatic arena of ideological production—atheism—the term "stagnation" is deceptive.

The state's turn to the social sciences as a tool of governance makes the Brezhnev era ideological transformations visible. Indeed, for the Soviet social sciences, the early Brezhnev period has been described as a "second birth" and a "golden age."[5] Two factors made the resurrection of the Soviet social sciences possible. The first is that the years between Khrushchev's dismissal in October 1964 and the consolidation of Brezhnevism in the late 1960s were a time of behind-the-scenes reforms. Much of this reformism revolved around discussions about the ways in which Soviet reality departed from proclamations about progress towards Communism. In fact, this effort to bridge the gap between Communist ideology and Soviet reality began under Khrushchev, when the ideological apparatus turned to "concrete social research" (*konkretnye sotsial'nye issledovaniia*) to gather data on Soviet society in order to address various economic and social problems.

Also contributing to the revival of the social sciences were the dramatic economic, demographic, and cultural transformations that had begun in the mid-1950s.[6] Soviet citizens were becoming younger as well as more urban, educated, and wealthy—developments that were rapidly transforming Soviet society. Soviet people had more private space, leisure time, and opportunities for consumption, and therefore greater autonomy in shaping their lives. Tellingly, the first "concrete social research" projects focused on byt. A study of village life in the Gorky region—carried out by the "new forms of labor and byt" sector formed in the Institute of Philosophy of the Academy of Sciences in 1960—examined the ways that economic and political transformations affected everyday life in the countryside.[7] Soon after, a sociological laboratory opened in Leningrad to study "the person and his work," which examined labor and leisure patterns of the urban population.[8] But the question that interested the party most was why Soviet citizens were becoming alienated from Communist ideals, and why ideological work seemed to have little impact on this state of affairs. Over the course of the late Soviet period, the ideological establishment continued to create institutes and laboratories, hoping that more and better information on the population would allow it to better "see" Soviet society, to borrow anthropologist James C. Scott's famous formulation.[9]

The party also signaled its continued commitment to the social sciences by issuing multiple decrees that called on social scientists to take a more active role in ideological work.[10] At an Ideological Commission meeting held from November 15 to 18, 1965, to discuss the social sciences, the official philosopher Petr Fedoseev (1908–90)—then the vice president of the Soviet Academy of Sciences and a member of the party's Central Committee—expressed the "desirability" of creating an institute for sociological research, signaling, in the bureaucratic language of the time, that the subject was already on the party's agenda.[11] Fedoseev's suggestion was supported by Mitin, who argued that in this department, the Soviet Union was lagging behind not just the capitalist but also other socialist bloc countries. "In America," Mitin noted, "250 million dollars are spent on sociological research each year, and there are 25,000 sociologists."[12] For those in doubt about the need for sociological research, Mitin wryly proposed that "a brigade be sent . . . to the Kirov factory in Leningrad in order to really study how the formation of the new man is going."[13]

The intimate connection between social scientists, the ideological establishment, and the political elite made the social context in which the Soviet social sciences developed peculiar. To carry out sociological studies, sociologists required the cooperation of local party organs, and when the results of these studies departed from party orthodoxy, local officials would quickly withdraw their support, as happened when the Gorky study showed that the thesis about the convergence of intellectual and physical labor, and city and countryside, was unsubstantiated by the reality of Soviet rural life. After mobilizing the social sciences, then, the party found itself in a predicament about how to handle the apparent departures between Marxist-Leninist ideology and Soviet reality.

While the "fathers"—the historical materialists—decried any conclusions that undermined the party dogma, the "sons" increasingly identified with the professional ethos of the social scientist. Increasingly, their commitment to the truth of their data began to overshadow their commitment to the truth of Marxism-Leninism, which in turn complicated their mission: to make Communist ideology into Soviet reality.

## *A Home for Soviet Atheism*

The INA was founded to bring the social sciences to bear on the religious question, and it pursued this task by systematizing the study of religion, developing atheist theory, and coordinating atheist work on the ground. It trained graduate students to conduct fieldwork, and, in turn, INA graduate students were supposed to train local cadres to conduct atheist work. The institute also organized conferences, seminars, and publications in order to disseminate research findings and party directives from the center to the country's peripheries. Initially, the party allotted the INA thirteen employees. This cohort of newly minted atheist experts came both from party and Komsomol organs, and from universities and research institutes, including the Department of Atheism at Moscow State University, and the Institutes of Philosophy, History, and Ethnography of the Soviet Academy of Sciences.[14]

The leadership of the INA was decided over the course of 1964. Considering the significance of the INA for the development of Soviet atheism, religious studies, and the party's understanding of and approaches to religion, it is worth examining the figures who made up the center of the atheist apparatus in greater detail. Frantsev proposed Aleksandr Okulov (1908–93), the deputy director of the Institute of Philosophy and a professor of philosophy at the AON, for the position of director. Pavel Kurochkin (1925–81) and Lev Mitrokhin (1930–2005) were proposed as deputy directors. A short time later, Frantsev added the candidacy of Vladimir Evdokimov (1923–69), who until then worked in the Central Committee.[15] The choice of Okulov to lead the INA is unsurprising. At the time of his appointment, Okulov—who began as a logger in the Kirov region in the late 1920s, but quickly moved into cultural enlightenment and party work—had an established career as a party philosopher, working within both the AN and the AON since 1951. By education, Okulov was a journalist (he attended the Moscow School of Journalism from 1934 to 1937), which, in the Soviet context, put him in the sphere of propaganda and ideology. He had also served as the editor of the journal *Problems of Philosophy* between 1959 and 1960. All of this made him a reliable political choice to lead the country's new center of atheist work.[16]

The proposed candidates for deputy director—Kurochkin and Evdokimov—were members of a younger generation who came of age professionally in the postwar period. Kurochkin had served in the Red Army from 1938 to 1945, became a party member in 1946, and was educated in the party schools in Novgorod and Leningrad between 1945 and 1951. In the 1950s, Kurochkin had worked in the Novgorod regional party apparatus, and in 1959, entered the graduate program in the Philosophy Department of the AON, where he, like Okulov, received a teaching position upon graduation. In the decade before the establishment of the institute, Kurochkin's work had focused on both the theory and practice of religion and atheism. He had produced eight publications on the subject, and had also served as a member of Znanie's Methodological Council for the Propaganda of Scientific Atheism.[17] Evdokimov, meanwhile, had come to the INA after working in the party apparatus as an assistant to Il'ichev, who headed the party's Ideological Commissions under Khrushchev. He had focused on philosophy, but not on religion and atheism in particular.[18] As the INA's two deputy directors, Kurochkin oversaw scholarly research, whereas Evdokimov was charged with overseeing the practical aspects of atheist work.[19]

To coordinate research and atheist work, the INA formed a Scientific Council, which reported to the party's Central Committee and, in turn, received and disseminated the party's ideological directives.[20] On the ground, the call to connect research and policy, ideology and reality, and theory and practice propelled the creation of "local bases" (*opornye punkty*) that operated as regional centers for both sociological research and cadre training. Their primary objective was to study local religiosity in order to formulate policies that would improve atheist work on the ground. A council ran each local base, receiving directives from both the INA and regional party organs, and in turn reported back with results. The institute would then report on the activities of local bases by coordinating conferences and publishing research findings in internal reports, bulletins, and journal articles, access to which was largely restricted to atheist cadres. Within two years, the INA had established forty local bases across the Soviet Union, many of which were in major urban centers, or areas with high concentrations of religious communities (such as western Ukraine).[21]

Besides serving as the Soviet Union's center for atheist research, the INA was also charged with running the country's top graduate program in the study of religion and atheism. The institute brought together philosophers, historians, and ethnographers, along with party and government functionaries, to train a new generation of atheist cadres. Most of those who eventually became part of the atheist apparatus initially knew little about religion, though of course many were baptized and had encountered religiosity in some form—a religious family member or classmate, or proximity to a local religious community—during their childhood or youth. Most also had little prior interest in religion, or enthusiasm for atheist work, although there were, of course, exceptions—like Iurii Zuev, who recalls rushing past the guards in the AON building to enroll in the INA graduate program after reading about it in the newspaper.[22] But for the most part, the late Soviet generation of professional atheists found themselves in atheist work by chance.[23] For some, the interest in religion was sparked by an unexpected encounter with a religious believer.[24] For others, atheist work was a stepping stone to career advancement or an advanced degree. For others still, it was simply an opportunity to get out of the provinces and move to the city. The INA's graduate students arrived from different parts of the country, usually by referral of their local Komsomol or party organs. Their research was overseen by the Central Committee's "curators" on religious questions (such as Emil Lisavtsev) who directed graduate students to research topics in which the party had a particular interest, such as trends in religious ritual observance, or the process of secularization under Soviet conditions.[25] In gathering material for their dissertations, students often coordinated research through the INA's local bases.[26] They brought their local knowledge to bear on the theoretical training they received in Moscow, and then brought their theoretical training back to the provinces by conducting fieldwork and training local cadres. The goal was to create a mutually beneficial relationship; whereas the ideological establishment needed data on the religious landscape, local cadres needed the center's access to data, methodological training, and political guidance.

## *Mapping Soviet Religiosity*

One of the first problems that the institute had to grapple with was the fact that enlightenment measures had not been able to meet the challenges posed by religious modernization. To address this, Frantsev proposed that the sociological analysis of contemporary religiosity should be the main task of atheist work: atheists had to speak with believers in order to learn about how the circumstances of their lives shaped their worldview. Citing Lenin's *Materialism and Empirio-Criticism*, a foundational text for the Marxist-Leninist conception of religion, Frantsev presented religion as the result of socialism's failures. "Lenin says that he set for himself the goal to discover what tripped people up," he declared. "So we need to find out what a person stumbles on as he walks along the Soviet path of life, what stones we need to remove from his path, what holes we need to fill, so that he would not stumble." The institute's research needed to illuminate why a believer turned to religion and what atheists could do to change this. Frantsev reminded cadres that whereas formerly atheists had focused primarily on exposing the reactionary political role of religion, the current objective was to "go much deeper, to touch on all sides and all levels of social consciousness where religion might make a nest (*gde mozhet gnezditsia religiia*)."[27]

As an example of the position to which atheists had to produce an adequate response, Frantsev discussed the writings of a West German Catholic theologian, who argued that science offers humankind only fragments of reality rather than a whole picture of the world. This left humankind searching for wholeness, yet whereas believers could "overcome the fragmentation [*razorvannost'*] of modern knowledge [and] modern science," the situation for atheists was more complicated.

> Comrades, if one is to translate this into the language of materialists, atheists, of warriors against such religious conceptions, then this means something along these lines: the clerical crowd [*popovshchina*] is trying to fill the empty spaces in knowledge, in science, is trying to rush into empty spaces, to fill these holes, these blank spots, of which there are ever fewer, in order to create a distorted religious worldview. We do not yet know if there is life on Mars. But this does not prevent us from saying that no devil, no miracle, no supernatural power is hiding in our not knowing. This conviction is given to us by the scientific materialist worldview.[28]

Atheists acknowledged that most ordinary people did not have this "conviction," and that in trying to inculcate it, atheists would have to move beyond denying devils and miracles, and understand religious experience.

The institute took stock of atheist work, outlined the shortcomings in previous practices, and set about defining the agenda for future research. Okulov noted that since the late 1950s, substantial work had been done on learning about the religiosity of the population. Institutes in the Soviet Academy of Sciences had organized expeditions around the country, and graduate students in the newly established departments of atheism at Moscow State University and Kiev State University also conducted fieldwork and gathered data.[29] Already in the mid-1960s, these findings had appeared in monographs and specialist journals, such as *Problems of Philosophy* (*Voprosy filosofii*) and *Soviet Ethnography* (*Sovetskaia etnografiia*). "All of this shows revitalization, a turn to the concrete study of the state of religiosity and atheist work," observed Okulov. Yet despite the evident intensification of atheists' efforts, Okulov insisted that "the general picture of the population's religiosity in our country remains, as before, unclear." Atheist work continued to be unsystematic, and there was little research into the effect of atheist propaganda on believers. The time had come to "bring clarity" to the Soviet spiritual landscape.[30]

The INA formed thematic research groups that brought together senior scholars, graduate students, and local cadres to focus on specific "problem" areas with the goal of coordinating atheist work across the country and bringing theory into conversation with practice.[31] The institute's early research investigated the activities of religious organizations and religiosity in specific localities, and posed questions about modern believers' conceptions of God and social relations (1964–65), reasons for the observance of religious rituals (1964), the nature of religious emotions (1964), the emotional influence of religious rituals (1964), and the reasons people broke with religion (1964).[32] INA studies analyzed Soviet people's social and cultural conditions; where and how often they went to church; how familiar they were with the history and dogma of their faith; what they thought of their local religious community and the priest; how much of their income they gave to the church, and how much they spent on religious items; and whether they observed rituals and, if so, which ones.[33] Even as atheists gathered more and better information, however, the disconnect persisted between what research studied and what atheists actually needed to know. The inherent tensions between the descriptive (research) and prescriptive (policy) functions of the institute—and between alarm about the present stage of ideological work and a cautionary approach to change—became more and more apparent.

## *In Search of a Spiritual Atheism*

Atheists recognized that they needed to determine the psychology behind religiosity and figure out how atheism could fulfill spiritual needs, but in order to do that, one of the primary questions atheists had to address was what exactly constituted atheism. At heart, the question was one that atheism had continuously asked. Beyond the rejection of religion, did atheism have its own positive content? To answer this question, atheists discussed how atheism related to other disciplines, such as philosophy, history, theology, and religious studies, and whether atheism (and the attending criticism of religion) was a constituent part of Marxist-Leninist philosophy or an independent discipline. An immediate area where this problem presented itself was in the debates about how the subject of scientific atheism should be taught in higher education.[34] The January 2, 1964, Central Committee decree had made scientific atheism a required course for students in universities and pedagogical institutes, but atheists could not even agree about which department should house the course, revealing the confusion around the subject even at the top. Nor was there consensus about what content should constitute the coursework. Should the course focus on the history of religion through a critical lens, trace the development of unbelief in philosophical thought, or examine how scientific advancements undermined religious conceptions of the world? Atheists also faced the practical question of who would teach it. Since the course had never been taught systematically in higher education, there were no trained instructors, which meant that most instructors for the new course had to be drafted from other disciplines and trained hastily to assume their new roles.[35] Few academic scientists, historians, or philosophers felt at home in the subject, and many resisted explicitly engaging in atheist propaganda. Scientists, for example, defended themselves from party criticism by arguing that their disciplines were implicitly, if not explicitly, atheist because they presented students with scientific knowledge—an assertion that went back to the early Soviet debates about whether Soviet education should be *antireligious* or simply *irreligious*, but which, by the late Soviet period, had exhausted itself as an adequate explanation.

In their attempt to work out a positive foundation for atheism, atheists criticized those definitions that emphasized negative components. Gubanov, for instance, drew an analogy between the terms "atheism" and "Communism," noting that as a category, Communism would suffer if it were defined only as the opposite of capitalism, although he did not go on to give a positive definition of Communism.[36] Philosopher Boris Grigorian, however, argued that the very essence of atheism was negative since it was founded in criticism. "It seems to me that we can speak of a certain critical spirit, a negative spirit, if you will, of our atheism as a science," Grigorian contended, and therefore "there is not one part, not one point in Marxism, which does not carry a critical character, that does not have, in some form or another, in your terms, a 'negative' form."[37] Nevertheless, even if atheists did not agree on the definition of atheism, there was general agreement that emphasizing the critical side of atheism had not been effective in transforming Soviet hearts, minds, and worldviews. Inga Kichanova, a young INA researcher, argued that this was because atheism had failed to account for religion's role in individual and social psychology. The problem of atheism, Kichanova proposed, was a "humanist" one—it came down to "determining ways to fill that need that forces a person to appeal for help not to social organizations but to otherworldly powers." As a form of humanism, atheism had to "create a harmonious spiritual world, which does not need to appeal to otherworldly powers."[38]

Some maintained that atheism should be seen as part of the broader discipline of philosophy, and to take seriously the individual person.[39] A young INA researcher, Irina Galitskaia, agreed that the origins of atheism were in the rejection of religion, but asserted that the time had come to "broaden" the definition to include "issues connected to human personality, man's relationship to life and himself—that is, those problems on which religion grows." Galitskaia observed that in Soviet philosophy, almost no research had been done on the subject of human personality. A person was looked at as "either the subject or object of cognition—that is, as a productive unit—but was not examined as a holistic personality, as had been done by Renaissance philosophy." Because the individual person had stayed on the margins of Soviet philosophical concerns, related issues—happiness, suffering, the meaning of life and death—had also been relegated to the periphery. "With us," Galitskaia remarked, "the tacit assumption is that a person should not suffer, that under Communism there will be no suffering." Instead, Soviet ethics preferred to concentrate on happiness. The results, Galitskaia observed, were often comical, since "in reality it is funny to insist that a person will not always suffer for one reason or another.

And religion uses this wonderfully and has managed to provide mankind with solace." Religion, unlike atheism, was able to offer solace in the face of trouble, grief, and especially death. This was especially evident if one examined the issue of immortality. Dialectical materialism asserted that humans are mortal, Galitskaia noted, "But what kind of solace is there when they say that you are mortal, but matter is eternal?" In Soviet philosophy, such issues had remained "completely unexamined," whereas religion "blossoms on them." She concluded that the subject matter of atheism was "not exactly philosophy, but maybe philosophical-ethical or psychological issues—those issues that concerned man and his attitude toward life."[40] "Perhaps atheist work [should] consist in the cultivation of a personality that will not seek personal meaning in religion," Galitskaia concluded.[41]

Galitskaia observed that Soviet atheism failed to address the search for personal meaning and need for solace in the face of suffering. If one considered the stakes of atheist work in this light, then figuring out how to fill this empty space was not just a scholastic concern but a practical one too. As Okulov put it, "In studying atheist work, we have to look at the degree to which our spiritual life is fulfilling, which parts of our ideological work function [and] which wheels are broken. We have to figure out where we lost people."[42] For the INA cadres charged with figuring out how to produce an atheist society, then, atheism was not a theoretical academic exercise but rather a practical question with real consequences.

## *The Atheist Family*

The ultimate goal of Soviet atheism was to achieve a society free of religion. Indeed, this was the title of the INA's first major sociological study on the secularization of Soviet society, conducted in the Penza region between 1967 and 1969.[43] In order to achieve this goal, though, atheists had to locate "those specific forms in which religiosity was preserved" and the mechanisms through which it was reproduced. This was critical because field data was beginning to undermine the long-held assumption that religion was the lot of grandmothers. Whereas the party had assumed that eventually the generation of grandmothers who filled Soviet churches would disappear and religion would die out with them, this hypothesis seemed less plausible as the churches filled with new generations of grandmothers.

To make sense of why secularization did not seem to be following the expected pattern, atheists had to understand where contemporary religiosity was being produced. The institute directed research in several directions: the size and makeup of religious communities among different confessions as well as dynamics of their religious life and organizational structure; ways in which religiosity manifested itself among different groups of people, broken down by age, gender, and socioeconomic categories; contemporary forms of religiosity among different confessional communities, and the significance these communities attributed to ritual life; and evolution of modern mass religious consciousness and ways in which religious conceptions were intertwined with scientific knowledge. Okulov urged researchers to pay attention not just to the statistical measures of religiosity but also to the qualitative transformation of religion under modern conditions. When religious worldviews transformed under the pressure of modernity, what died off and what remained? And were those elements that remained transformed to assume new functions? Frantsev, contended that in order to make sociological research more useful to atheist work, cadres had to place believers in their social context. He encouraged researchers to study religious psychology, asserting that interviews were more effective than surveys in providing access to the inner world of the Soviet person.[44] Another researcher suggested that rather than interviewing believers about religion directly, it was much more effective to ask questions about belief "by the by," amid general questions about the person's life.[45]

Yet studying religiosity in a broader context revealed a messy reality that defied clear categories. N. P. Alekseev, a graduate student at Moscow State University's Department of Scientific Atheism who studied rural religiosity on three collective farms in the Orel region, stated that the religious views of modern collective farm workers were "very simplified." Their religiosity, he argued, was the product of custom and tradition, not religious conviction. Alekseev reported that the vast majority—more than 90 percent—had icons in their homes, and 87 percent of those surveyed—both believers and unbelievers—took part in religious rituals.[46] In some regions, 60 percent baptized their children, and in others the figures ranged from 30 to 40 percent. One of the reasons behind such high statistics, Alekseev proposed, was that the clergy, even after the introduction of "extraordinary" legal measures, continued to "make money on the side" by performing rituals. For instance, ten children would be brought from the collective farm for baptism, but only one form would be registered. "Homegrown" priests would "go around the collective farm in the summer and baptize all the children." Indeed, baptism and other rites continued to be ubiquitous, despite the fact that many of those who observed religious rites were unbelievers. For Alekseev, the force of public opinion and social psychology explained this phenomenon. Many unbelievers, he put forth, did not find it "disgraceful" to participate in religious rituals because they lived in a social collective and therefore had to "have a place" within the community. Perhaps such an unbeliever was unhappy with this situation, but he had to "reckon with the opinion of his mother [and] mother-in-law." In short, Alekseev summed up, the modern collective farmer was religious because "this is how he was brought up by his mother—[because] 'the elders believed and we believe.'"[47]

Vadim Ol'shanskii, a researcher at the Institute of Philosophy's sector on "new forms of labor and byt," agreed that social psychology was central to understanding religion since one could not make sense of data on ritual observance without taking into account group dynamics. The pressure of the collective, he argued, was among the most important factors motivating people's religiosity.[48] Lev Mitrokhin, who specialized in religion and atheism at the Institute of Philosophy, observed that atheists also had to study the theologies of different confessions since "a person often expresses his views according to the canons of his religion [and] if you do not know these canons, then naturally your conclusions will not have any scientific value."[49] Okulov worried more generally about the poor quality of atheist cadres, and recommended that atheists coordinate their research with psychologists, philologists, sociologists, and philosophers. It was time, Okulov insisted, to "bring an end to the situation where atheist work takes the back seat [and] where it is considered the lot of defective people." Okulov pointed to the need to determine the practical effect of sociological research and atheist work. "We cannot isolate atheism from the whole of the spiritual life of our society," Okulov maintained, "and in general, we are speaking about the practical applicability of our research."[50]

The Orthodox-apostate-turned-public-atheist Duluman reported on a disturbing trend from his study of religiosity in Ukraine: many believers, it turned out, were young people born decades after the 1917 revolution and educated in Soviet schools.[51] What could explain the religiosity of the Soviet youth? Since the material conditions for religion did not "objectively" exist, Duluman observed, some "subjective" element must be transmitting these survivals to young people. Duluman considered this a failure of the Soviet school system and argued that teachers had to familiarize themselves with the family lives of their students by regularly visiting their homes.[52]

Findings like these led atheists to focus their attention on women and the elderly, who were no longer seen as just bearers of religious survivals but were now cast as dangerous channels through which religion was being reproduced.[53] Some proposed that the success of the atheist project hinged on work with women, since they not only made up the majority of believers but—as mothers and grandmothers who educated children in religious traditions, introduced them to the church, and insisted on the observance of religious rites—also were the primary vehicle for the transmission of religion across generations. Some proposed that women could be drawn into atheist work with lectures that covered topics aimed at their interests, such as child rearing or "the meaning of a woman's happiness." In Gorky, held up as a model of effective atheist work (and a city where women made up 80 percent of believers), the female activists of the House of Culture had organized a "Housewives Club," cozily called "Over a Cup of Tea."[54] The atheist component of the club's work was disguised within a broader emphasis on cultivating a more cultured and enlightened use of leisure time. Using folksy language, the invitation asked women to come to a "gathering over a cup of tea," during which they would be asked for their opinion on how to better organize leisure as well as given the opportunity to discuss anything that "[they] might like to know about life in the world."

The elderly, who had previously been seen as a lost cause and left outside the sphere of atheist work, also became a new target, since research revealed that the older generation had a critical influence on the upbringing of children. Since most parents worked and frequently depended on grandparents for childcare, grandparents could insist on baptism, sometimes even refusing to care for unbaptized grandchildren. A Gorky study that surveyed three thousand factory workers, for example, proposed that "the main reason for the execution of the ritual was the refusal of others to care for an unbaptized child."[55] Of those who baptized their children, only 8 percent identified as believers, and the majority were exemplary laborers, but more than 75 percent did not have access to regular childcare.

The older generation remained an unregulated repository of religious traditions and customs, even when the state fought to contain religious practices by limiting the spaces in which they could legally be conducted. M. K. Tepliakov, the leader of the institute's Voronezh base, asserted that the primary mechanism by which religion was disseminated was the "authoritarian family" and especially grandparents, who "using affection as a hook" (*na prieme laskovosti*), introduced religion into children's lives. The root of the problem, Tepliakov put forth, was that the elderly were socially isolated; even those who had once been exemplary workers weakened their ties with the labor collective once they retired. The Voronezh party organs had addressed this situation with some success by organizing an "elderly club," thereby making it into "a kind of helper to the party in deciding many issues." Local authorities—the director of the collective farm or secretary of the party committee—would visit with the club in order to seek advice on local affairs, and "the old folks would be very pleased" that their opinions were taken into account. The minimum, Tepliakov noted, "was to neutralize the religious influence that the elderly had on children in the family. But the main thing was to win the old folks over to our side."[56] Finally, what the study of religiosity among the elderly also brought home was that religion was not a static phenomenon but rather could have different meanings for the same individual over the course of their life.[57]

Increasingly, researchers suggested that atheism had to narrow its focus to the "microsphere"—to the local community and the family. Yet atheists were also aware that this microsphere could not be accessed through enlightenment measures. Atheists contended that spiritual life had to be approached through emotions. In order to explain "the mobility, disorderliness, [and] murkiness of most believers' religious consciousness," atheists had to turn their attention to the interior worlds of ordinary Soviet people—a project that many acknowledged was difficult because lived religion was mercurial, difficult to categorize, and, more often than not, left unarticulated. New approaches nevertheless suggested that rituals provided the best access to the spiritual worlds of Soviet people. Atheists argued that rituals supplied religion "not only with a base of support, but with well-known dissemination," and atheism needed to "create effective means to block this channel of religious influence."[58]

The influence of religious rituals on Soviet youth was especially troubling. An atheist cadre from Gorky named Stemakov reported that sociological findings from surveys of the socioeconomic status, cultural markers, and expressed motives of those who took part in rituals "significantly differ[ed] from traditional understandings." One survey showed that most adults bringing children to be baptized in the Orthodox Church were young (68 percent were between sixteen and forty-five) and highly skilled laborers (66.2 percent). Surveys of Catholic and Muslim ritual observance showed analogous results. The reasons most provided for baptizing children had less to do with articulated beliefs, and more to do with satisfying the wishes of friends and relatives as well as observing the norms of the local community. There was the notion, that baptism was "an ancient Russian ritual that one should observe" so as not to be "worse than others." Even more surprising was that the majority of these young workers (60 percent) had attended socialist birth rituals prior to baptizing their children and yet still did not understand the "harm" of participating in religious rites, which showed "the absence of any worldview barrier whatsoever against religious ideology and ritual observance." The result of this, Stemakov complained, was that it was unclear what atheists "must grab first, what they must target" (*za chto prezhde vsego ukhvatitsia, po chemu prezhde vsego bit'*).[59]

Overall, Soviet atheists faced a peculiar predicament. On the one hand, cadres noted that the future of atheist work "depended on the convictions of the youth," and while it was "difficult to reform" the elderly, Soviet youth needed to be "saved." On the other hand, youth religiosity was produced in the family. Even if youth participation in religious rituals was less "proof of the diffusion of religion, but to a greater degree, what 'mom and dad want,'" it still pointed to an absence of ideological conviction. And if the convictions of the youth were the "cardinal issue" in atheist work, atheists had little reason for complacency. "We cannot seriously speak about changing people's minds; these are exceptionally rare occurrences." For an "ordinary person" religion was, above all, an emotion, "and if this emotion has been formed, it is very difficult to replace it." But what was even more troubling was that for young people, religion was "a form of skepticism . . . a vacuum that is formed out of disillusionment with our ideological values."[60]

## *Elevated Words and Atheist Tears*

Studies of Soviet religiosity transformed atheists' understanding of the religious landscape and clarified ideological objectives. A consensus began to form about the function of religion in individual and social life, the crucial role played by the family, and the importance of psychological, emotional, aesthetic, and ritual elements. Religion, atheists observed, was not so much a system of views as a "system of feelings."[61] Mikhail Briman, an atheist journalist from the Komi ASSR, proposed that the strength of religion in contemporary society was that it was well adapted to "satisfy the interest of a person in himself [and atheists] needed to realize that a greater interest than the interest of a person in himself does not exist." Briman described an "unusual contest" conducted by the Syktyvkar newspaper *Red Banner*, in which readers were asked to keep a diary for one month in 1967 and then send the diary to the newspaper. "When this undertaking was just being born, there was a terrible discord among us," Briman shared. "Some said that no one would write with any sincerity, others said that in the best-case scenario, we would get six to ten diaries. Our experience with such appeals showed that they were limited to fifteen to twenty letters maximum, with the exception of answers to crossword puzzles, when we received thirty to forty. And here we have a diary, the most intimate thing of all, it would seem." Contrary to expectations, though, the staff was "amazed" to receive eighty-one diaries. According to Briman, their content followed a certain characteristic pattern: the diaries started with attempts to "please" the editors, but after the first two or three days, people "gradually became captivated and began to speak about themselves: about intimate issues, their loneliness, their illnesses, and so forth."[62] From the point of view of Marxism-Leninism, Briman's focus on emotions was peculiar, yet other atheists concurred. If atheists really looked at believers, another expert put forth, they would see that religion depends more on emotions than on belief.

The INA's deputy director, Evdokimov, argued that emotions and psychology play a "colossal role in the religious complex," and proposed that atheists "must constantly keep in mind that religion is not just ideology—if religion were only an ideology, only a worldview, our task would be easier. Religion is an ideological and emotional complex, it is a ceremonial complex that is closely tied to everyday life, which pierces byt, and all of this, of course, complicates our task." Evdokimov urged atheists to consider the "moral and aesthetic satisfaction, the emotional and aesthetic richness of religious experiences, the emotional satisfaction of visiting a church or a meeting of the [religious] community, of prayer, [and] of the commandments." He summed up this position by quoting one of the subjects of sociological research, who informed her interviewer that "love of God is necessary for us, not for God." Some also pointed out that the "greatest mass [of believers] were those whose belief manifested itself in the habit of performing rituals, [which was] mainly a psychological habit rather than a logical one."[63] The clergy manipulated this by awakening religious emotions through moving sermons, the aesthetic arrangement of services, and rituals in gilded churches. Religious experiences, atheists acknowledged, could bring congregations to tears. Atheist propaganda, on the other hand, was criticized for its anemic content and feeble delivery.

Since atheism's loss was perceived to be religion's gain, atheists underscored the urgency of improving atheist theory and methods. In order to be effective, atheist content had to be tied to brilliant forms and powerful delivery. The historian of atheism Mark Persits suggested that the success of an atheist lecture depended not so much on the content as on the lecturer. Whereas priests were trained in homiletics, however, some atheist lecturers read from their notes and would be better off inviting actors to read their lectures for them. In order to reach the audience, the lecturer had to be "distinguished by his . . . emotionality, should experience some kind of feeling rather than chew the cud. With us [atheists] it often happens like this: it's all the same to the [lecturer] whether he reads a lecture on atheism or a lecture on the benefits of kefir to elephants at the zoo. He absolutely does not think about what he is reading [and] is completely indifferent to the questions that make up the subject of his [lecture]. As a result, [it] is completely unsatisfying."[64] Persits's observation was supported by Iurii Krasovskii and Evgenii Riumin, whose study of the role of emotions in atheist work led them to assert that "the main objective of an atheist propagandist is to skillfully fill the ideological and emotional-psychological 'vacuum' that forms in the consciousness of believers after religious conceptions and emotions are destroyed."[65]

Atheist work had to strive toward a synthesis of reason and emotion. As Evdokimov noted, research of religious psychology revealed that believers' ties to religion could not just be explained away by social pressures and customs, although these factors were certainly important; believers also sought something personal in religion, "something elevated [and] spiritual" that helped them transcend the confines of earthly interests and concerns.

> Without fearing "elevated words," one can say that a believer seeks in religion the ideal of the beautiful and exalted, seeks the meaning of his life on earth [and] Truth and Justice. . . . What can we offer in place of the powerful emotional influence that, having formed over the course of centuries, is today used by the church? How deeply are we replowing the untrodden expanses of the virgin lands that have been left to us after many years of inactivity?[66]

The implication, of course, was that scientific atheism did not. The point was supported by Briman, who described how believers, after hearing his lecture on the meaning of life and death, approached him and said, incredulously, "You also think about such things? It turns out you atheists also think about death? How very strange."[67]

In returning to these themes, atheists were returning to a question that consistently haunted their work: the suspicion that the failures of atheism were symptomatic of ideological failures in general. As Evdokimov put it, "What concerns me in our practice is not only that [people] do not shed tears during lectures about the origins of religion but that [people] also do not shed tears during lectures on patriotism [or] the love of humanity. With us, people do not shed tears at any lectures at all. Which is why . . . we should be talking about the fact that our atheist emotional stock is simply a continuation and reflection of our general emotional stock."[68]

Atheists also found that their subjects could easily reconcile what atheists perceived to be contradictions. Duluman provided evidence for this when he described the "concrete, real reality" that cadres often encountered on the ground in a telling episode he shared with his colleagues:

> A group went to the village Beloozer'e in the Cherkassy region. I moved into the home of a young believer. I was told that he was a believer, but I did not say that I was an atheist. I am not conducting atheist work, but I see that here there is not even a trace of religiosity. In the evening they sit and play cards under the icons. I endured this for three days—in the sense that I do not see the relationship between cards and God—and then ask: "Why do you play cards under the icons?" And they answer: "Because we are very comfortable there!" And I say, but what about God, who is painted there? And the owner says: "Oh, [the icons] are used to it by now!"
>
> [Laughter in the hall]
>
> They say that they do not believe in God. I ask: "So do you go to church?"
>
> They answer: "Everybody goes and we go!"
>
> "Did you baptize your child?"
>
> "Everyone baptized and we baptized!"
>
> So I start to read a lecture—that this is savage, that savages conduct such rituals and so forth. The owner listened attentively and said that what I was telling him was very interesting, but then he declares, "Everyone is a savage, and I am a savage" (*Vse dikari, i ia dikar'*).
>
> [Laughter in the hall]
>
> I knew he did not like the priest and so I ask him, "How much did you pay the priest?" And he says that the priest is a parasite, that everything goes in his pocket, that when he baptized his child he paid three rubles to the bank and two to the priest. So I say: "You gave five rubles to a freeloader." And the owner says: "I hope he chokes on them!"
>
> I start appealing to parental feelings—meaning, "How did you allow your child to be dipped in cold water?" The owner answers: "But we made an agreement with the priest and he warmed the water!" I continue on that this is not hygienic, that there are bacteria in the water,

> that you are subjecting your child to danger, that [the child] might fall ill, catch something, but he asks me: "Were you baptized?"
>
> I answer: "I was."
>
> He declares: "And so was I. All of Mother Russia was baptized and look at how fine she turned out!"
>
> [Lively animation and laughter]
>
> And alongside this, people go to church, give money, support it. This is why it is difficult to determine whether they are believers or unbelievers.

Duluman concluded his story by pointing out, "Above all, criteria of religiosity . . . are necessary not only to 'separate the goats from the sheep' but also in order to know with whom we must conduct our work. Here we are not yet able to give an explanation of how to classify people."[69] The traditional spectrum, with the "religious fanatic" and "convinced believer," on one side, and the "unbeliever" and "convinced atheist," on the other, was no longer sufficient.

What is most striking about Duluman's retelling of his exchange with a rural believer is that he criticizes him not so much for his belief but rather for his lack of consciousness and discipline. Indeed, Duluman is much more concerned that the man is playing cards under an icon than the purported "believer" himself. What bothers Duluman about the scene he encounters in Beloozer'e is not that the man has icons in his home but that he is indifferent to the contradiction between his professed religious belief and his irreverent behavior. Soviet atheists, then, were disciplinarians in search not just of ideological adherence but also of a specific type of reason and consciousness. Religion, as they understood it, was about individual belief and internalized discipline. The believer's conduct had to correlate to the tenets of the faith. Yet what atheists saw was that the contradictions that were obvious to atheists were not obvious to believers.

Life, sociological research revealed, did not bend to the criteria demanded by atheist social scientists, which led atheist cadres to reexamine their assumptions and reconsider their categories. They understood that without figuring out a language to speak about the contradictory religiosity that actually existed on the ground, successful atheist work was impossible. Efforts to produce a typology of "belief" continued to occupy a central place in the institute's work. Conferences and seminars were filled with questions and proposals, but also with disagreements and debates, about how the atheists' new knowledge of the religious landscape could be applied in atheist work. These issues were critical because by the end of the 1960s, atheists had come to realize that it was not enough to destroy religious belief, and that an unbeliever was not the same as an atheist. As a result, some proposed that atheist work focus on the middle of the spectrum: religious doubters and passive atheists.

But just as there was confusion about what constituted a believer, there was also confusion about what made an atheist. As one Moscow atheist proposed, "an atheist is one who is absolutely not subject to any supernatural tendencies," including not only religious belief but also various forms of "mysticism."[70]

Yet the category that was growing most noticeably, especially among young people, was "indifference." Thus, the "atheist" had to be distinguished not just from the "believer" but also from someone who was indifferent to both religion and atheism.[71] Indifference emerged as a critical category of belief, and atheist cadres noted with alarm that it was the fastest-growing category on the spectrum.

## *Toward a Society Free of Religion*

A major turning point in the development of Soviet atheism was the Penza project—the first major sociological survey of the Soviet religious landscape, carried out in the central Russian region of Penza between 1967 and 1969.[72] Titled "Atheism and a Person's Spiritual World," the Penza project rested on the assumption that if the atheist apparatus could mobilize the social sciences, then it would finally produce an effective plan for achieving "a society free of religion." The hopes of Soviet atheists were quickly disappointed, however. Not only did the Penza project underscore their worries that atheist propaganda did not produce atheists; it suggested that modernization did not necessarily produce secularization. The Penza project also confirmed the existence of indifference as a critical factor in the spiritual and ideological composition of Soviet society. Whereas 58 percent of the 30,674 individuals surveyed identified themselves as unbelievers, only 11.1 percent of those surveyed identified themselves as convinced atheists.[73] The discovery of indifference brought to light the distinction between unbelief, on the one hand, and atheist conviction, on the other. Even when religiosity seemed to be declining, atheist conviction was not taking root in Soviet society, suggesting that even if Soviet people considered themselves unbelievers, atheism had not made great inroads into their spiritual world.

Indifference was problematic for many reasons. First, it undermined Soviet claims about the moral superiority of socialism over capitalism, and Soviet atheism over bourgeois atheism. Over the course of the 1960s, atheist theoreticians had come to insist that what distinguished "socialist atheism" from its "bourgeois" counterpart was the fact that it was not just negative but had a positive component as well—that is, Soviet atheism did not just show the falsehood of religious belief but also filled the spiritual world of the Soviet person with the true scientific atheist worldview. Second, indifference was a problem because it was observed above all among Soviet youth. Young people were "opting out" of official Soviet culture in favor of various countercultures, from the eclectic (the hippie movement, yoga, Hare Krishna, and what the Soviet establishment generally referred to as "mysticism") to the traditional, since in the Soviet context traditional religion also stood in opposition to official culture.[74] This meant that the Soviet system was not effectively transmitting socialist values to the next generation, and that put the survival of the entire enterprise at stake.[75]

As a new generation of Soviet atheists made sense of the material they gathered in their studies, it remained unclear how exactly the social sciences could advance the mission of creating a mass atheist society. Viktor Pivovarov, an INA researcher and leader of the Penza project, observed that conducting surveys to determine religiosity presented numerous difficulties. "If we determine that the complex of religious consciousness, of religious behavior, is the basis of sociological research, then what do we mean by religious consciousness? We take belief in God, belief in the immortality of the soul. But if this can even be formulated, how do we transfer the meaning of the investigation onto a document, and from a document, to a person's everyday consciousness?" Pivovarov also brought attention to another problem. Unlike other researchers, sociologists working on religion and atheism could not approach their subjects directly. Even though researchers were interested in religion and atheism, Pivovarov pointed out, they had "to mask this in some way" in their surveys. Pivovarov also noted that there was a disconnect between what atheists were asked to research and their ability to explain what they actually found on the ground. "Sometimes, what is demanded of a sociological research project is something that the given project cannot provide," Pivovarov observed. "For instance, in Penza, a report was demanded on the reasons for religiosity. But the reasons for religiosity were not studied in Penza."[76] Instead, researchers in Penza searched for evidence of secularization in order to provide practical advice to atheist cadres about how to produce a "society free of religion."

By the late 1960s, though, one thing was apparent: everyone involved was frustrated with atheist work. The party leadership was frustrated because atheists continued to spin their wheels. Lisavtsev, the INA's curator inside the Central Committee, complained at a 1971 meeting that atheists were asking the same questions over and over, yet offered no answers. Atheist researchers were frustrated because the more professional experience they gained, and the more they encountered lived religion, the more their two roles—atheist activist and social scientist—came into conflict. Among atheist cadres, there was a growing distance between those who understood atheism as primarily the theoretical and social-scientific study of religion, and those who largely saw it as the mission of converting Soviet people to the scientific materialist worldview. Was the purpose of atheism to understand religion or produce atheist conviction? The two, of course, were seen as inherently related; it was necessary to understand religion in all its complexity in order to produce a program that would effectively instill atheist conviction. But as the years went by, atheists became increasingly interested in religion along with what it revealed about the social and cultural transformations taking place in Soviet society, and less confident in the propaganda mission of atheist work.

Indeed, leading cadres and researchers in both the ideological and academic establishments remained unclear about the foundations of atheist work, and even disagreed on the fundamental question of what exactly constituted atheism.[77] Inside universities, there was discord about whether scientific atheism should be an independent discipline or incorporated into an existing discipline, such as history or philosophy, and, if so, which one.[78] Indeed, there was not even consensus on whether scientific atheism should be a required part of the university curriculum at all. In summarizing the dilemma, Il'ia Pantskhava, the chair of the Department of Atheism at Moscow State University, quoted the philosopher Teodor Oizerman, who argued against incorporating atheism into the Department of Philosophy: "Scientific Communism, sociology, ethics, aesthetics, [and] atheism are not philosophical disciplines. With regard to atheism, the profile of this discipline is completely unclear to me. If you take away dialectical and historical materialism, then the only thing that remains of it is history."[79]

There was general agreement that atheist work consisted of two component parts—the negative (criticism of religion) and positive (affirmation of atheism)—but when pressed, few could articulate what positive atheism actually was or who was responsible for inculcating it into Soviet society in order to make it "free of religion." Dmitrii Ugrinovich, a professor of philosophy at Moscow State University, saw the criticism of religion as a form of "religious studies" (*religiovedenie*), and argued that the task of academics was to make sense of religion rather than produce atheism. Ugrinovich urged others to work out atheism's positive content, implying that the production of positive atheism—whatever it may entail—was not the work of scholars.[80] Still, even as the purpose of the atheist mission remained unclear, the institute continued to research religion and in this sense moved toward a better understanding of the process of secularization. But the professionalization of INA researchers and their gradual transformation from atheist activists into atheist social scientists put the institute in a peculiar predicament, the nature of which was underscored by Lisavtsev, who complained that the INA had to "seriously rework" its research plan "so that it becomes the plan of the Institute of Scientific Atheism, and not the Institute of Religious Studies."[81]

## *Conclusion*

The mobilization of the social sciences in the service of the atheist project revealed a complex ideological landscape that continuously challenged the party's understanding of religion. As atheists became social scientists, their experiences in the field showed them that religion was not just about "belief" but also about practice, emotion, community, and experience. Setting out to overcome a religion that was believed, atheists ran up against a religion that was lived. And the problem with lived religion was precisely that it was a world distinct, if not apart, from religious dogma and institutions. Rather than being confined to specific spaces and texts (which could be regulated and disciplined by church and state authorities), lived religion was domesticated, dispersed, and therefore often beyond the party's reach. When atheists went to the people, they tried to explain why a Soviet person who was loyal to Soviet power and did not go to church or even believe in God—but still had icons in the home and baptized children—nevertheless fell short of the Communist ideal of atheist conviction. They encountered ordinary people who had difficulty understanding why they had to actively renounce religion and profess atheism in order to be considered full members of Soviet society.

But Soviet studies of religion also reveal that atheists were aware of their limitations and sincerely grappled with the shortcomings of atheist work. As atheism was theorized and applied on a large scale, its goals and methods changed: while initially success was measured by decline in religiosity, by the late 1960s, indifference emerged as a central concern. Indifference revealed a lack of individual conviction in Communism and made evident that the party was losing its grasp on Soviet society. More problematically, the prevalence of indifference among Soviet youth meant that the Communist system of values was not being reproduced in the next generation. Indeed, when the ideological establishment studied the convictions of Soviet people, what worried them in particular were young people who lacked commitment to the Soviet project, even as they expertly performed the language and rituals of official ideology in public. Indifference, for the ideological establishment, was above all a failure of ideological discipline. Their solution, from the 1960s through the 1980s, was the development of a system of ideological socialization that inculcated Soviet values through a system of atheist, ethical, aesthetic, international, and patriotic upbringing. Even as this system became more expansive and complex, however, there was little to indicate that it produced atheist or Communist conviction. As Alexei Yurchak shows in his study of the last Soviet generation, young people could both accept the Soviet ideological universe as normal and have no illusions that it described their lived experience.[82]

If the objective of the Soviet project was secularization—an institutional separation between politics and religion, the decline of religious authority, and the disappearance of religion from the public and private lives of individuals—then indifferent subjects should have been considered a sign of success. Yet on the contrary, indifference came to worry the party more than religious belief. After decades of trying to overcome religion, Soviet atheists began to think differently about why religion posed a problem to the Communist project. The ideological establishment no longer saw religion as a problem primarily because it was a political enemy or even alien ideology. Instead, religion was now understood above all as a spiritual problem. The ideological establishment began to focus on the spiritual development of Soviet society and saw the production of the "socialist way of life" (*sotsialisticheskii obraz zhizni*) as the final battleground for the Soviet soul—because it assumed that the political and ideological battles had already been won.

CHAPTER SIX

# The Communist Party between State and Church

## SOVIET ATHEISM AND SOCIALIST RITUALS

> How precious are the old institutions, the old traditions, the old customs! The people guard them as the ark of the covenant of its forefathers. But how often has history shown that popular governments do not value but regard them as an old garment of which they must be rid. Rulers condemn them without mercy, or re-cast them in new forms, and expect a new spirit to animate them at once. Their expectations are seldom fulfilled.
>
> —KONSTANTIN POBEDONOSTSEV, "THE SPIRITUAL LIFE" (1898)

ON JANUARY 2, 1956, around the same time that the Central Committee learned about Stone Zoia of Kuibyshev, it also received another curious report, this one from the head of the Soviet Writers' Union, the writer Aleksei Surkov (1899–1983). In it, Surkov described a letter that the union received from T. I. Kubrikova, an elderly woman from Saratov, asking Soviet writers to create new socialist rituals to replace the religious rites cast aside by the revolution. Surkov characterized Kubrikova's letter as both naïve and poignant:

> This letter . . . might seem primitive and even somewhat funny. And yet the questions posed by the letter have worried the people for all the years following the October Revolution. In fact, nothing was given to the people in exchange for the colorful church rituals that formalize the birth, marriage, and death of a human being—rituals that affect the imagination.[1]

Surkov wrote that since the Writers' Union was a professional organization and could not address such ideological questions, he was bringing it to the Central Committee. But the Central Committee also did not want to take up the ritual question, and informed Surkov that "manufacturing everyday rituals and disseminating them in a directed fashion was not advisable." Instead, the party instructed Surkov to inform Kubrikova that "satisfying her request does not appear to be possible."[2] This exchange—between a Soviet citizen, a prominent writer, and the party's Central Committee—provides a window into how the party understood its role in Soviet spiritual life. Indeed, the party's response speaks to the low priority it still assigned to the ritual question in

1956 and points to confusion about who was responsible for addressing the spiritual needs of Soviet society.

For most Soviet citizens at the beginning of the Khrushchev era, when Kubrikova wrote her letter, the public experience of marriage, the birth of a child, or the death of a loved one was confined to the bureaucratic procedure of registering the event at the civil registry bureau, the ZAGS. Afterward, of course, most people celebrated or commemorated these occasions at home among family and friends, yet it is striking that for decades, the presence of Soviet Communism in the most significant transitions in people's lives was limited to the act of registering the change in civil status. This was true whether the person was an ordinary worker or member of the political elite. As Khrushchev's son-in-law, Aleksei Adzhubei, remembered of his 1949 marriage to Khrushchev's daughter, Rada, "The idea of a marriage ceremony was completely foreign to the Khrushchevs. This only made Rada and me happy. On August 31, 1949, accompanied by Vasilii Bozhko of Khrushchev's security forces, we went to the district ZAGS and received the necessary stamps in our passports."[3] Even as Soviet Communism filled public life, it remained marginal in some of the most important moments in the private lives of Soviet people.

Under Khrushchev, this situation changed drastically and in many surprising ways. It became unacceptable for Soviet people to experience birth, marriage, and death simply as the bureaucratic registration of a change in civil status. Rituals went from being considered a meaningless vestige of a former way of life to the impetus for the creation of new ritual spaces, services, and material attributes, ritual art and songs, trained professionals and specialized methodologies, and, of course, socialist rituals themselves. If at the beginning of the Khrushchev era, when Kubrikova sent her letter, socialist rituals could still be seen as an unimportant issue that could be ignored, by the time Brezhnev replaced Khrushchev as the party's general secretary, socialist rituals were considered the party's most powerful weapon in the battle against religion and thus central to ideological work. As the ideological establishment confronted the ideological vacuum threatening Soviet society, they came to believe that atheism's prospects hinged on how effectively Soviet Communism could address Kubrikova's request.

## *From Church to State: The Secularization of Soviet Life*

One of modernity's central stories is that the work of caring for the people shifts from the church to the state.[4] How individuals experience rites of passage underscores this transformation. In the Soviet case, this process was more swift and radical than elsewhere in Europe.[5] Whereas before the revolution, religious institutions and clergy oversaw both the administrative and ritual aspects of life-cycle transitions, after the revolution, the Bolsheviks' creation of a government bureaucracy to register changes in civil status placed birth, marriage, and death under the jurisdiction of the state.[6] This transfer was a critical component of the party's secularization program. The new regime specified that "[m]arriages conducted through religious rites and with the participation of spiritual figures give no rights or obligations if they are not registered in the prescribed way," and only civil acts registered by the ZAGS were legally recognized.[7] By taking over the management of birth, marriage, and death from religious institutions, the Bolsheviks sought to undermine religion's symbolic power and thereby marginalize it in social life. Indeed, this goal was made explicit by Deputy Justice Commissar Nikolai Krylenko, who described the new legislation as a weapon whose "spearhead is pointed against church marriage in order to destroy its authority in the eyes of the masses."[8] At the same time, the ZAGS, as a tool of secularization, was destructive rather than constructive. It remained, above all, a bureaucratic organ that simply recorded changes in civil status—a process that is elegantly captured in Dziga Vertov's film *Man with a Movie Camera* (1929), which shows a procession of people at the ZAGS office registering marriages, births, divorces, and deaths in quick succession. The role of the ZAGS, then, was to enforce Soviet legal norms; it was not to solemnify rites of passage or endow life with meaning.

Whether anyone should take over the ritual side of life-cycle transitions, and if so, what these new socialist rituals would look like, remained unclear.[9] Some within the socialist camp, like Bonch-Bruevich, saw the development of secular rites as the natural outcome of the separation of church and state. After the revolution, Bonch-Bruevich wrote, Soviet people would have the option to mark these transitions either "in the civic way," or "in the old way, with the clergy."[10] Others remained ambivalent about whether the revolution should have its own rituals or, indeed, whether rituals had any place in the new world at all. In fact, these debates had begun before 1917. On one end were those who saw rituals as inherently primitive and backward, and sought to eradicate religious holidays, rituals, rites, and even military oaths. Their vision was of a society devoid of senseless ritual acts and freed from the base craving for spectacle. As Iaroslavskii recounted at the first congress of the League of the Godless in 1925, one fervent Bolshevik, in his war against what he called "Communist double-belief [*dvoeverie*]," even willed his corpse to a soap factory to be made into soap.[11] Others saw rituals as a vestige of the old way of life out of which the masses would eventually mature and maintained that the party should satisfy the popular need for ritual as a transitional measure. In the meantime, it was better that these be "our" socialist rituals, cleansed of mystical and supernatural elements, than "their" religious ones. Others still pointed to the existence of rituals in different cultures across history in order to suggest that rituals in general were not inherently retrograde but a historically specific manifestation of a universal human experience. They argued that, given the transformative potential of ritual experience, it was in the party's best interests to offer the people its own rituals.[12] In the first years after the revolution, as the Bolsheviks debated the place of rituals in the new Communist byt, Soviet people continued to fall in love and get married, form families and have children, grow old and die, and this mundane but persistent social fact continued to pose the ritual question.

However, even as they denounced the old way of life along with the institutions, beliefs, and practices that ordered it, the Bolsheviks were not quick to offer meaningful replacements.[13] A 1928 painting titled *In the District ZAGS* illustrates the early Soviet vision of the new byt. Saturated in a deep red hue, the painting depicts a rural couple—the groom still in his Red Army uniform—merrily registering their union in a dark ZAGS office as their comrades looked on.[14] Inasmuch as there were efforts to introduce socialist rituals in the early Soviet period, they were the work of a small number of ritual enthusiasts who experimented with socialist baptisms ("octoberings"), weddings, and funerals. These "red rituals" were coordinated through local soviets and party and Komsomol cells, and usually took place in the factories and collective farms where the individual worked. The rituals themselves were solemn, ascetic, and stripped of ornate ritual elements, and often became a platform for antireligious propaganda rather than as a commemoration of a rite of passage. Moreover, even though the party propagandized early socialist ritual efforts in the press, their awkward implementation often made them the object of satire rather than a model for emulation. In a 1935 *Pravda* article, for example, the popular writers Il'ia Il'f and Evgenii Petrov parodied a socialist birth ceremony, describing how the chair of the local soviet presented each newborn with a red satin blanket, for which he would "exact payment" by "standing above the crib of the infant, [and] read[ing] a two-hour report on the international situation," while the "adults smoked dejectedly." Then, when the chair finished his report, "everyone, with a feeling of awkwardness, went home," where "of course, everything went back to normal. . . . But the feeling of dissatisfaction remained for a long time."[15] Stories like this highlighted the disparity between the lofty ideological aims of socialist rituals and the ways in which their execution fell short.

Over the course of the early Soviet period, then, the Bolsheviks created a litany of political rituals that shaped the symbolic organization of public life, yet spent little effort trying to provide socialist alternatives to the religious rituals and traditions that shaped private life and communal experience. Despite revolutionary dreams of remaking society and human nature, their sporadic attempts to introduce socialist rites into everyday life were

FIGURE 6.1. Mikhail M. Cheremnykh, "You Are Waiting in Vain at the Church Door, Priest—We Live Wonderfully without Icons and God!" (*U tserkovnogo poroga zhdesh' pop, naprasno; bez ikon i boga my zhivem prekrasno*). Moscow-Leningrad, Izd-vo "Isskustvo," 1939. GMIR, Inv. no. B-1202-IV, used with permission.

largely unsuccessful, and the question of how to transform religious rites and beliefs into socialist rituals and convictions remained unanswered. In fact, after the failures of these initial attempts, the Bolsheviks stopped asking the question.

By the end of the 1930s, as Stalin turned away from atheism, even episodic enthusiasm for socialist rituals largely died out. With the consolidation of Stalinist culture, public festivals were promoted as the authentic expression of Soviet identity, whereas private rites were depicted as a holdover of religious backwardness and bourgeois sentimentality. This sentiment is captured in a 1939 antireligious poster that shows the world split in half between religion (on the left, in darkness) and socialism (on the right, in light). On the left, a priest kneels on the ground next to a price list for weddings, baptisms, and funerals; on the right, a young Soviet couple (now dressed in neat middle-class fashion rather than army uniforms) looks down at the priest with benevolent condescension as young people dance in front of the cultural club in the background. Below, the slogan reads, "You are waiting in vain at the church door, priest. We live wonderfully without icons and God!" (see figure 6.1).[16] Of course, behind the propaganda, many Soviet people's lives remained connected to religion, whereas socialist rituals, and the new Communist byt more

FIGURE 6.2. ZAGS staff of Moscow's Kievskii district congratulate newlyweds. A. Agapov, January 1956. GBU "TsGA Moskvy," no. 1-19838, used with permission.

broadly, remained something they encountered in propaganda posters rather than experienced in their everyday lives.

After the war, the profile of the ZAGS began to change. A 1946 decree instructed the ZAGS to make the registration of civil acts into a solemn ceremony by making ZAGS spaces more beautiful and improving the training of ZAGS officials. In part, these reforms reflected the party's mission to regenerate Soviet society after the trauma of war by strengthening the Soviet family, the foundations of which had been shaken as spouses died, children were orphaned, and new unions were formed without old ones being broken.[17] By transforming the ZAGS from a purely administrative into an "educational" (*vopsitatel'nyi*) organ, the party sought to connect each small Soviet family to the big Soviet family of the state.[18] But despite these intentions, there was little immediate change in the work of the ZAGS, and it was only in 1956, when the ZAGS was transferred from the jurisdiction of the Ministry of Internal Affairs to the executive committees of the local soviets, that reforms began to be implemented. Continuing the initiatives originally proposed in 1946, the ZAGS moved its offices out of police stations and raised the education and training requirements for ZAGS employees. The ZAGS also worked to improve the "solemnity" (*torzhestvennost'*) of civil acts, starting with such basic changes as scheduling separate hours for the registration of joyous occasions like birth and marriage, from less happy ones like divorce and death (see figure 6.2).[19] Finally, with the start of Khrushchev's antireligious campaign in the late 1950s, the ZAGS became much more connected with the ideological establishment, especially as it began to be involved in the production and inculcation of socialist rituals. In the forty years since the revolution, the profile and mission of the ZAGS had transformed: if in the early Soviet period the party used the ZAGS as a tool for secularization, then by the Khrushchev era the ZAGS had become a tool for the sacralization of Soviet life.

## *"Marriage Is a Serious Affair": The New Soviet Wedding*

Under Khrushchev, the Komsomol played an important role in resurrecting the ritual question, much as it had in the early Soviet period, when it was on the front lines of the battle for the new socialist byt. Not surprisingly, the Komsomol focused on rituals to mark the central events in the lives of young people: coming of age, marriage, and the birth of a child.[20] At the Thirteenth Komsomol Congress (April 15–18, 1958), Shelepin—Komsomol secretary and part of Khrushchev's team mobilizing for the antireligious campaign—spoke about the need for socialist rites of passage to accompany important milestones in the lives of Soviet youth:

> For thousands of years the people created a wedding ritual, but now everything has been far too simplified. We need to introduce our own good wedding rituals. The wedding should always remain in young people's memories. Maybe the couple should give solemn oaths to honestly carry out their spousal duties? Maybe we should wear wedding rings? There is nothing religious in this; it is just a commemoration and sign for others that a person is married. And marriage certificates should be beautiful, commemorative. [The] ZAGS buildings should be well maintained and well furnished. . . .
>
> Everyone knows that young people get their passports when they are sixteen. We should introduce a traditional ceremony to give them the passport, and it would be good if Communists and exemplary workers [came to this ceremony] to wish them well. We should also commemorate significant milestones in a young person's life such as school

graduation, the assignment of a professional specialization, the birth of a child, and leaving for military service.[21]

The Komsomol's discussions about new rituals that followed the congress touched on a number of ideological tropes then circulating in Soviet public life: marriage, the family, and morality; material welfare and improvements in the standards of living; the revived interest in folk and ethnic traditions; and, of course, the battle against religion.[22]

Indeed, the ritual project addressed the major demographic, social, and cultural transformations taking place in Soviet society as a result of rapid urbanization, growth of private housing, and the impact of de-Stalinization on political culture.[23] As young people became more autonomous and moved into their own apartments, the Komsomol drew attention to the moral value of marriage and the family, issuing reports like "The Problem of Regulating Marital and Familial Relations (Marriage Is a Serious Affair)."[24] Beginning married life with a solemn ceremony, the report proposed, underscored the significance that the party placed in marriage as an institution. The Komsomol's interest in the socialist ritual project also reflected the party's new attention to individual welfare and consumption. In his speech at the Komsomol congress, Shelepin drew attention not only to the need for ideologically edifying socialist rituals but also to more prosaic elements, like the need for dignified ritual spaces and available goods. Soviet youth, Shelepin argued, had the right to celebrate private happiness, and there was nothing ideologically incorrect in their desire for material comfort and tradition. Shelepin even wrote to Kliment Voroshilov, the chairman of the Presidium of the Supreme Soviet, requesting a three-day paid vacation for newlyweds.[25]

Shortly after the Komsomol Congress, Leningrad's Komsomol organization began to work with the local ZAGS organs to establish the first Soviet Wedding Palace, which opened its doors on December 1, 1959. Soon after, two more Wedding Palaces were opened in Moscow (the first at the end of 1960, and second in 1962), and dozens more were established across the USSR over the next three decades.[26] Komsomol, party, and cultural organizations invented new traditions, with model scenarios for the new Soviet wedding even taking into account such factors as the local ethnic and cultural context, and whether the wedding would take place in a village, provincial town, or major city.[27]

Socialist rituals also began to appear in the press, with some presenting them as a weapon in the battle against religion, and others returning to the question initially raised in the early Soviet period, of whether Soviet people needed rituals at all. In the summer of 1959, the Leningrad Komsomol newspaper *Smena* published a series of articles that presented socialist rituals as a way to instill Communist morality and "deal a blow to religion."[28] Meanwhile, on October 3, 1959, *Izvestiia* published an article that asked "Are Soviet

Rituals Needed?," initiating a debate that continued across several issues.[29] But by the end of the 1950s, with the antireligious campaign already under way, the debate was no longer about whether or not rituals should exist in Soviet society but instead about how rituals might better serve both the party's ideological goals and society's spiritual needs: Who would create them? How would they be inculcated? Was the process to be spontaneous or directed from above? What values should they embody? And what needed to be done for them to become an intrinsic part of Soviet life?

Once socialist rituals appeared in the press, readers began to send in questions and comments, opening up the conversation about socialist rituals to the broader Soviet public. These press debates about socialist rituals point to shifts in public opinion around the definition of Soviet values, and reflect the broader political, ideological, social, and cultural transformations of the Khrushchev era. In 1958, for example, a wedding greeting card printed in the newspaper *Soviet Culture* (*Sovetskaia kul'tura*) became the subject of a small scandal when its symbolic representation of the "good life"—depicted by the artist Leonid Vladimirskii as a house, car, three babies, and horseshoe, next to a black cat crossed out with thick red lines—was criticized by some readers as a betrayal of Soviet values. The character of the card's perceived ideological defects is best captured in a letter sent by A. Sheshin, to the satirical journal *Crocodile*. In his letter, Sheshin sarcastically congratulated the artist on his "defective goods," with the "depiction of 'happiness' in the form of a horseshoe, a house, three babies, and a car." The only thing missing "to complete the picture of petty bourgeois happiness [*meshchanskogo schast'ia*]," Sheshin observed, was "seven little elephants," referencing the decorative marble figurines that had become, in the Soviet cultural lexicon, a symbol of bourgeois philistinism.[30]

The artist's published response, however, points to his confidence that he was on the right side of the emerging culture war, which he underscored by pointing out that the entire 350,000 print run of the card had already been sold. "When we began work on this greeting card," Vladimirskii wrote, "we were sure that there will be certain people who will not like it, and who will rush to display their 'political principles' [*politichnost'*] and their 'fine tastes' by criticizing it," Vladimirskii wrote. "One could even say that in creating this card, we were consciously entering into a debate with those people, who remain prisoners of outdated ideas." Why, he asked, when the party was calling for "a great increase in the people's welfare," was it problematic to wish a Soviet person "a well-heeled life [*zazhitochnoi zhizni*]," if that life was the product of honest labor? Once upon a time, he pointed out, it was considered "petty bourgeois" to have a tree for the winter holidays, whereas "now we not only put up the tree but celebrate the Russian folk holiday Maslenitsa in the Moscow Palace of Sport for an entire week." "We stand for the joyous celebration

FIGURE 6.3. "The wedding of [ Valentina ] Tereshkova and [Andrian] Nikolaev," B. N. Iaroslavtsev, November 3, 1963. GBU "TsGA Moskvy," no. 0-99270, used with permission.

FIGURE 6.4. "Witness V. I. Gagarina signs the wedding registration book." B. N. Iaroslavtsev, November 3, 1963. GBU "TsGA Moskvy," no. 0-99271, used with permission.

of the Komsomol wedding, for grooms to give their brides wedding rings," he concluded. "Let the life of Soviet people become richer, more interesting, and fuller every year. Let us not fear the new, even if this new [life] uses old traditional forms."[31] For Vladimirskii, then, embracing both consumerism and tradition did not contradict Soviet values but rather reflected the new possibilities of Soviet modernity. In publishing such exchanges, the press offered Soviet people a new ideological framework that legitimated socialist rituals, including their most "traditional" and "bourgeois" elements.

But perhaps nothing sanctioned socialist rituals more powerfully than the public spectacle surrounding the wedding of cosmonauts Andrian Nikolaev and Valentina Tereshkova (see figure 6.3). Their wedding, on November 3, 1963, took place in the Moscow Wedding Palace, and was attended by prominent party, government, and cultural figures, including Khrushchev and the first man in space, Yuri Gagarin (see figure 6.4). Reported widely by a press eager to capture the birth of the "first cosmic family," coverage of the event described the component parts of the socialist wedding ritual in detail.[32] The Soviet reader learned that Tereshkova, despite being an international symbol of Soviet Communism's progressive views on gender, was dressed in a traditional white bridal gown, including a veil, and that the couple entered the hall of the Wedding Palace to the classical accompaniment of Tchaikovsky's *Piano*

*Concerto No. 1*. The ritual itself involved Tereshkova and Nikolaev signing the civil registry book and exchanging rings and a kiss, and they were presented with a wedding certificate by the chairman of the Moscow City Council. Following the official ceremony, the press reported, the newlyweds entered the banquet hall where, "according to the ancient custom, everyone raise[d] a glass to their happiness." Khrushchev congratulated the couple, and Gagarin gave a toast about how wonderful it was to see such "spiritually rich" people enter into a union.[33] Not long after the cosmonauts' wedding, on November 19, 1963, the socialist wedding ceremony of two workers from Moscow's Likhachev Factory was aired on Soviet television.[34] The socialist wedding ritual entered into Soviet public life.

## *Distracting Soviet People from Religion: Socialist Rituals as Atheist Weapons*

While the ritual project was introduced to the Soviet people through Komsomol initiatives, press discussions, and media events like the wedding of two cosmonauts, the ideological establishment developed socialist rituals behind closed doors in party, government, and cultural organizations. The Soviet Academy of Sciences studied the transformation of Soviet byt, paying particular attention to ritual culture.[35] Ethnographers, historians, and folklorists searched for and documented examples of socialist rituals that had emerged spontaneously across the USSR. Leningrad's GMIRA researchers did field work in the provinces, also searching for successful socialist rituals, as well as evidence of the decline of religious ritual observance,[36] and Moscow's Central House of Folk Arts (Tsentral'nyi Dom Narodnogo Tvorchestva imeni N. K. Krupskoi, or TsDNT) likewise sent amateur folklorists to the countryside to collect examples of socialist weddings and collective farm holidays. Besides gathering examples of organic socialist rituals, ethnographers and folklorists also studied religious rituals in order to liberate them from their religious meaning by unveiling their pre-Christian roots.[37] The TsDNT and Znanie held a conference on "Soviet Holidays, Folk Traditions, and Their Role in Overcoming Religious Survivals" from October 25 to 27, 1960, which for the first time brought together party, government, and cultural institutions to discuss the production and inculcation of socialist rituals as a centralized project.[38] Followed by several republican and union-wide conferences on socialist rituals, these measures initiated the birth of what can be called the socialist ritual complex.

From the outset, it was the antireligious campaign that gave the socialist ritual project political momentum. As the paltry results of antireligious initiatives revealed that religion could not be overcome by either force or argument, socialist rituals came to be seen as atheism's best weapon. But rituals also became increasingly important to atheist work because they were central to how the party understood religion, seeing in ritual observance the best measure of religious vitality, as well as one of the most significant sources of church income. The socialist ritual project, therefore, had two aims: to weaken the church and religion by undermining religious rites, and to buttress the party and Communism by effecting the ideological and spiritual transformation of Soviet society.

To weaken the church, CAROC put pressure on the Orthodox Church to implement internal reforms, which the church did in 1961. CAROC made sure that the initiative had the appearance of coming from the church itself, so as to uphold the fiction of the Soviet separation of church and state. As Kuroedov—the new chair of CAROC—explained in his report to the party's Central Committee, he had "convinced Patriarch Aleksii to give a directive to the church administration to transfer the clergy to salary under the pretext that this would put an end to various misunderstandings between the clergy and local finance organs about taxation."[39] Under the guidance of CAROC, the Orthodox Church made the clergy into salaried employees—a deliberate strategy to lower religious ritual observance, ostensibly by removing the clergy's "material incentive" to officiate rites. It also required individuals who turned to the church for baptisms, marriages, and funerals to register their personal information with the parish administration to create disincentives for those who did not want an official record of their religious observance. Moreover, the permission of both parents was now required to baptize a child, and baptizing a child without parental permission was categorized as an infringement on the conscience of atheist parents. What this meant, in practice, was that it became much more difficult for grandmothers to baptize grandchildren in secret, although often the supposed secrecy was a way to give parents deniability in order to protect them from potential repercussions. As one CAROC plenipotentiary noted, requiring documentation allowed one city soviet to find out about eleven Communists who had baptized their children, and even though four of them initially denied that they had given permission for the baptism, their signatures on the receipts proved their complicity.[40] Introducing the above measures also gave the council information about believers who could then be targeted more effectively for "educational work."[41]

To illustrate the reform's economic impact on the church, Kuroedov explained that whereas before the reforms the fees for rites were paid to the priest, creating a "material interest in performing as many rituals as possible," the reforms would "paralyze the material stimulus for increasing rituals." He noted that, before the reforms, each of the four priests of the Smolensk Church in Leningrad earned eleven hundred to thirteen hundred rubles each month—adding that this amount did not include undeclared income, and was about ten times higher than the average Soviet salary—but that now the church set clerical salaries at one hundred to five hundred rubles in major cities, and eighty to two hundred rubles in rural areas. Kuroedov also reviewed the clergy's responses to the reforms, reporting that while most had reacted "loyally" to the new state of affairs, those who had a "longer view" understood that the reforms weakened the church. He reported that, in a letter to the patriarch, the metropolitan of Krasnodar wrote that "the transfer of the clergy to salaries will undermine the initiative of the clergy in performing their spiritual duties, which will become a real help to atheist work, which is being conducted in all directions. All of this will lead to the decline of the church, and I can see no measures that would prevent this." A Leningrad priest, meanwhile, was reported to have said, "Now I have no need to try and conduct as many rituals as possible and stress my health. If before we had an interest in holding daily services, now the less there are the better." Another priest maintained that if he "could have foreseen that he would be earning 150 to 200 rubles per month, of which 100 to 130 remain after taxes," he would have never entered the seminary.[42]

However, CAROC soon learned that even these restrictions were not insurmountable obstacles. Over the course of 1962, the council met to discuss the reasons for the "tenacity of religious rites," and why administrative measures did not lead to a significant decline in religious vitality."[43] Noting the ineffectiveness of both church reforms and antireligious measures, CAROC now proposed that the reason that religious rites did not disappear under the pressure of administrative restrictions was because there were no attractive socialist alternatives:

> Almost everywhere, religious rituals are not opposed with captivating, emotionally saturated civic rituals. The registration of births and marriages in most cases takes place prosaically, formalistically, in inappropriate spaces, which does not reflect either the importance or solemnity of these events. It is no coincidence that certain citizens perform religious rituals after registering marriage and birth at the ZAGS, even though they are in essence unbelieving people. Our composers, writers, and artists still have not created songs, pictures, and scenarios connected with Soviet civic rituals.[44]

To address these issues, CAROC recommended that local party organs "systematically work on the inculcation of rituals into the registration of civil acts, executing this work with ethnic and local specificities and traditions in mind." More specifically, the council proposed that local organs adopt the Leningrad model, and create ritual commissions—comprising representatives from party, soviet, Komsomol, trade union, and social and cultural organizations—to assist the ZAGS in improving civil registrations.[45] In January 1963, CAROC brought together representatives from the council, party, Ministry of Culture, Znanie, and Ministry of Justice (which oversaw the ZAGS) to discuss "work on distracting the population from taking part in religious rites by inculcating Soviet rituals."[46]

To be sure, CAROC's claim that religion persisted because "religious rituals are not opposed with beautiful Soviet rituals" was convenient because it shifted the burden away from the council itself.[47] But it also underscored the bigger lesson that scientific atheism was ultimately inadequate to the task of ideological conversion. This gave the socialist ritual project a particular urgency, and, by the end of the Khrushchev era, placed socialist rituals prominently on the party's agenda—which, given the party's dismissive response to Kubrikova's request for socialist rituals only a few years earlier, speaks to the significant transformations taking place within the Soviet ideological apparatus.

## *From State to Church: The Sacralization of Soviet Life*

In the history of the Soviet Communist Party's engagement with religion, there was a moment when it began to understand both religion and atheism differently. It began when the Ideological Commission met in the fall of 1963 to make sense of why religion remained part of Soviet life while atheism struggled to reach the Soviet soul. Even though there was anxiety about atheist prospects, there was still optimism that with the necessary political will and resources, former misconceptions and approaches could be corrected, and the atheist project would succeed. Socialist rituals were central to this calculation. While various initiatives to "distract" the population from religious rites and produce socialist rituals had been discussed since the late 1950s, it was not until the political establishment began to appreciate the stakes of the competition with the church that the ritual project got the political will and resources to be implemented on a grand scale.

In November 1963, the Ideological Commission gathered to discuss socialist rituals, and the commission's chair, Il'ichev, invited officials from around the country to report on progress. The secretary of the Leningrad party committee, Iurii Lavrikov, shared that in 1959, around 25 percent of marriages and 30 percent of births were accompanied by a religious ceremony, and the number of religious funerals was "very high." When Leningrad officials tried to understand the reality behind the numbers, they found that the statistics were high because of "people who observe religious rituals but, as a rule, do not believe." To address "this category of people," party cadres believed only one measure would work: "to oppose religious rites with our Soviet rituals."[48] Since socialist rituals were already being introduced in the city—the first Wedding Palace had opened in 1959, followed by another in 1962, and the construction of the "Maliutka" (*Little Baby*) palace for birth registration ceremonies was already under way—Lavrikov also shared how socialist rituals changed the city's religious observance, reporting that after the opening of the Wedding Palaces, the number of religious weddings declined from 25 to 0.24 percent, so that, "In essence the religious ritual was brought to naught."[49]

These statistics made an impression on the ideological establishment. They suggested that the socialist wedding was an unqualified success, and socialist rituals could, indeed, be a powerful weapon. The audience showered Lavrikov with questions: How many Wedding Palaces were already open, and could they accommodate the demand? What about the birth registration ritual? What did the ritual specialist say to the parents? What did they give to the parents in honor of the newborn? How much did it all cost? In response, Lavrikov shared that socialist birth registration rituals were also destined for success. To illustrate the component parts of the ceremony, Lavrikov described the birth certificates handed out during the registration ritual as well as the medals awarded to newborns, which showed a monument to Lenin at the Finland Station on the front, and had a space for the child's name under the text "Born in Leningrad" on the back.[50] Lavrikov also addressed the question of cost, informing his audience that the birth registration ceremony cost one ruble and six kopeks, and included the medal and a greeting card. Il'ichev wanted to know if the state covered the cost or if the parents had to pay, to which Lavrikov answered that the parents paid, and "happily." Il'ichev's response—that this is "correct"—elicited protest among the audience. Yet Lavrikov pointed out that "the baptism ritual costs three to five rubles, without the candle and other attributes, so in essence it can sometimes cost ten rubles, which is to say that [the clergy] siphon [*vykachivaiut*] significant sums just for the ritual." In comparison, the socialist birth registration was "reasonable, not too expensive, and very important for the atheist education of workers."[51]

On the whole, Lavrikov explained, Leningrad ritual specialists "tr[ied] to create a ritual that could elevate people aesthetically in this solemn moment—that is, a ritual that could completely counter that splendor that parents encounter when they show up at the church with their children."[52] Once the Maliutka Palace opened, the number of baptisms declined sharply.

> There was even an incident like this: we get a call from the Leningrad ZAGS headquarters and they ask us, "What's going on, why has the birth rate suddenly declined?" But this could be explained very easily. People, knowing that in a few days registrations will be marked [with a socialist ritual], with a medal, waited to register the birth of their child according to the old method of the ZAGS.[53]

But Lavrikov nonetheless admitted that the ritual was still "far from complete." Leningrad party cadres continued to strive to make the rituals "correspond to the spirit of our age," but were also frustrated by the lack of central guidance. Lavrikov proposed that "since this work is being carried out in many cities in the Soviet Union, the time has come to synthesize [it] on the state level, to select all the best practices, the most interesting and beautiful aspects . . . in order to recommend for inculcation on a government scale a ritual that could successfully counter the church."[54] In order for socialist rituals to successfully "distract" Soviet people from the church, they had to be coordinated from the center, but have support from the highest organs of power.

Il'ichev agreed that socialist rituals were still in the early stages of development. They were being introduced episodically in diverse locations and lacked a shared theoretical foundation. For example, while in Leningrad newborns were being awarded medals with "Born in Leningrad" stamped on the back, in Krasnodar, "they do not give medals but a letter that congratulates the newborn and lists all the principles of the Moral Code of the Builders of Communism."[55] This idea—of newborns receiving letters with the principles of the Communist Moral Code—solicited laughter among the ideological elite in the conference hall, but Il'ichev reminded them that the stakes of the project were serious. Indeed, the simple fact that party bureaucrats should convene to discuss, in the minutest detail, how to commemorate the birth of a child in an appropriate socialist fashion is noteworthy. The Soviet ideological establishment was beginning to see the danger of losing the competition with the religion. As Aleksei Puzin (1904–87), chair of CARC, put it, "The question of children is the question of the life and death of the church. The church will die if it is unable to capture the souls of the next generation."[56] The reverse, of course, was also true, raising the question of what the failure of socialist rituals would mean for Soviet atheism, and for Soviet Communism.

The socialist ritual complex, born from discussions within the Central Committee's Ideological Commission, was institutionalized with two decrees that came out shortly thereafter, the first from the Central Committee, and the second from the Council of Ministers. The first, the January 2, 1964 Central Committee decree, "On Measures for Strengthening the Atheist Education of the Population," called for improvement in atheist work, of which socialist rituals were a component party. The second, the February 18, 1964 RSFSR Council of Ministers decree, "On the Inculcation of New Civic Rituals into Soviet Byt," established a central council to oversee the socialist ritual project.[57]

The goals articulated in the ritual decree as well as the establishment of the Council for the Development and Inculcation of New Civic Rituals into Everyday Life speak to the scope envisioned for the project. Formed under the auspices of the RSFSR Ministry of Justice (which oversaw the work of the ZAGS), the council was chaired by the lawyer Aleksei Kruglov, chair of the Juridical Commission of the RSFSR Council of Ministers, and Nikolai Belyk, the supervisor of the RSFSR Juridical Commission's ZAGS department.[58] It also gathered an impressive array of representatives from government, party, and cultural institutions, including the Ministry of Culture, the Ministry of Municipal Affairs, as well as the Writers', Composers', and Artists' Unions, the All-Russian Theatrical Society, and the Council of Ministers Committee on Cinematography.[59] The decree instructed local government officials to establish volunteer commissions to assist in the dissemination of socialist rituals, and to "activate" the work of existing volunteer commissions for "controlling the observance of laws on religious cults." Municipal authorities were instructed to allocate "well-furnished" ritual spaces for ZAGS offices, such as Palaces of Culture, clubs, and conference halls, and to include the construction of Wedding Palaces in their urban planning. The RSFSR Ministry of Trade was instructed to create "specialized stores" to sell goods intended for newlyweds, such as wedding dresses, suits, and wedding rings, and the RSFSR Economic Council was to increase the production of such goods. The RSFSR Ministry for the Preservation of Social Order was instructed to develop the passport ceremony. The State Planning Committee (Gosplan) was instructed to issue 55.9 tons of paper for the production of ceremonial registry books. Finally, the decree also instructed municipal authorities to clean up cemeteries and "improve the organization of civic funerals." The RSFSR Ministry of Municipal Affairs was ordered to work with the State Committee for Construction in the Soviet Union (Gosstroi) on producing models for "mourning pavilions," and with Gosplan on "preparing objects necessary for the funerary ritual." The Committee on Cinematography was instructed to produce three short films on the subject in the coming year and to "regularly show solemn civic rituals in cine-journals."[60]

The Ministry of Culture (RSFSR) featured prominently in the initial phases of the socialist ritual project, and its role was to "ensure the active participation of cultural institutions in the organization and putting on of folk holidays and inculcation of contemporary rituals," cover ritual efforts in its journals *Cultural Enlightenment Work* (*Kul'turno-prosvetitel'naia rabota*) and *Librarian* (*Bibliotekar'*), and participate in the creation of a ritual "repertoire" alongside the Composers' and Writers' Unions. The Ministry of Culture also organized the first all-union conference on socialist rituals, held in Moscow in May 1964. This conference, chaired by Vladimir Stepakov (1912–87)—one of the Central Committee's "curators" of religion and atheism—gathered specialists from across the country to present the socialist ritual project to the Soviet public.[61] It also ignited a flurry of activity: the creation of amateur and professional arts groups to produce rituals; the formation of councils and volunteer groups to disseminate them; and the establishment of commissions of professional atheists, sociologists, and ethnographers to analyze their successes and failures. As is typical of Soviet campaigns, once the party signaled that socialist rituals were a political priority, they were suddenly everywhere.

One of the more remarkable aspects of the party's mobilization to "expel all survivals of the past from [the Soviet] byt and family relations" was its ambition. This was evident not just in the envisioned scope of socialist rituals and the scale of resources mobilized, but also in the fact that the Council of Ministers decree initially instructed the ritual commission to present its proposals for socialist rituals three months after it was formed. The ultimate aim of the

FIGURE 6.5. "'Strong family-strong state': Solemn act of registering newlyweds in the Gorky Palace of Culture, conducted by the directorate of the Palace of Weddings No. 1, ZAGS division (Moscow)." Moscow House of Scientific Atheism, June 4, 1977. GBU "TsGA Moskvy," no. 1-52311, used with permission.

socialist ritual project was to create an emotional bond with each Soviet person from the cradle to the grave.[62] The scope of public rituals was expanded as state, professional, and calendar holidays became an even more pronounced part of Soviet life. The first and most developed category, state rituals, was already a central part of Soviet culture, with celebrations of the anniversary of the October Revolution and May Day among the most important events of the Soviet calendar. In the 1960s, these mass holidays were joined by new celebrations of critical moments in the patriotic narrative—most prominently the commemoration of Soviet victory in the Second World War on May 9.[63] The second category of public rituals, those connected to labor, also became more common, with celebrations created to mark every stage of professional life—from induction into the working class to professional achievements, the celebration of family "labor dynasties" (when multiple generations of one family worked in one enterprise), and retirement. Special days were devoted to celebrate different professions (from teachers and doctors to coal miners and cosmonauts), and enterprises regularly participated in "socialist competitions" to earn glory for the enterprise and privileges for their employees. Indeed, in the late Soviet period, professional holidays were intended to weave labor even

FIGURE 6.6. "Before the solemn registration of newborns at the Moscow Palace of Happiness." Moscow House of Scientific Atheism, 1960s. GBU "TsGA Moskvy," no. 1-52311, used with permission.

more intimately into individual life as a central marker of identity—a goal underscored by another new phenomenon: the commemoration of professional identity in Soviet cemeteries. In the 1970s, it was common for gravestones to depict not just the heroic labor of military leaders in uniform or cosmonauts in their helmets but also the labor of less obviously heroic professions—scientists with their instruments, doctors in their lab coats, geologists with their field gear, and professional sports coaches with hockey sticks crisscrossing their grave. Public rituals in the third category, those centered around the seasonal calendar, were intended to replace religious holidays (such as Christmas, Easter, and the Trinity) with rituals that celebrated the changing of seasons and harvest cycle, placing stress on the pagan origins and folk elements of seasonal holidays as well as sacred value of rural agriculture.

But the most dramatic development was the creation and dissemination of Soviet rites of passage to accompany every significant moment in individual and family life. The registration of newborns was to be accompanied by elaborate ceremonies that symbolically incorporated the infant into the Soviet community (see figure 6.6). Numerous coming-of-age rituals would mark young people's lives. These would begin with the holiday of the "first bell" to mark the start of school, continue with induction into Communist youth organizations like the Octoberists and Komsomol, and conclude with the passport ceremony, when they would be given their first Soviet passports and thus be recognized as full citizens of the Soviet state (see figure 6.7). Soviet couples could be married with a new socialist ceremony, which might take place in a new kind space invented for the occasion, the Wedding Palace or Palace of Happiness. There, couples would be reminded about the seriousness of their union by a ZAGS official dressed in a special ceremonial costume and trained as a ritual specialist in order to give the event the requisite solemnity. After the ZAGS official's speech, the couple would exchange rings, kiss, and sign their names in an official civil registry book—an act that marked the legal recognition of their union by the state. Following the official ceremony, the ritual continued with the couple's tour of the city's most important historic and patriotic sites, such as the Lenin monument, Eternal Flame, and Tomb of the Unknown Soldier. When the union lasted, the couple celebrated important milestones, like silver and gold wedding anniversaries.

At the outset of the ritual campaign, the ideological establishment's optimism that socialist rituals could solve ideological problems, including religion, bordered on audacity. A year later, when the ritual commission gathered for a weeklong conference to evaluate progress, the mood was more measured. In the year since it was established, Belyk, the commission's co-chair reported, it had created 148 ritual commissions across the RSFSR, from which

FIGURE 6.7. Soviet ceremony for the presentation of the Soviet passport. Moscow House of Scientific Atheism, 1970s. GBU "TsGA Moskvy," no. 1-52306, used with permission.

it received reports, and through which it could introduce and coordinate new initiatives. It had also produced proposals for socialist birth, wedding, and passport ceremonies, and had begun work on the socialist funeral. With Gosstroi, it had worked out architectural plans for Palaces of Happiness that could be built across the country and used for "all events in the personal life of the Soviet person."[64] The municipal authorities were cleaning up cemeteries and had begun work on socialist funerary pavilions and Gosplan had allocated a hundred buses to be used for funerals.

The council also reviewed the material attributes of socialist rituals, such as the design of marriage certificates and the uniform to be worn by ritual officiants. To "create a solemn atmosphere" during socialist rituals, the council proposed that officiants wear a state symbol, like the emblem of their republic, on a "heraldic chain."[65] But Belyk also noted difficulties with the material side of ritual production. In order to produce beautiful marriage certificates, for instance, artists had to participate in the project and the state needed to allocate more resources (six hundred thousand rubles extra each year) to the ZAGS to cover expenses. Moreover, Belyk noted, it was difficult to create "a government document that would satisfy the creative unions and at the same time answer those demands that are placed on government documents."[66] In general, Belyk repeatedly drew attention to the fact that the creative intelligentsia was not participating in the ritual project, and that socialist rituals had a "weak emotional intensity" as a result.[67] Film studios were not making enough films on rituals, and the most "venerable" composers avoided taking part in ritual production. The council had sent two letters to the Composers' Union asking for help in creating music for the socialist funeral, but its letters went unanswered. "We, of course, understand that creative work is a subtle and very difficult affair," Belyk complained. "But it appears that there are Communists in the administration of the Composers' Union who need to understand that it is difficult for us without them, that without well-qualified people [we cannot] create a good civil funeral ceremony."[68]

To address this deficit of creative power, the council had turned to the Ministry of Culture, which began to organize contests for the best new socialist rituals. But ultimately, Belyk insisted, it would take party pressure. "It is absolutely essential that party organs issue directives to creative unions in order to force . . . writers, composers, and artists to work more actively on ritual themes." Without the creative intelligentsia, he warned, it would be difficult to create effective rituals and train ritual specialist with the necessary "oratory mastery."[69] The issue with cadres was a problem not just of quality, but of quantity. ZAGS administrators complained that they did not have the "strength" to register births with a socialist ceremony, since many district ZAGS offices only had one employee, and even where there were more officials, they were unprepared to conduct new socialist rituals, since they had "never been taught how."[70]

The diverse results of the initial efforts to introduce socialist rituals reveal that the project's goals were interpreted differently, and its implementation depended on the enthusiasm and abilities of local cadres, as well as on how these mapped onto local culture. In Iaroslavl', a region known for its high religiosity and dense network of churches, the high rates of ritual observance (in 1960, 60 percent of newborns were baptized, with some districts as high as 78 to 84 percent) declined after local activists had introduced socialist rituals. As a Iaroslavl' party official shared with the ritual commission, "Reporting to the patriarchate at the end of 1964, the new archbishop of Iaroslav-Rostov, Sergii, had to constitute the following, and I quote: 'Unfortunately, I must note that irreligiosity is developing intensively in the eparchy. This can be confirmed by the decline in the sacraments of marriage and baptism, and especially baptism.' "[71]

An atheist from Krasnodar named Sidorov reported that local atheists had created a socialist ritual council in 1963, and as a result of their work, "most towns and villages have begun to celebrate the registration of newborns, marriage, days of commemorating the fallen and the dead, the first paycheck, [and] induction into the working class" with the new socialist ritual. In order to "inflict the most harm to the defenders of religion," the council had focused on the birth registration ceremony, "since the positions of the church are especially strong in this department."[72] Since the council began its work, Sidorov continued, "baptisms and church weddings have almost disappeared," and the earnings of the Krasnodar eparchy fell by 21 percent.[73] Sidorov also explained that the council's work did not stop at the official registration but instead continued in the efforts of local atheists to "influence the entire wedding celebration [*svadebnoe gulianie*]" so that there would be no "ancient traditions, habits, rooted in the Kuban [region], which offend the dignity of the Soviet person."[74] It was "no secret," Sidorov observed, that sometimes "we have the [socialist] marriage registration ceremony, but the newlyweds are met at home by old men and women with icons, and everything goes in the old way." According to custom, Sidorov shared, locals would "climb on the roof and sit on the chimney while the food for the wedding is being prepared in the oven (forcing the parents to pay a bribe in vodka), dress like gypsies and shoot at chickens on the third day of the wedding, or bathe the parents of the newlyweds in puddles or roll them around in the snow [until] they pay a bribe." To root out these "savage customs," the atheist council would meet with the couple and their parents before the wedding to discuss the socialist ritual, and if they refused to "exclude these outdated traditions," then the council would inform them that "there cannot be a [new socialist] wedding."[75] While some atheists sought to incorporate "folk customs" into socialist rituals to make them more "authentic," others—as in the Krasnodar example—saw socialist rituals as a disciplinary instrument to expel the backward customs of the "old way."

But the most striking aspect of the socialist ritual project was that the ideological establishment explicitly discussed it as a competition between "us" (the party, atheist apparatus, and atheists) and "them" (religious institutions, clergy, and believers). As one cadre put it,

> Look how well thought out everything is in the Christian religion! If you take rituals: a person is born, they baptize him; he goes to school, another ritual; lives some more, wedding, again a ritual; [then] confession, funeral—meaning, a person is constantly under the influence of religion. And what is our influence over our people, how do we deal with this part of it? Since I am myself an atheist, I can say, that . . . we do not have a unified system. Why not? If a person is born, we have to do something nice, give him some sort of program that would guide him later on, so that this young person would grow up and see that someone wrote him this letter and he should not forget about it. And when this young man grows up, comes of age and goes to receive his passport, then during the passport ceremony he will be reminded that he fulfilled this program. And then we will again meet him during his wedding. Then our influence will be from a person's birth to the end of his life.[76]

Whereas everything in Christianity had been "worked out over the course of years," atheist work happened in "fits and starts," and lacked a "system that would correctly influence the formation of the scientific atheist worldview."[77] Belyk concurred that while atheists were struggling to produce socialist rituals, "the church is taking measures to actualize its own rituals, improves the makeup of the choirs, modernizes the baptism and wedding ritual, [and] introduces services for the dead that can be observed in absentia [*zaochnoe otpevanie*]."[78] In the Kursk region, 50 percent of newborns were baptized, while only 19.5 percent had a socialist birth ceremony. In Iaroslavl', where the churches were "working very intensively," one district had a baptism rate of 118.8 percent—which meant that local clergy were baptizing not just local newborns but also newborns from other districts as well as local children who had not been baptized as newborns.[79]

Not all reports were so grim. Nevertheless, as the ritual project became institutionalized over the course of the late Soviet period, the ideological establishment became increasingly doubtful that socialist rituals could achieve atheist goals.

## *What's Behind the Cross?*

In October 1981, Eduard Filimonov, the deputy director of the INA, was asked by the editors of *Izvestiia* to respond to a letter from a Soviet citizen seeking clarity about the status of religion and religious rituals in Soviet life. In his letter the author, P. Kovalev, remembered that his grandmother and her friends had gone to church when he was a child, but he wondered "why even certain Komsomol and party members baptize their children." Even if the "hypocrisy" of such behavior was evident, Kovalev was still not sure how to make sense of the "so-called fashion for crosses and icons, with which certain people decorate the 'red corners' of their apartments." Is it fashion—he asked—or a failure in the upbringing of Soviet youth? These questions, Kovalev wrote, "worried" him. What worried him more, however, was that when he tried to raise these issues among his friends and acquaintances, his questions "elicit[ed] a smile among some of them, as if it's nonsense."[80] Kovalev's letter—and perhaps just as significantly, *Izvestiia*'s publication of it—spoke to both the changes in attitudes toward religion taking place in Soviet society as well as increasing confusion within the ideological establishment about how to make sense of these transformations and present them to the public.

Filimonov's reply to Kovalev's letter captures some of this ambivalence. Filimonov reassured Kovalev that in a "developed socialist society," atheism "has become one of the inseparable parts of the spiritual world of the Soviet person," even if there are still people who have not been able to "master the scientific atheist worldview." At the same time, it was "impossible not to agree with the author of the letter" that there were "certain defects in the moral and ethical upbringing of [Soviet] youth." For some, the atheist education they received in school did not "turn into firm convictions" along with "an active life philosophy on religion and its rituals." Instead of secular paintings or engravings, youngsters were putting icons on their walls, wearing crosses, visiting "historical monuments of a cult character," and reading literature on religious art and architecture—all of which these fashionable Soviet youngsters saw as a sign of "good form." Therefore, even if the new interest in religion was real, Filimonov assured Kovalev that it should be interpreted not as evidence of religious convictions or a sign of "religious revival" but rather as an unhealthy fashion. He explained that sociological studies had revealed a "paradoxical" finding: that among those who baptize their children, believers are in the minority. "In other words, this ritual is observed—and supports the material and moral position of the church—by people who, as the saying goes, do not believe in either god or the devil." Those who baptize their children, Filimonov explained, do not believe in God or supernatural forces, and have a negative attitude toward the church and religion as an institution, but see in baptism "a beautiful popular tradition." Baptism, for them, is "a game, a spectacle," simply an occasion for a celebration and feast, and "no one thinks about the fact that this ritual, no matter what innovations the clergy introduces into it, remains a religious ritual that affirms the idea of sinfulness, of insignificance before god. In other words, ideas, incompatible with the moral principles of the Soviet way of life."[81]

Yet Filimonov explained that even if this new religiosity was not a sign of religious convictions among Soviet youth, it spoke to the "well-known

FIGURE 6.8. "Even those without principles—it's no secret—have 'principles': when it's convenient, they say 'there is no god!,' when it's convenient, they go to church" (*U bezprintsipnykh—ne secret—est' tozhe printsip vrode: udobno—skazhut "boga net!," udobno—v tserkov' skhodiat*). Image by V. Kiunnap, poem by V. Alekseev. Leningrad: Izd-vo "Khudozhnik RSFSR," 1975. GMIR, Inv. no. A-6156/5-IV, used with permission.

worldview confusion in the heads of certain young people, of their absence of taste, or more precisely, their philistine tastes, or what is now called by the fashionable word—kitsch." Most of these youngsters "see in the cross [they wear around their necks] simply a beautiful object" that has little connection with Christian religion. Moreover, "these young 'crossbearers' . . . are convinced that fashion has no connection to a person's convictions and worldview." Even if their religiosity was not evidence of religious revival, therefore, it was evidence of their spiritual emptiness. As Filimonov put it, "Behind the little 'x' [cross] one can see a little 'o' [zero]—moral and spiritual." It is telling that in Filimonov's discussion of the place and significance of ritual in Soviet society, he makes only passing mention of the socialist ritual project, noting only that even though socialist rituals "occasionally lack emotionality [and] aesthetic appeal," they nevertheless "facilitate the displacement" of religious rituals "from the sphere of the family and everyday life."[82]

The creative intelligentsia, though, remained at best ambivalent about the socialist ritual project and indeed even criticized socialist rituals in the press. Emblematic of this genre was "Paper Flowers," A. Petukhov's 1969 review of literature about the socialist ritual project.[83] Petukhov made his ambivalence about socialist rituals clear. He pointed out that, to begin with, there was no consensus about what exactly they were intended to achieve. Whereas for some, socialist rituals were the next stage of the progress of cultural and material development, for others rituals were an essential and necessary part of human life since without them life becomes "common, desiccated, prosaically gray" (*obydennoi, vyshchelochennoi, prozaicheski seroi*). Still others, Petukhov continued, saw in rituals a solution to various social problems, from alcoholism to the exodus of Soviet youth from the countryside. In short, Petukhov ironically observed, "Holidays and rituals seem to be a universal means to solve the most difficult social problems." Petukhov acknowledged the great power of rituals in general, "which are worked out over many generations," but wondered about the efficacy of new socialist rituals, which were "born of the fantasies and will of enthusiasts only recently."[84] Indeed, Petukhov asked how new socialist rituals were even to be judged. Did success simply depend on whether the ritual gathered a large audience, and, if so, how was it different from any other "organized performance," such as a concert, game show, or even traveling circus? Or did people have to become participants in order for the ritual to be more than a mere spectacle? After all, Petukhov pointed out, oftentimes "such holidays fell through, failed to come off, and like an unsuccessful concert, called forth a feeling of disappointment, dissatisfaction, and disillusionment." A "thought-up" socialist ritual, created in a committee and implemented from above, "is not yet a ritual but simply a staging, a play, which might be interesting and even beautiful, but no more."[85] In any case, Petukhov concluded, these "created and 'revived'" rituals "leave no trace" on the lives and byt of Soviet people, who "accept these novelties, oversaturated with 'educational elements,' with calm and indifference, wondering at the naïveté of those who hope [with socialist rituals] to kill two birds with one stone: to make our 'common, desiccated, prosaically gray' life more beautiful, and at the same time cleanse the people's consciousness of survivals of the past."[86]

In another article, the writer Leonid Zhukhovitskii wrote that church weddings "call forth fairly deep emotional experiences," whereas the form of civil registrations were "pretty awkward." Describing a recent experience watching a short film about the new Soviet wedding rituals, he observed that much of the time the audience was laughing "not loudly, not joyfully—but more likely out of discomfort."[87] Meanwhile, the ethnographer Iulian Bromlei (1921–80) drew attention to the consumerist elements of new socialist rituals. The Soviet wedding, he argued, "reviv[ed] mercantilist attitudes," becoming an event in which "it is not done to invite less than a hundred guests." Soviet people, Bromlei continued, spend their entire savings on such weddings, even taking out loans that take years to repay. He also wondered about the reasons behind the tenacity of baptisms. There, he wrote, "do not seem to have anything attractive about them for our young contemporaries," and were unhygienic and dangerous to the health of the child to boot—and yet "many people baptize all the same." Finally, Bromlei stressed the particular "danger" posed by death. "This occasion, as no other, remains the sphere of the sharpest clash with religion," he noted, since it sometimes even brought people to "reconsider worldview foundations."[88]

By the late 1970s, faith in the transformative potential of the socialist rituals had waned. Filimonov himself mentioned part of the reason, when in referring to the lack of aesthetic power of socialist rituals, was simply repeating a criticism that had by then become part of the narrative. The creative intelligentsia, after all, had never truly signed on to the project, which instead had to rely on the enthusiasm of amateurs and efforts of officials working in the ideological and cultural establishments. In fact, the creative intelligentsia was becoming more vocal in its skepticism about not only the strategies used by the state to inculcate socialist rituals but also the very purpose of the ritual project—the "displacement" of religious rites from the everyday lives of Soviet citizens. Finally, as the party continued to invest in the project and socialist rituals became widespread, a more complicated problem emerged. To the great frustration of the ideological establishment, Soviet people adopted new socialist rituals, but they often adopted them as an addition to the religious rite rather than its replacement.

## *Conclusion*

Beginning in the Khrushchev era, the party mobilized tremendous resources and expertise to ritualize every sphere of Soviet life. A state that in the 1950s questioned whether Soviet people had any need for rituals at all ended up producing a ritual complex that embraced the totality of the human experience. By the end of the Soviet period, many socialist rituals had become important parts of Soviet life—so much so, in fact, that it is now difficult to imagine Soviet life without them. Yet the adoption of socialist rituals, and their eventual ubiquity in Soviet life, hides the story of their peculiar origins. Socialist rituals were a state project, created by specific individuals in committees that were established to disseminate them to a large and diverse population. As a project, socialist rituals were intended to fulfill concrete ideological objectives: to exorcize religion in order to produce a Soviet community with a distinct and shared way of life.[89]

Soviet atheists initially saw socialist rituals as the best solution to the problem of religion, which the party had not been able to solve through political repression, administrative restrictions, or scientific enlightenment. But Soviet atheists did not just see rituals as an instrument in political socialization; rather, many considered rituals a phenomenon that performed an important social and spiritual function that had been inadequately addressed by Soviet Communism. In their struggle to overcome religion, they learned that what keeps people connected to religion is not only belief but also the aesthetic, psychological, emotional, communal, and spiritual components of religious experience. As a result, atheists came to see the transformative experience of rituals—which they spent great resources to weave into the Soviet social fabric—as central to creating an atheist worldview and socialist way of life.

But socialist rituals never lived up to the many expectations that atheists had placed on them. It was clear that even when socialist rituals succeeded as rituals—that is, when they were widely adopted, as in the case of the socialist wedding—they still failed as atheist weapons. Rather than produce atheist conviction, they revealed Soviet people's ideological flexibility. Despite the widespread adoption of many socialist rituals, atheists continued to believe that they were losing the battle against religion. Religion had institutions, trained cadres, a coherent ideology, aesthetic appeal, and established traditions, whereas atheists were just beginning the experiment. The main advantage of the church was that it was—already—a church.

CHAPTER SEVEN

# The Socialist Way of Life

## SOVIET ATHEISM AND SPIRITUAL CULTURE

> Religion ought to be based on certainty. Its aim, its effects, its usages collapse as soon as the firm conviction of its truths is erased from the mind.
>
> —PIERRE BAYLE, *HISTORICAL AND CRITICAL DICTIONARY*

IN 1969, VLADIMIR TENDRIAKOV—the most prominent public atheist among the creative intelligentsia—found himself in trouble with the party's Central Committee for a novella he published in *Science and Religion*. Titled *Apostolic Mission* (*Apostol'skaia komandirovka*), the novella follows the spiritual crisis of a young Soviet man in the late 1960s.[1] The protagonist is in his late thirties, works as a writer for a popular science journal, and lives in Moscow in a private apartment with his wife and daughter. He is the archetype of the late Soviet urban technical intelligentsia: young, educated, and materially comfortable—the embodiment of the Soviet dream. And yet, Tendriakov tells us, the young man is a "spiritual invalid." The protagonist renounces his professional, social, and familial obligations, and decides to leave Moscow to embark on a spiritual quest, destination unknown. When we encounter him, he is in line at a Moscow train station to buy a ticket out of town. While he waits, he sees a young hippie walking down the street with cans tied to his leg, but as others in line condemn the passerby as a "parasite," the protagonist remains quiet with his own "secret": he has become a religious believer. Though he does not wear his secret tied to his leg, he nevertheless feels a kinship with the "parasite" and considers him his spiritual "relative," since they both find themselves on the margins of the official Soviet narrative. Tendriakov's protagonist embodies the Soviet project's most cherished values, but he rejects those in favor of Communism's imagined "other": religion. He is the new Soviet person turned inside out.

What leads to the protagonist's spiritual crisis is an awareness of something missing: a transcendent moral and spiritual framework that can accommodate and forgive human weakness. This becomes crystallized when his neighbor Ritochka, a woman who has managed to incur the wrath of the housing committee with her tumultuous—and public—personal life, pleads with him to speak on her behalf during the upcoming comrade's court convened to judge her immoral conduct. Rather than show compassion and support, the protagonist does nothing, and the next day learns that Ritochka has committed suicide. Reflecting on his own moral cowardice—"I did not stop it, even though I could have," he thinks—the young man is brought to a spiritual crisis that eventually leads him to buy a one-way ticket out of Soviet life.[2] Interestingly, it is from Ritochka that we learn the young man's name: Yuri.

Yuri's spiritual crisis, however, has deeper origins than his role in Ritochka's unfortunate fate. It began when he and his wife, the beneficiaries of Khrushchev's housing campaign, got their own separate apartment. Instead of satisfying him, his new material comfort created new expectations and further unmet desires. He became entangled in the pursuit of everyday "needs"—furniture, decorations, and home improvement projects—but he no longer understood the purpose of his ceaseless striving. Alienated and depressed, Yuri started to question the source of his spiritual emptiness, and wonder whether there may not be more to life than career advancement and material comfort.

Yuri's search for meaning takes him to a small village in the Russian provinces, where he rents a bed in the home of an elderly woman whose religiosity offers the only comfort in her otherwise-unfortunate life. As he continues to search for truth, he gets into heated debates with both the young village priest and local religious "fanatic" (whose effort during Stalin's cultural revolution to stop the demolition of the village church earned her two decades in a labor camp). Yuri spends his days at the collective farm digging ditches and trying to explain to the befuddled farmers why he would renounce the comforts of the Soviet dream to do manual labor in a forsaken Soviet village. He asks himself the same question, but struggles to find an adequate answer, and returns to Moscow after several weeks, realizing that the answers he seeks cannot be found in religion.

By ultimately bringing Yuri back into the Soviet fold, Tendriakov, on the face of it, conformed to the master narrative of Soviet Communism, yet he still found himself censured by the Communist Party. From the party's perspective, not only did the biographical trajectory of Tendriakov's hero—whose journey took him from city to village, modernity to backwardness, and knowledge to faith—put the progressive telos of Soviet Communism in question, his ultimate return to atheism seemed inauthentic. As the Central Committee report noted, in *Apostolic Mission*, "Atheists are portrayed as unattractive people [and] the hero's conversion to religion looks more convincing than his return to atheism."[3] Rather than finding fulfillment in the material and spiritual promises of Soviet Communism, Tendriakov's protagonist turns to religion.[4] True, eventually he sees the error of his ways and rejects the religious answers to his questions, but he never makes it to the other shore: atheist conviction.

The spiritual crisis of Tendriakov's protagonist is, in many ways, a microcosm of the spiritual crisis of Soviet atheism, and points to the broader crisis within late Soviet Communism. If in 1967, as the Soviet Union celebrated the fiftieth anniversary of the October Revolution, Brezhnev was still giving speeches about the Soviet Union being in the process of the "full-scale construction of Communism," after 1968, the Soviet project faced a qualitatively different political and ideological landscape.[5] By the 1970s, the developments that had underpinned Soviet optimism—political and cultural liberalization, economic growth and increased material welfare, and the scientific technological revolution and space conquest—were all reaching their limits. The economy had hit a plateau. Science, technology, and even cosmic conquest were no longer as novel, or liberating, as they had seemed when Gagarin became the first human in space in 1961—especially when, by the end of the decade, American astronauts (as opposed to Soviet cosmonauts) landed on the moon. As it became clear that Khrushchev's promise that Communism would be built within a generation was not going to take place on the timeline proposed, ideological utopianism receded farther into the past, and was replaced by the ideological malaise of Brezhnevism.

Within this broader context, the party increasingly read Soviet citizens' attitudes on religion and atheism as a critical barometer of their broader commitment to Soviet Communism. Armed with the tools of the social sciences and fruits of sociological studies, the party had a more robust portrait of Soviet society than ever before and found two trends to be particularly worrisome. The first was the growing indifference of the Soviet youth to ideological and worldview questions in general, and to religion and atheism in particular. The second was the growing interest in religion as national culture and spiritual heritage among certain segments of Soviet society—a trend that was led by the creative intelligentsia, but threatened to contaminate young people. As the party worked to produce a unified Soviet society of convinced atheists, conscious Communists, and committed patriots, the production of the socialist way of life was seen as a critical tool for overcoming ideological indifference and cultivating atheist conviction, especially among the Soviet youth. After all—as the party recognized with increasing anxiety—the future of Soviet Communism depended on whether it could reproduce itself in the next generation.

## *The Socialist Way of Life as a Spiritual Project*

By the end of the 1960s, the Soviet political establishment had not only backed away from ideological utopianism; it had lost its tolerance for reformist discourse more broadly—especially when debates about the meaning and future of Communism took place in the public square rather than the closed world of bureaucratic committees. Brezhnev made clear his intolerance of dissent from the Soviet party line in 1968 on the streets of Prague, when the Prague Spring—Czechoslovakia's attempt to challenge Soviet ideological hegemony and propose an alternative, "socialism with a human face"—was brought to an end by a Soviet-led military intervention. While the Soviet Union's violent suppression of the Prague Spring solved an immediate political problem by consolidating Brezhnev's power both in the Communist bloc abroad and Soviet Communist Party at home, it produced another, ultimately more difficult, dilemma: the growing disconnect between Communist ideology and Soviet society. The disillusionment of 1968 transformed many optimistic reformers across the Communist bloc into pessimistic dissidents or disengaged cynics.[6] Struggling to contain the fallout of new political challenges and disappointed expectations, the party continued to rely on ideology to manage and shape Soviet society. By the time the Central Committee held its Twenty-Fourth Party Congress in March 1971, the party had produced a new ideological formula—developed socialism—which attempted to reconceptualize the social contract that bound Soviet citizens to Communism, reaffirm the correctness of the party's chosen historical course, and address the complex political, economic, and social realities of late Soviet life.[7]

Brezhnev described developed socialism as a distinct historical stage in the development of Communism, in which the focus increasingly shifted to the necessary transformation of the Soviet economy to meet consumer demands. Continuing Khrushchev's rhetoric on Communism's commitment to improving the quality of life of Soviet citizens, Brezhnev explained that whereas in the early years of Soviet power, economic resources had to be focused on heavy industry—since "the very existence of the young Soviet state" depended on it—mature socialist society could shift priorities and channel the economy toward "the resolution of tasks related to the improvement of the well-being of the Soviet people." Higher living standards, Brezhnev noted, were a precondition for further development, since advanced production depended on "how fully material and spiritual requirements can be satisfied."[8] Developed socialism was therefore not just about fulfilling economic goals but also about developing the character of Soviet citizens. In the service of this project, the party reaffirmed its commitment to the formation of the new Soviet person whose "Communist morality and outlook are consolidated in constant and uncompromising struggle with survivals of the past."[9] A Central Committee resolution, "On the Intensification of Atheist Work among the Population," followed shortly after, on July 16, 1971. In it, the party criticized party members for their toleration of religion and accommodation of religiosity in their own lives, and clarified that the party's criticism of "administrative excesses" against religious organizations and believers did not mean that it had abandoned its commitment to atheism. Even with the new political détente between the cold war adversaries the party emphasized that just as there could not be neutrality in the ideological battle between Communism and capitalism, there could be no neutrality on the religious question.

In the late Soviet period, atheism increasingly came to be read as a weathervane of Soviet progress toward Communism, which kept religion at the center of ideological work. As a domestic problem, religion continued to be cast as a tenacious holdover in Soviet people's consciousness that needed to be overcome with atheist work. As a foreign problem, religion was denounced as a weapon cynically used by the enemies of Communism for political ends—above all, to disorient young people with alien values and undermine the unity of Soviet society. Under Brezhnev, however, religion came to be seen as a predominantly spiritual—as opposed to a political or ideological—problem. If the political threat of religious institutions was defused under Stalin, and ideological threat of religious belief was the focus of atheist work under Khrushchev, then under Brezhnev religion came to be perceived as a threat because it underscored the weakness of the party's claims on Soviet spiritual life. Religion became less about institutions and beliefs, and more about culture, tradition, and everyday life. To address religion as a spiritual problem, the atheist establishment expanded the boundaries of what constituted atheism. This new kind of atheism—a spiritual atheism—had to address tradition and heritage, lived experience and spiritual needs, and produce its own cosmology and way of life.

The party recognized that given the new political situation, it needed to address old issues in new ways. This shifted the focus of atheist work to the cultivation of the socialist way of life—a project that emerged in the 1970s within the framework of developed socialism and remained central to Soviet ideological discourse until Gorbachev's introduction of perestroika in 1985. As a concept, the socialist way of life had coalesced over the course of the 1960s within the ideological establishment's debates about the place and nature of byt in the project of building Communism, but it entered into official party discourse at the Twenty-Fifth Party Congress in 1976.[10] In his speech, Brezhnev characterized the socialist way of life as "an atmosphere of genuine collectivism and comradeship, solidarity, the friendship of all the nations and peoples of our country, which grows stronger from day to day, and moral health that makes us strong and steadfast."[11] By the end of the 1970s, the socialist way of life was at the center of ideological discourse, with more than 150 studies on its development and characteristics, and numerous party seminars and conferences devoted to topics like the Socialist Way of Life and Contemporary Ideological War (Moscow, 1974), Socialist Way of Life and Ideological Work (Kiev, 1977), and Socialist Way of Life and Formation of Ideological Convictions among the Youth (Vilnius, 1977).[12]

A defining characteristic of the socialist way of life was its opposition to the bourgeois and, more specifically, American way of life. Indeed, the American Exhibition held in Moscow in 1959, which foregrounded the ideological significance of consumption—perhaps most prominently in the famous "Kitchen Debate" between Khrushchev and Vice President Richard Nixon—was titled "The American Way of Life."[13] The socialist way of life, then, was the product of both internal developments within Soviet ideology, and of the Cold War, which pitted the opposing sides—Communism and capitalism—against one another not just as political and economic systems but as moral orders.[14] As the party philosopher Fedoseev put it, "The competition of socialism and capitalism is not limited only to technological and economic indicators; it includes also the sphere of social ideals and morals, the person's way of life."[15] But before long, as it became clear that the Soviet Union could not win the competition with the American consumer economy, and fell further behind in the race to produce material abundance, Soviet ideology began to frame the superiority of the socialist way of life predominantly in moral and spiritual terms. Even if Soviet citizens were still waiting for their promised single-family apartments, Soviet women had not yet been liberated from housework by household appliances, and central planning had not yet produced a consumer paradise, the Soviet Union surpassed the West in its commitment to collectivism, internationalism, and humanism. Whereas capitalism offered unfair competition, rapacious and irrational consumerism, social anomie, and spiritual emptiness, Communism offered rational consumption, collective cooperation, and spiritual fulfillment through creative labor and leisure.[16]

Yet assertions about the moral and spiritual superiority of the socialist way of life hid the party's anxiety about material shortages, which became all the more dangerous against the background of Soviet people's rising material expectations.[17] The youth, of course, were considered to be most vulnerable to the seduction of consumerism, and thus most in need of ideological guidance. In order to fortify Soviet youth to withstand the corruption of not only material but also spiritual consumerism, the party increasingly articulated the goal of ideological work to be the production of conviction. This was all the more necessary once détente had given way, with the election of Ronald Reagan as the US president, to a renewed ideological standoff with the Soviet Union's Cold War enemy. As a 1982 Central Committee report, "The Formation of Conviction in the Superiority of Socialism in the Contemporary Ideological Battle," put it, Communism's enemies expended a great deal of energy arguing for the moral superiority of capitalism and "putting the positive values of socialism in question."[18] In this context, the inculcation of the socialist way of life was necessary "so that every Soviet person understood deeply, with their whole soul and heart, the historical correctness of socialism."[19]

## *The New God-Seekers*

On April 8, 1970, at a conference at the INA, Iosif Kryvelev (1906–91)—a veteran atheist with roots in the prewar League of the Militant Godless—shared that at a recent meeting of the editorial board of *Science and Religion*, Tendriakov, author of *Apostolic Mission* and also a member of the journal's editorial board, had announced that he "hates militant atheism." Kryvelev found it troubling that a prominent Soviet writer known for works criticizing religion expressed an antipathy toward what Kryvelev considered to be the necessary foundation of Soviet atheism: its militancy. As Kryvelev informed the INA's scientific council, "We would like for all the members of the editorial board to love militant atheism and for themselves to be militant atheists."[20] By 1970, however, Tendriakov was not a lone or marginal voice in his criticism but instead emblematic of an emerging ambivalence about Soviet atheism, even within the atheist apparatus. Indeed, in the context of the political demobilization and ideological disorientation of the late Soviet period, it was Kryvelev's *militant* atheism that was becoming increasingly marginal.

One of the most pressing questions that faced the Soviet ideological establishment in the Brezhnev era was how to manage the creative intelligentsia's growing interest in religion as a repository of spiritual heritage and national tradition. In Russia, this impulse emerged in the 1950s with the Village Prose movement, whose authors decried the desecration of Russian rural life. Depicting the dying countryside in nostalgic tones, Village Prose literature asked whether the loss of traditional culture and the rural way of life was not too high a price to pay for modernity. For writers like Vladimir Soloukhin (1924–97), the ravaged countryside became a symbol of the deep wound that Soviet modernization had inflicted on Russian national culture, and he used powerful images of abandoned churches and destroyed icons as well as forgotten religious customs and rites to make the alienation of modern Soviet people from their national roots concrete and visible.

The questions and themes raised in Village Prose had a clear resonance, especially among some members of the Soviet intelligentsia. As early as 1960, a number of prominent cultural figures initiated a public debate about the place of Russian history and culture in modern Soviet life, setting the stage for what the anthropologists Zhanna Kormina and Sergei Shtyrkov call "the ideology of Soviet retrospectivism."[21] In an article titled "Those Who Forgot Their Roots," writer Iurii Chaplygin questioned the morality of Russian cultural amnesia, while historian Dimitrii Likhachev's article "In the Name of the Future" called on the Soviet public to preserve national monuments—which in the Russian context inherently meant Russian Orthodox spaces and objects—as a civic and patriotic duty.[22] Over the course of the 1960s, the intelligentsia mobilized Soviet society to participate in new cultural initiatives, such as historical preservation and cultural tourism.[23]

For the party, the intelligentsia's god-seeking—whether in the form of literary production or cultural advocacy—presented a serious challenge. What was especially problematic about the intelligentsia's turn to religion was that it cast the historical rupture and cultural amnesia of Soviet modernity within a narrative of national decline.[24] In this way, it became intertwined with an emerging nationalist discourse, and struck a dissonant chord that was difficult to reconcile with the well-worn official narrative that cast religion and the old way of life as something to be discarded on the forward march to Soviet Communism.[25]

As Soviet society's growing interest in spiritual heritage became more apparent, the party tried to address it in two ways. The first approach was to direct, co-opt, and, when necessary, discipline its most threatening expressions.[26] The party used covert strategies to "neutralize" the influence of problematic figures among the creative intelligentsia. For example, a 1976 KGB report on the "Russophile" painter Il'ia Glazunov (1930–2017), who was getting unwelcome foreign attention, suggested that perhaps it would be "advisable" to "involve him in some civic activity, such as the creation of a museum of Russian furniture in Moscow."[27] But the most explicit and successful example of the party's effort to co-opt the public interest in religious and spiritual heritage was the creation of the All-Russian Society for the Preservation of Monuments of History and Culture (Vserossiiskoe Obshchestvo Okhrany Pamiatnikov Istorii i Kul'tury, or VOOPIiK) in 1965.[28] In many ways, the VOOPIiK, which eventually became one of the largest Soviet civic organizations (counting fifteen million members by 1985), was a response to the creative intelligentsia's increasingly vocal denunciation of ideological iconoclasm.[29] Though it lacked the power to make policy and ultimately remained under the control of the state, its activities—from tourism to education and restoration—provided the opportunity for Soviet people to encounter religious objects and spaces, and created the space for a public conversation about religion in Soviet life.

The party's second strategy sought to appropriate the symbolic capital of religion by transforming it into an ideologically acceptable form—namely, culture. To do this, the ideological establishment tried to articulate the difference between a healthy interest in spiritual heritage and an ideologically suspect "idealization" of religion. *Science and Religion*, for example, attempted to direct public interest in spiritual heritage into more innocuous channels by offering new rubrics like "The Holy Sites of Our Motherland" (*Sviatyni nashei rodiny*). As Anatolii Ivanov, the journal's editor through most of the Brezhnev era, explained, "The main task is to develop research into the spiritual values of the past, in which the religious and the aesthetic are deeply intertwined, in order to free everything historically and aesthetically valuable of its religious wrapping."[30] As Ivanov noted, it was crucial to distinguish between religion as unscientific worldview and religion as culture, because "the interest of Soviet people and especially the youth [in these subjects] has grown sharply," and the journal needed "to give people the right orientation on these far from simple questions."[31] Within the framework of Soviet Communism, religion could be reconciled with Soviet life as a cultural artifact, but not as a living faith and dynamic social institution.

Arguably the biggest conceptual hurdle in the ideological establishment's effort to incorporate spiritual heritage into the official Soviet narrative was atheism itself. At a meeting to discuss *Science and Religion*, historian A. V.

Mel'nikova highlighted the intimate link between religion and culture, and challenged atheists to consider how atheism could oppose religion's traditions, aesthetics, and emotional appeal. "Religion uses everything to defend itself," Mel'nikova warned. "Everything created by humanity . . . is presented by our enemies as the achievement of religion, as proof of its high and influential place in the history of humanity. We need to oppose this with something."[32] The problem for Soviet atheists—one they readily acknowledged—was that in contrast to religion, they were latecomers to the ideological battlefield. Moreover, even if atheists could neutralize religion by reframing it as a cultural artifact, they also had to articulate atheism's positive role in spiritual culture by producing a narrative that gave atheism historical continuity and cultural authenticity.[33]

To do this, Soviet atheism required a robust creative apparatus to produce a compelling atheist culture. But while in theory the party had an army of intelligentsia cadres, in practice it consistently failed to mobilize creative power for atheist work.[34] The scientific intelligentsia had always disappointed the ideological establishment with its lack of enthusiasm for atheist work, and the creative intelligentsia was even worse. The ideological establishment lamented that not only did the creative intelligentsia stand "on the sidelines" of the atheist project; it also produced work that created a positive image of religion in Soviet society. Indeed, in a 1971 report to the Central Committee titled "On Flawed Estimations of Religion and Atheism in Certain Works of Literature and Art," the INA noted that the intelligentsia was not just sympathetic to religion but portrayed it as the center of the country's spiritual heritage as well. This was evident in the "growing interest in idealistic philosophers" (such as Vladimir Soloviev and Sergei Bulgakov), a revived interest in tourism to sacred places, and an "uncritical" view of religion in certain works of contemporary literature, like Vera Panova's (1905–73) *The Legend of Feodosia* (*Skazanie o feodosii*, 1967) as well as Soloukhin's *Native Beauty, Why We Need to Study and Preserve Historical Monuments* (*Rodnaia krasota, dlia chego nado izuchat' i berech' pamiatniki stariny*, 1966) and *Letters from a Russian Museum* (*Pis'ma iz Russkogo muzeia*, 1967).[35] Soloukhin, the report underscored, even went so far as to call atheists "iconoclasts" in a Soviet publication.

More troubling still, from the party's perspective, was the fact that the intelligentsia's attitude seemed to be spreading, so that "in certain circles, it is becoming 'fashionable,' a sign of good form, to have an icon in one's apartment, . . . to glorify the 'historical accomplishments' of the church and 'moral merits' of religion, and conversely, express irony and even distaste toward atheism."[36] As the literary critic Feliks Kuznetsov put it in a 1972 article in *Science and Religion*, "As our material problems find solutions, questions of moral upbringing and spiritual values become more important." Soviet writers searched for answers, but "not always successfully," instead finding themselves entangled in "antihistorical, nonclass illusions about our historical past and present, the patriarchal peasantry and that abstraction—the 'national spirit.'"[37] Even those few among the creative intelligentsia who had participated in the atheist project under Khrushchev, like Tendriakov, were becoming estranged from the atheist project.

In the 1950s and 1960s, Tendriakov had occupied a peculiar place in Soviet literature by producing atheist works in the Village Prose genre.[38] Though also focused on rural themes, Tendriakov's works had a decidedly different message than most of his contemporaries. Unlike writers such as Soloukhin, who cast rural life as a repository of authentic spirituality and national heritage, Tendriakov portrayed idyllic images of village culture and nostalgia for religious traditions as a misguided effort to escape from modernity into a world destined to die out.[39] But while Tendriakov had started out as a champion of Soviet atheism, by the late 1960s he had become an increasingly vocal critic of the atheist project, producing works like *Apostolic Mission* that questioned the material and spiritual values of Soviet Communism, and even denouncing militant atheism. Following the unfortunate *Science and Religion* meeting where he clashed with Kryvelev over militant atheism, Tendriakov sent a letter to the Central Committee outlining his criticism of Soviet atheism in full. In it, Tendriakov argued that atheist militancy could have dangerous political consequences, and instead called for greater cooperation with believers in the project of unifying Soviet society. "So-called 'militant atheism' in its existing form," Tendriakov wrote, was "harmful" and "dangerous" because it alienated believers, creating divisions and tensions that could undermine social solidarity. In decades of atheist work, "we, alas, have not been able to overcome god," whereas the number of believers continued to grow, from twenty, thirty, or forty million, to perhaps as many as a hundred million. Who were these millions, Tendriakov asked, "Our enemies, enemies of our order, our politics? Or after all, not?"[40]

What should the party do about the fact that millions of its citizens remained religious? So far, Tendriakov wrote, the party's approach had relied above all on repressive administrative measures carried out by poorly trained atheist cadres. Such cadres were "not only ignorant on religious questions but often consider[ed] this ignorance an achievement." And since such an atheist was both uninformed and incompetent, the only thing that remained for them to do was to "sneak away, hide, stay silent, and quietly kick the enemy with their administrative boot." But, Tendriakov asked, did not the threat of such militant atheism outweigh its benefits? Since "no one doubts that the contemporary believer is not an enemy," and since religion continued to be an important part of the lives of millions of Soviet citizens, Tendriakov argued that not taking this into account would amount to "criminal carelessness." He described his conversations with students, artists, writers, and scientists, who, while not themselves believers, sympathized with religion.

Tendriakov maintained that atheist aggression would lead "uninformed observers" to think that "in the battle of atheism and religion, the truth is on the side of religion." This, in turn, would give rise to a growing number of people "sympathetic" to religion, "of whom there are several times more than believers themselves." Is it not better, then, "to support [religion] since it carries to the masses human ideals, even if primitive ones?" The primary goal of Soviet religious policy, Tendriakov proposed, should be to "unite with believers on the basis of common human norms of morality and justice, which are shared by religion and Communism."[41]

In his report to the Central Committee "On the Occasion of V. F. Tendriakov's Assessment of the State of Contemporary Atheist Work," the INA's director, Okulov, conceded that Tendriakov was correct about Soviet society's growing interest in religion, but he disagreed with his assessment that this new sympathetic attitude was "the result of deviations in the battle against religion." Okulov explained to the Central Committee that Tendriakov lost faith in the atheist mission because he did not understand the full complexity of the secularization process. "The process of overcoming religion turned out to be, for a whole host of reasons, more complicated and long lasting than was expected back when atheism in our country was becoming a mass phenomenon," noted Okulov. While the "general tendency" has followed the pattern of decline, it was "a complicated process, which in certain periods and certain conditions, does not exclude a certain increase in believers." Hence, overcoming religion "does not only move along the path of believers becoming atheists but [also] on the path of religious views becoming deformed and diluted." Because he did not appreciate the complexity of secularization, Okulov argued, Tendriakov presented religion as "something that has an almost-mystical vitality, power, and tenacity." Tendriakov's thinking was driven by the "logic of capitulation to religion," which leads in the end to its continued preservation. If taken to its logical conclusion, "we should be thinking not about overcoming religion but [instead] about 'cementing society,' divided among believers and unbelievers." But grounding atheist work only in universal moral principles, Okulov explained, ignored not only the "worldview functions" of Marxist atheism but also its class essence, contradicting the Marxist-Leninist model of historical development. In trying to reduce Marxist philosophy simply to "anthropology, axiology, to only humanistic problems," Tendriakov was proposing to "throw the theory and laws of the objective development of the world overboard." For Okulov, the Soviet project could not make such accommodations with religion. Indeed, he emphatically disagreed with Tendriakov's position that administrative repression posed the greatest danger to Soviet Communism, asserting instead that "the more serious threat emerging today is the benign, conciliatory attitude toward religion, which creates the foundations for the activation of the church [and] emergence among certain parts of the intelligentsia of God-seeking tendencies."[42]

Since the intelligentsia had tremendous moral authority in Soviet society, it had significant influence—which in turn could lead the Soviet youth astray.

Yet even if the party could criticize Tendriakov and the creative intelligentsia for their "unmilitant" position on religion, it could not make the issues they raised disappear. Moreover, although the redefinition of religion in Soviet public discourse was partly driven by the intelligentsia's cultural production and social mobilization, the party itself contributed to the process, too, since in its effort to control the emerging enthusiasm for spiritual heritage, it sanctioned religion in public life in the form of culture. As Kormina and Shtyrkov note, this reframing of religion in ideologically acceptable terms—that is, in the secular form of museum expositions and historic monuments—"nevertheless brought into the public sphere a positive image of objects of religious origin."[43]

The Brezhnev era, then, was a critical turning point in religion's place in Soviet Communism. Catriona Kelly, in her study of "socialist churches" in the Soviet period, shows how under Brezhnev, churches were redefined from being vestiges of a shameful and backward past (and therefore, in their desacralized form, best transformed into socially beneficial spaces like libraries, clubs, or even storage facilities for agricultural products) to becoming sacred sites of national memory that society had an obligation to preserve for future generations.[44] This "recoding" of religious symbols and objects "into a language acceptable for Soviet propaganda" was not just the work of the creative intelligentsia. It was also the work of a broad network of Soviet cultural cadres—from museum specialists, tour guides, and enlightenment lecturers, to the staff of local libraries and Houses of Culture—who saw the objective of the Soviet person's encounter with religious culture to be the cultivation of "aesthetic and patriotic emotions," rather than religious or nationalist sympathies or commitments.[45] This blurring of boundaries between religion as "Russian culture" and "Russian Orthodoxy," however, created space to contest the meaning of religion and destabilize the official Soviet narrative.

## *Soviet Youth as Spiritual Consumers*

On April 16, 1971, shortly after the Twenty-Fourth Party Congress, the Leningrad Komsomol organization convened a seminar to discuss how the latest party pronouncements should direct atheist work with Soviet youth.[46] Among those chosen to address the audience of young propaganda cadres were two prominent Leningrad atheists: Mikhail Shakhnovich (1911–92), professor of scientific atheism at Leningrad State University, and Nikolai Gordienko (1929–2011), chair of the Department of Scientific Atheism at Herzen Pedagogical Institute.[47] Shakhnovich had begun his career during the militant cultural milieu of the early Soviet period and was one of the founders of Leningrad's GMIRA, where he remained in the role of deputy director for decades.[48]

Gordienko, on the other hand, was a product of the Khrushchev era, carried by the antireligious campaign to become a prominent atheist author (including of the textbook *Foundations of Scientific Atheism*). Both Shakhnovich and Gordienko had expertise in religion along with experience in atheist work targeting young people, and they spoke to their Komsomol audience about why religion was still part of Soviet life and the demands that the new era of developed socialism placed on the Komsomol.

For Shakhnovich, the continued existence of religion in the Soviet Union was the product of two problems: the subversive efforts of the capitalist opponent to use religion to undermine Soviet power, and the ideological demobilization of Soviet society in general and Soviet youth in particular. Fifty years after the revolution, Shakhnovich explained, there were no more exploiting classes, no internal enemies of Communism, but religion remained a weak link—an alien ideology inside Soviet borders. Religion, then, was a central tool in the global "war of ideas" because it was the channel through which the capitalist world could sow divisions within Soviet society. But the continued existence of religion in Soviet life also had an internal cause: the spiritual emptiness and ideological indifference of Soviet youth. Unlike Shakhnovich's generation, which had been forged by the revolution, Stalin's Five-Year Plan, and the war, the new generation had grown up in the relative political stability and material comfort of the 1950s and 1960s. The youth had been infected by the consumerist fetishization of things (*veshchism*), and had begun to "worship goods in and of themselves."[49] As a result, Soviet youth had become spiritually empty. They no longer cared about building Communism; all that mattered was "acquisitiveness, acquiring things," in the name of which they were "willing to sacrifice anything." Shakhnovich qualified this contention by saying that while for some the corruption of consumerism turned material satisfaction into an end in itself, for others the resulting spiritual emptiness produced despair. It was in seeking refuge from this spiritual emptiness that some young people mistakenly turned to religion. The power of religion, then, was no longer in its truth but rather in its function. "Religion does not argue over whether God created the earth in six days or six million years," Shakhnovich explained. "It puts the question deeper, about the meaning of human existence, about a person's relationship to social reality"—which was why young people could master the scientific knowledge they acquired in Soviet schools and still turn to religion to find spiritual meaning. In this way, religion distracted Soviet youth "from earthly affairs," instead focusing their attention on the world beyond and thereby blinding them to the possibility of "building paradise" in this world.

Given this, what was the mission of the Komsomol? Shakhnovich observed that the transformation of ideologically undetermined young people into conscious Communists would not happen on its own. It required active ideological intervention. It was incorrect to think, Shakhnovich asserted, "that honest, saintly people, who will build Communist society appear all on their own." And just as the new person would not simply appear, survivals would not merely disappear. Shakhnovich noted that those who thought that there could be no more survivals after half a century of Soviet life missed the point.

> They think that everything depends on whether a person lived before 1917 or not, and that if someone is eighteen to twenty years old right now, then he cannot have any survivals since he does not even know this past. In reality, the situation is quite different. People can live in socialist society, but have the consciousness not just of 1917 but [also] of the seventeenth century. There are people whose understanding of the world is so ignorant and backward that even in bourgeois society it would be considered a survival.

The purpose of atheist work was thus not to "divide people into believers and unbelievers, with the first building Communism and the second reaching for heaven," but rather to show both believers and unbelievers that "building Communism [is] the purpose of their life." Faith in Communism had to become an inner conviction—and only then would "illusions about heaven and the afterlife and the kingdom of heaven fade away and disappear."[50]

How did Shakhnovich propose to transform ideological indifference and spiritual searching into ideological conviction and spiritual wealth? To begin with, he argued that it was necessary to "replace the religious way of life with the Soviet way of life." Religious phenomena had to be confronted with Soviet ones—Easter with the all-union *subbotnik*, and baptism with the socialist registration of newborns—and this confrontation had to take place "not on the pages of a book but in real life." Yet Shakhnovich also maintained that it was not enough to replace one set of symbols and practices with another. Atheist conviction had to come from within.

> We have to strive for all people, and especially young people, to live a beautiful spiritual life. If a person understands his work as just chasing after a piece of bread and does not see beyond it the shining goal of his labor, does not acknowledge his obligation to his motherland, does not feel himself a part of the Soviet people, then he will feel his life to be empty, and this emptiness will lead him in one way or another to deformations. Maybe not straight to religion, but some kind of survivals will be resurrected inside him.

Since the spiritual refuge offered by religion was illusory, Komsomol cadres had to direct the spiritual searching of Soviet youth toward the socialist way of life, and the spiritual life of Soviet people had to be made "as rich as possible." All "scientific knowledge, art, and all the [cultural] wealth" had to be mobilized to "overcome religious survivals."[51] But freeing Soviet youth from survivals was not the end toward which ideological work was to be directed. It was the means through which the new Soviet person would come to see herself as a member of a unified Soviet community, and develop the conviction that this community was morally and spiritually above all other alternatives.

In reconstructing Shakhnovich's ideal, it is difficult not to see his efforts to reproduce his own ideological conviction in his audience as a missionary project. After all, the vision espoused was not about adherence to a prescribed set of norms but rather about an internal conversion to a comprehensive worldview in which building Communism was understood as the meaning of life. Indeed, reflecting later on his life's work, Shakhnovich described the Communist project as "our Reformation."[52] But equally notable is the growing divide between Shakhnovich, a member of the first Soviet generation forged in the militant culture of the 1920s and 1930s, and his audience, the Khrushchev generation, whose ideas about spiritual fulfillment were connected with values beyond Communist construction, and included satisfying leisure, private space, and material welfare. Whereas Shakhnovich and his generation were committed to Communism despite constant deprivation and shortages, the postwar generation was growing indifferent to Communist values despite relative abundance. For Shakhnovich, then, atheist work with Soviet youth was about ideological discipline, and the primary objective was to create a subject who could withstand the seduction of consumerism, in both its material and its spiritual forms.

Gordienko offered another interpretation of the obstacles that stood in the way of atheism's triumph over religion. He urged his audience to stop looking at religion in the abstract, and instead examine the concrete reasons behind why people turned to religion for answers, solutions, and fulfillment. To illustrate his point, Gordienko shared the results of a recent sociological study. In order to understand the religious motivations of Leningraders, local cadres studied what happened at the chapel of the "notorious" Blessed Kseniia, one of the most popular religious figures in Leningrad.[53] Even though the chapel itself had been turned into a workshop and storage space in the Soviet period, locals continued to leave notes with prayers addressed to Blessed Kseniia. When local atheists gathered and studied these notes, Gordienko informed his audience, they found that people turned to religion for "purely everyday affairs":

> What do people ask of her? If we leave aside the notes of believers that say simply "Kseniia, pray for me," then the content of the notes is quite concrete. For example: I am applying to university, help me to pass the exams; dear Kseniia, I am planning to apply for a chauffeur license, help me; I want to get into the textile institute, help me and I will believe in you; or dear Kseniia, my son has started to drink and got tied up with bad people, help him get out of it; my daughter's husband is a drunk, help her, and so forth.[54]

Gordienko proposed that the notes people left for Blessed Kseniia were "a cry of the soul," but were in essence no different than "petitions to local authorities [*mestkom*]." For those "who have gotten mixed up in life" and could not find a solution to their problems in the Soviet system, Blessed Kseniia became an alternate "local authority," another channel through which their appeal might be heard and resolved.

Gordienko argued that the more atheists helped people in need, "the less they will need to appeal to the supernatural." Komsomol cadres should see "the creation of friendly, sincere relationships—what in comrade Brezhnev's report was called the creation of a comradely atmosphere"—as itself a form of atheist work. Moreover, atheist work had to extend to those whose worldview position was undetermined—the "waiverers" and indifferent—since their lack of conviction made them ideologically and spiritually vulnerable. "It is from this gray mass that people are recruited into seminaries," Gordienko explained, and the Komsomol's mission was to bring this gray mass of indifferent Soviet youth into the socialist way of life.[55]

That the party perceived the gray mass of indifferent youth as a serious political problem can be seen in the growing attention and resources it was devoting to the problem. This was evident, on the one hand, in the party's commissioned studies of the demographic, social, and cultural profile of Soviet youth, and, on the other hand, in the intensification and expansion of projects concerned with their ideological upbringing. Increasingly, the traditional education young people received in schools and universities was accompanied by extracurricular disciplinary efforts that included, alongside atheist education, patriotic and military education (to instill civic unity) as well as international education (to combat nationalism).

To understand the spiritual world of Soviet youth and find the channels through which they could be guided in the correct direction, the INA conducted a two-year study on "the process of forming atheist convictions among students," the findings of which Okulov reported to the Central Committee in 1974.[56] Okulov observed that while the majority of Soviet young people were "free of religious survivals," the situation was more complicated beneath the surface, since oftentimes indifference toward religion was connected with "an indifference to worldview questions as a whole—with a peculiar kind of spiritual and ideological emptiness [*bezdukhovnost'* and *bezideinost'*], with the mistaken view that the most important goal in a person's life is professional advancement and nothing else."[57]

Other young people had an "accommodating attitude" toward manifestations of religiosity, and especially toward religious holidays and rituals. The report noted that among those surveyed, "it turned out that a certain part of the student body sees in religious rituals and holidays a folk custom . . . that preserves national traditions and emotions [and] establishes a connection between the past and the present." This "worrisome" trend was part of the broader discovery of surprising patterns in the transformation of Soviet religiosity. "There are instances when certain students, formerly unbelievers or indifferent to religion, begin to exhibit interest in religious views and religious rituals," Okulov noted, and this interest is often born of a "mistaken moral and worldview 'searching.'" Moreover, Okulov noted, religious organizations capitalized on this searching. They spread the "mistaken view" that "religion is the only repository of morality," which even under socialism "regulates moral behavior, above all in the sphere of personal morality." But for the party, the most worrisome trend was that young people's interest in religion sometimes became a form of "rebellion [*frondism*] that aspires to originality," which could in turn lead to ideological demobilization and even political dissent.[58]

The lion's share of the blame for the persistence of religiosity among Soviet youth was attributed to the influence of the intelligentsia. On Soviet television as well as in Soviet films and novels, artists "idealized" religious ceremonies and traditions, which "revive[d] a certain fashion for religious rituals, symbols, and religious objects—icons, crosses, and so forth." Surveys of humanities students showed that they were especially susceptible to "idealizing" religion on aesthetic grounds, since their admiration for "those masterpieces that are historically tied to religion" led to "the unjustified positive appraisal of religion's role in history and culture, in the development of society, and doubts about the necessity of atheist work." One student explained that depictions of religion in contemporary films and works of art "give aesthetic satisfaction both to the believer and unbeliever." Their "fancies," the report argued, were evidence of "ideological immaturity, an amorphous worldview and moral convictions, and sometimes of a low spiritual culture." This was all the more worrying because it was precisely arts and humanities students who should have been "the reserve of our creative intelligentsia, which is supposed to develop and propagandize art from the position of the scientific materialist, socialist worldview." Perhaps most disturbing was that a "certain section of the intelligentsia"—such as Soloukhin—tried to "pass the religious for the national," which led to religion becoming not just fashion but also "an expression of antisocialist and nationalist attitudes."[59]

Finally, the report turned its focus to the ideological establishment itself. Not only did atheist education in schools and universities still leave much to be desired, but the very focus of atheist work had been misdirected. While atheists concentrated on believers, they had overlooked those young people who "consider themselves unbelievers, have a negative attitude to the religious worldview, [and] are unfamiliar with religious rituals, but do not yet have the necessary scientific atheist knowledge and convictions." These young people were unbelievers, but they lacked atheist conviction, and thus were "unable to guard against clerical and sectarian propaganda, sometimes even [falling] under its pernicious influence."[60]

As a whole, the report produced an ambivalent portrait of Soviet youth. Some young people idealized religion for its cultural and aesthetic value; others rejected religion as such, but their consciousness was "littered with various kinds of superstitions"; a third group was indifferent to religion, but this indifference extended to worldview and ideological questions in general; while for a fourth group, the interest in religion was connected with nationalism, which threatened to become a rebellion against the socialist way of life. What tied these different categories together was the absence of "a deep and unified scientific materialist worldview and firm atheist convictions."[61] Increasingly, the atheist apparatus saw indifference not just as a social problem but as a political one, too. That indifference was especially prevalent among the youth only underscored its political threat, since it suggested that the Soviet system was not effectively transmitting its values to the next generation.

Over the course of the 1970s, the figure of the indifferent youth became an important concern for the party and thus a central trope in ideological debates.[62] Two characteristics marked someone as ideologically indifferent. The first was a "neutral" position on religion that expressed itself as "nonintervention" in religious questions, grounded in the view that either the person "knows little about the issue" or "does not have conviction in what he knows, and therefore cannot or will not defend his views."[63] But more than neutrality, the defining characteristic of ideological indifference was spiritual consumerism, which manifested above all in unbelievers observing religious rites. Iurii Gurov, one of the most prolific authors on the subject of youth indifference, offered examples of the ways in which indifference underpinned unprincipled behavior: a Komsomol girl who went to get baptized on a dare in exchange for a kilogram of candy, or an engineer who, for "mercenary reasons," had a church wedding because his in-laws promised him a car.[64] For other young people, Gurov explained, religious practice had become a form of entertainment, simply "another pretext to have some fun," and they went to church "as they would to the theater or a holiday party."[65] To underscore his point, he quoted an Orthodox priest who complained that young people "come to church as if to a circus: made up and dressed up. They laugh in the church. They do not know the prayers and do not want to repeat them after the priest. What is the point of such a baptism? They see it as a secular and not a church affair."[66]

The spiritual consumerism and indifference of Soviet youth also became a common trope in satirical articles, cartoons, and propaganda posters. One poster depicted a couple leaving a church while, off to the side, a young woman cried to her mother, "But he gave me his Komsomol word that he would marry me!" A short poem accompanied the image, noting that the young man should have chosen long ago whether he would be a religious devotee (*bogomolets*) or member of the Komsomol.[67] Another poster showed a young man straddling a divided world, with modernity on one side (portrayed as a modern cityscape bathed in light) and backwardness on the other (illustrated by a church cast in darkness). Whereas modernity meant getting married in a Wedding Palace and registering your newborn at the ZAGS office with a socialist ceremony, the poster showed that alongside these socialist rituals, the young man also got married and baptized his child in a church. Beneath, the slogan reads, "A hypocrite lives his whole life between the heavens and the earth [*Tak i zhivet khanzha inoi, vsiu zhizn' mezh nebom i zemlei*]" (see figure 7.1).[68]

While some construed the passive participation of unbelievers in religious rites as harmless, Gurov explained that such behavior reflected an undeveloped political consciousness. Komsomol members who identified as unbelievers or even militant atheists showed by their participation in religious rites that their atheism was "only words that have not yet become convictions or a life program."[69] They would be cured only once they internalized the atheist values that would make it impossible for them to act against their convictions.

As Soviet atheists grappled with the problem of ideological indifference, they sought to broaden the scope of atheist work. "Atheist education cannot just be reduced to work among believers," one atheist commented at a meeting of the INA's local bases. "It carries broader functions, the whole population needs it, and it seems that we should include [within it] the cultivation of atheist conviction." An atheist from Stavropol' outlined the problem in greater detail:

> We are missing criteria for atheist conviction. Why are we all atheists? A person says, "I do not believe in God" and is considered an atheist. But can a person be considered a convinced atheist if he thinks that atheist work in our country is not an urgent issue, that religious issues are the lot of just a few people? People who say, "You know what, atheism can wait, we have more urgent matters." Can we really consider such people convinced atheists?! From such views, there is but one step to actions like baptizing a son or daughter, or having [a son] circumcised, and when you ask [them] how this happened, you hear that this "atheist" was on a business trip, and the child was taken to the village and everything was done without his agreement. And it is possible to find thousands of such excuses. This is what the degree of atheist conviction consists of, so that such things could never happen. . . . You get a paradoxical situation . . . when a famous writer does something like this. But how many are there who are not famous and who have such opinions, and in certain circles expound the view that atheism is not particularly urgent?[70]

Once the ultimate goal of atheist work became the production of atheist conviction, atheists envisioned the process in two stages. The first stage—which

FIGURE 7.1. A. Tsvetkov, "This Is How a Hypocrite Lives His Life—Between Heaven and Earth" (*Tak i zhivet khanzha inoi, vsiu zhizn' mezh nebom i zemlei*). Poem by A. Vnukov. Moscow: Plakat, 1970s.

had guided atheist work thus far—focused on "overcoming the reproduction of religiosity."[71] Paradoxically, it was the very success of this first stage that had produced indifference and required the second stage of atheist work: replacing indifference with atheist conviction. Gurov explained that indifference, as a social phenomenon, was "contradictory." On the one hand, "it is the result of the enormous work, done under the direction of our party, to tear religious believers away from religion—which can be evaluated as a positive phenomenon." On the other hand, it is "the result of insufficiencies of atheist work in the upbringing of irreligious youth," and, as such, is a "negative phenomenon that gets in the way of the confirmation of young people's civic and ideological-political consciousness and activism." Gurov noted that whereas unbelief was passive, the task of atheist work was to produce a militant position, since "to stand firmly on atheist positions means to decisively, mercilessly, and most important, consciously and consistently break with the neutral [and] compromising attitude to religion and [religious] practices."[72]

What exactly constituted atheist conviction? Gurov argued that the "knowledge" acquired through education and enlightenment was not enough. To illustrate this point, he shared the story of a Baptist university student who received a perfect score on her scientific atheism exam. When asked how she could reconcile her mastery of scientific atheism with her religious beliefs, she replied that she had been tested on her knowledge of the material, but that "not once was anyone interested in my views on the issues. They evaluated my knowledge, not my convictions."[73] In order for passive unbelief to become active atheism, knowledge had to be "united with the emotional factor," so that there would be "confidence in the truth of this knowledge," and based on this knowledge, there would emerge "a negative stereotype about religion and religious practices." Knowledge, Gurov observed, had to be transformed into an "atheist worldview position and set of convictions," so that these convictions would, in the words of Marx and Engels, become "bonds, from which it would be impossible to break free without tearing apart one's own heart."[74] A person with atheist conviction would not "confuse a religious rite with a national tradition, the religious with the national, [because] he assumes a precise class and party position in relationship to any religious idea and any religious rite."[75] This atheism, in the words of another theorist of indifference, Soloviev, was "not some sort of bugbear [*zhupel*] aimed against religion" but rather "an important aspect of the spiritual world of an educated, cultured person that manifests in an active life position [and] the conscious, creative participation . . . in the battle for all that is progressive." The "main marker of a Soviet person's authentic atheism" was "the confirmation through behavior, deeds, and the entire way of life of the true values of socialism."[76]

If indifference was the space in which alien ideas, practices, and commitments could take root and flourish, then atheist conviction needed to fill this space with a firm worldview position. For a person with atheist conviction, contradictions between beliefs, words, and deeds were impossible. This made the production of atheist conviction—especially among youth—critical to the production of Communist conviction—and hence the reproduction of Soviet Communism.[77]

## *Unmilitant Atheism*

Over the course of the Brezhnev era, consensus about what atheism was, how it should be implemented—or indeed its role in the greater project of building Communism—began to come apart. Sociological studies revealed that despite decades of administrative restrictions and propaganda campaigns, religion—both in its traditional forms and in new spiritual and religious movements—remained a fact of Soviet life. Okulov shared statistics compiled by the CRA that showed that "despite the intensification" of atheist work during the 1960s, religiosity was on the rise in as many as thirty regions in the country, including Moscow. "The church is not laying down its arms and not leaving the field of battle," Okulov warned, and therefore atheists could not "fall into a state of anabiosis."[78]

By the 1970s, the picture looked even worse. In even the most developed regions in the country—Moscow, Gorky, Kharkov, Penza, and Kursk, among others—as many as 40 to 50 percent of newborns were being baptized, yet as Okulov acknowledged, "We are unable to give serious, concrete recommendations that could significantly enrich our propaganda."[79] Of even greater concern was the fact that religion seemed to be revitalizing—it was not just being reproduced inside religious communities but also attracting outsiders, including young people. Some even entered clerical life, which meant that not only was the clergy was reproducing itself but it was becoming younger. The vitality of the church meant that "millions of people are still drawn to religion. In Moscow region every other newborn is baptized. In certain regions, this percentage is higher and growing. We need to make sense of this, because this is a big, serious problem for government and dialectics."[80] Forced to revisit the familiar question of why, after more than fifty years of Soviet power, religion survived and even thrived in such a "cultured and politically developed country," the atheist establishment sought new answers.[81]

The problem, however, was not so much with the answer as with the question. As atheists acquired a more robust portrait of Soviet religious life through sociological studies, they became more vocal about the fact that Marxist-Leninist historical materialism failed to explain the reality they encountered on the ground. To begin with, religion had a much more complicated relationship with economic development than the Marxist model had proposed. Whereas Marxism presented religion as a product of poverty, atheists noted that spiritual needs often increased with material well-being. Indeed, an atheist from Moldova reported that religiosity was highest in rich villages:

"Comrades! What is going on here? We attempted to study economic markers of the village, and came to the conclusion that with the rise in the well-being of Soviet people, with high levels of material satisfaction, with the improvement of the quality of life, [Soviet people's] spiritual needs also rise, and we must satisfy them."[82] The believer also did not have the fixed characteristics still being reproduced in atheist propaganda. As atheists devoted more attention to the "spiritual profile" of the modern Soviet believer, it became clear that believers were not necessarily socially marginal elements—alcoholics, parasites, or sectarians—but instead could be exemplary workers, respected members of their community, and even party members.[83] They were young as well as old; men as well as women; members of the intelligentsia as well as the "unenlightened" masses; urban dwellers living in central Soviet cities as well as rural folk from the country's distant peripheries.

Atheists also learned that to find religion, they did not need to go on ethnographic expeditions to distant villages, because religion was hiding in plain sight even in the center of the Soviet Union. The Moscow city CRA plenipotentiary Aleksei Plekhanov reported that between 1971 and 1976, more than four hundred thousand religious rites—baptisms, marriages, and funerals—had been registered in the city of Moscow alone.[84] These figures did not include those Muscovites who did not register rites or registered them in other regions in order to avoid problems at home.[85] The statistics also did not factor in other participants in the rite, who also fell under religious influence. Plekhanov pointed out that even if just four people—the parents and godparents—took part in a religious ceremony, then between January and September 1976 alone, eighty thousand Soviet citizens participated in religious rites in Moscow. And religious rites were not the only evidence of religiosity in the city. An inspection of atheist work in Moscow's Krasnogvardeiskii district turned up "holy wells" in the city's Kolomenskii Park, to which believers would make "pilgrimages" to procure "holy water." Local officials tried to put an end to this by filling the springs with concrete, but time and again the wells were reopened and people returned. Plekhanov produced photographs surreptitiously taken at the site as proof.[86] By the 1970s, then, atheists had to concede that religion was not a marginal survival on the edges of modernity but rather a complex, living part of Soviet life—even in Moscow, the very center of Soviet Communism.

The area where things were especially unclear—and that highlighted the tensions within the atheist project—was the problem of rituals. Even with the widespread introduction of socialist rituals, young people continued to observe religious rites and atheists did not know what to do when they "encountered this question in practice": "So we know that the [socialist] wedding ritual is very necessary and very good, but it is not as solemn and festive as in the church, even if there is some emotion and solemnity in it. And what about other rituals? It should not be just atheists who work on these issues."[87] Still, behind the customary official denunciations of religious rituals, including reminders to party and Komsomol members about their charter obligations, in practice those charged with disciplining ideological infractions were often more ambivalent. *Pravda* editorials continued to criticize those who "publicly supported atheism yet behind closed doors participated in religious rites" for their ideological passivity, but behind closed doors, the party's own position was inconsistent.[88]

At a 1967 conference of directors of Houses of Atheism, one participant asked Lisavtsev, one of the Central Committee's curators on religious questions, whether it was still permitted to criticize Communists for observing religious rites, and "how to best handle such a delicate affair." Lisavtsev pointed out that the party's position on the matter was clear: "With regard to this delicate issue there is a directive from Lenin. He is for expelling those who participate in religious rituals from the party. As for publications, we have never shied away from openly criticizing our own deficiencies. This speaks of our strength, not of our weakness."[89] Yet while the party toed the party line, cadres within the CRA—a government institution—were less categorical. Faced with a similar question at an atheist seminar, CRA deputy chair Ivan Brazhnik was more hesitant. "I can cite many examples where Komsomol cards are presented [at a baptism] because there is no other document, and one must present documents at a baptism," Brazhnik observed. "There are many incidents of unreligious parents baptizing children, the reasons [behind this] are varied, and responses in such incidents should likewise be varied. There is one level of demands and punishment for Communists and Komsomol members, and another for those not in the party." But when asked whether a party member should fulfill the dying wish of his believing father or mother to be "buried with a priest," Brazhnik answered, "I think that he should."[90] In an even more telling example, Plekhanov reported to CRA chair Kuroedov that in 1974, a Moscow CRA official had a religious funeral for his father in Moscow's Troitskaia church that was attended by several council officials.[91] The problem of rituals, then, tested individual commitments to the party's ideological dictates, even among the very people whose role it was to overcome religion and inculcate atheism.[92]

While the INA struggled to reformulate the atheist mission in response to new social and political realities, local cadres criticized the center for failing to provide guidance. Atheists attending INA conferences to get practical advice usually came away disappointed. At one conference, the chair of the atheist council at Moscow's "Red Banner" factory complained that while INA atheists posed questions and relayed information, they did not offer answers.[93] A Komsomol cadre from Moscow observed, "From the point of view of Marxism, religion stems from poverty and ignorance; however, today we are rich and live relatively well, but people continue to go to God."[94] At another conference, an atheist from the Moscow regional party committee asked about criteria of religiosity, and whether religiosity should be measured by church income, rituals, or the presence of icons.[95] Atheist cadres also complained about stagnation in the development of atheist theory and methods. An Estonian atheist noted that atheist material still in circulation from the Khrushchev era, from atheist books to lecture programs, was unusable, no new atheist material was being produced.[96] Another Znanie lecturer, a school principal from Zagorsk, agreed: "Take a plan from ten years ago, and you will see the same points that appear in current plans. Why? Because people do not know what to do, or rather, they know *what* to do, but they do not know *how* [to do it]." Life, she concluded, "demands concrete answers to concrete questions."[97]

It was also becoming less clear how much importance the party really invested in atheist work. Okulov asserted that even as the party made statements about the need to cultivate the scientific worldview, atheism remained a low priority for local party organs. He described the situation central atheists typically encountered when they spoke with local party officials on their trips to the provinces: "We come to the party organization and ask who is responsible for atheist work. They name Ivan Ivanovich. And why him, and not someone else? Oh, because if you assign organization work to Ivan Ivanovich, he will mess it all up. If you give him political enlightenment, he will also mess it up. But with atheism there is nothing to do, so we assigned it to him." Or as another atheist remarked, "[Local cadres] say, 'Who cares about religion? [If you mess it up] no one will scold you about it, whereas for something else they will.'" As a result, despite the "enormous energy and resources" devoted to cadre training, the atheist apparatus still lacked quality cadres.[98]

Both central and local atheists were frustrated because the party's position on religion continued to oscillate, which meant that they frequently found themselves on the wrong side of the party line. As one atheist put it, one day you could denounce a believer as a "religious fanatic" and the next day find yourself accused of "violating freedom of conscience."[99] Indeed, the overall sentiment of the atheist establishment was summed up by Evdokimov, the INA's deputy director, who relayed that after a recent meeting, one local cadre exclaimed that if before at least the general direction of atheist work was "more or less clear," then "now nothing at all is clear."[100]

Finally, atheists also began to find their two roles—as party propagandists and social scientists—increasingly difficult to reconcile. At a 1979 atheist seminar, Kurochkin, one of the INA's deputy directors, asked whether the "connection of party organizations to atheist issues and [problem of] overcoming religion did not appear too rigid and straightforward," and proposed that atheist work should move away from "overemphasizing" the religious question.[101] In part, this was a call for a greater stress on positive atheism as distinct from antireligious propaganda. But Kurochkin's attention to how atheist work "appeared" also reflects the atheists' growing awareness of the changing global political landscape, which—with the consolidation of the human rights movement and its emphasis on religious freedom in the Communist bloc—brought more and more international attention to religion in the USSR.[102]

## *Militant Religion*

By the end of the 1970s, a new problem emerged alongside ideological indifference as an urgent concern for the Soviet state: the return of religion to public life. Religion had become both visible and politically contested on the world stage, appearing in diverse contexts, from the rise of the religious right in the United States to the religious mobilization around human rights (especially following the adoption of the Helsinki Accords in 1975), the Vatican's growing political engagement with the Communist bloc and election of the Polish bishop Karol Wojtyla as Pope John Paul II in 1978, and the Islamic revolution in Iran in 1979.[103] For the Soviet Communist Party, this made apparent that religion could still mobilize society to political action. Even if these developments originated beyond Soviet borders, they created the fear that foreign religious mobilizations would infect Soviet citizens, especially those perceived to be vulnerable to ideological diversion: Baptists, Jehovah's Witnesses, Seventh-day Adventists, Lithuanian and Ukrainian Catholics, and Muslims, many of whom were concentrated in the border regions.

Once religion had returned to politics and public life on the world stage, the party had no choice but to take it seriously. That it actually did so is evident in, among other things, the opening of filial branches of the INA in politically sensitive areas. The first branch was established in 1977 in Kiev, in part because Ukraine, as the most religious and religiously diverse republic in the USSR, was considered the best platform for the production of atheist propaganda to counter the "bourgeois-clerical propaganda" flowing into the country.[104] The second branch—in Tashkent, Uzbekistan was established in 1980 in response to the 1979 Islamic revolution in Iran and Soviet Union's war with Afghanistan. Finally, the third filial branch—in Vilnius, Lithuania was established in 1983 to address the growing influence of the Catholic Church in the Communist bloc, and in particular, John Paul II's role in mobilizing Poland's Solidarity movement (which had politically paralyzed the Polish Communist Party in 1980–81) with his 1979 visit to Poland. For the rest of the Soviet period, the INA's filial branches served as party think tanks that provided reports and proposals that shaped how the Central Committee understood and approached the new phenomenon of public religions.[105]

The Soviet state's growing alarm about religion as a political force abroad also mapped onto other anxieties, including increasingly robust and vocal domestic nationalisms, and the escalation of Cold War tensions.[106] Reflecting these new concerns, party pronouncements on atheism and ideological conviction now included direct statements on the necessity of countering domestic nationalisms and foreign efforts to subvert the unity of Soviet society. An April 26, 1979, Central Committee decree, titled "On the Further Improvement of Ideological and Politico-Educational Work," explicitly combined atheist education with international education in its effort to address the threat of nationalism, and noted in particular the importance of ideological work among children, who, under the influence of their families, formed "distorted ideas" about the connection between religious and national identity.[107] On September 22, 1981, the party issued a secret Central Committee decree, "On the Intensification of Atheist Education," which called for the cultivation of atheist conviction in order to fortify Soviet society against alien ideological influences.[108] A 1982 AON report to the Central Committee, "The Formation of Conviction in the Advantages of Socialism in the Contemporary Ideological Battle," noted that the "strategists of anti-Communism" focus their energies on undermining faith in the "advantages of socialism."[109]

Brezhnev's death, on November 10, 1982—and the rise to power of his immediate successors, Yuri Andropov (until his death on February 9, 1984) and Konstantin Chernenko (until his death on March 10, 1985)—brought no significant changes in the official position on religion and atheism. In his role as general secretary, Andropov—who had spent the previous two decades policing dissent in his role as head of the KGB—reaffirmed the party's commitment to overcoming religion. Indeed, at the Central Committee's June 1983 Plenum on ideology, Andropov denounced religious dissidents for "proclaiming a national religious revival as an alternative to Marxist-Leninist ideology," and warned those assembled that "a part of the people remains under the influence of religion—a part that, so to speak, is not that small."[110] Even the young and energetic future reformer Gorbachev, in the role of chief party ideologist under Chernenko, maintained the party line, stressing the need to "overcome centuries-old survivals, prejudices, and customs in people's consciousness."[111]

Following Gorbachev's election to the post of general secretary in March 1985, Znanie held a series of closed roundtables to discuss three topics: socialist rituals, atheism, and the place of religion—and the Russian Orthodox Church in particular—in Soviet life. The first of these, "The Development and Actualization of Socialis t Ritualism in Developed Socialist Society" (April 4–5, 1985), took stock of socialist rituals since their introduction. Participants continued to cast rituals as central to the "spiritual culture of socialism" that reflected "the main characteristics of the socialist way of life, traditions, and customs of the Soviet people who are creating a new Communist civilization." In their ideal form, socialist rituals were supposed to "function as a means of regulating social life, the actualization of the methods for organizing production, labor, and various forms of collective relations—in short, to encompass all spheres of the spiritual life of our people." Socialist rituals were also supposed to cultivate atheist conviction, "effectively combine national forms with international content," and serve as the "most effective means for the socialization of new generations of socialist society . . . by transferring to them the moral and aesthetic qualities of life of our people." Yet, as one participant noted, even after twenty years, the impact of socialist rituals remained unclear, so that while "some see [socialist rituals] as a new mode of decoration or fashion, others expect that rituals will solve all problems of upbringing, even ones that have nothing to do with them."[112]

Above all, it was difficult to measure the effect of socialist rituals. While socialist rituals had undoubtedly become a major project—in Ukraine, for example, there were more than two hundred thousand cadres working in the socialist ritual complex—atheists acknowledged that it was "no secret" that socialist birth ceremonies, weddings, and funerals were often followed by religious rites. "What are these people looking for in religious rituals?" one atheist asked. "These are things that we must weigh, measure, and try to understand."[113] If the main purpose of socialist rituals was to "facilitate the displacement of religious rituals," then the result—Soviet people's "syncretic" and "parallel" adoption of socialist rituals alongside religious rites—certainly cast doubt on the project's success. Socialist rituals were supposed to assist in the "formation of [socialist] social and spiritual qualities," and "confirm the values of the socialist way of life," but instead, atheists observed, the result confirmed popular "indifferentism to atheism and religion."[114]

When atheists convened several months later to discuss "Current Issues of Atheist Upbringing in Conditions of Contemporary Ideological Warfare" (October 30–31, 1985), there was an open pessimism about atheist prospects. Filimonov, one of the INA's deputy directors, admitted that their faith in secularization had been misplaced:

> One of the realities of contemporary life is that contrary to overly optimistic predictions, the process of the transformation of social consciousness, which is tied to its liberation from church and religious influence, is not developing all that quickly. Unfortunately, this truth has somehow only become clear in the minds of scholars, both here and in other countries, not all that long ago. . . . The victory of the scientific materialist worldview in our society and successes of atheist education give no reason for self-satisfaction. After all, religion and religious organizations have significant opportunities for the preservation of their positions, and even for their temporary activation and revitalization.

Filimonov shared that while rural Orthodoxy continued to decline, along with Soviet rural life more broadly, urban congregations were growing and church income had increased more than 300 percent in the previous few years. Furthermore, statistics on religious rites did not "reflect the true state of affairs," and the actual level of religious observance was several times higher than what appeared in the official data. For example, one thing that remained hidden behind the statistics was the fact that in the previous four years, baptisms of school-age children had increased significantly, as had the number of adult baptisms. "How can we explain this?" Filimonov asked. "After all, we are not talking about infants, but about schoolchildren who could have been taken to the church to be baptized earlier."[115]

The international context around the approaching millennium of the Christianization of Rus,' Filimonov observed, created especially favorable conditions for the Russian Orthodox Church to be more active in Soviet society and more visible in public life. This added a third component to Soviet atheist work; alongside overcoming religion and forming atheist conviction, atheists were now to focus on addressing "efforts to use religion for political ends as a weapon in the ideological war." The INA's Kiev branch had been charged with this problem, and its director, Aleksandr Onishchenko, shared the ways in which atheists in Ukraine had mobilized "atheist counterpropaganda" to address foreign attempts to politicize the millennium. Their task, Onishchenko argued, was to prevent Western "clerical propaganda" from successfully "penetrating" into the USSR and "fomenting anti-Soviet hysteria." At the same time, Onishchenko stressed that the Russian Orthodox Church was patriotic, although he did not exclude the possibility that it would use the occasion of the millennium's global audience to advance its own agenda. Nevertheless, he noted, "The absolute majority of the clergy and absolute majority of believers in no shape or form share the positions of the foreign clerical centers. They have no antisocial goals and reject the anti-Sovietism of bourgeois-clerical propaganda." Therefore, atheists needed to combine counterpropaganda against foreign subversion with "positive propaganda" that "shows atheism in all the richness of its content and forms." Soviet atheism, Onishchenko concluded, "is the expression, the reflection, the embodiment of deep spiritual values, founded on the scientific worldview [and] it has more claim to spirituality than religion."[116]

Where, then, did this leave the church in contemporary Soviet life? This question became the subject of Znanie's final roundtable, held on December 15 and 16, 1985. The underlying concern of the discussion was how to frame the growing presence of the Russian Orthodox Church in Soviet society, and to clarify what role it should play in "activating the human factor" by mobilizing believers. In a report on the "everyday consciousness of contemporary Orthodox believers," one participant shared that sociological studies showed that Orthodox believers, on the whole, lacked strong religious convictions and were unversed in the theological precepts of the faith. This meant that their Orthodoxy was primarily cultural; contemporary believers, he posited, saw

Orthodoxy as the foundation of tradition and community and expressed their belonging primarily through the observance of religious rites, especially rites of passage. This meant that Orthodox believers "relatively rarely spread their religious creed, and their religious influence on others is usually limited to their family."[117]

The church, on the other hand, was more cause for concern. As former priest turned public atheist Chertkov reported, the church was becoming more engaged with social issues that fell "beyond the boundaries of religious questions," and expressed itself more openly on Soviet political developments. Moreover, it was emphatic about its own patriotism and the need to cultivate patriotism among the clergy and Orthodox parishioners.[118] The church's new social engagement, especially when expressed in the language of patriotism, placed the Soviet state in a complicated position—particularly given the attention to the issue abroad. In his presentation, Grigorii Zharinov, the longtime CRA plenipotentiary in Leningrad, outlined the costs and benefits of allowing the church into Soviet public life. He noted that the church did "necessary and useful" work in the international arena, especially in helping to discredit anti-Soviet "insinuations about human rights, and the supposed repression of believers and clergy in our country."[119] Likewise, the church was doing beneficial work in helping to address social problems at home—corruption, drunkenness, and immoral behavior—and Zharinov argued that "it would be absurd if we excluded it, with its influence on a significant part of our citizens, and its potential to influence the significant amount of religious followers abroad." At the same time, Zharinov observed that the benefits of the church's work on the international stage were offset by the fact that this raised its authority at home, thereby creating "the illusion that the church itself is necessary and useful."[120]

The Russian Orthodox Church, meanwhile, saw the rise of the young, energetic, and reform-minded Gorbachev to the post of general secretary as an opportunity to play a more active and visible role in Soviet public life. On December 17, 1985—the day following Znanie's roundtable on the role of the church in Soviet society—Metropolitan Aleksii (Ridiger) sent Gorbachev a letter outlining his vision. The cooperation between church and state, Aleksii wrote, did not have to be limited only to the international arena:

> The law on the separation of the church from the state—the foundational principle on which our relations are constructed—does not mean that the church exists outside the state, or that believing citizens [exist] outside Soviet society. On the contrary, the church is tied to the state in thousands of visible and invisible threads. . . . In short, the separation of the church from the state does not exclude cooperation between us; on the contrary, only under these conditions of separation can we have genuine cooperation.[121]

Aleksii assured the Soviet leader that the interests of the church could not be separated from the interests of the Soviet people, and that as a result, the church could and should play a more prominent role in Soviet social life. Aleksii proposed that "the main directions of our cooperation" would be the church's contribution to "patriotic and civic education, to the strengthening of the unity of our society, which is so necessary in the difficult current international situation." He noted that de facto, the church was already doing this work. But he suggested that the church could "more actively and decisively combat the various social vices and illnesses—alcoholism, moral depravity, and egoism—to strengthen the family as an essential foundation of Soviet society, and defend the spiritual and moral health of the people."[122]

After the letter was discussed by members of the party Politburo, the metropolitan's offer was rejected. Soon after, he was dismissed from his position as the head of internal church affairs and transferred from Moscow to Leningrad. With this, the party reminded the church that its domain was "satisfying the religious needs of believers," not solving social or political problems.[123]

In effect, the religious question, especially as it regarded the status of the Russian Orthodox Church, exposed the central conundrum facing the party as it embarked on perestroika: How should it approach the religious question, when the nature of the question itself depended on whether one examined it through the lens of politics or ideology? As Zharinov put it, "We need to distinguish politics from ideology. Although politics and ideology cannot be divided, with regard to this question we reward the church for its peace-building efforts, and this is not an ideological question but [rather] a political one. As for the sphere of ideology, religion remains, as it has always been, our ideological enemy. We have never hidden this and we should not hide it now."[124] The question of how the Soviet establishment should position itself on religion reflected the intrinsic tension between ideology and politics in the Soviet project, and raised the question of whether it was possible to divorce ideology and politics within Soviet Communism. When the party weighed the costs and benefits of bringing the Russian Orthodox Church into Soviet public life in 1985, it decided to maintain the status quo. By 1988, when Gorbachev decided to meet with Patriarch Pimen in the Kremlin in anticipation of the upcoming Orthodox millennium, the party had arrived at a different conclusion.

## *Conclusion*

In the fall of 1979, the INA sent a young atheist sociologist named Remir Lopatkin to Czechoslovakia to attend an atheist symposium and survey the state of religious affairs and atheist work following the "crisis" of 1968. On his return, Lopatkin reported that while the Czechoslovak Communist Party had "on the whole managed to overcome the repercussions [of the crisis] in the sphere of religious relations," there was still cause for concern. Guided by a secret 1973 Czechoslovak Communist Party decree that "stipulated the involvement of believers and the progressively oriented clergy into the process of consolidating society," local atheists were working on "neutralizing the activity of the reactionary part of the clergy and laypeople [and] rebuffing the intrigues of the church in emigration as well as pressure from the Vatican." They had organized "tight control over the activity of the churches," and intensified efforts to train cadres, inculcate the scientific worldview, and promote socialist rituals. Lopatkin reported that sociological studies of the religious landscape of Czechoslovakia revealed a decline in religiosity; the "vast majority" of religious organizations "[stood] on loyal positions," and the majority of believers "conscientiously [took] part in the construction of developed socialist society." Nevertheless, Lopatkin noted, the "religious question" in Czechoslovakia remained "complicated and acute." The 1968 crisis revealed that "in certain conditions the church can act as an active antisocialist force," and for some, including segments of the intelligentsia, "religiosity continues to act as a kind of 'internal emigration,' the rejection of the socialist way of life." Moreover, dissidents organized around the "so-called 'Charter-77'" sought to "form an alliance with the church," and foreign clerical circles tried to use the ideological disorientation of Czech society "toward imperialist goals."[125]

But Lopatkin also highlighted the ideological confusion within the Czechoslovak atheist apparatus, noting that "certain worrisome tendencies among atheist cadres strike a dissonant chord." At the symposium, he reported, "unexpectedly one of the most significant discussions was about the seemingly long-ago decided question of what to call our academic discipline: scientific atheism or religious studies." But behind this supposedly "academic" debate, Lopatkin explained, was "a certain ideological dissociation between those who stood on the side of a party-oriented scientific atheism that includes religious studies as a component part, and those who stood for the pseudo-objective, ideologically undetermined 'science of religion' with a clear slouching toward positivism." Lopatkin maintained that, while on the surface, these discussions might seem far removed from urgent political issues, a similar situation had been observed shortly before 1968, and that "the ensuing events showed [that] behind this position there can hide a negative attitude toward Marxism and socialism." This was "especially worrisome" because "these pseudo-objective attitudes are characteristic above all for younger scholars and graduate students." Young atheist cadres showed an unhealthy interest in the legacy of Tomas Masaryk, the "revisionists" of 1968, and the work of Western sociologists, and made "statements along the lines of 'we need to cleanse sociology of ideology.'" A Czech colleague had even told him in confidence that "one graduate student at the Institute of Atheism in Brno signed Charter-77 and is planning to emigrate, and another illegally escaped abroad."[126]

Lopatkin's reflections on the fragile ideological situation of post-1968 Czechoslovakia through an atheist lens speak to the ways in which the developments of the late Communist period forced the Soviet Communist establishment to reconsider the relationship between politics, ideology, religion, and atheism. In the fragile political climate of post-1968 Czechoslovakia—and not only there—religiosity came to be read not just as a manifestation of an attachment to a dying spiritual culture that could eventually be banished with atheist enlightenment and socialist rituals but as a political statement of opposition to the socialist way of life. This atmosphere made one's position on an academic question—such as whether scientific atheism was a component of the party's work in Communist upbringing (ideology) or the academic study of religion (sociology)—politically significant. The fact that young atheist cadres wanted to cleanse sociology of ideology—and that some among them wanted out of the socialist project as a whole—made one's position on religion and atheism a sign of political commitment to Communism.

Until the 1970s, then, the atheists' main concern was that secularization was not moving as quickly as Marxism-Leninism had predicted, but there was still confidence that secularization embodied the logic of history, and that history ended with the disappearance of religion and arrival of Communism. Over the course of the 1970s, a number of developments began to erode this confidence. First, the increasingly complex portrait of Soviet spiritual life emerging from social-scientific studies complicated existing conceptions of religion and introduced indifference as a distinct position on the spectrum of belief. Second, the continued ineffectiveness of atheist work contributed to the growing frustration of atheist cadres with their contradictory roles as both agents of ideological transformation and social scientists. Third, the creative intelligentsia's persistent refusal to participate in the atheist project, compounded by its growing interest in religious heritage and spiritual questions, made manifest its alienation from the party and its ideology. Finally, Soviet youth—from the party's perspective—were becoming increasingly consumerist, in both the material sense (in their fetishizing of Western consumer goods) and the spiritual sense (in their growing indifference to worldview questions).

For the party, the intelligentsia and youth—and the relationship between the two—became the primary focus of ideological work in the late Soviet period, because the party believed that the intelligentsia's god-seeking had a pernicious influence on the next generation. By the 1980s, the party added another issue to its growing list of concerns: Soviet society's turn to the emerging marketplace of religions, ideologies, spiritualities, and countercultures. Whereas in the 1970s atheists were still concentrating most of their efforts on overcoming indifference, by the time Gorbachev became general secretary of the Soviet Communist Party in 1985, religion had become a political problem for Soviet Communism—again.

In the end, however, the biggest disappointment for Soviet atheists was Soviet people, because they never managed to live up to the atheist ideal of disciplined conviction in the scientific atheist worldview and socialist way of life. As one atheist put it at Znanie's 1985 roundtable on scientific atheism, "These people are not of a very high spiritual level. . . . They want to take more and more. Worldview positions and concepts do not apply to them. We think our own spiritual world is the spiritual world of these people. They are our people, good people—but they remain on the level of byt, where there is no worldview, only spontaneous everyday consciousness."[127] Unlike atheists themselves, most ordinary Soviet people never managed to internalize atheist conviction or embrace the socialist way of life—and therefore always kept Communism out of reach.

CONCLUSION

# Utopia's Orphan

## SOVIET ATHEISM AND THE DEATH OF THE COMMUNIST PROJECT

FROM JUNE 5 to 12, 1988, the Orthodox millennium was publicly celebrated in Moscow, with celebrations continuing through the month of June across the USSR. The millennium celebrations had all the symbolic trappings of political patronage, with a number of the events taking place in important Soviet institutions, like the Bolshoi Theater, and attended by prominent officials and public figures, including Andrei Gromyko, the chairman of the Presidium of the Supreme Soviet; Konstantin Kharchev, the chair of the CRA; Vadim Medvedev, the curator of religious affairs in the Communist Party's Central Committee; and Gorbachev's wife, Raisa (see figure C.1).[1] Kharchev even secured a ZIL limousine—a mode of transportation reserved for the political elite—to transport Patriarch Pimen to the celebration events, thereby signaling to both the Soviet public and the political establishment itself that the new course on religion had been officially sanctioned.[2] The millennium was also widely covered in the press and on television—to the great surprise of the Soviet audience accustomed to seeing religion depicted as a world of backward old women and fanatical sectarians.[3] For the first time since the October Revolution, religion was cast as a legitimate part of the country's past, and, perhaps more importantly, a normal part of its present.[4]

### *Enter Religion*

It is tempting to see the shift in the Soviet position on religion and atheism as part of the broader story of perestroika liberalization, but this is misleading. Indeed, when Gorbachev assumed the post of general secretary in 1985, he gave the party no reason to doubt the sincerity of his belief that Communism was the best of all possible systems, and that the political task of the day was

FIGURE C.1. Celebration in honor of the millennium of the Baptism of Rus' at the Bolshoi Theater. Among those on stage are representatives of the Russian Orthodox Church, Patriarch Pimen (Izvekov), Metropolitan Filaret (Varkhomeev), and Metropolitan Iuvenalii (Poiarkov); representatives of other religious confessions of the USSR; Raisa Gorbacheva, wife of Mikhail Gorbachev; the head of the Soviet government, Andrei Gromyko; and representatives of Soviet institutions engaged with religious questions, including Konstantin Kharchev, chair of the Council of Religious Affairs of the USSR Council of Ministers, and Vadim Medvedev, curator of religious affairs in the Communist Party's Central Committee. June 10, 1988, Moscow. Image no. 18828454, Alexander Sentsov for ITAR-TASS, used with permission.

to remove the obstacles that stood in the way of the Communist ideal finally becoming a reality. But perestroika was not just an economic and political program; it was a call for moral and spiritual renewal. When Gorbachev denounced the "stagnation" of the Brezhnev era, he was referring not only to declining economic performance but also to the pervasive corruption, cynicism, and anomie that had become the unspoken norm of Soviet life. The party's stress on overcoming ideological indifference and cultivating conviction underscores that by 1985 it was well aware that it was losing Soviet society, and that economic and political reforms would work only if Soviet citizens could be inspired to again believe in the system—a goal that the party described as "activating the human factor." Even as Gorbachev embarked on perestroika, his position on religion and atheism remained consistent with that of his predecessors. Even as Gorbachev diagnosed the moral decay and spiritual sickness of Soviet society, he did not initially posit religion as a remedy. The party had loosened its grip on the economy and society, but it had not abandoned its commitment to atheism.

Despite the significance of the millennium for the Orthodox Church, the question of how much public attention it would receive continued to remain unanswered. Though the church had formed a jubilee commission to plan the millennium in 1980, and the Soviet state made the highly symbolic gesture of returning Moscow's Danilov Monastery to the church in 1983, the official line was that the celebration of the Orthodox millennium would be a strictly religious affair. Behind the scenes, however, the party continued to debate how to position itself on the millennium, especially since, as the Soviet Union's ideological foes in the West consistently pointed out, the Baptism of Rus' in 988 was the origin not just of Orthodox Christianity but of Russian statehood. This placed the party in an awkward position, since it needed to either acknowledge the political continuity between Soviet Communism and Russia's prerevolutionary past, or reject the sacred origins of Russian statehood. As Gorbachev embarked on perestroika in 1986, he remained silent about his position on an event that many at home saw as the bedrock of Russian history and many abroad were watching as a litmus test for the sincerity of perestroika reforms.[5]

In the first years after Gorbachev's election, the party sent no signals that it planned to devote public attention to the celebration of the approaching millennium. If anything, it sought to minimize public attention to the event. Shortly after Gorbachev's election in March 1985, the Central Committee met to discuss counterpropaganda measures to deflect attention from the millennium, especially from abroad. Aleksandr Yakovlev—deputy head of the party's propaganda department and the future ideological "architect" of perestroika—informed his audience that the Vatican was trying to "strengthen its influence" in the country and "[Karol] Wojtyla dreams of coming to the USSR with political ambitions." While Yakovlev highlighted the danger of foreign attention on the millennium, Nikolai Ryzhkov—then the chairman of the Soviet Council of Ministers—warned against mobilizing a public counterpropaganda campaign, noting that the party had to have a "balanced, calm approach so as not to attract particular attention to this event." Kharchev, who had just been appointed CRA chair following Kuroedov's retirement in 1984, also noted the risks of politicizing the millennium, pointing out that "the object" of foreign propaganda was not so much the Soviet believer but the Orthodox Church, which hostile foreign powers wanted to "push off its loyal position vis-à-vis the [Soviet] government."[6] In trying to manage the millennium, the Soviet political establishment struggled to balance the competing objectives of the party and government at home, and the delicate place of the religious question in the international arena.

While the party continued its efforts to neutralize "bourgeois-clerical propaganda," the meaning of the millennium was spiraling out of its control. On June 2, 1985, when Pope John Paul II issued the encyclical *Slavorum Apostoli* (Apostles to the Slavs)—commemorating Saints Cyril and Methodius, who had brought Christianity to the Slavs in the ninth century—the party took notice of the numerous ways in which the pope used the occasion to address the contemporary situation. In the encyclical, John Paul II promoted a Europe united by common Christian origins; presented Cyril and Methodius as "the fathers of both the Christianity [of the Slavs] and their culture"; and made an emphatic distinction between the nation, which represented the people, and the state, which he cast as an artificial entity the moral legitimacy of which was grounded in ensuring the people's well-being (and not the other way around). The party also took note that the pope paid particular attention to religious anniversaries, noting Poland's millennium in 1966, but bringing particular attention to the "millennium of the baptism of Saint Vladimir, Grand Duke of Kiev," which, he pointedly observed, would be celebrated "in a few years—in 1988 to be exact."[7] In response, the party's Secretariat adopted a secret decree, "On Countering Foreign Clerical Propaganda Connected with the One Thousandth Anniversary of the Introduction of Christianity in Rus'," in September 1985,[8] and instructed the Moscow and Kiev branches of the INA to intensify counterpropaganda measures and address the "activation of Orthodox clergy inside the country by foreign religious centers."[9]

Through 1986 and 1987, even as the floodgates of glasnost opened Soviet public life to a plurality of voices, including religious voices, the party remained committed to atheism. In February 1986, at the Twenty-Seventh Party Congress, Gorbachev urged party members to be vigilant when under the guise of a national "uniqueness" (*samobytnost'*), certain works of literature and art portrayed religion in idyllic tones. Gorbachev reminded the audience that religion was opposed to "our ideology, the socialist way of life, and the scientific worldview." Indeed, he portrayed indifference to religion and atheism as a symptom of the broader crisis afflicting Soviet society, and insisted that "stagnation is intolerable in a sphere like atheist education."[10] The new party program, adopted at the congress, still devoted a section to "Atheist Upbringing," and the new Party Charter still obligated party members to "conduct decisive work against religious prejudices."[11] On another occasion, Egor Ligachev, Gorbachev's conservative opponent in the Central Committee, proclaimed that "sometimes certain individuals, on meeting infringements of the norms of socialist morality, begin to mutter that it would be desirable to show tolerance for religious ideas [and] return to religious morality. But they forget the essential truth of Marxism: that religion is far from the source of a person's morality."[12] An editorial published on the front page of *Pravda* on September 28, 1986, criticized "certain writers" for "occasionally 'flirt[ing] with God [and] objectively facilitating the revival of god-seeking ideas," and affirmed that "the Leninist principle of the class-party approach to religion as a false system of views top to bottom remains in effect."[13]

As the millennium neared, and the political arena under perestroika became increasingly more complex, the party nevertheless continued to reiterate the official line on religion—even as it became apparent that much of Soviet society was no longer listening. In February 1987, the CRA sent a secret circular informing its regional plenipotentiaries that in the lead-up to the millennium, the Moscow patriarchate would publish Bibles, religious literature, and photo albums, and even make a documentary showing religious life in the USSR in a positive light. The goal of all this was to "dispel the myth, produced by bourgeois propaganda, about the absence of freedom of conscience in the USSR, dispel the lies of clerical and anti-Soviet organizations that aim to discredit the politics of the Communist Party and the Soviet government in relation to religion, the church and believers, [and] flame nationalist attitudes." The Moscow patriarchate was also "taking measures to inform foreign circles about freedom of conscience in our country and the preparations for the thousandth anniversary of the 'baptism of Rus'.'" At the same time, the council warned, the church was trying to "strengthen its authority" at home by "drawing parallels" between the millennium of Orthodox Christianity and Russian history in order to show that "the church has always been 'with the people.'"[14] The task of local officials was to minimize the impact of the church on Soviet society, while, at the same time, continuing to allow the church to play its part in countering anti-Soviet propaganda abroad, which accused the Soviet Union of violating the rights of believers.

The party also remained committed to countering attempts to cast the millennium as a pivotal event in Russian history or Orthodoxy as the center of Russian culture. Writing in the party journal *Kommunist* in December 1987, historian Aleksandr Klibanov and philosopher Lev Mitrokhin acknowledged the importance of these questions, especially with the "approach of the millennium of the introduction of Christianity in Rus'," but they cautioned against getting carried away by the "unhealthy frenzy inflamed by church apologists, as well as those unscrupulous foreign dilettantes who serve subversive ideological centers in the West."[15] In another 1987 article, Yakovlev conceded that "the acceptance of Christianity helped Kievan Rus' to develop links with the contemporary civilization," and that therefore "the church played a certain educative role that should not be belittled." But he also categorically denied the centrality of religion to Russian culture. "[T]hey say: let god have what is god's; let the church have what is the church's; but we Marxists have the whole truth," Yakovlev wrote. "And from this point of view we must decisively repudiate any attempt to portray Christianity as the "mother" of Russian culture.[16] Kharchev, meanwhile, continued to insist on the strictly religious character of the millennium, arguing, in a November 1987 article in *Science and Religion*, that it was "a holiday of various Christian confessions that exist in our country," and not a "national holiday" (*obshchenarodnyi prazdnik*).[17] In the first months of 1988, the party continued to train cadres in how to counter ideological diversions. The Moscow City party organization organized training sessions at the Moscow House of Political Enlightenment in January 1988, and in February held a two-day conference on "intensifying atheist education in contemporary conditions" to debrief party cadres about the upcoming millennium.[18]

In this context, Gorbachev's decision to meet with Patriarch Pimen on April 29, 1988, which announced the state's embrace of the millennium as a national celebration, was unexpected not just for foreign observers and Soviet society, but even within the party apparatus itself.[19] Kharchev's subsequent comments depict the decision as driven by the desire to right the wrongs of the Soviet past,[20] but there are also reasons to see it as a political calculation that responded to a more immediate concern: the crisis of perestroika. Gorbachev had just emerged from the so-called "Nina Andreeva Affair," a conservative offensive against perestroika orchestrated by Ligachev, in which, on March 13, 1988, the conservative newspaper *Soviet Russia* (*Sovetskaia Rossiia*) published a letter by a Leningrad chemistry teacher named Nina Andreeva arguing that glasnost and perestroika had gone too far in denouncing Soviet history and values. Timed to come out when both Gorbachev and Yakovlev, the party's principal reformers, were out of the country, the letter, titled "I Cannot Forsake My Principles," cynically cited Gorbachev's own speech at the February Plenum of the Central Committee in which he stated that "in the spiritual sphere, and perhaps primarily here, [the party], in its actions, must be guided by our Marxist-Leninist principles. Principles [with which] we must not part under any circumstances."[21] Following this call, Andreeva argued, meant putting an end to those same reforms initiated by Gorbachev, which disoriented Soviet youth and threatened the moral unity of Soviet society. Andreeva's letter, and the media and public debates around it, became a flash point in the escalating contest between party liberals and conservatives about the scope and course of reforms.[22]

Looking ahead, Gorbachev was undoubtedly also mindful of Reagan's upcoming visit to the Soviet Union for the Moscow Summit, held May 29 to

June 3, 1988. Though the official agenda of the summit was intermediate-range nuclear arms, the religious question was always prominent in Reagan's engagements with the "evil empire," and was especially so with the upcoming millennium.[23] Indeed, during his visit, Reagan met with Soviet religious dissidents at the US embassy in Moscow and visited the Danilov Monastery, the main site of the millennium celebrations.[24] It is necessary, then, to also place Gorbachev's reversal on the religious question in its immediate political context. With the Nina Andreeva Affair behind him in March, and the Moscow Summit with Reagan approaching in May, Gorbachev decided to meet with Patriarch Pimen—a decision made just weeks before the official reception on April 29, 1988.[25]

Speaking to party cadres at the Moscow Higher Party School shortly after the patriarch's visit to the Kremlin, Kharchev explained the new party line on religion to his confused audience as a political strategy: "Remember the Leninist idea, that politics begins when you start to talk in terms of millions. . . . The church has survived, and has not only survived, but has rejuvenated itself. And the question arises: Which is more useful to the party—someone who believes in God, someone who believes in nothing at all, or someone who believes in both God and Communism? I think we should choose the lesser evil." Kharchev also shared that he had received numerous complaints about the extensive coverage of religious themes in the Soviet media, but that in the new political reality, people had to start to think about religion and the church as a "normal" part of Soviet life.[26] These backroom maneuvers reveal that even as Gorbachev reversed course on religion, the political establishment continued to see the Orthodox Church primarily as a loyal institution that could be used as a political tool, and assumed that even once religion entered Soviet public life, the party would remain in control. But by 1989, when the Soviet Union held its first multiparty elections, Patriarch Pimen and Metropolitan Aleksii, as well as nearly 300 clergymen (190 of them from the Russian Orthodox Church), were elected to the Congress of People's Deputies[27]—something that would have been unthinkable before 1988, never mind before perestroika. Religion had entered politics.

For the party, the return of religion to politics and public life was unexpected because it ran counter to the telos underpinning Soviet Communism, which posited that religion would inevitably decline and disappear. Over the course of the twentieth century, this set of assumptions developed within the framework of secularization theory, which held that as society became more industrial, bureaucratic, urban, educated, and diverse, religion would become less significant—both for society as a whole and in the lives of individuals. Religion would withdraw from the public sphere and become a meaningful phenomenon only in private life, eventually losing its relevance even in that narrow set of experiences. For almost a century, the secularization model remained the dominant framework for understanding the relationship between religion and modernity, reaching its apotheosis in the 1960s, when both secular and religious observers in capitalist as well as socialist worlds agreed that the death of religion was both inevitable and imminent—even as some decried and others celebrated it.[28] Over the course of the 1970s and 1980s, however, social scientists (in both the capitalist and socialist worlds) lost their certainty about the nature of religion or its future in the modern world, and by the 1990s had become increasingly vocal about the inadequacy of the secularization model to explain religion in the modern world. Indeed, in some cases the same people who had devoted their careers to understanding secularization published works discussing the ways in which the thesis proved wrong.[29]

The ideological and political transformations that followed the public celebration of the Orthodox millennium were radical and swift. At the Nineteenth Party Conference (June 28–July 1, 1988), held just a few weeks after the millennium celebration, Gorbachev proceeded to separate Communist ideology and Soviet politics, noting, "We do not hide our position on the religious worldview as an unscientific, unmaterialist [worldview]. But this is not a foundation for disrespecting the spiritual world of believing people."[30] This separation was further underscored by Viktor Garadzha, director of the INA, in a report on the millennium sent to the Central Committee's Propaganda Department on August 1, 1988. Garadzha maintained that the party had effectively moved the millennium "beyond the boundaries of a strictly church holiday," and cast it as an event that had "an important cultural-historical and political significance." He also noted that the party's initial efforts to "limit" the celebration and "assign it a strictly religious character" had been a mistake that allowed foreign "bourgeois-clerical propaganda" to gain "ideological capital."[31] At the same time, Garadzha observed that the scope of millennium celebrations had disoriented rank-and-file party cadres. It had also mobilized conservative antiperestroika elements, who "under the flag of fighters for 'militant atheism'" now accused the party itself of god-seeking tendencies as well as "flirting with religion and the church." Soviet society, however, had definitively turned away from atheism. Public opinion studies following the millennium showed that 41.4 percent of those surveyed believed atheist work did more harm than good, 34.3 percent believed it was useless, and only 24.3 percent saw any point to it at all. For Garadzha, this underscored the fact that Gorbachev's meeting with the patriarch and subsequent celebration of the millennium had a "cardinal significance," and constituted the "official recognition of the fact that religious organizations should and must find their place in solving the problems that face [Soviet] society."[32]

In 1989, the party reflected further on the "atheist aspect of the party's work on the ideological provisioning of perestroika," acknowledging the need not just to reform atheist approaches, but to reconsider the Marxist position on the meaning of religion in socialist society. Religiosity, the report stated, remained a mass phenomenon, and was "represented among practically all social and national spheres." Even if "on the whole" Soviet society could be considered secular, "the myth about socialism as a society free of religion pushe[d] us toward attempts to overcome religion." While in theory this was supposed to be done through "ideological influence and reeducation of believers into atheists," in practice it usually led to "administrative-command methods." It was clear now that this form of atheist work "is not only ineffective but [also] not infrequently connected with serious political and ideological costs." In light of the "socialist pluralism of opinions," continued religiosity of the masses, and "active work of religious organizations," the report proposed that it was essential to "clearly delineate the two aspects of the party's relationship to religion and the church—the political and the worldview—in order to exclude the possibility of transferring the worldview opposition of Marxism to religion into the realm of political confrontation between Communists and believers." In short, if religion was here for the "long-term perspective," it was essential to "ensure the consolidation of society on a platform of renewing socialism"—a task that required "the cooperation of believers and unbelievers [and] normal state-church relations."[33]

In 1989, the party also studied the "ideals and value orientations of Soviet youth," surveying 10,549 Soviet young people across the USSR in order to measure whether or not they had "preserved their commitment to the Communist ideal." They did not. The party learned that in conditions of ideological and political pluralism, Soviet youth did not view the "historical choice" of 1917 with any "ideological-political unity." Soviet youth had largely abandoned class values and embraced universal values, and had a "polycentric moral consciousness." The Communist idea, on the other hand, did not "sit well," and only 9 percent of the young people surveyed had "conviction in the truth of one of Marxism-Leninism's foundational theses about the inevitability of the transition of all countries [to Communism]."[34] By 1990, the party had to concede that Soviet society had been ideologically unmoored from Communism. In the great battle for the hearts and souls of humankind, the party had lost.

So where did this leave atheism? In December 1988, Filimonov, the INA's deputy director and head of Znanie's atheist section, observed that atheists found themselves in a "strange" situation:

> The return to Leninist principles in relations with religion is viewed as a concession to religion. . . . We support perestroika, we support the rejection of customary stereotypes, but a question arises as a result: Should atheist propaganda exist or not? Should we battle religion? What should we do about the very meaning of "scientific atheism"? Should we get rid of it or replace it with something else? There are many questions, and we need to answer them.[35]

Over the course of the Soviet period, Soviet atheists tried to respond to these questions, at different times and in different ways. In the process, they learned

FIGURE C.2. Installation at the Moscow Planetarium by artists Kirill Ass and the Blue Soup Group on April 12, 1999, to mark the coincidence of the Orthodox Christian Easter and Cosmonautics Day. S. N. Pominov, April 12, 1999. GBU "TsGA Moskvy," no. 0-7027; used with permission.

about their opponent and the nature of religion, about themselves and the nature of atheism, and about the relationship between the two. Over the course of 1989 and 1990, Znanie held long, soul-searching debates about what the political transformations of perestroika meant for the future of Soviet atheism. Some insisted that atheists needed to reject "those stereotypes that we ourselves created," while others questioned whether it was wise to reject all parts of their "heritage." One atheist even posited that "it is now clear to everyone that we never had socialism and the system in which we exist is itself the reason that religious issues have become so strained." Some wondered whether Znanie should have an atheist section at all. Shortly after, Znanie's atheist section changed its name to the section of "religious studies and free thought."[36]

As the Soviet experiment wound down, Znanie's journal, *Science and Religion,* went from being a platform for Soviet atheism to becoming a mechanism of religious revival.[37] Indeed, many of the journal's atheist efforts over the course of the late Soviet period had unintended consequences. The journal was the first Soviet periodical to give voice to religion by printing conversations with believers. On the journal's pages, readers learned about the history of religion, sacred spaces and places, and religious rites.[38] The journal also became a vehicle for the transformation of atheists themselves. As atheists tried to make sense of the late Soviet ideological and spiritual landscape, *Science and Religion* continued to search for positive content in an effort "not to leave [the] reader spiritually empty."[39] In their attempt to improve atheist work, atheists became more educated about the history of religion and the contemporary religious landscape, which led them to part with ideological stereotypes and ask new questions—though it is telling that even after extensive discussions about changing the journal's title to reflect atheism's new concern with worldview and spiritual themes, the journal ultimately kept the title *Science and Religion*.[40] In 1991, Znanie lost its two primary centers of atheist work, the Moscow House of Scientific Atheism and the Moscow Planetarium. The House of Scientific Atheism became the House of Spiritual Heritage and was closed shortly thereafter over a property dispute.[41] The Moscow Planetarium was privatized and fell into disrepair. On April 12, 1999, when Cosmonautics Day happened to coincide with the Russian Orthodox Easter, a group of Russian artists covered the planetarium's cupola in red with the letters "KhV"—for "Christ Is Risen!" (*Khristos voskrese*)—painted across the front (see figure C.2).[42] In 1991, the INA became the Institute of Religious Studies—and was liquidated soon after, along with the Soviet Communist Party.

## *Exit Atheism*

In 1879, in response to a question posed by a *Chicago Tribune* reporter about whether he and his followers would like to see religion "destroyed, root and branch," Marx replied, "We know . . . that violent measures against religion are nonsense; but this is an opinion: as Socialism grows, religion will disappear."[43] As the Soviet experiment unfolded, this Marx quote—which appeared regularly in atheist publications, speeches, and reports—began to sound more ominous than prophetic. If religion was still alive in the Soviet Union, it was hard not to wonder about the Soviet Union's progress toward Communism, and indeed, about the very prospects of Communism. Over the course of its history, Soviet atheism was a tool to clear the way for the new world—to sweep away all that was old, backward, and false in order to make space for all that was new, progressive, and true. Atheism's role was to exorcize alien commitments, ideas, and ways of life so as to consolidate Soviet Communism's political, ideological, and spiritual authority. Within this framework, atheism assumed different definitions and functions over the course of the Soviet period, which reflected how the party understood the nature of the threat that religion posed to the Soviet project.

In the early Soviet period, when the party's hold on political power was precarious and the survival of the revolution was at stake, the Bolsheviks addressed religion primarily as a political problem. The secular framework of Lenin's 1918 law separating religion from government and education was initially aimed at dislodging the Orthodox Church from its privileged position in Russian political life along with consolidating Bolshevik power over the central institutions of the modern state: the bureaucracy, law, and education. Yet what quickly became clear—through the mass popular resistance to the Bolsheviks' requisitioning of church property during the civil war and continued influence of the clergy through the 1920s—was that religion still remained a significant social force. Thus, even after the Orthodox Church in effect gave up claims to political autonomy with Metropolitan Sergii's declaration of loyalty to Soviet power in 1926, the Bolsheviks continued to perceive religion as a political threat because it could mobilize ordinary people against the revolution and Soviet power.

The 1929 decree on religious associations adopted during Stalin's First Five-Year Plan was intended to undermine religion's social power by removing it from public life. Henceforth religion was not just separated from the bureaucracy, law, and education but also prohibited from performing any form of charity or social work, as well as religious education. The 1929 decree limited religious activity to liturgical practice within the walls of the church, thereby removing religion from public life. In this context, atheist work under Lenin and Stalin—although it had multiple components, including scientific enlightenment and the battle for the new Communist byt—was above all an anticlerical project. The militant atheism of the early Soviet period, which reached its apogee with the "Godless Five-Year Plan" during Stalin's cultural revolution, was intended to undermine the authority of the church as an institution and clear Soviet public space of religion's symbolic influence. By the time Stalin reconstituted the Orthodox Church in 1943, at the height of the Second World War, religion had been largely excised from Soviet public life and the church had no political power beyond the function assigned to it by the Soviet state. Militant atheism became unnecessary and could be retired.

When, following Stalin's death in 1953, Khrushchev returned to the religious question, religion was reconstituted as an ideological problem. After the antireligious campaign mobilized in July 1954 led to administrative "excesses" against the clergy and believers, the party issued a decree on November 10, 1954, clarifying that religion was no longer considered a political enemy but rather an alien ideology. Since both the Orthodox Church and believers were now considered "patriotic," religion no longer threatened Soviet power politically, but it still had the power to corrupt Soviet minds and in this way thwart further progress. Within Khrushchev's project of building Communism, religion needed to be eradicated in order to bring Soviet society to Communist consciousness.

Since the primary site of the battle against religion was now within the Soviet person, the militant atheism of the early Soviet period was discarded in favor of scientific atheism. The objective of atheist work under Khrushchev was to produce the scientific-materialist worldview, and to this end, the state employed two strategies. The first strategy—orchestrated through the government bureaucracies charged with managing religious affairs—closed religious spaces, disbanded religious communities, and severely limited the scope of church activity by placing new legal restrictions and financial burdens on both religious institutions and clergy. The second strategy—orchestrated through party organs and social organizations like Znanie—spread scientific enlightenment through formal and informal education, the press, and public lectures. The results were mixed. By the end of the campaign in 1964, more than half the country's religious spaces had been closed, and the Soviet people's enthusiasm for Soviet space conquest suggested that they embraced scientific enlightenment. Yet as atheists learned when they began to survey Soviet society, closing churches did not bring the expected decline in religious rites or church income, and scientific enlightenment did not necessarily produce atheist worldviews. For Soviet atheists, the lesson of Khrushchev's antireligious campaign was that many Soviet people had little trouble reconciling science and religion, or (un)belief with (religious) practice. Many continued to rely on religion for moral norms, traditions, and rites of passage. Religion, then, continued to shape communities, families, and individuals.

The experiences of the Khrushchev era forced atheists to reevaluate how they understood religion and what they hoped to achieve with atheism, leading Soviet atheism to shift to a positive atheism in the Brezhnev era. Rather than simply focusing on negative strategies, atheists concentrated on inculcating atheist conviction and the "socialist way of life." Atheist work turned to moral and spiritual questions. Znanie's atheist journal, *Science and Religion*, itself the product of Khrushchev's antireligious campaign, held extensive discussions about reforming the journal into a publication centered on worldview concerns, and even considered changing its title to "The World of Man." Atheist work also started to turn away from its focus on belief toward rituals and everyday life. Under Brezhnev, the party invested significant resources into the production of socialist rituals and new Communist byt—returning to projects that emerged in the early Soviet period, but were abandoned in the late 1930s. In the context of "developed socialism," socialist rituals were seen not only as the spiritual foundation of the socialist way of life, but also as the best mechanism for the production of ideological conviction. Finding themselves in the unexpected role of spiritual caretakers, Soviet atheists shifted their attention inward, to the interior worlds of ordinary Soviet people. This turn reflected their recognition that in order for Soviet atheism to succeed, it would have to address new kinds of questions and move into new kinds of spaces.

This transformation in the party's understanding of both religion and atheism over the course of the Soviet period is reflected in the shifting locus of atheist work. If early Soviet militant atheism targeted the physical space of the church—with churches repurposed for other uses (libraries, clubs, or even storage facilities), turned into museums, or demolished—then the enlightenment focus of scientific atheism moved atheist work into the lecture hall and planetarium. When, under Brezhnev, atheists began to see religion primarily as a spiritual phenomenon grounded in everyday life, atheist work moved into the private sphere. As atheists came to see the home and family as the center of religious conservation and reproduction, ritual spaces—such as the new Wedding Palaces—came to be considered the most important sites for atheist work.

Finally, as it became apparent that religion was not succumbing to the Marxist laws of historical development, atheists had to assume a new role and become not just propaganda cadres but social scientists as well. As the party mobilized disciplines like sociology and ethnography to study religion and secularization, the ideological establishment's understanding of the Soviet spiritual landscape became more nuanced and complex. The most significant and surprising development that atheists discovered when they began to study Soviet society was indifference as a distinct position. For Soviet atheists, the fact of indifference came to be more unsettling than the fact of the continued existence of religion. Whereas believers could be engaged and converted, those who were indifferent had no interest in the questions at the heart of religion or atheism. They were disengaged from religious or ideological truth claims, and were unconcerned if their actions did not accord with their convictions, since they lacked firm convictions. That indifference was especially prevalent among Soviet youth only underscored the danger it posed for Soviet Communism and made the production of atheist conviction the central goal of late Soviet atheism.

Over the course of its history, Soviet atheism developed in conversation with religion in theory and through the direct engagement with religion in practice. It was through these engagements that atheism's contradictions became apparent, pointing to the deeper crisis within Soviet Communism. In its battle against religion as a political, ideological, and spiritual authority, Soviet atheism struggled to fill the sacred spaces it had cleared. Atheism's inability to address existential questions, meet spiritual needs, and produce atheist conviction among the masses created the perception that atheism was an empty space rather than a meaningful category. But whereas the discovery, in the 1970s, that Soviet people were indifferent to religion and atheism pointed to the failures of Soviet ideology, the discovery, in the 1980s, that these same Soviet people were turning to alternative spiritual, ideological, and even political commitments again made religion into a political problem.

The party's anxiety about indifference also reveals the central paradox of Soviet atheism: Soviet atheism was about not secularization or secularism but instead conversion. Soviet atheism was not secular because secularism can tolerate indifference. Indeed, it requires it. In order to leave the spheres of politics and public life to the state, and accept their spiritual commitments as an essentially private, secular subjects must have some degree of indifference toward both their own convictions and those of others. For Soviet atheism, however, the privatization of religion was never acceptable in the long term, and indifference and neutrality were unacceptable positions.[44] Under Stalin, the party deployed militant atheism to marginalize religion in politics and public life. Under Khrushchev, it mobilized scientific atheism to undermine religion's truth claims. Yet it was the campaign to exorcize religion from spiritual life that became the final frontier and decisive battle in the war against the old world. Winning this battle was the necessary precondition for the arrival of Communism. In the end, Soviet atheism ran up against a problem at the center of all revolutionary projects, whether secular or religious, that require moral transformation: how to attract and keep followers, instill a coherent set of convictions, and build a meaningful and self-reproducing community. By internalizing atheist conviction, Soviet society was supposed to become the Communist Party writ large. It fell far short of this ideal.

One could look at the story of the Cathedral of Christ the Savior as a palimpsest of the Soviet war against religion. Conceived in 1813 by Tsar Alexander I to commemorate Russia's 1812 victory over Napoleon, the cathedral became a symbol of Russian military might and civic patriotism.[45] Its central location, imposing size, and citation of ancient Russian architecture made it a powerful monument to the Russian nation—the imperial autocracy's answer to Europe's age of nationalism. On December 5, 1931, at the height of the Cultural Revolution that accompanied Stalin's First Five-Year Plan, the Cathedral of Christ the Savior was blown by the Soviet authorities, its materials used for various socialist construction projects, including the Moscow Metro. In its place, the Bolsheviks planned to construct the Palace of Soviets, a colossal tower topped by an enormous statue of Lenin. The Palace of Soviets was meant to be a testament to the triumph of the new world built on the ruins of the old—a palace for the proletariat in place of the palaces of its oppressors.

In the first years following the destruction of the cathedral, Muscovites walking past the site were greeted by a sign painted on the fence proclaiming, "Instead of the hearth of opiate—a palace" (*Vmesto ochaga durmana—dvorets*).[46] But the proletariat never got the palace it was promised. When the war came in 1941, the steel foundations were melted down and the project was abandoned, leaving a crater in the center of Moscow. Then, in 1960, at the height of Khrushchev's antireligious campaign, the space was finally filled: with an enormous, heated outdoor swimming pool, which went on to be enjoyed by Muscovites for decades. But the cathedral's history did not end there. In 1988, the satirical journal *Crocodile* published a curious drawing, titled "Swimmer," that depicted a diving board above the pool's water, and upside down in the water's reflection, a triumphant Saint George in front of an image

FIGURE C.3. "Swimmer," Valerii Balabanov, *Krokodil*, no. 8 (1988): 8. The image shows a reflection, in the waters of the "Moskva" swimming pool, of Saint George in front of the Cathedral of Christ the Savior (destroyed by the Bolsheviks in 1931). The swimming pool had been put in the place of the cathedral in 1960, during Nikita Khrushchev's antireligious campaign. After the dissolution of the USSR, the Cathedral of Christ the Savior was rebuilt and reopened to the public in 1997.

of the Cathedral of Christ the Savior (see figure C.3). The drawing turned out to be prescient; after the end of Communism and the dissolution of the USSR, the Russian Orthodox Church restored the Cathedral of Christ the Savior in its original location and form.[47]

In many ways, then, the history of the Cathedral of Christ the Savior is an allegory for the fate of religion and atheism under Soviet Communism. The Bolsheviks saw the destruction of the symbols of the old world as a powerful statement about their vision for the future. But while their destruction of religious spaces, symbols, and traditions clearly transmitted the antireligious message, it did little to strengthen the people's bond to Soviet Communism. The fact that the cathedral had been destroyed ostensibly to make room for the Palace of Soviets, but that the palace never materialized, underscored the empty space that had been left behind. That the space remained empty for decades, only to be filled by a swimming pool—a space of modern leisure, but hardly a monument to the utopia promised by the revolution—speaks to Soviet atheism's struggle to fill the empty space it had created with its own meaning.

Why did the Soviet Communist Party orchestrate the divorce between Communism and atheism, and between the party's Communist ideology and political power? To answer these questions, it is necessary to return to the role that Communist ideology played in the Soviet project along with the role atheism played within Soviet Communism. For Soviet Communism, ideology performed two essential functions: theoretical and practical. In theory, Soviet ideology was the space in which Marxism-Leninism was worked out in response to changing historical conditions, and the task of ideology was to answer questions, address problems, and resolve contradictions as these emerged. In practice, ideology was the party's mechanism for producing a conscious Communist subject and harmonious Soviet community.

From the beginning, religion was a destabilizing force within Soviet Communism. As ideologically mobilized party cadres and citizen activists repeatedly reminded the party, religion was the only ideological alternative to Marxism-Leninism legally permitted to exist within the closed world of Soviet Communism. Until the 1970s, however, religion could still be folded into the ideological narrative since it could still be construed as dying out. The return of religion—first to Soviet culture, with the intelligentsia's "spiritual turn" under Brezhnev; then to the mass media, with the appearance of positive portrayals of religion on television and in the press under Gorbachev; and finally to public life, with the officially sanctioned celebration of the millennium in 1988—disrupted the internal logic of the Soviet Communism.[48] The return of religion also made atheism seem like an increasingly alien element. Whereas in the 1970s atheists had put forward the convinced atheist as a counterpoint to the indifferent youth, by the late 1980s convinced atheists came to be perceived as a dogmatic sect, marginal—indeed foreign—to the body politic.

Religion's return undermined a system that relied on the constant public articulation of the official narrative for its moral and political legitimacy. Ideological coherence was central to the integrity of Soviet Communism, and atheism was essential to this integrity because it delegitimated competing claims to authority and consolidated the party's claims to a monopoly on truth. By 1988, however, the Soviet establishment was well aware of atheism's conceptual contradictions and practical inefficacy. The party lost confidence that Marxist-Leninist ideology could bridge the gulf between the Communist Party and Soviet society. Atheism proved unable to help the party address the social crisis overwhelming Soviet society or combat the increasing precariousness of its monopoly on power. Nevertheless, the Soviet Communist Party tried to remain ideologically committed to atheism even after 1988. What changed was that it now separated the party's atheist platform from how the state ought to position itself vis-à-vis religion—which is to say, it had given up its monopoly on truth. The Soviet Communist Party's abandonment of atheism and sanctioning of religion destabilized the coherence of Marxist-Leninist ideology, which in turn undermined the legitimacy of the party, which had always defined itself against the political, ideological, and spiritual claims of religion, and viewed the decline of religion as a measure of progress toward Communism. Soviet atheism therefore did not die; it was abandoned by a political project that came to see it as useless to the broader goal of consolidating political, ideological, and spiritual authority. Soviet atheism was abandoned in the divorce of party and state, becoming utopia's orphan.

In important ways, the history of Soviet atheism sheds light on one of the most complicated relationships in Soviet history: the relationship between party and state. The common use of the term "party-state" to describe the Soviet political order suggests that the state was not itself a meaningful political entity. And, to a large degree, this is true, in that for much of the Soviet period, political decision making was concentrated in the top echelons of the Communist Party, with the state operating largely as the executor of the party's will. And yet, the state was never truly subsumed by the party. It remained institutionally autonomous, an autonomy buttressed by the legal separation of party and government organs. Even if this separation was a legal fiction (since power was concentrated in the party), it created the conditions for the party's downfall. When the party and its ideology lost social support and ideological legitimacy, it became a politically meaningless institution—a fact that was illustrated by Gorbachev's formal dissolution of the USSR after it had already ceased to exist as a meaningful geographical and political reality, since it had dissolved into independent states, including an autonomous Russian state. This independent Russian state, it turned out, was both new but old. It was a fledgling democracy, but one that could also claim to be an ancient polity with a millennial pedigree that gave it moral legitimacy—a narrative that in some ways insulated the Russian state from the complexity of its own history. This narrative was supplied by Orthodoxy and consecrated by the public celebration of the anniversary of the Baptism of Rus' in 1988, a moment that has come to be referred to as the "Second Baptism of Rus'."[49] The erection of a statue to Grand Prince Vladimir in the center of Moscow in 2016 was simply the visual culmination of this political narrative.[50] It made manifest the Russian state's rejection of the new world that had been declared in 1917 and its embrace of the old world, the chief value of which was precisely that it was old.

Gorbachev's sanctioning of religion by officially embracing the Orthodox millennium was politically meaningful—and consequential.[51] Reflecting back on the year 1988, the writer Anatolii Strelianskii remarked, "There came a moment when the number one Soviet poet—[Andrei] Voznesensky—and the number one Soviet singer—[Alla] Pugacheva—understood that they could wear a cross around their neck and nothing would happen to them because of it." In the words of one contemporary observer, religion returned to public life, "not through the service entrance, but through the front door."[52] The sanctioned return of religion to public life bolstered the moral authority of the state, but it undermined the Soviet Communist Party, which found itself increasingly marginal to the emerging ideological and political landscape.[53] Soviet Communism's break with atheism in favor of universal values and ideological pluralism signaled the end of the party's monopoly on truth, ideological coherence, and thus moral authority and political legitimacy. The Soviet Communist Party gave up the faith and became simply a political party, no longer seeking to make windows into the human soul.

# NOTES

## *Introduction*

Epigraph: GARF, f. A-561, op. 1, d. 3163, l. 9.

1. Press coverage of the meeting was published in the main party and government newspapers, *Pravda* and *Izvestiia*, as well as the *Journal of the Moscow Patriarchate*. See "Vstrecha General'nogo sekretaria TsK KPSS M. S. Gorbacheva s Patriarkhom Moskovskim i vseia Rusi Pimenom i chlenami Sinoda Russkoi pravoslavnoi tserkvi," *Pravda*, April 30, 1988, 1–2; "Vstrecha General'nogo sekretaria TsK KPSS M. S. Gorbacheva s Patriarkhom Moskovskim i vseia Rusi Pimenom i chlenami Sinoda Russkoi pravoslavnoi tserkvi," *Izvestiia*, April 30, 1988, 1–2; "Vstrecha General'nogo sekretaria TsK KPSS M. S. Gorbacheva s Patriarkhom Moskovskim i vseia Rusi Pimenom i chlenami Synoda Russkoi Pravoslavnoi Tserkvi," *Zhurnal Moskovskoi Patriarkhii*, July 1988, 2–6. It is worth noting that press coverage intended for Soviet citizens placed the article in the bottom-left corner under a dry, neutral title that simply stated the fact of the meeting. *Moskovskie Novosti*, whose audience was foreign, featured it at the top of the page and offered a more compelling title, "Common History, One Fatherland" (*Obshchaia istoriia, odno otechestvo*). This difference in presentation was also reflected in the images that accompanied the articles. Whereas the Soviet audience saw an official meeting with the participants seated around a large round table, the foreign audience saw an intimate close-up of Gorbachev in conversation with Pimen as the other members of the Synod looked on, smiling.

2. There were, in fact, two separate laws passed in October 1990, the first, Law on Freedom of Conscience and Religious Organizations (*Zakon o svobode sovesti i religioznykh organizatsiiakh*), on October 1, 1990, for the USSR, and the second, Law on Freedom of Confession (*Zakon o svobode veroispovedanii*), on October 25, 1990, for the RSFSR. After the dissolution of the USSR, it was the RSFSR law that served as the foundation for the Russian Federation's religious policy. On the 1990 laws as well as the ways in which they informed the subsequent legislation in Russia, see Marat Shterin and James Richardson, "Local Laws Restricting Religion in Russia: Prosecutors of Russia's New National Law," *Journal of Church and State* 40 (1998): 319–41.

3. Jonathan Z. Smith famously wrote that "religion is solely the creation of the scholar's study. It is created for the scholar's analytic purposes by his imaginative acts of comparison and generalization." See Jonathan Z. Smith, *Imagining Religion: From Babylon to Jonestown* (Chicago: University of Chicago Press, 1982), xi. Echoing Smith, E. Valentine Daniel writes, "After almost twenty years of resisting the idea, I have come to the conclusion that religion is not a human universal. It never was. In this rapidly globalizing world it might some day become one. But it isn't one yet." See E. Valentine Daniel, "The Arrogation of Being by the Blind-Spot of Religion," *International Studies in Human Rights* 68 (2002): 31.

4. Donald Lopez Jr. notes that this perspective has produced "the generally unquestioned assumption that adherents of a given religion, any religion, understand that adherence in terms of belief." Donald S. Lopez Jr., "Belief," in *Critical Terms for Religious Studies*, ed. Mark C. Taylor (Chicago: University of Chicago Press, 1998), 21.

5. Jonathan Z. Smith, "Religion, Religions, Religious," in Taylor, *Critical Terms for Religious Studies*, 269. In religious studies, this definition of religion as "belief" is the product of colonialism, the Reformation, the Enlightenment, or the emergence of the social sciences during Europe's "long" nineteenth century. Yet regardless of the specific narrative,

the consensus is that when we speak about "religion," we invoke a concept that is European in origin, Protestant Christian in form, and modern by definition. See Catherine Bell, "Paradigms Behind (and Before) the Modern Concept of Religion," *History and Theory* 45, no. 4 (2006): 27–46; Leora Batnitzky, *How Judaism Became a Religion: An Introduction to Modern Jewish Thought* (Princeton, NJ: Princeton University Press, 2011). On the colonial and early modern origins of religion, see Smith, "Religion, Religions, Religious"; Talal Asad, *Genealogies of Religion: Discipline and Reasons of Power in Christianity and Islam* (Baltimore: Johns Hopkins University Press, 1993); Peter Gottschalk, *Religion, Science, and Empire: Classifying Hinduism and Islam in British India* (Oxford: Oxford University Press, 2013). On the nineteenth-century roots of world religions, see Tomoko Masuzawa, *The Invention of World Religions: Or, How European Universalism Was Preserved in the Language of Pluralism* (Chicago: University of Chicago Press, 2005), 2.

6. Alexis de Tocqueville, *The Old Regime and the French Revolution* (New York: Anchor Books, 1983), 13. There is a robust literature on religion and the French Revolution, but the Russian case has not yet been studied to the same extent. See Suzanne Desan, *Reclaiming the Sacred: Lay Religion and Popular Politics in Revolutionary France* (Ithaca, NY: Cornell University Press, 1990); Mona Ozouf, *Festivals and the French Revolution* (Cambridge, MA: Harvard University Press, 1991); Dale K. Van Kley, *The Religious Origins of the French Revolution: From Calvin to the Civil Constitution, 1560–1791* (New Haven, CT: Yale University Press, 1999); Daniel Schonpflug and Martin Schulze Wessel, eds., *Redefining the Sacred: Religion in the French and Russian Revolutions* (Frankfurt am Main: Lang, 2012).

7. Arthur Koestler, *The God That Failed* (New York: Harper, 1950); Eric Voegelin, *Political Religion* (1938; repr., Lewiston, NY: Edwin Mellen, 1986); Waldemar Gurian, *Bolshevism: An Introduction to Soviet Communism* (Notre Dame, IN: University of Notre Dame Press, 1952).

8. Philippe Burrin, "Political Religion: The Relevance of a Concept," *History and Memory* 9, nos. 1–2 (Fall 1997): 321–49; Emilio Gentile, "Political Religion: A Concept and Its Critics—A Critical Survey," *Totalitarian Movements and Political Religions* 6, no. 1 (2005): 19–32.

9. On Bolshevik millenarianism, see Yuri Slezkine, *The House of Government: A Saga of the Russian Revolution* (Princeton, NJ: Princeton University Press, 2017).

10. Pius XI, "Divini Redemptoris" (March 19, 1937). All citations are drawn from the official English-language translation of the encyclical: http://www.vatican.va/holy_father/pius_xi/encyclicals/documents/hf_p-xi_enc_19031937_divini-redemptoris_en.html. On the importance of Soviet atheism to interwar anti-Communism, see Todd H. Weir, "The Christian Front against Godlessness: Anti-secularism and the Demise of the Weimar Republic, 1928–1933," *Past & Present* 229, no. 1 (2015): 201–38; Giuliana Chamedes, "The Vatican, Nazi-Fascism, and the Making of Transnational Anti-communism in the 1930s," *Journal of Contemporary History* 51, no. 2 (2016): 261–90. On the Cold War mobilization of religion against Communism, see Jonathan P. Herzog, *The Spiritual-Industrial Complex: America's Religious Battle against Communism in the Early Cold War* (Oxford: Oxford University Press, 2011).

11. On the relationship between science and ideology under Stalin, see Ethan Pollock, *Stalin and the Soviet Science Wars* (Princeton, NJ: Princeton University Press, 2006). Even in debates about the nature of "political religion" and "totalitarianism," however, the interactions of science, religion, and atheism in Soviet Communism have rarely been examined together. On science, religion, and ideology, see Michael David-Fox, "Religion, Science, and Political Religion in the Soviet Context," *Modern Intellectual History* 8, no. 2 (2011): 471–84. For a new study that puts these subjects in conversation, see Paul Betts and Stephen A.

Smith, eds., *Science, Religion and Communism in Cold War Europe* (Basingstoke: Palgrave Macmillan, 2016).

12. Sonja Luehrmann, "Was Soviet Society Secular? Undoing Equations between Communism and Religion," in *Atheist Secularism and Its Discontents*, ed. Tam T. T. Ngo and Justine B. Quijada (Basingstoke: Palgrave Macmillan, 2015), 140.

13. Nikolai Berdiaev, Sergei Bulgakov, Semen Frank, Mikhail Gershenzon, and Aleksandr Izgoev, *Vekhi (Landmarks)* (New York: M. E. Sharpe, 1994).

14. Petr Struve, ed., *Iz glubiny: Sbornik statei o russkoi revoliutsii* (1918; repr., Moscow: Novosti, 1999).

15. Nicolas Berdyaev, *The Origin of Russian Communism* (1937; repr., Ann Arbor: University of Michigan Press, 1960), 158. See also Nikolai Berdiaev, *The Russian Revolution* (Ann Arbor: University of Michigan Press, 1961).

16. René Fülöp-Miller, *The Mind and Face of Bolshevism: An Examination of Cultural Life in Soviet Russia* (New York: Harper & Row, 1965), ix, 71–72.

17. On Russian émigré philosophers and anti-Communism during the Cold War, see Christopher Stroop, "The Russian Origins of the So-Called Post-secular Moment: Some Preliminary Observations," *State, Religion and Church* 1, no. 1 (2014): 59–82.

18. For examples of scholarship that emphasizes antireligious repression, see Bohdan Bociurkiw and John Strong, eds., *Religion and Atheism in the USSR and Eastern Europe* (Toronto: University of Toronto Press, 1975); Michael Bourdeaux, *Opium of the People: The Christian Religion in the USSR* (London: Faber and Faber, 1965); Michael Bourdeaux, *Patriarch and Prophets: Persecution of the Russian Orthodox Church Today* (London: Mowbrays, 1975); Michael Bourdeaux, Michael Rowe, and International Committee for the Defense of Human Rights in the USSR, *May One Believe—in Russia? Violations of Religious Liberty in the Soviet Union* (London: Darton, Longman & Todd, 1980); Walter Kolarz, *Religion in the Soviet Union* (London: Macmillan, 1969); Dimitrii V. Pospielovskii, *A History of Marxist-Leninist Atheism and Soviet Antireligious Policies* (New York: St. Martin's, 1997); and Paul Froese, *The Plot to Kill God: Findings from the Soviet Experiment in Secularization* (Berkeley: University of California Press, 2008). Sonja Luehrmann offers an analysis of the ways in which early studies of religion in the Soviet Union constituted a form of Cold War activism. See Sonja Luehrmann, *Religion in Secular Archives: Soviet Atheism and Historical Knowledge* (New York: Oxford University Press, 2015), esp. chap. 4, "Counter-Archives: Sympathy on Record."

19. For literature that privileges atheism in the framework of ideology, see David E. Powell, *Antireligious Propaganda in the Soviet Union: A Study in Mass Persuasion* (Cambridge, MA: MIT Press, 1975); James Thrower, *Marxist-Leninist "Scientific Atheism" and the Study of Religion and Atheism in the USSR* (New York: Mouton, 1983); Richard Stites, *Revolutionary Dreams: Utopian Vision and Experimental Life in the Russian Revolution* (New York: Oxford University Press, 1989); Glennys Young, *Power and the Sacred in Revolutionary Russia: Religious Activists in the Village* (University Park: Pennsylvania State University Press, 1997); Daniel Peris, *Storming the Heavens: The Soviet League of the Militant Godless* (Ithaca, NY: Cornell University Press, 1998); William B. Husband, *"Godless Communists": Atheism and Society in Soviet Russia, 1917–1932* (DeKalb: Northern Illinois University Press, 2000); Valerii Alekseev, *"Shturm nebes" otmeniaetsia? Kriticheskie ocherki po istorii bor'by s religiei v SSSR* (Moscow: Rossiia molodaia, 1992). Arto Luukkanen addresses both ideology and governance, though in separate books. See Arto Luukkanen, *The Religious Policy of the Stalinist State. A Case Study: The Central Standing Commission on Religious Questions, 1929–1938* (Helsinki: Suomen Historiallinen Seura, 1997); Arto Luukkanen, *The Party of Unbelief: The Religious Policy of the Bolshevik Party, 1917–1929* (Helsinki: Societas Historiae Finlandiae, 1994).

20. Stephen Kotkin, *Magnetic Mountain: Stalinism as a Civilization* (Berkeley: University of California Press, 1995); Igal Halfin, *Stalinist Confessions: Messianism and Terror at the Leningrad Communist University* (Pittsburgh: University of Pittsburgh Press, 2009); Halfin, *From Darkness to Light: Class, Consciousness, and Salvation in Revolutionary Russia* (Pittsburgh: University of Pittsburgh Press, 2000); Jochen Hellbeck, *Revolution on My Mind: Writing a Diary under Stalin* (Cambridge, MA: Harvard University Press, 2006).

21. For works that extend into the postwar period, see John Anderson, *Religion, State and Politics in the Soviet Union and Successor States* (Cambridge: Cambridge University Press, 1994); Sonja Luehrmann, *Secularism Soviet Style: Teaching Atheism and Religion in a Volga Republic* (Bloomington: Indiana University Press, 2011); Luehrmann, *Religion in Secular Archives*; Catherine Wanner, ed., *State Secularism and Lived Religion in Soviet Russia and Ukraine* (New York: Oxford University Press, 2012); Ulrike Huhn, *Glaube und Eigensinn: Volksfrömmigkeit zwischen orthodoxer Kirche und Sowjetischem Staat, 1941 bis 1960* (Wiesbaden: Harrassowitz Verlag, 2014); Emily B. Baran, *Dissent on the Margins: How Soviet Jehovah's Witnesses Defied Communism and Lived to Preach about It* (Oxford: Oxford University Press, 2014); Catriona Kelly, *Socialist Churches: Radical Secularization and the Preservation of the Past in Petrograd and Leningrad, 1918–1988* (DeKalb: Northern Illinois University Press, 2016). In a noteworthy departure from much of the Anglophone scholarship, Russian scholars who work on religion in the USSR underscore the institutional distinctions between the government and party approaches to religion. See Tatiana Chumachenko, *Church and State in Soviet Russia: Russian Orthodoxy from World War II to the Khrushchev Years*, trans. and ed. Edward E. Roslof (Armonk, NY: M. E. Sharpe, 2002); Mikhail V. Shkarovskii, *Russkaia pravoslavnaia tserkov' pri Staline i Khrushcheve (gosudarstvenno-tserkovnye otnosheniia v SSSR v 1939–1964 godakh)* (Moscow: Krutitskoe patriarshee podvor'e, 1999); Shkarovskii, *Russkaia Pravoslavnaia Tserkov' v XX veke* (Moscow: Veche, Lepta, 2010); Mikhail I. Odintsov and Tatiana A. Chumachenko, *Sovet po delam Russkoi pravoslavnoi tserkvi pri SNK (SM) SSSR i Moskovskaia patriarkhiia: epokha vzaimoseistviia i protivostoianiia, 1943–1965* (Saint Petersburg: Rossiiskoe ob"edinenie issledovatelei religii, 2013).

22. On Orthodoxy, see Edward E. Roslof, *Red Priests: Renovationism, Russian Orthodoxy, and Revolution, 1905–1946* (Bloomington: Indiana University Press, 2002); Nathaniel Davis, *A Long Walk to Church: A Contemporary History of Russian Orthodoxy* (Boulder, CO: Westview, 2003); Scott M. Kenworthy, *The Heart of Russia: Trinity-Sergius, Monasticism, and Society after 1825* (Oxford: Oxford University Press, 2010); Sergei Firsov, *Vlast' i ogon': Tserkov' i sovetskoe gosudarstvo, 1918–nachalo 1940–kh gg* (Moscow: Pravoslavnyi Sviato-Tikhonovskii Gumanitarnyi Universitet, 2014). On Baptism and Protestantism, see Catherine Wanner, *Communities of the Converted: Ukrainians and Global Evangelism* (Ithaca, NY: Cornell University Press, 2007); Heather J. Coleman, *Russian Baptists and Spiritual Revolution, 1905–1929* (Bloomington: Indiana University Press, 2005); Tat'iana Nikol'skaia, *Russkii protestantizm i gosudarstvennaia vlast' v 1905–1991 godakh* (Saint Petersburg: European University Press, 2009); Alexander Kashirin, "Protestant Minorities in the Soviet Ukraine, 1945–1991" (PhD diss., University of Oregon, 2010). On Islam, see Yaacov R'oi, *Islam in the Soviet Union: From the Second World War to Gorbachev* (London: Hurst, 2000); Eren Murat Tasar, "Soviet and Muslim: The Institutionalization of Islam in Central Asia, 1943–1991" (PhD diss., Harvard University, 2010); Shoshana Keller, *To Moscow, Not Mecca: The Soviet Campaign against Islam in Central Asia, 1917–1941* (Westport, CT: Praeger, 2001); Adeeb Khalid, *Islam after Communism: Religion and Politics in Central Asia* (Berkeley: University of California Press, 2007); Michael Kemper, *Studying Islam in the Soviet Union* (Amsterdam: Vossiuspers UvA, 2009); Galina Yemelianova,

*Russia and Islam: A Historical Survey* (Basingstoke: Palgrave, 2002). On Judaism, see Zvi Y. Gitelman, *Jewish Nationality and Soviet Politics: The Jewish Sections of the CPSU, 1917–1930* (Princeton, NJ: Princeton University Press, 1972), 298–318; Judith Deutsch Kornblatt, *Doubly Chosen: Jewish Identity, the Soviet Intelligentsia, and the Russian Orthodox Church* (Madison: University of Wisconsin Press, 2004); Anna Shternshis, *Soviet and Kosher: Jewish Popular Culture in the Soviet Union, 1923–1939* (Bloomington: Indiana University Press, 2006), 1–43; Mordechai Altshuler, *Religion and Jewish Identity in the Soviet Union, 1941–1964* (Waltham, MA: Brandeis University Press, 2012), 1–22, 90–116, 205–314; Elissa Bemporad, *Becoming Soviet Jews: The Bolshevik Experiment in Minsk* (Bloomington: Indiana University Press, 2013), 112–44; Yohanan Petrovsky-Shtern, *Lenin's Jewish Question* (New Haven, CT: Yale University Press, 2010).

23. For literature that privileges the framework of secular governance, see Wanner, *State Secularism and Lived Religion*, 1–26; Luehrmann, *Secularism Soviet Style*; Ngo and Quijada, *Atheist Secularism and Its Discontents*; Marian Burchardt, Monika Wohlrab-Sahr, and Matthias Middell, "Multiple Secularities beyond the West: An Introduction," in *Multiple Secularities beyond the West: Religion and Modernity in the Global Age*, ed. Marian Burchardt, Monika Wohlrab-Sahr, and Matthias Middell (Berlin: De Gruyter, 2015), 1–15.

24. For an overview of the debates surrounding the politics of secularism, see Phil Zuckerman and John R. Shook, "Introduction: The Study of Secularism," in *The Oxford Handbook of Secularism*, ed. Phil Zuckerman and John R. Shook (New York: Oxford University Press, 2017), 1–17.

25. Asad, *Genealogies of Religion*; Winnifred Fallers Sullivan, *The Impossibility of Religious Freedom* (Princeton, NJ: Princeton University Press, 2005); Michael Warner, Jonathan Van Antwerpen, and Craig J. Calhoun, *Varieties of Secularism in a Secular Age* (Cambridge, MA: Harvard University Press, 2010); Saba Mahmood, *Religious Difference in a Secular Age: A Minority Report* (Princeton, NJ: Princeton University Press, 2015); Elizabeth Shakman Hurd, *The Politics of Secularism in International Relations* (Princeton, NJ: Princeton University Press, 2007); Charles Taylor, *A Secular Age* (Cambridge, MA: Harvard University Press, 2007); Linell E. Cady and Elizabeth Shakman Hurd, "Comparative Secularisms and the Politics of Modernity: An Introduction," in *Comparative Secularisms in a Global Age*, ed. Linell E. Cady and Elizabeth Shakman Hurd (New York: Palgrave Macmillan, 2010), 3–24; Bruce R. Berglund and Brian Porter, eds., *Christianity and Modernity in Eastern Europe* (Budapest: Central European University Press, 2010).

26. Asad, *Genealogies of Religion*, 207. Mayanthi L. Fernando observes that with the advent of the secular, belief emerges as "the authentic site of religion." See Mayanthi L. Fernando, *The Republic Unsettled: Muslim French and the Contradictions of Secularism* (Durham, NC: Duke University Press, 2014), 166.

27. Wanner, for example, suggests that governance offers a more productive approach to understanding Soviet secularism, since "it is the historically shifting needs of governance that provoke the ups and downs of intensity of religious sentiment and shifting understandings as to what constitutes belief and appropriate practice." See Wanner, *State Secularism and Lived Religion*, 9.

28. Ngo and Quijada, *Atheist Secularism and Its Discontents*, 7. For comparative studies of secularism that seek to broaden the spectrum of what constitutes the "secular" and point to the limitations of equating secularism with liberalism, see Rajeev Bhargava, ed., *Secularism and Its Critics* (New Delhi: Oxford University Press, 1998).

29. Juliane Fürst, *Stalin's Last Generation: Soviet Post-war Youth and the Emergence of Mature Socialism* (Oxford: Oxford University Press, 2010); Donald J. Raleigh, *Soviet Baby Boomers: An Oral History of Russia's Cold War Generation* (New York: Oxford University Press, 2013); Dina Fainberg and Artemy Kalinovsky, eds., *Reconsidering Stagnation in the*

*Brezhnev Era: Ideology and Exchange* (Lanham, MD: Lexington Books, 2016). One area that has made a particularly valuable contribution to the analysis of late socialist ideology is the study of the media under late socialism. See Thomas C. Wolfe, *Governing Soviet Journalism: The Press and the Socialist Person after Stalin* (Bloomington: Indiana University Press, 2005); Paulina Bren, *The Greengrocer and His TV: The Culture of Communism after the 1968 Prague Spring* (Ithaca, NY: Cornell University Press, 2010); Kristin Roth-Ey, *Moscow Prime Time: How the Soviet Union Built the Media Empire That Lost the Cultural Cold War* (Ithaca, NY: Cornell University Press, 2011); Christine E. Evans, *Between Truth and Time: A History of Soviet Central Television* (New Haven, CT: Yale University Press, 2016).

30. Oleg Kharkhordin, *The Collective and the Individual in Russia* (Berkeley: University of California Press, 1999); Alexei Yurchak, *Everything Was Forever until It Was No More: The Last Soviet Generation* (Princeton, NJ: Princeton University Press, 2006) and his translated and revised Aleksei Iurchak, *Eto bylo navsegda, poka ne konichilos': Poslednee sovetskoe pokolenie* (Moscow: Novoe Literaturnoe Obozrenie, 2014); Sergei I. Zhuk, *Rock and Roll in the Rocket City: The West, Identity, and Ideology in Soviet Dniepropetrovsk, 1960–1985* (Baltimore: Johns Hopkins University Press, 2010); Anatoly Pinsky, ed., *Posle Stalina: Pozdnesovetskaia sub"ektivnost', 1953–1985* (Saint Petersburg: Izdatel'stvo Evropeiskogo universiteta v Sankt-Peterburge, 2017).

31. Peter Kenez, *The Birth of the Propaganda State: Soviet Methods of Mass Mobilization, 1917–1929* (New York: Cambridge University Press, 1985); David Brandenberger, *Propaganda State in Crisis: Soviet Ideology, Indoctrination, and Terror under Stalin, 1927–1941* (Cambridge, MA: Harvard University Press, 2002).

32. On the inner workings of the Communist Party, see Nikolai Mitrokhin, *Russkaia Partiia: Dvizhenie russkikh natsionalistov v SSSR. 1953–1985 gg.* (Moscow: Novoe Literaturnoe Obozrenie, 2003); Nikolai Mitrokhin, "Back-office Mikhaila Suslova ili kem i kak proizvodilas' ideologiia Brezhnevskogo vremeni," *Cahiers du monde russe* 54, no. 3 (2013): 409–40; Caroline Humphrey, "The 'Creative Bureaucrat': Conflicts in the Production of Soviet Communist Party Discourse," *Inner Asia* 10, no. 1 (2008): 5–35.

33. Karl Marx, "Contribution to the Critique of Hegel's *Philosophy of Right:* Introduction [1844]," in *The Marx-Engels Reader*, 2nd ed., ed. Robert Tucker (New York: Norton, 1978), 54.

34. Karl Marx, "Theses on Feuerbach [1845]," in Tucker, *Marx-Engels Reader*, 145.

35. Karl Marx and Friedrich Engels, "The German Ideology (1845–1846)," in Tucker, *Marx-Engels Reader*, 158.

36. Marx, "Contribution to the Critique," 59.

37. Ibid., 54.

38. Ibid., emphasis original.

39. Friedrich Engels, "Socialism: Utopian and Scientific," in Tucker, *Marx-Engels Reader*, 725–27.

40. Auguste Comte, "The Positive Philosophy," in *Introduction to Contemporary Civilization in the West* (New York: Columbia University Press, 1961), 2:767–91.

41. Gareth Stedman Jones, "Religion and the Origins of Socialism," in *Religion and the Political Imagination*, ed. Ira Katznelson and Gareth Stedman Jones (Cambridge: Cambridge University Press, 2010), 171–89. Stedman Jones proposes that socialism was "the outcome of a critique, not so much of the state, as of the church, and of the unsuccessful revolutionary attempts to find a replacement for it" (174–75).

42. Marx, "Contribution to the Critique," 40.

43. Karl Marx and Frederick Engels, "Manifesto of the Communism Party (Extracts from Chapters II and III)," in *Karl Marx and Friedrich Engels on Religion* (Mineola, NY: Dover, 2008), 88.

44. Vladimir Lenin, "Sotsializm i religiia," in *Lenin ob ateizme, religii, i tserkvi (Sbornik statei, pisem i drugikh materialov)* (Moscow: Mysl', 1969), 43, 46.

45. Ibid., 43.

46. Ibid., 44–45.

47. Ibid., 45.

48. Ibid., 46–47.

49. Richard Stites notes that Gorky, in his *Confession* (1907), coined the terms "God-seeking" and "God-building," while Lunacharskii was the "real innovator" behind God-building, providing a comprehensive treatment in *Religion and Socialism* (1908–11). See Stites, *Revolutionary Dreams*, 102–3.

50. Vladimir Lenin to Maxim Gorky, November 13–14, 1913, in *Polnoe sobranie sochinenii*, 5th ed. (Moscow, 1958–65), 48:226–29.

51. David Myers, "Marx, Atheism and Revolutionary Action," *Canadian Journal of Philosophy* 11, no. 2 (1981): 317–18.

52. Emelian Iaroslavskii, *Kak rodiatsia, zhivut i umiraiut bogi i bogini* (Moscow: Sovetskaia Rossiia, 1959), 7.

53. The term "byt" is famously difficult to translate. As literary scholar Irina Gutkin notes, byt is derivative of verb "to be," and was initially used to designate material objects like household belongings. By the beginning of the nineteenth century, "the word came to mean more generally a combination of customs and mores manifest in the forms of everyday life characteristic of a given social milieu." See Irina Gutkin, *The Cultural Origins of the Socialist Realist Aesthetic, 1890–1934* (Evanston, IL: Northwestern University Press, 1999), 81.

54. After Stalin's rapprochement with religion during the war, this work fell to the Council on the Affairs of the Russian Orthodox Church (CAROC) and the Council on the Affairs of Religious Cults (CARC), which in 1965 were united into the Council for Religious Affairs (CRA).

55. The Soviet security apparatus underwent numerous reforms over the course of the Soviet period, and included, in chronological order, the All-Russian Extraordinary Commission for the Struggle with Counter-Revolution and Sabotage (VChK or Vecheka), Joint State Political Directorate (OGPU), People's Commissariat for Internal Affairs (NKVD), People's Commissariat for State Security (NKGB), and Committee for State Security (KGB). See Julie Fedor, *Russia and the Cult of State Security: The Chekist Tradition, from Lenin to Putin* (New York: Routledge, 2013).

56. For an overview of the population of the Russian Empire by confession according to the 1897 census, see Paul W. Werth, *The Tsar's Foreign Faiths: Toleration and the Fate of Religious Freedom in Imperial Russia* (Oxford: Oxford University Press, 2014), 4, 37. According to the 1897 census (with select revisions), Orthodox and Old Believers made up 69.4 percent of the empire (89,377,000 adherents), Muslims 10.8 percent (13,907,000), Roman Catholics 9.0 percent (11,468,600), Protestants 5.0 percent (6,390,800), Jews 4.1 percent (5,228,700), Armenians 0.9 percent (the exact number of adherents was not recorded), and Pagans 0.7 percent (719,900).

57. Yuri Slezkine, "The USSR as a Communal Apartment, or How a Socialist State Promoted Ethnic Particularism," *Slavic Review* 53, no. 2 (1994): 414–52.

## *Chapter 1: The Religious Front*

1. Paul W. Werth, *The Tsar's Foreign Faiths: Toleration and the Fate of Religious Freedom in Imperial Russia* (Oxford: Oxford University Press, 2014). For an overview of imperial Russia's confessional landscape, see ibid., 12–29. See also Robert P. Geraci and Michael

Khodarkovsky, eds., *Of Religion and Empire: Missions, Conversion, and Tolerance in Tsarist Russia* (Ithaca, NY: Cornell University Press, 2001); Robert D. Crews, "Empire and the Confessional State: Islam and Religious Politics in Nineteenth-Century Russia," *American Historical Review* 108, no. 1 (2003): 50–83; Crews, *For Prophet and Tsar: Islam and Empire in Russia and Central Asia* (Cambridge, MA: Harvard University Press, 2006); Theodore R. Weeks, *Nation and State in Late Imperial Russia: Nationalism and Russification on the Western Frontier, 1863–1914* (DeKalb: Northern Illinois University Press, 2008); Mikhail Dolbilov, *Russkii krai, chuzhaia vera: Etnokonfessional'naia politika imperii v Litve i Belorussii pri Aleksandre II* (Moscow: Novoe Literaturnoe Obozrenie, 2010); Eileen Kane, *Russian Hajj: Empire and the Pilgrimage to Mecca* (Ithaca, NY: Cornell University Press, 2015).

2. Paul W. Werth, "In the State's Embrace? Civil Acts in an Imperial Order," *Kritika: Explorations in Russian and Eurasian History* 7, no. 3 (2006): 433–58; Charles Steinwedel, "Making Social Groups, One Person at a Time: The Identification of Individuals by Estate, Religious Confession, and Ethnicity in Late Imperial Russia," *Documenting Individual Identity: The Development of State Practices in the Modern World*, ed. Jane Caplan and John Torpey (Princeton, NJ: Princeton University Press, 2001), 67–82.

3. On "Official Nationality" and the ambiguity of the term "narodnost'," see Nicholas Riasonovsky, *Russian Identities: A Historical Survey* (New York: Oxford University Press, 2005), 133, 141.

4. Simon Franklin and Jonathan Shepard, *The Emergence of Rus 750–1200* (London: Longman, 1998), 367–69. Historians Franklin and Shephard write that the lands of the Rus' were "afflicted by the decay of feudal disunity," which led to "catastrophic disintegration" (367–68). But they also pose the question of whether early Kiev Rus' was "an entity or a plurality" (369). Their answer is that it was both: "It was no unitary state, it had no fixed hierarchy of power, no central structure of administration, no institutional atrophy to stunt local economic initiatives. On the other hand, there were clearly affinities between the dynastic lands which set them apart—collectively—from their neighbours" (369). See also Alexis P. Vlasto, *The Entry of the Slavs into Christendom: An Introduction to the Medieval History of the Slavs* (Cambridge: Cambridge University Press, 1970).

5. Georgii P. Fedotov, *The Russian Religious Mind*, vol. 2 (Cambridge, MA: Harvard University Press, 1966), 22.

6. On the role of religious discipline in the consolidation of the early modern state, see Philip S. Gorski, *The Disciplinary Revolution: Calvinism and the Rise of the State in Early Modern Europe* (Chicago: University of Chicago Press, 2003).

7. On Peter's church reforms, see James Cracraft, *The Church Reform of Peter the Great* (Stanford, CA: Stanford University Press, 1971). On the Holy Synod, see John D. Basil, *Church and State in Late Imperial Russia: Critics of the Synodal System of Church Government (1861–1914)* (Minneapolis: University of Minnesota Press, 2005). The nature of the "symphonic" relationship between the Russian Orthodox Church and Russian state remains deeply contested. For two opposing views, see Richard Pipes, "The Church as Servant of the State," in *Russia under the Old Regime* (New York: Penguin, 1974), 221–45; Gregory L. Freeze, "Handmaiden of the State? The Church in Imperial Russia Reconsidered," *Journal of Ecclesiastical History* 36, no. 1 (1985): 82–102. Freeze offers the most forceful argument against seeing the church as the state's handmaiden. Yet I follow Vera Shevzov, among others, in seeing the state as setting the parameters of church activity, even if it was not directly involved in every aspect of church affairs. See Vera Shevzov, *Russian Orthodoxy on the Eve of Revolution* (New York: Oxford University Press, 2004), 15–17.

8. On state efforts to discipline superstition in imperial Russia, see Simon Dixon, "Superstition in Imperial Russia," *Past & Present* 199 (2008): 207–28; Viktor Zhivov, "Dist-

siplinarnaia revoliutsiia i bor'ba s sueveriem v Rossii XVIII veka: 'provaly' i ikh posled-stviia," in *Antropologiia revoliutsii: Sbornik statei po materialam XVI Bannykh chtennii zhurnala "Novoe literaturnoe obozrenie,"* ed. Irina Prokhorova, Aleksandr Dmitriev, Il'ia Kikulin, and Maria Maiofis (Moscow: Novoe Literaturnoe Obozrenie, 2009), 327–61.

9. Zhivov, "Distsiplinarnaia revoliutsiia i bor'ba," 352.

10. Alexander V. Muller, trans and ed., *The Spiritual Regulation of Peter the Great* (Seattle: University of Washington Press, 1972), 10, cited in Shevzov, *Russian Orthodoxy*, 16n21.

11. Nadieszda Kizenko, "Hand in Hand: Church, State, Society, and the Sacrament of Confession in Imperial Russia" (forthcoming). I am grateful to Nadieszda Kizenko for sharing her unpublished manuscript with me.

12. Chris J. Chulos, *Converging Worlds: Religion and Community in Peasant Russia, 1861–1917* (DeKalb: Northern Illinois University Press, 2003), 5; Moshe Lewin, "Popular Religion in Twentieth-Century Russia," in *The World of the Russian Peasant: Post-emancipation Culture and Society*, ed. Ben Eklof and Stephen Frank (Boston: Unwin Hyman, 1990), 155–68.

13. Reginald E. Zelnik, "'To the Unaccustomed Eye': Religion and Irreligion in the Experience of St. Petersburg Workers in the 1870s," *Russian History* 16, nos. 2–4 (1989): 297–326; Mark D. Steinberg, "Workers on the Cross: Religious Imagination in the Writings of Russian Workers, 1910–1924," *Russian Review* 53, no. 2 (April 1994): 213–39; Page Herrlinger, *Working Souls: Russian Orthodoxy and Factory Labor in St. Petersburg, 1881–1917* (Bloomington, IN: Slavica, 2007).

14. On lived Orthodoxy, see Shevzov, *Russian Orthodoxy*; Christine Worobec, "Lived Orthodoxy in Imperial Russia," *Kritika: Explorations in Russian and Eurasian History* 7, no. 2 (2006): 329–50.

15. Paul W. Werth, "The Emergence of 'Freedom of Conscience' in Imperial Russia," *Kritika: Explorations in Russian and Eurasian History* 13, no. 3 (2012): 585–610; Randall A. Poole, "Religious Toleration, Freedom of Conscience, and Russian Liberalism," *Kritika: Explorations in Russian and Eurasian History* 13, no. 3 (2012): 611–34; Victoria Frede, "Freedom of Conscience, Freedom of Confession, and 'Land and Freedom' in the 1860s," *Kritika: Explorations in Russian and Eurasian History* 13, no. 3 (2012): 561–84.

16. As historian Geoffrey Hosking notes, the "symphonic" relationship of the Orthodox Church with the imperial state, while bestowing it with privileges and protections, also put it in a "double bind": "It had the advantages of being the established church, but also the disadvantages of not being able to order its own principles." The bureaucratization of the church distanced it from the lives of ordinary people, and at the same time charged it with "fulfill[ing] functions delegated to it by the imperial state whose priorities were not its own." See Geoffrey Hosking, "The Russian Orthodox Church and Secularisation," in *Religion and the Political Imagination*, ed. Ira Katznelson and Gareth Stedman Jones (Cambridge: Cambridge University Press, 2010), 117.

17. Alexander Etkind, *Khlist: Sects, Literature and Revolution* (Moscow: New Literary Review, 1998); Laura Engelstein, *Castration and the Heavenly Kingdom: A Russian Folktale* (Ithaca, NY: Cornell University Press, 2003); Sergei I. Zhuk, *Russia's Lost Reformation: Peasants, Millennialism, and Radical Sects in Southern Russia and Ukraine, 1830–1917* (Baltimore: Johns Hopkins University Press, 2004).

18. Laura Engelstein, *Slavophile Empire: Imperial Russia's Illiberal Path* (Ithaca, NY: Cornell University Press, 2009), 92–94; Werth, *Tsar's Foreign Faiths*, 187–88, 195.

19. Werth, *Tsar's Foreign Faiths*, 230–32, 239.

20. Victoria Frede, *Doubt, Atheism, and the Nineteenth-Century Russian Intelligentsia* (Madison: University of Wisconsin Press, 2011), 11, 35. On religious and ideological

commitments among the prerevolutionary Russian intelligentsia, see also Christopher Read, *Religion, Revolution and the Russian Intelligentsia, 1900–1912* (London: Palgrave Macmillan, 1979); Laurie Manchester, *Holy Fathers, Secular Sons: Clergy, Intelligentsia, and the Modern Self in Revolutionary Russia* (DeKalb: Northern Illinois University Press, 2008). On the "crisis of value" among Russian-educated society at the turn of the century, see the introduction to Bernice Glazer Rosenthal and Martha Bochachevsky-Chomiak, eds., *A Revolution of the Spirit: Crisis of Value in Russia, 1890–1924*, trans. Marian Schwartz (New York: Fordham University Press, 1990), 1–40.

21. Vladimir Lenin, "Sotsializm i religiia," in *Lenin ob ateizme, religii, i tserkvi (Sbornik statei, pisem i drugikh materialov)* (Moscow: Mysl', 1969), 45.

22. "Dekret o zemle," in *Dekrety Sovetskoi vlasti* (Moscow: Gos. izd-vo polit. literatury, 1957), 1:17–19.

23. "Dekret o grazhdanskom brake, o detiakh i o vedenii knig aktov sostoianiia," in *Sobranie uzakonenii i rasporiazhenii pravitel'stva za 1917–1918 gg. Upravlenie Sovnarkoma SSSR* (Moscow, 1942), 161–63.

24. "Dekret Soveta Narodnykh Komissarov. Ob otdelenii tserkvi ot gosudarstva i shkoly ot tserkvi," in *Sobranie uzakonenii i rasporiazhenii*, 286–87. The first version of the decree, which was passed three days later with some alterations, was titled "Decree on Freedom of Conscience, Church, and Religious Organizations" (January 20, 1918). See "Dekret o svobode sovesti, tserkovnykh i religioznykh obshchestvakh," in *Dekrety Sovetskoi vlasti*, 1:373–74.

25. "Dekret Soveta Narodnykh Komissarov. Ob otdelenii tserkvi ot gosudarstva i shkoly ot tserkvi," in *Sobranie uzakonenii i rasporiazhenii*, 286.

26. On the argument that the early antireligious campaigns were aimed above all at the Orthodox Church, see Georgii Mitrofanov, *Istoriia Russkoi Pravoslavnoi Tserkvi: 1900–1927* (Saint Petersburg: Satis, 2002).

27. In fact, the first years of Soviet power have been called a "golden age" of Russian sectarianism. For an overview of this trope, see Heather J. Coleman, *Russian Baptists and Spiritual Revolution, 1905–1929* (Bloomington: Indiana University Press, 2005), 154, 196, 224.

28. Vladimir Lenin, "Proekt programmy nashei partii" (1899), in *Lenin ob ateizme, religii, i tserkvi*, 17–18.

29. Vladimir Bonch-Bruevich, "O religii, religioznom sektanstve i tserkvi," in *Izbrannye sochineniia*, vol. 1 (Moscow, 1959), 33. On the Bolsheviks and sectarianism, see Aleksandr Etkind, "Russkie sekty i sovetskii kommunizm: Proekt Vladimira Bonch Bruevicha," *Minuvshee: Istoricheskii al'manakh* 19 (1996): 275–319.

30. After the fall of the autocracy, the Provisional Government allowed the Orthodox Church to convene the Church Council, which met over the course of 1917–18. See Aleksandr A. Safonov, *Svoboda sovesti i modernizatsiia veroispovednogo zakonodatel'stva Rossiiskoi imperii v nachale XX v* (Tambov: Izdatel'stvo R. V. Pershina, 2007).

31. A. Vvedenskii, *Tserkov' i gosudarstvo* (Moscow: Mospoligraf "Krasnyi Proletarii," 1923), 115, cited in Nathaniel Davis, *A Long Walk to Church: A Contemporary History of Russian Orthodoxy* (Boulder, CO: Westview, 2003), 2.

32. Once Patriarch Tikhon declared his loyalty to the Soviet regime, the Bolshevik support for Renovationism subsided. See Edward E. Roslof, *Red Priests: Renovationism, Russian Orthodoxy, and Revolution, 1905–1946* (Bloomington: Indiana University Press, 2002); Mikhail V. Shkarovskii, *Obnovlencheskoe dvizhenie v Russkoi Pravoslavnoi Tserkvi XX veka* (Saint Petersburg: Izd. Nestor, 1999).

33. Natalia Krivova, *Vlast' i Tserkov' v 1922–1925 gg.: Politburo i GPU v bor'be za tserkovnye tsennosti i politicheskoe podchinenie dukhovenstva* (Moscow: AIRO-XX, 1997); Jonathan W. Daly, "'Storming the Last Citadel': The Bolshevik Assault on the Church, 1922,"

in *The Bolsheviks in Russian Society: The Revolution and the Civil Wars*, ed. Vladimir N. Brovkin (New Haven, CT: Yale University Press, 1997), 236–59; James Ryan, "Cleansing *NEP* Russia: State Violence against the Russian Orthodox Church in 1922," *Europe-Asia Studies* 9 (2013): 1807–26.

34. *Izvestiia TsK KPSS*, no. 4 (1990): 193. On Lenin's letter, see Roslof, *Red Priests*, 66–67.

35. Vladimir Lenin, "O znachenii voinstvuiushchego materializma" (1922), in *Polnoe sobranie sochinenii*, 5th ed. (Moscow, 1958–65), 45:23–33.

36. Ibid., 45:23.

37. Ibid., 45:24.

38. Ibid., 45:24.

39. Ibid., 45:26.

40. Ibid., 45:26.

41. Aleksei Beglov, *V poiskakh bezgreshnykh katakomb: Tserkovnoe podpol'e v SSSR* (Moscow: Izdatel'skii sovet Russkoi Pravoslavnoi Tserkvi i Arefa, 2008).

42. Davis, *Long Walk to Church*, 4–5. Metropolitan Sergii's declaration of loyalty to Soviet power produced a schism within the Russian Orthodox Church that shaped relations with the Russian Orthodox Church Abroad for the rest of the twentieth century.

43. Beglov, *V poiskakh bezgreshnykh katakomb*, 19.

44. Beglov writes that already in 1922, the Bolsheviks realized that "shifting the borders of legality can be used as a powerful weapon" to subordinate the church, yet it became clear that as the legal borders of religious life were narrowed, more and more people would be pushed into the catacombs. Ibid., 39.

45. On Stalin's shift on religion during the New Economic Policy (NEP), see Igor A. Kurliandskii, "Stalin i religioznyi vopros v politike bol'shevistskoi vlasti (1917–1923)," *Vestnik PSTGU* 5 (48): 72–84; Igor A. Kurliandskii, *Stalin, vlast' i religiia* (Moscow: Kuchkovo Pole, 2011).

46. Lev Trotsky, "Ne o 'politike' edinoi zhiv chelovek," in *Voprosy byta: Epokha "kul'turnichestva" i ee zadachi* (Moscow: Gosizdat, 1923), 7.

47. Robert Greene, *Bodies Like Bright Stars: Saints and Relics in Orthodox Russia* (DeKalb: Northern Illinois University Press, 2010), 122–59; Steven A. Smith, "Bones of Contention: Bolsheviks and the Struggle against Relics, 1918–1930," *Past & Present* 204, no. 1 (2009): 155–94.

48. Victoria Bonnell, *Iconography of Power: Soviet Political Posters under Lenin and Stalin* (Berkeley: University of California Press, 1997).

49. Larry E. Holmes, *The Kremlin and the Schoolhouse: Reforming Education in Soviet Russia, 1917–1953* (Bloomington: Indiana University Press, 1991), 3–4.

50. Anatoly Lunacharsky, *On Education: Selected Articles and Speeches* (Moscow, 1981), 168–69, cited in Holmes, *Kremlin and the Schoolhouse*, 5n12. On Lunacharsky's work, see Sheila Fitzpatrick, *The Commissariat of Enlightenment: Soviet Organization of Education and the Arts under Lunacharsky (October 1917–1921)* (Cambridge: Cambridge University Press, 1970).

51. Holmes, *Kremlin and the Schoolhouse*, 5, 11–12.

52. Larry E. Holmes, "Fear No Evil: Schools and Religion in Soviet Russia, 1917–1941," in *Religious Policy in the Soviet Union*, ed. Sabrina P. Ramet (New York: Cambridge University Press, 1993), 134.

53. Ibid., 135.

54. Ibid., 131–32.

55. Jeffrey Brooks argues that for many intellectuals involved in the enlightenment project, the battle was against superstition rather than religion, and points out that priests

and teachers were allied with authors of popular literature in the task of enlightening the population. Superstition was "clearly not equated" with religion, "nor was atheism considered a necessary concomitant to the rational world view." See Jeffrey Brooks, *When Russia Learned to Read: Literacy and Popular Literature, 1861–1917* (Princeton, NJ: Princeton University Press, 1985), 251. James Andrews shows that the scientific intelligentsia saw the eradication of religion not necessarily as an end in itself but instead as a means for overcoming nonscientific thinking. James T. Andrews, *Science for the Masses: The Bolshevik State, Public Science, and the Popular Imagination in Soviet Russia, 1917–1934* (College Station: Texas A&M University Press, 2003), 104–5, 172.

56. Early antireligious museums were frequently improvised, and depending on one's criteria for designating an exhibit a "museum," there were anywhere from thirty to several hundred antireligious museums in the Soviet Union by the 1930s. It is also worth noting that there was a distinct tension between preservationism, which promoted turning churches into museums and religious objects into cultural artifacts, and iconoclasm, which sought to desecrate religious spaces and objects. See Crispin Paine, "Militant Atheist Objects: Anti-religion Museums in the Soviet Union," *Present Pasts* 1 (2009): 61–76; Adam Jolles, "Stalin's Talking Museums," *Oxford Art Journal* 28, no. 3 (2005): 429–55. On Leningrad's State Museum of the History of Religion (Gosudarstvennyi Muzei Istorii Religii, or GMIR), see Igor J. Polianski, "The Antireligious Museum: Soviet Heterotopia between Transcending and Remembering Religious Heritage," in *Science, Religion and Communism in Cold War Europe*, ed. Paul Betts and Stephen A. Smith (Basingstoke: Palgrave Macmillan, 2016), 253–73; Mariana M. Shakhnovich and Tatiana V. Chumakova, *Muzei istorii religii Akademii nauk SSSR i rossiiskoe religiovedenie (1932–1961)* (Saint Petersburg: Nauka, 2014), 15. On preservationism within antireligious museums, see Maria E. Kaulen, *Muzei-khramy i muzei-monastyri v pervoe desiatiletie Sovetskoĭ vlasti* (Moscow: Luch, 2001).

57. "Krematsiia v bor'be s religioznymi predrassudkami," *Bezbozhnik*, no. 9 (1928): 10–11.

58. Victoria Smolkin-Rothrock, "The Contested Skies: The Battle of Science and Religion in the Soviet Planetarium," in *Soviet Space Culture: Cosmic Enthusiasm in Socialist Societies*, ed. Eva Maurer, Julia Richers, Monica Rüthers, and Carmen Scheide (Basingstoke: Palgrave Macmillan, 2011), 57–78.

59. *Sovremennaia arkhitektura*, no. 3 (1927): 79.

60. Catherine Cooke, *Russian Avant-Garde: Theories of Art, Architecture, and the City* (London: Academy Editions, 1995), 133–35.

61. TsAGM, f. 1782, op. 3, d. 183, l. 7.

62. Early Soviet enlightenment publications saw an important role for astronomy in the battle of science and religion. For representative publications from this genre, see works by Grigorii A. Gurev, such as *Pravda o neve: Antireligioznye besedy s krest'ianami o mirozdanii* (Leningrad: Priboi, 1931), *Kopernikovskaia eres' v proshlom i nastoiashchem i istoriia vzaimootnoshenii nauki i religii* (Leningrad: GAIZ, 1933), *Nauka i religiia o vselennoi* (Moscow: OGIA, 1934), *Nauka o vselennoi i religiia: kosmologicheskie ocherki* (Moscow: OGIZ, 1934); and those of Nikolai Kamenshchikov, such as *Chto videli na nebe popy, a chto videm my* (Moscow: Ateist, 1930), and *Astronomiia bezbozhnika* (Leningrad: Priboi, 1931).

63. TsAGM, f. 1782, op. 3, d. 183, l. 7. The recollection about Iaroslavskii is by Ivan Shevliakov, who lectured at the planetarium for more than forty years, becoming the most senior lecturer of the Moscow Planetarium. See "Legendy planetariia: K 115-letiiu stareishego lektora Planetariia I. F. Shevliakova," http://www.planetarium-moscow.ru/about/legends-of-the-planetarium/detail.php?ID=2429.

64. Aleksey Gan, "Novomu teatru—novoe zdanie," *Sovremennaia arkhitektura*, no. 3 (1927): 80–81.

65. B. A. Vorontsov-Veliaminov, *Astronomicheskaia Moskva v 20e gody—Istoriko-astronomicheskie issledovaniia, vyp. 18* (Moscow: Nauka, 1986); Viktor N. Komarov and K. A. Portsevskii, *Moskovskii planetarii* (Moscow: Moskovskii rabochii, 1979). On Tsander's propaganda of space travel and his role in early scientific societies, see Asif A. Siddiqi, "Imagining the Cosmos: Utopians, Mystics, and the Popular Culture of Spaceflight in Revolutionary Russia," *Osiris* 23, no. 1 (2008): 260–88. On the philosophical genealogy of Soviet space travel, see Michael Hagemeister, "Konstantin Tsiolkovsky and the Occult Roots of Soviet Space Travel," in *The New Age of Russia: Occult and Esoteric Dimensions*, ed. Michael Hagemeister, Birgit Menzel, and Bernice Glatzer Rosenthal (Munich: Verlag Otto Sagner, 2012), 135–50.

66. Lev Trotsky, "Chtob perestroit' byt, nado poznat' ego," in *Voprosy byta*, 38. For a discussion of Trotsky's engagement with the problem of byt, see Aleksandr Reznik, "Byt ili ne byt? Lev Trotskii, politika, i kul'tura v 1920-e gody," *Neprikosnovennyi zapas*, no. 4 (2013): 88–106.

67. The Bolsheviks understood that religiosity was a pervasive social fact that had to be managed if it was not to become an obstacle to the revolution—as it did in 1918, during a standoff between the Bolsheviks and priests in the city of Perm, when the clergy's refusal to perform rites brought the life of the city to a standstill, until the Bolsheviks deprived the clergy of food rations and forced them to return to their duties. See Anna D. Sokolova, "Nel'zia, nel'zia novyh liudei horonit' po-staromu!," *Otechestvennye zapiski* 56, no. 5 (2013), http://www.strana-oz.ru/2013/5/nelzya-nelzya-novyh-lyudey-horonit-po-staromu.

68. Andrei Belyi, *Na rubezhe dvukh stoletii* (Moscow: Khudozhestvennaia literatura, 1989), 36, cited in Irina Gutkin, *The Cultural Origins of the Socialist Realist Aesthetic, 1890–1934* (Evanston, IL: Northwestern University Press, 1999), 85n8. On the cultural and ideological ideas of the creative intelligentsia, see also Olga Matich, *Erotic Utopia: The Decadent Imagination in Russia's Fin de Siècle* (Madison: University of Wisconsin Press, 2005).

69. Roman Jakobson, "On a Generation That Squandered Its Poets," in *Major Soviet Writers: Essays in Criticism*, ed. Edward Brown (New York: Oxford University Press, 1973), 10–11, cited in Gutkin, *Cultural Origins of the Socialist Realist Aesthetic*, 88n20.

70. Michael David-Fox, *Revolution of the Mind: Higher Learning among the Bolsheviks, 1918–1929* (Ithaca, NY: Cornell University Press, 1997), 101–17.

71. For debates about byt and the family as these relate to family law, see Ia. Brandenburgskii, ed., *Sem'ia i novyi byt: spory o proekte novogo kodeksa zakonov o sem'e i brake* (Moscow: Gos. izd-vo, 1926). Interestingly, there were even organizations created as laboratories of the new byt, such as the Association for the Study of the Contemporary Revolutionary Everyday (Assotsiatsiia po izucheniiu sovremennogo revoliutsionnogo byta), founded in 1922. Gutkin, *Cultural Origins of the Socialist Realist Aesthetic*, 91.

72. Lev Trotsky, "Sem'ia i obriadnost'," in *Voprosy byta*, 59–62.

73. Lev Trotsky, "Vodka, tserkov' i kinematograf," in *Voprosy byta*, 43–48.

74. Trotsky, "Sem'ia i obriadnost'," 59.

75. Ibid., 59.

76. Lev Trotsky, "O zadachakh derevenskoi molodezhi," in *O novom byte* (Moscow: Novaia Moskva, 1924), 14–15.

77. On byt, see Gutkin, *Cultural Origins of the Socialist Realist Aesthetic*; Natalia B. Lebina, *Povsednevnaia zhizn' sovetskogo goroda: normy i anomalii: 1920–1930 gody* (Saint Petersburg: Letnii Sad, 1999); Vladlen Izmozik and Natalia Lebina, *Peterburg sovetskii: "novyi chelovek" v starom prostranstve, 1920–1930e gody* (Saint Petersuburg: Kriga, 2010);

Elizabeth Wood, *The Baba and the Comrade: Gender and Politics in Revolutionary Russia* (Bloomington: Indiana University Press, 2000); Eric Naiman, *Sex in Public: The Incarnation of Early Soviet Ideology* (Princeton, NJ: Princeton University Press, 1997); Vadim Volkov, "The Concept of Kul'turnost': Notes on the Stalinist Civilizing Process," in *Stalinism: New Directions*, ed. Sheila Fitzpatrick (New York: Routledge, 2000), 210–30; Christina Kiaer and Eric Naiman, eds., *Everyday Life in Early Soviet Russia: Taking the Revolution Inside* (Bloomington: Indiana University Press, 2006).

78. David-Fox, *Revolution of the Mind*, 101.

79. David-Fox notes that Trotsky's "Ikh moral' i nasha" (published in *Biullen' oppozitsii*, no. 68–69 [August–September 1938]) was "one of the most forceful arguments ever made for the Bolshevik class-based conception of morality." Ibid., 102n48.

80. Emelian Iaroslavskii, *Bibliia dlia veruiushchikh i neveruiushchikh* (Leningrad: Lenizdat, 1975); Ivan Skvortsov-Stepanov, "Mysli o religii" (1922), in *Izbrannye ateisticheskie proizvedeniia*, ed. Vladimir Zybkovets (Moscow, 1959), 299–331.

81. Aron Sol'ts, "Bytovoi front," *Bezbozhnik u stanka*, no. 1 (1923): 2.

82. Section 13 of the Bolshevik Party Program. See *Programma Rossiiskoi kommunisticheskoi partii (bol'shevikov): priniata 8-m s"ezdom 18–23 marta 1919 g* (Moscow: Kommunist, 1919).

83. Nikolai Bukharin and Evgenii Preobrazhenskii, *Azbuka kommnizma. Populiarnoe ob'iasnenie programmy rossiiskoi kommunisticheskoi partii (1919)* (Khar'kov: Gos. Izd., 1925).

84. Emelian Iaroslavskii, "Dan' predrassudkam," in *O religii* (Moscow: Gospolitizdat, 1957), 21–29, published in *Pravda* on June 7, 1919, and July 24, 1919, respectively.

85. Iaroslavskii, "Dan' predrassudkam," 23.

86. Ibid., 25.

87. Ibid., 29.

88. Ibid., 27.

89. Ibid., 28.

90. "O postanovke antireligioznoi propagandy i o narushenii punkta 13 Programmy (Postanovlenie TsK VKP[b] 1921 g)," in *O religii i tserkvi* (Moscow, 1965), 58.

91. Emelian Iaroslavskii, "Mozhno li prozhit' bez very v boga?," in *O religii*, 100–108, published in *Pravda*, June 1, 1924.

92. Ibid., 104–5.

93. Ibid., 106.

94. Ibid., 106.

95. Emelian Iaroslavskii, "Zadachi i metody antireligioznoi propagandy sredi vzroslykh i detei," in *O religii*, 109–29, written in 1924.

96. Ibid., 122.

97. Ibid., 139–40.

98. Emelian Iaroslavskii, "O lenintse, sem'e, i religii," in *O religii*, 132–41, written in 1925.

99. Ibid., 132.

100. Ibid., 136.

101. Ibid., 138.

102. Emelian Iaroslavskii, "Chego partiia trebuet ot kommunistov v lichnom bytu?," in *O religii*, 254–62, published in *Pravda*, August 10, 1933.

103. Ibid., 254–56.

104. Ibid., 255–57.

105. Beglov, *V poiskakh bezgreshnykh katakomb*, 32.

106. Catherine Wanner, introduction to *State Secularism and Lived Religion in Soviet Russia and Ukraine* (New York: Oxford University Press, 2012), 12.

107. It did not help that when given the freedom to vote, peasants frequently elected religious activists to village councils, which undermined the Bolsheviks' already-tenuous grasp on the countryside. See Glennys Young, *Power and the Sacred in Revolutionary Russia: Religious Activists in the Village* (University Park: Pennsylvania State University Press, 1997), 255–70.

108. Young, *Power and the Sacred*, 255.

109. Ibid., 255–56.

110. Ibid., 270.

111. Gregory L. Freeze, "Subversive Atheism: Soviet Antireligious Campaigns and the Religious Revival in Ukraine in the 1920s," in Wanner, *State Secularism and Lived Religion*, 27–62.

112. Nikolai Bukharin, *Izbrannye sochineniia* (Moscow, 1927), 24; Aleksei Rykov, "Religiia—vrag sotsialisticheskogo stroitel'stva. Ona boretsia s nami na kul'turnoi pochve," in *Stenogramma X s"ezda Sovetov* (Moscow, 1928), 191. See also Nikolai Bukharin, "Rekonstruktivnyi period i bor'ba s religiiei. Rech' na II Vsesoiuznom s"ezde bezbozhnikov," *Revoliutsiia i kul'tura*, no. 12 (1929): 4.

113. Daniel Peris, *Storming the Heavens: The Soviet League of the Militant Godless* (Ithaca, NY: Cornell University Press, 1998), 127.

114. Beglov, *V poiskakh bezgreshnykh katakomb*, 35. See also Gregory L. Freeze, "The Stalinist Assault on the Parish, 1929–1941," in *Stalinismus vor dem Zweiten Weltkrieg: Neue Wege der Forschung*, ed. Manfred Hildermeier (Munich: Oldenburg Verlag, 1998), 209–32.

115. In fall 1928, the NKVD was instructed to wage war on religion and the pace of church closures picked up. Whereas 134 churches were closed in 1927, by 1929 the state had closed approximately 1,000. Mikhail V. Shkarovskii, *Russkaia Pravoslavnaia Tserkov' v XX veke* (Moscow: Veche, Lepta, 2010), 119.

116. On Stalinist culture, see David L. Hoffman, *Stalinist Values: The Cultural Norms of Soviet Modernity, 1917–1941* (Ithaca, NY: Cornell University Press, 2003); Karen Petrone, *Life Has Become More Joyous, Comrades: Celebrations in the Time of Stalin* (Bloomington: Indiana University Press, 2000); Jeffrey Brooks, *Thank You, Comrade Stalin! Soviet Public Culture from Revolution to Cold War* (Princeton, NJ: Princeton University Press, 2000); David Brandenberger, *National Bolshevism: Stalinist Mass Culture and the Formation of Modern Russian National Identity, 1931–1956* (Cambridge, MA: Harvard University Press, 2002).

117. Iosif Eliashevich, "Chego my zhdem ot II S"ezda," *Antireligioznik*, no. 6 (1929): 59–62.

118. Daniel Peris, "The 1929 Congress of the Godless," *Europe-Asia Studies* 43, no. 4 (1991): 711–32.

119. Shkarovskii, *Russkaia Pravoslavnaia Tserkov' v XX veke*, 120–21.

120. Ibid., 123–26.

121. Beglov, *V poiskakh bezgreshnykh katakomb*, 35–36.

122. Mikhail I. Odintsov and Tatiana A. Chumachenko, *Sovet po delam Russkoi pravoslavnoi tserkvi pri SNK (SM) SSSR i Moskovskaia patriarkhiia: epokha vzaimoseistviia i protivostoianiia, 1943–1965* (Saint Petersburg: Rossiiskoe ob"edinenie issledovatelei religii, 2013), 23.

123. As historian Hiroaki Kuromiya writes, in 1937–38, Stalin enacted "an almost wholesale killing of the clergy." See Hiroaki Kuromiya, "Why the Destruction of Orthodox Priests in 1937–1938," *Jahrbücher für Geschichte Osteuropas* 55 (2007): 87.

124. Shkarovskii, *Russkaia Pravoslavnaia Tserkov' v XX veke*, 126.

125. Ibid., 127.

126. See N. M. Matorin and A. Nevsky, *Programma dlia izucheniia bytovogo pravoslaviia* (Leningrad, 1930), cited in Mariana M. Shakhnovich and Tatiana V. Chumakova, "N. M. Matorin i ego programma izucheniia narodnoi religioznosti," *Religiovedenie*, no. 4 (2012): 191–93.

127. On the 1937 Soviet census, see Francine Hirsh, *Empire of Nations: Ethnographic Knowledge and the Making of the Soviet Union* (Ithaca, NY: Cornell University Press, 2005), 276–92.

128. Felix Corley, "Believers' Responses to the 1937 and 1939 Soviet Censuses," *Religion, State, and Society* 22, no. 4 (1994): 403.

129. The fact that the results of the census were not made public until 1990, and many of those who carried out the census were repressed during the terror, underscores the importance of these statistics for the Soviet leadership. See Valentina Zhiromskaia, Igor Kiselev, and Iurii Poliakov, *Polveka pod grifom "sekretno": Vsesoiuznaia perepis' naseleniia 1937 goda* (Moscow: Nauka, 1996), and Andrei Volkov, "Iz istorii perepisi naseleniia 1937 goda," *Vestnik statistiki*, no. 8 (1990): 45–56.

130. Corley, "Believers' Responses," 412.

131. Rossiiskii Gosudarstvennyi Arkhiv Ekonomiki, f. 7486, op. 37, d. 61, l. 45, cited in Lynn Viola, *Peasant Rebels under Stalin: Collectivization and the Culture of Peasant Resistance* (New York: Oxford University Press, 1999), 59.

132. Mikhail I. Odintsov, "Veroispovednaia politika sovetskogo gosudarstva v 1939–1958 gg.," in *Vlast' i tserkov' v SSSR i stranakh vostochnoi evropy, 1939–1958 (diskussionnye aspekty)* (Moscow: Institut slavianovedeniia RAN, 2003), 7–10; Steven M. Miner, *Stalin's Holy War: Religion, Nationalism, and Alliance Politics, 1941–1945* (Chapel Hill: University of North Carolina Press, 2003), 22.

133. Beglov, *V poiskakh bezgreshnykh katakomb*, 34.

134. Sergei Bakhrushin, "K voprosu o kreshchenii Rusi," *Istorik-Marksist*, no. 2 (1937): 40–77. On Bakhrushin's article as the foundation of the Soviet Vladimir narrative, see Simon Franklin, "988–1988: Uses and Abuses of the Millennium," *World Today* 44, no. 4 (April 1988): 66.

135. Donald Ostrowski, "The Christianization of Rus' in Soviet Historiography: Attitudes and Interpretations (1920–1960)," *Harvard Ukrainian Studies* 11, nos. 3–4 (1987): 446–47.

136. See David Brandenberger, *Propaganda State in Crisis: Soviet Ideology, Indoctrination, and Terror under Stalin, 1927–1941* (Cambridge, MA: Harvard University Press, 2002). In his study of the Stalinist ideological establishment, Brandenberger argues that the inability to produce a compelling official history was central to the crisis of Bolshevik propaganda under Stalin.

137. The nature of the Russian nationalist revival under Stalin is contested. Nicholas Timasheff's classic work describes the abandonment of utopianism for more traditional values in the mid-1930s as a "great retreat," while David Brandenberger labels it "national bolshevism" and presents it as a political strategy rather than a return to a previous order. See Nicholas Timasheff, *The Great Retreat: The Growth and Decline of Communism in Russia* (New York: E. P. Dutton, 1946), and Brandenberger, *National Bolshevism*, 1–2.

138. Arto Luukkanen, *The Religious Policy of the Stalinist State. A Case Study: The Central Standing Commission on Religious Questions, 1929–1938* (Helsinki: Suomen Historiallinen Seura, 1997).

139. Peris, *Storming the Heavens*, 8–9.

140. Peris, *Storming the Heavens*, 118–20.

141. Ibid., 119.

142. Ibid., 108.

143. Shkarovskii, *Russkaia Pravoslavnaia Tserkov' v XX veke*, 128.

144. Daniel Peris, "'God Is Now on Our Side': The Religious Revival on Unoccupied Soviet Territory during World War II," *Kritika: Explorations in Russian and Eurasian History* 1, no. 1 (2008): 97–118. On religious policies in German-occupied territories during the war, see Odintsov, "Veroispovednaia politika," 20.

145. On Sergii's June 22, 1941, address to Soviet people, see Tatiana A. Chumachenko, *Church and State in Soviet Russia: Russian Orthodoxy from World War II to the Khrushchev Years*, trans. and ed. Edward E. Roslof (Armonk, NY: M. E. Sharpe, 2002), 4.

146. On the patriotic wartime activity of the church and its contributions to the defense funds, see Odintsov and Chumachenko, *Sovet po delam Russkoi pravoslavnoi*, 56–66, 72. On Protestants, see Alexander Kashirin, "Protestant Minorities in the Soviet Ukraine, 1945–1991" (PhD diss., University of Oregon, 2010), 11.

147. Of the 950 open churches in the RSFSR on the eve of the war, only about one-third actually functioned. See Odintsov and Chumachenko, *Sovet po delam Russkoi pravoslavnoi*, 32. On the reversal of Soviet religious policy during the Second World War, see Mikhail V. Shkarovskii, *Russkaia pravoslavnaia tserkov' i sovetskoe gosudarstvo v 1943–1964 godakh: ot 'premiriia' k novoi voine* (Saint Petersburg: DEAN + ADIA-M, 1995); Miner, *Stalin's Holy War*; Tatiana Volokotina, ed., *Vlast' i tserkov' v vostochnoi evrope, 1944–1953: Dokumenty rossiiskikh arkhivov* (Moscow: Rosspen, 2009), 1:11–12.

148. Odintsov and Chumachenko, *Sovet po delam Russkoi pravoslavnoi*, 84–85.

149. Mikhail Odintsov, "I. Stalin: Tserkov' mozhet rasschityvat' na vsestoronniuiu podderzhku pravitel'stva," *Disput* 3 (1991): 152.

150. GARF, f. 6991, op. 1, d. 1, ll. 1–10, in *Russkie patriarkhi XX veka: Sud'by otechestva na stranitsakh arkhivnykh dokumentov* (Moscow: Izdatel'stvo RAGS, 1999), 283–91.

151. On church openings and registrations, see Postanovlenie SNK SSSR, "O poriadke otkrytiia tserkvei" (November 28, 1943), GARF, f. 5446, op. 1, d. 221, ll. 3–5, cited in Olga Vasil'eva, Ivan I. Kudriavtsev, and Liudmilma A. Lykova, eds., *Russkaia Pravoslavnaia Tserkov' v gody Velikoi Otechestvennoi Voiny 1941–1945 gg.: Sbornik dokumentov* (Moscow: Izdatel'stvo Krutitskogo podvo'ia, 2009), 263–65. The historian Igor Kurliandskii refers to Stalin's rapprochement with religious organizations as a "legalization of religion." See Kurliandskii, *Stalin, vlast' i religiia*, 531.

152. GDA SBU, f. 9, d. 17. l. 287.

153. Ibid., 289.

154. Ibid., 289.

155. Odintsov, "Veroispovednaia politika," 7.

156. Ibid., 11–20.

157. Regina Laukaityte, "The Orthodox Church in Lithuania during the Soviet Period," *Lithuanian Historical Studies* 7 (2002): 67–94; Bohdan Bociurkiw, *The Ukrainian Greek Catholic Church and the Soviet State, 1939–1950* (Edmonton: Canadian Institute of Ukrainian Studies Press, 1996), 65–69.

158. Shkarovskii, *Russkaia Pravoslavnaia Tserkov' v XX veke*, 5.

159. RGASPI, f. 17, op. 125, d. 506, ll. 110–18, 120–22, cited in Volokotina, *Vlast' i tserkov' v vostochnoi evrope*, 1:518.

160. Yaacov R'oi, *Islam in the Soviet Union: From the Second World War to Gorbachev* (London: Hurst, 2000); Adeeb Khalid, *Islam after Communism: Religion and Politics in Central Asia* (Berkeley: University of California Press, 2007).

161. Tat'iana Nikol'skaia, *Russkii protestantizm i gosudarstvennaia vlast' v 1905–1991 godakh* (Saint Petersburg: European University Press, 2009), 135–42.

162. Mikhail Shkarovskii, "Staliniskaia religioznaia politika i Russkaia Pravoslavnaia Tserkov' v 1943–1953 godakh," *Acta Slavica Iaponica* 27 (2009): 1–27.

163. Peris, "'God Is Now on Our Side,'" 107.

164. Ibid., 108–9.

165. Ibid., 114.

166. Ibid., 111–12.

167. Shkarovskii, "Staliniskaia religioznaia politika," 7. A number of Russian historians also see the state-sanctioned return of the religion to Soviet life under Stalin as a "normalization" of church-state relations in the Soviet Union. For example, in their scholarship, Chumachenko and Odintsov characterize the late Stalin period as a period of normalization.

168. As Brandenberger argues, the Bolsheviks ultimately failed to find a solution that reconciled these competing objectives, and the nationalist revival became the answer to the ideological crisis produced by the destruction of the Soviet pantheon during the Great Terror of 1936–38. See Brandenberger, *Propaganda State in Crisis.*

169. Peris, "'God Is Now on Our Side,'" 115–16.

170. Luukkanen, *Religious Policy of the Stalinist State.*

171. Shkarovskii stresses the foreign policy value of the Russian Orthodox Church on the world stage, and writes that "Moscow patriarchate was viewed by the leadership of the USSR above all as an instrument in foreign policy—more or less important in different periods." Mikhail V. Shkarovskii, *Russkaia pravoslavnaia tserkov' pri Staline i Khrushcheve (gosudarstvenno-tserkovnye otnosheniia v SSSR v 1939–1964 godakh)* (Moscow: Krutitskoe patriarshee podvor'e, 1999), 201.

172. Peris, "'God Is Now on Our Side,'" 102. As Peris notes in his study of wartime religious revival, "That hundreds of thousands if not millions of Russians in areas never occupied by the Germans were willing to identify themselves publicly in one way or another with Orthodoxy testifies to the frailty of the atheistic official edifice created over the previous several decades . . . which provided dramatic testimony to the Bolshevik failure to assert the absolute supremacy of Soviet symbols, spaces, rites, associations, and morality over those inherited from Orthodox culture. . . . [T]he regime's claim to permanence paled in comparison with Orthodoxy's claim, and the invocation of God proved necessary when the reliance on Soviet power seemed insufficient. . . . While many Orthodox saw little contradiction in placing their faith in both the Soviet state and Orthodoxy, this solace counted as an undeniable failure for a regime that had originally demanded exclusive ideological allegiance." Ibid., 102.

173. Fedor Oleshchuk, "Kommunisticheckoe vospitanie mass i preodolenie religioznykh predrassudkov," *Bolshevik*, no. 9 (1939): 38–48.

174. Peris, "'God Is Now on Our Side,'" 115.

## *Chapter 2: The Specter Haunting Soviet Communism*

Epigraph: "Otchet Tsentral'nogo Komiteta KPSS XXII S"ezdu Kommunisticheskoi Partii Sovetskogo Soiuza, Doklad Pervogo sekretaria TsK tovarishcha N. S. Khrushcheva 17 Oktiabria 1961 goda," *Pravda*, October 18, 1961, 11.

1. RGANI, f. 5, op. 16, d. 753, l. 19.

2. On "Stone Zoia" of Kuibyshev, see Ulrike Huhn, *Glaube und Eigensinn: Volksfrömmigkeit zwischen orthodoxer Kirche und Sowjetischem Staat, 1941 bis 1960* (Wiesbaden: Harrassowitz Verlag, 2014), 309–23. The Orthodox Church conducted its own investigation and published a pamphlet, *The Standing of Zoia.* The legend continues to evolve into the present day, inspiring religious folklore, art, and even a blockbuster film, *Miracle (Chudo),* in 2009.

3. RGANI, f. 5, op. 16, d. 753, l. 19.

4. "Dikii sluchai," *Volzhskaia kommuna*, January 24, 1956, 3.

5. RGANI, f. 5, op. 16, d. 753, l. 19.

6. TsDAGO, f. 1, op. 70, d. 2577, ll. 79–81. Another famous instance from the Khrushchev era was the "Libokhorskoe" miracle, which took place on July 20, 1963, in western Ukraine. As the CAROC report recounted, as the "sun was setting and multicolored rainbows were sparkling on the glass," someone exclaimed that they saw an image of the Mother of God on the window of a church. News quickly spread, and soon more than three hundred people were praying in front of the church. Before long, visions of the Virgin began to be reported in other locations. A much darker incident appears in another CAROC report, in which a woman was accused of putting spells on a family using specific objects. The family burned the objects, killed the woman, and then hung her in the barn in an effort to pass it off as a suicide. See TsDAGO, f. 1, op. 31, d. 1235, ll. 46–47. On popular religiosity, see Robert Orsi, "Everyday Miracles: The Study of Lived Religion," in *Lived Religion in America: Toward a History of Practice*, ed. David D. Hall (Princeton, NJ: Princeton University Press, 1997), 3–21.

7. Joan Delaney Grossman, "Khrushchev's Antireligious Policy and the Campaign of 1954," *Europe-Asia Studies* 24, no. 3 (1973): 374–86. For the July 7, 1954, and November 10, 1954, resolutions, see *Zakonodatel'stvo o religioznykh kul'takh: Sbornik materialov i dokumentov* (Moscow, 1971), 34, 40–45.

8. Stephen V. Bittner, *The Many Lives of Khrushchev's Thaw: Experience and Memory in Moscow's Arbat* (Ithaca, NY: Cornell University Press, 2008), 12; Polly Jones, *Myth, Memory, Trauma: Rethinking the Stalinist Past in the Soviet Union, 1953–70* (New Haven, CT: Yale University Press, 2013).

9. On the shift from mobilizational strategies shifting from coercion to persuasion during the Khrushchev era, see Polly Jones, ed., *The Dilemmas of De-Stalinization: Negotiating Cultural and Social Change in the Khrushchev Era* (New York: Routledge, 2006). On Soviet citizens' efforts to maintain faith in the Communist project, see Iurii Aksiutin, *Khrushchevskaia "ottepel'" i obshchestvennye nastroeniia v SSSR v 1953–1964 gg* (Moscow: Rosspen, 2004); Ludmilla Alexeyeva and Paul Goldberg, *The Thaw Generation: Coming of Age in the Post-Stalin Era* (Pittsburgh: University of Pittsburgh Press, 1993); Vladislav Zubok, *Zhivago's Children: The Last Russian Intelligentsia* (Cambridge, MA: Belknap, 2009).

10. *Programma Kommunisticheskoi Partii Sovetskogo Soiuza priniata XXII s'ezdom KPSS* (Moscow: Izdatel'stvo politicheskoi literatury, 1971). See also William Taubman, *Khrushchev: The Man and His Era* (New York: Norton, 2003), 508–9; Alexander Titov, "The 1961 Party Program and the Fate of Khrushchev's Reforms," in *Soviet State and Society under Nikita Khrushchev*, ed. Melanie Ilic and Jeremy Smith (New York: Routledge, 2009), 8–25.

11. As Titov notes, "Competition with the USA was one of the main reference points in the Programme." See Titov, "1961 Party Program," 12.

12. Tatiana A. Chumachenko, *Church and State in Soviet Russia: Russian Orthodoxy from World War II to the Khrushchev Years*, trans. and ed. Edward E. Roslof (Armonk, NY: M. E. Sharpe, 2002), 148; Andrew B. Stone, "'Overcoming Peasant Backwardness': The Khrushchev Antireligious Campaign and the Rural Soviet Union," *Russian Review* 67 (2008): 298. The professional atheist Evgraf Duluman referred to the antireligious campaign as Khrushchev's "idée fixe" and indicated Khrushchev was personally invested in the religious question. Evgraf Duluman, interview with author, Kiev, February 10, 2009.

13. Sergei Khrushchev, *Khrushchev Nikita. Reformator. Trilogiia ob otse* (Moscow: Vremia, 2010); Aleksei Adzhubei, *Krushenie illiuzii* (Moscow: Interbuk, 1991).

14. "N. S. Khrushchev Interviewed by Correspondent from French newspaper Le Figaro," *Pravda* and *Izvestiia*, March 27, 1957, 1–2. See also "N. S. Khrushchev Interview with

Newspaper Chain Director W. R. Hearst," *Current Digest of the Post-Soviet Press* 9, no. 46 (December 25, 1957): 10–17.

15. *Pravda*, March 27, 1958, cited in John Anderson, *Religion, State and Politics in the Soviet Union and Successor States* (Cambridge: Cambridge University Press, 1994), 15.

16. Mikhail V. Shkarovskii, *Russkaia pravoslavnaia tserkov' pri Staline i Khrushcheve (gosudarstvenno-tserkovnye otnosheniia v SSSR v 1939–1964 godakh)* (Moscow: Krutitskoe patriarshee podvor'e, 1999), 382. Khrushchev's claim was often mentioned during my interviews with former atheist cadres.

17. *Pravda*, October 18, 1961; *XXII S'ezd KPSS* (Moscow: Politizdat, 1962), 411.

18. Iosif Stalin, "Otchetnyi doklad XVII s"ezdu partii o rabote TsK VKP(b)," in *Sochineniia* (Moscow, 1942–46), 13:308–9. The United States recognized the USSR diplomatically on November 16, 1933.

19. Mikhail V. Shkarovskii, *Russkaia Pravoslavnaia Tserkov' v XX veke* (Moscow: Veche, Lepta, 2010), 429–30. According to Shkarovskii, the number of functioning Orthodox churches had remained relatively stable in the immediate postwar period, reaching a postwar apex in 1949 with 14,477, and slightly declining thereafter, to 14,273 (1950), 13,867 (1951), 13,740 (1952), 13,508 (1953), 13,422 (1954), and 13,376 (1955). That was followed by 13,417 (1956), 13,430 (1957), 13,414 (1958), 13,324 (1959), 13,008 (1960), 11,572 (1961), 10,149 (1962), 8,580 (1963), 7,873 (1964), and 7,551 (1965), at which point it stabilized again and remained in the 7,000 range until 1981.

20. Chumachenko, *Church and State in Soviet Russia*, 127.

21. For the most comprehensive study of Znanie, see Michael Froggatt, "Science in Propaganda and Popular Culture in the USSR under Khrushchëv (1953–1964)" (DPhil thesis, University of Oxford, 2006). See also James T. Andrews, "Inculcating Materialist Minds: Scientific Propaganda and Anti-religion in the USSR during the Cold War," in *Science, Religion and Communism in Cold War Europe*, ed. Paul Betts and Stephen A. Smith (Basingstoke: Palgrave Macmillan, 2016), 105–25.

22. Mikhail I. Shakhnovich, *Sueverie i nauchnoe predvidenie* (Leningrad: Lenizdat, 1945); B. A. Vorontsov-Veliaminov, *Vselennaia* (Moscow: Gostekhizdat, 1947).

23. Mikhail V. Shkarovskii, *Russkaia Pravoslavnaia Tserkov' i sovetskoe gosudarstvo v 1943–1964 godakh: Ot "peremiriia" k novoi voine* (Saint Petersburg: DEAN + ADIA-M, 1995), 46; Chumachenko, *Church and State in Soviet Russia*, 121–22.

24. Chumachenko goes so far as to argue that the stability of postwar church-state relations depended on Stalin personally, since his disapproval of aggressive policies toward the church kept the situation stable as long as he was alive. The last attempt to attack the church in the Stalin era, which took place in 1948–49 and peaked with the so-called Saratov Affair, was derailed by Stalin's intervention. GARF, f. 6991, op. 1, d. 451, ll. 162–67, cited in Chumachenko, *Church and State in Soviet Russia*, 96–100, 125. See also RGASPI, f. 17, op. 132, d. 10, l. 26.

25. RGANI, f. 5, op. 16, d. 542, ll. 124–26, cited in Shkarovskii, *Russkaia Pravoslavnaia Tserkov' v XX veke*, 351.

26. Ibid.

27. Chumachenko, *Church and State in Soviet Russia*, 125–26.

28. Joan Delaney Grossman, "Leadership of Antireligious Propaganda in the Soviet Union," *Europe-Asia Studies* 24, no. 3 (1973): 217.

29. Mariana M. Shakhnovich and Tatiana V. Chumakova, *Muzei istorii religii Akademii nauk SSSR i rossiiskoe religiovedenie (1932–1961)* (Saint Petersburg: Nauka, 2014); V. N. Sherdakov, "Muzei istorii religii i ateizma v sisteme nauchno-ateisticheskoi propagandy," *Voprosy nauchnogo ateizma* 19 (1976): 97–106.

30. Grossman, "Leadership of Antireligious Propaganda"; Iu. Kogan, "V. D. Bonch-Bruevich i nauchno-atiesticheskaia rabota AN SSSR (1946–1955)," *Voprosy istorii religii i ateizma* 12 (1964): 11–21.

31. It produced only the first issue of a planned multivolume series, titled *Problems in the History of Religion and Atheism* (*Voprosy istorii religii i ateizma*).

32. Mariana M. Shakhnovich, "Muzei istorii religii AN SSSR i otechestvennoe religiovedenie," *Religiovedenie*, no. 4 (2008): 150–58.

33. Arkhiv Presidenta Rossiiskoi Federatsii (APRF), f. 3. op. 60, d. 14. l. 90, cited in V. V. Kornev, "Presledovaniia Russkoi Pravoslavnoi Tserkvi v 50-60-x godax XX veka," in *Ezhegodnaia bogoslovskaia konferentsiia PSTBI: Materialy 1997 g.* (Moscow: PSTGU, 1997), 214.

34. RGANI, f. 5, op. 16, d. 650, ll. 18–21, cited in Shkarovskii, *Russkaia Pravoslavnaia Tserkov' v XX veke*, 352.

35. ARAN, f. 498, op. 1, d. 2, ll. 1–11. On Bonch-Bruevich's role in the revival of atheism, see also Shkarovskii, *Russkaia Pravoslavnaia Tserkov' v XX veke*, 350–52.

36. Chumachenko notes that for the church authorities and clergy, the revival of antireligious propaganda was "completely unexpected." Metropolitan Nikolai decried the scope implied by the new party line, telling CAROC, "If antireligious propaganda was previously part of the party's work, in this new era it has taken on a governmental character since the state demands that students depart from schools as atheists, that army officers force their soldiers to reject religious belief, and so forth. One concludes that all believers are lumped together with people who oppose state policy." GARF, f. 6991, op. 1, d. 1118, l. 153, cited in Chumachenko, *Church and State in Soviet Russia*, 129. See also Shkarovskii, *Russkaia Pravoslavnaia Tserkov' v XX veke*, 128.

37. On the connection between Khrushchev's agricultural policies and the attack on cultural "backwardness" in the countryside, see Stone, " 'Overcoming Peasant Backwardness.' "

38. *Zakonodatel'stvo o religioznykh kul'takh*, 34.

39. RGANI, f. 5, op. 16, d. 705, ll. 40–48.

40. RGANI, f. 5, op. 34, d. 112, l. 105. For a discussion of efforts to replace local feast days with Soviet labor holidays on the same collective farm, see RGASPI, f. 556, op. 15, d. 96.

41. RGANI, f. 5, op. 16, d. 650, ll. 21–22.

42. RGANI, f. 5, op. 16, d. 664, ll. 41–63.

43. Ibid., 58–59.

44. "Shire razvernut' nauchno-ateisticheskuiu propagandu," *Pravda*, July 24, 1954, 2; "Svet protiv t'my," *Pravda*, August 4, 1954. Articles about clergy drunkenness became so common that the patriarch appealed to clergy members to preach against drunkenness in their sermons. See Chumachenko, *Church and State in Soviet Russia*, 131.

45. V. Knyp, *Trud*, August 22, 1954, 22.

46. Sergei Krushinskii, "Svet protiv t'my: Ob odnom vazhnom no zapushchennom uchastke vospitatel'noi raboty," *Pravda*, August 4, 1954, 2–3.

47. RGANI, f. 5, op. 16, d. 650, l. 22.

48. R. Saakov, " 'Chudesa' v sele Ivanovke," *Komsomol'skaia Pravda*, February 20, 1954, 3.

49. Ibid.

50. "Shire razvernut' nauchno-ateisticheskuiu propagandu," *Komsomol'skaia Pravda*, June 13, 1954, 1.

51. A. Skrypnik, "Vo chto oboshlos' bogomol'e," *Komsomol'skaia Pravda*, August 21, 1954, 2.

52. Ibid. See also "Nauka i religiia neprimirimy," *Komsomol'skaia Pravda*, July 1, 1954, 2–3.

53. RGANI, f. 5, op. 16, d. 669, l. 149.

54. Ibid., 162–63.

55. RGANI, f. 5, op. 33, d. 53, l. 151. See also Chumachenko, *Church and State in Soviet Russia*, 131; Shkarovskii, *Russkaia Pravoslavnaia Tserkov' v XX veke*, 351.

56. GARF, f. 6991, op. 1, d. 1116, l. 7, cited in Chumachenko, *Church and State in Soviet Russia*, 133.

57. Chumachenko, *Church and State in Soviet Russia*, 134–35.

58. *O religii i tservki: sbornik dokumentov* (Moscow: Izd-vo polit. litry, 1965), 77–82.

59. On the persecution of sectarians and confessions of foreign origin, see Hiroaki Kuromiya, *Conscience on Trial: The Fate of Fourteen Pacifists in Stalin's Ukraine, 1952–1953* (Toronto: University of Toronto Press, 2012); Emily B. Baran, *Dissent on the Margins: How Soviet Jehovah's Witnesses Defied Communism and Lived to Preach about It* (Oxford: Oxford University Press, 2014).

60. RGANI, f. 5, op. 16, d. 689.

61. RGANI, f. 5, op. 16, d. 705, l. 47, 116.

62. RGANI, f. 5, op. 16, d. 689, l. 117.

63. Ibid., 21, 114–15, 116.

64. ARAN, f. 498, op. 1, d. 4, ll. 16–18.

65. Shkarovskii, *Russkaia Pravoslavnaia Tserkov' v XX veke*, 429–31.

66. Chumachenko, *Church and State in Soviet Russia*, 137.

67. Ibid., 139.

68. RGANI, f. 5, op. 30, d. 240, l. 22.

69. GARF, f. A-561, op. 1, d. 398, ll. 16, 21.

70. RGANI, f. 5, op. 33, d. 90, l. 10.

71. Ibid.

72. RGANI, f. 5, op. 33, d. 53, l. 67, 78.

73. RGANI, f. 5, op. 33, d. 54, ll. 3–4.

74. Ibid. Since fees collected for religious rites and the sale of religious objects were among the most important sources of church income, the church had earned 667 million rubles in 1957, as compared to 180 million in 1948.

75. RGANI, f. 5, op. 33, d. 53, ll. 93–97. On Trushin's long career, see Edward E. Roslof, "'Faces of the Faceless': A. A. Trushin Communist Over-Procurator for Moscow, 1943–1984," *Modern Greek Studies Yearbook* 18–19 (2002–3): 105–25.

76. RGANI, f. 5, op. 33, d. 53, l. 97.

77. Ibid., 97. Bulganin (1895–1975) was initially Khrushchev's ally in the struggle with Malenkov, and replaced Malenkov as the chair of the Council of Ministers from 1955 until 1958. On Malenkov's and Bulganin's meetings with the patriarch in 1954–56, see Chumachenko, *Church and State in Soviet Russia*, 137–40.

78. RGANI, f. 5, op. 16, d. 754, ll. 103–9.

79. Ibid., 102–4.

80. Chumachenko, *Church and State in Soviet Russia*, 143–44.

81. RGANI, f. 5, op. 33, d. 53, ll. 34–44.

82. Chumachenko, *Church and State in Soviet Russia*, 144.

83. RGANI, f. 5, op. 33, d. 53, ll. 39–40.

84. Ibid., 44.

85. Alexander Titov, "Partiia protiv gosudarstva: reforma apparata TsK KPSS pri Nikite Khrushcheve," *Neprikosnovennyi zapas* 83, no. 3 (2012): 155–66.

86. Shkarovskii, *Russkaia Pravoslavnaia Tserkov' v XX veke*, 357.

87. Ibid., 361.

88. Chumachenko, *Church and State in Soviet Russia*, 148–49.

89. RGANI, f. 5, op. 33, d. 91, ll. 23–29.

90. Ibid. Chumachenko writes that Shapovnikova's letter provided a "certain stimulus" for the revival of the antireligious campaign. Chumachenko, *Church and State in Soviet Russia*, 159–60.

91. Anderson, *Religion, State and Politics*, 24–25.

92. Tatiana A. Chumachenko, "Sovet po delam Russkoi pravoslavnoi tserkvi pri SNK (SM) SSSR: 1954–1965 gg" (PhD diss., Lomonosov Moscow State University, 2011), 371.

93. On the practice of refusing registration as an antireligious measure, see Nadezhda A. Beliakova, "Vlast' i religioznye ob'edineniia v 'pozdnem' SSSR: problema registratsii," *Otechestvennaia istoriia* 4 (2008): 124–30; Irina I. Maslova, "Sovet po delam religii pri Sovete ministrov SSSR i Russkaia pravoslavnaia tserkov' (1965–1991 gg.)," in *Gosudarstvo i tserkov' v XX veke: Evoliutsiia vzaimootnoshenii, politicheskii i sotsiokul'turnyi askpekty*, ed. A. I. Filimonova (Moscow: Librokom, 2012), 78–106.

94. Chumachenko, *Church and State in Soviet Russia*, 161; Shkarovskii, *Russkaia Pravoslavnaia Tserkov' v XX veke*, 362.

95. The Komsomol was studying youth religiosity and atheist work already in 1957. See RGASPI-m, f. 1, op. 32, d. 845. On Soviet youth in the postwar era, see Zubok, *Zhivago's Children*, 23, 33–40; Juliane Fürst, "Friends in Private, Friends in Public: The Phenomenon of the Kampaniia among Soviet Youth in the 1950s and 1960s," in *Borders of Socialism: Private Spheres of Soviet Russia*, ed. Lewis H. Siegelbaum (New York: Palgrave Macmillan, 2006), 135–53; Juliane Fürst, *Stalin's Last Generation: Soviet Post-war Youth and the Emergence of Mature Socialism* (Oxford: Oxford University Press, 2010); Donald J. Raleigh, *Soviet Baby Boomers: An Oral History of Russia's Cold War Generation* (New York: Oxford University Press, 2013).

96. RGANI, f. 5, op. 33, d. 58.

97. RGASPI-m, f. 1, op. 32, d. 757; RGANI, f. 5, op. 33, d. 53, ll. 83–88.

98. On atheism in Soviet schools, see Michael Froggatt, "Renouncing Dogma, Teaching Utopia: Science in Schools under Khrushchev," in Jones, *Dilemmas of De-Stalinization*, 250–67.

99. RGANI, f. 5, op. 33, d. 53, ll. 126–29.

100. On popular religiosity, see Alexander Panchenko, "Popular Orthodoxy in Twentieth-Century Russia: Ideology, Consumption and Competition," in *National Identity in Soviet and Post-Soviet Culture*, ed. Mark Bassin and Catriona Kelly (Cambridge: Cambridge University Press, 2012), 321–40. See also Sergei Alymov, "The Concept of the 'Survival' and Soviet Social Science in the 1950s and 1960s," *Forum for Anthropology and Culture* 9 (2013): 157–83.

101. Sergei Shtyrkov, "Prakticheskoe religiovedenie vremen Nikity Khrushcheva: respublikanskaia gazeta v bor'be s 'religioznymi perezhitkami' (na primere Severo-Osetinskoi ASSR)," in *Traditsii narodov Kavkaza v meniaiushchemsia mire: preemstvonnost' i razryvy v sotsiokul'turnyk praktikakh*, edited by A. A. Karpov (Saint Petersburg: Izd. Peterburgskoe Vostokovedenie, 2010), 306–43.

102. Ibid., 314.

103. On the new emphasis on lived religion in the Khrushchev era, see ibid., 314.

104. Sergei Shtyrkov, "Oblichitel'naia etnografiia epokhi Khrushcheva: bol'shaia ideologiia i narodnyi obychai (na primere Severo-Osetinskoi ASSR)," *Neprikosnovennyi zapas* 65, no. 1 (2009): 147–61.

105. Ibid.

106. RGANI, f. 5, op. 16, d. 650, l. 20.

107. GARF, f. 6991, op. 1, d. 227, ll. 71–80, cited in Iurii P. Zuev and Vil'iam V. Shmidt, eds., *Nasledie: Istoriia gosudarstvenno-konfessional'nykh otnoshenii v Rossii (X-nachalo XXI veka)* (Moscow: Izd-vo. RAGS, 2010), 138, 142.

108. *Klikushi* is sometimes translated as "shriekers" in English. On the phenomenon of *klikushestvo*, see Christine D. Worobec, *Possessed: Women, Witches, and Demons in Imperial Russia* (DeKalb: Northern Illinois University Press, 2001).

109. Chumachenko, *Church and State in Soviet Russia*, 154–55.

110. On holy springs being a source of venereal disease, see RGASPI-m, f. 1, op. 32, d. 1198, ll. 21–41. Stone also describes a spring in the Soletskii district of the Novgorod region being drained in order to "fight malarial mosquitoes." Stone, "'Overcoming Peasant Backwardness,'" 303.

111. RGANI, f. 5, op. 33, d. 91, ll. 111–12.

112. GARF, f. 6991, op. 1, d. 1747, ll. 19–20, cited in Chumachenko, "Sovet po delam Russkoi pravoslavnoi tserkvi," 379.

113. Volodimir Kuroedov, interview by Viktor Yelenskii, *Lyudina i svit*, series 8–12, no. 2, (1991), http://risu.org.ua/ua/library/periodicals/lis/lis_91/lis_91_02/37636/.

114. Ibid.

115. Chumachenko, "Sovet po delam Russkoi pravoslavnoi tserkvi," 381.

116. Shkarovskii, *Russkaia Pravoslavnaia Tserkov' v XX veke*, 373–74.

117. The seminaries in Saratov, Stavropol, Minsk, Volyna (Lutsk), and Kiev were closed during the antireligious campaign. Among the monasteries closed was the Monastery of the Caves in Kiev, considered by many to be the center of Orthodox Christianity. Chumachenko, *Church and State in Soviet Russia*, 187–88. On antimonastic measures, see also Sabrina P. Ramet, *Nihil Obstat: Religion, Politics, and Social Change in East-Central Europe* (Durham, NC: Duke University Press, 1998), 233–34.

118. For statistics of church closures, see Nathaniel Davis, "The Number of Orthodox Churches before and after the Khrushchev Antireligious Drive," *Slavic Review* 50, no. 3 (1991): 614; Chumachenko, *Church and State in Soviet Russia*, 187–88. The ethnographer Kira Tsekhanskaia cites 13,372 functioning churches at the beginning of 1959, and 8,314 in 1963. See Kira Tsekhanskaia, "Russia: Trends in Orthodox Religiosity in the Twentieth Century (Statistics and Reality)," in *Religion and Politics in Russia: A Reader*, ed. Marjorie Mandelstam Balzer (Armonk, NY: M. E. Sharpe, 2010), 9.

119. Maria V. Redko, "Realization of the State Religious Policy of the Krasnoyarsk Kray in 1954–1964 (on the Example of the Russian Orthodox Church)," *Journal of Siberian Federal University* 1, no. 3 (2010): 154.

120. The income of local parishes increased, as did the number of religious rites performed. Ibid., 155.

121. Ibid., 155. For example, the price of candles in candle workshops was increased twentyfold, yet increasing the price of candles for sale was banned, resulting in the profit on candles dropping from 84,857 rubles in 1957 to 76,684 rubles in 1959.

122. Ibid., 157.

123. K. Iu. Popova, "Religioznye ob'edineniia v Orenburgskoi oblasti v 1960–1980-e gg: problema registratsii," in *Orenburgskii krai: istoriia, traditsii, kul'tura: sbornik*, ed. G. I. Biushkin (Orenburg, 2009), 88–92. Popova writes that by the end of the Soviet period, the majority of churches in the Orenburg region were in the cities. See also Redko, "Realization of the State Religious Policy," 157.

124. RGASPI, f. 556, op. 25, d. 191, ll. 226–30.

125. Ibid., 226.

126. Ibid., 227.

127. Ibid., 228.

128. Ibid.

129. Ibid., 231.

130. RGASPI-m, f. M-1, op. 34, d. 130, ll. 31–32.

131. Ibid.

132. Ibid.

133. Karl Marx and Friedrich Engels, "Manifesto of the Communist Party," in *The Marx-Engels Reader*, 2nd ed., ed. Robert Tucker (New York: Norton, 1978), 473.

134. "Spravka V. G. Furova o besede s Patriarkhom Aleksiem, June 10, 1961," in *Pis'ma i dialogi vremen "khrushchevskoi ottepeli" (Desiat' let iz zhizni patriarkha Aleksiia, 1955–1964 gg.)*, ed. Mikhail Odintsov, *Otechestvennye arkhivy*, no. 5 (1994): 72.

135. On the coexistence of optimistic pronouncements alongside material hardships in the Khrushchev era, see Elena I. Zubkova, *Obshchestvo i reformy, 1945–1964* (Moscow: Rossiia molodaia, 1993); Elena I. Zubkova, *Russia after the War: Hopes, Illusions, and Disappointments, 1945–1957* (Armonk, NY: M. E. Sharpe, 1998); Iurii Aksiutin and Aleksandr Pyzhikov, *Poststalinskoe obshchestvo: problema liderstva i transformatsiia vlasti* (Moscow: Nauchnaia kniga, 1999); Elena Zubkova, *Poslevoennoe sovetskoe obshchestvo: politika i povsednevnost': 1945–1953* (Moscow: Rosspen, 2000); Aksiutin, *Khrushchevskaia "ottepel'"*; Rudolf G. Pikhoia, *Moscow, Kreml', vlast'. Sorok let posle voiny: 1945–1985* (Moscow: Astrel', 2007).

136. RGANI, f. 5, op. 33, d. 215, l. 145.

## *Chapter 3: Cosmic Enlightenment*

1. "Titov Gives World Fair Extra Thrill," *Washington Post*, May 6, 1962, A16; "Saw Nothing in Space to Lead Him to Believe God Exists, Titov Says," *Washington Post*, May 7, 1962, A3; "Titov, Denying God, Puts His Faith in the People," *New York Times*, May 7, 1962, 2.

2. "Glenn Didn't Expect to See God in Space," *Hartford Courant*, May 11, 1962, 4; Lawrence M. Hassett, "Titov and God," *Hartford Courant*, May 12, 1962, 14; Helen W. Morales, "Could Titov Know God?" *Los Angeles Times*, May 12, 1962, B4; Louis Cassels, "Religion in America," *Chicago Defender*, May 26, 1962, 8; Gertrude Wilson, "Attack on God," *New York Amsterdam News*, June 2, 1962, 11; "Bishop Raps Titov's Sally about God," *Washington Post*, June 7, 1962, C17. See also John Glenn and Nick Taylor, *John Glenn: A Memoir* (New York: Bantam Books, 1999), 288; James Gilbert, *Redeeming Culture: American Religion in an Age of Science* (Chicago: University of Chicago Press, 1997), 39.

3. As historian Slava Gerovitch writes, "Both sides viewed the space race as a proxy for the Cold War, and both sides chose to personify the technological competition with a human space explorer. . . . Both in the United States and the Soviet Union, the main reasons for building piloted ships were political rather than technological or scientific." Slava Gerovitch, *Soviet Space Mythologies: Public Images, Private Memories, and the Making of a Cultural Identity* (Pittsburgh: University of Pittsburgh Press, 2015), 67.

4. Numerous accounts exist on the political and technological dimensions of the space race in the context of the Cold War. See Matthew Brzezinski, *Red Moon Rising: Sputnik and the Hidden Rivalries That Ignited the Space Age* (New York: Times Books, 2007); Nicholas Daniloff, *The Kremlin and the Cosmos* (New York: Knopf, 1972); Walter A. McDougall, *The Heavens and the Earth: A Political History of the Space Age* (New York: Basic Books, 1985); Asif A. Siddiqi, *Sputnik and the Soviet Space Challenge* (Gainesville: University Press of Florida, 2003); Von Hardesty and Gene Eisman, *Epic Rivalry: The Inside Story of the Soviet and American Space Race* (Washington, DC: National Geographic Society, 2007). On the intimate connection between science and religion in space travel, see Roger D. Launius, "Escaping Earth: Human Spaceflight as Religion," *Astropolitics* 11, nos. 1–2 (2013): 45–64.

5. As Gerovitch writes, "Soviet space myths showed remarkable similarity to their U.S. Counter-parts, with proper substitution: The New Soviet Man for the 'right stuff,' and the superiority of socialism for the superiority of capitalism." Gerovitch, *Soviet Space Mythologies*, xiv.

6. Roger D. Launius, "Heroes in a Vacuum: The Apollo Astronaut as Cultural Icon," *Florida Historical Quarterly* 87, no. 2 (Fall 2008): 174–209.

7. C. L. Sulzberger, "Foreign Affairs: Paradise and Old Noah Khrushchev," *New York Times*, September 9, 1961, 18.

8. "Presidential Prayer Breakfast," *New York Times*, March 2, 1962, 3. On the role of religion in the Cold War, see T. Jeremy Gunn, *Spiritual Weapons: The Cold War and the Forging of an American National Religion* (Westport, CT: Praeger, 2008); Jonathan P. Herzog, *The Spiritual-Industrial Complex: America's Religious Battle against Communism in the Early Cold War* (Oxford: Oxford University Press, 2011); James C. Wallace, "A Religious War? The Cold War and Religion," *Journal of Cold War Studies* 15, no. 3 (2013): 162–80.

9. Gilbert, *Redeeming Culture*, 298–99.

10. Ibid., 226.

11. On religious responses to human space travel, see Ryan Jeffrey McMillen, "Space Rapture: Extraterrestrial Millennialism and the Cultural Construction of Space Colonization" (PhD diss., University of Texas at Austin, 2004).

12. Peter L. Berger, *The Sacred Canopy: Elements of a Sociological Theory of Religion* (Garden City, NY: Doubleday, 1967), 112–13.

13. On the religious crisis of the 1960s, see Hugh McLeod, *The Religious Crisis of the 1960s* (Oxford: Oxford University Press, 2007).

14. Cathleen Lewis, "The Birth of the Soviet Space Museums: Creating the Earthbound Experience of Spaceflight during the Golden Years of the Soviet Space Programme, 1957–1968," *Showcasing Space* 6 (2005): 148–50.

15. There are numerous hagiographic accounts of Soviet cosmonauts. Insider accounts, by engineers in the space program or cosmonauts themselves, were especially popular, such as Titov's biography of Gagarin. See German Stepanovich Titov, *Pervyi kosmonavt planety* (Moscow: Znanie, 1971). Children's books were also a popular genre. On the myth of Gagarin, see Trevor Rockwell, "The Molding of the Rising Generation: Soviet Propaganda and the Hero Myth of Iurii Gagarin," *Past Imperfect* 12 (2006): 1–34.

16. "Piat' let shturmu kosmosa," *Nauka i religiia*, no. 10 (October 1962): 3–8.

17. Ibid.

18. "Address of the Central Committee of the KPSS, the Presidium of the Supreme Soviet, and the Government of the Soviet Union," *Komsomol'skaia Pravda*, April 13, 1961, 1.

19. "Estafeta pokolenii," *Nauka i religiia*, no. 9 (September 1962): 4.

20. "Piat' let shturmu kosmosa," *Nauka i religiia*, no. 10 (October 1962): 5.

21. Ibid.

22. "Piat' let shturmu kosmosa," *Nauka i religiia*, no. 10 (October 1962): 7.

23. Yuri Gagarin, *Doroga v kosmos* (Moscow: Pravda, 1961), 171. Although Gagarin's book was almost certainly ghostwritten, the claim that he made these statements became part of popular folklore. For example, the historian of Soviet science Loren Graham recalls that a pamphlet with Gagarin's comment was sold in the antireligious bookstore of the St. Sergius monastery in Sergeev Posad/Zagorsk. See Loren R. Graham, *Moscow Stories* (Bloomington: Indiana University Press, 2006), 178.

24. Louis Cassels, "Religion in America," *Chicago Defender*, May 26, 1962, 8; "Gherman Titov, Soviet Cosmonaut, Comments at World's Fair, Seattle, Washington, May 6, 1962," *Seattle Daily Times*, May 7, 1962, 2.

25. German Titov, "Vstretil li ia boga?" *Nauka i religiia*, no. 1 (January 1962): 10. The tradition of cosmonauts pronouncing on religion continued, with the cosmonaut Georgii Beregovoi also contributing to the genre. See Georgii T. Beregovoi, *"Shagi po zemle, shagi v kosmose," Ia—ateist: 25 otvetov na vopros "Pochemu vy ateist?"* (Moscow: Izdatel'stvo politicheskoi literatury, 1980), 32–39.

26. Numerous accounts in the atheist essay collection *Why We Broke with Religion* (*Pochemu my porvali s religiiei*) (Moscow: Gospolitizdat, 1964) featured space travel as a decisive turning point in the believer's break with religion.

27. Stites notes that Gagarin's brother said that the cosmonaut received hundreds of letters from former believers testifying to their atheist conversions. Richard Stites, *Russian Popular Culture: Entertainment and Society since 1900* (New York: Cambridge University Press, 1992), 175.

28. "1000 Pisem," *Nauka i religiia*, no. 2 (February 1960): 8.

29. For letters from former believers who renounced religion after Gagarin's flight, see "Kak zhe bog? Obzor pisem," *Izvestiia*, May 23, 1961, 4.

30. The editorial cites other believers who "came to the same conclusion" as Danilova, and also shares the conversion story of a priest, Pavel Darmanskii, who felt his belief called into doubt during a scientific atheist lecture on astronomy. "Piat' let shturmu kosmosa," *Nauka i religiia*, no. 10 (October 1962): 8.

31. Danilova's letter was originally published in "Kak zhe bog? Obzor pisem," *Izvestiia*, May 23, 1961, 4. It is also cited in P. V. Liakhotskii, *Zavoevanie kosmosa i religiia* (Groznyi: Checheno-Ingushskoe knizhnoe izdanie, 1964), 64–68; V. Bazykin, "V nebesakh chelovek, a ne bog," *Sovetskie profsoiuzy*, no. 13 (1961): 28. For other conversion stories, see also *Komsomol'skaia Pravda*, August 13, 1962; "Estafeta pokolenii," *Nauka i religiia*, no. 9 (September 1962): 5. See also K. K. Gabova, ed., *Zavoevanie neba i vera v boga. Sbornik statei* (Moscow: Znanie, 1964).

32. RGASPI, f. 599, op. 1, d. 211, ll. 116–21.

33. Ibid., 117–18.

34. Ibid., 121.

35. E. Gurov, *Krokodil*, no. 9 (March 30, 1965): 3. On the deployment of the cosmonaut for political satire, see John Etty, "Comic Cosmonaut: Space Exploration and Visual Satire in Krokodil in the Thaw," in *Russian Aviation, Space Flight, and Visual Culture*, ed. Vlad Strukov and Helena Goscilo (New York: Routledge, 2016), 89–115.

36. A. Vasilenka (artist), *Voiovnichii ateist*, no. 7 (1961): 17–18.

37. See inside cover of *Nauka i religiia*, no. 1 (1959).

38. GARF, f. 9547, op. 1, d. 1210, l. 34.

39. RGASPI, f. 606, op. 4, d. 119, l. 58. For comparison, the circulation of the popular science journal *Science and Life* was 167,000 in 1961. By 1963, it almost tripled to 475,000, and by 1964 Znanie received permission to raise circulation to 750,000 and felt confident enough to request that the figure be raised to one million. GARF, f. 9547, op. 1, d. 1310, ll. 29–30, 62; GARF, f. 9547, op. 1, d. 1371, l. 54.

40. TsAGM, f. 709, op. 1, d. 177, l. 75.

41. Ibid.

42. TsAGM, f. 709, op. 1, d. 177, l. 75. In 1959, the Moscow Planetarium earned 1,906,000 rubles, while its expenditures constituted 2,071,000 rubles—that is, it had a deficit of 165,000 rubles.

43. GARF, f. A-561, op. 1, d. 492.

44. In 1974, planetariums across the USSR hosted 3,586,000 lectures on science, of which 897,000 were on atheism. This includes lectures conducted beyond planetarium

buildings by "mobile" planetariums. See Iurii K. Fishevskii, "Obshchestvo 'Znanie' i propaganda nauchnogo mirovozzrenia," *Voprosy nauchnogo ateizma* 19 (1976): 76. See also Viktor Komarov, "Planetarii i propaganda ateisticheskikh znanii," *Voprosy nauchnogo ateizma* 19 (1976): 115–26.

45. Some prominent examples include the Gorky (Nizhnyi Novgorod) Planetarium, opened in 1948 in the space of the Alekseevskaia Church of the Blagoveshchenskii Monastery; the Barnaul Planetarium, opened in 1950 in the space of the Krestovozdvizhenskaia Church; and the Kiev Planetarium, the oldest in Ukraine, opened in 1952 in the space of the Aleksandr Cathedral.

46. GARF, f. 9547, op. 1, d. 1324, ll. 53–54.

47. Viktor N. Komarov and V. V. Kaziutinskii, eds., *Voprosy mirovozzreniia v lektsiiakh po astronomii: Sbornik* (Moscow: Znanie, 1974). See also Boris M. Mar'ianov, *Otvoevannoe nebo* (Moscow: Moskovskii rabochii, 1971); Boris M. Mar'ianov, *Voprosy mirovozzrenia v lektsiiakh po astronomii: Sbornik* (Moscow: Znanie, 1974).

48. Komarov and Chertkov even coauthored atheist literature. See Viktor N. Komarov and Aleksei B. Chertkov, *Besedy o religii i ateizme* (Moscow: Prosveshchenie, 1975).

49. In 1963, the cosmonauts Andriian Nikolaev and Titov lectured at the Moscow Planetarium. GARF, f. 9547, op. 1, d. 1324, l. 9.

50. For a description of enlightenment work in the Khar'kov planetarium, see the memoirs of lecturer Natal'ia Bershova, "Esli zvezdy zazhigaiut . . . (Zapiski lektora Khar'kovskogo Planetariia," http://kharkov.vbelous.net/planetar/index.htm.

51. GARF, f. 9547, op. 1, d. 1324, ll. 28–31.

52. Ibid., 16.

53. Mark B. Mitin, "O soderzhanii i zadachakh nauchno-ateisticheskoi propagandy v sovremennykh usloviiakh," in *Nauka i religiia: Sbornik stenogramm lektsii, prochitannykh na Vsesoiuznom soveshchanii-seminare po nauchno-ateisticheskim voprosam* (Moscow: Znanie, 1958), 17.

54. Gustav Naan, "Chelovek, bog i kosmos," *Nauka i religiia*, no. 2 (1961): 6.

55. Ibid., 7.

56. GARF, f. 9547, op. 1, d. 1048, l. 14.

57. Ibid.

58. GARF, f. 9547, op. 1, d. 1324, ll. 26–27.

59. GARF, f. 9547, op. 1, d. 1048, l. 15.

60. TsAGM, f. 1782, op. 3, d. 183.

61. Ibid., 4.

62. Ibid., 6.

63. Ibid., 7.

64. GARF, f. A-561, op. 1, d. 492, ll. 25–28.

65. Ibid., 36–39.

66. GARF, f. 9547, op. 1, d. 1048, l. 22.

67. RGANI, f. 71, op. 1, d. 15, l. 171.

68. Ibid.

69. Ibid., 151–53.

70. RGASPI, f. 606, op. 4, d. 37, l. 31.

71. RGASPI, f. 606, op. 4, d. 156, l. 29.

72. Ibid.

73. Ibid., 47.

74. Ibid., 48.

75. Ibid., 139.

76. RGANI, f. 5, op. 55, d. 72, l. 53.

77. RGASPI, f. 606, op. 4, d. 126, ll. 33–34.

78. RGASPI, f. 606, op. 4, d. 37, l. 85.

79. Viktor N. Komarov and V. V. Kaziutinskii, eds., *Voprosy mirovozzreniia v lektsiiakh po astronomii: Sbornik* (Moscow: Znanie, 1974), 4.

80. RGASPI, f. 606, op. 4, d. 133.

81. Max Weber, "Science as a Vocation," in *From Max Weber: Essays in Sociology*, ed. and trans. H. H. Gerth and C. Wright Mills (New York: Oxford University Press, 1946), 129–56. Speech at Munich University (1918), published as "Wissenschaft als Beruf," in *Gesammlte Aufsaetze zur Wissenschaftslehre* (Tubingen, 1922), 524–55.

82. Weber, "Science as a Vocation," 154–55.

## *Chapter 4: The Ticket to the Soviet Soul*

1. GARF, f. A-561, op. 1, d. 399, l. 54. The story is titled "Orator" (not "The Death of a Civil Servant," as per Gubanov).

2. Ibid., 51.

3. Ibid., 54.

4. While there had been earlier attempts to create a new party program (in the mid-1930s, 1939, and 1947), none of these had come to fruition. A new commission was formed for the task in 1952, at the Nineteenth Party Congress, but Stalin's death and the subsequent struggle for leadership again left the project without a clear direction. See Alexander Titov, "The 1961 Party Program and the Fate of Khrushchev's Reforms," in *Soviet State and Society under Nikita Khrushchev*, ed. Melanie Ilic and Jeremy Smith (New York: Routledge, 2009), 8–25.

5. Alfred B. Evans, *Soviet Marxism-Leninism: The Decline of an Ideology* (Westport, CT: Praeger, 1993), 105, 89–91; Deborah A. Field, *Private Life and Communist Morality in Khrushchev's Russia* (New York: Peter Lang, 2007).

6. Tom Casier, "The Shattered Horizon: How Ideology Mattered to Soviet Politics," *Studies in East European Thought* 51 (1999): 35–59; Aleksandr Fokin, *"Kommunizm ne za gorami": obrazy budushego u vlasti i naseleniia SSSR na rubezhe 1950–1960kh godov* (Cheliabinsk: Entsiklopediia, 2012).

7. Karl Marx, "The German Ideology," in *Karl Marx: Selected Writings*, ed. David McLellan, 2nd ed. (New York: Oxford University Press, 2000), 185.

8. RGASPI, f. 556, op. 25, d. 191.

9. On the mobilization of public opinion studies and sociology in the Khrushchev era, see Vladimir Shlapentokh, *Soviet Public Opinion and Ideology: Mythology and Pragmatism in Interaction* (Westport, CT: Praeger, 1986); Vladimir Shlapentokh, *The Politics of Sociology in the Soviet Union* (Boulder, CO: Westview, 1987); Boris Firsov, *Istoriia sovetskoi sotsiologii 1950–1980-kh godov* (Saint Petersburg: Evropeiskii universitet v Sankt Peterburge, 2001); Gennadii S. Batygin and C. F. Iarmoliuk, eds., *Rossiskaia sotsiologiia shestidesiatykh godov v vospominaniiakh i dokumentakh* (Saint Petersburg: Russkii Khristianskii Gumanitarnyi Institut, 1999).

10. RGANI, f. 5, op. 30, d. 409, ll. 112–23. The party's Ideological Commission received a record numbers of letters on ideological questions after the Twenty-Second Party Congress: 5,950 between January and June 1962.

11. The Institute of Public Opinion (Institut obshestvennogo mnenia) under *Komsomol'skaia Pravda* was headed by Boris Grushin. See Boris A. Grushin, *Chetyre zhizni Rossii v zerkale oprosov obshchestvennogo mneniia: ocherki massovogo soznaniia rossiian vremen Khrushcheva, Brezhneva, Gorbacheva i Eltsina v 4-kh knigakh* (Moscow: Progress-Traditsiia, 2001).

12. On the Ideological Commissions, see Titov, "1961 Party Program"; Stephen V. Bittner, "Ideologicheskie komissii TsK KPSS, 1958–1964: Dokumenty (review)," *Kritika: Explorations in Russian and Eurasian History* 3 no. 2 (2002): 356–61.

13. See Steve E. Harris, *Communism on Tomorrow Street: Mass Housing and Everyday Life after Stalin* (Baltimore: Johns Hopkins University Press, 2013); Christine Varga-Harris, *Stories of House and Home: Soviet Apartment Life during the Khrushchev Years* (Ithaca, NY: Cornell University Press, 2015); Susan E. Reid, "Communist Comfort: Socialist Modernism and the Making of Cosy Homes in the Khrushchev-Era Soviet Union," *Gender and History* 21, no. 3 (2009): 465–98; Paulina Bren and Mary Neuburger, eds., *Communism Unwrapped: Consumption in Cold War Eastern Europe* (New York: Oxford University Press, 2012).

14. Nikita Khrushchev, "Providing People with Earthly Goods, Not Promising Them Heavenly Rewards," *Voiovnichii ateist* 2 (1961): inside cover. Speech made on January 17, 1961, at the Central Committee Plenum on agriculture.

15. On the development of the concept of the "Soviet person" in Soviet philosophy, see Edward Swiderski, "From Social Subject to 'Person': The Belated Transformation in Latter-Day Soviet Philosophy," *Philosophy of the Social Sciences* 23, no. 2 (1993): 199–227; Regula M. Zwahlen, "The Lack of Moral Autonomy in the Russian Concept of Personality: A Case of Continuity across the Pre-Revolutionary, Soviet, and Post-Soviet Periods?," *State, Religion and Church* 2, no. 1 (2015): 19–43.

16. The virtues to be embodied by the new Soviet person in the "Moral Code of the Builders of Communism" included patriotism ("devotion to the cause of Communism, love of the socialist homeland, and the socialist countries"), internationalism ("friendship and brotherhood of all peoples of the USSR, intolerance of national and racial animosity"), work ethic ("conscientious labor for the good of society" and "a high sense of public duty, intolerance of the violations of the public interest"), collectivism ("comradely mutual assistance" and "humane relations and mutual respect"), the moderation of desire ("an uncompromising attitude to injustice, parasitism, dishonesty, careerism, and moneygrubbing"), family values ("mutual respect in the family and concern for the upbringing of children"), commitment to Communism (and an "uncompromising attitude" toward its enemies), and morality ("honesty and truthfulness, moral purity, guilelessness and modesty in public and private life").

17. RGASPI, f. 586, op. 1, d. 7; RGASPI, f. 586, op. 1, d. 8.

18. RGASPI, f. 586, op. 1, d. 8, 1. 4.

19. RGASPI, f. 586, op. 1, d. 7, ll. 9–11.

20. RGASPI, f. 586, op. 1, d. 10, l. 8.

21. Ibid., l. 2. A number of studies on the participation of the Soviet public in the project of redefining socialism show that the public did not always necessarily push for liberalization and indeed often focused on policing deviance. See Sheila Fitzpatrick, "Social Parasites: How Tramps, Idle Youth, and Busy Entrepreneurs Impeded the Soviet March to Communism," *Cahiers du Monde russe et soviétique* 47, no. 1–2 (2006): 1–32; Polly Jones, "From the Secret Speech to the Burial of Stalin: Real and Ideal Responses to De-Stalinization," in *The Dilemmas of De-Stalinization: Negotiating Cultural and Social Change in the Khrushchev Era*, ed. Polly Jones (New York: Routledge, 2006), 41–63; Susanne Schattenberg, "'Democracy' or 'Despotism'? How the Secret Speech was Translated into Everyday Life," in *The Dilemmas of De-Stalinization: Negotiating Cultural and Social Change in the Khrushchev Era*, ed. Polly Jones (New York: Routledge, 2006), 64–79; Oleg Kharkhordin, *The Collective and the Individual in Russia* (Berkeley: University of California Press, 1999), 279–302.

22. *Programma Kommunisticheskoi Partii Sovetskogo Soiuza priniata XXII s'ezdom KPSS* (Moscow: Izdatel'stvo politicheskoi literatury, 1971).

23. As Mitrokhin writes, "Speaking of the communicative practices of work within [the party's Central Committee], we see that the ordering and selection of 'Soviet' cultural symbols were not based on any sort of written instructions or a rigid and fixed system (codex) of ideological norms. De-facto they existed in the minds of their carriers. At each level of the vertical hierarchy the bureaucrat worked out the borders of what is and is not allowed, checking with the position of higher-ups, noting the opinions of colleagues and experts, but also guided by his own conceptions of what was permitted by his professed ideology, which he associated with Marxism-Leninism." See Nikolai Mitrokhin, "Back-office Mikhaila Suslova ili kem i kak proizvodilas' ideologiia Brezhnevskogo vremeni," *Cahiers du monde russe* 54, no. 3 (2013): 409–40.

24. Ibid. On ideological production, see also Mikhail Nemtsev, "K istorii sovetskoi akademicheskoi distsipliny 'Osnovy nauchnogo kommunizma,'" *Idei i idealy* 27, no. 1 (2016): 23–38; Caroline Humphrey, "The 'Creative Bureaucrat': Conflicts in the Production of Soviet Communist Party Discourse," *Inner Asia* 10, no. 1 (2008): 5–35; Sonja Luehrmann, "The Modernity of Manual Reproduction: Soviet Propaganda and the Creative Life of Ideology," *Cultural Anthropology* 26, no. 3 (2011): 363–88.

25. "O zadachakh partiinoi propagandy v sovremennykh usloviiakh," *Kommunist* 1 (1960): 12.

26. Ibid.

27. RGASPI, f. 623, op. 1, d. 246 and d. 267.

28. RGASPI, f. 623, op. 1, d. 202, l. 68.

29. Ibid., 66.

30. Ibid., 83.

31. See Evgraf Duluman, "How I Became an Atheist," *Komsomol'skaia Pravda*, March 17, 1957, 1, and Aleksandr Osipov, "Otkaz ot religii—edisntvenno pravel'nyi put': Pis'mo v redaktsiiu," *Pravda*, December 6, 1959, 4. Shortly after publishing "How I Became an Atheist," Duluman published a book-length version of his conversion, titled *Why I Stopped Believing in God*, where he expanded his story for Soviet readers. See Evgraf K. Duluman, *Pochemu ia perestal verit' v boga: Rasskaz byvshego kandidata bogosloviia* (Moscow: "Molodaia gvardiia," 1957). Likewise, Osipov published *My Response to Believers* (*Moi otvet veruiushchim*), where he answered letters from clergy and believers, as well as from members of the Soviet collective welcoming him into the fold. See Aleksandr A. Osipov, *Moi otvet veruiushchim* (Leningrad: Lenizdat, 1960). In our interview, Duluman said he filled stadiums during his lectures and discussed the outpouring of letters in response to his publications, but his popularity as a lecturer is also confirmed by archival materials. For example, a report in the Ukrainian Central Communist Party archives, "On Short-Comings in Scientific Atheist Propaganda and Measures for Its Improvement," describes a lecture by Duluman and another former student at the Odessa Theological Seminary, A. V. Mokhortov, at the grand opening of the Stalino House of Atheism as having been so successful that "the hall could not fit all of those who wanted to attend." See TsDAGO, f. 1, op. 31, d. 1470, l. 27. A lecture by Aleksandr Osipov at the Gorky House of Atheism attracted 1,500 people. See RGASPI, f. 606, op. 4, d. 68, l. 87.

32. GARF, f. 9547, op. 1, d. 1310, l. 85.

33. GARF, f. 9547, op. 1, d. 1048, l. 5. On Znanie's work in the 1940s to 1960s, see Vasilii Zaichikov, *Akademiia millionov: O rabote Vsesoiuznogo obshchestva "Znanie"* (Moscow: Znanie, 1967) and Vladimir Mezentsev, *Znanie—narodu (K 25-letiiu Vsesoiuznogo obshchestva "Znanie")* (Moscow: Znanie, 1972). By the late 1960s, Znanie claimed more than 2.5 million members.

34. GARF, f. 9547, op. 1, d. 1048, ll. 8–27.

35. Ibid., 9.

36. GARF, f. 9547, op. 1, d. 1310, l. 27.

37. Ibid., 10.
38. Ibid., 13–14.
39. GARF, f. A-561, op. 1, d. 375, l. 22.
40. GARF, f. A-561, op. 1, d. 406, l. 58.
41. Ibid.
42. Ibid.
43. Ibid., 59.
44. Ibid., 60.
45. Ibid., 61.
46. Ibid., 62.
47. Ibid., 63.
48. Ibid., 64.
49. GARF, f. 9547, op. 1, d. 1353, ll. 190–96.
50. Ibid., 193.
51. Ibid., 194–95.
52. Ibid., 195.
53. Ibid., 193.
54. Ibid., 195–96.
55. Ibid.
56. Ibid., 79–92.
57. GARF, f. A-561, op. 1, d. 676, l. 17.
58. GARF, f. A-561, op. 1, d. 281, ll. 43–44, 56–61.
59. Ibid.
60. RGANI, f. 5, op. 30, d. 409, l. 116.
61. *Ustav KPSS* (Moscow: Izdatel'stvo politicheskoi literatury, 1961), 6.
62. GARF, f. A-561, op. 1, d. 283, ll. 35–36.
63. Ibid.
64. Ibid.
65. Ibid., 26.
66. GARF, f. A-561, op. 1, d. 281, ll. 45, 47–48.
67. Ibid., 56.
68. Ibid., 58.
69. Ibid., 61.
70. Ibid., 59–60.
71. Ibid.
72. Gagarin (1895–1960) was the first chair of the Institute of Red Professors in Moscow State University's Philosophy Department. Gagarin's career was devoted to philosophy in the sphere of education and party work. He was also one of the first atheist philosophers in the Soviet Union. In the early 1920s, he worked in the Smolensk regional party committee and was editor of the journal *Doloi bogov (Away with the Gods)*. He began to teach philosophy in 1925 at the Saratov Party School, and studied at the IKP from 1928 to 1933. In 1935, Gagarin became the chair of the Philosophy Department at the Moscow Institute of Philosophy, Literature, and History. In 1939, he defended one of the first doctoral dissertations in philosophy in the Soviet Union, titled "The Ideological Front of Class War in Russia in 1917," for which Iaroslavskii served as an opponent. See *Vestnik Moskovskogo universiteta. Filosofiia* 7, no. 5 (1999): 87–97. On Gagarin's career at Moscow State University, see *Vestnik Moskovskogo universiteta. Filosofiia* 7, no. 5 (1996): 79–94; Teodor Oizerman, "Sovetskaia Filosofiia v seredine 40kh-nachale 50-kh godov: Filosofskii fakul'tet MGU," *Chelovek*, no. 2 (2007): 50–62.

73. GARF, f. A-561, op. 1, d. 402, ll. 39–40.

74. Ibid.

75. GARF, f. A-561, op. 1, d. 399, ll. 11–12.

76. GARF, f. 9547, op. 1, d. 1314. Other Khrushchev era Znanie conferences on morality, aesthetics, and spiritual development included "The Moral Code of the Builders of Communism" (ibid., dd. 1311–12), "The Role of Literature and Art in Communist Upbringing" (ibid., d. 1313), and "Principles of the Formation and Development of the Spiritual Life of Communist Society" (ibid., d. 131).

77. RGASPI, f. 606, op. 1, d. 458, ll. 50–51.

78. Ibid., 209–10.

79. Ibid., 344–45.

80. Ibid., 279–81.

81. Ibid., 308, emphasis added.

82. The Ideological Commission was formed by decree of the Presidium of the Central Committee of the Communist Party on November 23, 1962, and existed until its dissolution on May 4, 1966. Before chairing the Ideological Commission, Il'ichev was the head of the Central Committee's Propaganda and Agitation department (1958–61). After Khrushchev's departure, he was removed from top party posts, and was the Deputy Minister of Foreign Affairs from 1965 until 1989. On Il'ichev's career, see Aleksandr A. Fursenko, ed., *Prezidium TsK KPSS 1954–1964: Chernovye protokol'nye zapisi zasedanii, stenogrammy, postanovleniia*, vol. 1 (Moscow: Rosspen, 2004), 1225; and Mikalai Zian'kovich, *Samye zakrytye liudi: entsiklopedia biografii* (Moscow: OLMA-Press, 2002), 205–9. For a political biography of Mikhail Suslov, see Roi Medvedev and Dimitrii Ermakov, *"Seryi kardinal": M.A. Suslov, Politicheskii portret* (Moscow: Respublika, 1992); and Serge Petroff, *The Red Eminence: A Biography of Mikhail A. Suslov* (Clifton, NJ: Kingston Press, 1988).

83. On worldview, see Todd H. Weir, "Säkularismus (Freireligiöse, Freidenker, Monisten, Ethiker, Humanisten)," in *Handbuch Religionsgeschichte des 20. Jahrhunderts im deutschsprachigen Raum*, ed. Lucian Hoelscher and Volkard Krech (Paderborn: Schönigh, 2016), 6/2:189–218.

84. Todd H. Weir, "The Riddles of Monism: An Introductory Essay," in *Monism: Science, Philosophy, Religion, and the History of a Worldview*, ed. Todd H. Weir (Basingstoke, UK: Palgrave Macmillan, 2012), 13.

85. RGANI, f. 72, op. 1, d. 9, l. 29.

86. *Plenum Tsentral'nogo Komiteta Kommunisticheskoi Partii Sovetskogo Soiuza, 18–21 June 1963: Stenograficheskii otchet* (Moscow: Izdatel'stvo Politicheskoi Literatury, 1964), 6–8.

87. Ibid., 17.

88. Ibid., 20–25.

89. RGANI, f. 72, op. 1, d. 9, l. 7

90. Ibid., 23, 19, 21.

91. Ibid., 25.

92. Ibid., 60.

93. Ibid., 46.

94. Ibid., 63.

95. Ibid., 48, 60.

96. Ibid., 35–36, 42.

97. Ibid., 29.

98. Leonid Il'ichev, "Formirovanie nauchnogo mirovozzreniia i ateisticheskoe vospitanie," *Kommunist* 1 (1964): 23–46.

99. For examples of Khrushchev-era literature on byt, see O. Kuprin, *Byt—ne chastnoe delo* (Moscow: Politizdat, 1959); M. I. Lifanov, ed., *Za kommunisticheskii byt* (Leningrad: Obshchestvo po rasprostraneniiu politicheskikh i nauchnykh znanii RSFSR, 1963); Vladimir G. Shtiuka, *Byt i religiia* (Moscow: Mysl', 1966).

100. It is noteworthy, for example, that the new Family Code of 1969 explicitly addressed socialist rituals. See Iuridicheskaia komissiia pri Sovete Ministrov RSFSR, *Kodeks o brake i sem'e RSFSR: ofitsial'nyi tekst* (Moscow: "Iuridicheskaia literatura," 1969), 8.

101. RGANI, f. 72, op. 1, d. 15, ll. 121–22.

102. Ibid., 261–62.

103. Ibid., 203.

104. Ibid., 290.

105. Ibid., 288.

106. Ibid., 291.

107. Ibid.

108. GARF, f. 9547, op. 1, d. 1371, l. 60. Indeed, Zaichikov and Mezentsev's letter came in the aftermath of a purge of the journal's editorial board, when Mezentsev was brought in to replace the journal's original (reportedly liberally inclined) editor, Petr Kolonitskii, who had also been in charge of the working group that drafted the party's position on religion for the Third Party Program (RGASPI, f. 586, op. 1, d. 10). Mezentsev served as the executive editor of *Science and Religion* from 1964 to 1968.

109. GARF, f. 9547, op. 1, d. 1371, l. 60.

110. Ibid., 2–3.

111. For an account of how the party apparatus influenced the journal's work, see "Dva chlena redkollegii zhurnala byli rabotnikamki Tsk KPSS': Beseda Nikolaia Mitrokhina s Ol'goi Timofeevnoi Brushlinskoi," *Neprikosnovennyi zapas*, no. 3 (2008), http://magazines.russ.ru/nz/2008/3/dv15-pr.html. Olga Brushlinskaia (b. 1934) graduated from the Department of Journalism of Moscow State University in 1956. Her career with *Science and Religion* began in 1970 as a correspondent who specialized in Islam. Starting in 1975, she headed the Islam division of the journal. In 2001, she became the journal's executive secretary, and in 2007 its editor in chief.

112. Olga Brushlinskaia, interview with author, Moscow, December 7, 2008.

113. GARF, f. 9547, op. 1, d. 1371, l. 61.

114. Attempts to rename the journal were taken up in 1963, 1964, and 1965. See ibid., 2–3, and GARF, f. 9547, op. 1, d. 1447.

115. GARF, f. 9547, op. 1, d. 1447, ll. 2–3.

116. Ibid., 16–17.

117. GARF, f. 9547, op. 1, d. 1310, l. 29.

118. In 1966, the INA began publishing its own journal, *Problems of Scientific Atheism* (*Voprosy nauchnogo ateizma*), which was devoted to atheist theory and methods and aimed at cadres.

119. GARF, f. 9547, op. 1, d. 1310, l. 17.

120. Ibid., 23–24. Movses M. Grigorian (1905–95) rose up through the party's educational institutions as a historian of philosophy, and was likewise active in the party and Komsomol propaganda apparatus. In 1934, he graduated from the Institute of Red Professors in Moscow and worked in the Institute of Philosophy of the Soviet Academy of Sciences until the war, and then from 1946 to 1948. From 1948 until 1964, he taught in the Philosophy Department of the Academy of Social Sciences (AON), and in 1964 was transferred to the newly established Institute of Scientific Atheism (INA), where he worked until 1975. He published one of the main atheist textbooks in the USSR. See Movses M. Grigorian, *Kurs lektsii po istorii ateizma* (Moscow: Mysl', 1970).

121. Ibid., 10.

122. On the "balancing act between the need to impose authority and the need to elicit involvement," see Stephen Lovell, "Broadcasting Bolshevik: The Radio Voice of Soviet Culture, 1920s–1950s," *Journal of Contemporary History* 48, no. 1 (2013): 94. This dilemma is also central to the story of Soviet television. See Christine E. Evans, *Between Truth and Time: A History of Soviet Central Television* (New Haven, CT: Yale University Press, 2016).

123. GARF, f. 9547, op. 1, d. 1310, l. 9.

124. Ibid., 30.

125. GARF, f. 9547, op. 1, d. 1447, ll. 11–13.

126. Ibid., 19–20, 22.

127. Ibid., 19–21. On Stel'makov's Komsomol work, see RGASPI-m, f. 1, op. 32, d. 1198, ll. 2–20.

128. GARF, f. 9547, op. 1, d. 1447, ll. 14, 19–21.

129. RGASPI, f. 606, op. 4, d. 52, l. 91.

130. Ibid., 30.

131. Ibid., 10–11.

132. Ibid. See also Anatolii S. Ivanov, "Zhurnal 'Nauka i religiia'—vazhnoe zveno v ateisticheskom vospitanii," *Voprosy nauchnogo ateizma* 19 (1976): 82–96. Ivanov, the executive editor of *Science and Religion* from 1968 to 1982, worked in the Central Committee apparatus prior to coming to the journal. "The work [of the journal] is indivisible from the broader process of the development of atheism in the country; it was the reflection [of atheist work] and at the same time was one of its component parts. The successes that resulted from the efforts of scholars in working out atheist theory elevated the quality of the journal's materials. The journal's formulation of the most important issues in atheist theory and practice helped raise the level on which these issues were worked out." Ivanov, "Zhurnal 'Nauka i religiia,'" 82.

133. Ivanov, "Zhurnal 'Nauka i religiia,'" 84.

134. For examples of publications engaging in life questions, see Boris Grigor'ian, "Dlia chego zhivet chelovek?," *Nauka i religiia*, no. 7 (1964): 62–69, which was published under the rubric "A conversation about the meaning of life" (*Razgovor o smysle zhizni*). The magazine also published readers' letters on the meaning of life. See, for example, "O zhizni, o shchast'e," *Nauka i religiia*, no. 3 (1965): 8–9, and "V chem radost', i sila, i shchast'e?," *Nauka i religiia*, no. 6 (1965): 33–35. See also Sergei F. Anisimov, *Nauka i religiia o smysle zhizni: Otvety na voprosy* (Moscow: Znanie, 1964); Sergei F. Anisimov and Grigorii A. Gurev, *Problema smysla zhizni v religii i ateizme* (Moscow: Znanie, 1981).

135. Iurii Frantsev and Iurii Filonovich, "Filosofskii kamen," *Izvestiia*, September 19, 1965, 5, cited in David E. Powell, *Antireligious Propaganda in the Soviet Union: A Study in Mass Persuasion* (Cambridge, MA: MIT Press, 1975), 2.

136. RGASPI, f. 606, op. 4, d. 14, ll. 1–7. Boris T. Grigorian (1928–95) specialized in the critique of so-called "bourgeois philosophy," publishing works such as Boris T. Grigorian, *Sotsiologiia religii ili apologiia religii?* (Moscow: Nauka, 1962). He graduated from the History Department at MGIMO in 1952, and went on to work for numerous academic and popular publications, serving as the deputy editor of *Science and Religion* from 1959 to 1965. From 1965 until his death in 1993, Grigorian worked in the Institute of Philosophy of the Soviet Academy of Sciences. I am grateful to Felix Corley for clarifying Grigorian's biography.

## *Chapter 5: "We Have to Figure Out Where We Lost People"*

Epigraph: *Chekhov. Il'f. Dovlatov. Iz zapisnykh knizhek*, ed. Aleksandr Shkliarinskii (New York: Alexandria, 1999), 17.

1. RGASPI, f. 606, op. 4, d. 14, ll. 62–67. For an internal history of the INA, see Iurii P. Zuev, "Institut nauchnogo ateizma (1964–1991)," *Voprosy religii i religiovedeniia. Antologiia otechestvennogo religiovedeniia* 1 (2009): 9–34; Iurii P. Zuev and Vil'iam V. Shmidt, "Ot instituta nauchnogo ateizma k kafedre gosudarstvenno konfessional'nykh otnoshenii: stanovlenie religiovedcheskoi shkoly (1964–1991, 1992–2010)," *Voprosy religii i religiovedeniia. Antologiia otechestvennogo religiovedeniia* 1 (2010): 15–28.

2. RGASPI, f. 606, op. 4, d. 18, l. 6.

3. Mariana M. Shakhnovich and Tatiana V. Chumakova, *Muzei istorii religii Akademii nauk SSSR i rossiiskoe religiovedenie (1932–1961)* (Saint Petersburg: Nauka, 2014), 53. Frantsev was transferred from GMIR to the Communist Party apparatus.

4. Indeed, a recent history of the Soviet Communist Party describes the Brezhnev era as a succession of party congresses where nothing substantial happened: "After the Twenty-Third Congress [in 1968] the rest of the congresses of the Brezhnev epoch contained no surprises and were carried out in a routinized fashion." See *Istoriia Kommunisitcheskoi partii Sovetskogo Soiuza* (Moscow: Rosspen, 2014), 324.

5. As one observer writes, "The sociology of the 1950s and 1960s existed without a 'residence permit' under the roof of historical materialism and other social sciences." See G. S. Batygin and C. F. Iarmoliuk, eds., *Rossiiskaia sotsiologiia shestidesiatykh godov v vospominaniakh i dokumentakh* (Saint Petersburg: Izdatel'stvo Russkogo gumanitarnogo universiteta, 1999), 9. See also Vladimir Shlapentokh, *The Politics of Sociology in the Soviet Union* (Boulder, CO: Westview, 1987); Ol'ga Sveshnikova, "Iubilei Gerodota: Shestidesiatnicheskoe proshloe v zerkale sovremennoi sotsiologii," *Novoe Literaturnoe Obozrenie* 98 (2009): 97–110. Sociology was officially institutionalized as a separate university discipline only in 1986, when students could major in sociology at the university.

6. On the spiritual malaise of rural youth, see Lewis H. Siegelbaum and Leslie Page Moch, *Broad Is My Native Land: Repertoires and Regimes of Migration in Russia's Twentieth Century* (Ithaca, NY: Cornell University Press, 2014), 134.

7. The sector was led by Gennadii V. Osipov. See Gennadii V. Osipov, "My zhili naukoi," in Batygin and Iarmoliuk, *Rossiiskaia sotsiologiia shestidesiatykh*, 95–109.

8. The city of Leningrad was a forerunner in the revival of sociology. See Asalkhan O. Boronoev, ed., *Sotsiologiia v Leningrade—Sankt-Peterburg vo vtoroi polovine 20 veka* (Saint Petersburg: Izdatel'stvo SPbGU, 2007); Asalkhan O. Boronoev, "Sociological Research in Leningrad–St. Petersburg (1960s–1990s), *Sociological Research* 48, no. 5 (September–October 2009): 45–54. On sociological studies of religion conducted by GMIR, see Nikolai P. Krasnikov, "Predvaritel'nye rezul'taty izucheniia religioznykh verovanii i obriadnosti," in *Konkretnye issledovaniia sovremennykh religioznykh verovanii (metodika, organizatsiia, rezul'taty)* (Moscow: Mysl', 1967), 129–37.

9. James C. Scott, *Seeing Like a State: How Certain Schemes to Improve the Human Condition Have Failed* (New Haven, CT: Yale University Press, 1998).

10. The Central Committee issued two decrees on the relationship between ideology and the social sciences, "On Measures for the Further Development of the Social Sciences and Raising Their Role in Communist Construction" (August 1967) and "On Measures for the Improvement in the Training of Theoretical Cadres of the Academy of Social Sciences of the TsK KPSS" (November 1970). On the birth and history of the discipline of Scientific Communism, see Mikhail Nemtsev, "K istorii sovetskoi akademicheskoi distsipliny 'Osnovy nauchnogo kommunizma,'" *Idei i idealy* 27, no. 1 (2016): 23–38.

11. RGANI, f. 5, op. 35, d. 210, ll. 21, 31–33, cited in Marina G. Pugacheva, "Institut konkretnykh sotsial'nykh isledovanii Akademii Nauk, 1968–1972 gody," *Sotsiologicheskii zhurnal* 2 (1994): 158–72.

12. Ibid., 202.

13. ARAN, f. 499, op. 1, d. 438, l. 41, cited in Pugacheva, "Institut konkretnykh," 159n4.

14. RGANI, f. 5, op. 55, d. 70. In general, these institutions were not enthusiastic about losing their religion specialists. On the history of the late Soviet study of religion, see Mariana M. Shakhnovich, "Otechestvennoe religiovedenie 20–80kh godov XX veka: Ot kakogo nasledstva my otkazyvaemsia," in *Ocherki po istorii religiovedeniia*, edited by Shakhnovich (Saint Petersburg: Izd-vo S.-Peterb. un-ta, 2006), 181–97; Mikhail Iu. Smirnov, "Religiovedenie v Rossii: problema samoidentifikatsii," *Vestnik Moskovskogo universiteta. Filosofiia* 1 (2009): 90–106.

15. On Soviet religious studies, including the work of the INA, see Iurii P. Zuev, "Dinamika religioznosti v Rossii v XX veke i ee sotsiologicheskoe izuchenie," in Viktor I. Garadzha, *Sotsiologiia religii* (Moscow, 1995), 187–210.

16. RGASPI f. 606, op. 2, d. 25, l. 2.

17. Ibid., l. 5.

18. At the time of his untimely death in 1969, Evdokimov was working on a study of conceptions of religion in socialist society. See Vladimir I. Evdokimov, "Utopicheskii sotsializm o religii v 'ideal'nom obshchestve,'" *Voprosy nauchnogo ateizma* 12 (1971): 167–96. On Evdokimov's career, see Nikolai Mitrokhin, "'Obydennoe soznanie liubit prostye resheniia . . .': Beseda Nikolaia Mitrokhina s Vladimirom Aleksandrovichem Saprykinym," *Neprikosnovennyi zapas* 3, 59 (2008), http://magazines.russ.ru/nz/2008/3/sa14.html.

19. Of the three nominations, Mitrokhin was the one not chosen for the post. He was also the one whose background was more connected with academic than party institutions. Mitrokhin received his degree in 1953 from the Department of Philosophy at Moscow State University, where he continued as a graduate student until 1956. In 1958, he joined the Institute of Philosophy as a junior researcher in the scientific atheism sector. Of the nominees, Mitrokhin had the most ambivalent relationship with atheist work. In his recollections, he describes his initial involvement in atheist propaganda, as a Znanie lecturer, as the result of financial difficulties after the arrest of his father in 1950. He ascribes his choice to work in scientific atheism at the Institute of Philosophy to the influence of Aleksandr Klibanov (1910–84), a prominent scholar of religious sectarianism with whom Mitrokhin conducted fieldwork and co-authored several articles. As a candidate, Mitrokhin had the weakest party record. He joined the party in 1961, the same year he left the Institute of Philosophy to work in the Komsomol as the Deputy Chief of the Propaganda-Agitation Department. There, for two years, Mitrokhin reported on the religious situation in the country, focusing on youth and sectarians. Mitrokhin's Komsomol work concentrated on religion and atheism. In the early 1960s, he authored numerous reports on youth religiosity and sectarianism for the Komsomol Central Committee. See RGASPI-m, f. 1, op. 32, d. 1111 and RGASPI-m, f. 1, op. 32, d. 1150. Archival sources do not provide an answer about why Mitrokhin's candidacy for the post of deputy director was not approved—though it is possible to speculate that his party experience may have been deemed insufficient, and the fact that he returned to the Institute of Philosophy, after his time in the Komsomol, to work in the sector of Western Philosophy may have also played a part. Mitrokhin's own rejection of the post is also not out of the question, as his later writings and interviews reveal his ambivalence on the subject of atheist education, despite his close professional ties with this field throughout his life. Indeed, in an interview given toward the end of his life, Mitrokhin avoided direct discussion of scientific atheism, and when asked directly about his specialization, he answered simply that he "did not consider [him]self to be a 'scientific atheist' but a philosopher of religion." On Mitrokhin's views of atheist work and his role in the atheist project, see Lev N. Mitrokhin, "O vremeni I o sebe," in *Religiia I kul'tura (filosofskie ocherki)* (Moscow: IF RAN, 2000), 9–37.

20. RGASPI, f. 606, op. 4, d. 1. For example, in the first year of its existence, the INA took part in several topical conferences coordinated by the Central Committee: in

Leningrad, on the improvement of organization and content of atheist work; in Kiev, on work among believers in rural areas; and in Riga, on work among Catholics and Lutherans in the Baltic republics.

21. RGASPI, f. 606, op. 4, d. 119, l. 192. By 1974, there were forty-seven. In the RSFSR, these included Moscow and the Moscow region, Vladimir, Gorky, Penza, Perm, Vologda, Voronezh, Ivanovo, Kazan', Krasnodar, Briansk, Chuvashiia, Dagestan, Mordovia, Orel, Novgorod, Pskov, Riazan', Stavropol', Tomsk, Cheliabinsk, Checheno-Ingushetiia, and Iaroslavl', among others. The INA also coordinated research across the USSR's republics. In Ukraine, bases were established in Kiev, Ivano-Frankovsk, Dnepropetrovsk, Odessa, and Uzhgorod. In Belarus there were bases in Minsk and Brest. There were also bases in Kazakhstan, Uzbekistan, Georgia, Tadzhikistan, Kyrgyzstan, Lithuania, Latvia, and Estonia, and Karelia.

22. Iurii Zuev, interview with author, Moscow, June 23, 2011.

23. My profile of INA cadres, and the late Soviet cohort of professional atheists more generally, is based on numerous interviews with former employees and graduate students of the institute, as well as those who interacted with the institute professionally. Vladimir Glagolev, interview with author, Moscow, June 27, 2011; Remir Lopatkin, interview with author, Moscow, June 23, 2011; Nadezhda Nefedova, interview with author, Moscow, June 25, 2011; Mikhail Odintsov, interview with author, Moscow, June 27, 2011; Zul'fiia Tazhurizina, interview with author, Moscow, June 25, 2011; Nikolai Zakovich, interview with author, Kiev, February 5, 2009; Zuev, interview; Viktor Garadzha, interview with author, Moscow, May 31, 2012. On the biographies of professional atheists, see also Nikolai Mitrokhin, "'Otvetstvennyi rabotnik TsK KPSS Vladimir Saprykin': kar'era odnogo sovetskogo professional'nogo ateista," in *Chelovek I lichnost' v istorii Rossii, konets XIX–XX vek: Materialy mezhdunarodnogo kollokviuma* (St. Petersburg: Nestor-Istoriia, 2012), 613–26; and Victoria Smolkin-Rothrock, "'The Confession of an Atheist Who Became a Scholar of Religion': Nikolai Semenovich Gordienko's Last Interview," *Kritika: Explorations in Russian and Eurasian History* 15, no. 3 (Summer 2014): 596–620.

24. Lopatkin, interview; Zakovich, interview.

25. That the Central Committee directed the work of the institute's graduate students was confirmed in my interviews with INA graduates, including Zuev, who writes that the party oversaw their studies and careers. Students were assigned a research project when they were accepted into the graduate program, and often placed in professional positions by the Central Committee personnel department after completing their studies. Some INA graduates wound up in academic work, but many went into party work. Over the course of the institute's existence, 120 students completed its graduate program, 200 defended candidate-level dissertations, and 40 defended doctoral-level dissertations.

26. Lopatkin, interview; Zakovich, interview.

27. RGASPI, f. 606, op. 4, d. 14, ll. 62–67; RGASPI, f. 606, op. 4, d. 18, l. 6.

28. RGASPI, f. 606, op. 4, d. 14, ll. 4–6.

29. RGASPI, f. 606, op. 4, d. 19, l. 76.

30. Ibid., 76–77. Some of the earliest sociological research on Soviet religiosity took place from 1959 to 1961. A group at the Institute of History of the Soviet Academy of Sciences, directed by the historian of religion Aleksandr I. Klibanov, conducted research expeditions to study the religious life of sectarians in the Tambov, Lipetsk, and Voronezh regions. Likewise, a group of graduate students in scientific atheism from Moscow State University went to the Orel region to study local religiosity. Igor N. Iablokov, interview with author, Moscow, June 24, 2011. Klibanov published prolifically on religious sectarianism. See Aleksandr I. Klibanov, *Reformatsionnye dvizheniia v Rossii* (Moscow: Nauka, 1960); Aleksandr I. Klibanov, *Istoriia religioznogo sektantstva v Rossii* (Moscow: Nauka, 1965);

Aleksandr I. Klibanov, *Konkretnye issledovaniia sovremennykh religioznykh verovanii* (Moscow: Nauka, 1967); Aleksandr I. Klibanov, *Religioznoe sektantsvo I sovremennost': sotsiologicheskie I istoricheskie ocherki* (Moscow: Nauka, 1969); Aleksandr I. Klibanov, *Religioznoe sektantstvo v proshlom I nastoiashchem* (Moscow: Nauka, 1973).

31. RGASPI, f. 606, op. 4, d. 1, ll. 3–8. On later changes and additions, see RGASPI, f. 606, op. 4, d. 4, ll. 18–19.

32. The subjects studied more systematically by the institute's first research groups also reveal the state's interests and priorities. These included "the character and degree of the religiosity of Soviet believers," "features of the battle between science and religion in contemporary conditions," "moral progress and religion," "tendencies in the development of religious ideology and organizations in capitalist countries," "preconditions for and paths toward fully overcoming religion," "the effectiveness of various forms of atheist education" (later renamed "forms and methods of atheist propaganda"), "the atheist education of the emerging generation," and "bourgeois atheism and free thought at the present stage," added a year later, in 1965. On the INA's early studies of Soviet religiosity, see Miriam Dobson, "The Social Scientist Meets the 'Believer': Discussions of God, the Afterlife, and Communism in the Mid-1960s," *Slavic Review* 74, no. 1 (2015): 79–103.

33. RGASPI, f. 606, op. 4, d. 56, ll. 67–68.

34. RGASPI, f. 606, op. 4, d. 12.

35. Smolkin-Rothrock, "Confession of an Atheist Who Became a Scholar of Religion."

36. RGASPI, f. 606, op. 4, d. 12.

37. RGASPI, f. 606, op. 4, d. 12, ll. 16–17.

38. Ibid., 28. This shift from scientistic to humanistic discourse in the social sciences was accompanied by the shift from the collective to the individual as the object of analysis within Soviet philosophy and sociology. See Aleksandr Bikbov, *Grammatika poriadka: istoricheskaia sotsiologiia poniatii, kotorye meniaiut nashu real'nost'* (Moscow: Izdatel'skii dom Vysshei Shkoly Ekonomiki, 2014).

39. Galitskaia's scholarly interests focused on atheism and religion in youth education. See Irina A. Galitskaia, ed., *Molodezh' I ateizm* (Moscow: Mysl', 1971).

40. RGASPI, f. 606, op. 4, d. 12, ll. 35–36.

41. Ibid., 36.

42. RGASPI, f. 606, op. 4, d. 19, l. 80.

43. Pavel Kurochkin, ed., *K obshchestvu, svobodnomu ot religii: Protsess sekuliarizatsii v usloviiakh sotsialisticheskogo obshchestva* (Moscow: Mysl', 1970).

44. RGASPI, f. 606, op. 4, d. 18, ll. 7, 9.

45. Ibid., 14.

46. RGASPI, f. 606, op. 4, d. 37, l. 47.

47. RGASPI, f. 606, op. 4, d. 18, l. 23–24.

48. RGASPI, f. 606, op. 4, d. 19, ll. 58–66.

49. Ibid., 28.

50. Ibid., 85, 78.

51. Evgraf Duluman, Boris Lobovik, and Vladimir Tancher, *Sovremennyi veruiushchii: Sotsial'no psikhologicheskii ocherk* (Moscow: Politizdat, 1970).

52. RGASPI, f. 606, op. 4, d. 80.

53. Tamara Dragadze, "The Domestication of Religion under Soviet Communism," in *Socialism: Ideals, Ideologies, and Local Practice*, ed. C. M. Hann (London: Routledge, 1993), 148–56.

54. RGASPI, f. 606, op. 4, d. 68, ll. 80–82.

55. RGASPI, f. 606, op. 4, d. 56, l. 103.

56. RGASPI, f. 606, op. 4, d. 72, ll. 42–45.

57. On the ways in which the role of religion changes over the course of a person's life, see Douglas Rogers, *The Old Faith and the Russian Land: A Historical Ethnography of Ethics in the Urals* (Ithaca, NY: Cornell University Press, 2009).

58. RGASPI, f. 606, op. 4, d. 56, l. 71.

59. RGASPI-m, f. 1, op. 34, d. 129, ll. 8–13; RGASPI-m, f. 1, op. 34, d. 108, l. 28.

60. RGASPI-m, f. 1, op. 34, d. 108, ll. 14, 28.

61. RGASPI, f. 606, op. 4, d. 67, l. 62.

62. Ibid., 31–35.

63. RGASPI, f. 606, op. 4, d. 75, l. 10.

64. RGASPI, f. 606, op. 4, d. 67, l. 41.

65. RGASPI-m, f. 1, op. 34, d. 131, l. 40.

66. RGASPI, f. 606, op. 4, d. 67, ll. 9–10.

67. RGASPI, f. 606, op. 4, d. 67, l. 31.

68. RGASPI, f. 606, op. 4, d. 67, l. 29.

69. RGASPI, f. 606, op. 4, d. 80, ll. 53–56.

70. Ibid., 88.

71. There has thus far been little Anglophone scholarship on "indifference" as a concept and category. Tara Zahra's analysis of indifference in the context of nationalism is illuminating with regard to the phenomenon of religious indifference. See Tara Zahra, "Imagined Noncommunities: National Indifference as a Category of Analysis," *Slavic Review* 69, no. 1 (2010): 93–119. On religious indifference, see Yves Lambert, "New Christianity, Indifference and Diffused Spirituality," in *The Decline of Christendom in Western Europe, 1750–2000*, ed. Hugh McLeod and Ustorf Werner (New York: Cambridge University Press, 2003), 63–78.

72. Lopatkin, interview. See also the interview with Saprykin, who also participated in the Penza study. Mitrokhin, "'Obydennoe soznanie.'"

73. RGASPI, f. 606, op. 4, d. 92, ll. 46–47.

74. On the Hare Krishna movement in the USSR, see John Anderson, "The Hare Krishna Movements in the USSR," *Religion in Communist Lands* 14, no. 3 (1986): 316–17; Joseph Kellner, "The End of History: Radical Responses to the Soviet Collapse" (PhD diss., University of California, Berkeley, 2018).

75. Hugh McLeod observes this disintegration of moral consensus and the rise of various countercultures and individualized spiritualities, especially among young people, beginning in the 1960s, and describes the "religious crisis of the 1960s" as the end of Christendom. See Hugh McLeod, *The Religious Crisis of the 1960s* (Oxford: Oxford University Press, 2007), 134–36, 147.

76. RGASPI, f. 606, op. 4, d. 114, ll. 23, 26, 28.

77. RGASPI, f. 606, op. 4, d. 103, ll. 80–81.

78. RGASPI, f. 606, op. 4, d. 62, ll. 8–15.

79. RGASPI, f. 606, op. 4, d. 62, l. 15. Pantskhava (1906–86) formed the Department of the History and Theory of Atheism at Moscow State University in 1959, where he spent more than twenty years. He specialized in dialectical materialism and wrote on worldview themes, such as the meaning of life, death, and immortality. See Il'ia D. Pantskhava, *Zhizn', Smert' i Bessmertie* (Moscow, 1966); Pantskhava, *Chelovek, ego zhizn' i bessmertie* (Moscow, 1967); Pantskhava, *O smerti i bessmertii* (Moscow, 1972).

80. RGASPI, f. 606, op. 4, d. 103, l. 15. Ugrinovich (1923–90) was a professor of philosophy at Moscow State University. For a brief overview of his professional career, see A. P. Alekseev, A. M. Korshunov, and P. A. Rachkov, "Kafedra filosofii gumanitarnykh fakul'tetov: Itogi 50-letiia i novye zadachi," *Vestnik Moskovskogo universiteta. Filosofiia* 7, no. 6 (2003): 3–20.

81. RGASPI, f. 606, op. 4, d. 103, l. 57.

82. See Aleksei Iurchak, *Eto bylo navsegda, poka ne konichilos': Poslednee sovetskoe pokolenie* (Moscow: Novoe Literaturnoe Obozrenie, 2014), 165–254, 255–310 (chap. 3, "Ideologiia naiznanku," and chap. 4, "Vnenakhodimost' kak obraz zhizni").

## *Chapter 6: The Communist Party between State and Church*

Epigraph: Konstantin P. Pobedonostsev, "The Spiritual Life," in *Reflections of a Russian Statesman* (Ann Arbor: University of Michigan Press, 1965), 184.

1. RGANI, f. 5, op. 36, d. 14, l. 3.

2. Ibid., 4.

3. Aleksei Adzhubei, *Krushenie illiuzii* (Moscow: Interbuk, 1991), 16.

4. Thomas W. Laqueur's *The Work of the Dead* chronicles this story, relating it in particular to the management of death. See Laqueur, *The Work of the Dead: A Cultural History of Mortal Remains* (Princeton, NJ: Princeton University Press, 2015), esp. 305–9.

5. Paul W. Werth, "In the State's Embrace? Civil Acts in an Imperial Order," *Kritika: Explorations in Russian and Eurasian History* 7, no. 3 (2006): 440. As Werth notes, the adoption of civil registration in Europe "typically involved political struggles" (France with the revolution, England in 1836, and Germany in 1875), where it was part of Bismarck's Kulturkampf against the Catholic Church. By the late nineteenth century, civil registration had been adopted in most of Europe, "rendering Russia's strongly confessional system increasingly exceptional."

6. Record keeping in the Russian Empire began as part of Peter the Great's modernization program in 1722, when Peter decreed that the Orthodox Church had to keep records of the Orthodox population. Requirements of other confessions followed later, with Catholics in 1826, Muslims in 1828, Lutherans in 1832, Jews in 1835, and Old Believers in 1874. See Werth, "In the State's Embrace? Civil Acts in an Imperial Order," 433–58.

7. "Kodeks zakonov ob aktakh grazhdanskogo sostoianiia," SU, 1918, 76/77-118, par. 52, as cited in Elizabeth A. Wood, *The Baba and the Comrade: Gender and Politics in Revolutionary Russia* (Bloomington: Indiana University Press, 1997), 51n17.

8. Nikolai V. Krylenko, *Proekt kodeksa o brake i sem'e* (Moscow, 1926), 6, cited in Wood, *Baba and the Comrade*, 52n18.

9. Vladimir I. Brudnyi, *Obriady vchera i segodnia* (Moscow: Nauka, 1968), 65–70.

10. Vladimir D. Bonch-Bruevich, "Otdelenie tserkvi ot gosudarstva," in *Deiateli Oktiabria o religii i tserkvi* (Moscow: Mysl', 1968), 13, cited in Anna D. Sokolova, "Transformatsiia pokhoronnoi obriadnosti u russkikh v XX–XXI vv (Na materialakh Vladimirskoi oblasti)" (PhD diss., Institute of Ethnography and Anthropology of the Russian Academy of Sciences, 2013), 53.

11. The term *dvoeverie* was typically used in a disparaging fashion to refer to the syncretic religiosity of ordinary people, which combined Christian precepts with folk customs. Emelian Iaroslavskii, "Kak vesti antireligioznuiu propaganda. Doklad, prochitannyi 20-go aprelia na 1-m Vsesoiuznom s'ezde korrespondentov gaz. 'Bezbozhnik' i Obshchestva druzei gazety 'Bezbozhnik'" (Moscow: Izdatel'stvo Bezbozhnik, 1925), 21, cited in Sokolova, "Transformatsiia pokhoronnoi obriadnosti," 57.

12. For an example of this debate, see Vikentii V. Veresaev, *Ob obriadakh starykh i novykh (k khudozhestvennomu oformleniiu byta)* (Moscow: Novaia Moskva, 1926). For a criticism of Veresaev's position, see Lev N. Voitolovskii, "O krasnykh obriadakh (Po povodu stat'i V. Veresaeva 'K khudozhestvennomu oformleniiu byta,'" *Krasnaia nov'* (March 1926): 174–82.

13. Irina Gutkin, *The Cultural Origins of the Socialist Realist Aesthetic, 1890–1934* (Evanston, IL: Northwestern University Press, 1999), 95. For scholarship on rituals in the early Soviet period, see Richard Stites, *Revolutionary Dreams: Utopian Vision and Experimental Life in the Russian Revolution* (New York: Oxford University Press, 1989), 109–12; James Von Geldern, *Bolshevik Festivals, 1917–1920* (Berkeley: University of California Press, 1993); Daniel Peris, *Storming the Heavens: The Soviet League of the Militant Godless* (Ithaca, NY: Cornell University Press, 1998), 86–92; Katerina Clark, *Petersburg: Crucible of Cultural Revolution* (Cambridge, MA: Harvard University Press, 1995); Karen Petrone, *Life Has Become More Joyous, Comrades: Celebrations in the Time of Stalin* (Bloomington: Indiana University Press, 2000); Malte Rolf, *Soviet Mass Festivals, 1917–1991* (Pittsburgh: University of Pittsburgh Press, 2013). On the post-Stalin period, see Christel Lane, *The Rites of Rulers: Ritual in Industrial Society—The Soviet Case* (New York: Cambridge University Press, 1981); Christopher Binns, "The Changing Face of Power: Revolution and Accommodation in the Soviet Ceremonial System, Part I," *Man* 14, no. 4 (December 1979): 585–606; Binns, "The Changing Face of Power: Revolution and Accommodation in the Soviet Ceremonial System, Part II," *Man* 15, no. 1 (March 1980): 170–87; Vladimir V. Glebkin, *Ritual v sovetskoi kul'ture* (Moscow: Ianus-K, 1998); Elena Zhidkova, "Sovetskaia obriadnost' kak al'ternativa obriadnosti religizonoi," *Gosudarstvo, Religiia i Tserkov' v Rossii i za Rubezhom*, nos. 3–4 (2012): 408–29. On the broader European context of ritual production, see Eric Hobsbawm and Terence Ranger, *The Invention of Tradition* (New York: Cambridge University Press, 1984).

14. Aleksandr V. Moravov (1878–1951), "V Volostnom ZAGSe," 1928, State Tretiakov Gallery.

15. Il'ia Ilf and Evgenii Petrov, *The Twelve Chairs*, trans. John H. C. Richardson (Evanston, IL: Northwestern University Press, 1997); Il'ia Ilf and Evgenii Petrov, "Mat" (1935), in *Sobranie Sochinenii*, vol. 3 (Moscow: Gos. Izd. Khud. Lit., 1961), 382–88.

16. Mikhail M. Cheremnykh, "You Are Waiting in Vain at the Church Door, Priest—We Live Wonderfully without Icons and God!" (*U tserkovnogo poroga zhdesh' pop, naprasno; bez ikon i boga my zhivem prekrasno*), Moscow-Leningrad, Izd-vo "Isskustvo," 1939, GMIR, Inv. no. B-1202-IV, used with permission.

17. On postwar pronatalist campaigns and efforts to rebuild the Soviet family, see Mie Nakachi, "Replacing the Dead: The Politics of Reproduction in the Postwar Soviet Union, 1944–1955" (PhD diss., University of Chicago, 2008); Mie Nakachi, "Gender, Marriage, and Reproduction in the Postwar Soviet Union," in *Writing the Stalin Era: Sheila Fitzpatrick and Soviet Historiography*, ed. Golfo Alexopoulos, Julie Hessler, and Kiril Tomoff (Basingstoke: Palgrave Macmillan, 2011), 101–16; Edward D. Cohn, "Sex and the Married Communist: Family Troubles, Marital Infidelity, and Party Discipline in the Postwar USSR, 1945–64," *Russian Review* 68, no. 3 (2009): 429–50.

18. See January 8, 1946, RSFSR Council of Ministers decree "On Measures for the Regularization of Acts of Civil Status."

19. By the late 1960s, ZAGS organs were understood as administrative bureaucracies that also "perform[ed] a significant educational and prophylactic (*vospitatel'nuiu i profilakticheskuiu*) work among the population," which included consultations about the significance of marriage and the inculcation of new rituals into the byt of Soviet people. See K. L. Emel'ianova, "Nekotorye voprosy sovershenstvovaniia deiatel'nosti organov ZAGS," *Pravovedeniie* 4 (1968): 101–3.

20. On Summer Youth Days and Komsomol activities in the Baltics, see RGASPI-m, f. 1, op. 32, d. 959, ll. 136–47; Genadii Gerodnik, *Dorogami novykh traditsii* (Moscow, 1964).

21. RGASPI, f. M-1, op. 32, d. 959; Aleksandr N. Shelepin, *Otchetnyi doklad Tsentral'nogo Komiteta Vsesoiuznogo leninskogo kommunisticheskogo soiuza molodezhi XIII s"ezdu komsomola (15 aprelia 1958 g.)* (Moscow: Molodaia gvardiia, 1958), 37–38.

22. Sergei Shtyrkov, "'V gorode otkryt Dvorets schast'ia': Bor'ba za novuiu sovetskuiu obriadnost' vremen Khrushcheva," in *Topografiia schast'ia: etnograficheskie karty moderna. Sbornik statei*, ed. Nikolai Ssorin-Chaikov (Moscow: Novoe literaturnoe obozrenie, 2013), 261–75.

23. On Khrushchev era housing reforms and their effect on Soviet everyday life and society, see Steve E. Harris, *Communism on Tomorrow Street: Mass Housing and Everyday Life after Stalin* (Baltimore: Johns Hopkins University Press, 2013); Christine Varga-Harris, *Stories of House and Home: Soviet Apartment Life during the Khrushchev Years* (Ithaca, NY: Cornell University Press, 2015).

24. RGASPI-m, f. 1, op. 32, d. 940, ll. 37–92.

25. Ibid., 30.

26. The first Moscow Wedding Palace was opened on December 15, 1960. See TsAGM, f. 2511, op. 1.

27. On reports of ZAGS work "on distracting the population from taking part in religious rituals by way of inculcating civic rituals," see RGASPI-m, f. 1, op. 32, d. 940, ll. 118–37, 150–69, and RGASPI-m, f. 1, op. 32, d. 1040, ll. 98–104.

28. A. Kamaev and A. Kulikov, "O trekh momentakh," *Smena*, August 26, 1959, 3. See also the discussion of new socialist rituals in *Smena*, August 13, 1959; *Smena*, September 11, 1959.

29. Aleksandr Usakovskii, "Nuzhny li sovetskie obriady?," *Izvestiia*, October 3, 1959, 6; Evgenii Kriger, "Spor prodolzhaetsia," *Izvestiia*, December 5, 1959, 2. In November 1959, the Herzen Pedagogical Institute in Leningrad also had an organized dispute about the place of rituals in Soviet society under the rubric "Soviet Traditions and Rituals Must Help Us Educate the Person of the Future." See Petr P. Kampars and Nikolai M. Zakovich, *Sovetskaia grazhdanskaia obriadnost'* (Moscow: Mysl', 1967), 33.

30. RGASPI-m, f. 1, op. 32, d. 940, ll. 174–76. This exchange takes place between one Levina, writing on behalf of a group of "lovers of soviet postcards," and the artist, Vladimirskii.

31. RGASPI-m, f. 1, op. 32, d. 1151, ll. 173–74.

32. "Bol'shogo shchast'ia vam, geroi-kosmonavty! Serdechnye pozdravleniia novobrachnym—Valentine Tereshkovoi i Andrianu Nikolaevu," *Pravda*, November 4, 1963, 1; "Ruka ob ruku—na zemle i v kosmose!," *Izvestiia*, November 4, 1963, 1.

33. Ibid.

34. TsAGM, f. 709, op. 1, d. 48, l. 8.

35. RGASPI, f. 606, op. 4, d. 36. The Institute of Ethnography of the Soviet Academy of Sciences worked on new socialist rituals, and the ethnographer (and professional atheist) Kryvelev published numerous articles on the subject in *Sovetskaia Etnografiia*. See, for example, Iosif A. Kryvelev, "Preodolenie religiozno-bytovykh perezhitkov u narodov SSSR," *Sovetskaia etnografiia*, no. 4 (1961): 30–43, and Iosif A. Kryvelev, "O formirovanii i rasprostranenii novykh obychaev i prazdnikov u narodov SSSR," *Sovetskaia etnografiia*, no. 6 (1963): 16–24.

36. TGALI, f. 195, op. 1, d. 251.

37. GARF, f. A-628, op. 2, d. 1111.

38. GARF, f. A-628, op. 2, d. 1106.

39. Ibid.

40. GARF, f. 6991, op. 1, d. 1942, l. 12, cited in Tatiana A. Chumachenko, "Sovet po delam Russkoi pravoslavnoi tserkvi pri SNK (SM) SSSR: 1954–1965 gg" (PhD diss., Lomonosov Moscow State University, 2011), 424–26.

41. Ibid.

42. RGANI, f. 5, op. 35, d. 215, l. 136.

43. Ibid., 137.

44. Ibid., 135.

45. GARF, f. 6991, op. 1, d. 2038, ll. 22–94, cited in Chumachenko, "Sovet po delam Russkoi pravoslavnoi tserkvi," 426.

46. Ibid.

47. GARF, f. 6991, op. 1, d. 1942.

48. RGANI, f. 72, op. 1, d. 9, ll. 134–35.

49. Ibid., 135.

50. Ibid., 138.

51. Ibid., 138–40.

52. Ibid.

53. Ibid., 136–37.

54. Ibid., 136–37.

55. RGANI, f. 72, op. 1, d. 15, ll. 121–22.

56. Ibid., 197–99.

57. RGASPI, f. 556, op. 25, d. 191, ll. 26–36; GARF, f. A-259, op. 1, d. 1952, ll. 118–22.

58. Shortly before being appointed to the council, Belyk had published a letter to the editor in *Komsomol'skaia Pravda* on the topic of socialist rituals. See Nikolai Belyk, "V etot torzhestvennyi den' . . . : Pis'mo v redaktsiiu," *Komsomol'skaia Pravda*, July 31, 1963: 2.

59. Council members included the deputy minister of culture (V. V. Gordeev), deputy of the Ministry of the Preservation of Social Order (A. Ia. Kudriavtsev), deputy head of the Ministry of Municipal Affairs (L. N. Shakunov), first deputy director of the Council of Ministers State Committee on Cinematography (Mikhail A. Solov'ev), first deputy director of the Council of Ministers State Committee on Print (V. K. Grudinin), secretary of the Moscow city ispolkom (Anatolii M. Pegov), secretary of the Leningrad city council (N. D. Khristoforov), first deputy chair of the Soviet Writers' Union (Sergei V. Sartakov), secretary of the Composers' Union (Anatolii G. Novikov), secretary of the Artists' Union (Boris K. Smirnov), and a member of the Presidium of the All-Russian Theatrical Society (Nikolai V. Petrov).

60. GARF, f. A-259, op. 1, d. 1952, ll. 118–22.

61. Vladimir I. Stepakov, *Novye prazdniki i obriady—v narodnyi byt* (Moscow, 1964). In his pamphlet, Stepakov notes that the church was no access to the public sphere, so if religion is continuing to be reproduced, it is in the home, and through rituals. He cites the *Journal of the Moscow Patriarchate* characterization of rituals as "the door to religion." Ibid., 5.

62. Christel Lane's *Rites of Rulers* remains the most comprehensive treatment of the various kinds of rituals introduced in the Soviet period.

63. Nina Tumarkin, *The Living and the Dead: The Rise and Fall of the Cult of World War II in Russia* (New York: Basic Books, 1994).

64. RGASPI, f. 606, op. 4, d. 38, l. 99.

65. Ibid., 97.

66. Ibid., 99.

67. Ibid., 102.

68. Ibid., 107.

69. Ibid., 102, 105–6.

70. Ibid., 103, 107.

71. Ibid., 67.

72. Ibid., 40–41.

73. Ibid., 45.

74. Ibid., 42–44.

75. Ibid., 44.

76. Ibid., 12–14.

77. Ibid., 14.

78. RGASPI, f. 606, op. 4, d. 38, l. 102. On the Orthodox Church's response to Soviet ritual efforts as well as its own work to modernize rituals, see Natalia Shlikhta, "'Ot traditsii k sovremennosti': pravoslavnaia obriadnost' i prazdniki v usloviiakh antireligioznoi bor'by (na materialakh USSR, 1950-e–1960-e gg.)," *Gosudarstvo, Religiia i Tserkov' v Rossii i za Rubezhom*, nos. 3–4 (2012): 380–407.

79. RGASPI, f. 606, op. 4, d. 38, l. 103.

80. Eduard Filimonov, "Besedy po vashei pros'be: Chto proiskhodit s religiei, ee obriadami i traditsiiami v nashi dni," *Izvestiia*, October 8, 1981, 3.

81. Ibid.

82. Ibid.

83. A. Petukhov, "Bumazhnye tsvety," *Novyi mir*, no. 6 (1969): 272–77. The article reviewed the vast literature on socialist rituals that began to emerge in the mid-1960s, which included books like Vladimir A. Rudnev, *Kommunisticheskomu bytu—novye traditsii* (Leningrad: Lenizdat, 1964); Emil Lisavtsev, *Novye sovetskie traditsii* (Moscow: Izd-vo "Sov. Rossiia," 1966); Anatolii N. Filatov, *O novykh i starykh obriadakh* (Moscow: Profizdat, 1967); Dmitrii M. Ugrinovich, *Obriady: za i protiv* (Moscow: Politizdat, 1975); Iurii Bokan' and Vladimir G. Sinitsyn, *Nashi prazdniki: (Sov., obshchegos., trud., voin., molodezh. i semeino-bytovye prazdniki, obriady, ritualy)* (Moscow: Politizdat, 1977); and Iosif A. Kryvelev, *Traditsionnye i novye obriady v bytu narodov SSSR* (Moscow: Nauka, 1981).

84. Petukhov, "Bumazhnye tsvety," 272–73.

85. Ibid., 275.

86. Ibid., 277.

87. Leonid Zhukhovitskii, "Tri zadachi s odnim resheniem," *Molodoi Kommunist*, December 1978, 7–12.

88. Iulian V. Bromlei, "Prazdnik bez prazdnika: simvoly nravstvennykh tsennostei," *Literaturnaia gazeta*, August 31, 1978, 12. An article in *Komsomol'skaia Pravda* likewise criticized weddings, which the editors argued had come to "recall petty-bourgeois, merchant-class" (*kupechesko-meshchanskie razguly*). See "Vokrug svad'by," *Komsomol'skaia Pravda*, January 26, 1978, 2–3.

89. For comparative cases of the socialist ritual project in Eastern Europe, see Heléna Tóth, "Shades of Grey: Secular Burial Rites in East Germany," in *Changing European Death Ways*, ed. Eric Venbrux and Thomas Quartier (Münster: LIT Verlag, 2013), 141–64; Heléna Tóth, "Writing Rituals: The Sources of Socialist Rites of Passage in Hungary, 1958–1970," in *Science, Religion and Communism in Cold War Europe*, ed. Paul Betts and Stephen A. Smith (Basingstoke: Palgrave Macmillan, 2016), 179–203; Zsuzsanna Magdo, "The Socialist Sacred: Atheism, Religion, and Mass Culture in Romania, 1948–1989" (PhD diss., University of Illinois at Urbana-Champaign, 2016).

## *Chapter 7: The Socialist Way of Life*

Epigraph: Pierre Bayle, *Historical and Critical Dictionary: Selections*, trans. Richard H. Popkin (Indianapolis: Hackett, 1991), 195.

1. Vladimir Tendriakov, "Apostol'skaia komandirovka," in *Sobranie Sochinenii*, vol. 4 (Moscow: Khudozhestvennaia literatura, 1980), 230–420, originally serialized in *Nauka i religiia*, nos. 8–10 (1969).

2. Ibid., 253–54.

3. RGASPI, f. 606, op. 2, d. 46, ll. 2–14; RGASPI, f. 606, op. 4, d. 98, ll. 9–21.

4. Tendriakov, "Apostol'skaia komandirovka," 259.

5. Alfred B. Evans, *Soviet Marxism-Leninism: The Decline of an Ideology* (Westport, CT: Praeger, 1993), 105.

6. On the fallout of 1968, see Paulina Bren, *The Greengrocer and His TV: The Culture of Communism after the 1968 Prague Spring* (Ithaca, NY: Cornell University Press, 2010); Jonathan Bolton, *Worlds of Dissent: Charter 77, the Plastic People of the Universe, and Czech Culture under Communism* (Cambridge, MA: Harvard University Press, 2012). On the Soviet dissident movement, see Philip Boobbyer, *Conscience, Dissent, and Reform in Soviet Russia* (New York: Routledge, 2005), 75–93; Benjamin Nathans, "The Dictatorship of Reason: Aleksandr Vol'pin and the Idea of Rights under 'Developed Socialism,'" *Slavic Review* 66, no. 4 (2007): 630–63. On the onset of pessimism, see John Bushnell, "The 'New Soviet Man' Turns Pessimist," *The Soviet Union since Stalin*, ed. Stephen F. Cohen, Alexander Rabinowitch, and Robert S. Sharlet (London: Macmillan, 1980), 179–99.

7. On developed socialism, see Evans, *Soviet Marxism-Leninism*; Mark Sandle and Edwin Bacon, eds., *Brezhnev Reconsidered* (New York: Palgrave Macmillan, 2002).

8. Leonid Il'ich Brezhnev, *Otchetnyi doklad TK KPSS XXIV s'ezdu Kommunisticheskoi partii Sovetskogo Soiuza* (Moscow: Politizdat, 1972), 3:235, cited in Alfred B. Evans, "The Decline of Developed Socialism: Some Trends in Recent Soviet Ideology," *Soviet Studies* 38, no. 1 (January 1986): 3, 4n13.

9. *The 24th Party Congress of the CSPU—Documents* (Moscow, 1971), 100–101.

10. Vasilii I. Kas'ianenko notes that until the end of the 1960s, there were no specialized studies of the socialist way of life and the first monograph on the subject was Vladimir G. Sinitsyn, *Sovetskii obraz zhizni* (Moscow: Sovetskaia Rossiia, 1969). See Vasilii I. Kas'ianenko, "Istoriografiia sotsialisticheskogo obraza zhizni v SSSR," *Voprosy istorii*, no. 1 (1980): 3–20. In this way, there is a direct continuity from Sinitsyn's earlier publications on byt to his later ones on the socialist way of life. See Vladimir G. Sinitsyn, *Byt epokhi stroitel'stva kommunizma* (Cheliabinsk: Cheliabinskoe knizhnoe izd-vo, 1963); Vladimir G. Sinitsyn, *O sovetskom obraze zhizni* (Moscow, 1967); Vladimir G. Sinitsyn, *Obraz zhizni, dostoinyi cheloveka (V pomoshch' lektoru: bibliotechka "sovetskii obraz zhizni")* (Moscow: Znanie, 1970); Vladimir G. Sinitsyn, "In Lieu of an Introduction," in *The Soviet Way of Life* (Moscow: Progress Publishers, 1974), 7–24. See also Grigorii E. Glezerman, "Lenin i formirovaniia sotsialisticheskogo obraza zhizni," *Kommunist*, no. 1 (1974): 105–18.

11. Leonid Brezhnev, "Otchet Tsentral'nogo Komiteta KPSS i ocherednye zadachi partii v oblasti vnutrennei i vneshnei politiki," speech at the Twenty-Fifth Congress of the CPSU, February 1976, in *Leninskim kursom* (Moscow: Politizdat, 1976), 5:493, cited in Evans, *Soviet Marxism-Leninism*, 142.

12. Kas'ianenko, "Istoriografiia sotsialisticheskogo obraza zhizni v SSSR," 4.

13. Greg Castillo, *Cold War on the Home Front: The Soft Power of Midcentury Design* (Minneapolis: University of Minnesota Press, 2010), viii.

14. On Cold War competition in the sphere of consumption, see also Laura A. Belmonte, *Selling the American Way: US Propaganda and the Cold War* (Philadelphia: University of Pennsylvania Press, 2013).

15. Petr N. Fedoseev, "Konstitutsiia SSSR i sotsialisticheskii obraz zhizni," *Kommunist* 2 (1978): 61, cited in Evans, *Soviet Marxism-Leninism*, 142.

16. Historian Paulina Bren observes a similar rhetoric in Czechoslovakia, where the "socialist way of life" was cast as "a calm and quiet life, removed from the tumultuousness of both 1968 politics and late twentieth century capitalism. The message was that [it] was potentially able to challenge and even surpass capitalism not by offering the same or better material commodities (for it could not) but by offering an unmatchable 'quality of life.'" See Paulina Bren, "Mirror, Mirror, on the Wall . . . Is the West the Fairest of Them All?

Czechoslovak Normalization and Its (Dis) Contents," *Kritika: Explorations in Russian and Eurasian History* 9, no. 4 (2008): 844.

17. On consumption in the Brezhnev era, see James R. Millar, "The Little Deal: Brezhnev's Contribution to Acquisitive Socialism," *Slavic Review* 44, no. 4 (Winter 1985): 694–706; Natalya Chernyshova, *Soviet Consumer Culture in the Brezhnev Era* (Abingdon, UK: Routledge, 2013), 43–70; Luminita Gatejel, "Appealing for a Car: Consumption Policies and Entitlement in the USSR, the GDR, and Romania, 1950s–1980s," *Slavic Review* 75, no. 1 (2016): 122–45; Serguei Oushakine, "'Against the Cult of Things': On Soviet Productivism, Storage Economy, and Commodities with No Destination," *Russian Review* 73, no. 2 (2014): 198–236.

18. RGASPI, f. 606, op. 2, d. 311, ll. 1–2.

19. Ibid., 1.

20. RGASPI, f. 606, op. 4, d. 95, ll. 69–75.

21. Jeanne Kormina and Sergei Shtyrkov, "'Eto nashi iskonno russkoe, i nikuda nam ot etogo ne det'sia': predystoriia postsovetskoi desekuliarizatsii," in *Izobretenie religii v postsovetskoi Rossii*, ed. Jeanne Kormina, Alexander Panchenko, and Sergei Shtyrkov (Saint Petersburg: Evropeiskii universitet v Sankt-Peterburge, 2015), 12. On the "historical turn" in Soviet culture, see Denis Kozlov, "The Historical Turn in Late Soviet Culture: Retrospectivism, Factography, Doubt, 1953–1991," *Kritika: Explorations in Russian and Eurasian History* 3 (2000): 577–600.

22. Iurii Chaplygin, "Nepomniashie rodstva," *Literatura i zhizn'*, February 20, 1960, 2; Dimitrii S. Likhachev, "Vo imia budushchego," *Literatura i zhizn'*, March 11, 1960, 2. For a discussion about the resonance of Chaplygin's invocation of "those who forgot their roots," see Kormina and Shtyrkov, "'Eto nashe iskonno russkoe'"; Catriona Kelly, *Socialist Churches: Radical Secularization and the Preservation of the Past in Petrograd and Leningrad, 1918–1988* (DeKalb: Northern Illinois University Press, 2016), 197.

23. On the revived interest in cultural heritage, see Victoria Donovan, "'Going Backwards, We Stride Forward': Kraevedenie Museums and the Making of Local Memory in North West Russia, 1956–1981," *Forum for Anthropology and Culture*, no. 7 (2011): 211–30; Victoria Donovan, "'How Well Do You Know Your Krai?' The Kraevedenie Revival and Patriotic Politics in Late Khrushchev-Era Russia," *Slavic Review* 74, no. 3 (2015): 464–83. On the emergence of cultural tourism in the 1960s, see Sanami Takahashi, "Obraz religioznogo landshafta v SSSR 1965–1985 gody (na primere Solovetskogo muzeia-zapovednika)," *Vestnik Evrazii*, no. 4 (2008): 9–26.

24. On conservative discourse among the nationalist intelligentsia, see Anna Razuvalova, *Pisateli "derevenshchiki": literatura i konservativnaia ideologiia 1970-kh godov* (Moscow: Novoe literaturnoe obozrenie, 2015). See also Josephine von Zitzewitz, "The 'Religious Renaissance' of the 1970s and Its Repercussions on the Soviet Literary Process" (DPhil thesis, University of Oxford, 2009).

25. On the revival of nationalism in the late Soviet period, see Yitzhak M. Brudny, *Reinventing Russia: Russian Nationalism and the Soviet State, 1953–1991* (Cambridge, MA: Harvard University Press, 1998); Nikolai Mitrokhin, *Russkaia Partiia: Dvizhenie russkikh natsionalistov v SSSR. 1953–1985 gg.* (Moscow: Novoe Literaturnoe Obozrenie, 2003); Vladislav Zubok, *Zhivago's Children: The Last Russian Intelligentsia* (Cambridge, MA: Belknap, 2009), 226–69.

26. The party's effort to discipline nationalists applied to both the nationalist writers outside the political establishment and nationalist sympathizers within it. The most prominent conflict around this issue was the downfall of Aleksandr Yakovlev, a rising star in the party's propaganda department and the future "architect of perestroika," over his criticism

of nationalist themes in Soviet literature. See Aleksandr Yakovlev, "Protiv antiistorizma," *Literaturnaia Gazeta*, November 15, 1972, 4–5.

27. RGANI, f. 5, op. 64, d. 87, ll. 54–57. The report was authored by the then head of the KGB, Yuri Andropov, and sent to the party Central Committee on October 8, 1976. Il'ia Glazunov became a major figure in the Russian nationalist intelligentsia. See Il'ia Glazunov, "Doroga k tebe," *Molodaia Gvardiia*, no. 6 (1966): 236–71.

28. On the VOOPIiK, see Kelly, *Socialist Churches*, chap. 6.

29. Brudny, *Reinventing Russia*, 69–70.

30. Anatolii S. Ivanov, "Zhurnal 'Nauka i religiia'—vazhnoe zveno v ateisticheskom vospitanii," *Voprosy nauchnogo ateizma* 19 (1976): 89.

31. Ibid., 90.

32. GARF, f. 9547, op. 1, d. 1447, l. 26.

33. Ivanov, "Zhurnal 'Nauka i religiia,'" 90.

34. For example, the state organized events through artist unions, such as a conference titled, "Science, Literature, and Art against Religion," held in March 1964 at the Central House of Writers, the proceedings of which were published in *Science and Life* (*Nauka i zhizn'*). See "Nauka, literatura, i isskustvo protiv religii," *Nauka i zhizn'* 6 (1964): 14–20.

35. Vladimir A. Soloukhin, *Rodnaia krasota (dlia chego nado izuchat' i berech' pamiatniki stariny)* (Moscow: Sovetskii khudoznik, 1966); Vladimir A. Soloukhin, "Chernye doski. Zapiski nachinaiushchego kollektsionera," *Moskva* 1 (1969): 129–87; Vladimir A. Soloukhin, "Pis'ma iz Russkogo muzeia," in *Slovo zhivoe i mertvoe* (Moscow: Sovremennik, 1976), 226–321. Soloukhin increasingly found himself the subject of official rebuke. In 1972, for instance, his piece "Grass" (*Trava*), serialized in *Science and Life* in 1972, criticized the use of artificial fertilizer in Soviet agriculture, and the Central Committee criticized Soloukhin and the journal's editors for failing to distinguish between the capitalist and socialist use of fertilizer in agricultural production. See Vladimir A. Soloukhin, "Ob oshibochnoi publikatsii v zhurnale 'Nauka i zhizn,'" November 30, 1972, in RGANI, f. 5, op. 64, d. 87, ll. 54–57.

36. RGASPI, f. 606, op. 4, d. 98, l. 3, 1.

37. Feliks Kuznetsov, "Sovetskaia literatura i dukhovnye tsennosti: zametki kritika," *Nauka i religiia* 11 (1972): 54–55.

38. On Tendriakov's early work in the Village Prose genre, see J. G. Garrard, "Vladimir Tendriakov," *Slavic and East European Journal* 9, no. 1 (1965): 1–18; Kathleen F. Parthé, *Russian Village Prose: The Radiant Past* (Princeton, NJ: Princeton University Press, 1992). Over the course of the past two decades of his career, Tendriakov's private writings became increasingly concerned with moral themes. See Vladimir Tendriakov, "Tysiacha pervyi raz o nravstvennosti," *Zvezda*, no. 12 (2003), http://magazines.russ.ru/zvezda/2003/12/tendr-pr.html.

39. Tendriakov's novella *The Miracle Worker* was one of the most popular pieces of atheist fiction of the post-Stalin period, and was also made into a play and film.

40. RGASPI, f. 606, op. 2, d. 43, ll. 111–27, 116.

41. Ibid., 118, 116.

42. Ibid., 114–15, 116, 118, 120, 121–23, 125, 114.

43. Kormina and Shtyrkov, "'Eto nashe iskonno russkoe,'" 10. See also Postanovlenie Soveta Ministrov RSFSR no. 473, "O sostoianii i merakh uluchsheniia okhrany pamiatnikov istorii i kul'tury v RSFSR," May 24, 1966, cited in ibid., 18n12.

44. Kelly, *Socialist Churches*, 228–30, 245.

45. Kormina and Shtyrkov, "'Eto nashe iskonno russkoe,'" 15–16; Kelly, *Socialist Churches*, 235.

46. TsGAIPD, f. K-598, op. 27, d. 328, ll. 13–19.

47. For a biographical portrait and interview with Gordienko, see Victoria Smolkin-Rothrock, "The Confession of an Atheist Who Became a Scholar of Religion: Nikolai Semenovich Gordienko's Last Interview," *Kritika: Explorations in Russian and Eurasian History* 15, no. 3 (Summer 2014): 596–620.

48. Mikhail Shakhnovich was a prolific atheist author whose career and publications spanned almost the entirety of the Soviet period. See Mikhail I. Shakhnovich, *Sotsial'naia suchshnost' Talmuda* (Leningrad: 1929); Shakhnovich, *Russkaia tserkov' v bor'be s naukoi* (Leningrad: Gazetno-zhurnal'noe knizhnoe izdatel'stvo, 1939); Shakhnovich, *Sueverie i nauchnoe predvidenie* (Leningrad: Lenizdat, 1945); Shakhnovich, *Ot sueverii k nauke* (Moscow: Molodaia Gvardiia, 1948); Shakhnovich, *Lenin i problemy ateizma* (Moscow: Izdatel'stvo Akademii nauk SSSR, 1960); Shakhnovich, *Sovremennaia mistika v svete religii* (Leningrad: Nauka, 1965); Shakhnovich, *Kommunizm i religiia* (Leningrad: Obshchestvo "Znanie" RSFSR, 1966); Shakhnovich, *Mistika pered sudom nauki* (Moscow: Obshchestvo "Znanie," 1970); Shakhnovich, *Proiskhozhdenie filosofii i ateizm* (Leningrad: Nauka, 1973); Shakhnovich, *Novye voprosy ateizma: Sotsiologicheskie ocherki* (Leningrad: Lenizdat, 1973); Shakhnovich, *Kritika religioznykh istolkovanii ekologicheskikh problem* (Moscow: Izd. "Znanie," 1985); Shakhnovich, *Bibliia v sovremennoi bor'be idei* (Leningrad: Lenizdat, 1988).

49. On *veshchism*, see Oushakine, "'Against the Cult of Things,'" 222–23.

50. TsGAIPD, f. K-598, op. 27, d. 328, ll. 13–15.

51. Ibid., 18–19.

52. As historian Glennys Young observes, "That Bolshevism for some was a product and even extension of their religious sensibility is not at variance with the still vehement anticlericalism of Party and Komsomol members. In fact, it in part explains such anticlericalism. For those implicitly taking the ascetic saint as their internal model would have no doubt been very disappointed in the all too imperfect conduct of drunken, greedy priests. They very well may have even viewed certain antireligious acts as a kind of purification of religiosity; indeed, speaking retrospectively, Mikhail Shakhnovich, who served as an antireligious correspondent in the 1920s, characterized the antireligious campaign as 'our reformation.'" Glennys Young, *Power and the Sacred in Revolutionary Russia: Religious Activists in the Village* (University Park: Pennsylvania State University Press, 1997), 92n61.

53. On the cult of Blessed Kseniia, see Jeanne Kormina and Sergei Shtyrkov, "St. Xenia as a Patron of Female Social Suffering," in *Multiple Moralities and Religions in Post-Soviet Russia*, ed. Jarrett Zigon (New York: Berghahn Books, 2011), 168–90; Jeanne Kormina and Sergey Shtyrkov, "Believers' Letters of Advertising: St. Xenia of Petersburg's 'National Reception Centre,'" *Politicheskaia nauka* 2 (2012): 49–72.

54. TsGAIPD, f. K-598, op. 27, d. 328, l. 41.

55. Ibid.

56. RGASPI, f. 606, op. 2, d. 130, ll. 116–23.

57. Ibid., 116–17.

58. Ibid.

59. Ibid., 117–18.

60. Ibid., 118–19.

61. Ibid., 119.

62. Iurii S. Gurov, "Sekuliarizatsiia molodezhi—zakonomernyi protses dukhovnogo rosta lichnosti v usloviiah sotsial'nogo progressa," in *Dukhovnyi rost lichnosti v period stroitel'stva kommunizma* (Cheboksary: Izd-vo Chuvash. gos. un-ta, 1971); Gurov, "Mirovozzrencheskii indifferentizm i formirovanie nauchno-ateisticheskih vzgliadov u molodezhi," in *Ateisticheskoe vospitanie: opyt i zadachi* (Cheboksary: Chuvash. kn. izd-vo, 1974); Gurov, "Mirovozzrenie i mirovozzrencheskii indifferentism," in *Formirovanie nauchnogo*

*mirovozzreniia* (Cheboksary: Izd-vo Chuvash.gos.un-ta, 1977); Gurov, "O preodolenii iavlenii indifferentizma v otnoshenii religii i ateizma sredi uchashcheis'a molodezhi," in *Informatsionnyi biulleten' Instituta nauchnogo ateizma*, no. 17 (Moscow: AON KPSS, 1977); Gurov, *Molodezhi—Ateisticheskaia ubezhdennost'* (Moscow, 1977); Gurov, "Prichiny mirovozzrencheskogo indifferentizma sredi chasti neveruiushchei molodezhi: Na materialakh Chuvashskoi ASSR," *Nauchnyi ateizm: Voprosy teorii i praktiki* (Perm': Perm. gos. ped. in-t, 1979); Gurov, "Rol' trudovogo kollektiva v priodolenii mirovozzrencheskogo indifferentizma i formirovanii ateisticheckoi ubezhdennosti molodykh liudei," in *Trudovoi kollektiv i razvitie lichnosti* (Cheboksary: Izd-vo Chuvash. gos. un-ta, 1981); Gurov, "Preodolenie indifferentizma v voprosakh ateizma i religii kak odin iz aspektov formirovaniia dukhovnoi kul'tury molodezhy," in *Ateizm i sotsialisticheskaya kul'tura: Materialy nauchnoi konferentsii "Ateizm i duhovnaia ku'tura razvitogo sotsializma"* (Ioshkar-Ola: Mariiskoe kn. Izd-vo, 1982); Gurov, *Ot bezrazlichiia—k ubezhdennosti (Aktual'nye problemy ateisticheskogo vospitaniia molodezhi)* (Cheboksary, 1982); Gurov, *Formirovanie ateisticheskoi ubezhdennosti u molodezhi* (Moscow: O-vo Znanie RSFSR, 1984); Gurov, *Molodezhi—Ateisticheskaia ubezhdennost'* (Omsk, 1984); Gurov, "Preodolenie indifferentizma—aktual'nye problemy povysheniia effektivnosti ateisticheskogo vospitaniia molodezhy," in *Aktual'nye problemy obespecheniia effektivnosti nauchno-ateisticheskoi raboty* (Cheboksary: Izd-vo Chuvash.gos.un-ta, 1986); Gurov, "Preodolenie mirovozzrencheskogo indifferentizma—vazhnoe uslovie aktivizatsii chelovecheskogo faktora," in *Filosofskie aspekty vyrabotki nauchnogo mirovozzreniia* (Cheboksary: Izd-vo Chuvash.gos.un-ta, 1986); Gurov, *Molodezhy—mirovozzrencheskuiu zrelost'* (Moscow: Sovetskaia Rossiia, 1987).

63. Gurov, *Molodezhi—ateisticheskaia ubezhdennost'*, 14–16.

64. The story of the engineer was originally published in "Ne pridali znacheniia," *Sovetskaia Rossiia*, January 19, 1983, cited in ibid., 12.

65. Ibid., 16.

66. G. E. Kudriashov, *Dinamika polisinkreticheskoi religioznosti* (Cheboksary, 1974), 178, cited in Gurov, *Formirovanie ateisticheskoi ubezhdennosti u molodezhi*, 12.

67. "The young man should have chosen long ago! Either he's a Komsomol or a [religious] devotee!" (*Parniu nado by davno, vybrat' chto nibud' odno! Ili komsomolets, ili bogomolets!*) (Moscow: Plakat, 1970s).

68. A. Tsvetkov, "This Is How a Hypocrite Lives His Life—Between Heaven and Earth" (*Tak i zhivet khanzha inoi, vsiu zhizn' mezh nebom i zemlei*) (Poem by A. Vnukov) (Moscow: Plakat, 1970s).

69. Gurov, *Formirovanie ateisticheskoi ubezhdennosti u molodezhi*, 10.

70. RGASPI, f. 606, op. 4, d. 105, ll. 10, 25–26.

71. Gurov, *Formirovanie ateisticheskoi ubezhdennosti u molodezhi*, 4.

72. Ibid., 4–5.

73. Gurov, *Molodezhi—ateisticheskaia ubezhdennost'*, 57.

74. Karl Marx and Friedrich Engels, *Sochineniia*, 2nd ed. (Moscow: Gosudarstvennoie izdatel'stvo politicheskoi literatury, 1955), 1:118, cited in Gurov, *Formirovanie ateisticheskoi ubezhdennosti u molodezhi*, 20.

75. Gurov, *Formirovanie ateisticheskoi ubezhdennosti u molodezhi*, 21.

76. Vladimir S. Soloviev, *Po puti dukhovnogo progressa: Nekotorye itogi povtornykh sotsiologicheskikh issledovanii problem byta, kul'tury, natsional'nykh traditsii, ateizma i verovanii Mariiskoi ASSR* (Ioshkar Ola: Mariiskoe knizhnoe izdatel'stvo, 1987), 141.

77. RGASPI, f. 606, op. 2, d. 311, ll. 1–7.

78. RGASPI, f. 606, op. 4, d. 72, ll. 76–77.

79. RGASPI, f. 606, op. 4, d. 103, ll. 13–14.

80. RGASPI, f. 606, op. 4, d. 106, l. 104.

81. RGASPI, f. 606, op. 4, d. 103, l. 14.

82. RGASPI, f. 606, op. 4, d. 105, ll. 77–78.

83. For sociological studies of the "spiritual profile of the contemporary believer" carried out in Ukraine between 1958 and 1968, see Evgraf Duluman, Boris Lobovik, and Vladimir Tancher, *Sovremennyi veruiushchii: Sotsial'no psikhologicheskii ocherk* (Moscow: Politizdat, 1970).

84. TsAGM, f. 3004, op. 1, d. 101, l. 166.

85. RGASPI, f. 606, op. 4, d. 105, ll. 51–2.

86. TsAGM, f. 3004, op. 1, d. 104, ll. 202–4.

87. RGASPI, f. 606, op. 4, d. 106, l. 42.

88. Aleksandr Okulov, "Ateisticheskoe vospitanie," *Pravda*, January 14, 1972, 3–4.

89. RGASPI, f. 606, op. 4, d. 68, ll. 4–8.

90. RGASPI-m, f. 1, op. 34, d. 130, l. 52.

91. TsAGM, f. 3004, op. 1, d. 99, l. 56.

92. RGASPI-m, f. 1, op. 34, d. 129, ll. 34–35.

93. RGASPI, f. 606, op. 4, d. 105, l. 27.

94. Ibid., 45.

95. RGASPI, f. 606, op. 4, d. 72, l. 53–56.

96. Ibid., 56.

97. Ibid., 33; RGASPI, f. 606, op. 4, d. 106, l. 37.

98. RGASPI, f. 606, op. 4, d. 105, l. 13, 89.

99. RGASPI, f. 606, op. 4, d. 72, l. 72–73.

100. RGASPI-m, f. 1, op. 34, d. 129, l. 48.

101. RGASPI, f. 606, op. 4, d. 224, ll. 3–4.

102. As Samuel Moyn observes, during the Cold War there was a "tendency for human rights, with a special focus on a privileged right of religious freedom, to be identified more and more with the fate of Christianity in a world in which Communism claimed to incarnate secularism." See Samuel Moyn, *The Last Utopia: Human Rights in History* (Cambridge, MA: Belknap, 2012), 72.

103. Peter L. Berger, ed., *The Desecularization of the World: Resurgent Religion and World Politics* (Grand Rapids, MI: Eerdmans, 1999).

104. According to the statistics of the CRA, in the mid-1980s, 60 percent of Orthodox parishes were located in Ukraine, and it was home to 50 percent of the country's sectarians and 25 percent of its unregistered religious communities. GARF, f. 9547, op. 1, d. 3663.

105. On the "deprivatization" of religion, see José Casanova, *Public Religions in the Modern World* (Chicago: University of Chicago Press, 1994).

106. On the centrality of religion in Reagan's anti-Communism, see, for example, Andrew Preston, *The Sword of the Spirit, the Shield of Faith: Religion in American War and Diplomacy* (New York: Knopf, 2012), 579–86.

107. See "O dal'neishem uluchshenii ideologicheskoi, politico-vospitatel'noi raboty," in *KPSS o formirovanii novogo cheloveka: Sbornik dokumentov i materialov (1965–1981)* (Moscow: Politizdat, 1982), 286–99. This decree was the product of an all-union conference, titled "Formation of an Active Life Position: Practices and Problems of Moral Upbringing." See "Formirovaniie aktivnoi zhiznennoi pozitsii: opyt i aktual'nye problemy nravstvennogo vospitaniia," in *KPSS o formirovanii novogo cheloveka*, 501–3. Children's upbringing was especially emphasized in Muslim areas. See Yaacov Ro'i, "The Task of Creating the New Soviet Man: 'Atheistic propaganda' in the Soviet Muslim Areas," *Europe-Asia Studies* 36, no. 1 (1984): 26–44. The stress on Russian language and culture as the solution to the problem of competing nationalisms is also worth noting. See the May 22,

1979, all-union conference: "Russkii iazyk—iazyk druzhby i sotrudnichestva narodov SSSR," in *KPSS o formirovanii novogo cheloveka*, 503–4. Addressing the problem of nationalism on the sixtieth anniversary of the Soviet Union, Andropov stated that "it is necessary to remember that in the spiritual heritage, traditions, and byt of each nation, there is not only good but also bad, obsolete. And from here, the task is to not conserve this bad but [instead] to liberate from all that has outlived itself and goes against the norms of Soviet community life [*obshchezhitiia*], socialist morality, and our Communist ideals." See Iurii V. Andropov, *Shest'desiat let SSSR* (Moscow: Politizdat, 1982), 13.

108. RGASPI, f. 606, op. 2, d. 396. The decree was discussed in an INA report to the Central Committee. See also Viktor Yelensky, "The Revival before the Revival: Popular and Institutionalized Religion in Ukraine on the Eve of the Collapse of Communism," in *State Secularism and Lived Religion in Soviet Russia and Ukraine*, ed. Catherine Wanner (New York: Oxford University Press, 2012), 302–30.

109. RGASPI, f. 606, op. 2, d. 311, ll. 1–2.

110. *Materialy Plenuma Tsentral'nogo Komiteta KPSS. 14–15 iunia 1983 goda* (Moscow: Politizdat, 1983). See also Valerii Alekseev, *"Shturm nebes" otmeniaetsia? Kriticheskie ocherki po istorii bor'by s religiei v SSSR* (Moscow: Rossiia molodaia, 1992), 263. On the KGB's efforts to manage religion in the USSR, see Christopher Andrew and Vasili Mitrokhin, *The Sword and the Shield: The Mitrokhin Archive and the Secret History of the KGB* (New York: Basic Books, 2000), 493. Egor K. Ligachev and Filipp D. Bobkov, the deputy head of the KGB and the official in charge of religious questions, were considered the hard-liners on the religious question.

111. Alekseev, *"Shturm nebes" otmeniaetsia?*, 265.

112. GARF, f. 9547, op. 1, d. 3660, ll. 5, 20, 25, 26–27.

113. Ibid., 8, 21–22.

114. GARF, f. 9547, op. 1, d. 3661, ll. 12–13, 15, 13.

115. GARF, f. 9547, op. 1, d. 3663, ll. 11–13. The figure given for schoolchildren is thirty-nine thousand, and for adults, forty-seven thousand.

116. Ibid., 20, 73–75, 79.

117. GARF, f. 9547, op. 1, d. 3664, ll. 13–16.

118. Ibid., 44–45.

119. Ibid., 60–61.

120. GARF, f. 9547, op. 1, d. 3665, l. 58.

121. Valerii Legostaev, who worked in the party apparatus under Egor Ligachev, writes that Metropolitan Aleksii's letter was distributed among the members of the Politburo. See Valerii Legostaev, "Aleksii's Letter to Gorbachev" (October 8, 1999), http://flb.ru/info/4265.html.

122. Ibid.

123. On Metropolitan Aleksii's 1985 letter to Gorbachev, see *Izvestiia*, March 2, 1992, cited in Anatolii Krasikov, "Russkaia Pravoslavnaia Tserkov': Ot sluzhby gosudarevoi k ispytaniiu svobodoi," in *Novye tserkvi, starye veruiushie—starye tserkvi, novye veruiushie*, ed. Kimmo Kaariainen and Dmitrii Furman (Moscow: Letnii sad, 2007), 160; Mikhail V. Shkarovskii, *Russkaia Pravoslavnaia Tserkov' v XX veke* (Moscow: Veche, Lepta, 2010), 401; Aleksei L. Beglov, Olga Iu. Vasilieva, and Andrei V. Zhuravskii, eds., *Russkaia Pravoslavnaia Tserkov': XX v.* (Moscow: Izd. Sretenskogo monastyria, 2008), 578.

124. GARF, f. 9547, op. 1, d. 3665, l. 61.

125. RGASPI, f. 606, op. 2, d. 256, ll. 32–37.

126. Ibid., 36–37. The anthropologists Alexander Panchenko describes the last generation of the Soviet urban intelligentsia and youth as "spiritual seekers" whose "invisible religion" encompassed a "peculiar mixture of New Age beliefs, utopian expectations, and

totalistic forms of social control." See Alexander A. Panchenko, "Morality, Utopia, Discipline: New Religious Movements and Soviet Culture," in *Multiple Moralities and Religions in Post-Soviet Russia*, ed. Jarrett Zigon (New York: Berghahn Books, 2011), 120–22. On the late Soviet spiritual landscape, see also Juliane Fürst, "Introduction: To Drop or Not to Drop?," in *Dropping Out of Socialism: The Creation of Alternative Spheres in the Soviet Bloc*, ed. Juliane Fürst and Josie McLellan (New York: Lexington Books, 2017), 1–20; Joseph Kellner, "The End of History: Radical Responses to the Soviet Collapse" (PhD diss., University of California, Berkeley, 2018).

127. GARF, f. 9547, op. 1, d. 3660, l. 53.

## *Conclusion: Utopia's Orphan*

1. Helen Bell and Jane Ellis write that at the opening event of the jubilee, held at the Danilov Monastery, one foreign guest even found himself standing next to a cosmonaut. They also note that the prominence of the state's role in the celebrations subsequently became a point of criticism among religious dissidents. As one religious activist put it, the events were attended by "the kind of people who get tickets to the Bolshoi." See Helen Bell and Jane Ellis, "The Millennium Celebrations of 1988 in the USSR," *Religion in Communist Lands* 16, no. 4 (1988): 322. For a detailed description of the millennium celebrations, see Michael Bourdeaux, *Gorbachev, Glasnost & the Gospel* (Toronto: Hodder & Stoughton, 1990), 42–64.

2. In an interview, Kharchev clarified the significance of the ZIL limousine, noting that originally the patriarch was supposed to be chauffeured in a Volga. He explained that "back then, [government] ministers drove in Volgas, but only party functionaries drove in ZILs, and there were only about ten of them in all of Moscow." See the interview of Andrei Mel'nikov with Konstantin Kharchev, "Perestroika nadelila Tserkov' pravami, a obiazannostiami ne uspela: Predsedatel' Soveta po delam religii v 1984–1989 godakh vspominaet i otsenivaet reform v otnosheniiakh gosudarstva i veruiushchikh," *NG-Religii*, June 3, 2015, http://www.ng.ru/ng_religii/2015-06-03/1_perestroika.html. On the shifts in church-state relations in the late Soviet period, see Nikolai Mitrokhin, "Russkaia Pravoslavnaia Tserkov' v 1990 godu," in *1990: Opyt izucheniia nedavnei ustorii. Sbornik statei i materialov*, ed. Aleksandr Dmitriev, Maria Maiofis, Il'ia Kukulin, Oksana Timofeeva, and Abram Reitblat (Moscow: Novoe Literaturnoe Obozrenie, 2011), 300–349; Viktor Yelensky, "Religiia i perestroika v Ukraine," *Liudina i svit*, December 10, 2003, http://www.religare.ru/2_7596_1_21.html.

3. For example, Gordienko, an adviser for the state committee formed to plan the millennium, described his relatives' shock at seeing him discussing religion on television. Nikolai S. Gordienko, interview with author, Saint Petersburg, June 17, 2011.

4. One of the most important symbolic events in the millennium celebrations was the return, in a televised ceremony, of part of Kiev's Monastery of the Caves, which had been closed in 1961, during Khrushchev's antireligious campaign. See Bourdeaux, *Gorbachev, Glasnost & the Gospel*, 49.

5. William van den Bercken, "Holy Russia and the Soviet Fatherland," *Religion in Communist Lands* 15, no. 3 (1987): 264–77; van den Bercken, "The Rehabilitation of Christian Ethical Values in the Soviet Media," *Religion in Communist Lands* 17, no. 1 (1989): 6–7; John B. Dunlop, "The Russian Orthodox in the Millennium Year: What It Needs from the Soviet State," *Religion in Communist Lands* 16, no. 2 (1988): 100–116; John Anderson, *Religion and the Soviet State: A Report on Religious Repression in the USSR on the Occasion of the Christian Millennium* (Washington, DC: Puebla Institute, 1988).

6. RGANI, f. 89, op. 25, d. 10, ll. 1–3.

7. Pope John Paul II, "Slavorum Apostoli" (June 2, 1985), http://w2.vatican.va/content/john-paul-ii/en/encyclicals/documents/hf_jp-ii_enc_19850602_slavorum-apostoli.html.

8. RGANI, f. 89, op. 25, d. 10, ll. 1–3.

9. RGASPI, f. 606, op. 2, d. 396, 45–46.

10. *Sovetskaia Rossiia*, February 26, 1986, cited in Valerii Alekseev, *"Shturm nebes" otmeniaetsia? Kriticheskie ocherki po istorii bor'by s religiei v SSSR* (Moscow: Rossiia molodaia, 1992), 266.

11. *Programma Kommunisticheskoi partii Sovetskogo Soiuza* (Moscow: Politizdat, 1986), 125; *Ustav Kommunisticheskoi partii Sovetskogo Soiuza* (Moscow: Politizdat, 1986), 6.

12. Egor K. Ligachev, *Izbrannye rechi i stat'i* (Moscow, 1989), 133, cited in Alekseev, *"Shturm nebes" otmeniaetsia?*, 267.

13. "Vospityvat' ubezhdennykh ateistov," *Pravda*, September 28, 1986, 1.

14. LCVA, f. 181, ap. 3, b. 3130, ll. 51–67. The circular was sent to the chairs of the Ukrainian and Armenian CRAs as well as the CRA's plenipotentiaries across the USSR.

15. Aleksandr Klibanov, Lev Mitrokhin, "Istoriia i religiia," *Kommunist*, no. 12 (1987): 92.

16. Aleksandr N. Iakovlev, "Dostizhenie kachestvenno novogo sostoianiia sovetskogo obshchestva i obshchestvennye nauki," *Vestnik Akademii Nauk SSSR*, no. 6 (1987): 69. Basing his analysis on his interview with Lisavtsev, the Central Committee's curator of religion and atheism, Shkarovskii writes that when the party again raised the question of the approaching millennium at the end of 1987, the tone had softened. When the idea of organizing another propaganda campaign against the millennium was raised, Gorbachev sided with Kharchev, telling the party elite, "Let's not hurt the church's feelings; it's patriotic." See Mikhail V. Shkarovskii, *Russkaia Pravoslavnaia Tserkov' v XX veke* (Moscow: Veche, Lepta, 2010), 401.

17. Konstantin Kharchev, "Garantii svobody," *Nauka i religiia* 11 (1987): 23.

18. TsAOPIM, f. 4, op. 220, d. 2384, ll. 107–23; TsAOPIM, f. 4, op. 220, d. 2374.

19. That Gorbachev's reversal was unexpected was emphasized in several interviews with former employees of the CRA. Mikhail Odintsov, interview with author, Moscow, June 27, 2011; German Mikhailov, interview with author, Moscow, June 5, 2013. On the surprise about the Soviet reversal in the West, Jane Ellis, the editor of the journal *Religion in Communist Lands*, wrote that "the official celebration of the Millennium of the Baptism of Rus' . . . took place in conditions of far greater freedom than anyone could have predicted even a few months beforehand." Cited in Bell and Ellis, "Millennium Celebrations," 292.

20. Konstantin Kharchev, interview in *Ogonek*, no. 21 (May 1988): 26–28. For Kharchev's shifting views, see also Kharchev, "Garantii svobody," and Kharchev, "Utverzhdaia svobodu sovesti," *Izvestiia*, January 27, 1988, 3.

21. Nina Andreeva, "Ne mogu postupat'sia printsipami," *Sovetskaia Rossiia*, 13 March 1988, 2.

22. On the politics behind the Nina Andreeva Affair, see Archie Brown, *The Gorbachev Factor* (New York: Oxford University Press, 1996), 172–75; Simon Cosgrove, "Ligachev and the Conservative Counter-Offensive in Nash Sovremennik 1981–1991: A Case Study in the Politics of Soviet Literature" (PhD diss., University of London, School of Slavonic and East European Studies, 1998), 229–78; David Remnick, *Lenin's Tomb: The Last Days of the Soviet Empire* (New York: Random House, 1993), 70–85; Kevin O'Connor, *Intellectuals and Apparatchiks: Russian Nationalism and the Gorbachev Revolution* (Lanham, MD: Lexington Books, 2006), 101–22.

23. On Reagan's attitudes on religious affairs in the Soviet Union, see Suzanne Massie, *Trust but Verify: Reagan, Russia, and Me* (Rockland: Maine Authors Publishing, 2013), 134–42, 349–57.

24. Bourdeaux, *Gorbachev, Glasnost & the Gospel*, 45–46.

25. In our conversations, Odintsov, Mikhailov, and Kharchev underscored the contingency of these developments. For example, Odintsov, Kharchev's assistant in the CRA, described the meeting between Gorbachev and the patriarch as a last-minute maneuver orchestrated from within the CRA, which had been gradually pushing for "normalization" in church-state relations. Odinstov, interview; Mikhailov, interview.

26. *Russkaia mysl'*, May 20, 1988, 4, cited in Bell and Ellis, "Millennium Celebrations," 323. See also "Religiia i perestroika [iz sokrashennoi zapisi doklada predsedatelia Soveta po delam religii K. M. Kharcheva na vstreche s prepodavateliami VPSh] (konets marta 1989 g.)," in *Russkaia pravoslavnaia tserkov' v sovetskoe vremia: Materialy i dokumenty po istorii otnoshenii mezhdu gosudarstvom i Tserkov'iu*, ed. Gerd Shtriker, vol. 2 (Moscow: Propilei, 1995).

27. David E. Powell, "The Revival of Religion," *Current History* 90 (October 1991): 329.

28. For an overview of the secularization debate, see Steve Bruce, ed., *Religion and Modernization: Sociologists and Historians Debate the Secularization Thesis* (New York: Oxford University Press, 1992); David Martin, *On Secularization: Towards a Revised General Theory* (Aldershot, UK: Ashgate, 2005). For a critique of secularization theory, see Rodney Stark, "Secularization, R.I.P.," *Sociology of Religion* 60 (1999): 249–73. For a more balanced approach, see Philip S. Gorski and Ateş Atinordu, "After Secularization?," *Annual Review of Sociology* 34 (2008): 55–85.

29. The most prominent example is Peter Berger, who published *The Sacred Canopy* (1967), perhaps one of the foundational texts of secularization theory. In the introduction to his 1999 edited volume, he conceded that "the assumption that we live in a secularized world is false." See Peter L. Berger, "The Desecularization of the World: A Global Overview," in *The Desecularization of the World: Resurgent Religion and World Politics*, ed. Berger (Grand Rapids, MI: Eerdmans, 1999), 2–3.

30. *Materialy XIX Vsesoiuznoi konferentsii KPSS* (Moscow: Politizdat, 1988), 41.

31. RGASPI, f. 606, op. 2, d. 497, l. 18.

32. Ibid., 19–20, 27.

33. RGASPI, f. 606, op. 2, d. 525, ll. 2–9.

34. RGASPI, f. 606, op. 2, d. 549, ll. 2–8.

35. GARF, f. A-561, op. 1, d. 3047, l. 1.

36. GARF, f. A-561, op. 1, d. 3178, l. 4, 17.

37. Olga Brushlinskaia, interview with author, Moscow, December 7, 2008.

38. Mark Smirnov and Pavel Krug, "V zashchitu svobodomysliia: Ispolnilos' polveka zhurnalu 'Nauka i religiia,'" *Nezavisimaia gazeta*, October 21, 2009, http://www.ng.ru/ng_religii/2009-10-21/2_magazine.html.

39. Ibid.

40. Reflecting on her long career with *Science and Religion*, Brushlinskaia, a journalist at *Science and Religion* since the 1970s and the journal's editor in chief in the post-Soviet period, noted, "This was not the *Militant Atheist* of Emelian Iaroslavskii's time. Of course, we defended the advantages of the scientific approach. But in comparison with the customary Soviet agitprop, this was a true breakthrough." As Brushlinskaia put it, "We would ask atheist propagandists back then whether they knew what they were fighting against. Oftentimes they did not even have the necessary understanding about the lives of believers. And besides, you have to be certain that the believer, who becomes an atheist thanks to you, will be happier for it." Brushlinskaia, interview.

41. Nadezhda Nefedova, interview with author, Moscow, June 25, 2011.

42. K. Ass, K. Vytuleva, A. Dobrov, D. Lebedev, O. Sarsikian, "KhV 1999. Aktsiia." See Irina Kulik, "Aktsiia 'KhV 1999'," Moscow Art Magazine no. 25, http://xz.gif.ru/numbers/25/hv-1999/.

43. "Karl Marx: Interviews with the Corner-Stone of Modern Socialism," *Chicago Tribune*, January 5, 1879, 7.

44. Soviet atheism's intolerance of indifference underscores the problem of equating Soviet atheism with secularism. Secularism is fundamentally a project of the liberal state. It defines religion as individual belief, situates it in the private sphere, and protects religion as freedom of conscience, while regulating and disciplining it when it transgresses beyond those parameters and makes political claims.

45. E. I. Kirichenko, *Khram Khrista Spasitelia v Moskve* (Moscow: Planeta, 1992).

46. "80 let so dnia vzryva Khram Khrista Spasitelia" (December 5, 2011). http://xxc.ru/ru/news/index.php?id=160.

47. On the politics of the construction, destruction, and reconstruction of the Cathedral of Christ the Savior, see Andrew Gentes, "The Life, Death and Resurrection of the Cathedral of Christ the Saviour," *History Workshop Journal* 46 (1998): 63–95; Dmitri Sidorov, "National Monumentalization and the Politics of Scale: The Resurrections of the Cathedral of Christ the Saviour in Moscow," *Annals of the Association of American Geographers* 90, no. 3 (2000): 548–72; Kathleen E. Smith, *Mythmaking in the New Russia: Politics and Memory during the Yeltsin Era* (Ithaca, NY: Cornell University Press, 2002), 102–30.

48. On people's shock at certain ideas being permitted in public life during glasnost, see also Aleksei Iurchak, *Eto bylo navsegda, poka ne konichilos': Poslednee sovetskoe pokolenie* (Moscow: Novoe Literaturnoe Obozrenie, 2014), 203.

49. This was the title of a 2013 documentary produced by Metropolitan Ilarion (Alfeyev) of Volokolamsk, a member of the Holy Synod of the Russian Orthodox Church and the chairman of its Department of External Church Relations. It was aired on July 22, 2013, on the Russian television channel "Rossiia-1" to mark the 1025th anniversary of the Baptism of Rus'.

50. Shaun Walker, "From One Vladimir to Another: Putin Unveils Huge Statue in Moscow," *Guardian*, November 4, 2016, https://www.theguardian.com/world/2016/nov/04/vladimir-great-statue-unveiled-putin-moscow.

51. Historian Simon Franklin highlights both the power and ambivalence of the Russian Orthodox millennium as a symbol. As Franklin writes, "What is the significance of the millennium? The smug response is to say: nothing, there is no significance. From the historian's point of view the thousandth year can mean no more than the 738th year or the 2304th year. Millennia, like all anniversaries, do not mark any peculiarly coherent segmentation of linear time. They are symbols, excuses, opportunities to legitimise the present by laying claim to or rejecting the past. The smug response is true, but inadequate. Symbols are real enough for those who live by them, and mere superciliousness will not render them miraculously impotent. Yet in the case of this millennium, if bland historicism means that one is simply excluded from the feast, then blind symbolism leads to an embarrassment of invitations. For the millennium is not one celebration but many; not a single decorous parade, but a battleground." See Simon Franklin, "988–1988: Uses and Abuses of the Millennium," *World Today* 44, no. 4 (April 1988): 65.

52. "Namedni: 1988," http://www.namednitv.ru/online/namedni_1988_smotret_online.html.

53. On religion in the post-Soviet period, see Irina Papkova, *The Orthodox Church and Russian Politics* (New York: Oxford University Press, 2011); Geraldine Fagan, *Believing in Russia: Religious Policy after Communism* (New York: Routledge, 2013); John P. Burgess, *Holy Rus': The Rebirth of Orthodoxy in the New Russia* (New Haven, CT: Yale University Press, 2017).

# BIBLIOGRAPHY


## *Archives*

### MOSCOW, RUSSIA

ARAN: Arkhiv Rossiiskoi Akademii Nauk.
GARF: Gosudarstvennyi arkhiv Rossiiskoi Federatsii.
GBU "TsGA Moskvy": Gosudarstvennoe biudzhetnoe uchrezhdenie "Tsentral'nyi gosudarstvennyi arkhiv Moskvy," Fotoarkhiv (formerly Tsentral'nyi arkhiv elektronnykh i audiovizual'nykh dokumentov Moskvy).
RGANI: Rossiiskii gosudarstvennyi arkhiv noveishei istorii.
RGASPI: Rossiiskii gosudarstvennyi arkhiv sotsial'no-politicheskoi istorii.
RGASPI-m: Rossiiskii gosudarstvennyi arkhiv sotsial'no-politicheskoi istorii-m (formerly Tsentr khraneniia dokumentov molodezhnykh organizatsii).
TsAGM: Tsentral'nyi arkhiv goroda Moskvy.
TsAOPIM: Tsentral'nyi arkhiv obshchestvenno-politicheskoi istorii Moskvy.

### SAINT PETERSBURG, RUSSIA

GMIR: Gosudarstvennyi muzei istorii religii.
TsGAIPD: Tsentral'nyi gosudarstvennyi arkhiv istoriko-politicheskikh dokumentov.
TsGALI-SPb: Tsentral'nyi gosudarstvennyi arkhiv literatury i isskustva.

### KIEV, UKRAINE

GDA SBU: Galuzevii derzhavnii arkhiv sluzhby bezpeky Ukrainy.
TsDAGO: Tsentral'nii derzhavnii arkhiv gromads'kikh ob'ednan' Ukraini.
TsDAVO: Tsentral'nii derzhavnii arkhiv vishchikh organiv vladi ta upravlinnia Ukraini.

### VILNIUS, LITHUANIA

LCVA: Lietuvos centrinis valstybes archyvas.
LYA: Lietuvos ypatingajame archyve.

## *Interviews*

Brushlinskaia, Olga. Interview with author. Moscow, December 7, 2008.
Duluman, Evgraf. Interview with author. Kiev, February 10, 2009.
Garadzha, Viktor. Interview with author. Moscow, May 31, 2012.
Glagolev, Vladimir. Interview with author. Moscow, June 27, 2011.
Gordienko, Nikolai. Interview with author. Saint Petersburg, June 17, 2011.
Iablokov, Igor. Interview with author. Moscow, June 24, 2011.
Lopatkin, Remir. Interview with author. Moscow, June 23, 2011.
Mikhailov, German. Interview with author. Moscow, June 5, 2013.

Nefedova, Nadezhda. Interview with author. Moscow, June 25, 2011.
Odintsov, Mikhail. Interview with author. Moscow, June 27, 2011.
Smirnov, Mikhail. Interview with author. Saint Petersburg, June 16, 2011.
Tazhurizina, Zul'fiia. Interview with author. Moscow, June 25, 2011.
Zakovich, Nikolai. Interview with author. Kiev, February 5, 2009.
Zuev, Iurii. Interview with author. Moscow, June 23, 2011.

## *Periodicals*

*Agitator*
*Antireligioznik*
*Bezbozhnik*
*Bezbozhnik u stanka*
*Bezbozhnyi byt*
*Bolshevik*
*Chicago Defender*
*Chicago Tribune*
*Disput*
*Hartford Courant*
*Iunost'*
*Izvestiia*
*Klub i revoliutsiia*
*Kommunist*
*Komsomol'skaia Pravda*
*Krasnaia nov'*
*Krokodil*
*Kul'turno-prosvetitel'naia rabota*
*Literatura i zhizn'*
*Literaturnaia gazeta*
*Los Angeles Times*
*Mirovedenie*
*Molodaia Gvardiia*
*Molodoi Kommunist*
*Moskva*
*Nauka i religiia*
*Nauka i zhizn'*
*New York Amsterdam News*
*New York Times*
*NG-Religii*
*Novyi mir*
*Ogonek*
*Partiinaia zhizn'*
*Pravda*
*Religion in Communist Lands*
*Revoliutsiia i kul'tura*
*Revoliutsiia i tserkov*
*Seattle Daily Times*
*Smena*
*Sotsiologicheskie issledovaniia*
*Sovetskaia etnografiia*

*Sovetskaia Rossiia*
*Sovetskie profsoiuzy*
*Sovremennaia arkhitektura*
*Trud*
*Vestnik Akademii Nauk SSSR*
*Vestnik Moskovskogo universiteta. Filosofiia*
*Voiovnichii ateist*
*Voprosy filosofii*
*Voprosy istorii religii i ateizma*
*Voprosy nauchnogo ateizma*
*Voprosy religii i religiovedeniia*
*Washington Post*
*Zhurnal Moskovskoi Patriarkhii*

## *Published Works*


Adzhubei, Aleksei. *Krushenie illiuzii.* Moscow: Interbuk, 1991.

Akademiia Nauk SSSR. *Nravstvennye printsipy stroitelia kommunizma.* Moscow: Mysl', 1965.

Aksenov, Vladimir Stepanovich. *Organizatsiia massovykh prazdnikov trudiashchikhsia, 1918–1920: uchebnoe posobie po kursu "Istoriia massovykh prazdnikov."* Leningrad: Leningradskii gos. in-t kul'tury im. N.K. Krupskoi, 1974.

Aksiutin, Iurii. *Khrushchevskaia "ottepel'" i obshchestvennye nastroeniia v SSSR v 1953–1964 gg.* Moscow: Rosspen, 2004.

Aksiutin, Iurii, and A. V. Pyzhikov. *Poststalinskoe obshchestvo: problema liderstva i transformatsiia vlasti.* Moscow: Nauchnaia kniga, 1999.

Alekseev, Valerii A. *"Shturm nebes" otmeniaetsia? Kriticheskie ocherki po istorii bor'by s religiei v SSSR.* Moscow: Rossiia molodaia, 1992.

Alekseeva, L. *Sovremennye prazdniki i obriady v derevne.* Moscow: Profizdat, Bibliotechka sel'skogo profsoiuznogo aktivista, 1968.

Alexeyeva, Ludmilla, and Paul Goldberg. *The Thaw Generation: Coming of Age in the Post-Stalin Era.* Pittsburgh: University of Pittsburgh Press, 1993.

Altshuler, Mordechai. *Religion and Jewish Identity in the Soviet Union, 1941–1964.* Waltham, MA: Brandeis University Press, 2012.

Alymov, Sergei. "The Concept of the 'Survival' and Soviet Social Science in the 1950s and 1960s." *Forum for Anthropology and Culture* 9 (2013): 157–83.

Anderson, John. "The Hare Krishna Movements in the USSR." *Religion in Communist Lands* 14, no. 3 (1986): 316–17.

———. *Religion and the Soviet State: A Report on Religious Repression in the USSR on the Occasion of the Christian Millennium.* Washington, DC: Puebla Institute, 1988.

———. *Religion, State and Politics in the Soviet Union and Successor States.* Cambridge: Cambridge University Press, 1994.

Andrew, Christopher, and Vasili Mitrokhin. *The Sword and the Shield: The Mitrokhin Archive and the Secret History of the KGB.* New York: Basic Books, 2000.

Andrews, James T. "Inculcating Materialist Minds: Scientific Propaganda and Anti-religion in the USSR during the Cold War." In Betts and Smith, *Science, Religion and Communism in Cold War Europe*, 105–25.

———. *Red Cosmos: K. E. Tsiolkovskii: Grandfather of Soviet Rocketry.* College Station: Texas A&M University Press, 2009.

———. *Science for the Masses: The Bolshevik State, Public Science, and the Popular Imagination in Soviet Russia, 1917–1934.* College Station: Texas A&M University Press, 2003.

Andropov, Iurii V. *Shest'desiat let SSSR*. Moscow: Politizdat, 1982.

Anisimov, Sergei F. *Nauka i religiia o smysle zhizni: Otvety na voprosy*. Moscow: Znanie, 1964.

Anisimov, Sergei F., and Grigorii A. Gurev. *Problema smysla zhizni v religii i ateizme*. Moscow: Znanie, 1981.

Aptekman, D. M. *Ateisticheskii potentsial sovetskogo obriada i prazdnika*. Moscow: Znanie, 1987.

Asad, Talal. *Genealogies of Religion: Discipline and Reasons of Power in Christianity and Islam*. Baltimore: Johns Hopkins University Press, 1993.

Baidukov, Georgii. *Russian Lindbergh: The Life of Valery Chkalov*. Translated by Peter Belov. Edited by Von Hardesty. Washington, DC: Smithsonian Institution Press, 1991.

Bailes, Kendall E. *Technology and Society under Lenin and Stalin: Origins of the Soviet Technical Intelligentsia, 1917–1941*. Princeton, NJ: Princeton University Press, 1978.

Bakhrushin, Sergei. "K voprosu o kreshchenii Rusi." *Istorik-Marksist*, no. 2 (1937): 40–77.

Balina, Marina, and Evgeny Dobrenko, eds. *Petrified Utopia: Happiness Soviet Style*. New York: Anthem Press, 2009.

Baran, Emily B. *Dissent on the Margins: How Soviet Jehovah's Witnesses Defied Communism and Lived to Preach about It*. Oxford: Oxford University Press, 2014.

Basil, John D. *Church and State in Late Imperial Russia: Critics of the Synodal System of Church Government (1861–1914)*. Minneapolis: University of Minnesota Press, 2005.

Batnitzky, Leora. *How Judaism Became a Religion: An Introduction to Modern Jewish Thought*. Princeton, NJ: Princeton University Press, 2011.

Batygin, Gennadii S., and C. F. Iarmoliuk, eds. *Rossiskaia sotsiologiia shestidesiatykh godov v vospominaniiakh i dokumentakh*. Saint Petersburg: Russkii Khristianskii Gumanitarnyi Institut, 1999.

Bayle, Pierre. *Historical and Critical Dictionary: Selections*. Translated by Richard H. Popkin. Indianapolis: Hackett, 1991.

Beglov, Aleksei. *V poiskakh bezgreshnykh katakomb: Tserkovnoe podpol'e v SSSR*. Moscow: Izdatel'skii sovet Russkoi Pravoslavnoi Tserkvi i Arefa, 2008.

Beglov, Aleksei L., Olga Iu. Vasilieva, and Andrei V. Zhuravskii, eds. *Russkaia Pravoslavnaia Tserkov': XX v.* Moscow: Izd. Sretenskogo monastyria, 2008.

Beliakova, Nadezhda A. "Evoliutsiia otnoshenii vlasti i khristianskikh denominatsii v Belorusii, Ukraine, i respublikakh Pribaltiki v poslednei chetverti XX—nachala XXI vv." PhD dissertation, Moscow State University, 2009.

———. "Vlast' i religioznye ob'edineniia v 'pozdnem' SSSR: problema registratsii." *Otechestvennaia istoriia* 4 (2008): 124–30.

Bell, Catherine. "Paradigms Behind (and Before) the Modern Concept of Religion." *History and Theory* 45, no. 4 (2006): 27–46.

Bell, Helen, and Jane Ellis. "The Millennium Celebrations of 1988 in the USSR." *Religion in Communist Lands* 16, no. 4 (1988): 292–328.

Belmonte, Laura A. *Selling the American Way: US Propaganda and the Cold War*. Philadelphia: University of Pennsylvania Press, 2013.

Belyi, Andrei. *Na rubezhe dvukh stoletii*. Moscow: Khudozhestvennaia literatura, 1989.

Bemporad, Elissa. *Becoming Soviet Jews: The Bolshevik Experiment in Minsk*. Bloomington: Indiana University Press, 2013.

Berdiaev, Nikolai. *The Russian Revolution*. Ann Arbor: University of Michigan Press, 1961.

Berdiaev, Nikolai, Sergei Bulgakov, Semen Frank, Mikhail Gershenzon, and Aleksandr Izgoev. *Vekhi (Landmarks)*. New York: M. E. Sharpe, 1994.

Berdyaev, Nicolas. *The Origin of Russian Communism*. 1937; repr., Ann Arbor: University of Michigan Press, 1960.

Beregovoi, Georgii T. *"Shagi po zemle, shagi v kosmose," Ia—ateist: 25 otvetov na vopros "Pochemu vy ateist?"* Moscow: Izdatel'stvo politicheskoi literatury, 1980.

Berger, Peter L. "The Desecularization of the World: A Global Overview." In *The Desecularization of the World: Resurgent Religion and World Politics*, edited by Peter L. Berger, 1–18. Grand Rapids, MI: Eerdmans, 1999.

———. *The Sacred Canopy: Elements of a Sociological Theory of Religion* Garden City, NY: Doubleday, 1967.

Berglund, Bruce R., and Brian Porter, eds. *Christianity and Modernity in Eastern Europe*. Budapest: Central European University Press, 2010.

Bershova, Natal'ia. "Esli zvezdy zazhigaiut . . . (Zapiski lektora Khar'kovskogo Planetariia." http://kharkov.vbelous.net/planetar/index.htm.

Betts, Paul, and Stephen A. Smith, eds. *Science, Religion and Communism in Cold War Europe*. Basingstoke: Palgrave Macmillan, 2016.

Bhargava, Rajeev, ed. *Secularism and Its Critics*. New Delhi: Oxford University Press, 1998.

Bikbov, Aleksandr. *Grammatika poriadka: istoricheskaia sotsiologiia poniatii, kotorye meniaiut nashu real'nost'.* Moscow: Izdatel'skii dom Vysshei Shkoly Ekonomiki, 2014.

Binns, Christopher. "The Changing Face of Power: Revolution and Accommodation in the Soviet Ceremonial System, Part I." *Man* 14, no. 4 (December 1979): 585–606.

———. "The Changing Face of Power: Revolution and Accommodation in the Soviet Ceremonial System, Part II." *Man* 15, no. 1 (March 1980): 170–87.

Bittner, Stephen V. "Ideologicheskie komissii TsK KPSS, 1958–1964: Dokumenty (review)." *Kritika: Explorations in Russian and Eurasian History* 3 no. 2 (2002): 356–61.

———. *The Many Lives of Khrushchev's Thaw: Experience and Memory in Moscow's Arbat*. Ithaca, NY: Cornell University Press, 2008.

Bociurkiw, Bohdan. "Religion and Atheism in Soviet Society." In *Aspects of Religion in the Soviet Union*, edited by Richard H. Marshall, Jr. and Thomas Bird, 45–60. Chicago: University of Chicago Press, 1970.

———. *The Ukrainian Greek Catholic Church and the Soviet State, 1939–1950*. Edmonton: Canadian Institute of Ukrainian Studies Press, 1996.

Bociurkiw, Bohdan, and John Strong, eds. *Religion and Atheism in the USSR and Eastern Europe*. Toronto: University of Toronto Press, 1975.

Bokan', Iurii, and Vladimir G. Sinitsyn. *Nashi prazdniki: (Sov., obshchegos., trud., voin., molodezh. i semeino-bytovye prazdniki, obriady, ritualy)*. Moscow: Politizdat, 1977.

Bolton, Jonathan. *Worlds of Dissent: Charter 77, the Plastic People of the Universe, and Czech Culture under Communism*. Cambridge, MA: Harvard University Press, 2012.

Bonch-Bruevich, Vladimir. *Izbrannye sochineniia*. Vol. 1. Moscow, 1959.

Bonnell, Victoria. *Iconography of Power: Soviet Political Posters under Lenin and Stalin*. Berkeley: University of California Press, 1997.

Boobbyer, Philip. *Conscience, Dissent, and Reform in Soviet Russia*. New York: Routledge, 2005.

Boronoev, Asalkhan O. "Sociological Research in Leningrad–St. Petersburg (1960s–1990s)." *Sociological Research* 48, no. 5 (September–October 2009): 45–54.

———, ed. *Sotsiologiia v Leningrade—Sankt-Peterburg vo vtoroi polovine 20 veka*. Saint Petersburg: Izdatel'stvo SPbGU, 2007.

Bourdeaux, Michael. *Gorbachev, Glasnost & the Gospel*. Toronto: Hodder & Stoughton, 1990.

———. *Opium of the People: The Christian Religion in the USSR*. London: Faber and Faber, 1965.

———. *Patriarch and Prophets: Persecution of the Russian Orthodox Church Today*. London: Mowbrays, 1975.

Bourdeaux, Michael, Michael Rowe, and International Committee for the Defense of Human Rights in the USSR. *May One Believe—in Russia? Violations of Religious Liberty in the Soviet Union*. London: Darton, Longman & Todd, 1980.

Brandenberger, David. *National Bolshevism: Stalinist Mass Culture and the Formation of Modern Russian National Identity, 1931–1956*. Cambridge, MA: Harvard University Press, 2002.

———. *Propaganda State in Crisis: Soviet Ideology, Indoctrination, and Terror under Stalin, 1927–1941*. New Haven, CT: Yale University Press, 2011.

Brandenburgskii, Ia., ed. *Sem'ia i novyi byt: spory o proekte novogo kodeksa zakonov o sem'e i brake*. Moscow: Gos. izd-vo, 1926.

Bren, Paulina. *The Greengrocer and His TV: The Culture of Communism after the 1968 Prague Spring*. Ithaca, NY: Cornell University Press, 2010.

———. "Mirror, Mirror, on the Wall . . . Is the West the Fairest of Them All? Czechoslovak Normalization and Its (Dis) Contents." *Kritika: Explorations in Russian and Eurasian History* 9, no. 4 (2008): 831–54.

Bren, Paulina, and Mary Neuburger, eds. *Communism Unwrapped: Consumption in Cold War Eastern Europe*. New York: Oxford University Press, 2012.

Breslauer, George W. *Khrushchev and Brezhnev as Leaders: Building Authority in Soviet Politics*. Boston: Allen & Unwin, 1982.

———. "Khrushchev Reconsidered." In Cohen, Rabinowitch, and Sharlet, *Soviet Union since Stalin*, 50–70.

Brezhnev, Leonid Il'ich. *O kommunisticheskom vospitanii trudiashchikhsia: Rechi i stat'i*. Moscow: Izdatel'stvo Politicheskoy Literatury, 1974.

———. *Otchetnyi doklad TK KPSS XXIV s'ezdu Kommunisticheskoi partii Sovetskogo Soiuza*. Moscow: Politizdat, 1972.

Brooks, Jeffrey. *Thank You, Comrade Stalin! Soviet Public Culture from Revolution to Cold War*. Princeton, NJ: Princeton University Press, 2000.

———. *When Russia Learned to Read: Literacy and Popular Literature, 1861–1917*. Princeton, NJ: Princeton University Press, 1985.

Brown, Archie. *The Gorbachev Factor*. New York: Oxford University Press, 1996.

Bruce, Steve, ed. *Religion and Modernization: Sociologists and Historians Debate the Secularization Thesis*. New York: Oxford University Press, 1992.

Brudny, Yitzhak M. *Reinventing Russia: Russian Nationalism and the Soviet State, 1953–1991*. Cambridge, MA: Harvard University Press, 1998.

Brudnyi, Vladimir I. *Obriady vchera i segodnia*. Moscow: Nauka, 1968.

Brzezinski, Matthew. *Red Moon Rising: Sputnik and the Hidden Rivalries That Ignited the Space Age*. New York: Times Books, 2007.

Bukharin, Nikolai. *Izbrannye sochineniia*. Moscow: 1927.

Bukharin, Nikolai, and Evgenii Preobrazhenskii. *Azbuka kommnizma. Populiarnoe ob'iasnenie programmy rossiiskoi kommunisticheskoi partii (1919)*. Khar'kov: Gos. Izd., 1925.

Burchardt, Marian, Monika Wohlrab-Sahr, and Matthias Middell. "Multiple Secularities beyond the West: An Introduction." In *Multiple Secularities beyond the West: Religion and Modernity in the Global Age*, edited by Marian Burchardt, Monika Wohlrab-Sahr, and Matthias Middell, 1–15. Berlin: De Gruyter, 2015.

Burgess, John P. *Holy Rus': The Rebirth of Orthodoxy in the New Russia*. New Haven, CT: Yale University Press, 2017.

Burrin, Philippe. "Political Religion: The Relevance of a Concept." *History and Memory* 9, nos. 1–2 (Fall 1997): 321–49.

Bushkovitch, Paul. *Religion and Society in Russia: The Sixteenth and Seventeenth Centuries*. New York: Oxford University Press, 1992.

Bushnell, John. "The 'New Soviet Man' Turns Pessimist." In Cohen, Rabinowitch, and Sharlet, *Soviet Union since Stalin*, 179–99.

Cady, Linell E., and Elizabeth Shakman Hurd. "Comparative Secularisms and the Politics of Modernity: An Introduction." In *Comparative Secularisms in a Global Age*, edited by Linell E. Cady and Elizabeth Shakman Hurd, 3–24. New York: Palgrave Macmillan, 2010.

Caplan, Jane, and John Torpey, eds. *Documenting Individual Identity: The Development of State Practices in the Modern World*. Princeton, NJ: Princeton University Press, 2001.

Casanova, José. *Public Religions in the Modern World*. Chicago: University of Chicago Press, 1994.

Casier, Tom. "The Shattered Horizon: How Ideology Mattered to Soviet Politics." *Studies in East European Thought* 51 (1999): 35–59.

Castillo, Greg. *Cold War on the Home Front: The Soft Power of Midcentury Design*. Minneapolis: University of Minnesota Press, 2010.

Chamedes, Giuliana. "The Vatican, Nazi-Fascism, and the Making of Transnational Anticommunism in the 1930s." *Journal of Contemporary History* 51, no. 2 (2016): 261–90.

Chernyshova, Natalya. *Soviet Consumer Culture in the Brezhnev Era*. Abingdon, UK: Routledge, 2013.

Chulos, Chris J. *Converging Worlds: Religion and Community in Peasant Russia, 1861–1917*. DeKalb: Northern Illinois University Press, 2003.

Chumachenko, Tatiana A. *Church and State in Soviet Russia: Russian Orthodoxy from World War II to the Khrushchev Years*. Translated and edited by Edward E. Roslof. Armonk, NY: M. E. Sharpe, 2002.

———. "Sovet po delam Russkoi pravoslavnoi tserkvi pri SNK (SM) SSSR: 1954–1965 gg." PhD dissertation, Lomonosov Moscow State University, 2011.

Clark, Jonathan C. D. "Secularization and Modernization: The Failure of a 'Grand Narrative.'" *Historical Journal* 55 (2012): 161–91.

Clark, Katerina. *Petersburg: Crucible of Cultural Revolution*. Cambridge, MA: Harvard University Press, 1995.

Cohen, Stephen F., Alexander Rabinowitch, and Robert S. Sharlet, eds. *The Soviet Union since Stalin*. London: Macmillan, 1980.

Cohn, Edward D. "Sex and the Married Communist: Family Troubles, Marital Infidelity, and Party Discipline in the Postwar USSR, 1945–64." *Russian Review* 68, no. 3 (2009): 429–50.

Coleman, Heather J. *Russian Baptists and Spiritual Revolution, 1905–1929*. Bloomington: Indiana University Press, 2005.

Comte, Auguste. "The Positive Philosophy." In *Introduction to Contemporary Civilization in the West*, vol. 2, 767–91. New York: Columbia University Press, 1961.

Cooke, Catherine. *Russian Avant-Garde: Theories of Art, Architecture, and the City*. London: Academy Editions, 1995.

Corley, Felix. "Believers' Responses to the 1937 and 1939 Soviet Censuses." *Religion, State, and Society* 22, no. 4 (1994): 403–17.

Cosgrove, Simon. "Ligachev and the Conservative Counter-Offensive in Nash Sovremennik 1981–1991: A Case Study in the Politics of Soviet Literature." PhD dissertation, University of London, School of Slavonic and East European Studies, 1998.

Cracraft, James. *The Church Reform of Peter the Great*. Stanford, CA: Stanford University Press, 1971.

Crews, Robert D. "Empire and the Confessional State: Islam and Religious Politics in Nineteenth-Century Russia." *American Historical Review* 108, no. 1 (2003): 50–83.

———. *For Prophet and Tsar: Islam and Empire in Russia and Central Asia*. Cambridge, MA: Harvard University Press, 2006.

Daly, Jonathan W. "'Storming the Last Citadel': The Bolshevik Assault on the Church, 1922." In *The Bolsheviks in Russian Society: The Revolution and the Civil Wars*, edited by Vladimir N. Brovkin, 236–59. New Haven, CT: Yale University Press, 1997.

Daniel, E. Valentine. "The Arrogation of Being by the Blind-Spot of Religion." *International Studies in Human Rights* 68 (2002): 31–54.

Daniloff, Nicholas. *The Kremlin and the Cosmos*. New York: Knopf, 1972.

David-Fox, Michael. "Religion, Science, and Political Religion in the Soviet Context." *Modern Intellectual History* 8, no. 2 (2011): 471–84.

———. *Revolution of the Mind: Higher Learning among the Bolsheviks, 1918–1929*. Ithaca, NY: Cornell University Press, 1997.

Davis, Nathaniel. *A Long Walk to Church: A Contemporary History of Russian Orthodoxy*. Boulder, CO: Westview, 2003.

———. "The Number of Orthodox Churches before and after the Khrushchev Antireligious Drive." *Slavic Review* 50, no. 3 (1991): 612–20.

*Deianiia Sviashchennogo Sobora Pravoslavnoi Rossiiskoi Tserkvi 1917–1918 gg*. 3 vols. Moscow: Izdatel'stvo Sobornogo Soveta, 1918. Facsimile reprint, Moscow: Izdatel'stvo Novospasskogo monastyria, 1994.

*Dekrety Sovetskoi vlasti*. Vol. 1. Moscow: Gos. izd-vo polit. literatury, 1957.

Desan, Suzanne. *Reclaiming the Sacred: Lay Religion and Popular Politics in Revolutionary France*. Ithaca, NY: Cornell University Press, 1990.

Dixon, Simon. "Superstition in Imperial Russia." *Past & Present* 199 (2008): 207–28.

Dobson, Miriam. "The Social Scientist Meets the 'Believer': Discussions of God, the Afterlife, and Communism in the Mid-1960s." *Slavic Review* 74, no. 1 (2015): 79–103.

Dolbilov, Mikhail. *Russkii krai, chuzhaia vera: Etnokonfessional'naia politika imperii v Litve i Belorussii pri Aleksandre II*. Moscow: Novoe Literaturnoe Obozrenie, 2010.

Dolgikh, F. I., and A. P. Kurantov. *Kommunisticheskoe vospitanie i religiia*. Moscow: Voennoe Izdatel'stvo Oborony SSSR, 1964.

Donovan, Victoria. "'Going Backwards, We Stride Forward': Kraevedenie Museums and the Making of Local Memory in North West Russia, 1956–1981." *Forum for Anthropology and Culture*, no. 7 (2011): 211–30.

———. "'How Well Do You Know Your Krai?' The Kraevedenie Revival and Patriotic Politics in Late Khrushchev-Era Russia." *Slavic Review* 74, no. 3 (2015): 464–83.

Dragadze, Tamara. "The Domestication of Religion under Soviet Communism." In *Socialism: Ideals, Ideologies, and Local Practice*, edited by C. M. Hann, 148–56. London: Routledge, 1993.

Duluman, Evgraf K. *Pochemu ia perestal verit' v boga: Rasskaz byvshego kandidata bogosloviia*. Moscow: "Molodaia gvardiia," 1957.

Duluman, Evgraf K., Boris Lobovik, and Vladimir Tancher. *Sovremennyi veruiushchii: Sotsial'no psikhologicheskii ocherk*. Moscow: Politizdat, 1970.

Dunlop, John B. *The Faces of Contemporary Russian Nationalism*. Princeton, NJ: Princeton University Press, 1983.

———. *The New Russian Nationalism*. New York: Praeger, 1985.

———. *The Rise of Russia and the Fall of the Soviet Empire*. Princeton, NJ: Princeton University Press, 1993.

———. "The Russian Orthodox in the Millennium Year: What It Needs from the Soviet State." *Religion in Communist Lands* 16, no. 2 (1988): 100–116.

Emel'ianova, K. L. "Nekotorye voprosy sovershenstvovaniia deiatel'nosti organov ZAGS." *Pravovedeniie* 4 (1968): 101–3.

———. *Pervyi v strane*. Leningrad: Lenizdat, 1964.

Engels, Friedrich. "Socialism: Utopian and Scientific." In Tucker, *Marx-Engels Reader*, 683–717.

Engelstein, Laura. *Castration and the Heavenly Kingdom: A Russian Folktale*. Ithaca, NY: Cornell University Press, 2003.

———. "Holy Russia in Modern Times: An Essay on Orthodoxy and Cultural Change." *Past & Present* 173 (2001): 129–56.

———. *Slavophile Empire: Imperial Russia's Illiberal Path*. Ithaca, NY: Cornell University Press, 2009.

Etkind, Alexander. *Khlist: Sects, Literature and Revolution*. Moscow: New Literary Review, 1998.

———. "Russkie sekty i sovetskii kommunizm: Proekt Vladimira Bonch Bruevicha." *Minuvshee: Istoricheskii al'manakh* 19 (1996): 275–319.

Etty, John. "Comic Cosmonaut: Space Exploration and Visual Satire in Krokodil in the Thaw." In *Russian Aviation, Space Flight, and Visual Culture*, edited by Vlad Strukov and Helena Goscilo, 89–115. New York: Routledge, 2016.

Evans, Alfred B. "The Decline of Developed Socialism: Some Trends in Recent Soviet Ideology." *Soviet Studies* 38, no. 1 (January 1986): 1–23.

———. *Soviet Marxism-Leninism: The Decline of an Ideology*. Westport, CT: Praeger, 1993.

Evans, Christine E. *Between Truth and Time: A History of Soviet Central Television*. New Haven, CT: Yale University Press, 2016.

Fadeev, E. T. *O cheloveke, kosmose i boge*. Moscow: Znanie, 1965.

Fagan, Geraldine. *Believing in Russia: Religious Policy after Communism*. New York: Routledge, 2013.

Fainberg, Dina, and Artemy Kalinovsky, eds. *Reconsidering Stagnation in the Brezhnev Era: Ideology and Exchange*. Lanham, MD: Lexington Books, 2016.

Fedor, Julie. *Russia and the Cult of State Security: The Chekist Tradition, from Lenin to Putin*. New York: Routledge, 2013.

Fedotov, Georgii P. *The Russian Religious Mind*. Vol. 2. Cambridge, MA: Harvard University Press, 1966.

Fernando, Mayanthi L. *The Republic Unsettled: Muslim French and the Contradictions of Secularism*. Durham, NC: Duke University Press, 2014.

Field, Deborah A. *Private Life and Communist Morality in Khrushchev's Russia*. New York: Peter Lang, 2007.

Filatov, Anatolii N. *O novykh i starykh obriadakh*. Moscow: Profizdat, 1967.

Firsov, Boris M. *Istoriia sovetskoi sotsiologii 1950–1980-kh godov*. Saint Petersburg: Evropeiskii universitet v Sankt Peterburge, 2001.

Firsov, Sergei L. *Vlast' i ogon': Tserkov' i sovetskoe gosudarstvo, 1918–nachalo 1940-kh gg*. Moscow: Pravoslavnyi Sviato-Tikhonovskii Gumanitarnyi Universitet, 2014.

Fitzpatrick, Sheila. *The Commissariat of Enlightenment: Soviet Organization of Education and the Arts under Lunacharsky (October 1917–1921)*. Cambridge: Cambridge University Press, 1970.

———. *The Cultural Front. Power and Culture in Revolutionary Russia*. Ithaca, NY: Cornell University Press, 1992.

———. "Social Parasites: How Tramps, Idle Youth, and Busy Entrepreneurs Impeded the Soviet March to Communism." *Cahiers du Monde russe et soviétique* 47, nos. 1–2 (2006): 377–408.

Fokin, Aleksandr. *"Kommunizm ne za gorami": obrazy budushego u vlasti i naseleniia SSSR na rubezhe 1950–1960kh godov*. Cheliabinsk: Entsiklopediia, 2012.

Franklin, Simon. "988–1988: Uses and Abuses of the Millennium." *World Today* 44, no. 4 (April 1988): 65–68.

Franklin, Simon, and Jonathan Shepard. *The Emergence of Rus 750–1200*. London: Longman, 1998.

Frede, Victoria S. *Doubt, Atheism, and the Nineteenth-Century Russian Intelligentsia*. Madison: University of Wisconsin Press, 2011.

———. "Freedom of Conscience, Freedom of Confession, and 'Land and Freedom' in the 1860s." *Kritika: Explorations in Russian and Eurasian History* 13, no. 3 (2012): 561–84.

Freeze, Gregory L. "All Power to the Parish? The Problem and Politics of Church Reform in Late Imperial Russia." In *Social Identities in Revolutionary Russia*, edited by Madhavan K. Palat, 174–208. London: Macmillan, 2001.

———. "Counter-reformation in Russian Orthodoxy: Popular Response to Religious Innovation, 1922–1925." *Slavic Review* 2 (1995): 305–39.

———. "From Dechristianization to Laicization: State, Church, and Believers in Russia." *Canadian Slavonic Papers* 1 (2015): 6–34.

———. "Handmaiden of the State? The Church in Imperial Russia Reconsidered." *Journal of Ecclesiastical History* 36, no. 1 (1985): 82–102.

———. *The Parish Clergy in Nineteenth-Century Russia: Crisis, Reform, Counter-Reform*. Princeton, NJ: Princeton University Press, 1983.

———. *The Russian Levites: Parish Clergy in the Eighteenth Century*. Cambridge, MA: Harvard University Press, 1977.

———. "The Stalinist Assault on the Parish, 1929–1941." In *Stalinismus vor dem Zweiten Weltkrieg: Neue Wege der Forschung*, edited by Manfred Hildermeier, 209–32. Munich: Oldenburg Verlag, 1998.

———. "Subversive Atheism: Soviet Antireligious Campaigns and the Religious Revival in Ukraine in the 1920s." In Wanner, *State Secularism and Lived Religion in Soviet Russia and Ukraine*, 27–62.

———. "Subversive Piety: Religion and the Political Crisis in Late Imperial Russia." *Journal of Modern History* 68 (1996): 308–50.

Froese, Paul. *The Plot to Kill God: Findings from the Soviet Experiment in Secularization*. Berkeley: University of California Press, 2008.

Froggatt, Michael. "Renouncing Dogma, Teaching Utopia: Science in Schools under Khrushchev." In Jones, *Dilemmas of De-Stalinization*, 250–67.

———. "Science in Propaganda and Popular Culture in the USSR under Khrushchëv (1953–1964)." DPhil thesis, University of Oxford, 2006.

Fülöp-Miller, René. *The Mind and Face of Bolshevism: An Examination of Cultural Life in Soviet Russia*. New York: Harper & Row, 1965.

Fursenko, Aleksandr A., ed. *Prezidium TsK KPSS 1954–1964: Chernovye protokol'nye zapisi zasedanii, stenogrammy, postanovleniia*. Vol. 1. Moscow: ROSSPEN, 2004.

Fürst, Juliane. "The Arrival of Spring? Changes and Continuities in Soviet Youth Culture and Policy between Stalin and Khrushchev." In Jones, *Dilemmas of De-Stalinization*, 135–53.

———. "Friends in Private, Friends in Public: The Phenomenon of the Kampaniia among Soviet Youth in the 1950s and 1960s." In Siegelbaum, *Borders of Socialism*, 135–53.

———. "Introduction: To Drop or Not to Drop?" In *Dropping Out of Socialism: The Creation of Alternative Spheres in the Soviet Bloc*, edited by Juliane Fürst and Josie McLellan, 1–20. New York: Lexington Books, 2017.

———. *Late Stalinist Russia: Society between Reconstruction and Reinvention*. New York: Routledge, 2006.

———. *Stalin's Last Generation: Soviet Post-war Youth and the Emergence of Mature Socialism*. Oxford: Oxford University Press, 2010.

Gabova, K. K., ed. *Zavoevanie neba i vera v boga. Sbornik statei*. Moscow: Znanie, 1964.

Gagarin, Yuri. *Doroga v kosmos*. Moscow: Pravda, 1961.

Galitskaia, Irina A., ed. *Molodezh' i ateizm*. Moscow: Mysl', 1971.

Garrard, J. G. "Vladimir Tendriakov." *Slavic and East European Journal* 9, no. 1 (1965): 1–18.

Gatejel, Luminita. "Appealing for a Car: Consumption Policies and Entitlement in the USSR, the GDR, and Romania, 1950s–1980s." *Slavic Review* 75, no. 1 (2016): 122–45.

Gentes, Andrew. "The Life, Death and Resurrection of the Cathedral of Christ the Saviour." *History Workshop Journal* 46 (1998): 63–95.

Gentile, Emilio. "Political Religion: A Concept and Its Critics—A Critical Survey." *Totalitarian Movements and Political Religions* 6, no. 1 (2005): 19–32.

Geppert, Alexander C. T. "Flights of Fancy: Outer Space and the European Imagination, 1923–1969." In *Societal Impact of Spaceflight*, ed. Steven J. Dick and Roger D. Launius, 585–99. Washington, DC: National Aeronautics and Space Administration, History Division, 2007.

Geraci, Robert P., and Michael Khodarkovsky, eds. *Of Religion and Empire: Missions, Conversion, and Tolerance in Tsarist Russia*. Ithaca, NY: Cornell University Press, 2001.

Gerodnik, Genadii. *Dorogami novykh traditsii*. Moscow, 1964.

Gerovitch, Slava. *Soviet Space Mythologies: Public Images, Private Memories, and the Making of a Cultural Identity*. Pittsburgh: University of Pittsburgh Press, 2015.

Gilbert, James. *Redeeming Culture: American Religion in an Age of Science*. Chicago: University of Chicago Press, 1997.

Gitelman, Zvi Y. *Jewish Nationality and Soviet Politics: The Jewish Sections of the CPSU, 1917–1930*. Princeton, NJ: Princeton University Press, 1972.

Glebkin, Vladimir V. *Ritual v sovetskoi kul'ture*. Moscow: Ianus-K, 1998.

Glenn, John, and Nick Taylor. *John Glenn: A Memoir*. New York: Bantam Books, 1999.

Gorlizki, Yoram. "Too Much Trust: Regional Party Leaders and Local Political Networks under Brezhnev." *Slavic Review* 3 (2010): 676–700.

Gorski, Philip S. *The Disciplinary Revolution: Calvinism and the Rise of the State in Early Modern Europe*. Chicago: University of Chicago Press, 2003.

Gorski, Philip S., and Ateş Atinordu. "After Secularization?" *Annual Review of Sociology* 34 (2008): 55–85.

Gottschalk, Peter. *Religion, Science, and Empire: Classifying Hinduism and Islam in British India*. Oxford: Oxford University Press, 2013.

Graham, Loren R. *Moscow Stories*. Bloomington: Indiana University Press, 2006.

Greene, Robert. *Bodies Like Bright Stars: Saints and Relics in Orthodox Russia*. DeKalb: Northern Illinois University Press, 2010.

Grigorian, Boris T. *Sotsiologiia religii ili apologiia religii?* Moscow: Nauka, 1962.

Grigorian, Movses M. *Kurs lektsii po istorii ateizma*. Moscow: Mysl', 1970.

Grossman, Joan Delaney. "Khrushchev's Antireligious Policy and the Campaign of 1954." *Europe-Asia Studies* 24, no. 3 (1973): 374–86.

———. "Leadership of Antireligious Propaganda in the Soviet Union." *Studies in Soviet Thought* 12, no. 3 (1972): 213–30.

Grushin, Boris A. *Chetyre zhizni Rossii v zerkale oprosov obshchestvennogo mneniia: ocherki massovogo soznaniia rossiian vremen Khrushcheva, Brezhneva, Gorbacheva i Eltsina v 4-kh knigakh*. Moscow: Progress-Traditsiia, 2001.

Grushin, Boris A., and V. Chikin. *Ispoved' pokoleniia*. Moscow: Molodaia gvardiia, 1962.

Gunn, T. Jeremy. *Spiritual Weapons: The Cold War and the Forging of an American National Religion*. Westport, CT: Praeger, 2008.

Gurev, Grigorii A. *Ateizm Charlza Darvina*. Leningrad: AN SSSR, 1941.

———. *Darvinizm i ateizm: populiarnye ocherki*. Moscow: GIZ, 1930.

———. *Kopernikovskaia eres' v proshlom i nastoiashchem i istoriia vzaimootnoshenii nauki i religii.* Leningrad: GAIZ, 1933.

———. *Mir Bezbozhnika.* Leningrad: Priboi, 1931.

———. *Nauka i religiia o vselennoi.* Moscow: OGIA, 1934.

———. *Nauka o vselennoi i religiia: kosmologicheskie ocherki.* Moscow: OGIZ, 1934.

———. *Pravda o neve: Antireligioznye besedy s krest'ianami o mirozdanii.* Leningrad: Priboi, 1931.

Gurian, Waldemar. *Bolshevism: An Introduction to Soviet Communism.* Notre Dame, IN: University of Notre Dame Press, 1952.

Gurov, Iurii S. *Formirovanie ateisticheskoi ubezhdennosti u molodezhi.* Moscow: O-vo Znanie RSFSR, 1984.

———. "Mirovozzrencheskii indifferentizm i formirovanie nauchno-ateisticheskih vzgliadov u molodezhi." In *Ateisticheskoe vospitanie: opyt i zadachi.* Cheboksary: Chuvash. kn. izd-vo, 1974.

———. "Mirovozzrenie i mirovozzrencheskii indifferentism." In *Formirovanie nauchnogo mirovozzreniia.* Cheboksary: Izd-vo Chuvash.gos.un-ta, 1977.

———. *Molodezhi—Ateisticheskaia ubezhdennost'.* Moscow, 1977.

———. *Molodezhi—Ateisticheskaia ubezhdennost'.* Omsk, 1984.

———, ed. *Molodezhi—Ateisticheskuiu ubezhdennost': sbornik.* Moscow: Molodaia gvardiia, 1977.

———. *Molodezhy—mirovozzrencheskuiu zrelost'.* Moscow: Sovetskaia Rossiia, 1987.

———. *Novye sovetskie traditsii, prazdniki i obriady.* Cheboksary: Chuvashskoe knizhnoe izd-vo, 1990.

———. "O preodolenii iavlenii indifferentizma v otnoshenii religii i ateizma sredi uchashcheis'a molodezhi." In *Informatsionnyi biulleten' Instituta nauchnogo ateizma*, no. 17. Moscow: AON KPSS, 1977.

———. *Ot bezrazlichiia—k ubezhdennosti (Aktual'nye problemy ateisticheskogo vospitaniia molodezhi).* Cheboksary, 1982.

———. "Preodolenie indifferentizma—aktual'nye problemy povysheniia effektivnosti ateisticheskogo vospitaniia molodezhy." In *Aktual'nye problemy obespecheniia effektivnosti nauchno-ateisticheskoi raboty.* Cheboksary: Izd-vo Chuvash.gos.un-ta, 1986.

———. "Preodolenie indifferentizma v voprosakh ateizma i religii kak odin iz aspektov formirovaniia dukhovnoi kul'tury molodezhy." In *Ateizm i sotsialisticheskaya kul'tura: Materialy nauchnoi konferentsii "Ateizm i duhovnaia ku'tura razvitogo sotsializma."* Ioshkar-Ola: Mariiskoe kn. Izd-vo, 1982.

———. "Preodolenie mirovozzrencheskogo indifferentizma—vazhnoe uslovie aktivizatsii chelovecheskogo faktora." In *Filosofskie aspekty vyrabotki nauchnogo mirovozzreniia.* Cheboksary: Izd-vo Chuvash.gos.un-ta, 1986.

———. "Prichiny mirovozzrencheskogo indifferentizma sredi chasti neveruiushchei molodezhi: Na materialakh Chuvashskoi ASSR." In *Nauchnyi ateizm: Voprosy teorii i praktiki.* Perm': Perm. gos. ped. in-t, 1979.

———. "Rol' trudovogo kollektiva v priodolenii mirovozzrencheskogo indifferentizma i formirovanii ateisticheckoi ubezhdennosti molodykh liudei." In *Trudovoi kollektiv i razvitie lichnosti.* Cheboksary: Izd-vo Chuvash. gos. un-ta, 1981.

———. "Sekuliarizatsiia molodezhi—zakonomernyi protses dukhovnogo rosta lichnosti v usloviiah sotsial'nogo progressa." In *Dukhovnyi rost lichnosti v period stroitel'stva kommunizma.* Cheboksary: Izd-vo Chuvash. gos. un-ta, 1971.

Gutkin, Irina. *The Cultural Origins of the Socialist Realist Aesthetic, 1890–1934.* Evanston, IL: Northwestern University Press, 1999.

Hagemeister, Michael. "Konstantin Tsiolkovsky and the Occult Roots of Soviet Space Travel." In *The New Age of Russia: Occult and Esoteric Dimensions*, edited by Michael Hagemeister, Birgit Menzel, and Bernice Glatzer Rosenthal, 135–50. Munich: Verlag Otto Sagner, 2012.

———. "Russian Cosmism in the 1920s and Today." In *The Occult in Russian and Soviet Culture*, edited by Bernice Glatzer Rosenthal, 185–202. Ithaca, NY: Cornell University Press, 1997.

Halfin, Igal. *From Darkness to Light: Class, Consciousness, and Salvation in Revolutionary Russia*. Pittsburgh: University of Pittsburgh Press, 2000.

———. *Stalinist Confessions: Messianism and Terror at the Leningrad Communist University*. Pittsburgh: University of Pittsburgh Press, 2009.

———. *Terror in My Soul: Communist Autobiographies on Trial*. Cambridge, MA: Harvard University Press, 2003.

Hardesty, Von, and Gene Eisman. *Epic Rivalry: The Inside Story of the Soviet and American Space Race*. Washington, DC: National Geographic Society, 2007.

———. *Red Phoenix: The Rise of Soviet Air Power, 1941–1945*. Washington, DC: Smithsonian Institution Press, 1982.

Harris, Steve E. *Communism on Tomorrow Street: Mass Housing and Everyday Life after Stalin*. Baltimore: Johns Hopkins University Press, 2013.

Hellbeck, Jochen. *Revolution on My Mind: Writing a Diary under Stalin*. Cambridge, MA: Harvard University Press, 2006.

Herrlinger, Page. *Working Souls: Russian Orthodoxy and Factory Labor in St. Petersburg, 1881–1917*. Bloomington, IN: Slavica, 2007.

Herzog, Jonathan P. *The Spiritual-Industrial Complex: America's Religious Battle against Communism in the Early Cold War*. Oxford: Oxford University Press, 2011.

Higham, Robin, John T. Greenwood, and Von Hardesty, eds. *Russian Aviation and Air Power in the Twentieth Century*. Portland, OR: Frank Cass, 1998.

Hirsh, Francine. *Empire of Nations: Ethnographic Knowledge and the Making of the Soviet Union*. Ithaca, NY: Cornell University Press, 2005.

Hobsbawm, Eric, and Terence Ranger. *The Invention of Tradition*. New York: Cambridge University Press, 1984.

Hoffman, David L. *Stalinist Values: The Cultural Norms of Soviet Modernity, 1917–1941*. Ithaca, NY: Cornell University Press, 2003.

Holmes, Larry E. "Fear No Evil: Schools and Religion in Soviet Russia, 1917–1941." In Ramet, *Religious Policy in the Soviet Union*, 131–36.

———. *The Kremlin and the Schoolhouse: Reforming Education in Soviet Russia, 1917–1953*. Bloomington: Indiana University Press, 1991.

Hosking, Geoffrey. "The Russian Orthodox Church and Secularisation." In Katznelson and Jones, *Religion and the Political Imagination*, 112–31.

Huhn, Ulrike. *Glaube und Eigensinn: Volksfrömmigkeit zwischen orthodoxer Kirche und Sowjetischem Staat, 1941 bis 1960*. Wiesbaden: Harrassowitz Verlag, 2014.

Humphrey, Caroline. "The 'Creative Bureaucrat': Conflicts in the Production of Soviet Communist Party Discourse." *Inner Asia* 10, no. 1 (2008): 5–35.

Hurd, Elizabeth Shakman. *The Politics of Secularism in International Relations*. Princeton, NJ: Princeton University Press, 2007.

Husband, William B. *"Godless Communists": Atheism and Society in Soviet Russia, 1917–1932*. DeKalb: Northern Illinois University Press, 2000.

Iaroslavskii, Emelian. *Bibliia dlia veruiushchikh i neveruiushchikh*. Leningrad: Lenizdat, 1975.

———. *Kak rodiatsia, zhivut i umiraiut bogi i bogini.* Moscow: Sovetskaia Rossiia, 1959.

———. *O religii.* Moscow: Gospolitizdat, 1957.

Il'f, Il'ia, and Evgenii Petrov. *Dvenadtsat' stul'ev. Zolotoi telenok.* Moscow: Eksmo, 2006.

———. "Mat." In *Sobranie Sochinenii*, vol. 3, 382–88. Moscow: Gos. Izd. Khud. Lit., 1961.

———. *The Twelve Chairs.* Translated by John H. C. Richardson. Evanston, IL: Northwestern University Press, 1997.

Ilic, Melanie, Susan E. Reid, and Lynne Attwood, eds. *Women in the Khrushchev Era.* New York: Palgrave Macmillan, 2004.

Ilic, Melanie, and Jeremy Smith, eds. *Soviet State and Society under Nikita Khrushchev.* New York: Routledge, 2009.

*Istoriia Kommunisitcheskoi partii Sovetskogo Soiuza.* Moscow: Rosspen, 2014.

Iurchak, Aleksei. *Eto bylo navsegda, poka ne konichilos': Poslednee sovetskoe pokolenie.* Moscow: Novoe Literaturnoe Obozrenie, 2014.

Iuridicheskaia komissiia pri Sovete Ministrov RSFSR. *Kodeks o brake i sem'e RSFSR: ofitsial'nyi tekst.* Moscow: "Iuridicheskaia literatura," 1969.

*Iz"iatie tserkovnykh tsennostei v Moskve v 1922 g.* Edited by A. Mazyrin. Moscow: Izdatel'stvo Pravoslavnogo Sviato-Tikhonovskogo gumanitarnogo universiteta, 2006.

Izmozik, Vladlen, and Natalia Lebina. *Peterburg sovetskii: "novyi chelovek" v starom prostranstve, 1920–1930e gody.* Saint Petersuburg: Kriga, 2010.

Jolles, Adam. "Stalin's Talking Museums." *Oxford Art Journal* 28, no. 3 (2005): 429–55.

Jones, Polly, ed. *The Dilemmas of De-Stalinization: Negotiating Cultural and Social Change in the Khrushchev Era.* New York: Routledge, 2006.

———. "From the Secret Speech to the Burial of Stalin: Real and Ideal Responses to De-Stalinization." In Jones, *Dilemmas of De-Stalinization*, 41–63.

———. *Myth, Memory, Trauma: Rethinking the Stalinist Past in the Soviet Union, 1953–70.* New Haven, CT: Yale University Press, 2013.

Kääriäinen, Kimmo. *Discussion on Scientific Atheism as a Soviet Science, 1960–1985.* Helsinki: Suomalainen Tiedeakatemia Akateeminen Kirjakauppa, 1989.

Kamenshchikov, Nikolai. *Astronomicheskie zadachi dlia iunoshestva.* Moscow: GIZ, 1923.

———. *Astronomiia bezbozhnika.* Leningrad: Priboi, 1931.

———. *Chto videli na nebe popy, a chto videm my.* Moscow: Ateist, 1930.

———. *Nachal'naia astronomiia.* Moscow: GIZ, 1924.

Kampars, Petr P., and Nikolai M. Zakovich. *Sovetskaia grazhdanskaia obriadnost'.* Moscow: Mysl', 1967.

Kane, Eileen. *Russian Hajj: Empire and the Pilgrimage to Mecca.* Ithaca, NY: Cornell University Press, 2015.

Kashevarov, A. N. *Gosudarstvo i tserkov': Iz istorii vzaimootnoshenii sovetskoi vlasti i russkoi pravoslavnoi tserkvi, 1917–1946.* Saint Petersburg: Sankt-Peterburgskii gosudarstvennyi tekhnicheskii universitet, 1995.

———. *Pravoslavnaia rossiiskaia tserkov' i sovetskoe gosudarstvo 1917–1922.* Moscow: Izdatel'stvo Krutitskogo podvor'ia, 2005.

Kashirin, Alexander. "Protestant Minorities in the Soviet Ukraine, 1945–1991." PhD dissertation, University of Oregon, 2010.

Kas'ianenko, Vasilii I. "Istoriografiia sotsialisticheskogo obraza zhizni v SSSR." *Voprosy istorii*, no. 1 (1980): 3–20.

Katznelson, Ira, and Gareth Stedman Jones, eds. *Religion and the Political Imagination.* Cambridge: Cambridge University Press, 2010.

Kaulen, Maria E. *Muzei-khramy i muzei-monastyri v pervoe desiatiletie Sovetskoĭ vlasti.* Moscow: Luch, 2001.

Keller, Shoshana. *To Moscow, not Mecca: The Soviet Campaign against Islam in Central Asia, 1917–1941*. Westport, CT: Praeger, 2001.

Kellner, Joseph. "The End of History: Radical Responses to the Soviet Collapse." PhD dissertation, University of California, Berkeley, 2018.

Kelly, Catriona. *Socialist Churches: Radical Secularization and the Preservation of the Past in Petrograd and Leningrad, 1918–1988*. DeKalb: Northern Illinois University Press, 2016.

Kemper, Michael. *Studying Islam in the Soviet Union*. Amsterdam: Vossiuspers UvA, 2009.

Kenez, Peter. *The Birth of the Propaganda State: Soviet Methods of Mass Mobilization, 1917–1929*. New York: Cambridge University Press, 1985.

Kenworthy, Scott M. *The Heart of Russia: Trinity-Sergius, Monasticism, and Society after 1825*. Oxford: Oxford University Press, 2010.

Khalid, Adeeb. *Islam after Communism: Religion and Politics in Central Asia*. Berkeley: University of California Press, 2007.

Kharkhordin, Oleg. *The Collective and the Individual in Russia: A Study of Practices*. Berkeley: University of California Press, 1999.

Khrushchev, Sergei. *Khrushchev Nikita. Reformator. Trilogiia ob otse*. Moscow: Vremia, 2010.

Kiaer, Christina, and Eric Naiman, eds. *Everyday Life in Early Soviet Russia: Taking the Revolution Inside*. Bloomington: Indiana University Press, 2006.

Kirichenko, E. I. *Khram Khrista Spasitelia v Moskve*. Moscow: Planeta, 1992.

Kizenko, Nadieszda. "Hand in Hand: Church, State, Society, and the Sacrament of Confession in Imperial Russia." Forthcoming.

Klibanov, Aleksandr I. *History of Religious Sectarianism in Russia (1860s–1917)*. Translated by Ethel Dunn. Edited by Stephen Dunn. New York: Pergamon Press, 1982.

———. *Istoriia religioznogo sektantstva v Rossii*. Moscow: Nauka, 1965.

———. *Konkretnye issledovaniia sovremennykh religioznykh verovanii*. Moscow: Nauka, 1967.

———. *Reformatsionnye dvizheniiia v Rossii*. Moscow: Nauka, 1960.

———. *Religioznoe sektantstvo v proshlom i nastoiashchem*. Moscow: Nauka, 1973.

———. *Religioznoe sektantsvo i sovremennost': sotsiologicheskie i istoricheskie ocherki*. Moscow: Nauka, 1969.

Kline, George L. *Religious and Anti-religious Thought in Russia*. Chicago: University of Chicago Press, 1968.

Klumbytė, Neringa, and Gulnaz Sharafutdinova, eds. *Soviet Society in the Era of Late Socialism, 1964–1985*. Lanham, MD: Rowman & Littlefield, 2012.

Koestler, Arthur. *The God That Failed*. New York: Harper, 1950.

Kolarz, Walter. *Religion in the Soviet Union*. London: Macmillan, 1969.

Komarov, Viktor N. *Kosmos, bog i vechnost' mira*. Moscow: Gozpolitizdat, 1963.

Komarov, Viktor N., and Aleksei B. Chertkov. *Besedy o religii i ateizme*. Moscow: Prosveshchenie, 1975.

Komarov, Viktor N., and V. V. Kaziutinskii, eds. *Voprosy mirovozzreniia v lektsiiakh po astronomii: Sbornik*. Moscow: Znanie, 1974.

Komarov, Viktor N., and K. A. Portsevskii. *Moskovskii planetarii*. Moscow: Moskovskii rabochii, 1979.

Kormina, Jeanne. "Ispolkomy i prikhody: religioznaia zhizn' Pskovskoi oblasti v pervuiu poslevoennuiu piatiletku." *Neprikosnovennyi zapas* 3, no. 59 (2008). http://magazines.russ.ru/nz/2008/3/ko11.html.

Kormina, Jeanne, and Sergei Shtyrkov. "Believers' Letters of Advertising: St. Xenia of Petersburg's 'National Reception Centre.'" *Politicheskaia nauka* 2 (2012): 49–72.

———. "'Eto nashi iskonno russkoe, i nikuda nam ot etogo ne det'sia': predystoriia postsovetskoi desekuliarizatsii." In *Izobretenie religii v postsovetskoi Rossii*, edited by Jeanne Kormina, Alexander Panchenko, and Sergei Shtyrkov, 7–45. Saint Petersburg: Evropeiskii universitet v Sankt-Peterburge, 2015.

———. "St. Xenia as a Patron of Female Social Suffering." In Zigon, *Multiple Moralities and Religions in Post-Soviet Russia*, 168–90.

Kornblatt, Judith Deutsch. *Doubly Chosen: Jewish Identity, the Soviet Intelligentsia, and the Russian Orthodox Church*. Madison: University of Wisconsin Press, 2004.

Kornev, V. V. "Presledovaniia Russkoi Pravoslavnoi Tserkvi v 50–60-x godax xx veka." In *Ezhegodnaia bogoslovskaia konferentsiia PSTBI: Materialy 1997 g*, 212–17. Moscow: PSTGU, 1997.

Kotkin, Stephen. *Magnetic Mountain: Stalinism as a Civilization*. Berkeley: University of California Press, 1995.

Kozlov, Denis. "The Historical Turn in Late Soviet Culture: Retrospectivism, Factography, Doubt, 1953–91." *Kritika: Explorations in Russian and Eurasian History* 3 (2000): 577–600.

———. *The Readers of Novyi Mir: Coming to Terms with the Stalinist Past*. Cambridge, MA: Harvard University Press, 2013.

Kozlov, Denis, and Eleonory Gilburd, eds. *The Thaw: Soviet Society and Culture during the 1950s and 1960s*. Toronto: University of Toronto Press, 2013.

Kozlov, Vladimir A. *Massovye besporiadki v SSSR pri Khrushcheve i Brezhneve: 1953–nachalo 1980-kh gg*. Novosibirsk: Sibirskii khronograf, 1999.

*KPSS o formirovanii novogo cheloveka: Sbornik dokumentov i materialov (1965–1981)*. Moscow: Politizdat, 1982.

Krasikov, Anatolii. "Russkaia Pravoslavnaia Tserkov': Ot sluzhby gosudarevoi k ispytaniiu svobodoi." In *Novye tserkvi, starye veruiushie—starye tserkvi, novye veruiushie*, edited by Kimmo Kaariainen and Dmitrii Furman, 134–229. Moscow: Letnii sad, 2007.

Krasnikov, Nikolai P. "Predvaritel'nye rezul'taty izucheniia religioznykh verovanii i obriadnosti." In *Konkretnye issledovaniia sovremennykh religioznykh verovanii (metodika, organizatsiia, rezul'taty)*, 129–37. Moscow: Mysl', 1967.

Krivova, Natalia. *Vlast' i tserkov' v 1922–1925 gg.: Politburo i GPU v bor'be za tserkovnye tsennosti i politicheskoe podchinenie dukhovenstva*. Moscow: AIRO-XX, 1997.

Kryvelev, Iosif A. *Traditsionnye i novye obriady v bytu narodov SSSR*. Moscow: Nauka, 1981.

Kuprin, O. *Byt—ne chastnoe delo*. Moscow: Politizdat, 1959.

Kurliandskii, Igor A. "Stalin i religioznyi vopros v politike bol'shevistskoi vlasti (1917–1923)." *Vestnik PSTGU* 5 (48): 72–84.

———. *Stalin, vlast' i religiia*. Moscow: Kuchkovo Pole, 2011.

Kurochkin, Pavel, ed. *K obshchestvu, svobodnomu ot religii: Protsess sekuliarizatsii v usloviiakh sotsialisticheskogo obshchestva*. Moscow: Mysl', 1970.

Kuromiya, Hiroaki. *Conscience on Trial: The Fate of Fourteen Pacifists in Stalin's Ukraine, 1952–1953*. Toronto: University of Toronto Press, 2012.

———. "Why the Destruction of Orthodox Priests in 1937–1938." *Jahrbücher für Geschichte Osteuropas* 55 (2007): 86–93.

Lamanskaia, Nina B. "Gosudarstvennaia politika po otnosheniiu k religii i veruiushchim v 1954–1964 gg. (Na materialakh Krasnoiarskogo kraia)." Khakasskii gosudarstvennyi universitet imeni N. F. Katanova, 2004.

Lambert, Yves. "New Christianity, Indifference and Diffused Spirituality." In *The Decline of Christendom in Western Europe, 1750–2000*, edited by Hugh McLeod and Ustorf Werner. New York: Cambridge University Press, 2003.

Lane, Christel. *Christian Religion in the Soviet Union: A Sociological Study*. Albany: State University of New York Press, 1978.

———. *The Rites of Rulers: Ritual in Industrial Society—The Soviet Case.* New York: Cambridge University Press, 1981.

LaPierre, Brian. "Private Matters or Public Crimes: The Emergence of Domestic Hooliganism in the Soviet Union, 1939–1966." In Siegelbaum, *Borders of Socialism*, 191–207.

Laqueur, Thomas W. *The Work of the Dead: A Cultural History of Mortal Remains.* Princeton, NJ: Princeton University Press, 2015.

Laukaityte, Regina. "The Orthodox Church in Lithuania during the Soviet Period." *Lithuanian Historical Studies* 7 (2002): 67–94.

Launius, Roger D. "Escaping Earth: Human Spaceflight as Religion." *Astropolitics* 11, nos. 1–2 (2013): 45–64.

———. "Heroes in a Vacuum: The Apollo Astronaut as Cultural Icon." *Florida Historical Quarterly* 87, no. 2 (Fall 2008): 174–209.

Lebina, Natalia B. "Deiatel'nost' 'voinstvuiushchikh bezbozhnikov' i ikh sud'ba." *Voprosy Istorii* 5–6 (1996): 154–57.

———. *Povsednevnaia zhizn' sovetskogo goroda: normy i anomalii: 1920–1930 gody.* Saint Petersburg: Letnii Sad, 1999.

Legostaev, Valerii. "Aleksii's Letter to Gorbachev." October 8, 1999. http://flb.ru/info/4265.html.

Lenin, Vladimir I. *Polnoe sobranie sochinenii.* 5th ed., vol. 48. Moscow, 1958–65.

———. "Sotsializm i religiia." In *Lenin ob ateizme, religii, i tserkvi (Sbornik statei, pisem i drugikh materialov.* Moscow: Mysl', 1969.

Lewin, Moshe. "Popular Religion in Twentieth-Century Russia." In *The World of the Russian Peasant: Post-emancipation Culture and Society*, edited by Ben Eklof and Stephen Frank, 155–68. Boston: Unwin Hyman, 1990.

Lewis, Cathleen. "The Birth of the Soviet Space Museums: Creating the Earthbound Experience of Spaceflight during the Golden Years of the Soviet Space Programme, 1957–1968." *Showcasing Space* 6 (2005): 148–50.

———. "The Red Stuff: A History of the Public and Material Culture of Early Human Spaceflight in the U.S.S.R." PhD dissertation, George Washington University, 2008.

Liakhotskii, P. V. *Zavoevanie kosmosa i religiia.* Groznyi: Checheno-Ingushskoe knizhnoe izdanie, 1964.

Lifanov, M. I., ed. *Za kommunisticheskii byt.* Leningrad: Obshchestvo po rasprostraneniiu politicheskikh i nauchnykh znanii RSFSR, 1963.

Lisavtsev, E. *Novye sovetskie traditsii.* Moscow: Izd-vo "Sov. Rossiia," 1966.

Lopez, Donald S., Jr. "Belief." In Taylor, *Critical Terms for Religious Studies*, 21–35.

Lovell, Stephen. "Broadcasting Bolshevik: The Radio Voice of Soviet Culture, 1920s–1950s." *Journal of Contemporary History* 48, no. 1 (2013): 94.

———. *Russia in the Microphone Age: A History of Soviet Radio, 1919–1970.* Oxford: Oxford University Press, 2015.

Luehrmann, Sonja. "The Modernity of Manual Reproduction: Soviet Propaganda and the Creative Life of Ideology." *Cultural Anthropology* 26, no. 3 (2011): 363–88.

———. *Religion in Secular Archives: Soviet Atheism and Historical Knowledge.* New York: Oxford University Press, 2015.

———. *Secularism Soviet Style: Teaching Atheism and Religion in a Volga Republic.* Bloomington: Indiana University Press, 2011.

———. "Was Soviet Society Secular? Undoing Equations between Communism and Religion." In Ngo and Quijada, *Atheist Secularism and Its Discontents*, 134–51.

Lunacharsky, Anatoly. *On Education: Selected Articles and Speeches.* Moscow, 1981.

Luukkanen, Arto. *The Party of Unbelief: The Religious Policy of the Bolshevik Party, 1917–1929.* Helsinki: Societas Historiae Finlandiae, 1994.

———. *The Religious Policy of the Stalinist State. A Case Study: The Central Standing Commission on Religious Questions, 1929–1938*. Helsinki: Suomen Historiallinen Seura, 1997.

Magdo, Zsuzsanna. "The Socialist Sacred: Atheism, Religion, and Mass Culture in Romania, 1948–1989." PhD dissertation, University of Illinois at Urbana-Champaign, 2016.

Mahmood, Saba. *Religious Difference in a Secular Age: A Minority Report*. Princeton, NJ: Princeton University Press, 2015.

Manchester, Laurie. *Holy Fathers, Secular Sons: Clergy, Intelligentsia, and the Modern Self in Revolutionary Russia*. DeKalb: Northern Illinois University Press, 2008.

Mandelstam Balzer, Marjorie, ed. *Religion and Politics in Russia: A Reader*. Armonk, NY: M. E. Sharpe, 2010.

Mar'ianov, Boris M. *Otvoevannoe nebo*. Moscow: Moskovskii rabochii, 1971.

———. *Voprosy mirovozzrenia v lektsiiakh po astronomii: Sbornik*. Moscow: Znanie, 1974.

Martin, David. *On Secularization: Towards a Revised General Theory*. Aldershot, UK: Ashgate, 2005.

Marx, Karl. "Contribution to the Critique of Hegel's *Philosophy of Right*: Introduction." In Tucker, *Marx-Engels Reader*, 53–65.

———. "The German Ideology." In *Karl Marx: Selected Writings*, 2nd ed., edited by David McLellan. New York: Oxford University Press, 2000.

———. "Theses on Feuerbach." In Tucker, *Marx-Engels Reader*, 143–45.

Marx, Karl, and Friedrich Engels. "The German Ideology." In Tucker, *Marx-Engels Reader*, 146–200.

———. "Manifesto of the Communist Party." In Tucker, *Marx-Engels Reader*, 473.

———. *Sochineniia*. 2nd ed. Moscow: Gosudarstvennoie izdatel'stvo politicheskoi literatury, 1955.

Maslova, Irina I. "Sovet po delam religii pri Sovete ministrov SSSR i Russkaia pravoslavnaia tserkov' (1965–1991 gg.)." In *Gosudarstvo i tserkov' v XX veke: Evoliutsiia vzaimootnoshenii, politicheskii i sotsiokul'turnyi askpekty*, edited by A. I. Filimonova, 78–106. Moscow: Librokom, 2012.

———. *Sovetskoe gosudarstvo i Russkaia Pravoslavnaia Tserkov': politika sderzhivaniia (1964–1985 gg.)*. Moscow, 2005.

———. *Veroispovednaia politika v SSSR: povorot kursa (1985–1991 gg.)*. Moscow, 2005.

Massie, Suzanne. *Trust but Verify: Reagan, Russia, and Me*. Rockland: Maine Authors Publishing, 2013.

Masuzawa, Tomoko. *The Invention of World Religions: Or, How European Universalism was Preserved in the Language of Pluralism*. Chicago: University of Chicago Press, 2005.

*Materialy Plenuma Tsentral'nogo Komiteta KPSS. 14–15 iunia 1983 goda*. Moscow: Politizdat, 1983.

*Materialy XIX Vsesoiuznoi konferentsii KPSS*. Moscow: Politizdat, 1988.

*Materialy XXII S'ezda KPSS*. Moscow: 1961.

Matich, Olga. *Erotic Utopia: The Decadent Imagination in Russia's Fin de Siècle*. Madison: University of Wisconsin Press, 2005.

Maurer, Eva, Julia Richers, Monica Rüthers, and Carmen Scheide, eds. *Soviet Space Culture: Cosmic Enthusiasm in Socialist Societies*. Basingstoke: Palgrave Macmillan, 2011.

Mawdsley, Evan, and Stephen White. *The Soviet Elite from Lenin to Gorbachev: The Central Committee and Its Members, 1917–1991*. New York: Oxford University Press, 2000.

McDougall, Walter A. *The Heavens and the Earth: A Political History of the Space Age*. New York: Basic Books, 1985.

McLeod, Hugh. *The Religious Crisis of the 1960s*. Oxford: Oxford University Press, 2007.

———. *Secularisation in Western Europe, 1848–1914*. New York: St. Martin's, 2000.

McLeod, Hugh, and Werner Ustorf, eds. *The Decline of Christendom in Western Europe, 1750–2000*. Cambridge: Cambridge University Press, 2003.

McMillen, Ryan Jeffrey. "Space Rapture: Extraterrestrial Millennialism and the Cultural Construction of Space Colonization." PhD dissertation, University of Texas at Austin, 2004.

Medvedev, Roi, and Dimitrii Ermakov. *"Seryi kardinal": M.A. Suslov, Politicheskii portret*. Moscow: Respublika, 1992.

Mezentsev, Vladimir A. *Znanie—narodu (K 25-letiiu Vsesoiuznogo obshchestva "Znanie")*. Moscow: Znanie, 1972.

Millar, James R. "The Little Deal: Brezhnev's Contribution to Acquisitive Socialism." *Slavic Review* 44, no. 4 (Winter 1985): 694–706.

Miner, Steven M. *Stalin's Holy War: Religion, Nationalism, and Alliance Politics, 1941–1945*. Chapel Hill: University of North Carolina Press, 2003.

Mitin, Mark B. "O soderzhanii i zadachakh nauchno-ateisticheskoi propagandy v sovremennykh usloviiakh." In *Nauka i religiia: Sbornik stenogramm lektsii, prochitannykh na Vsesoiuznom soveshchanii-seminare po nauchno-ateisticheskim voprosam*. Moscow: Znanie, 1958.

Mitrofanov, Georgii. *Istoriia Russkoi Pravoslavnoi Tserkvi: 1900–1927*. Saint Petersburg: Satis, 2002.

Mitrokhin, Lev N. "O vremeni i o sebe." In *Religiia i kul'tura (filosofskie ocherki)*. Moscow: IF RAN, 2000.

Mitrokhin, Nikolai. "Back-office Mikhaila Suslova ili kem i kak proizvodilas' ideologiia Brezhnevskogo vremeni." *Cahiers du monde russe* 54, no. 3 (2013): 409–40.

———. "'Obydennoe soznanie liubit prostye resheniia . . .': Beseda Nikolaia Mitrokhina s Vladimirom Aleksandrovichem Saprykinym." *Neprikosnovennyi zapas* 59, no. 3 (2008). http://magazines.russ.ru/nz/2008/3/sa14.html.

———. "'Otvetstvennyi rabotnik TsK KPSS Vladimir Saprykin': kar'era odnogo sovetskogo professional'nogo ateista." In *Chelovek i lichnost' v istorii Rossii, konets XIX–XX vek: Materialy mezhdunarodnogo kollokviuma*, 613–26. Saint Petersburg: Nestor-Istoriia, 2012.

———. "Religioznost' v SSSR v 1954–1965 godakh glazami apparata TsK KPSS." *Neprikosnovennyi zapas* 5, no. (2010). http://magazines.russ.ru/nz/2010/5/re8.html.

———. *Russkaia Partiia: Dvizhenie russkikh natsionalistov v SSSR. 1953–1985 gg*. Moscow: Novoe Literaturnoe Obozrenie, 2003.

———. "Russkaia Pravoslavnaia Tserkov' v 1990 godu." In *1990: Opyt izucheniia nedavnei ustorii. Sbornik statei i materialov*, edited by Aleksandr Dmitriev, Maria Maiofis, Il'ia Kukulin, Oksana Timofeeva, and Abram Reitblat, 300–349. Moscow: Novoe Literaturnoe Obozrenie, 2011.

Moyn, Samuel. *The Last Utopia: Human Rights in History*. Cambridge, MA: Belknap, 2012.

Myers, David. "Marx, Atheism and Revolutionary Action." *Canadian Journal of Philosophy* 11, no. 2 (1981): 317–18.

Naan, Gustav I. *Chelovek, bog i kosmos*. Moscow: Sovetskaia Rossiia, 1963.

Naiman, Eric. *Sex in Public: The Incarnation of Early Soviet Ideology*. Princeton, NJ: Princeton University Press, 1997.

Nakachi, Mie. "Gender, Marriage, and Reproduction in the Postwar Soviet Union." In *Writing the Stalin Era: Sheila Fitzpatrick and Soviet Historiography*, edited by Golfo Alexopoulos, Julie Hessler, and Kiril Tomoff, 101–16. Basingstoke: Palgrave Macmillan, 2011.

———. "Replacing the Dead: The Politics of Reproduction in the Postwar Soviet Union, 1944–1955." PhD dissertation, University of Chicago, 2008.

Nathans, Benjamin. "The Dictatorship of Reason: Aleksandr Vol'pin and the Idea of Rights under 'Developed Socialism.'" *Slavic Review* 66, no. 4 (2007): 630–63.

Nemtsev, Mikhail. "K istorii sovetskoi akademicheskoi distsipliny 'Osnovy nauchnogo kommunizma.'" *Idei i idealy* 27, no. 1 (2016): 23–38.

Ngo, Tam T. T., and Justine B. Quijada, eds. *Atheist Secularism and Its Discontents*. Basingstoke: Palgrave Macmillan, 2015.

———. "Introduction: Atheist Secularism and Its Discontents." In Ngo and Quijada, *Atheist Secularism and Its Discontents*, 1–26.

Nikol'skaia, Tat'iana. *Russkii protestantizm i gosudarstvennaia vlast' v 1905–1991 godakh*. Saint Petersburg: European University Press, 2009.

O'Connor, Kevin. *Intellectuals and Apparatchiks: Russian Nationalism and the Gorbachev Revolution*. Lanham, MD: Lexington Books, 2006.

Odintsov, Mikhail Ivanovich. *Gosudarstvo i tserkov' (Istoriia vzaimootnoshenii, 1917–1938 gg.)*. Moscow: Znanie, 1991.

———. "Veroispovednaia politika sovetskogo gosudarstva v 1939–1958 gg." In *Vlast' i tserkov' v SSSR i stranakh vostochnoi evropy, 1939–1958 (diskussionnye aspekty)*, 7–68. Moscow: Institut slavianovedeniia RAN, 2003.

Odintsov, Mikhail I., and Tatiana A. Chumachenko. *Sovet po delam Russkoi pravoslavnoi tserkvi pri SNK (SM) SSSR i Moskovskaia patriarkhiia: epokha vzaimoseistviia i protivostoianiia, 1943–1965*. Saint Petersburg: Rossiiskoe ob"edinenie issledovatelei religii, 2013.

Oizerman, Teodor. "Sovetskaia Filosofiia v seredine 40kh-nachale 50-kh godov: Filosofskii fakul'tet MGU." *Chelovek*, no. 2 (2007): 50–62.

*O religii i tservki: sbornik dokumentov*. Moscow: Izd-vo polit. litry, 1965.

Orsi, Robert. *Between Heaven and Earth: The Religious Worlds People Make and the Scholars Who Study Them*. Princeton, NJ: Princeton University Press, 2007.

———. "Everyday Miracles: The Study of Lived Religion." In *Lived Religion in America: Toward a History of Practice*, edited by David D. Hall, 3–21. Princeton, NJ: Princeton University Press, 1997.

Osipov, Aleksandr A. *Moi otvet veruiushchim*. Leningrad: Lenizdat, 1960.

Osipov, Gennadii V. "My zhili naukoi." In *Rossiiskaia sotsiologiia shestidesiatykh godov v vospominaniakh i dokumentakh*, edited by G. S. Batygin and C. F. Iarmoliuk, 95–109. Saint Petersburg: Izdatel'stvo Russkogo gumanitarnogo universiteta, 1999.

Ostrowski, Donald. "The Christianization of Rus' in Soviet Historiography: Attitudes and Interpretations (1920–1960)." *Harvard Ukrainian Studies* 11, nos. 3–4 (1987): 444–61.

Oushakine, Serguei. "'Against the Cult of Things': On Soviet Productivism, Storage Economy, and Commodities with No Destination." *Russian Review* 73, no. 2 (2014): 198–236.

Ozouf, Mona. *Festivals and the French Revolution*. Cambridge, MA: Harvard University Press, 1991.

Paert, Irina. "Demystifying the Heavens: Women, Religion and Khrushchev's Anti-religious Campaign, 1954–64." In Ilic, Reid, and Attwood, *Women in the Khrushchev Era*, 203–21.

Paine, Crispin. "Militant Atheist Objects: Anti-religion Museums in the Soviet Union." *Present Pasts* 1 (2009): 61–76.

Panchenko, Alexander. "Morality, Utopia, Discipline: New Religious Movements and Soviet Culture." In Zigon, *Multiple Moralities and Religions in Post-Soviet Russia*, 119–45.

———. "Popular Orthodoxy in Twentieth-Century Russia: Ideology, Consumption and Competition." In *National Identity in Soviet and Post-Soviet Culture*, edited by Mark Bassin and Catriona Kelly, 321–40. Cambridge: Cambridge University Press, 2012.

Pantskhava, Il'ia D. *Chelovek, ego zhizn' i bessmertie*. Moscow, 1967.

———. *O smerti i bessmertii*. Moscow, 1972.

———. *Zhizn', smert' i bessmertie*. Moscow: 1966.

Papkova, Irina. *The Orthodox Church and Russian Politics*. New York: Oxford University Press, 2011.

Parthé, Kathleen F. *Russian Village Prose: The Radiant Past*. Princeton, NJ: Princeton University Press, 1992.

Peris, Daniel. "'God Is Now on Our Side': The Religious Revival on Unoccupied Soviet Territory during World War II." *Kritika: Explorations in Russian and Eurasian History* 1, no. 1 (2008): 97–118.

———. "The 1929 Congress of the Godless." *Europe-Asia Studies* 43, no. 4 (1991): 711–32.

———. *Storming the Heavens: The Soviet League of the Militant Godless*. Ithaca, NY: Cornell University Press, 1998.

Petroff, Serge. *The Red Eminence: A Biography of Mikhail A. Suslov*. Clifton, NJ: Kingston Press, 1988.

Petrone, Karen. *Life Has Become More Joyous, Comrades: Celebrations in the Time of Stalin*. Bloomington: Indiana University Press, 2000.

Petrov, E. *Kosmonavty*. Moscow: Krasnaia zvezda, 1963.

Petrovsky-Shtern, Yohanan. *Lenin's Jewish Question*. New Haven, CT: Yale University Press, 2010.

Pikhoia, Rudolf G. *Moscow, Kreml', vlast'. Sorok let posle voiny: 1945–1985*. Moscow: Astrel', 2007.

Pinsky, Anatoly, ed. *Posle Stalina: Pozdnesovetskaia sub"ektivnost', 1953–1985*. Saint Petersburg: Izdatel'stvo Evropeiskogo universiteta v Sankt-Peterburge, 2017.

Pipes, Richard. "The Church as Servant of the State." In *Russia under the Old Regime*, 221–45. New York: Penguin, 1974.

*Pis'ma i dialogi vremen "khrushchevskoi ottepeli" (Desiat' let iz zhizni patriarkha Aleksiia, 1955–1964 gg.)*. Edited by Mikhail Odintsov. *Otechestvennye arkhivy*, no. 5 (1994): 72.

*Plenum Tsentral'nogo Komiteta Kommunisticheskoi Partii Sovetskogo Soiuza, 18–21 June 1963: Stenograficheskii otchet*. Moscow: Izdatel'stvo Politicheskoi Literatury, 1964.

Pobedonostsev, Konstantin P. "The Spiritual Life." In *Reflections of a Russian Statesman*. Ann Arbor: University of Michigan Press, 1965.

Polianski, Igor J. "The Antireligious Museum: Soviet Heterotopia between Transcending and Remembering Religious Heritage." In Betts and Smith, *Science, Religion and Communism in Cold War Europe*, 253–73.

Pollock, Ethan. *Stalin and the Soviet Science Wars*. Princeton, NJ: Princeton University Press, 2006.

Poole, Randall A. "Religious Toleration, Freedom of Conscience, and Russian Liberalism." *Kritika: Explorations in Russian and Eurasian History* 13, no. 3 (2012): 611–34.

Pope John Paul II. "Slavorum Apostoli." June 2, 1985. http://w2.vatican.va/content/john-paul-ii/en/encyclicals/documents/hf_jp-ii_enc_19850602_slavorum-apostoli.html.

Pope Pius XI. "Divini Redemptoris." March 19, 1937. http://www.vatican.va/holy_father/pius_xi/encyclicals/documents/hf_p-xi_enc_19031937_divini-redemptoris_en.html.

Popova, K. Iu. "Religioznye ob'edineniia v Orenburgskoi oblasti v 1960–1980-e gg: problema registratsii." In *Orenburgskii krai: istoriia, traditsii, kul'tura: sbornik*, edited by G. I. Biushkin, 88–92. Orenburg, 2009.

Pospielovskii, Dimitrii V. *A History of Marxist-Leninist Atheism and Soviet Antireligious Policies*. New York: St. Martin's, 1987.

———. *The Orthodox Church in the History of Russia*. Crestwood, NY: St. Vladimir's Seminary Press, 1998.

———. *The Russian Church under the Soviet Regime, 1917–1982*. Crestwood, NY: St. Vladimir's Seminary Press, 1984.

———. *Russkaia pravoslavnaia tserkov' v XX veke*. Moscow: Respublika, 1995.

———. *Soviet Antireligious Campaigns and Persecutions*. New York: St. Martin's, 1988.

———. *Soviet Studies on the Church and the Believer's Response to Atheism*. New York: St. Martin's, 1988.

———. *Totalitarizm i veroispovedanie*. Moscow: Bibleisko-bogoslovskii institut sv. Apostola Andreia, 2003.

*Postanovlenie Tsentral'nogo Komiteta KPSS*. Moscow: Gospolitizdat, 1960.

Powell, David E. *Antireligious Propaganda in the Soviet Union: A Study of Mass Persuasion*. Cambridge, MA: MIT Press, 1975.

———. "The Revival of Religion." *Current History* 90 (October 1991): 329.

Preston, Andrew. *The Sword of the Spirit, the Shield of Faith: Religion in American War and Diplomacy*. New York: Knopf, 2012.

*Programma Kommunisticheskoi Partii Sovetskogo Soiuza*. Moscow: Politizdat, 1986.

*Programma Kommunisticheskoi Partii Sovetskogo Soiuza priniata XXII s'ezdom KPSS*. Moscow: Izdatel'stvo politicheskoi literatury, 1971.

*Programma Rossiiskoi kommunisticheskoi partii (bol'shevikov): priniata 8-m s"ezdom 18–23 marta 1919 g*. Moscow: Kommunist, 1919.

Pugacheva, Marina G. "Institut konkretnykh sotsial'nykh isledovanii Akademii Nauk, 1968–1972 gody." *Sotsiologicheskii zhurnal* 2 (1994): 158–72.

Raines, John C., ed. *Marx on Religion*. Philadelphia: Temple University Press, 2002.

Raleigh, Donald J. *Soviet Baby Boomers: An Oral History of Russia's Cold War Generation*. New York: Oxford University Press, 2013.

Ramet, Sabrina P. *Nihil obstat: Religion, Politics, and Social Change in East-Central Europe*. Durham, NC: Duke University Press, 1998.

———, ed. *Religious Policy in the Soviet Union*. New York: Cambridge University Press, 1993.

Razuvalova, Anna. *Pisateli "derevenshchiki": literatura i konservativnaia ideologiia 1970-kh godov*. Moscow: Novoe literaturnoe obozrenie, 2015.

Read, Christopher. *Religion, Revolution and the Russian Intelligentsia, 1900–1912*. London: Palgrave Macmillan, 1979.

Redko, Maria V. "Realization of the State Religious Policy of the Krasnoyarsk Kray in 1954–1964 (on the Example of the Russian Orthodox Church)." *Journal of Siberian Federal University* 1, no. 3 (2010): 154–58.

Reid, Susan E. "Cold War in the Kitchen: Gender and the De-Stalinization of Consumer Taste in the Soviet Union under Khrushchev." *Slavic Review* 61, no. 2 (2002): 211–52.

———. "Communist Comfort: Socialist Modernism and the Making of Cosy Homes in the Khrushchev-Era Soviet Union." *Gender and History* 21, no. 3 (2009): 465–98.

Remnick, David. *Lenin's Tomb: The Last Days of the Soviet Empire*. New York: Random House, 1993.

Reznik, Aleksandr. "Byt ili ne byt? Lev Trotskii, politika, i kul'tura v 1920-e gody." *Neprikosnovennyi zapas*, no. 4 (2013): 88–106.

Riasonovsky, Nicholas. *Russian Identities: A Historical Survey*. New York: Oxford University Press, 2005.

Rockwell, Trevor. "The Molding of the Rising Generation: Soviet Propaganda and the Hero Myth of Iurii Gagarin." *Past Imperfect* 12 (2006): 1–34.

Rogers, Douglas. *The Old Faith and the Russian Land: A Historical Ethnography of Ethics in the Urals*. Ithaca, NY: Cornell University Press, 2009.

R'oi, Yaacov. *Islam in the Soviet Union: From the Second World War to Gorbachev*. London: Hurst, 2000.

———. "The Task of Creating the New Soviet Man: 'Atheistic Propaganda' in the Soviet Muslim Areas." *Europe-Asia Studies* 36, no. 1 (1984): 26–44.

Rolf, Malte. *Das sowjetische Massenfest.* Hamburg: Hamburger Edition, 2006.

———. *Soviet Mass Festivals, 1917–1991.* Pittsburgh: University of Pittsburgh Press, 2013.

Rosenthal, Bernice Glazer, and Martha Bochachevsky-Chomiak, eds. *A Revolution of the Spirit: Crisis of Value in Russia, 1890–1924.* Translated by Marian Schwartz. New York: Fordham University Press, 1990.

Roslof, Edward E. "'Faces of the Faceless': A. A. Trushin Communist Over-Procurator for Moscow, 1943–1984." *Modern Greek Studies Yearbook* 18–19 (2002–3): 105–25.

———. *Red Priests: Renovationism, Russian Orthodoxy, and Revolution, 1905–1946.* Bloomington: Indiana University Press, 2002.

Roth-Ey, Kristin. *Moscow Prime Time: How the Soviet Union Built the Media Empire That Lost the Cultural Cold War.* Ithaca, NY: Cornell University Press, 2011.

Rudnev, Vladimir A. *Kommunisticheskomu bytu—novye traditsii.* Leningrad: Lenizdat, 1964.

*Russkaia pravoslavnaia Tserkov' v sovetskoe vremia (1917–1991). (Materialy i dokumenty po istorii otnoshenii mezhdu gosudarstvom i Tserkov'iu).* 2 vols. Moscow, 1995.

*Russkie patriarkhi XX veka: Sud'by otechestva na stranitsakh arkhivnykh dokumentov.* Moscow: Izdatel'stvo RAGS, 1999.

Ryan, James. "Cleansing *NEP* Russia: State Violence against the Russian Orthodox Church in 1922." *Europe-Asia Studies* 9 (2013): 1807–26.

Rykov, Aleksei. "Religiia—vrag sotsialisticheskogo stroitel'stva. Ona boretsia s nami na kul'turnoi pochve." In *Stenogramma X s"ezda Sovetov,* 191. Moscow, 1928.

Safonov, Aleksandr A. *Svoboda sovesti i modernizatsiia veroispovednogo zakonodatel'stva Rossiiskoi imperii v nachale XX v.* Tambov: Izdatel'stvo R. V. Pershina, 2007.

Sandle, Mark, and Edwin Bacon, eds. *Brezhnev Reconsidered.* New York: Palgrave Macmillan, 2002.

Schattenberg, Susanne. "'Democracy' or 'Despotism'? How the Secret Speech Was Translated into Everyday Life." In Jones, *Dilemmas of De-Stalinization,* 64–79.

Schonpflug, Daniel, and Martin Schulze Wessel, eds. *Redefining the Sacred: Religion in the French and Russian Revolutions.* Frankfurt am Main: Lang, 2012.

Scott, James C. *Seeing Like a State: How Certain Schemes to Improve the Human Condition Have Failed.* New Haven, CT: Yale University Press, 1998.

Shakhnovich, Mariana M. "Muzei istorii religii AN SSSR i otechestvennoe religiovedenie." *Religiovedenie,* no. 4 (2008): 150–58.

———. "Otechestvennoe religiovedenie 20–80kh godov XX veka: Ot kakogo nasledstva my otkazyvaemsia." In *Ocherki po istorii religiovedeniia,* ed. Mariana M. Shakhnovich, 181–97. Saint Petersburg: Izd-vo S.-Peterb. un-ta, 2006.

Shakhnovich, Mariana M., and Tatiana V. Chumakova. *Muzei istorii religii Akademii nauk SSSR i rossiiskoe religiovedenie (1932–1961).* Saint Petersburg: Nauka, 2014.

———. "N. M. Matorin i ego programma izucheniia narodnoi religioznosti." *Religiovedenie,* no. 4 (2012): 191–93.

Shakhnovich, Mikhail I. *Bibliia v sovremennoi bor'be idei.* Leningrad: Lenizdat, 1988.

———. *Kommunizm i religiia.* Leningrad: Obshchestvo "Znanie" RSFSR, 1966.

———. *Kritika religioznykh istolkovanii ekologicheskikh problem.* Moscow: Izd. "Znanie," 1985.

———. *Lenin i problemy ateizma.* Moscow: Izdatel'stvo Akademii nauk SSSR, 1960.

———. *Mistika pered sudom nauki.* Moscow: Obshchestvo "Znanie," 1970.

———. *Novye voprosy ateizma: Sotsiologicheskie ocherki.* Leningrad: Lenizdat, 1973.

———. *Ot sueverii k nauke.* Moscow: Molodaia Gvardiia, 1948.

———. *Proiskhozhdenie filosofii i ateizm.* Leningrad: Nauka, 1973.

———. *Russkaia tserkov' v bor'be s naukoi.* Leningrad: Gazetno-zhurnal'noe knizhnoe izdatel'stvo, 1939.

———. *Sotsial'naia suchshnost' Talmuda.* Leningrad, 1929.

———. *Sovremennaia mistika v svete religii.* Leningrad: Nauka, 1965.

———. *Sueverie i nauchnoe predvidenie.* Leningrad: Lenizdat, 1945.

Shelepin, Aleksandr N. *Otchetnyi doklad Tsentral'nogo Komiteta Vsesoiuznogo leninskogo kommunisticheskogo soiuza molodezhi XIII s"ezdu komsomola (15 aprelia 1958 g.).* Moscow: Molodaia gvardiia, 1958.

Shevzov, Vera. *Russian Orthodoxy on the Eve of Revolution.* New York: Oxford University Press, 2004.

Shkarovskii, Mikhail V. *Obnovlencheskoe dvizhenie v Russkoi Pravoslavnoi Tserkvi XX veka.* Saint Petersburg: Izd. Nestor, 1999.

———. *Russkaia pravoslavnaia tserkov' i sovetskoe gosudarstvo v 1943–1964 godakh: Ot "peremiriia" k novoi voine.* Saint Petersburg: DEAN + ADIA-M, 1995.

———. *Russkaia pravoslavnaia tserkov' pri Staline i Khrushcheve (gosudarstvenno-tserkovnye otnosheniia v SSSR v 1939–1964 godakh).* Moscow: Krutitskoe patriarshee podvor'e, 1999.

———. *Russkaia Pravoslavnaia Tserkov' v XX Veke.* Moscow: Veche, Lepta, 2010.

———. "Staliniskaia religioznaia politika i Russkaia Pravoslavnaia Tserkov' v 1943–1953 godakh." *Acta Slavica Iaponica* 27 (2009): 1–27.

Shlapentokh, Vladimir. *The Politics of Sociology in the Soviet Union.* Boulder, CO: Westview, 1987.

———. *Public and Private Life of the Soviet People: Changing Values in Post-Stalin Russia.* New York: Oxford University Press, 1989.

———. *Soviet Intellectuals and Political Power: The Post-Stalin Era.* New York: I. B. Tauris, 1990.

———. *Soviet Public Opinion and Ideology: Mythology and Pragmatism in Interaction.* New York: Praeger, 1986.

Shlikhta, Natalya. "'Orthodox' and 'Soviet': On the Issue of the Identity of Christian Soviet Citizens (1940s–Early 1970s)." *Forum for Anthropology and Culture* 11 (2015): 140–64.

———. "'Ot traditsii k sovremennosti': pravoslavnaia obriadnost' i prazdniki v usloviiakh antireligioznoi bor'by (na materialakh USSR, 1950-e–1960-e gg.)." *Gosudarstvo, Religiia i Tserkov' v Rossii i za Rubezhom,* nos. 3–4 (2012): 380–407.

Shterin, Marat, and James Richardson. "Local Laws Restricting Religion in Russia: Prosecutors of Russia's New National Law." *Journal of Church and State* 40 (1998): 319–41.

Shternshis, Anna. *Soviet and Kosher: Jewish Popular Culture in the Soviet Union, 1923–1939.* Bloomington: Indiana University Press, 2006.

Shtiuka, Vladimir Georgievich. *Byt i religiia.* Moscow: Mysl', 1966.

Shtyrkov, Sergei. "Oblichitel'naia etnografiia epokhi Khrushcheva: bol'shaia ideologiia i narodnyi obychai (na primere Severo-Osetinskoi ASSR)." *Neprikosnovennyi zapas* 65, no. 1 (2009): 147–61.

———. "Prakticheskoe religiovedenie vremen Nikity Khrushcheva: respublikanskaia gazeta v bor'be s 'religioznymi perezhitkami' (na primere Severo-Osetinskoi ASSR)." In *Traditsii narodov Kavkaza v meniaiushchemsia mire: preemstvonnost' i razryvy v sotsiokul'turnyk praktikakh,* edited by A. A. Karpov, 306–43. Saint Petersburg: Izd. Peterburgskoe Vostokovedenie, 2010.

———. "'V gorode otkryt Dvorets schast'ia': Bor'ba za novuiu sovetskuiu obriadnost' vremen Khrushcheva." In *Topografiia schast'ia: etnograficheskie karty moderna. Sbornik statei*, edited by Nikolai Ssorin-Chaikov, 261–75. Moscow: Novoe literaturnoe obozrenie, 2013.

Siddiqi, Asif A. "Imagining the Cosmos: Utopians, Mystics, and the Popular Culture of Spaceflight in Revolutionary Russia." *Osiris* 23, no. 1 (2008): 260–88.

———. *Sputnik and the Soviet Space Challenge*. Gainesville: University Press of Florida, 2003.

Sidorov, Dmitri. "National Monumentalization and the Politics of Scale: The Resurrections of the Cathedral of Christ the Saviour in Moscow." *Annals of the Association of American Geographers* 90, no. 3 (2000): 548–72.

Siegelbaum, Lewis H., ed. *Borders of Socialism: Private Spheres of Soviet Russia*. New York: Palgrave Macmillan, 2006.

Siegelbaum, Lewis H., and Leslie Page Moch. *Broad Is My Native Land: Repertoires and Regimes of Migration in Russia's Twentieth Century*. Ithaca, NY: Cornell University Press, 2014.

Sinitsyn, Vladimir G. *Byt epokhi stroitel'stva kommunizma*. Cheliabinsk: Cheliabinskoe knizhnoe izd-vo, 1963.

———. *Obraz zhizni, dostoinyi cheloveka (V pomoshch' lektoru: bibliotechka "sovetskii obraz zhizni")*. Moscow: Znanie, 1970.

———. *O sovetskom obraze zhizni*. Moscow: Znanie, 1967.

———. *Sovetskii obraz zhizni*. Moscow: Sovetskaia Rossiia, 1969.

———. *The Soviet Way of Life*. Moscow: Progress Publishers, 1974.

Skvortsov-Stepanov, Ivan. "Mysli o religii" (1922). In *Izbrannye ateisticheskie proizvedeniia*, edited by Vladimir Zybkovets, 299–331. Moscow, 1959.

Slezkine, Yuri. *The House of Government: A Saga of the Russian Revolution*. Princeton, NJ: Princeton University Press, 2017.

Slezkine, Yuri. "The USSR as a Communal Apartment, or How a Socialist State Promoted Ethnic Particularism." *Slavic Review* 53, no. 2 (1994): 414–52.

Smirnov, G. L. *Formirovanie novogo cheloveka—programnaia tsel' KPPS*. Moscow: Znanie, 1983.

Smirnov, Mark, and Pavel Krug. "V zashchitu svobodomysliia: Ispolnilos' polveka zhurnalu 'Nauka i religiia.'" *Nezavisimaia gazeta*, October 21, 2009. http://www.ng.ru/ng_religii/2009-10-21/2_magazine.html.

Smirnov, Mikhail Iu. "Religiovedenie v Rossii: problema samoidentifikatsii." *Vestnik Moskovskogo universiteta. Filosofiia*, no. 1 (January–February 2009): 90–106.

Smith, Jonathan Z. *Imagining Religion: From Babylon to Jonestown*. Chicago: University of Chicago Press, 1982.

———. "Religion, Religions, Religious." In Taylor, *Critical Terms for Religious Studies*, 269–84.

Smith, Kathleen E. *Mythmaking in the New Russia: Politics and Memory during the Yeltsin Era*. Ithaca, NY: Cornell University Press, 2002.

Smith, Stephen A. "Bones of Contention: Bolsheviks and the Struggle against Relics, 1918–1930." *Past & Present* 204, no. 1 (2009): 155–94.

Smolkin-Rothrock, Victoria. "The Confession of an Atheist Who Became a Scholar of Religion: Nikolai Semenovich Gordienko's Last Interview." *Kritika: Explorations in Russian and Eurasian History* 15, no. 3 (Summer 2014): 596–620.

———. "The Contested Skies: The Battle of Science and Religion in the Soviet Planetarium." In Maurer et al., *Soviet Space Culture*, 57–78.

*Sobranie uzakonenii i rasporiazhenii pravitel'stva za 1917–1918 gg. Upravlenie Sovnarkoma SSSR*. Moscow: 1942.

Sokolova, Anna D. "Nel'zia, nel'zia novyh liudei horonit' po-staromu!" *Otechestvennye zapiski* 56, no. 5 (2013). http://www.strana-oz.ru/2013/5/nelzya-nelzya-novyh-lyudey-horonit-po-staromu.

———. "Transformatsiia pokhoronnoi obriadnosti u russkikh v XX–XXI vv (Na materialakh Vladimirskoi oblasti)." PhD dissertation, Institute of Ethnography and Anthropology of the Russian Academy of Sciences, 2013.

Soloukhin, Vladimir A. "Pis'ma iz Russkogo muzeia." In *Slovo zhivoe i mertvoe*, 226–321. Moscow: Sovremennik, 1976.

———. *Rodnaia krasota (dlia chego nado izuchat' i berech' pamiatniki stariny)*. Moscow: Sovetskii khudoznik, 1966.

Soloviev, Vladimir S. *Po puti dukhovnogo progressa: Nekotorye itogi povtornykh sotsiologicheskikh issledovanii problem byta, kul'tury, natsional'nykh traditsii, ateizma i verovanii Mariiskoi ASSR*. Ioshkar Ola: Mariiskoe knizhnoe izdatel'stvo, 1987.

Stalin, Iosif. *Sochineniia*. Vol. 13. Moscow, 1942–46.

Stark, Rodney. "Secularization, R.I.P." *Sociology of Religion* 60 (1999): 249–73.

Stedman Jones, Gareth. "Religion and the Origins of Socialism." In Katznelson and Jones, *Religion and the Political Imagination*, 171–89.

Steinberg, Mark D. "Workers on the Cross: Religious Imagination in the Writings of Russian Workers, 1910–1924." *Russian Review* 53, no. 2 (1994): 213–39.

Steinberg, Mark D., and Catherine Wanner, eds. *Religion, Morality, and Community in Post-Soviet Societies*. Bloomington: Indiana University Press, 2008.

Steinwedel, Charles. "Making Social Groups, One Person at a Time: The Identification of Individuals by Estate, Religious Confession, and Ethnicity in Late Imperial Russia." In Caplan and Torpey, *Documenting Individual Identity*, 67–92.

Stepakov, Vladimir I. *Novye prazdniki i obriady—v narodnyi byt*. Moscow, 1964.

Stites, Richard. *Revolutionary Dreams: Utopian Vision and Experimental Life in the Russian Revolution*. New York: Oxford University Press, 1989.

———. *Russian Popular Culture: Entertainment and Society since 1900*. New York: Cambridge University Press, 1992.

Stone, Andrew B. "'Overcoming Peasant Backwardness': The Khrushchev Antireligious Campaign and the Rural Soviet Union." *Russian Review* 67 (2008): 297–320.

Stroop, Christopher. "The Russian Origins of the So-Called Post-secular Moment: Some Preliminary Observations." *State, Religion and Church* 1, no. 1 (2014): 59–82.

Struve, Petr, ed. *Iz glubiny: Sbornik statei o russkoi revoliutsii*. 1918. Reprint, Moscow: Novosti, 1999.

Sullivan, Winnifred Fallers. *The Impossibility of Religious Freedom*. Princeton, NJ: Princeton University Press, 2005.

Sveshnikova, Ol'ga. "Iubilei Gerodota: Shestidesiatnicheskoe proshloe v zerkale sovremennoi sotsiologii." *Novoe Literaturnoe Obozrenie* 98 (2009): 97–110.

Swiderski, Edward. "From Social Subject to 'Person': The Belated Transformation in Latter-Day Soviet Philosophy." *Philosophy of the Social Sciences* 23, no. 2 (1993): 199–227.

Takahashi, Sanami. "Church or Museum? The Role of State Museums in Conserving Church Buildings, 1965–85." *Journal of Church and State* 3 (2009): 502–17.

———. "Obraz religioznogo landshafta v SSSR 1965–1985 gody (na primere Solovetskogo muzeia-zapovednika)." *Vestnik Evrazii*, no. 4 (2008): 9–26.

Tasar, Eren Murat. "Soviet and Muslim: The Institutionalization of Islam in Central Asia, 1943–1991." PhD dissertation, Harvard University, 2010.

Taubman, William. *Khrushchev: The Man and His Era*. New York: Norton, 2003.

Taylor, Charles. *A Secular Age*. Cambridge, MA: Harvard University Press, 2007.

Taylor, Mark C., ed. *Critical Terms for Religious Studies*. Chicago: University of Chicago Press, 1998.

Tendriakov, Vladimir. "Apostol'skaia komandirovka." In *Sobranie Sochinenii*, vol. 4, 230–420. Moscow: Khudozhestvennaia literatura, 1980.

———. "Tysiacha pervyi raz o nravstvennosti." *Zvezda*, no. 12 (2003). http://magazines.russ.ru/zvezda/2003/12/tendr-pr.html.

Thrower, James. *Marxist-Leninist "Scientific Atheism" and the Study of Religion and Atheism in the USSR*. New York: Mouton, 1983.

Timasheff, Nicholas. *The Great Retreat: The Growth and Decline of Communism in Russia*. New York: E. P. Dutton, 1946.

Titov, Alexander. "The 1961 Party Program and the Fate of Khrushchev's Reforms." In Ilic and Smith, *Soviet State and Society under Nikita Khrushchev*, 8–25.

———. "Partiia protiv gosudarstva: reforma apparata TsK KPSS pri Nikite Khrushcheve." *Neprikosnovennyi zapas* 83, no. 3 (2012): 155–66.

Titov, German Stepanovich. *Pervyi kosmonavt planety*. Moscow: Znanie, 1971.

Tocqueville, Alexis de. *The Old Regime and the French Revolution*. New York: Anchor Books, 1983.

Tóth, Heléna. "Shades of Grey: Secular Burial Rites in East Germany." In *Changing European Death Ways*, edited by Eric Venbrux and Thomas Quartier, 141–64. Münster: LIT Verlag, 2013.

———. "Writing Rituals: The Sources of Socialist Rites of Passage in Hungary, 1958–1970." In Betts and Smith, *Science, Religion and Communism in Cold War Europe*, 179–203.

Trotsky, Lev. *O novom byte*. Moscow: Novaia Moskva, 1924.

———. *Voprosy byta: epokha "kul'turnichestva" i ee zadachi*. Moscow: Gosizdat, 1923.

Tsekhanskaia, Kira V. "The Icon in the Home: The Home Begins with the Icon." In Mandelstam Balzer, *Religion and Politics in Russia*, 18–30.

———. "Russia: Trends in Orthodox Religiosity in the Twentieth Century (Statistics and Reality)." In Mandelstam Balzer, *Religion and Politics in Russia*, 3–17.

Tucker, Robert C., ed. *The Marx-Engels Reader*. 2nd ed. New York: Norton, 1978.

Tumarkin, Nina. *Lenin Lives! The Lenin Cult in Soviet Russia*. Cambridge, MA: Harvard University Press, 1983.

———. *The Living and the Dead: The Rise and Fall of the Cult of World War II in Russia*. New York: Basic Books, 1994.

*The 24th Party Congress of the CSPU—Documents*. Moscow, 1971.

Ugrinovich, Dmitrii M. *Obriady: za i protiv*. Moscow: Politizdat, 1975.

Uhl, Katharina Barbara. "Building Communism: The Young Communist League during the Soviet Thaw Period, 1953–1964." DPhil thesis, University of Oxford, 2014.

*Ustav Kommunisticheskoi partii Sovetskogo Soiuza*. Moscow: Politizdat, 1986.

*Ustav KPSS*. Moscow: Izdatel'stvo politicheskoi literatury, 1961.

Vail', Petr, and Aleksandr Genis. *60–e: Mir sovetskogo cheloveka*. Moscow, Novoe literaturnoe obozrenie, 2001.

van den Bercken, William. "Holy Russia and the Soviet Fatherland." *Religion in Communist Lands* 15, no. 3 (1987): 264–77.

———. *Ideology and Atheism in the Soviet Union*. New York: Mouton de Gruyter, 1989.

———. "The Rehabilitation of Christian Ethical Values in the Soviet Media." *Religion in Communist Lands* 17, no. 1 (1989): 6–7.

Van Kley, Dale K. *The Religious Origins of the French Revolution: From Calvin to the Civil Constitution, 1560–1791*. New Haven, CT: Yale University Press, 1999.

Varga-Harris, Christine. *Stories of House and Home: Soviet Apartment Life during the Khrushchev Years*. Ithaca, NY: Cornell University Press, 2015.

Vasil'eva, Olga, ed. *Istoriia religii v Rossii*. Moscow, 2004.

Vasil'eva, Olga, Ivan I. Kudriavtsev, and Liudmilma A. Lykova, eds. *Russkaia Pravoslavnaia Tserkov' v gody Velikoi Otechestvennoi Voiny 1941–1945 gg.: Sbornik dokumentov*. Moscow: Izdatel'stvo Krutitskogo podvo'ia, 2009.

Veresaev, Vikentii V. *Ob obriadakh starykh i novykh (k khudozhestvennomu oformleniiu byta)*. Moscow: Novaia Moskva, 1926.

Viola, Lynn. *Peasant Rebels under Stalin: Collectivization and the Culture of Peasant Resistance*. New York: Oxford University Press, 1999.

Vlasto, Alexis P. *The Entry of the Slavs into Christendom: An Introduction to the Medieval History of the Slavs*. Cambridge: Cambridge University Press, 1970.

Voegelin, Eric. *Political Religion*. 1938. Reprint, Lewiston, NY: Edwin Mellen, 1986.

Volkov, Andrei. "Iz istorii perepisi naseleniia 1937 goda." *Vestnik statistiki*, no. 8 (1990): 45–56.

Volkov, Vadim. "The Concept of Kul'turnost'. Notes on the Stalinist Civilizing Process." In *Stalinism: New Directions*, ed. Sheila Fitzpatrick, 210–30. New York: Routledge, 2000.

Volokotina, Tatiana, ed. *Vlast' i tserkov' v vostochnoi evrope, 1944–1953: Dokumenty rossiiskikh arkhivov*. Moscow: ROSSPEN, 2009.

Von Geldern, James. *Bolshevik Festivals, 1917–1920*. Berkeley: University of California Press, 1993.

von Zitzewitz, Josephine. "The 'Religious Renaissance' of the 1970s and Its Repercussions on the Soviet Literary Process." DPhil thesis, University of Oxford, 2009.

Vorontsov-Veliaminov, B. A. *Astronomicheskaia Moskva v 20e gody—Istoriko-astronomicheskie issledovaniia, vyp. 18*. Moscow: Nauka, 1986.

———. *Vselennaia*. Moscow: Gostekhizdat, 1947.

Vvedenskii, A. *Tserkov' i gosudarstvo*. Moscow: Mospoligraf "Krasnyi Proletarii," 1923.

Wallace, James C. "A Religious War? The Cold War and Religion." *Journal of Cold War Studies* 15, no. 3 (2013): 162–80.

Wanner, Catherine. *Communities of the Converted: Ukrainians and Global Evangelism*. Ithaca, NY: Cornell University Press, 2007.

———, ed. *State Secularism and Lived Religion in Soviet Russia and Ukraine*. New York: Oxford University Press, 2012.

Ward, Christopher J. *Brezhnev's Folly. The Building of BAM and Late Soviet Socialism*. Pittsburgh: University of Pittsburgh Press, 2009.

Warner, Michael, Jonathan Van Antwerpen, and Craig J. Calhoun. *Varieties of Secularism in a Secular Age*. Cambridge, MA: Harvard University Press, 2010.

Weber, Max. "Science as a Vocation." In *From Max Weber: Essays in Sociology*, edited and translated by H. H. Gerth and C. Wright Mills, 129–56. New York: Oxford University Press, 1946.

Weeks, Theodore R. *Nation and State in Late Imperial Russia: Nationalism and Russification on the Western Frontier, 1863–1914*. DeKalb: Northern Illinois University Press, 2008.

Weir, Todd H. "The Christian Front against Godlessness: Anti-secularism and the Demise of the Weimar Republic, 1928–1933." *Past & Present* 229, no. 1 (2015): 201–38.

———. "The Riddles of Monism: An Introductory Essay." In *Monism: Science, Philosophy, Religion, and the History of a Worldview*, edited by Todd H. Weir, 1–45. Basingstoke: Palgrave Macmillan, 2012.

———. "Säkularismus (Freireligiöse, Freidenker, Monisten, Ethiker, Humanisten)." In *Handbuch Religionsgeschichte des 20. Jahrhunderts im deutschsprachigen Raum*, edited by Lucian Hoelscher and Volkard Krech, 6/2:189–218. Paderborn: Schönigh, 2016.

Werth, Paul W. "The Emergence of 'Freedom of Conscience' in Imperial Russia." *Kritika: Explorations in Russian and Eurasian History* 13, no. 3 (2012): 585–610.

———. "In the State's Embrace? Civil Acts in an Imperial Order." *Kritika: Explorations in Russian and Eurasian History* 7, no. 3 (2006): 433–58.

———. *The Tsar's Foreign Faiths: Toleration and the Fate of Religious Freedom in Imperial Russia.* Oxford: Oxford University Press, 2014.

Wolfe, Thomas C. *Governing Soviet Journalism: The Press and the Socialist Person after Stalin.* Bloomington: Indiana University Press, 2005.

Wood, Elizabeth. *The Baba and the Comrade: Gender and Politics in Revolutionary Russia.* Bloomington: Indiana University Press, 2000.

Worobec, Christine D. "Lived Orthodoxy in Imperial Russia." *Kritika: Explorations in Russian and Eurasian History* 7, no. 2 (2006): 329–50.

———. *Possessed: Women, Witches, and Demons in Imperial Russia.* DeKalb: Northern Illinois University Press, 2001.

*XXII S'ezd KPSS.* Moscow: Politizdat, 1962.

Yelensky, Viktor. "Religiia i perestroika v Ukraine." *Liudina i svit,* December 10, 2003. http://www.religare.ru/2_7596_1_21.html.

———. "The Revival before the Revival: Popular and Institutionalized Religion in Ukraine on the Eve of the Collapse of Communism." In Wanner, *State Secularism and Lived Religion in Soviet Russia and Ukraine,* 302–30.

Yemelianova, Galina. *Russia and Islam: A Historical Survey.* Basingstoke: Palgrave, 2002.

Young, Glennys. *Power and the Sacred in Revolutionary Russia: Religious Activists in the Village.* University Park: Pennsylvania State University Press, 1997.

Yurchak, Alexei. *Everything Was Forever until It Was No More: The Last Soviet Generation.* Princeton, NJ: Princeton University Press, 2006.

Zahra, Tara. "Imagined Noncommunities: National Indifference as a Category of Analysis." *Slavic Review* 69, no. 1 (2010): 93–119.

Zaichikov, Vasilii N. *Akademiia millionov: O rabote Vsesoiuznogo obshchestva "Znanie."* Moscow: Znanie, 1967.

*Zakonodatel'stvo o religioznykh kul'takh: Sbornik materialov i dokumentov.* Moscow, 1971.

Zelnik, Reginald E. "'To the Unaccustomed Eye': Religion and Irreligion in the Experience of St. Petersburg Workers in the 1870s." *Russian History* 16, nos. 2–4 (1989): 297–326.

Zhidkova, Elena. "Sovetskaia obriadnost' kak al'ternativa obriadnosti religizonoi." *Gosudarstvo, Religiia i Tserkov' v Rossii i za Rubezhom,* nos. 3–4 (2012): 408–29.

Zhiromskaia, Valentina, Igor Kiselev, and Iurii Poliakov. *Polveka pod grifom "sekretno": Vsesoiuznaia perepis' naseleniia 1937 goda.* Moscow: Nauka, 1996.

Zhivov, Viktor. "Distsiplinarnaia revoliutsiia i bor'ba s sueveriem v Rossii XVIII veka: 'provaly' i ikh posledstviia." In *Antropologiia revoliutsii: Sbornik statei po materialam XVI Bannykh chtennii zhurnala "Novoe literaturnoe obozrenie,"* edited by Irina Prokhorova, Aleksandr Dmitriev, Il'ia Kikulin, and Maria Maiofis, 327–61. Moscow: Novoe Literaturnoe Obozrenie, 2009.

Zhuk, Sergei I. *Rock and Roll in the Rocket City: The West, Identity, and Ideology in Soviet Dniepropetrovsk, 1960–1985.* Baltimore: Johns Hopkins University Press, 2010.

———. *Russia's Lost Reformation: Peasants, Millennialism, and Radical Sects in Southern Russia and Ukraine, 1830–1917.* Baltimore: Johns Hopkins University Press, 2004.

Zian'kovich, Mikalai. *Samye zakrytye liudi: entsiklopedia biografii.* Moscow: Olma-Press, 2002.

Zigon, Jarrett, ed. *Multiple Moralities and Religions in Post-Soviet Russia.* New York: Berghahn Books, 2011.

Zubkova, Elena I. *Obshchestvo i reformy, 1945–1964.* Moscow: Rossiia molodaia, 1993.

———. *Poslevoennoe sovetskoe obshchestvo: politika i povsednevnost': 1945–1953*. Moscow: Rosspen, 2000.

———. *Russia after the War: Hopes, Illusions, and Disappointments, 1945–1957*. Translated and edited by Hugh Ragsdale. Armonk, NY: M. E. Sharpe, 1998.

Zubok, Vladislav. *Zhivago's Children: The Last Russian Intelligentsia*. Cambridge, MA: Belknap, 2009.

Zuckerman, Phil, and John R. Shook. "Introduction: The Study of Secularism." In *The Oxford Handbook of Secularism*, edited by Phil Zuckerman and John R. Shook, 1–17. New York: Oxford University Press, 2017.

Zuev, Iurii P. "Dinamika religioznosti v Rossii v XX veke i ee sotsiologicheskoe izuchenie." In *Sotsiologiia religii*, ed. V. I. Garadzha, 187–210. Moscow, 1995.

———. "Institut nauchnogo ateizma (1964–1991)." *Voprosy religii i religiovedeniia. Antologiia otechestvennogo religiovedeniia* 1 (2009): 9–34.

Zuev, Iurii P., and Vil'iam V. Shmidt, eds. *Nasledie: Istoriia gosudarstvenno-konfessional'nykh otnoshenii v Rossii (X-nachalo XXI veka)*. Moscow: Izd-vo. RAGS, 2010.

———. "Ot instituta nauchnogo ateizma k kafedre gosudarstvenno konfessional'nykh otnoshenii: stanovlenie religiovedcheskoi shkoly (1964–1991, 1992–2010)." *Voprosy religii i religiovedeniia. Antologiia otechestvennogo religiovedeniia* 1 (2010): 15–28.

Zwahlen, Regula M. "The Lack of Moral Autonomy in the Russian Concept of Personality: A Case of Continuity across the Pre-Revolutionary, Soviet, and Post-Soviet Periods?" *State, Religion and Church* 2, no. 1 (2015): 19–43.

# INDEX

Page numbers in italics refer to photographs or illustrations.